THE PRACTICE OF
SILVICULTURE

THE PRACTICE OF
SILVICULTURE

DAVID MARTYN SMITH

Associate Professor of Silviculture, Yale University

SEVENTH EDITION

The continuation of a work published as a
first edition in March 1921, by Ralph C. Hawley

1962

John Wiley & Sons, Inc., New York · London · Sydney

PREFACE

This is the first time that an edition of *The Practice of Silviculture* has not appeared under the authorship of Professor Ralph C. Hawley, who has turned his attention from the guidance of communities of trees in the forest to those of human beings in the desert. Perhaps the most important premise of all previous editions has been his contention that silvicultural practice is based on economic as well as biological considerations; this philosophy is pursued still further in this seventh edition.

When the sixth edition was written, a deliberate attempt was made to leave no statement unsupported by at least an inkling of the reasoning behind it. The accelerating developments in forest science and American practice during the last eight years have made it possible to proceed with such analysis to an extent which gratifies as much as it whets the appetite for more. This line of attack is based on the belief that the most powerful tool of forestry is the analytical reasoning of its practitioners.

The book is intended primarily for use in North American forestry schools and in courses integrated with those others that comprise the normal curriculum of instruction in professional forestry. Therefore, an attempt has been made to elucidate the principles of silviculture, which are really independent of geography, almost entirely in terms of American practice. A secondary purpose is to provide the harried practitioner of forestry with a synoptic review of recent developments in silviculture.

The lists of references at the ends of the chapters are designed mainly to provide the reader with points of departure for the kind of further inquiry that is a necessary antidote to the sweeping and infectious generalizations that are diseases of textbooks. The references chosen are usually those deemed most likely to be accessible to the student and thus come more from the recent American literature than from older material or that published abroad. Consequently there are many instances in which the original sources have not been credited.

I am indebted to Professor Hawley for the wealth of ideas and material expressive of them that has been inherited from the forty-year history of this book. Thanks are due Professor David R. M. Scott for reviewing the chapters on thinning, and Messrs. Ernest A. Kurmes, D. Peter Loucks, and Edward J. Dimock II for critical editorial assistance. The opportunity to make selections of illustrations from the collections of the U. S. Forest Service, American Forest Products Industries, and other organizations credited in the text has been invaluable. Finally, I am humbly grateful to the host of foresters on whose thoughts, experience, and investigations this book is based.

DAVID M. SMITH

New Haven, Connecticut
June, 1962

CONTENTS

CHAPTER 1

Silviculture
and its place in forestry

Silviculture has been variously defined as: the art of producing and tending a forest; the application of the knowledge of silvics in the treatment of a forest; the theory and practice of controlling forest establishment, composition, and growth. The subject matter of silvicultural practice consists of the various treatments of forest stands that may be applied to maintain and enhance their productivity. The duties of the forester with respect to silviculture are to analyze the natural and economic factors bearing on each stand under his care and then to devise and conduct the treatments most appropriate to the objective of management.

Silviculture occupies a position in forestry somewhat analogous to that of agronomy in agriculture, in that it is concerned with the technical details of crop production. Like forestry itself, silviculture is an applied science which rests ultimately upon the more fundamental natural and social sciences. The immediate foundation of silviculture in the natural sciences is the field of silvics, which deals with the laws underlying the growth and development of single trees and of the forest as a biological unit. In silviculture, information from silvics is applied to the production of forest crops, and technical procedures are developed for the scientific tending and reproducing of these crops.

In a broad sense silviculture is often regarded as including both silvics and its practical application. The present book, as its name *The Practice of Silviculture* implies, does not include the field of silvics. However, it is taken for granted that those who read this book have already acquired some grasp of silvics.

1

It is in the practice of silviculture that much of the growing store of scientific knowledge about forests is applied. As Muelder (1959) pointed out, knowledge derived from formal research can be put to effective use only by practicing foresters who are alert to new developments and understand them. The efficient practice of silviculture, whether it be crude or elaborate, demands as much knowledge of such fields as ecology, plant physiology, entomology, and soil science (to name but a few) as a forester can acquire. If it were otherwise, there would be scant need for college-trained foresters.

The competent forester must maintain contact with forest science and the results of formal research. He cannot, however, depend upon these sources for ready-made solutions to silvicultural problems. Skillful practice itself is a continuing and informal kind of research in which new ideas are constantly applied and old ideas tested for validity. The observant and inquiring forester will find many of his questions about silviculture answered by the results of accidents of nature and earlier treatments of the forest.

The practice of silviculture is concerned with the economic as well as the biological aspects of forestry. The implicit objective of forestry is to make the forest useful to man. Since all management of the forest is, therefore, aimed at economic objectives, it is almost impossible to separate the biological aspects from the economic. The mere fact that the silviculturist grows trees so that they will be useful rather than merely vigorous from the physiological standpoint automatically introduces an economic purpose.

The Purpose of Silviculture

Silviculture is normally directed at the creation and maintenance of the kind of forest that will best fulfill the objectives of the owner. Returns from silviculture are generally thought of in terms of timber production, although it is not uncommon for owners to have other goals. The growing of wood may, in fact, have low priority among these objectives or none at all. The essential thing is that the objectives should be clearly defined and the treatment shaped to their attainment. In this book greatest emphasis is placed upon the production of wood crops because this is the most common objective and also because the treatments involved are better developed and ordinarily more intricate than those aimed at other goals.

The forester should work for the good of the forest as an entity, not for the sake of the forest itself, but to ensure that it will remain a permanently productive source of goods and benefits to the owner and to society.

Improving on Nature through Silviculture

The most magnificent forests that are ever likely to develop in North America were present at the time of settlement and grew without assistance from man. Furthermore, under reasonably favorable conditions, forests may remain productive even after long periods of mistreatment. Therefore, it is logical to consider why foresters should attempt to direct any of the powerful natural forces at work in the forest. The reasons are economic and mainly involve attempts to produce more useful forests than nature can and to do so in far less time.

The purely natural forest is governed by no purpose unless it be the unceasing struggle of all the component plant and animal species to perpetuate themselves. A purpose not existing in nature is introduced by human preference for certain species and for individuals thereof that have particular useful characteristics. Examination usually shows that whenever forests of highest utility have developed in nature it was the result of a fortuitous set of circumstances followed by a long period of growth.

The time required for growth was not a factor in utilizing virgin forests because no one had to pay any costs of holding land while the trees were growing. In managed forests the rate at which value is produced, and not the final value, is the important factor. Unmanaged or mismanaged forests, like poorly treated farm lands, do not yield products of the kind, amount, or value that might be grown. The forester increases the rate of production by properly tending the wild forest and establishing new forests on vacant areas.

The managed forest is more productive than the unmanaged or mismanaged forest because of the advantages gained through attainment of the following objectives of silvicultural practice:

Control of composition. Inferior species appear in almost any forest. One objective of silviculture is to restrict the composition of a stand to those species that are most suited to the location from the economic as well as the biological standpoint. This almost invariably means that the total number of species in a managed forest is less than that which could occur there under purely natural conditions. Since the inferior species flourish at the expense of the desirable, every reasonable effort should be made to keep them in check. The primary means by which species composition can be controlled is through regulating the severity of cuttings and the characteristics of the seedbeds during periods when new stands are being created by natural regeneration. In this manner environmental conditions can be adjusted to favor development of the stages of plant succession most nearly dominated by the desired species.

Regulation of natural succession by itself is not always enough to provide adequate control over stand composition. It is frequently necessary to supplement this approach by direct attack on the undesirable species. Cutting, poisoning, controlled burning, or regulated grazing may be used to restrict the competition and seed production of undesirable species. The desirable species can be favored in more positive fashion by planting them.

Crooked, misshapen, and defective trees (even though of valuable species) are apt to accumulate in the forest not under silvicultural treatment and retard the development of better individuals.

Control of stand density. Improperly managed forests are commonly too densely or too sparsely stocked with trees. If timber production is an objective, both extremes are detrimental and have the final effect of reducing the value of the crop produced. Deficient stocking is most prevalent in the early life of a stand and results from inadequate provision for regeneration; the unoccupied spaces are unproductive and trees in such stands are often too branchy to produce good timber. Excessively dense stocking causes the wood production of the stand to be distributed over so many individual trees that none can grow at the optimum rate. One should seek to provide and maintain just enough trees to stock the area properly at each stage of the life of the stand.

Restocking of unproductive areas. Without proper management many areas of land potentially suited to growth of forests tend to remain unstocked with trees. Fires, destructive logging, and ill-advised clearing of land for agriculture have already created many large, open areas that can be put back into immediate timber production only by planting or artificial seeding. Temporary, but nonetheless important, reductions in production can result from poor cutting practices that produce conditions unfavorable to immediate natural regeneration and resumption of growth.

Protection and salvage. In unmanaged stands, severe losses are commonly caused by such damaging agencies as insects, fungi, fire, and wind, as well as by the loss of merchantable trees through competition. Substantial increases in production may be achieved merely by salvaging material that might otherwise be lost. Proper control of damaging agencies can result in further increases in production. Forest protection often involves modification of silvicultural techniques in addition to more spectacular direct measures. Adequate protection should be extended to all forests, even the poorest, because fire and insect outbreaks developing in relatively worthless stands often spread into valuable adjacent areas.

Control of length of rotation. In any given situation there is an optimum size and age to which timber should be grown. Premature cutting is a common type of mismanagement in which trees are harvested before they have reached their optimum value. Trees allowed to grow beyond optimum size decline in value because of decay or difficulty of handling, or merely because further increase in value ceases to provide an acceptable rate of return on the investment represented by the value of the trees. Under proper management, the optimum size or age is carefully determined and the trees harvested accordingly. The period of years required to grow a crop of timber to this specified condition of either economic or natural maturity is known as the **rotation.** Proper regulation of stand density can shorten the rotation by making the crop trees grow to the desired size at an earlier age.

Facilitating the harvesting, management, and use of the forest. In the unmanaged forest timber, like gold in the hills, is where one finds it; the greater the amount extracted, the more difficult and expensive it becomes to find and extract more. In the managed forest it is possible to plan the growth of stands so that any use of them is on a more efficient, economical, and predictable basis. It becomes possible not only to produce good stands but also to have them so located and of such composition by species and age classes that the cost of transporting products from them is kept under control. The recent tendency of some forest products to be priced off the market has taken place in spite of the introduction of all kinds of labor-saving machinery for harvesting. It is due in part to the necessity of going to ever less accessible unmanaged forests to find timber of ever dwindling quality. The vicious cycle can be halted only by growing good stands on sites readily accessible to convenient harvesting.

Protection of site and indirect benefits. Proper management of forest lands often provides benefits that have little to do with production of wood. In fact, many forests are managed primarily for other purposes, although wood production is rarely inconsistent with these objectives. The techniques employed for improving the habitat of wildlife and grazing animals in the forest are essentially silvicultural. To a more limited extent, the same is true of measures designed to maintain the aesthetic beauty of forests used for recreation.

The relationship between silviculture and watershed management is coming to be of primary importance. Interception of precipitation by dense, untreated forests can, on the one hand, cause appreciable reductions in the water yield of an area. Excessively drastic treatment may, on the other hand, induce erosion or compaction of the soil which in turn reduces the capacity of the forest soil to store water. The resultant irregularities of stream flow and siltation can have a variety of disastrous consequences downstream. The damage done to the forest soil by erosion and compaction can also cause well-nigh irreparable reductions in the growing capacity of forest lands.

Silviculture as an Imitation of Nature

Silviculture is usually a combination of improvement upon and limitation of natural processes of forest growth. If knowledge of both economic and natural factors were perfect, it would always be possible to determine how far to move from the purely natural toward the degree of artificiality exemplified by intensive agriculture. Since one is not clairvoyant enough to know all the economic consequences of natural laws or to foretell all future fluctuations of the economy, there is bound to be uncertainty about how far to depart from nature. Some departure is certain; even a so-called wilderness area that is imperfectly protected from fire and used for limited recreational purposes ceases to be wholly natural. If the forest were created for the express benefit of man and natural processes reacted to his changing demands, it would be advisable and require no great silvicultural effort to follow nature closely.

Some silvicultural measures depart very far from natural precedent. These usually involve the introduction of exotic species or the creation of communities of native species unlike anything that might come into existence naturally. Departures of this sort cannot be condemned out of hand but should be viewed with reservations until they have been tested over long periods. Otherwise, most of the choices can be thought of in terms of the degree to which natural succession is accepted or arrested, pursued or reversed.

Preoccupation with natural plant succession has sometimes led to the erroneous assumption that sound forestry consists entirely of presiding passively over the majestic progress of succession. According to this philosophy, the primary goal of silviculture should be to encourage the development of stable, climax types that are held to be, by their very nature, superior to earlier successional stages. The importance of thorough knowledge of the natural succession on a given kind of site lies in the fact that it shows how fast and in what manner the composition of existing stands is being or may be altered by natural processes. With this information the forester can determine whether and by what means he can control the succession. The fact that he must know the course of natural succession does not indicate that he should necessarily allow it to proceed.

Economic factors ultimately decide the silvicultural policy to be followed on any given area; the objective is to operate so that the value of benefits derived from a forest exceeds by the widest possible margin the value of efforts expended. The most profitable forest type is not necessarily the one with the greatest potential growth or that which can be harvested at lowest cost. One must also consider the silvicultural costs of growing the crop and the prospective losses to the damaging agencies. In fact, it is usually the inroads of insects, fungi, and atmospheric agencies that ultimately show where silvicultural policy has run afoul of the laws of nature. The majority of the best choices are imitations of those natural communities, not necessarily or even commonly climax communities, that have grown well in nature.

It is not entirely safe to accept the success of modern agriculture as justification for highly artificial kinds of silviculture. The environment of a cultivated field is much more thoroughly modified and readily controlled than that of a forest stand. Furthermore, forest crops must survive winter and summer over a long period of years while most agricultural crops need survive only through a single growing season. One disastrous year harms the production of but one year with an annual crop but can destroy the accumulated production of many years in a stand of trees. Any silvicultural application of refinements borrowed from agriculture must be combined with *all* the kinds of measures appropriate to the intensity of agriculture imitated. Forestry can profitably borrow much more than it ever has from the science on which modern agriculture is based, but there is little place for uncritical imitation.

Many of the unpromising kinds of deviation from nature can be eliminated simply by exercise of knowledge and reason. The residue of uncertainty can be resolved only by trial and error, cautiously and objectively conducted. Any departure from nature that still looks good at the end of a rotation is probably sound.

The best approach to the matter is to determine which stage of successional development is most desirable in a given situation. In the Pacific Northwest, for example, the forester must often decide whether to perpetuate pure stands of Douglas-fir or allow them to be succeeded by western hemlock. In the Lake Region, he may have to choose between the pioneer aspen association and later stages like the spruce-fir association. In the South, he must determine whether to let old-field stands of loblolly pine revert to hardwoods. Several generalizations of wide, but not universal, application may be introduced at this point.

In the first place, the most valuable commercial species in any region tend to be relatively intolerant trees representative of the early or intermediate stages in natural succession. Such species as pines, Pacific Coast Douglas-fir, yellow-poplar, and ash definitely fall in this category. It is no coincidence that species of this kind are important commercially because they are the ones most likely to lose their lower branches through natural pruning. It is also significant that some of them are adapted to reproduce mostly after major disturbances that occur infrequently. If they are to survive from one major disturbance to another they must be long-lived; as a result they are likely to develop the economically desirable attributes of large size and resistance to decay or other relatively minor sources of damage. Late successional forest types, characterized by species such as hemlock, true firs, and beech, are frequently composed of branchy trees which produce less valuable wood. Because of their shade tolerance they can reproduce almost continuously so the ability of individuals to endure for long periods is not so crucial in the survival of the species. Of course, many pioneer species have even less capacity for individual survival; however, they usually exhibit good natural pruning and the necessity that they grow rapidly to seed-bearing age is an economically desirable attribute.

Natural succession proceeds most rapidly and vigorously on the better sites, that is, on soils that are both moist and well aerated. Here it is sometimes impossible to resist natural succession without expensive silvicultural treatments. Furthermore, such sites are, at any stage of succession, hospitable to the growth of such a large assortment of species that silvicultural treatment becomes complicated and difficult. These considerations have the paradoxical effect of making silviculture most profitable on sites of intermediate quality where uncomplicated stands can be maintained without strenuous effort. In fact, on poor sites it may occasionally be virtually impossible for succession to proceed beyond an intermediate stage, which is sometimes referred to as a **physiographic climax.** For example, stands of both jack and red pine occasionally represent valuable physiographic climaxes on certain dry, sandy soils in the Lake Region.

It has also been claimed that late successional types may be more resistant to, and more cheaply protected from, fire, insects, fungi, and atmospheric agencies than earlier stages. This advantage results more from the diversity of species and age classes in a climax type than it does from position in the successional scale. Similar advantages can prevail in mixed stands with a variety of age classes that are still typical of earlier successional stages.

The point is often advanced that natural communities are in a stable and favorable equilibrium with the physical and biological environment. Actually any kind of stand is in dynamic equilibrium with its environment. Perfect stability and complete favorability do not exist, so one must think in terms of relative degrees of each quality. For example, the balance achieved by long-continued natural processes, operating more or less at random, is not necessarily more favorable to the trees than to the organisms that feed upon them. The more artificial equilibrium produced by prudent silviculture is likely to be less stable but ought to be more favorable from the standpoint of the integrated effect of all economic factors relevant to the particular circumstances. If the dynamic equilibrium created by treatment ultimately balances at a condition of economic disaster, the silviculture was hardly prudent.

The naturalistic doctrine of silviculture did not arise from any clearly demonstrated disadvantages of early stages of natural forest succession. It developed largely from disappointments with attempts to create unnatural types, particularly with exotic species or those not indigenous to the sites involved. The most extreme manifestation of this viewpoint is, in some respects, merely an unwarranted extension of a sound observation.

The classic example of violation of the ecological principles of silviculture is the widely cited and frequently misinterpreted "Saxon spruce sickness" which appeared in the lowlands of east central Germany early in this century. In this region the financial charms of spruce pulpwood had induced foresters to convert degraded stands of hardwoods to pure plantations of Norway spruce. The first crops were excellent, but successive crops commonly grew less and less vigorously. All kinds of explanations were proposed, and a widespread impression developed that pure stands of conifers in particular and tampering with natural succession in general were universally responsible for "deterioration of the soil." However, a thorough analysis of the difficulty [Krauss et al., 1939] has shown it to be neither mysterious nor the basis for sweeping generalizations.

In the first place, spruce was introduced into the lowlands from the moister and cooler climate of neighboring mountains. Furthermore, the decline in vigor occurred only on very heavy, clay soils. After the old root canals of the hardwoods had closed, internal soil drainage became very poor. The soils were then so moist and poorly aerated in the spring that the spruce became even more shallow rooted than normally. Therefore, during the summer, when the low rainfall was further reduced in effectiveness by interception, the spruce suffered from drought. The situation grew progressively worse as more of the old root canals became closed. In other words, this particular difficulty was not mysterious and was confined to soils rich in clay; it could not even be said that planting of spruce was out of the question on all sites in the locality.

The famous experience in Saxony has an important lesson for foresters everywhere but not to the extent that one may say that "they have found in Europe that repeated crops of pure conifers cause site deterioration." What it does show is that proper aeration of the soil is necessary for good growth of trees and that shallow-rooted species allow internal drainage to deteriorate on soils with a high clay content. The little leaf disease of shortleaf pine on badly eroded clay soils on the Piedmont Plateau of the Southeast (Zak, 1961) is a more spectacular example of the same sort of thing in American experience.

The important thing to note about this illustration is that such problems can eventually be explained in terms of definite ecological factors. It is far better to base practice on available knowledge than to ignore it and proceed on a mystic philosophy founded on vaguely suspected influences of unknown agencies. Where lack of knowledge hampers practice there is clear need for the critical observations essential to both formal research and intelligent practice. Knowledge is, after all, a cheap commodity when compared to the values wasted when operations are conducted in ignorance.

The Field of Silvicultural Practice

The subject matter of the practice of silviculture is logically divided into three parts defined as:

Methods of reproduction, treatment of the stand during the period of regeneration or establishment. (See Fig. 1-1.)

In every stand the time comes, sooner or later, when it is desired to harvest all or a portion of the timber and to replace the trees removed with others of a new generation. The act of replacing old trees, either naturally or artificially, is called **regeneration** or **reproduction** and these two words, which are entirely synonymous in this usage, also refer to the new growth that develops. **Advance repro-**

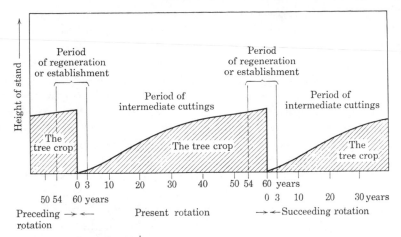

Fig. 1-1. The relationship between the period of regeneration and the period of intermediate cuttings for a sequence of even-aged stands managed on a 60-year rotation according to the shelterwood system.

duction or **regeneration** is that which appears before any special measures are undertaken to establish new growth. **Reproduction** or **regeneration cuttings** are made with the two purposes of removing the old trees and creating environmental conditions favorable for establishment of reproduction. The period over which they extend is known as the **regeneration** or **reproduction period.** Reproduction cuttings range from one to several in number, and the regeneration period may extend from less than 5 years to more than 50 years. In truly uneven-aged stands, handled under the selection system, regeneration is always underway in some part of the stands. The period of regeneration begins when preparatory measures are initiated and does not end until young trees have become established in acceptable numbers and are fully adjusted to the new environment. The **rotation** is the period during which a single crop or generation is allowed to grow.

Intermediate cuttings, treatment of the stand during that portion of the rotation not included in the period of regeneration. (See Fig. 1-1.)

After a new stand is established, a long period ensues during which the crop grows and passes through various stages until it is mature and ready, in its turn, to be harvested and replaced by a succeeding generation. The various cuttings made during development from the reproduction stage to maturity are termed **intermediate cuttings.**

They have as their object the improvement of the existing stand, regulation of growth, and provision of early financial returns, without any effort directed at regeneration.

Intermediate cuttings that are aimed primarily at controlling the growth of stands through adjustments in stand density are called **thinnings.** Those conducted to regulate the composition by species and improve the quality of very young stands are **release cuttings;** cuttings made in older stands for the same purposes are **improvement cuttings;** those that involve only the branches are **prunings.**

Those kinds of intermediate cutting that involve an outright investment are sometimes referred to as **stand improvement.** Many kinds of intermediate cutting can now be accomplished without actually cutting down trees. Therefore, usage of the word "cutting" is now often correct only if viewed in a traditional and figurative sense.

Protection of the stand against injuries of many kinds. The more important are fire, insects, fungi, animals, and atmospheric agencies. This subject leads into various specialized fields, such as fire control, entomology, pathology, and zoology. Protection should be as much a part of applied silviculture as harvesting, regenerating, and tending the crop. The details of successful silvicultural practice for a given species are often determined by the requirements necessary to reduce injuries. Where protective measures fail or are inadequate it is sometimes desirable to conduct **salvage cuttings** to recover the values represented by damaged trees or stands.

The Role of Cutting in Silviculture

The techniques of silviculture proceed on the basic assumption that the vegetation on any site normally tends to extend itself aggressively to occupy the available growing space. The limit on growing space is usually set by the availability of light from the sun, of water and inorganic nutrients from the soil, or carbon dioxide from the atmosphere. In a general way the available amount of growing space is set by the most limiting of these factors, although an abundant supply of one factor can partially offset deficiency of another.

If the vegetation nearly fills the growing space, the only way that the forest can be altered or controlled is by killing trees and other plants. In reproduction cutting this is done to provide room for the establishment of new trees; in intermediate cutting, to promote the growth of desirable trees already in existence. Paradoxical as it may seem, and repugnant as it may be to certain influential segments of public opinion, useful forests are created and maintained chiefly by the temporary destruction of judiciously chosen parts of them. The axe and other means of killing trees can be used for the construction as well as the destruction of the forest. The importance of cutting as a means of harvesting wood for human use should not obscure its role as the major means by which forests are established and tended.

Preoccupation with the trees should not cause one to overlook the lesser vegetation and the animals which are a part of the forest community. The animals ultimately depend on the vegetation for food and thus do not compete directly for the growing space. However, whether they be defoliating insects or carnivores that feed on herbivorous mammals, they can exert a major influence on the nature of the vegetation even as they are, in turn, controlled by it. The fauna and nonarborescent vegetation of the forest are as likely to respond to cutting as the trees.

Effect of cutting on stand structure. Cuttings affect the forest outwardly by determining the arrangement of the trees which are left standing and that of the new trees which appear. This arrangement is known as the **stand form** or **structure** and is best indicated by the profile of the tree crowns. The most important criterion of stand form is age distribution, three general types of which may be recognized: even-aged, stands with two age classes, and uneven-aged. In an **even-aged stand** (Fig. 1-2) all trees are the same age or at least of the same age class; a stand is considered even-aged if the difference in age between the oldest and youngest trees does not exceed 20 per cent of the length of the rotation. An **uneven-aged stand** contains at least three age classes intermingled intimately on the same area. **Stands with two age classes** represent an intermediate category. All gradations of age distribution may be found in nature or created by cuttings designed to make way for new age classes.

Distinction should be made between balanced and irregular uneven-aged stands (Fig. 1-2). A **balanced uneven-aged stand** consists of three or more different age classes, each of which occupy an approximately equal area; the age classes are also spaced at uniform intervals all the way from newly established reproduction to trees near rotation age. Such stands, once created, function as self-contained, sustained-yield units. **Irregular uneven-aged stands** do not contain all the age classes necessary to ensure that trees will arrive at rotation age at short intervals indefinitely. Uneven-aged virgin stands and stands which have been culled over without plan are almost always irregular in age distribution. In fact, irregular uneven-aged stands are common and may be highly desirable, so long as they are recognized and treated for what they are.

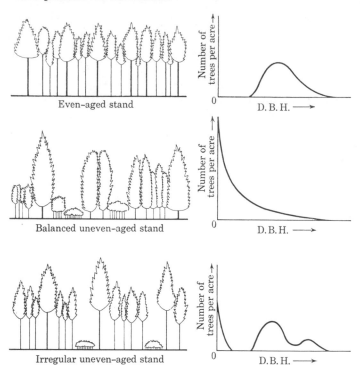

Fig. 1-2. Typical examples of three different kinds of age distribution, showing appearance of stands in vertical cross section and corresponding graphs of diameter distribution in terms of number of trees per acre.

   The profile of a stand is a good criterion of age distribution because trees of the same age grow in height at roughly the same rate, provided site conditions are uniform; those that do not keep pace are suppressed and disappear.   Therefore an even-aged stand tends to be almost smooth on top.   An uneven-aged stand is distinctly irregular in height; the greater the number of age classes, the more uneven the top of the canopy.   This is not, however, true of very old uneven-aged stands in many virgin forests.   Growth in height becomes so slow in old trees that irregularities in height of uneven-aged stands gradually smooth out as the trees approach a common level.   Actually relatively even-aged virgin forests of intolerant species are not uncommon; most of them, however, have occasional patches of reproduction where openings have developed in the old even-aged stands.
   The diameter growth of trees is more variable than their growth

in height.   Therefore, the trees in an even-aged stand are nowhere near as uniform in diameter as they are in height.   If one plots the number of trees in each diameter class over diameter for a given even-aged stand, the distribution approximates the normal, bell-shaped curve (Fig. 1-2).   The continual loss of small trees through suppression accounts for the typically abrupt slope of the left-hand side of the curve.   It should be borne in mind that even-aged stands always contain a wide range of diameter classes; age distribution of a stand cannot be determined merely from the *range* of diameter classes present.

Uneven-aged stands are composed essentially of small even-aged groups of different ages; the distribution of diameters in each group also fits a bell-shaped curve.   However, as each little even-aged group grows older the number of trees in it declines, rapidly at first and more slowly later on, until the point may even be reached where but 1 tree remains from 100 or more.   Therefore, the composite diameter distribution curve for a balanced uneven-aged stand (Fig. 1-2) is "J-shaped," if each age class occupies the same area.

If the age classes of an irregular uneven-aged stand differ widely in age, they are revealed as humps on the diameter distribution curve. The diameter distribution of each even-aged component broadens with age and will also be modified if the age class is composed of different species that grow at varying rates.

When direct determinations of age are made from counts of annual rings, allowance should be made for the fact that some long-lived, tolerant species may start as suppressed advance growth beneath older trees.   In such instances, the **effective age** is more important than the **chronological age** and equals the period since the trees were released. In other words, any core of fine growth rings around the pith is best discounted in assigning a tree to its proper age class.

Differences in age distribution are most easily recognized in pure stands and in mixed stands composed of very similar species.   Mixtures of dissimilar species can be very complicated; however, they often exhibit a **stratified** structure in which the species of most rapid height growth form the upper layer of the canopy and those of slowest juvenile height growth form the lower layers.   Ordinarily the uppermost species are least tolerant of shade and those of the lower stories are the most tolerant.   This kind of structure is most easily recognized if the mixed stands are also even-aged because the various strata are then most likely to be continuous.   Many of the mixed forests of North America, of both hardwoods and softwoods, are stratified in greater or lesser degree.

Effect of cutting on growing stock. Cutting not only controls the composition and form of forest stands but also the relationship between trees reserved for growth and the amount of growth available for cutting. It is important to understand the long-term, cumulative effect of cutting operations in building, or degrading, a forest.

Timber growing is one of the few kinds of creative processes in which both product and productive machinery are the same thing (Heiberg, 1945). The wood of the stem cannot be removed without destroying the machinery that produced it. A clear distinction must, therefore, be drawn between the trees that must be left to produce more wood and the surplus trees that can be regarded as product and harvested.

The trees that must be reserved somewhere in the forest to continue production are the **growing stock** or **forest capital.** The volume of wood that is grown in the future depends on the quantity and condition of growing stock that is maintained. Cuttings regulate the amount of this growing stock and its distribution within individual stands or among the varous stands that comprise the forest. The regulation of growing stock is of most crucial importance in silviculture when partial cuttings are applied within stands.

Relationship with Utilization

Any silviculture directed at the production of timber crops is pointless unless these crops can be harvested efficiently and utilized profitably. Preoccupation with the expensive processes of harvesting and utilization has, however, commonly led to reduction of forest productivity, which is the ultimate foundation of all forest industries. For this reason, it is better to formulate silvicultural procedures aimed at the development of highly productive stands and then modify the actual practices to meet nonsilvicultural problems than to proceed in the reverse order of logic.

Silviculture is expedited by advances in wood technology and harvesting procedures that enlarge opportunities for use of inferior trees. It is indeed argued that there will soon be no purpose in growing good trees because it will become entirely feasible to grind up wood of any species, size, and quality and reconstitute it into any kind of product that might be desired. Under these circumstances, the part of silviculture concerned with wood production might be reduced to such minimal measures as those necessary to grow sprouting hardwoods on short rotations; the most difficult and important problems of forestry might even become the management of watershed, wildlife, and recreational resources.

These things may come to pass, but there are ample reasons for doubting that they will or that the general economy would benefit from such developments. It would be a dereliction of duty on the part of the forestry profession if it allowed the timber resource and economy to drift into such impoverished circumstances. The products of future forests will be determined to an increasing extent by the way foresters manage the stands. The kinds of trees that are available in the forest inevitably limit the kinds of forest industries that can exist. The forestry profession is not completely at the mercy of economic trends in wood utilization because these trends depend fully as much on the condition of the forests as on anything else.

The process of collecting timber and transporting it to points of manufacture from widely dispersed locations is inherently inefficient. This handicap of forest industry is not going to be reduced by dealing with small, poor, or scattered trees. Furthermore, the possibility of *growing* timber profitably is much greater if the attributes of size, strength, and shape are mainly built into the growing wood rather than created by subsequent processing of fractionated wood. Otherwise profitable timber growing depends mainly on the existence of chronic deficiencies in the supply of raw wood which are still remote as far as North America is concerned. The uncertainties of the future can be faced most confidently with well-stocked stands of reasonably large trees of sufficient quality to be versatile as to use.

Relationship with Forest Management and Economics

The decisions that are made in silvicultural practice are based fully as much on economic considerations as upon the natural factors that govern the forest. There is no neatly defined point at which the two can be separated even for purposes of convenience in academic instruction.

Recognition of economic limitations substantially reduces the number of alternatives of silvicultural treatment that might logically be considered in the absence of such restrictions. Considerations involving such things as income taxes, mill requirements, and alternative investments in other parts of an enterprise may have a powerful effect on the silvicultural treatment of particular stands. Even though intelligent application of silviculture can make a positive contribution to the task, the solution of these problems is not really part of silviculture. They are instead dealt with in the field of forest management which is concerned both with the organization of collections of stands into integrated forests and the business aspects of the forestry enterprises thus created. Economics, as a social science applied in forestry, impinges at all levels from the consideration of the world forest economy down through the economics of the single forest enterprise to silvicultural attempts to maximize net returns from single trees.

It is important to note that silviculture and forest management are interdependent and not parallel, alternative approaches to the same problem.   Silviculture, because of its dominant concern for efficient application of the natural sciences, is not any less "practical" than forest management, with its tendency toward preoccupation with economic considerations.   No management plan is better than the silviculture it stipulates or any silvicultural treatment than the economic results it produces.

The stand and the forest.   The essential unit of silviculture is the little world of the **stand,** which is a contiguous group of trees sufficiently uniform in species composition, arrangement of age classes, and condition to be a homogeneous and distinguishable unit.   Forest management is primarily concerned with the **forest,** in a special sense meaning a collection of stands administered as an integrated unit. The forest, or some major sub-division thereof, is usually the smallest unit for which one can draw up logical plans designed to resolve the conflicting economic objectives and limitations implicit in any management program.

The distinction between stand and forest is important in connection with the regulation of the cut from the forest, which is one aspect of management.   The objective of this type of planning usually is achievement of a sustained, annual yield of products.   The forest, and not the stand, is the unit from which this sustained yield is sought. Management determines the volume of timber which should be removed from the whole forest in a given period; silvicultural principles should govern the sequence and manner in which individual stands are cut to produce the required volume.   The tendency to treat large groups of dissimilar stands as if they conformed to a uniform, hypothetical average should be studiously avoided.   However, an arbitrary decision must always be made regarding the minimum size of stand which can be regarded as a separate entity.

The size and number of stands recognized depends on the intensity of practice, the value of the stands, and the diversity of site conditions.   Where intensive forestry is feasible, stands as small as one acre may be recognized; under crude, extensive practice the same forest might be divided into units no smaller than several hundred acres.   The best policy is to recognize the smallest stands that can be conveniently delineated on the type maps used in administration.

Even after type maps have been put on paper the forester must still deal with variations that actually exist within each stand. From the technical standpoint, each portion is best treated separately, although acceptance of too many variations would eventually create a mosaic of conditions which would be awkward for both logging and administration.

Silviculture and the long-term economic viewpoint. The economic time-scale of forestry is so vast and unique that many investors regard it as a form of endeavor that is hardly economic at all. There is scarcely any part of forestry in which this issue is faced more squarely than in silviculture, especially when investments in establishing or treating young stands are involved. As a result there is an irrational tendency to evade the issue by condemning silviculture as an uneconomic and unessential part of forestry. The conflict is not between "silviculture" and "economics," but between the long-term economic viewpoint of forestry itself and the customary short-term outlook on financial matters.

The holding of land for future production of wood crops or other benefits involves silviculture even if nothing more is done than to let nature take its course and to harvest trees occasionally. Ownership incurs costs and these constitute investments in the future even if nothing is invested in treatments to increase future production. The question is not whether an owner is investing in silviculture because he already is, even if unintentionally; it is whether he is using his capacity for long-term investments in silviculture and other parts of his forest enterprise to optimum advantage.

Thoughts about silviculture are often clouded by regarding it as more of a moral and ethical matter than it really is (Muelder, 1960). The silviculture that an owner may cause to be practiced is simply one of the vehicles for whatever mixture of moral, ethical, social, and economic viewpoints he adopts. Silviculture becomes confused with morality because it is more likely than most other parts of forestry to require clear acceptance of a long-term economic viewpoint which, in turn, may erroneously be taken as purely a phenomenon of ethics rather than of economics.

It is, for example, common to characterize as "good" silviculture those programs of treatment that involve large investments in cultural measures and reserved growing stock. In this pattern of thought, the levels of silviculture grade on down to those termed "poor" in which immediate returns are paramount. Where the economic situation will not support the so-called "good" silviculture, this kind of thought can lead to the conclusion that "fair" or "poor" silviculture is really better than the "good." If one must speak of "good" silviculture it would seem better to think of it as that most skillful technique of stand management that best met the combination of natural and economic factors involved. In unfavorable circumstances, this might be a rather crude brand of silviculture.

Funds are rarely available for all the silvicultural work likely to prove profitable, so the forester must ensure that those which are invested are expended on the most remunerative lines of work possible. In any situation it is logical to apply first those treatments which will yield the greatest increase in value of benefits per dollar of investment. One then adds additional treatments of successively lower ratio of benefit to cost until the cumulative margin between the value of all benefits and all costs reaches a maximum (Fedkiw, 1960). This procedure is more easily described than done, and it requires successful intuition in addition to careful factual analysis. It is rare that this sequence of successive investments has actually been pursued to a point even close to that of maximum long-term profit. For example, Worrell (1956), in a comparison of the predicted monetary yields and various levels of investment in growing pines in the Georgia Piedmont, found that the most intensive and expensive kind of silviculture envisioned in his study would probably fall short of the level of maximum profit.

The first stage in the evolution of silvicultural practice (Spurr, 1960) is that in which continued production is actively sought but not to the extent that owners make cash investments in it. This "no-investment" silviculture places emphasis on treatments that can be accomplished by removing merchantable timber without significant increase in harvesting costs. Some forests are sufficiently easy to control that treatments made on this basis give reasonably good results. This kind of silviculture is practiced over wide areas and will doubtless continue to be for a long time. It rarely makes the ownership of forests very attractive financially. The idea of taking values out of the forest without really reinvesting anything in future production has a powerful appeal. It almost completely dominated American silviculture for decades and there are still many instances in which it is consciously or unconsciously regarded as the only feasible economic viewpoint about the treatment of forests.

Orderly policies of long-term investment in silviculture emerge if economic conditions and natural productivity are favorable, provided that adequate experience has accumulated. The kind and amount of investment is limited only by the economic law of diminishing returns. The actual amount expended on this kind of silviculture varies widely but is not likely to be trivial. The main characteristic is that long-term investments are not regarded with skepticism and are carried to whatever level is found to be adequately profitable.

The application of different policies regarding silvicultural investments is something that varies in time and place in complicated fashion. If the existence, cause, and logic of this pattern are not recognized both the application and analysis of silvicultural practice become hopelessly confused. If one becomes too much accustomed to one policy it becomes difficult to understand any other or to change to another when and where circumstances warrant.

Variations in intensity of practice. The amount of effort expended on the treatment and care of stands, that is, the **intensity** of silviculture, varies widely, depending chiefly on economic circumstances. The converse of **intensive** silviculture is **extensive** silviculture. The degree of intensity is usually estimated in terms of such things as the amount of money invested in cultural treatment, the frequency and severity of cuttings during the rotation, and the amount of concern accorded to future returns relative to immediate returns.

The appropriate intensity of silviculture varies with accessibility, markets, site quality, objective of management, and nature of ownership. The proper level often must be chosen for each stand because the application of a single degree of intensity will not give optimum results throughout a given forest, unless it is exceedingly small and uniform. The more favorable is the combined economic effect of all factors, the higher is the appropriate level of intensity of silviculture. The place for crude, extensive silviculture is found in remote areas, on poor sites, or where owners are not willing or able to make more than minimum investments.

In the past, American forests have been exploited in such a manner that the poorest and most ill-treated stands are often found on the best sites and in the most accessible areas, such as those along permanent roads. This situation, which is the reverse of that which should apply, results from the fact that the best and most conveniently located stands have been exploited first, most heavily, and most frequently. Ultimately silviculture of the highest intensity should be practiced in many of these situations rather than in the remote areas where the best forests now often grow. Permanent roads and good markets for a diversity of forest products do not automatically ensure optimum practice, but they are essential to intensive management.

The intensity of silviculture depends in large measure on the nature and objectives of ownership. Variations in the species and sizes of trees desired may necessitate different procedures on adjoining lands that are fundamentally similar. Stability or longevity of ownership also controls intensity of silviculture. Large corporations and public agencies, which are relatively immortal, are in a far better position to practice intensive silviculture than individuals or small corporations of uncertain stability.

The intensity of silviculture often depends on the extent to which the owner processes the wood grown in his forest. The closer he carries the product to the ultimate consumer, the greater is his ability to capture the values added by increases in intensity of practice in the woods. Prices for **stumpage,** that is, standing trees, rarely reflect all the values added to the product by silvicultural measures to improve the quality of wood. Therefore, the owner who is not in a position to do more than sell stumpage may not be able to practice silviculture as intensive as that suitable for owners who also harvest, manufacture, or sell the final product. This relationship is, however, modified by ability and willingness to make long-term investments. For example, public forestry agencies usually confine their operations to producing stumpage; they may, however, practice intensive silviculture without great concern for profit on their investments in order to discharge their long-term responsibilities to the national economy.

Financial analysis of silviculture. The financial techniques employed in measuring and predicting silvicultural accomplishment are part of forest management, valuation, and economics. A preliminary understanding of them is necessary because, both as detailed methods and as concrete expressions of economic viewpoints, they are indispensable to sound choices among the numerous silvicultural measures that might be applied in particular instances.

The returns from silvicultural treatment aimed at wood production are most objectively assessed in terms of the increase in stumpage values that is attributable to treatment. Where the silviculture is directed at production of benefits such as wildlife, recreation, and control of watersheds, the values are usually so intangible that the whole analysis tends to be highly intuitive.

One of the most peculiar and important problems of the financial analysis of silviculture results from the fact that many of the benefits are not reaped until many years after the investments in treatment are made. The act of waiting has a certain kind of cost so decisions between alternatives of treatment must be based on some means of comparing not only the values created by various treatments but the costs of waiting for varying periods to obtain the benefits. For example, it may be necessary to decide whether to invest $1.00 in a planting operation that will yield $20.00 in stumpage 50 years hence or in a precommercial thinning that will increase the value of wood harvested 10 years from now by $3.00.

The methods of comparing such differing alternatives employ the device of compound interest in the same sense used in connection with accounts in savings banks. If the appropriate rate of compound interest is known, it is possible to estimate both present values of future benefits and the future costs represented by present expenditures. Usually the procedure is to reduce all estimates of future costs and benefits to the present time so that various alternatives of procedure can be compared on the same basis. The rate of interest used depends on the circumstances, including the estimated risks and the compound-interest return available to the owner from alternative investments.

The following example, drawn from tables like those in textbooks like that of Chapman and Meyer (1947), illustrates the increase in the value of a $1.00 investment with time at 4 and 8 per cent compound interest:

Time, years	20	40	60	80
Value at 4%	$2.19	$4.80	$10.52	$23.05
Value at 8%	$4.66	$21.72	$101.26	$471.96

In other words, if one demands a 4 per cent return on the investment of $1.00 in planting made now, he is expecting a gross return of $10.52 on it 60 years hence. If the ultimate return *was* $10.52, it would be worth $1.00 to him now. To take a purely hypothetical example, if the $1.00 were invested in pruning rather than planting and yielded an increase in stumpage value of $101.26 at the end of 60 years, this would represent a return of 8 per cent and would clearly be a better investment. If $1.00 were invested in release cutting and produced an increase in value of $21.72 at 40 years, it would also represent an 8 per cent return and would have the same **present worth** as the pruning investment. However, it would be the better of the two alternatives because an investor would demand an indefinably larger interest rate on a 60-year investment than on a 40-year investment.

The techniques just illustrated find their only real utility in guiding choices between alternative long-term investments such as those involved in silviculture. They are not used in conventional accounting; in practice, silvicultural costs are usually charged against current income. The idea also has the defect of leading to the naive impression that it is actually possible to invest money at high rates of compound interest and effortlessly watch the funds mushroom decade after decade.

The delay between silvicultural treatments and their financial fruition is such that anything that can shorten the delay is beneficial. The inevitable existence of such delay forces diligent search for the modest inputs of effort that yield large benefits. Fortunately the natural productivity of the forest is plastic enough to respond to gentle guidance. However, it would be most remarkable if silviculture were the unique form of economic activity which yielded maximum profits with little or no outright investment. Owners of some forests may indeed find that the minimum costs of protection and other carrying charges exceed the value of benefits derived from such management.

Silviculture in Application

The practice of silviculture does not consist of rigid adherence to any set of simple or detailed rules of procedure. For example, there is no part of this book that could be safely used as a manual of operations. Many of the techniques of cutting are described in simplified form shorn of the myriad of refinements and modifications necessary to accommodate the special circumstances and local variations encountered in practice. Each procedure described is merely an illustration designed to demonstrate the application of a set of treatments designed to meet a uniform set of circumstances. Even though uniform stands have important advantages that make them worthy of creation, the stands encountered in the field may lack uniformity and thus call for variation in treatment.

Any consideration of silviculture covers a variety of treatments wider than is likely to be practiced in any locality at a particular time. In times when the forests of a locality are all immature, silvicultural practice may be limited to intermediate cuttings and anything connected with regeneration may be limited to the reforestation of vacant areas. In areas where it is customary to secure regeneration by planting, the forester may regard methods of natural regeneration only as matters of intellectual exercise. Where attention is for the time being concentrated on replacing old-growth forests with regeneration, consideration of intermediate cuttings may seem quite unessential. At times and places where economic conditions support only the crudest kind of extensive silviculture, intensive treatments may seem visionary indeed.

The subject matter of this book reflects a wide variation in intensity of silvicultural practice because an attempt is made to describe all known techniques that seem applicable in any significant forest area of North America within the foreseeable future. The procedures characteristic of the more intensive kinds of silviculture cannot be described as briefly as those associated with extensive silviculture and so get more attention. This does not mean that a management program must include a long series of different treatments to be silviculture. Some of the most astute silviculture is the kind conducted at low intensity in which much is accomplished with a very limited amount of treatment.

The student forester interested in only one particular region cannot safely restrict his attention to the kind of silviculture currently practiced there. Foresters move, times change, and ideas from other places are often as fruitful as the indigenous ones.

There are many places where the impractical of twenty years ago is now the routine, and may prove to be the naive and inadequate of two decades hence. Because of cutting and growth, the forests of a locality often change at the same rate and such change calls forth new methods of treatment. This is especially true in North America where the forests of most localities tend to be uniform either because they have been scarcely touched or because they were all cut over in a short space of time. This book may seem to contain more techniques and ideas than a forester might need in his professional lifetime. While some may go unused or go quickly out of date, there are really only enough to provide a starter.

It is not enough for the forester to know what to do and how to do it. The important questions in silviculture, whether they involve matters of natural or social science, start with the word "why." As in other applied sciences, action proceeds from the knowledge represented by the answer, or sometimes the merest inkling of an answer. The forester finds as many solutions in the woods as he finds in the printed word or from institutions of education or research, but he must learn to ask himself the questions that generate the solutions.

REFERENCES

Chapman, H. H., and W. H. Meyer. 1947. *Forest valuation.* McGraw-Hill, New York.

Fedkiw, J. 1960. Capital budgeting for acquisition and development of timberlands. *In:* Z. W. White (Ed.). Financial management of large forest ownerships. *Yale Univ. School of Forestry Bul.* 66. Pp. 1–45.

Heiberg, S. O. 1945. "Is forestry unique?" *J. Forestry* 43:294–295.

Krauss, G., et al. 1939. Standortsgemässe Durchführung der Abkehr von der Fichtenwirtschaft im nordwestsächsischen Niederland. *Tharandter forstliches Jahrb.* 90:481–715.

Muelder, D. W. 1959. How to make progress in California silviculture. *J. Forestry* 57:323–328.

Spurr, S. H. 1960. Progress in silviculture. *In:* H. Clepper and A. B. Meyer (Eds.). *American forestry, six decades of growth.* Society of American Foresters, Washington. Pp. 65–82.

Worrell, A. C. 1956. Optimum intensity of forest land use on a regional basis. *Forest Sci.* 2:199–240.

Zak, B. 1961. Aeration and other soil factors affecting southern pines as related to littleleaf disease. *USDA Tech. Bull.* 1248.

PART I

INTERMEDIATE CUTTING

CHAPTER 2

Thinnings and their effect on growth and yield

Cuttings made in immature stands in order to stimulate the growth of the trees that remain and to increase the total yield of useful material from the stand are termed **thinnings.** Surplus trees are removed for the purpose of concentrating the potential wood production of the stand on a limited number of selected trees. The total yield of the stand is augmented largely by the utilization of trees that would ultimately die of suppression; however, the value and utility of the final crop may be increased by virtue of the fact that the favored trees grow more rapidly than they would without thinning. The fundamental objectives of thinning are, in other words, (1) to redistribute the growth potential of the stand to optimum advantage and (2) to utilize all the merchantable material produced by the stand during the rotation.

The direct objective of thinning is the regulation of the distribution of growing space for the advantage of the existing crop; its objective is not the creation of vacancies for the establishment of a new crop. Simultaneous pursuit of both objectives often results neither in good regeneration nor in fullest realization of the potentialities of the present stand. However, regeneration is usually the most difficult step in silviculture. Consequently thinnings should be so conducted that the ultimate process of regeneration is facilitated or at least not rendered unduly difficult.

New growth may appear as a result of thinnings or even beneath stands that have had no treatment whatsoever. However, such new growth is not likely to be useful unless the desirable species are sufficiently tolerant to predominate in the understory. The new growth appearing during the period of intermediate cuttings often consists of shrubs and herbs or of arborescent species more tolerant and less valuable than those desired in the new crop. Since the existing stand must occupy the site completely if highest production is to be attained, the development of an understory represents a departure from the ideal objective of thinning. Therefore, thinnings should ordinarily be conducted so as to restrict rather than encourage this development. In any event, the gaps created in the crown canopy by proper thinnings are so small that they close before any of the plants of the understory have an opportunity to initiate rapid, sustained growth in height.

The general principles of thinning have been formulated for application in even-aged aggregations of trees. Although it is easiest to think in terms of even-aged stands, these principles also apply to the even-aged **groups** that make up the immature components of uneven-aged stands.

Natural Development of the Stand

The basis of the theory followed in thinning is found in the natural development of the stand. The typical stand starts life with a relatively large number of small trees, usually thousands or tens of thousands per acre. The number of trees decreases as they grow larger, at first rapidly but more slowly with each passing decade. When the stand is ready for reproduction cuttings, it has been reduced to a few hundred trees per acre or to even less than one hundred.

This continual diminution in numbers is primarily the result of a rigorous natural selection and is the expression of one of the most fundamental biological laws of silviculture. Those trees that are most vigorous or best adapted to the environment are most likely to survive the intense competition for light, moisture, and nutrients. However, the process is not entirely a steady and progressive selection of the fittest because it may be interrupted or temporarily reversed by natural accidents that eliminate trees purely at random. Furthermore, the individuals that are the fittest from the standpoint of natural selection are not necessarily the best from the forester's viewpoint.

Growth in height is the most critical factor in competition, although those trees that increase most rapidly in height are almost invariably the largest in all dimensions, especially in size of crown. As the weaker trees are crowded by their taller associates their crowns become increasingly misshapen and restricted in size; unless freed by the random accidents mentioned in the previous paragraph, such trees gradually become overtopped and ultimately die. In this constant attrition the weaker trees are progressively submerged and the strongest forge ahead. The process is known as **differentiation into crown classes**; four standard crown classes are recognized (Figs. 2-1 and 2-2).

Very few trees ever recover a dominant position after they have fallen behind in the race for the sky (Guillebaud and Hummel, 1949; Warrack, 1952). Once the crown of a tree has been reduced in size by the competition of its more vigorous neighbors it cannot always be restored to a dominant position by cultural treatment. Therefore, the most common policy followed in thinnings is to encourage the growth of the leading trees rather than to resuscitate those that have fallen behind.

The competition between trees for places in the crown canopy is readily visible and uncomplicated. The corresponding competition for growing space in the soil is also important, but more intricate and exceedingly difficult to observe. The roots can wander in quite devious patterns and form intraspecific root grafts. Through these root grafts adjacent trees can either nourish each other mutually or engage in subtle kinds of parasitism the patterns and results of which are obscure. Such effects become very significant if soil moisture or

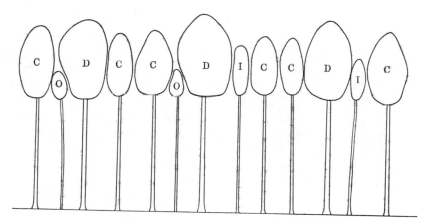

Fig. 2-1. The relative positions of trees in the different crown classes in an absolutely even-aged, pure stand that has not been thinned. The letters, D, C, I, and O, stand for dominant, codominant, intermediate, and overtopped crown classes.

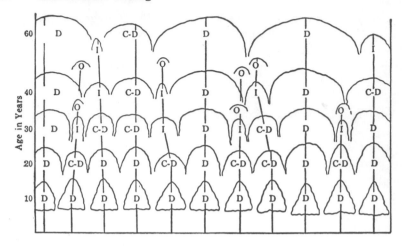

Fig. 2-2. The differentiation of a stand into crown classes with advancing age, illustrating the submergence, as a result of the struggle for existence, of trees that were initially dominant.

nutrients are in short supply. Usually competition for space in the crown canopy is more decisive because the foliage is the source of the raw material and energy on which the extension and activity of the roots depend.

The struggle for existence in dense, unthinned stands is so fierce as to reduce the growth and vigor of all the trees in the stand. Even those that express dominance and go on to become the largest and most vigorous survivors usually develop live crowns that are too short and narrow in proportion to the total height of the trees. The resultant reduction in diameter growth is not entirely disadvantageous because such trees are likely to be well pruned and may contain a high proportion of clear lumber. The severe competition also causes the stems to be straighter and more nearly cylindrical than they might be had the growing space been less restricted.

In the practice of thinning these advantages of competition between trees are at least partly preserved by refraining from thinnings so heavy that orchard-like stands of widely spaced trees develop. The primary objective is, however, to keep the more promising trees growing steadily by removing less desirable, neighboring trees before their competition becomes injurious. In accomplishing this purpose the number of trees per acre is reduced as it would be under purely natural conditions, but at a substantially more rapid rate. An ideal program of thinning might, for example, gradually reduce the number of trees in a stand so that it would have at 60 years the same number of trees and about the same average D.B.H. that it would normally attain at an age of 90 years.

Classification into Crown Classes

The outward signs of the struggle for existence are the relative position and condition of the tree crowns. Vigorous trees that have outstripped their neighbors occupy superior positions in the crown canopy and normally have the best chance of surviving competition in the future. The less vigorous occupy successively lower positions in the crown canopy until they succumb. Since thinnings are conducted to accelerate or modify the course of the struggle, the position of the crown is an important and convenient criterion in deciding which trees to cut and which to favor.

The crown classification most widely used in the practice of thinning in North America is as follows:

Dominant: Trees with crowns extending above the general level of the crown cover and receiving full light from above and partly from the side; larger than the average trees in the stand, and with crowns well developed but possibly somewhat crowded on the sides.

Codominant: Trees with crowns forming the general level of the crown cover and receiving full light from above but comparatively little from the sides; usually with medium-sized crowns more or less crowded on the sides.

Intermediate: Trees shorter than those in the two preceding classes but with crowns extending into the crown cover formed by codominant and dominant trees; receiving a little direct light from above but none from the sides; usually with small crowns considerably crowded on the sides.

Overtopped: Trees with crowns entirely below the general level of the crown cover, receiving no direct light either from above or from the sides. *Synonym:* "suppressed."

This crown classification is simple and fits the ordinary requirements of thinning practice. It has the drawback of being essentially qualitative; ultimately quantitative classifications, presumably based on crown dimensions, are likely to be developed. Various modifications have been applied to the general qualitative system. The dominant and codominant classes have, for example, been grouped as a single class (Champion and Griffith, 1948) or subdivided into several categories (Table 2-1).

In the classification given here, the intermediate and overtopped classes are well-defined and easily distinguished from the superior categories. However, it is difficult to draw a sharp line of distinction between the dominant and codominant classes. It would be desirable if the codominant class, which usually includes the majority of the main canopy trees, could be objectively subdivided into thrifty and less thrifty categories. Special recognition is sometimes given to a category of **super-dominant** trees which have so far outstripped their contemporaries as to develop excessively large branches or poor bole form.

The crown classification is applicable in uneven-aged stands only with respect to the small, uniform, even-aged components thereof; tree classifications useful for the description of other differences in such stands are discussed in Chapters 6 and 14. Complications also arise in certain mixed stands, both even- and uneven-aged, in which there are many species arranged in two or more layers with shade-tolerant species beneath those capable of more rapid growth in height; special consideration is given to stands of this kind in Chapter 16. The crown classification just presented best fits uniform stands with a single, well-defined main canopy composed of species of nearly the same rate of development. Anything growing in a stratum definitely below the main crown canopy is better considered part of the **understory** or of some subordinate layer of vegetation rather than as part of the overtopped crown class.

The selection of the trees to be favored and of those to be cut in thinnings is based not only on (1) the relative position and condition of the crown but also on (2) the health of the tree and (3) the condition and quality of the bole. In mixed stands the choice between species also affects the selection.

The correlation between crown class and health of trees within a pure, even-aged group is very high, except when some of the trees have recently been injured by agencies capable of reducing growth. If proper allowance is made for such injuries, crown classes may be regarded as adequate indices of health or vigor for thinnings designed primarily to favor dominant trees. This relationship does not always hold valid for other kinds of cutting in which it may be advantageous to apply a classification of vigor to trees released by cutting their larger neighbors. Hough and Taylor (1946) have, for example, found a formal classification of vigor useful in thinning previously untreated stands of northern hardwoods. In general, classification of trees according to vigor should be regarded as a refinement of the ordinary crown classes rather than as a substitute for them.

The correlation between crown class and condition of bole is less definite, particularly if the stand tends to depart from the even-aged condition. Trees that have grown into exceptionally vigorous dominants often develop coarse branches and poor form. Furthermore, injuries sufficient to deform the bole of a tree frequently have surprisingly little effect on its growth. The extent of natural pruning is also greater the lower the crown class.

It is difficult to generalize about the relationship between crown class and straightness of bole. There is, however, a tendency for trees with excurrent branching, like conifers, to have straighter stems when grown in a subordinate position than when they are strong dominants. Most hardwoods, on the other hand, develop deformed or shortened boles when grown in the lower crown classes. This difference is the result of the fact that most hardwoods, being relatively phototropic, tend to lean toward the light, while conifers, being almost exclusively geotropic, tend to grow vertically. In hardwood silviculture this situation presents a problem that is best attacked by seeking the prompt and dense reproduction required to produce uniform stands with dominants of good form.

In selecting trees to be removed in thinnings consideration should always be given to injuries affecting the condition of the bole and the health of the tree, even though subdivisions are not specifically set up in the classification for this purpose. The diminution of number of trees with advancing age is so great that there is rarely any necessity to formalize distinctions between relative degrees of imperfection among trees that ought to be removed in the earlier thinnings. In practical application of thinnings, the most important differences with regard to health and quality lie between the good trees and those that fall short of perfection.

It is occasionally useful to develop more elaborate classifications for special purposes. If a stand consists almost exclusively of imperfect trees, it may be desirable to classify the trees according to quality and vigor so that the improvement of the stand in successive thinnings may follow a rational sequence. Detailed classifications are also useful if marking for thinnings is to be done by inexperienced personnel. Additional refinements may be advantageous in research or in timber inventory.

Gevorkiantz, Rudolf, and Zehngraff (1943) proposed a more elaborate tree classification for aspen, jack pine, and red pine; a summary

Table 2-1. Summary of tree classification for aspen, jack pine, and second-growth red pine in the Lake States by Gevorkiantz, Rudolf, and Zehngraff (1943)

Progressive

1. Head dominants. Dominating surrounding trees with crowns definitely above the general level of the canopy.
2. Strong dominants. In competition with trees of the same crown class but of poorer development.

Provisional

Position and Relation to Surrounding Trees

3. Conditional dominants and codominants. Competing with trees of the same crown class and development and not in immediate danger of being crowded out.

Regressive

4. Weak dominants and codominants. Competing with trees of better development.
5. Intermediates. Competing with trees of higher crown class and development, occupying small holes in the canopy.
6. Suppressed. Trees definitely below the general level of the canopy.
0. Open-grown. Isolated trees.

Crown Density

a. Good crown. At least ⅔ filled, with foliage of healthy green color and normal size.
b. Medium crown.
c. Poor crown. Less than ⅓ filled or with foliage of poor color and of less than normal size.

Soundness

1. Sound
2. Diseased. With visible signs of fungus or insect damage.
3. Badly scarred or damaged. Fire scars, visible rot at base, dead top, etc.
4. Defective or cull.
5. Dying or dead.

Form

a. Good form. Straight boles and uniform, well-developed crowns.
b. Forked. Only when merchantability is affected.
c. Limby. Excessive limbiness affecting merchantability.
d. Crooked or bent. Too much lean or sweep.
e. "Whippers." Trees with small, narrow crowns whipping or injuring the crowns of neighboring trees.

Utility

S. Sawlog trees. (Subject to modification under different market conditions.)
  S^1 Usable for piling.
  S^2 Usable for mine timbers.
  S^3 Usable for lumber.
  S^4 Usable for box lumber and lagging.
P. Cordwood trees.
  P^1 Usable for pulpwood.
  P^2 Usable for poles, etc.
F. Fuelwood trees.

36

of this scheme is reproduced in Table 2-1. This system embraces virtually all of the considerations that might be involved in marking stands for thinning in the locality for which it is intended.

EFFECT OF THINNING ON GROWTH AND YIELD

A program of thinnings is essentially a series of temporary reductions made in stand density (measured in terms of basal area or some similar parameter) to maximize the net value of products removed during the whole rotation. Among the factors determining this net value are the quantity, quality, utility, and size of the products as well as the costs of harvesting and manufacture. Production in terms of quantity or volume of wood is usually considered to be the factor of greatest importance. In this connection, clear distinctions should be drawn between all the different ways in which the growth and yield of stands and trees are measured. Thinning practice cannot be adequately understood without a thorough comprehension of the relationships between the very different mensurational units in which growth can be evaluated.

In the following sections it will be shown how thinning can be used to increase the economic yield of a stand in spite of evidence that, in the biological sense, gross production of wood or of total dry matter is not subject to much alteration. If growth is measured in terms of volume or weight of all parts of the trees of a given stand or even in terms of the total amount of stem wood, it is usually found that artificial changes in stand density do not affect production unless the stand becomes very open or exceedingly dense. The faster diameter growth induced by thinning, however, increases the proportion of stem wood that is large enough for profitable use. The greater the extent to which processing costs restrict the proportion of total volume that is utilized, the more pronounced is this effect. Because of it, thinning can be used to increase the yield of *merchantable* volume even if the total production of wood remains essentially unaltered or actually suffers a slight reduction. For example, a thinning which resulted in no change in the production per acre of either total dry matter or *total* cubic-foot volume might effect a modest increase in the actual utilizable yield of tonnage or volume of pulpwood, a major increase in the board-foot volume, and an even greater increase in the real value of the yield.

The literature on the effect of stand density on growth is voluminous. Only a small portion is cited in the text and the reference list at the end of Chapter 3. Among the general references on the subject are those of Mar:Møller (1946, 1947), Baker (1950), Spurr (1952), Mar: Møller et al. (1954), Braathe (1957), Sakaguchi (1961), and Assmann (1961).

Production of Dry Matter by Stands

The populations of most organisms have a tendency to increase to the limit of the food available to them. Forests are probably more efficient than other plant communities in approaching full use of their food supply, even though they are far from perfect in this respect.

Stands of trees, like all green plants, make their own food by using solar energy to combine water from the soil and carbon dioxide from the air into glucose, the simple sugar that contributes most of the basic building materials for all the compounds that provide the trees with energy and structural material. The ultimate limits on production are set by the ability of the soil to supply water and chemical nutrients, the amount of carbon dioxide and light available, and the time during which temperature and other environmental conditions will permit photosynthesis and other essential processes.

In more concrete terms, the roots of a stand tend toward complete occupancy of the whole stratum of soil in which the supply of water and oxygen is sufficient in quantity and stability to allow them to persist. The foliar surface likewise tends to expand to form a complete crown canopy, unless severely limited by damaging agencies or unfavorable soil conditions. The available crown space is presumably fully occupied when the canopy has not only closed horizontally but also developed enough in the vertical that the lower branches die. Trees, being perennial rather than annual plants, easily live long enough to achieve this kind of nearly complete occupancy of the site.

It may take a dozen or more years for a new stand to achieve full occupancy of the site (Ovington, 1957). Once achieved, full or nearly full occupancy of the site is probably maintained by the stand until middle age, provided that no trees are lost to agencies other than suppression. Actually there is no direct, quantitative measure of the degree to which a stand of trees utilizes the site. The amount of accessory vegetation, especially that in any understory, provides an approximate indication of the extent to which the main stand falls short of full occupancy. From the evidence provided by such vegetation it is logical to conclude that a given generation of trees ultimately loses full command of the site. While these effects of age and other modifying influences must be kept in mind, most silvicultural practices can be viewed as attempts to modify plant communities which are at almost all times able to utilize nearly all the available growing space.

Stands of forest trees, of given species composition, tend to maintain the same amount of foliage so long as they fully occupy a given kind of site (Mar:Møller, 1946, 1947). If scattered trees are removed, the remaining trees expand their crowns and root systems; the amount of foliage and effective root surface soon returns to that which existed before treatment. Intraspecific root grafts may enable the residual trees to effect immediate capture of part of the root systems of cut trees.

According to Mar:Møller the amount of foliage maintained by closed stands of a given species not only remains constant with age but also shows little tendency to differ between sites. However, the evidence is somewhat contradictory, especially about the effect of site quality on the amount of foliage (Scott, 1955). It is probable that the deficiencies of moisture and nutrients associated with poorer sites sometimes limit the amount of foliage that can be supported. Annual fluctuations in leaf amount indicate an influence of climatic variation as well. It is also obvious that damaging agencies such as defoliators and even root rots directly or indirectly reduce the amount of foliage. In any event, it is clear that different species vary widely in the amount of foliage they maintain and the amount of carbohydrate and wood they produce.

In view of the fact that the amount of foliage tends to approach a constant, it is not surprising that stands of given species, age, and site class tend to produce the same average total tonnage of dry matter per acre in spite of moderately large differences in stand density caused by ordinary thinning. If the size of the manufacturing apparatus, the foliage, is nearly constant, the amount of carbohydrate produced will depend chiefly on the amount of raw material fed into it and the period and rate of operation allowed by the environment or, in other words, on the site quality.

Not all the carbohydrate produced by a stand is converted to permanent stem and root tissue. Some must be used for temporary tissues like leaves, small twigs, rootlets, and fruits or cones. A major portion is expended in respiration to supply energy to the leaves, roots, meristematic tissues, and other living parts of the trees.

The production of new tissues by a tree or stand of trees may be viewed as depending upon the relationship between the **photosynthetic** or foliar surface and the **aphotosynthetic** surface (Satoo and Senda, 1958). The aphotosynthetic surface is composed of the meristematic tissues of boles, branches, and roots; the growth of permanent tissues and respiration other than that of leaves and rootlets takes place at or near this surface. If the amount of foliage and carbohydrate produced by a stand are fixed quantities and the rootlets completely occupy the available soil space, the amount of new stem and root tissue laid down will be determined by the amount of carbohydrate left for the aphotosynthetic surface after the requirements of respiration are met. From this viewpoint, the goal of thinning could be looked upon as reducing the aphotosynthetic surface of a stand to the minimum consistent with maintenance of a full crown canopy and complete occupancy of the soil. An ideal balance at this level should theoretically give the highest diameter growth available without reduction of total growth per acre.

Estimates of the distribution of gross dry-matter production among the component uses have been prepared for whole stands by Mar: Møller, Müller, and Nielsen (1954) for European beech on good sites in Denmark and are shown in Fig. 2-3. These indicate that, at least with beech, respiration consumes more of the gross dry-matter production than is channeled into the permanent stem tissues. Respiration, being immediately essential to continued life, commands the highest priority in the carbohydrate metabolism of the trees.

The data in Fig. 2-3 also show that the gross production is not constant with age. It does not approach its maximum value until the stand achieves full occupancy of the site and the foliage weight becomes constant or at about the twenty-fifth year in this example. With further increase in age, however, the annual production of dry matter commences to dwindle even though foliage weight remains constant with age. Ovington (1957) observed a similar pattern of variation of dry-matter production with age in Scotch pine in England. The ultimate decrease in production with age has been observed in practically all organisms and poses an outstanding enigma of biology. In trees it is less pronounced than in most terrestrial organisms but the causes are obscure.

There is ample evidence that different species vary widely in their capacity to produce dry matter (Burger, 1929–53; Mar:Møller, 1946, 1947; Ovington, 1956; Ovington and Madgwick, 1959). Differences in this ability are related to shade tolerance, but can be thought of more precisely in terms of efficiency of photosynthesis. The efficient species manufacture more sugar at low light intensity than those less well adapted in this particular respect. Species with leaves of high chlorophyll content, often manifest by dark green foliage, tend to be

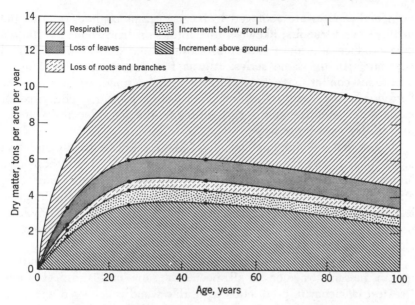

Fig. 2-3. An estimate, adapted from one by Mar:Møller, Müller, and Nielsen (1954), of the dry-matter budget of an even-aged stand of European beech during the course of about one rotation. The vertical distances between the curves define the amounts of dry matter expended for various functions. The total area below the lowest curve, for example, also defines the total weight of stems and permanent branches produced in 100 years.

relatively efficient. Efficiency is reduced by leaf arrangement to whatever extent that there is mutual shading among the leaves. The evergreen habit enables a given amount of foliage to function for a longer period than is the case with deciduous species.

The variations among species are well illustrated by estimates of the mean annual gross increment of dry matter (exclusive of roots) for 40- to 47-year-old stands of various species planted on comparable soils in England (Ovington and Pearsall, 1956). *Castanea sativa* and *Quercus robur,* deciduous species of only moderate shade tolerance, produced dry matter at an average annual rate of 1.7 and 1.8 tons per acre, respectively; *Fagus sylvatica,* a very tolerant hardwood, 2.3 tons per acre. As is usually the case, the evergreen conifers produced dry matter at a greater average rate: *Pinus silvestris,* 3.6; *Pinus nigra,* 4.2; *Pseudotsuga menziesii,* 4.4; and *Picea abies,* 3.4 to 4.2 tons per acre per year. Data from other localities indicated that even higher rates are achieved by very tolerant conifers such as the hemlocks and true firs; likewise, that intolerant hardwoods like *Betula alba* produce at a lower rate than those indicated above for oak and chestnut. In the same series, it was found that *Larix decidua,* a deciduous conifer, gave a production rate intermediate between the hardwoods and conifers, 2.7 tons per acre per year. The yield of moderately intensive mixed agriculture in the same locality was 2.0 tons of dry matter per acre.

Species that are high in efficiency of photosynthesis usually maintain more foliage than the less shade-tolerant species. Thus they have higher live crown ratios and produce a thicker canopy of foliage. In other words, species with efficient leaves are able to maintain more leaves and are thus able to use more light for even more carbohydrate production than the difference in efficiency of a unit of leaf surface alone would indicate.

Not all the trees of a stand use the carbohydrate that they manufacture in the same way nor are all species the same in this respect either. Greatest efficiency in production of usable wood is achieved when the amount that goes into the branches is small. Satoo and Senda (1958) found that within stands of a conifer, *Chamaecyparis obtusa,* trees of smaller D.B.H. and lower crown class produce distinctly less wood per unit of foliage than do those of higher crown class. Dominants and codominants were about equally efficient, although the most vigorous dominants had a tendency to put a slightly higher proportion of wood substance into branches and could thus be regarded as slightly less efficient than trees with crowns that had been somewhat more restricted. However, in comparable studies of an aspen (*Populus davidiana*), Satoo, Kunugi, and Kumekawa (1956) found that the proportion of total wood expended on branch construction increased with increasing diameter. The efficiency of production of stem wood is undoubtedly strongly influenced by the branching habit of the species, particularly when conifers are compared with typical hardwoods. At least among the conifers, however, it seems most likely that the greatest efficiency, in terms of yield of usable wood per unit of foliage, is achieved by the most vigorous codominants and those dominants that have not been allowed to develop coarse branches.

Effect of Thinning on Growth in Total Cubic Volume

The basic relationship between stand density (usually expressed as basal area) and total growth of stem wood has been studied for decades but remains so difficult to measure precisely that it has yet to be established with thorough reliability. The weight of evidence accumulates in favor of the somewhat surprising view that changes in stand density caused by moderate or light thinning do not significantly alter the total amount of dry matter or stem wood produced by a stand. It can at least be safely said that the variations in cubic-volume growth induced by thinning are usually too small to be of practical importance. This idea at least has the virtue of focusing attention on the economic advantages available from thinning which actually do not lie in increasing the total growth of stands.

The following broad and tentative generalization is thus taken as a reasonable approximation of the truth and as a basis for subsequent discussion:

The total production of cubic volume by a stand of given age and composition on a given site is, for all practical purposes, constant and optimum for a wide range of density of stocking. It can be decreased, but not increased, by altering the amount of growing stock to levels outside this range.

This hypothesis was expressed in graphical form by Langsaeter (1941) as shown in Fig. 2-4. It must be noted that this hypothesis

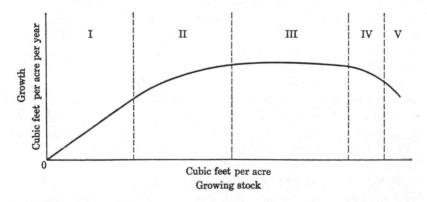

Fig. 2-4. The relationship between density of stocking, measured in cubic volume, and growth in cubic volume, as postulated by Langsaeter (1941). In Density Type I the trees stand so far apart that they do not influence each other and growth is directly proportional to the volume of growing stock. The effect of slight competition in Density Type II is indicated by a declining rate of increase in increment with respect to stand volume. In the broad range of stocking indicated by Density Type III, increment of cubic volume is virtually independent of variations in stocking; the usual objective of thinning is to keep the growing stock somewhere within this optimum range. In Density Types IV and V the effects of extreme competition are reflected in a decline in growth with increasing density.

cannot be regarded as valid unless the total production of wood in the boles of all the trees in a stand is counted as growth. Total production of cubic volume includes not only the wood in the tops of the stems but also the wood produced in trees that die of suppression.

It is also obvious that this hypothesis cannot hold for stands that are so heavily thinned that they do not soon regain full occupancy of the growing space. Neither can it hold for stands that are so dense or so sparse that the height growth of dominant trees suffers. The growth of very dense stands is presumably lowered because so little carbohydrate remains for stem growth after the demands for respiration and leaf formation are satisfied.

This hypothesis has been developed mainly by the work of Mar: Møller and others but is by no means universally accepted. The evidence is clouded by the tremendous variation that becomes obvious in the scatter of points representing the actual observations on which graphs like that in Fig. 2-4 are based. Some of these variations are due to such factors as genetic differences, differences in site quality or stand density *within* experimental thinning plots, and observational errors, especially those involving the effect of taper on stem volume. In fact, the hypothesis may even rest on nothing more than the fact that there is no universally demonstrable upward or downward trend in total growth with respect to moderate artificial decreases in stand density.

It was once believed that maximum growth was obtained at a single, high level of density in tightly closed stands; the so-called normal yield tables were supposed to define this level of density. It was because of this that the view once prevailed that removal of anything more than dead or dying trees would reduce production of total cubic volume.

Early in the present century, however, experiments with heavy thinning seemed to indicate that thinning actually caused an increase in production. This idea is valid enough when growth is measured in units of *merchantable* volume but appears to have resulted from various imprecisions of measurement as far as total growth is concerned. One of the sources of error was the temptation to regard growth in basal area as perfectly equivalent to growth in total cubic volume.

Growth in basal area is much more conveniently and accurately measured than that in volume and is a thoroughly adequate criterion for many purposes. However, it is a completely reliable index of cubic volume only when thinning does not cause changes in height growth or taper. Although height growth is not so affected, heavy thinning causes such a remarkable concentration of diameter growth in the lower portion of the stem as to lead to overestimates of diameter growth of as much as 20 per cent (Wiedemann, 1950–1).

If thinning is delayed until late in the rotation, as it often is in North America, the cubic-volume growth may decrease rather than remain unchanged (Smithers, 1954). Braathe (1957), on the other hand, stated that in cold, humid climates, like those of Scandinavia, this kind of delayed thinning often results in increase in growth, probably because thinning may cause accelerated release of nutrients from accumulations of raw humus. In any event, the basic hypothesis about the fundamental effect of thinning on cubic-volume growth is at best provisional and rests mainly on observations of thinnings that are commenced early in the rotation, are frequently repeated, and do not cause the stands to lose command of the site.

The next consideration involves the degree to which the relationship between stand density and gross production is affected by differences in species, age, and site.

There is reasonably good evidence that shade-tolerant species maintain maximum gross production at higher levels and over greater ranges of stand density than intolerant species. In other words, they are more plastic and probably should be kept at higher densities than stands of intolerant species. As was previously shown, their production is also higher, except that evergreen conifers are more productive than deciduous hardwoods even if the degree of shade tolerance seems comparable. These relationships are depicted very tentatively in Fig. 2-5; there is better evidence about the behavior of shade-tolerant species than intolerant species. It is possible, for example, that only the tolerant ones actually exhibit a range of stand density in which gross production is at a maximum. Some intolerant species may indeed ultimately be found to attain maximum gross production only at a single level of stand density.

If species and site are held constant, the lowest level of basal area consistent with maximum gross production probably increases gradually with age. It has been found that the heavy thinnings that give good production in young Norway spruce seem, if continued, to be associated with poorer increment when the stands become older (Holmsgaard, 1958). Løvengreen (1949), however, concluded that the annual increment of European beech on Danish Site II was essentially maximal between 100 and 150 square feet of basal area per acre at ages ranging from 40 to 120 years even though it declined markedly in actual amount with the increase in age. In other words, the level

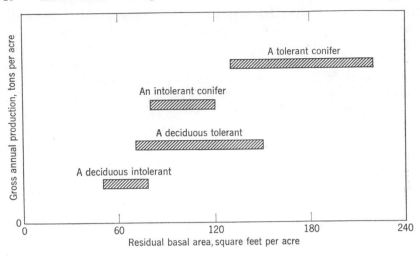

Fig. 2-5. A *tentative* estimate of the approximate relationship between the gross annual growth of middle-aged stands, equal in height but of distinctly different kinds of species, and the basal areas left in thinning. This graph is designed to give quantitative illustration of the hypothesis that in stands of shade-tolerant species optimum production can be maintained with greater stand densities and over broader ranges thereof than with intolerant species. There is no doubt that stands of shade-tolerant species arc, as shown, more efficient than those of intolerants or that evergreen conifers are likewise more productive than deciduous hardwoods even when site conditions are uniform. The bars show only the approximate ranges of residual basal area within which gross annual growth is presumed to be nearly constant and optimum.

of stand density that was optimum at one age was, in this instance, claimed to be optimum at other ages. The best that can be concluded is that the basal area remaining after thinning should either be the same at all ages or, more likely, should be increased gradually with age.

The extent to which optimum stand density varies with site quality is not clear. Mar:Møller (1946, 1947), on the basis of investigations of shade-tolerant species like Norway spruce and European beech, concluded that both the optimum stand density and the total amount of foliage produced by each of these species tended to remain the same on all sites. Other investigations (McClay, 1955; Smithers, 1954; Gruschow and Evans, 1959; and Nelson et al., 1961), especially with the intolerant American hard pines, indicate that the range of optimum density may be distinctly lower and narrower on poor sites than on good. In any event, if there are differences between sites it appears that optimum density would be higher on good sites than on poor and that such differences between sites would be more pronounced with intolerant than with shade-tolerant species.

Effect of Thinning on Economic Yield of Stands

The key to practical understanding of thinning procedures is knowledge of the ways in which they can be applied to increase the economic yield from a quantitatively unalterable capacity to produce wood. The general approach is to allocate the production to some optimum number of trees of highest potentiality for increase in value; the other trees are systematically removed in such sequence as to obtain maximum economic advantage from them. The various advantages that can be gained are summarized as follows:

1. Salvage of anticipated losses of merchantable volume
2. Increase in value from enhanced growth in tree diameter
3. Yield of income and control of growing stock during the rotation
4. Improvement of product quality
5. Opportunity to improve stand composition, to prepare for establishment of new crops, and reduce risk of damage.

Salvage of anticipated losses. The gross production of wood by a stand should not be confused with the actual yield in terms of usable volume removed in cuttings. Not all the cubic feet of wood produced by the growing stand remain stored on the stump until the end of the rotation. In fact, a high proportion of the total production will be lost from death and decay of the large numbers of trees which fail to survive the struggle for existence. From the economic standpoint, any part of this perishable volume which can be salvaged by removing doomed trees in thinnings represents an increase in the quantitative yield of the stand.

Studies by Worthington and Staebler (1961) indicate, for example, that in a normally stocked, unthinned stand of Douglas-fir on Site II the gross yield during a 100-year rotation would be 139,600 board feet per acre but that 27,000 board feet or 19 per cent of this would be lost to mortality caused by suppression alone. A similar situation would exist in any stand except one managed on such a short rotation that mortality was of no consequence or in one composed of decay-resistant species.

Thinnings designed to anticipate losses of volume through natural suppression represent the only reliable method of increasing yield of cubic volume from a stand. Only part of the prospective losses can be recovered, because it is inevitable that some, if not all, of the trees involved will be too small to be utilized and a portion of each stem is bound to be left in the woods. On the other hand, the volume removed in anticipation of loss need not come entirely from small trees of the suppressed and intermediate crown classes. In certain methods of thinning, it is possible to take out part of this volume in larger trees thus forestalling the death and stimulating the growth of their subordinates. This particular technique must be used carefully and then only in situations where the trees of the lower crown classes are still thrifty enough to respond to release.

Relationship between diameter and value of trees. Up to this point, the discussion of the effect of thinning on the quantitative yield of a stand has dealt with production of cubic volume. However, not all cubic feet of wood are equally valuable; other things being equal, those that come from large trees will tend to be of greater utility than those from small trees. One of the important objectives of most, but not all, kinds of thinning is to reduce the stocking of the stand in such manner that it eventually has a smaller number of trees, of larger average diameter, than it would have if it were not thinned.

The advantage of seeking this alteration in diameter distribution may be illustrated by the relationship of board-foot volume to total cubic-foot volume. Part of the reason why a cubic foot of wood in a large tree is more valuable than one in a small tree lies in the fact that it can be converted to square-edged lumber with a lower proportion of waste in slabs and edgings. The practice of measuring the volume of standing trees in board feet is largely confined to North America and is regarded as an incomprehensible joke in most other parts of the world. Although subject to errors of measurement, board-foot volume has the virtue of providing an objective expression of part of the variation in value resulting from differences in tree diameter.

The ratio of board feet to cubic feet would be 12 only if the stem of a tree were a square timber throughout its length and could be sliced into boards without any waste. Since the stem is round and tapering it cannot be cut into lumber without substantial loss both in mill-waste and in the upper parts of the stem which are too small or too knotty for saw logs. The ratio is, therefore, far less than 12, and varies with the diameter of the tree, the usable length of stem, and the standard of utilization. Curve A of Fig. 2-6 shows how this ratio varies with D.B.H. in loblolly pine, if total height, one of the factors that cannot be altered appreciably by thinning, is held constant at 90

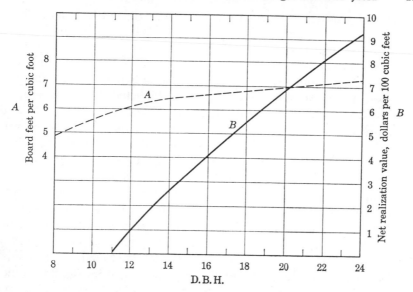

Fig. 2-6. The effect that variations in D.B.H. brought about by thinning might have on (*A*) board-foot/cubic-foot ratio and (*B*) net realization value per 100 cubic feet in a stand of loblolly pine, site index 80, at the end of a 70-year rotation. The board-foot/cubic-foot ratios in Curve *A* were computed from tables of the U. S. Forest Service (1929). Net realization values per 100 cubic feet (Curve *B*) were computed from the data of Reynolds, Bond, and Kirkland (1944) on conversion returns from the harvesting and manufacture of lumber from such a stand in 1935–1936.

feet. By this mode of representation it is possible to show the effects of differences in diameter induced by thinning if growth in height and total cubic feet per acre are unalterable.

The same general relationship between tree diameter and utility prevails between almost any unit of utilizable volume and the cubic-foot content of the entire tree. In fact, this is true even when merchantable volume is determined in cubic feet because the *usable* proportion of the total cubic content of the stem increases with the size of the bole.

The greatest and most nearly universal effect that tree diameter has on the value and utility of a fixed total cubic volume of wood lies in relationships that cannot be described purely in mensurational terms. Most important among these is the fact that a given unit of product can be harvested and manufactured more cheaply and profitably from large trees than from small ones.

If the product is lumber, an additional premium is attached to the greater dimensions and higher quality of material cut from large trees.

The combined effect of all these variables is exemplified by Curve *B* of Fig. 2-6. This curve shows how the net realization value per cubic foot of total volume varies with D.B.H. In other words, it indicates the net value of lumber, per tree, loaded for shipment at the mill, after all costs of harvesting and processing are deducted. This net value is expressed in terms of the total cubic-foot volume of the tree as it stood in the woods, regardless of what proportion of that total volume was actually utilized. Here again it is assumed that growth in height and production of total cubic volume remain constant regardless of treatment. The advantages of redistributing a fixed production of wood in such fashion as to increase the proportion of large trees should be self-evident. The same type of relationship between net value per cubic foot of total volume and the size of the tree prevails almost without regard for the kind of product or the unit of measurement, until the point is reached where the trees become too large to handle efficiently.

The 70-year-old stand of loblolly pine envisioned in Fig. 2-6 would, if fully stocked and unthinned, have trees of all sizes up to 24 inches D.B.H. (Meyer, 1942). It would have 154 trees per acre and an average D.B.H. of 12.6 inches; the average number of trees in the 24-inch class would be less than one per acre. The effect of properly conducted thinnings would probably have been to increase the proportion of trees attaining diameters of 16 to 24 inches and to reduce the total number to between 50 and 75 per acre. The prospect of producing many trees larger than 24 inches D.B.H. in 70 years would be slim unless the thinnings were very heavy and carried out with the deliberate intention of sacrificing total production of wood for the sake of growing trees of large diameter.

It should be obvious that the results of thinnings cannot be evaluated properly unless consideration is given to the sizes of trees produced rather than merely to the volume they represent. Different treatments are often tested simply by comparing the diameters of the trees of average basal area in the various stands. This method is adequate for the purpose if the comparisons are made between the average diameters of *equal* numbers of crop trees on each acre (Adams and Chapman, 1942). The procedure may, for example, take the form of comparing the average diameters of the 100 largest trees per acre. It must be borne in mind that the average diameter of a whole stand is automatically increased merely by removing some of the smaller trees.

In order to reap the rewards of cutting large trees late in the rotation it is necessary to cope with the high cost per unit volume of harvesting and utilizing small trees in earlier thinnings. This difficulty can be mitigated partly by using different equipment and logging methods for the small trees than are later used for the large. The kind of equipment that is most efficient for handling final-crop trees is not necessarily the best for the thinnings, ordinarily being heavier, more cumbersome, more costly, and more expensive to operate for a given length of time.

The problem can also be evaded by delaying the thinnings until the trees to be removed grow large enough to handle economically. Another evasion is to confine the first removals to any large or medium-sized trees of poor potentiality and ignore the small ones until they become larger. Trees that are destined never to be worth harvesting can be either left to die of suppression or killed by the cheapest means available.

The ideal solution is to manipulate the equipment and sequence of thinnings such that the equipment is matched with the sizes of trees to be removed and as many trees as possible are cut when they have grown into the range of diameter which can be harvested efficiently. The objective should be to maximize the return from harvesting the entire crop of one rotation rather than to minimize the cost of each separate operation in the whole sequence of cuttings.

If total cubic-volume growth remains almost constant over a wide range of stand density, it seems most logical that stand density should be reduced, at the time of each thinning, to the lowest at which nearly optimum production of cubic volume can be maintained. Justification exists for reducing density still further if yield of net value can be increased by the additional diameter growth obtained. The limit on this approach is usually set by the undesirable effects on tree form and the vigorous invasion of undesirable vegetation that can result from excessively heavy thinning. In some European countries there are laws against thinnings so heavy that cubic-volume production is reduced (Braathe, 1957); these are probably responsible for some of the traditional reluctance to thin heavily.

Yield of income and control of growing stock during rotation. An unthinned crop of trees is an asset that increases in value throughout the rotation but is otherwise uncontrollable and financially inaccessible. No tangible income is realized, yet the carrying charges and other expenses chargeable against the crop continue to accumulate. These can, of course, be compensated by income from the cutting of older stands that are harvested in the meantime. However, the situation can be very onerous if the whole forest is relatively young and lacking in stands ready for harvest. Under such circumstances, which are common in regions of depleted forests, thinnings and other intermediate cuttings may represent the only source of income for long periods.

A more general problem is the fact that any costs of establishing new crops are most logically charged against these crops. Whether these charges are carried at compound interest or not, it is far better to pay them off through income from thinnings than to carry them to the end of the rotation.

The problem of improving the return on large investments in growing stock is one of the most crucial in forest management. Growing stock that is merchantable but not yet mature has a liquidation value often considered an investment which ought to yield a reasonable rate of interest in the form of growth in value. All too commonly the rate of return from forest growing stock is not especially attractive when viewed in these terms. Thinning provides a means of reducing the value of the growing stock and increasing the value of the growth, thus increasing the rate of interest returned on the investment represented by the growing stock (Staebler, 1960a).

For example, a good growing stock that is not being thinned might be worth $1,000,000 yet give a net annual return from final harvest cuttings of only $40,000 or 4 per cent simple interest. It is by no means inconceivable that a thinning program could increase the return to $60,000 or 8 per cent on an investment in growing stock of only $750,000 on the same land. The reduction in growing stock is also an advantage if property taxes are levied on its value.

Thinning can also be visualized and employed as a technique by which those trees that cannot yield the desired rate of interest on their own value are converted into cash, leaving those which will increase in value at an acceptable interest rate (Fedkiw and Yoho, 1960). The average rate of return on the investment represented by the whole stand can thus be maintained at an interest rate at least as high as that desired. The trees most likely to continue yielding the desired rate for the longest time are those of highest quality and rate of growth. In a pure application of this approach, the first trees to be cut would be those of low quality or slowest growth, although they would not be cut until they had acquired a positive value.

Thinning also provides improved control over rotation length. The rotation necessary to grow trees of a given size can be shortened; larger and more valuable trees can be grown on rotations of fixed duration. On the other hand, short rotations do not necessarily have the financial virtue so often ascribed to them. If thinnings have produced enough return to amortize establishment costs, are yielding an adequate income, and are maintaining a good rate of growth, there is no need to rush headlong into the risk and expense of starting a new crop which will be some years in regaining full occupancy of the site. The logical financial rotation in unthinned stands is usually shorter than in thinned stands because the trees decelerate more rapidly in diameter growth and the accumulation of unsalvaged losses causes the mean annual increment to decline earlier and more rapidly (Worthington and Staebler, 1961). The shorter the rotation the greater is the average annual cost of establishing new crops for the forest as a whole.

Improvement in wood quality. The value of a fixed total production can be enhanced simply by favoring the trees of best potential quality and discriminating against the poor; *this effect of thinning on wood quality is vastly more important than any other.* The superior diameter growth induced by thinning usually improves wood quality because large trees tend to be of better quality than small ones. The general effect of thinning on wood quality is not harmful, in spite of much opinion and some evidence to the contrary. This matter can, however, be dealt with more effectively after considering the effect of thinning on the growth of individual trees.

Stand composition, regeneration, and protection. The opportunity to intervene in the development of the stand during the rotation is convertible into a number of other economic benefits. It enables continuing control of undesirable species not eliminated during the period of regeneration. If mixed stands of dissimilar species are being deliberately maintained, thinning may represent the only means of taking adequate advantage of those species that tend to mature earlier than the major components.

The long period of control over stand composition enables one to prepare for natural regeneration by reducing the seed source of undesirable species and fostering that of the good. Thinning also builds up the physiological vigor, mechanical strength, and seed production of the individual trees of the final crop so that there is wider choice among methods of regeneration cutting. Unthinned stands are likely to have to be replaced during an abbreviated period of establishment even when more gradual replacement might enable greater use of the financial potentialities of the crop.

A subsequent section of this chapter is devoted to the ways, in addition to salvage, by which thinning increases the strength and health of stands and thus reduces the total monetary loss to damaging agencies.

EFFECT OF THINNING ON
THE DEVELOPMENT OF THE TREE

Most of the advantages of thinning are obtained by increasing or at least regulating the amount of growing space into which the trees of the final crop can expand after each thinning. Furthermore, much of the potential value of a stand usually resides in a relatively small proportion of the trees. Therefore, the success of thinning, and indeed that of silvicultural treatment in general, depends on understanding the handling and development of individual trees.

Response of Crown and Root System

The amount of carbohydrate produced by a tree depends mainly on the size of the crown and the ability of the roots to supply it. When a tree is released in thinning, any prompt increase in growth is mainly the result of an increased supply of moisture and nutrients. The amount of foliage does not increase until there has been time for the crown to enlarge, although this delayed effect ultimately becomes the most important. The upper portions of the crown produce much more carbohydrate than the poorly lighted lower portions, so not all units of leaf surface are as productive as all others (Holsoe, 1951; Takahara, 1954). In fact, the crown surface area existing above the point of closure of the stand canopy is probably a better index of the productive capacity of the crown than the total surface.

The lateral extension of the roots is more rapid than that of the crown (Zahner and Whitmore, 1960). The roots do not have to support themselves like aerial branches so their extension is not limited by structural necessities. Consequently, they may extend into any unoccupied soil space even if this involves intermingling with or going around behind the root systems of other trees. If intraspecific root grafting exists, it is possible for a tree to incorporate part of the root system of an adjacent cut tree. It is very likely, in fact, that the trees of a pure stand ultimately exist as individuals only above ground and come, at least in part, to share a common root system (Bormann and Graham, 1959).

One rough but convenient index of the ability of the crown of a tree to nourish the remainder is the **live crown ratio,** which is the percentage of length of stem clothed with living branches. Ordinarily, a tree will grow satisfactorily if the live crown ratio is maintained at about 40 per cent (Holsoe, 1950; Chapman, 1953; Labyak and Schumacher,

1954). If the ratio is allowed to decrease to 30 per cent or less the general reduction in vigor will cause substantial loss of diameter growth. If the ratio is very low, the recovery after thinning will, at best, be delayed or the tree may even succumb.

The loss of trees with small crowns after thinning may be caused by insect attack, sunscald, or even the cutting of other trees which had formerly nourished the unthrifty through root grafts. The most important cause may be merely the increase in respiration induced by the sudden increase in temperature caused by exposure. If the respiratory demand is great enough very little carbohydrate will be left for renewal of vital tissues. However, unthrifty trees are usually eliminated by bark beetles and other biotic agencies before they actually starve to death. Such difficulties are avoided by selecting crop trees from the dominant and codominant classes with acceptable live crown ratios.

Effect of Thinning on Tree Dimensions

Diameter growth is a good first approximation of growth in volume only if it is multiplied by the circumference of the tree on which it is laid down and thus converted to growth in basal area. An annual ring of given thickness laid down on a 15-inch tree adds much more volume than on a 10-inch tree. Therefore, a tree is not declining in volume growth simply because its annual rings become thinner with advancing age. Conversely, the crown surface of the tree would have to expand very rapidly indeed to produce an ideal stem with annual rings of relatively great and uniform width.

A pronounced increase in diameter growth, although not unwelcome, is actually a sign that the tree should have been released much earlier. It is erroneous to assume that thinning should cause dominant crop trees to show a shift from narrow annual rings to wide. Such accelerations are likely to occur only when the growth of a tree has been seriously restricted by competition. In fact, the most spectacular response is likely to occur in the trees of the subordinate crown classes, provided that they have not been suppressed to the point where they fail to respond at all.

The pattern of diameter growth characteristic of a crop tree which has been periodically released in a series of timely thinnings is one in which the thickness of the growth rings decreases very slowly but steadily outward from the pith. In such trees the stimulation of growth resulting from thinning has the effect of forestalling sharp decelerations in diameter growth rather than that of remedying them after they have occurred.   In other words, the effects of judicious thinning cannot be detected by casual inspection of increment borings taken from dominant crop trees.   They will, however, be obvious if a comparison is made between the growth of dominant trees in thinned and unthinned stands.

Very light thinning may have no effect on diameter growth, yet it is not impossible by drastic thinning to produce a crop of trees of double the diameter that they might have attained in the same time without thinning.   In other words, the variation in diameter that can be induced by thinning is very wide.   However, the increase in final diameter of crop trees ordinarily anticipated from a series of thinnings is, very roughly, of the order of 20 per cent.

Stand density has very little effect on growth in height, except where the stand is extremely dense or so open that the trees are distinctly isolated (Lynch, 1958).   In very dense stands, height growth is reduced significantly.   In stands that are so open that the trees grow as isolated individuals, height growth is also likely to be reduced; the reasons are far from clear but appear to involve growth of branches and lower bole at the expense of height.   Staebler (1956) observed instances in which thinning caused temporary reductions of height growth of dominant Douglas-firs; slight increases are sometimes observed in other species.   Within the range of density involved in thinning, height growth of the main canopy trees remains nearly constant.

This would all be simple enough if each annual layer of wood was uniformly thick from top to bottom and homogeneous in composition. The pattern of development is much more complicated and is perhaps least bewildering if viewed in terms of the biological importance and functions of the stem.

It is logical to assume that the growth and other physiological processes will operate to increase ability of the tree to survive and that developments along this line will be limited chiefly by the capacity to produce carbohydrate.   Some functions are more crucial for survival than others and a schedule of priorities seems to exist.

Respiration comes first because the living tissues would perish immediately without it.   The greater the amount of crown surface per unit of living tissue the greater will be the proportion of carbohydrate left for formation of new tissues.   The amounts then used for the renewal of foliage and the extension of crown and root system depend mainly on the room for expansion that is made available by thinning or can be captured from less vigorous competitors.   Part of this process is growth in height, which is so important to the survival of competing trees that it commands high priority and is limited almost entirely by site quality. The production of seeds is also so vital that whenever it takes place it does so at the expense of some other functions. Another vital function that must be fulfilled is that of conduction of materials between crown and root through the xylem and phloem. Although the conductive tissue must be renewed annually most trees lay down far more than is actually necessary for this function. This can be verified by observing how small a "bridge" of tissues is necessary to maintain an imperfectly girdled tree in full vigor.

Most of the wood laid down in the stem and larger roots serves to support the crown. Although this is a crucial function it does not appear to have enough immediate survival value to command high priority. In any event, the extent to which provision is made for mechanical support seems to depend on the vigor of the tree and the amount of carbohydrate that remains after provision for more vital functions. The part of the growth that is of greatest economic concern is thus low enough on the scale of biological priority that it is subject to great variation. It is for this reason that growth in diameter of stems is so readily controllable by thinning or other means of regulating stand density and tree vigor.

The pattern in which wood is laid down on the bole is a rather complicated one most readily understood if the necessity of mechanical support is kept constantly in mind. The stem of a tree is a remarkable piece of structural engineering, being designed to support the weight of the crown and resist horizontal wind stresses without waste of material (Ylinen, 1954). If there were no horizontal stresses and the tree had only to support its own vertically acting weight, the bole would be cone-shaped above the base of the crown and almost cylindrical below the crown. Since the tree is always exposed to some wind, the stem actually takes the strongly tapered form of the modified paraboloid recognized in mensurational work. From the standpoint of engineering, the stem develops into a cantilever beam uniform in resistance to bending throughout its length. The amount of carbohydrate available probably determines the maximum horizontal stress the stem and roots are built to withstand.

The bending of the bole by wind causes at least some of the variation in vertical distribution of diameter-growth that is responsible for the tapering form of tree stems. Jacobs (1939) found, for example, that, if the bole of a tree was held rigid by guy-wires, the rapid growth in diameter that might normally occur at the base of the tree was transferred to the lowest point where the stem could bend. The point of greatest bending is the base of the tree and this is the reason for the development of the typical butt swell. However, the diameter growth at the base of the stem actually fluctuates between wider extremes than at any other point. If the tree is very vigorous or is suddenly exposed to increased bending by removal of adjacent trees, diameter growth at the base of the tree becomes very rapid, sometimes more so than at any higher level. If the tree has a very small crown and is in a densely closed stand, the level of *minimum* diameter growth is in the region of the butt swell, although the tree dies long before the swelling turns into a constriction.

The region of maximum diameter growth above the butt swell is consistently found in the lower portion of the crown (Duff and Nolan, 1953, 1957; Senda and Satoo, 1956; Yerkes, 1960). It is not clear whether this is because there is a secondary maximum of bending in this zone or because it is more richly nourished with carbohydrate moving downward from the vigorous branches above. In either case, the result conforms fairly closely to structural requirements; the good supply of carbohydrate may simply happen to provide a mechanism by which these requirements are met. No swelling develops at the base of the crown because this level of maximum diameter growth is always rising; the rate at which it rises must, however, affect the form of the bole.

As a result, the greatest effect of thinning on diameter growth occurs in the lower portion of the stem and tends to increase the degree of taper or decelerate the rate at which taper might otherwise decrease. The magnitude of the change is rather large if taper is evaluated by true form factor (Wiedemann, 1950–1) and small in terms of form quotient (or Girard form class).

It is important to note that the region of the butt swell extends above breast height, except in young trees, and that conventional measurements of diameter growth thus reflect the extreme variations described. Such measurements thus provide a very sensitive index of the vigor of the tree but a somewhat exaggerated idea of the magnitude of its effect on volume growth, especially when the growth is found to be very slow. For this reason growth in basal area (at breast height) does not always correspond to growth in cubic volume. Comparable measurements made at higher levels would be far less convenient but more reliable as indicators of volume growth.

Effect on Wood Quality

Further complexities arise because structural requirements are not met entirely by laying down wood of homogeneous density, structure, and strength. If wood were of absolutely homogeneous strength, trees would be much more tapering than they are. Instead the strength of the wood in a stem, at least in conifers, usually increases from the pith outward as well as from the top downward (Bethel, 1940; Bryant, 1951; Wellwood, 1952; McKimmy, 1959). The resistance to breakage at any point is determined largely by the product of the strength of the outermost fibers and the distance by which they are separated. The strength of the wood between is of little consequence other than in reducing the actual amount of bending caused by a given wind load.

When a conifer is young and short, the loads placed upon it are small and it usually produces the weak **juvenile** or **core wood.** However, during its period of active increase in size and height, the specific gravity and strength of wood laid down tend to increase. When a tree of almost any species reaches maturity and ceases to increase much in height or size of crown, the annual rings added to the bole become very thin and of low strength, representing little more than enough xylem to renew the water-conducting system. It is at least tempting to conclude that this situation develops because the load on the stem ceases to increase much with time.

The doctrine once prevailed and is still widely held (Paul, 1959) that the strength of wood was controlled by the rate at which it grew. According to this view, rapid growth produced strong wood in ring-porous hardwoods, weak wood in conifers, and caused no appreciable difference in the strength of diffuse-porous hardwoods. On the basis of this interpretation the stimulation of diameter growth of conifers by thinning was looked upon as a questionable practice that would lead to the production of light wood of low strength.

The actual effect of thinning on the strength of coniferous wood has not yet been investigated enough to yield positive conclusions. However, the idea that fast-grown conifers produced weak wood was based on little more than the observation that young trees had weak wood and grew rapidly whereas older trees grew more slowly and produced stronger wood. It is now clear that the effects of age and growth rate were being confounded and that the age when the wood was laid down was more nearly the controlling variable (Turnbull, 1948; Larson, 1957). In other words, if a conifer is made to grow rapidly by thinning, it produces a greater volume of the same kind of wood that might have been laid down without release rather than shifting to the production of weak wood (Spurr and Hsiung, 1954).

The relative proportion of early- and late-wood in the annual ring is a more reliable indicator of the strength and specific gravity of wood than ring width, although it may not reveal all of the subtle differences that exist in the characteristics of wood fibers. The time of the annual change from production of early-wood to that of late-wood appears to coincide with the cessation of the initial period of shoot elongation in the spring (Larson, 1960). Any treatments or site factors that prolong or increase diameter growth during the early summer increase the proportion of late-wood, which is produced mainly at that time (Paul, 1930; Larson, 1957). The proportion of late-wood also tends to increase with distance from the pith, at least in thrifty trees, but not sufficiently to account for all of the observed increase in strength and specific gravity.

The grading rules that exclude dimension stock of some conifers from good structural grades if it has, for example, less than six rings per inch or less than one-third late-wood appear valid to the extent that they discriminate against juvenile wood. The lower limit on proportion of late-wood seems sound but the restriction on ring count is at least questionable.

Those conifers, like the spruces and eastern white pine, that have no pronounced variation between early- and late-wood show considerable internal homogeneity of wood properties and adjust to structural demands more by increasing taper than by variations in wood strength (Spurr and Hsiung, 1954).

There are many aspects of the effect of thinning on the density and strength of wood that have yet to be elucidated, but there seems little reason to believe that thinning is likely to produce weaker wood. In fact, thinning is most likely to increase the proportion of strong wood in a tree by increasing the volume laid down at ages and sizes when strong wood is produced. This is especially true if rainfall or soil moisture remain favorable enough to stimulate growth of the late-wood.

The sudden and spectacular accelerations of growth resulting from delayed thinning do harm certain properties of wood (Paul, 1946) regardless of the properties of the new wood. There is a strong tendency for shake to occur at the point of acceleration. A board which contains both fast- and slow-grown wood is likely to warp and is not uniformly suitable to a given purpose. From the standpoint of both volume and quality production it is desirable to maintain the rate of diameter growth at a relatively steady rate directing most efforts against the decline in diameter growth associated with increasing age and size.

Thinnings that are heavy enough to cause major changes in the form and taper of boles may be detrimental as a consequence. If the logs are converted into lumber there is increased waste in slab-bing and the boards are more likely to be cross-grained. The trees may no longer meet the specifications for poles and piling if they taper too much or have excessively large branches high on the stems (Guilkey, 1958).

Thinning has a tendency to halt natural pruning and stimulate the development of large branches. If not remedied by artificial pruning, this effect will increase the size and number of knots in the wood. The only compensating effect is that the branches remain alive longer, thereby reducing the number of loose knots eventually produced. If a large amount of clear material is to be grown without artificial pruning, thinning should be delayed until natural pruning has pro-ceeded to the extent ultimately desired. Regardless of how the prun-ing is accomplished, it is prudent to set some realistic goal as to the length of branch-free bole that will be developed; the remaining upper portion of the stem should ordinarily be kept clothed with liv-ing branches. The contemplated length of clear bole should be greater the better the site and the longer the rotation because it de-pends on the ultimate height and live crown ratio. If one plans to grow trees 100 feet tall with a live crown ratio of 40 per cent, it is important to plan for the proper development of the 60-foot length below the live crown.

The criteria of quality for pulp depend on the pulping process and the characteristics desired in the product. In most circumstances the procedures necessary to produce strong wood of high density will be appropriate (Mitchell and Wheeler, 1960). Such would normally be the case if pulp high in most criteria of mechanical strength were de-sired. There is evidence that the fiber length of softwoods increases outward from the pith in the same manner as specific gravity but does not vary so much with height (Anderson, 1951; Spurr and Hyvarinen, 1954; Jackson, 1959; Wellwood, 1960). The proportion of cellulose, by weight relative to lignin and other constituents, is also less in the central core of juvenile wood than it is in outer portions of the stem; it apparently shows considerable genetic variation be-tween trees but is not correlated with wood density (Zobel and McElwee, 1958; Zobel, Webb, and Henson, 1959; Kennedy and Jaworsky, 1960). If the wood is of high density, the volume that must be harvested and processed for a given yield of pulp will be low.

All these desirable characteristics go with growing trees to at least moderate size and age as well as maintaining good volume growth after, rather than before, trees have ceased to produce juvenile wood. It would thus appear that the rotations and thinning procedures suitable for growing pulpwood of good quality should differ little from those for growing medium-sized sawlogs for structural timber.

Not all wood is grown for pulp or structural material. Sometimes the most valuable is that which is sufficiently soft and uniform in texture to be shaped and finished easily for millwork, furniture, plywood, veneer, and similar products. Homogeneity of properties and freedom from defect are more crucial characteristics than strength and density. This kind of material now comes mainly from the very fine-ringed wood of the outer portions of large, ancient trees.

The problems of producing such wood in the future arise with species in which there is a sharp contrast between early- and late-wood. Such species include the oaks and other ring-porous hardwoods as well as the hard pines and Douglas-fir among the conifers. Rotary-cut plywood veneer from Douglas-fir, for example, tends to fracture between early- and late-wood when peeled from wood with less than 10 rings per inch (Fleischer, 1949). If high-quality finish lumber or veneer are to be produced from such species, measures will probably have to be taken to restrict the rate of growth. Any thinning should be light; the prospects for success would be greatest with long rotations on sites or in regions where the supply of soil moisture becomes deficient early in the summer.

These difficulties are less serious with the diffuse-porous hardwoods and those conifers, like the spruces and soft pines, that show little contrast between early- and late-wood. The wood produced by vigorous, medium-sized trees of these species may be harder than desirable for some purposes but it is at least homogeneous. It is possible that they will ultimately represent the most reliable species to use for production of finish lumber and veneer products from managed forests.

The one kind of wood that is of low utility for almost all purposes is the juvenile wood, usually of rapid growth, found in the central core of most coniferous stems. It is soft, weak and usually full of small knots. Because of poor fiber characteristics it is also subject to warping and various kinds of fractures when dried. Juvenile wood forms mainly within the living crown so its amount depends more on the initial density of the stand than on the nature of the thinnings. The main thing is to arrange to grow as much as possible of the kind of wood desired after the formation of juvenile wood has ceased.

REFERENCES

Since many of the references for this chapter are again cited in the next chapter, the entire list has been placed at the end of Chapter 3 to avoid repetition.

CHAPTER 3

Methods and application of thinning

METHODS OF THINNING

Four distinct principles may be recognized in the methods that have been developed for determining which trees to remove and which to favor in thinnings. In each of the first three methods, the relative development or position of the crowns of the individual trees is the primary basis for selection. In the fourth, spacing of the stems is the first consideration. The four methods are: (1) **low thinning**, (2) **crown thinning**, (3) **selection thinning**, and (4) **mechanical thinning**. It is also useful to distinguish a fifth method, **free thinning**, which is actually a combination of the other four. It is often applicable in stands sufficiently irregular that two or more of the other methods are best suited to different parts of the same stand.

These methods of thinning will be considered in turn. A series of vertical profiles through stands is presented to illustrate the basic principles of the first three methods. It should be noted that sketches of this kind inevitably lack the depth of three-dimensional representation and, therefore, make the various grades of thinning look heavier than they do when actually applied in the woods. Each profile depicts a kind of stand for which the thinning method illustrated is especially appropriate.

Low Thinning

This technique, the oldest of thinning methods, is sometimes called "thinning from below" as well as the "ordinary" or "German" method. In low thinning, trees are removed from the lower crown classes. In the lightest of low thinnings only the overtopped trees would be removed; a somewhat heavier low thinning is made by cutting the intermediates as well as all of the overtopped trees; the heaviest would leave only the dominants and some of the thriftiest codominants. In a series of low thinnings, trees might conceivably be removed as they are gradually submerged below the crown class regarded as the lowest worth retaining.

Several grades of severity are recognized in low thinnings. These range from A-grade thinnings, the lightest, to D-grade thinnings, which are normally regarded as the heaviest low thinnings. None of these grades of low thinning are defined uniformly and precisely by all authorities. Conservative and radical interpretations of the four grades are contrasted in Table 3-1; Figs. 3-1 and 3-2 illustrate the radical interpretation. There has been a uniform tendency toward increasing the severity of low thinnings such that even the most radical kind of A-grade thinning is rarely practiced.

In low thinning the natural extermination of the lower crown classes is simulated and accelerated. The degree of acceleration depends on the grade of low thinning. So long as no codominant trees are removed, low thinnings result in little more than the salvage of trees which will inevitably die; competition among the remaining trees is alleviated only to the extent that root competition is reduced. The growth of the remaining trees is stimulated only if openings are made in the main canopy by cutting some of the codominants (Fig. 3-2). The once-prevalent idea that gaps should not be created in the crown canopy has been abandoned. The lighter grades of low thinning also involve the removal of distinctly limited volumes in relatively

Table 3-1.

| Grade | Trees Removed in a | |
| | Conservative | Radical |
	Application of the Low Thinning Principle	
A. Very light	Poorest overtopped	Overtopped
B. Light	Overtopped and poorest intermediate	Overtopped and intermediate
C. Moderate	Overtopped and intermediate	Overtopped, intermediate, and a few codominant
D. Heavy	Overtopped, intermediate, and many codominant	Overtopped, intermediate, and most of codominant

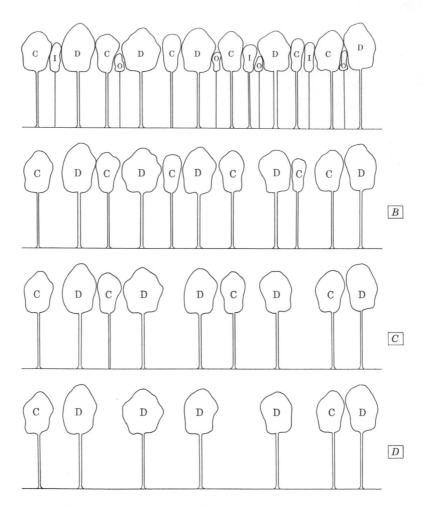

Fig. 3-1. The B, C, and D grades of low thinning as they might look if applied in a middle-aged stand of loblolly pine that had been rendered unusually uniform and thrifty by earlier thinning. The letters on the crowns denote crown classes; note that previous treatments have already promoted the crop trees to the dominant class. The uppermost sketch shows the stand before low thinning; the letters beside the other sketches denote the grade of low thinning illustrated; the nearly useless A grade is omitted.

small trees.   It is for these reasons that low thinnings lighter than the
C grade have fallen into disfavor.

Low thinnings are more likely to create vacancies in the lower
stratum of a stand than are those other kinds of thinning in which the
subordinate crown classes are left more or less intact.   Therefore,
they are somewhat less desirable than crown or selection thinnings in
situations where a troublesome understory is likely to develop.   It has
been found, for example, that low thinning tends to favor the permanent establishment of *Ribes* in the understory of the western white
pine type, whereas crown thinning does not (Moss and Wellner, 1953).

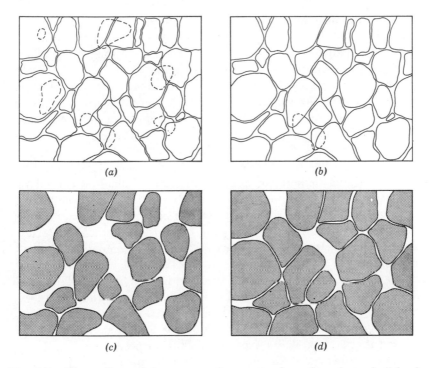

(a)   (b)

(c)   (d)

Fig. 3-2.   The outlines of the crowns of a previously unthinned stand of hardwoods as viewed from above.   Overtopped portions of the crowns of trees of
the lower crown classes are indicated by broken lines: (*a*) before thinning; (*b*)
after an A-grade thinning in which overtopped trees were removed leaving the
canopy unbroken; (*c*) immediately after a D-grade thinning in which overtopped,
intermediate, and many codominant trees were removed leaving each remaining
tree exposed on one or more sides; (*d*) the same stand 10 years after the D-grade
thinning showing the canopy so nearly completely closed that another thinning is
needed.

The subordinate vegetation that often appears after thinning may be undesirable or welcome, depending on its species and vigor. It is of little consequence if its growth is soon arrested by the re-establishment of a closed canopy. Understory vegetation of appropriate species may play an important role in wildlife management, for which purpose low thinning may be found superior to other thinning methods.

Sometimes subordinate vegetation may serve a useful function when the overstory does not make full use of the inorganic nutrients of the soil. At least part of the surplus that might otherwise be lost to the site by leaching can be kept in the nutrient cycle by the subordinate vegetation (Scott, 1955). The mixture of different kinds of leaf litter also stimulates decomposition. In Europe these effects are sometimes regarded as so important in safeguarding the soil and the nutrient capital that hardwood understories are deliberately sought, by planting if necessary, under some coniferous stands.

If the advance growth stimulated by thinning is of undesirable species it may be necessary to eliminate it when the time comes to establish a new crop. This difficulty is commonly encountered if the desirable overstory is of some early stage of plant succession. If this is the case, attempts should be made to add the elimination of the seed source of the undesirable species to the normal objectives of thinning. Under exceptional circumstances the difficulties caused by such unwanted vegetation may outweigh the benefits gained from thinning. Bamford and Little (1960) found this to be true in the Atlantic white-cedar type of the peat bogs of southern New Jersey. Under ordinary circumstances, however, if the site, climate, and stand composition are at all conducive to the establishment of advance growth, it will ultimately appear even without thinning. The main thing is that such developments should be anticipated and, where expedient, thinning programs should be adjusted so as to regulate the advance growth, restricting its development if it is undesirable and allowing its existence if it serves any useful purpose.

Advance growth of desirable species is a detriment only if, as with many hardwoods, it becomes so malformed before the end of the rotation that it must be eliminated to make room for better trees in the new crop. In other respects it is a fortuitous benefit of thinning.

The most serious drawback of low thinning lies in the fact that the smaller trees of the stand are removed and it is often difficult to utilize such trees profitably. It is frequently not until the latter part of the rotation that true low thinnings can be carried out at a profit. Low thinning is not likely to be worth while in young stands except where small material is merchantable or in cases where such treatment represents the soundest possible investment in the future value of the stand.

The greatest merit of low thinning lies in its inherent, logical simplicity and its close relationship to the natural course of development of the stand. A minimum of skill is necessary in selecting the trees to be removed, and an ample margin for error is present in the large number of dominants and codominants that are reserved.

The usefulness of low thinnings is greatest in stands where the trees of the subordinate crown classes are merchantable but have lost so much crown surface that they are no longer capable of responding to release rapidly. This condition is most likely to occur in stands of intolerant species, particularly those that have reached middle age. As soon as losses to suppression become imminent among trees of merchantable size the advantages of low thinning become much more compelling than when such losses are still confined to trees that cannot be utilized profitably.

Low thinnings are readily adaptable to their original purpose of salvaging prospective mortality but can be rather cumbersome as a means of encouraging the growth of the residual trees. A low thinning must be comparatively heavy if vacancies in the canopy are to be extended upward sufficiently to create openings for enlargement of the crowns of the crop trees. The removal of the subordinate crown classes during this process stimulates the growth of the remaining trees only to the extent that root competition is reduced. Although this may sometimes be effective in alleviating deficiencies of moisture and nutrients, it is more often found to be unnecessary as far as subsequent growth is concerned.

Crown Thinning

In order to overcome the limitations encountered in applying low thinnings, a method was developed in which trees are removed from the middle and upper portion of the range of crown and diameter classes rather than from the lower end. This technique is best referred to as **crown thinning**. It is also known as the "French" method of thinning because of its origin and early use in France. The terms "thinning from above," "high thinning," and "thinning in the dominant" have also been used for crown thinning, but these are too easily confused with selection thinning.

In crown thinning, trees are removed from the upper crown classes in order to open up the canopy and favor the development of the most promising trees of these same classes (Fig. 3-3). Most of the trees that are cut come from the codominant class, but any intermediate or dominant trees interfering with the development of potential crop trees are also removed. The trees to be favored are chosen, if possible from the dominants and, where necessary, from the codominants. Crown thinning favors nearly the same kinds of trees as low thinning but more by removing a few strong competitors than by wholesale elimination of the weak. Low thinning and crown thinning differ radically from selection thinning in which dominant trees are cut to favor the lesser crown classes.

Crown thinning is basically different from low thinning in two respects. First, no matter how lightly applied, the principal cutting is

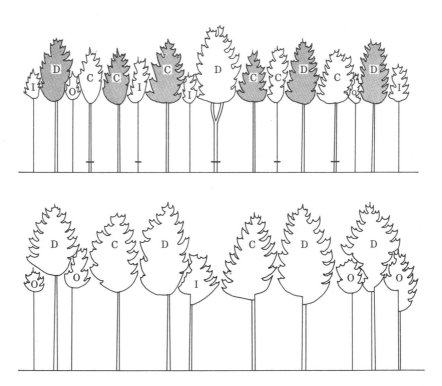

Fig. 3-3. The upper sketch shows a coniferous stand immediately before a single crown thinning. The trees to be cut are denoted by horizontal lines on the lower boles and those with shaded crowns are the crop trees. The lower sketch shows the same stand about 20 years after the crown thinning and reclosed to the point where a low thinning would be desirable.

made in the upper crown classes. Second, the bulk of the intermediate class and the healthier portion of the overtopped class remain after each thinning.

The question of whether individual dominant or codominant trees are favored is settled according to the relative potentialities of adjacent trees. If the choice lies between a promising codominant and mediocre dominant, the codominant is favored. A situation of this kind occurs most often where the codominant has a straighter, smoother bole and smaller branches than the dominant. Where all trees are of good health, form, and species, codominants interfering with the growth of dominants are removed, on the premise that position in the crown canopy is the best index of past and future vigor.

Theoretically, overtopped trees and intermediates that do not interfere with crop trees are not cut in crown thinning. In practice, there is little reason to leave such trees if they can be harvested profitably and their continued presence will add value neither to themselves nor to the stand as a whole. If many of the smaller trees are removed, the operation becomes an incomplete low thinning.

The immediate cash return from crown thinnings is greater than from low thinnings of equal severity, because the material removed is larger and of greater utility. The smaller trees of the subordinate classes, which would be removed in low thinnings, can be left to grow to larger size. Any losses of material too small to be utilized profitably are of no consequence.

One result of crown thinning is the division of the residual stand into two categories of trees. The first consists of the favored dominants and codominants, which are destined for removal either in reproduction cuttings or in later thinnings. The second category is made up of the subordinate trees, which are favored only by indirect action and are gradually removed as they grow up and interfere with the trees of the first group. After a series of crown thinnings it is possible that a stand of two distinct stories, but only one age class, may be created (Fig. 3-4). This development is not likely to be persistent unless the subordinate trees are of tolerant species. Actually it is common to have the lower story of trees vanish as a result of the combined attrition of natural suppression and a series of crown thinnings. Under such conditions, a program of crown thinnings pursued to its logical conclusion will be replaced almost automatically by low thinning. With some very intolerant species the first crown thinning may prove to be the last because of the failure of the subordinate trees to survive after release. A result of this kind represents poor judgment only if

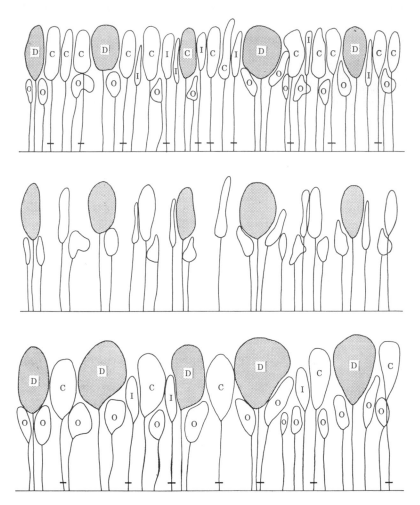

Fig. 3-4. Part of a series of crown thinnings in a mixed hardwood stand. The upper sketch shows the previously untreated stand immediately before the first crown thinning. The trees to be cut are denoted by horizontal lines on the lower boles and those with shaded crowns are the final crop trees. The middle sketch shows the stand immediately after the first thinning. The lower sketch shows it advanced to readiness for the second crown thinning. Note that a lower story, which is composed of relatively tolerant species, is being developed by these thinnings. Presumably a third crown thinning could be conducted in this stand.

the trees which die could have been utilized profitably at the time of thinning.

Crown thinning is more likely to decelerate the dying of the lower branches of the crop trees than most other kinds of thinning, being equalled in this respect only by the very heaviest grades of low thinning. This effect is beneficial if the crop trees have reached the size and age at which the live crown ratio should be increased but not if additional natural pruning is desirable. Deliberate use must be made of the actively competing trees in whittling off the crowns of the crop trees to the desired height. The lower branches of a tree succumb mostly because of being shaded from above. The crowns of the trees of subordinate classes may hasten the shedding of dead branches and hinder the sprouting of epicormic branches but they cannot affect living branches above them. Artificial pruning provides an alternative; however, offending branches are generally above the levels of conventional artificial pruning so the expense of cutting them off is justifiable only if the branches also persist long after death and knot-free wood commands a high premium.

Early thinning can usually be conducted so as to maintain good diameter growth while killing off the unwanted portions of the crowns if the necessity of combining the processes is properly anticipated. The difficulties can be rendered most acute by excessively heavy crown thinnings; the supply of active competitors left in light or moderate crown thinning provides ample maneuverability for attacking the problem. The delayed thinning regimes common under American conditions usually make it more difficult to maintain adequate live crown ratios than to reduce those that become excessive.

Merely by occupying the lower stratum of crown space, the subordinate trees left in crown thinnings restrict the development of undesirable vegetation in the understory. Therefore, once an adequate length of clear bole has been developed, it is possible to free the crowns of the favored trees more completely than would be advisable in low thinning. Any large gaps made in the canopy by eliminating rough dominants are given over to the growth of reasonably well-developed trees rather than to the uncertain prospects of regeneration.

The effect of the subordinate trees left after crown thinning could conceivably be undesirable if root competition were the most critical factor limiting growth. They are occasionally a hindrance in the work of cutting and transporting products within the stand.

One important advantage of crown thinning lies in the opportunity to stimulate the growth of selected crop trees without sacrificing quantity production. The favored trees grow to a given size in a shorter time, or to larger size in a given time, than they would with a regime of low thinnings, owing to the freedom for expansion of the crowns. Meanwhile any growing space not taken up by the selected trees is given over to the subordinates. Most evidence indicates that the total yield, in terms of cubic feet per acre, is no greater from crown thinnings than from a comparable series of low thinnings. With crown thinnings, however, this volume is harvested in fewer trees of greater average diameter than with low thinnings.

Crown thinning is a more flexible method than low thinning, and it demands greater skill on the part of the forester. Since it is not feasible to distinguish different grades of crown thinning, the severity of cutting must be regulated in terms of basal area or some other index of stand density.

There are at least two ways of applying crown thinnings. In one, the cutting in the upper crown classes is conducted uniformly throughout the stand. A generous, but not unlimited, number of the most promising trees on the area are released, without considering which of these will be carried to the end of the rotation. In the second, a conscious effort is made to select the relatively few trees that will form the final crop. In a young stand these trees will be far fewer than the number of promising trees on the area. Each thinning is then directed toward giving the few final crop trees (which may be ringed with paint or otherwise permanently designated) ample freedom on all sides.

The second method is particularly useful where markets for the products of thinnings or labor for making them is restricted. Treatment may be confined to the areas immediately adjoining the crop trees in such fashion that maximum advantage is secured from a given amount of work. The first method is the more useful under highly intensive practice where the objective is to increase the yield from thinnings to a maximum. If the first method is followed, the final crop trees should also be selected well before the end of the rotation so that there can be some continuity of purpose in their treatment.

When a stand is young and the trees are relatively small it is possible, although not necessarily desirable, to free the crowns of the crop trees on all sides without leaving very large gaps in the canopy. Holes up to a diameter one-third that of the crowns of the crop trees will usually close without undue delay. However, as the trees grow older and larger it becomes impossible to afford the crop trees such complete release without seriously reducing the stocking of the stand. Therefore, if large holes are inevitable, the strongest competitors of the crop trees should be cut and the rest left to be taken out in subsequent thinnings. The stage is eventually reached when a crop tree can be freed on but one side at the time of each thinning. The thinnings must also be less frequent in the later stages because it takes longer for the holes to close.

Crown thinning, if it is not started too early, normally embodies the best basic principles to follow in the development of good stands of hardwoods for saw timber and veneer logs (Fig. 3-5). The key to

Fig. 3-5. An even-aged mixture of black oak, other hardwoods, and shortleaf pine in the North Carolina Piedmont after a crown thinning. The crowns of the better dominant and codominant trees have been released by the removal of competing trees of inferior quality from the upper portion of the canopy. Except in the immediate foreground, the trees of the lower crown classes remain. (*Photograph by U. S. Forest Service.*)

success lies in the proper handling of individual stems, a process that is one of the essential guiding principles of crown thinning. Because they tend to be deficient in apical dominance, hardwoods are prone to develop low forks and crooks that may restrict the merchantable length which is usually all too short anyhow (Conover and Ralston, 1959). Because of their tendency to be phototropic, hardwoods are very likely to develop sweeping stems from having grown toward the source of one-sided illumination. The best way to avoid these difficulties is to grow the chosen trees as dominants throughout life. During the course of the rotation the trees that lapse into the codominant or lower crown classes are harvested, if merchantable, as soon as they cease to be of use in training the crop trees or are unlikely to show further increase in value.

Hardwood grading standards are so stringent that it is even more important to develop branch-free boles than it is with conifers. Careful handling of the competitors can cause the lower branches of the crop trees to die at the proper rate. The shedding of all but the largest dead branches is usually quite rapid but is even more rapid in the stable, moist environment induced by the presence of a subordinate layer of trees. The subordinates also restrict epicormic branching which can spoil the benefits of previous natural pruning. However, if the crop trees are kept dominant, epicormic sprouting is at a minimum.

Most hardwood stands are sufficiently variable that their optimum treatment becomes a sophisticated kind of free thinning strongly accented in the direction of crown thinning. Many of the so-called Danish thinnings (Zehngraff, 1950; Mar:Møller et al., 1954; Sabroe, 1954) are outstanding examples of very intensive application of this approach. The term "Danish thinning" is not as much a precise technical term as it is a hallmark of distinction attached to programs of frequent thinnings developed to a fine art under highly favorable economic conditions. Danish thinnings take a wide variety of forms in coniferous as well as hardwood stands.

Crown thinning often represents one of the most expeditious means of restricting the investment represented by value of growing stock without reducing the growth in value that represents the income on this investment. The codominants that are typically removed in crown thinning subtract more from the investment in growing stock than the smaller trees that would be removed in low thinning. At the same time the potential for increase in value remains essentially undiminished because the dominant trees are favored. Selection thinning, by removing numerous dominants, may reduce the investment more but it usually reduces the growth in value as well. If all of the trees in a stand are of good quality and value, differing mainly as to rate of growth, low thinning is likely to represent the logical way of manipulating the investment represented by the stand, because the dominants will increase in value most rapidly.

The principles of crown thinning can be followed in almost any situation where economic conditions are compatible with the application of thinning. This method provides such direct and consistent means of fostering and regulating the development of the chosen trees of the final crop that it has become very common. It is also sufficiently versatile in application that the details of procedure are subject to a wide variety of modifications; many of these modifications are recognizable as crown thinning only if the method is interpreted rather broadly.

Crown thinning works best, or at least can be repeated most often, in mixed stands or in pure stands of tolerant species; both kinds of stands are likely to have trees capable of forming a subordinate stratum. It can be applied at appropriate stages in handling pure stands of intolerant species, but must soon be succeeded by low thinnings if any use is to be made of the trees of the subordinate crown classes. One of the shortcomings of crown thinning is that it makes no provision for the ultimate disposition of the subordinates. This drawback is readily correctable by subsequent use of low thinning or other techniques; the subordinate stratum of trees is detrimental only where root competition is crucial.

Selection Thinning

This method of thinning differs radically in principle from the two methods already discussed. In selection thinning, dominant trees are removed in order to stimulate the growth of the trees of the lower crown classes (Figs. 3-6 and 3-8). The same kind of vigorous trees that are favored in crown and low thinning are the very ones that are likely to be cut in selection thinning. It is obvious then that selection thinning is suitable only for rather limited purposes and, if not carefully used, readily degenerates into high-grading.

There are really a number of different kinds of selection thinning and the method can be understood only in the light of these various approaches and the situations in which they are applicable. These approaches differ with respect to the objectives sought and the number of times this kind of thinning is repeated.

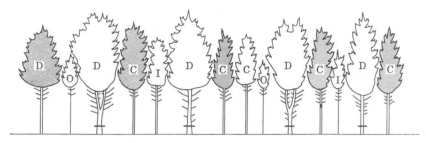

Fig. 3-6. A coniferous stand marked for a selection thinning aimed primarily at the elimination of rough, poorly formed dominants and the release of less vigorous trees of better form. The next thinning would not come until the large holes in the canopy had nearly closed and it could not logically be another selection thinning because the crop trees (*shaded crowns*) would then be the dominants.

In the first and most common approach, poorly formed dominants are eliminated in favor of satisfactory crop trees chosen from the highest possible level in the lower crown classes (Fig. 3-6). *There is no point in procrastinating about the removal of the kind of coarse dominants that become poorer and cause more harm to better trees the longer they are allowed to remain.* The removal of such trees takes advantage of the fact that codominant and intermediate trees as well as the smaller dominants often have smoother, straighter boles and smaller branches than the most vigorous dominants. This advantage can be pursued to absurdity because it is impossible to grow trees without branches regardless of how high the quality of the stems might be. Success hinges on the choice of trees for the final crop.

The trees selected for retention to the end of the rotation should have live crowns sufficiently deep to enable them to respond to release rapidly and then develop into thrifty, fast-growing individuals. Trees with live crown ratios less than 30 per cent are rarely suitable. In general, the more tolerant the species the greater is the possibility that appropriate trees can be found in the lower crown classes. The ability of trees of a given crown class to respond to release will also depend on the site and other factors peculiar to each locality.

Selection thinnings designed to improve the quality of the crop trees are best carried out as early as possible in the life of the stand and replaced by other thinning methods as soon as the crop trees approach the dominant position. Occasion arises for such treatment only where the irregularity and sparsity of initial stocking has caused rough dominants to develop (Fig. 3-7). An outstanding illustration is to be

Fig. 3-7. An old-field stand of loblolly pine in which a selection thinning has just been completed. Most of the trees removed were large, rough dominants that produced the kind of material typified by the butt log appearing in the foreground. The men are standing in front of a gap in the canopy created by the removal of trees of this kind. (*A. F. P. I. Photograph by South Carolina State Commission of Forestry.*)

found in stands of eastern white pine which have been attacked by the white pine weevil. Since the dominant trees are the ones most likely to be deformed by this insect, it is advantageous to remove them as soon as the straight, potential crop trees from the lower crown classes have attained a height equal to the desired log length.

This kind of treatment is best regarded as a necessary evil dictated by imperfect initial stand structure, especially with intolerant species. The importance of this point should not be minimized because so many valuable species are relatively intolerant. With such species, it is rare that any additional advantage can be secured from selection thinnings after rough dominant trees have been eliminated in favor of better codominants.

In the second approach (Fig. 3-8), selection thinnings are continued until the point is reached when further removals from the main canopy would open holes too large to be filled by the expansion of the crowns of the remaining trees. At that point attention is turned either to low thinning or, more often, to whatever measures are necessary for regeneration. The objective of this kind of treatment is not to develop large trees but to grow as many trees as possible to medium size for pulpwood, small saw logs, posts, poles, or piling. The procedure differs from diameter-limit cutting only to whatever extent discretion is exercised in choosing the trees to cut.

The stands with the greatest capacity to endure this kind of treatment are those composed of tolerant conifers, such as mixtures of spruce and fir. When the trees of the subordinate crown classes do not become deformed and retain the capacity to respond to release it is feasible to harness their potentiality for growth by means of selection thinnings. Even though large trees are not produced, few if any stems need be cut until they reach the size at which they can be handled profitably.

Selection thinnings can be continued, at least for a time, in stands of tolerant species without reducing the total cubic volume production below that obtainable with other methods of thinning. Mar:Møller and Holmsgaard (1947) found this to be true for about six repetitions of light selection thinning in Norway spruce in Denmark, although the residual stand finally became so reduced that reproduction began to appear (Braathe, 1957). It should be clearly recognized that this is not the kind of procedure that increases growth in terms of either board feet or value of saw timber. However, growth in terms of cords, merchantable cubic feet, or value of products sold in the round may not suffer unduly.

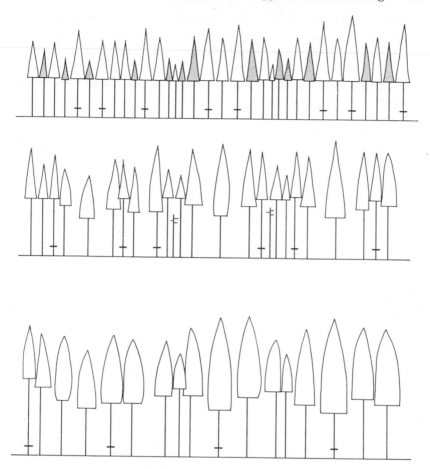

Fig. 3-8. A series of three selection thinnings in a stand of balsam fir and spruce being grown for pulpwood on a good site. Each sketch shows the stand immediately before a thinning. The trees with the shaded crowns in the first sketch are those that persist until the end of the rotation. The choice of trees to be removed in the second and third thinnings is somewhat modified by the necessity of avoiding enlargement of gaps caused by the earlier removal of dominants. The advanced reproduction that would undoubtedly become prominent by the time of the third thinning is not shown.

A program of repeated selection thinnings can have the virtue of holding the investment represented by merchantable growing stock at a low value. The value of the growth obtained then tends to return a high rate of interest on this part of the investment in the forestry enterprise. This can, of course, be an empty virtue if the annual cash return per acre is so low as to constitute a low rate of interest on the capital represented by the whole enterprise. The rotation will be very significantly prolonged, but if the overall returns can be kept high throughout the rotation this can actually be advantageous.

Species of low or intermediate shade-tolerance lack the ability to respond satisfactorily to very much repetition of selection thinning. If they are not extremely intolerant, stands of such species usually suffer no damage from one judicious selection thinning and may even be improved as far as stem quality is concerned. However, the second selection thinning is almost invariably the last that can be conducted without casting away most of the future growth potential of the stand. In stands of such species the less thrifty codominants and intermediates dwindle in vigor rapidly, with or without thinning; they may easily lose most of their crown surface and the ability to recover before the process of selection thinning can bring the top level of the canopy down to them.

Species that have a strong tendency to be negatively geotropic are better adapted to selection thinning than those that are inclined to be positively phototropic. In other words, selection thinning is more likely to prove successful with conifers, which tend to retain a single, vertical stem regardless of the effects of competition, than with most hardwoods. Selection thinnings have little place in hardwood management except as initial corrective action in elimination of rough dominants from young stands.

There is a third approach to selection thinning in which the technique is combined with simultaneous low thinning in order to enhance the vigor of the remaining trees. This usually has the effect of concentrating future production on the codominants and giving them room to expand their crowns and root systems to the side. Such treatment is of greatest advantage where the crowns of the codominants are unthrifty or where root competition is a crucial factor. It counteracts the baneful effects of selection thinning, but to a very limited extent. It is more useful in crowded, previously untreated stands than those that have been thinned before. Sometimes the supplementary low thinning is merely a means of harvesting merchantable subordinate trees that would serve no advantage if left. This combination of selection and low thinning, which could be regarded as a form of free thinning, cannot be repeated very often before prudence dictates a shift to low thinning or replacement by a new crop.

Almost all methods of selection thinning have a tendency to increase the possibility of losses to physical and biotic agencies. The trees that are released are likely to be of less than optimum vigor and to have rather weak and slender stems. Their reservation is, therefore, a calculated risk until they develop thriftier crowns and stronger stems.

In theory, the choices made in favor of unthrifty trees would appear undesirable from the genetic standpoint and discrimination against poorly formed trees, desirable. Although the selectivity may not be severe enough and the characteristics insufficiently heritable, it is prudent to assume that repeated selection thinning will prevent regeneration of the best genetic combinations.

One outstanding and insidious advantage of selection thinnings is that they are more likely to return an immediate profit than any other kind of thinning. The trees that are cut are the largest and ordinarily the most salable to be found in the stand at the time of cutting. This advantage is, however, gained at the expense of some others normally associated with thinning. The length of time required to grow the crop trees to a particular diameter is increased and the rate of growth in board-foot volume is decreased. If too many vigorous trees are eliminated, production in both tonnage and cubic volume will also dwindle.

The proportion of the cubic volume removed in any one selection thinning should generally be as low as possible. The heavier the thinning the greater is the reliance placed on growth in trees which characteristically show a delayed response to release and the more serious is the reduction in total growth of the stand. There is a tendency to make low thinnings and crown thinnings too light; the reverse is generally true of selection thinnings. The intervals between successive selection thinnings are longer than for thinnings of other kinds because the holes created by cutting dominants close so slowly.

The stratum of trees of the lower crown classes left in selection thinning has much the same effect as that left in crown thinning.

Selection thinnings bear only a superficial resemblance to the selection methods of regeneration employed in reproducing uneven-aged stands.- There is distinctly more to both techniques than merely cutting the big trees and leaving the little ones, although this is a characteristic feature of both. Selection thinnings are not more suitable for the even-aged aggregations of uneven-aged stands than other methods of thinning.

Actually the term, "selection" thinning, is merely the least confusing that might be applied to the method in question; it has, at least, never been applied to any other. All of the more grammatical and descriptive terms have unfortunately been applied rather indiscriminately to both crown and selection thinning.

There is a rather desperate sort of cutting, sometimes euphemistically described as one of the kinds of "selective cutting," which is best regarded, at least in its early stages, as selection thinning. Such cuttings involve attempts to extract the fullest potentialities for growth from the subordinate crown classes by successive cuttings of trees that have been brought to the dominant position. This often results from despair over the problem of replacing existing stands with desirable reproduction. Usually the source of concern is the active invasion of undesirable species of successional stages later than that represented by an existing stand of desirable species. If the problem is evaded by very light periodic cuttings of the largest trees, the residual stand grows poorly and the undesirable understory burgeons. One way to break this vicious cycle is to destroy the understory and open the overstory enough to allow reproduction of the desirable intolerant species.

This kind of cutting can also result from excessively single-minded concern about avoiding the high costs of harvesting small trees. Even more short-sighted is the policy of regarding the stand merely as a magic warehouse into which one ventures sporadically attempting to find trees that will meet the specifications for current orders. Both procedures ultimately leave stands of poor trees that cannot be moved economically by the most ingenious logging or the most astute salesmanship.

Mechanical Thinning

In the fourth general method of thinning, the trees to be cut or retained are chosen on the basis of a predetermined spacing or pattern with little or no regard for their position in the crown canopy. This technique can often be used to advantage in treating young stands that have not been thinned previously and are densely crowded. The arbitrary basis on which the trees are selected is justified in highly uniform stands that have not yet differentiated into crown classes; the same is true of stands that have many more dominants than are necessary to provide a fully stocked stand in the final stages of the rotation.

The technique of choosing trees to cut on a mechanical basis is often, although not invariably, followed in **precommercial thinnings** made purely as investments in the future growth of stands so young that none of the felled trees are extracted and utilized. **Commercial thinnings** are most simply defined as those in which all or part of the felled trees are extracted for useful products, regardless of whether their value is great enough to defray the cost of operation.

There are two general patterns that may be followed in mechanical thinning. In the first, referred to as **spacing thinning**, trees at fixed intervals of distance are chosen for retention and all others are cut. In the second, which is usually called **row thinning**, the trees are cut out in lines or narrow strips at fixed intervals throughout the stand. The rigidity of these specifications may be modified as occasion demands. In general, the justification for adherence to an arbitrary pattern decreases as the variation in size and quality of the trees increases.

Spacing thinnings are most commonly applied in seriously overcrowded stands that have developed from exceedingly dense natural reproduction. The simplest mode of application involves adherence to a rigid spacing. This approach can be modified by leaving the best tree in each square defined by the desired spacing. The amount of work involved can sometimes be reduced by removing only the active competitors of trees designated for release.

The principle of thinning to a predetermined spacing is ordinarily employed only in young stands. The technique is used for the first thinning and then usually discarded in favor of one of the other methods after the stand has differentiated into crown classes. The idea of thinning to a certain *average* spacing may, however, be followed in subsequent thinnings in order to control the severity of the cutting rather than the selection of trees to be reserved.

Row or line thinning, when applied in unmodified form, involves the same general principle as spacing thinning except that the trees are cut in narrow strips in order to facilitate the work. It has, for example, been found expeditious to thin densely crowded stands of slash pine saplings with rolling brush-cutters (McCulley, 1950). The trees are crushed down on strips 7 feet wide, leaving the trees in intervening bands 2 feet wide to form the crop. The same effect can be achieved with various other tractor-mounted devices (Fig. 3-9) or with hand-operated power saws designed for brush cutting (Dosen, Stoeckeler, and Kilp, 1957; Teeguarden and Gordon, 1959). In stands where large trees are intermingled with dense reproduction this kind of thinning can be carried out in crude but judicious fashion by felling or skidding timber across the overcrowded clumps.

Row thinning has been successfully used, with or without modifica-

Fig. 3-9. Mechanical thinning in a dense, stagnating stand of ponderosa pine, nearly 50 years old, in eastern Oregon. The trees in the cleared lanes (*right*) were crushed with a bulldozer, leaving the narrow strips of trees visible in the aerial photograph (*left*). Such treatment is crude but effective; the only serious danger is that *Ips* beetles will breed in the slash and attack the standing trees. (*Photographs by American Forest Products Industries.*)

tion, to facilitate the harvesting of products from dense, uniform stands that have not been thinned previously (Spurr, 1948). The first thinning carried out in a stand is almost invariably the most difficult because the congestion in the crown canopy creates problems in felling the trees and the close spacing of the residual stand impedes transportation of logs. Furthermore, the relatively small size of the trees results in high cost and low value per unit of volume removed. These problems have often made it virtually impossible to initiate conventional thinnings in the very stands that need them most.

In row thinnings it is possible to proceed in such a way that the trees are successively felled into the vacancies created by the cutting of adjacent trees. The products can then be easily removed along the lanes that have been cut through the stand, provided that care is taken to deposit the slash at the sides. This overcomes many of the objections, real or imaginary, which have been raised against the idea of thinning by woods labor. A second cycle of row thinnings is rarely necessary (or advisable) because of the improved accessibility resulting from the first.

Row thinnings are most readily applied in plantations that are already laid out in straight rows. In its purest form, this involves removal of every third row. Every residual tree is freed on one side and the removal of one-third of the stand is a good approximation of the normal severity of most thinnings in young stands. The removal of every other row would ordinarily be too severe. It is sometimes found that the spacing of the trees can be adjusted more satisfactorily in subsequent thinnings if the residual strips alternate in width between those that are two and those that are three rows wide.

The strips can also be shifted to go around especially desirable trees (Fig. 3-10). In closely spaced stands the lanes might be made two rows wide in order to allow the passage of equipment used in transportation. The severity of the thinning can be reduced by spacing the cut strips at wider intervals. This course would be desirable where the objective was to stimulate the growth of trees destined to be removed in the final crop without heavy expenditure of labor or the production of an excessive amount of small material for which there was a limited demand.

Row thinning is also effectively used in combination with other methods of thinning merely to create avenues of transportation (Luther and Cook, 1948). Rows are removed at fixed, predetermined intervals, usually such that four to seven rows are left in between and are subjected to some other method of thinning. This is the only kind of row thinning that is really justified in stands that have already differentiated into crown classes or have a limited number of potential crop trees.

There is no reason why any of these kinds of row thinning cannot be applied in dense, uniform stands of natural origin. In fact, the logging problems associated with the first thinning, done according to any method in any kind of stand, are reduced if the marking is done so that there are closely spaced avenues of access wide enough and sufficiently free of abrupt curves for use by the extraction equipment. It is sometimes possible to mark whole stands in this manner and with a high degree of selectivity simply by proceeding in gently sweeping and sinuous curves from one tree that ought to be cut to another, marking them as one goes along. If such special measures are taken in the first thinning, they do not have to be repeated because the avenues created remain useful for subsequent thinnings.

Row thinning leads to the development of oval or lop-sided crowns; this result is likely to be only temporary and of little consequence, especially if attention is given to developing symmetrical crowns in subsequent thinnings. The boles of the trees do not, in any event, become elliptical as a result of row thinning (Spurr, 1948).

The main disadvantages of arbitrary selection of the trees lie in the

Fig. 3-10. A row thinning in a 28-year-old plantation of red pine in Connecticut. Every third row of trees has been arbitrarily removed, except where the strips were shifted to go around especially promising trees. The opening in the canopy will close in about 6 years. (*Photograph by Yale University School of Forestry.*)

unfavorable effects of removing good trees and leaving poor ones in stands where there is substantial variation between individuals. The removal of an excessively high proportion of the dominant trees can have the same undesirable effects sometimes associated with selection thinning. As a consequence, row thinning is best carried out when the stand is young, before the dominants become restricted in number and the crowns of the trees so large that wide gaps result. Appropriate modifications of the technique often eliminate most of these disadvantages. As with all methods of cutting, row thinning must be conducted with discretion and will give poor results if applied indiscriminately.

It is likely that row thinning will become more important as progress is made in the development of equipment for complete mechanization of harvesting. Such equipment is not likely to be especially maneuverable, especially if tree-length logging is involved, so it may be anticipated that the trees will have to be removed along rather straight lines.

Free Thinning

Cuttings designed to release crop trees without regard for their position in the crown canopy are **free thinnings,** in the sense of being unrestricted by adherence to any one of the other methods of thinning. However, in any free thinning the mode of treatment accorded any one of the trees cut or released can be identified as representing one of the other four methods. The greatest need for combining several methods in a single thinning is encountered in stands that are somewhat irregular in age, density, or composition. Plantations are usually sufficiently uniform that free thinnings are unnecessary in them. According to Braathe (1957), the European view is that natural stands almost invariably present such a variety of conditions that they can be handled only by free thinning.

Technical terminology should convey as much meaning as possible. Therefore, vague terms like "free thinning" ought to be avoided if there is any reasonable possibility that one of the other terms might apply to a particular operation. It is more informative to use terms like "modified crown thinning" or "crown and selection thinning" than to throw all variants into a miscellaneous category. It should be noted that all of these terms refer to single operations and not sequences thereof. A program of treatment is not referred to as free thinning simply because crown thinnings are, for example, followed by low thinnings.

Conditions requiring free thinnings are most likely to exist at the time of the first thinning in previously untreated natural stands. This approach is distinctly advantageous for bringing a stand into shape for efficient production (Wahlenberg, 1952). If the objectives of the thinning program are clearly defined and consistently pursued the irregularities begin to fade and the likelihood increases that a logical thinning operation will conform to a single method. From the stand-point of efficiency of logging and administration, it is desirable to achieve regularity of treatment as soon as uniformity can be imposed without undue sacrifice of the growth potential of the stand.

A typical free thinning operation in an unevenly stocked but even-aged stand might simultaneously include: (1) selection thinning to eliminate scattered undesirable dominants, (2) crown thinning to re-lease crop trees drawn mainly from good dominants and secondarily from thrifty codominants in the more sparsely stocked portions, and (3) low thinning to salvage all merchantable overtopped trees throughout the stand and to thin the well-stocked portions to the se-verity of the D grade.

Quantitative Definition of Thinning Methods

The ratio d/D, where d is the average D.B.H. of trees removed in thinning and D, the average before thinning, is a useful and objective expression for the method of thinning (Hummel, 1953). This is espe-cially true if the method is varied. The ratio is more than 1.00 for se-lection thinning, less than 1.00 for other methods of thinning, and least for light low thinning.

APPLICATION OF THINNINGS

A schedule of thinning should be a systematic undertaking con-sistently followed until the period of regeneration on the basis of a definite plan leading to the production of the kind of material de-sired. Some of the details should remain flexible enough to be set-tled on the basis of conditions prevailing at the time of each operation but the goals should be changed only in event of major alterations in the long-term objectives of the management of the forest.

Three main considerations enter into the development of an ef-fective program of thinnings. It is first necessary to decide which method or methods of thinning should be employed at each stage of the rotation. The second consideration is the timing of the first and subsequent thinnings. Finally it is necessary to determine approxi-mately how much growing stock will be left after each thinning.

All these factors are interdependent, and their adjustment must be worked out in the light of the economic objectives and natural limi-tations that prevail in each situation. The relationship between the timing and the severity of the thinnings is especially close, because heavy thinnings cannot be repeated as frequently as lighter cuttings.

Choosing Methods of Thinning

Like any other silvicultural technique, each method of thinning is designed to solve some general type of problem encountered in the treatment of a stand. Although clarity demands that the descriptions of the methods be rigid, the procedures actually followed may be quite flexible. Even if allowance is made for the introduction of minor deviations from a standard technique, it is only under the least complicated circumstances that a single method can be followed through an entire thinning program.

If it is possible to thin a stand only once or twice a single method may be most applicable. On the other hand, the necessity of doing so much with such limited opportunity is likely to dictate simultaneous use of two or more methods in free thinning operations. This would be especially true if the stand was not very uniform.

The likelihood that repeated application of a single method might be found best for a long series of thinnings is rather limited, at least under American conditions. The stand would have to be very uniform so that the crop trees would be alike and treatment would not have to be varied in different parts of the stand. Then, if markets were excellent and if the crop trees were of good quality and always in a clearly dominant position, one might conceivably employ a simple series of low thinnings like that shown later in Fig. 3-13. A series of selection thinnings might be applicable to growing stands of very tolerant conifers for pulpwood, although there might be some problems of securing reproduction and disposing of unmarketable residual trees at the end of the rotation. With species of sufficient tolerance, it might be possible to apply a series of what could be called crown thinnings if the ultimate disposal of any lower layer of trees were not regarded as a deviation from the method.

Ordinarily the crown classes that should be removed to favor the crop trees and those that can be harvested profitably will change as a stand grows older. This calls for changes in the method of thinning even in the absence of differences in condition of various parts of the stand.

The high labor costs and low product values typical of American forestry make it necessary to pay close attention to the diameters of the trees removed. This factor introduces a more acute need for changes of thinning method than is apparent under less restrictive economic conditions. The diagrams shown in Fig. 3-11 illustrate the point that the four well-defined methods involve the removal of trees from different segments of the distribution of diameter classes in an

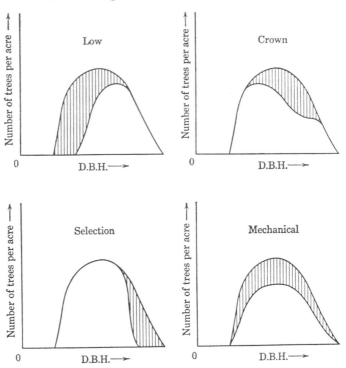

Fig. 3-11. Diameter distributions for the same even-aged stand showing, by cross-hatching, the parts that would be removed in the four different methods of thinning. In each case about one-third of the basal area is represented as having been removed. It is assumed that no overtopped trees are salvaged in the crown and selection thinnings, that the stands have not been treated previously, and that D.B.H. is closely correlated with crown class.

even-aged stand. From this it can be seen that if selection, crown, and low thinnings followed in succession as a stand grew older there would be some possibility of avoiding cutting trees when they were small. If removals from the dominant crown class are undesirable, the same can be accomplished by crown thinning that is followed with low thinning. Such measures are not perfect solutions to the problem because it is so difficult to make the trees of the lower crown classes increase rapidly in diameter. Mechanical methods like row thinning contribute to reduction of logging costs chiefly by facilitating the work; the choice of diameter classes removed is purely random so that both large and small trees will be represented in those cut.

The changes in thinning methods appropriate to developing good crop trees often follow the same sequence by which the costly logging of small trees is evaded. It is logical that any coarse dominants be removed in early selection thinnings. The enlargement of the crowns of crop trees is, in the early stages, most readily expedited and controlled by crown thinnings, provided that care is taken to avoid undue deceleration of natural pruning. Once the crop trees have been successfully promoted to clearly dominant position, their competitors can be removed in low thinnings. One might even start such a sequence with a mechanical thinning.

Such changes generally follow the principle of shifting the level from which trees are removed downward through the crown canopy. Although any one of the steps mentioned might be omitted from the sequence, it is rarely possible or advantageous to reverse the order. It is conceivable, however, that one could switch from low thinnings to crown or selection thinnings. Such a pattern might be useful if it were necessary to keep the canopy closed during early stages in order to hasten the death of lower branches. The compulsion to low thinning late in the rotation comes purely from the fact that the trees of the subordinate crown classes have usually reached the end of their usefulness and only the dominants or vigorous codominants retain much capacity for further increase in value.

The pattern of shifting the level of thinning downward through the canopy is discernable in many of the sophisticated European thinning regimes. One of the most intensive of these is the *Auslesedurchforstung*, literally "selective thinning," of Schädelin (1942) in which the choice of potential crop trees is made on the basis of branching habit and other characteristics early in the sapling stage and the chosen trees are released by light cleanings. Many of the so-called Danish thinnings follow the same pattern but rarely start so early in the rotation.

Even though a stand is uniform it is not necessarily desirable that each thinning operation follow the same pattern throughout the stand. For example, if the rotation is long and the thinnings start early, it may at 30 years be useful to accord different treatment to trees destined for removal at 60 years and those to be held for 100 years (Macdonald, 1961). The "short-rotation" trees may require complete release so that they will lose no more live crown surface and will grow rapidly during the remainder of their allotted time. Meanwhile, the "long-rotation" trees may be left somewhat crowded so that the attrition of their lower live branches will continue and their boles will not develop large branches or excessive taper. In general, when thinnings start early in the rotation, it is necessary to plan proper treatment not only for the final-crop trees but also for the rather numerous ones which can develop substantial value even if they are destined for somewhat earlier removal.

Timing of the First Thinning

In theory the first thinning can be carried out just as soon as the crowns or the root systems of individual trees close together and start to interfere with one another. Competition of this sort almost invariably commences early in the sapling stage in any but the most poorly stocked stands. The best single criterion for determining when to apply the first thinning is the live crown ratio of the potential crop trees. As long as a satisfactory ratio is maintained, a stand need not be thinned until the thinning will pay an immediate profit. If the live crown ratio is dropping toward a dangerously low point, a thinning may be required at a present financial loss as an investment for the future.

The various natural factors that affect the timing of the first thinning are considered in terms of their economic consequences. The owner's policy regarding long-term silvicultural investments is the basic factor influencing this particular decision. Where such investments cannot be made, the first thinning is delayed until it can be carried out with an immediate profit. Where funds for silvicultural investments are unlimited, the first thinning may be made as soon as the value of all the ultimate benefits, discounted to the present at compound interest, will equal the cost of the operation. There are, of course, a variety of positions that can be taken between these two extreme viewpoints. There are also situations unfavorable to intensive silviculture in which the appropriate time never arrives.

In precommercial thinning, it is desirable to proceed in such manner as to achieve the greatest possible increase in diameter growth with small amount of work. This line of attack differs from commercial thinning in which it is usually advantageous to harvest the highest possible proportion of those trees that will not contribute to the future increase in value of the stand.

One useful approach to precommercial thinning is that of "crop-tree thinning" in which only the trees likely to form the final crop are released. Usually most of the potential benefits are gained merely by eliminating the one or two most serious competitors of each crop tree. Reukema (1961) found, for example, that the cutting of additional competitors caused little further increase in diameter growth of Douglas-fir and that dominant trees responded better than those of lower crown classes. However, it is possible that the period of enhanced diameter growth is longer the more drastic the reduction of competition. If an investment is required to carry out the first thinning, it is desirable to make it heavy enough to ensure that no further treatment will be required before the stand reaches the stage where a profitable cutting can be made.

The cost of precommercial thinning can be substantially reduced by use of power-driven equipment or chemicals.

The policy of postponing the first thinning until it will return an immediate profit can be defended on the ground that many fine stands have developed in nature without treatment of any kind. In most stands, failure to thin should be looked upon as a lost opportunity rather than as an invitation to disaster. However, in many of these same stands the net return from the whole crop could be increased if an outright investment were made in thinning at the appropriate time. Zasada (1952), for example, described a case in which an investment in precommercial thinning in a 20-year-old stand of aspen almost tripled the stumpage value and was returned at a good rate of interest in the remaining 20 years of the rotation. The stand involved was typical of the majority of those encountered, because its development would have proceeded to an acceptable, although less profitable, outcome without thinning. It is significant that Webster (1960) concluded that precommercial thinning of hardwood stands would represent the most rewarding long-term silvicultural investment in the state forests of Pennsylvania.

A strong case can be made for investment in early thinning where the stand would deteriorate without treatment. The most important examples of this situation are to be found in very dense stands of natural reproduction which are likely to stagnate. This tendency is prevalent in hard pines such as lodgepole (Alexander, 1960), jack (Roe and Stoeckeler, 1950), red (Schantz-Hansen, 1952), slash (Gruschow, 1949), and ponderosa pine (Stage, 1958; Myers, 1958), as well as in balsam fir (Hart, 1961), although it can occur to some extent in almost any species. Stagnation of height growth and failure to express dominance are most common on poor sites and in species that can regenerate prolifically there. Certain species, however, appear to have sufficient genetic variability in vigor to express dominance even in dense stands; eastern white pine is a good example (Deen, 1933). The ability of trees in stagnated stands to respond to release decreases with the passage of time; therefore, no advantage is gained by delaying treatment.

There are instances in which stagnation or failure to express dominance has been overcome on poor sites by fertilization alone (Gessel, 1959), including one in which thinning itself was not effective (Heiberg and White, 1951).

The period that can be allowed to elapse between the time of crown closure and the first thinning is generally shorter in plantations than in naturally regenerated stands. The trees of planted stands are exceptionally uniform in age and spacing and, therefore, tend to be evenly matched in size and vigor. On the other hand, while competition is suddenly joined in planted stands the time of this development can be postponed by widening the initial spacing.

Another general situation in which ample justification can be found for investments in treatment of very young stands is, oddly enough, the reverse of stagnation. Differentiation into crown classes may proceed so far that certain dominants get too far ahead of their neighbors and develop into trees of poor form with little or no prospective value. If their removal is delayed until they can be cut profitably, the better subordinates may be lost or oppressed beyond the point of recovery.

Even if the untreated stand does not stagnate or develop into a collection of rough dominants, the stage is ultimately reached at which it may be dangerous or fruitless to initiate thinning or any other form of partial cutting. Even the dominants eventually reach the point where the crowns are reduced to small tufts at the tops of weak, slender stems. If trees of this kind are released by thinning they are likely to be killed or injured by biotic and atmospheric agencies; even at best, they respond to release only after a long delay. In other words, a situation can develop in which it is unwise to thin a stand even after the time has arrived when the operation would be immediately profitable. In such a stand, an investment in early thinning may represent the only way in which the financial benefits of later thinnings can be made available.

Special consideration should be given to early thinnings in situations where stands are seriously endangered by damage from wind or other mechanical agencies. The stout, tapering form of the boles of trees that are resistant to this sort of damage can be maintained only if thinnings are early and frequent. The longer the first thinning is postponed the greater is the risk that it will be followed by wholesale losses. Even if no thinning is carried out in such places, the risk of damage will gradually increase because the trees become taller and more slender with increasing age.

Early thinning is likewise advisable in places where the trees must be kept vigorous if they are to remain resistant to the ravages of those kinds of insects, fungi, and physiological disorders which attack trees weakened by competition. Trees that have just been released by long-delayed thinnings are generally very susceptible to such injuries.

The immediate financial advantages of postponing the first thinning should be carefully weighed against the danger of being trapped in a vicious cycle in which treatment becomes ever more necessary and ever more dangerous.

There are several other considerations that affect the timing of the first thinning. As has already been indicated, thinning is often delayed until natural pruning has proceeded to a satisfactory extent. Delayed thinning also tends to reduce the taper of the stems, rendering a higher proportion of them suitable for poles and other round products.

Other things being equal, the first thinning should be made earlier in stands of wide-crowned species than in those that have trees with characteristically narrow crowns. It can be delayed longer in stands of tolerant species than in those composed of intolerant trees. Thinnings become advantageous earlier in untreated stands than in those that have been subjected to cleaning or improvement cutting. In general, a stand in which the crop trees have been artificially pruned should be thinned almost immediately to ensure that the pruned trees survive and grow rapidly.

Timing of Subsequent Thinnings

The effects of a single thinning are not maintained indefinitely. After a few years, the gaps in the canopy close together and before long the same crowded condition that existed before thinning redevelops. As the crowns expand the number of trees that can occupy an acre to best advantage decreases and the surplus volume available for removal in the next thinning accumulates.

The rate of growth of the crop trees is the best single criterion for determining when thinnings should be repeated. It is logical to set some realistic rate of diameter growth as a goal and thin when the growth of the crop trees falls below it.

It is also likely to be necessary to wait until the volume that can be removed has accumulated enough to support a profitable operation. If the stand closes too tightly and diameter growth slows down too much before sufficient volume accumulates, it is a sign that the previous thinning was either too light or was not done in such manner as to give the crop trees enough room to grow. In this respect close attention must be paid to manipulation of the diameter distribution of trees destined to be removed in thinnings. If too many of the larger ones are cut at once, the next thinning may have to be postponed until long after the small trees have choked the crown canopy in the process of growing to merchantable size.

The proper balance between severity, method, and timing of thinnings is not an easy one to strike. This kind of adjustment is still highly intuitive because there are so many considerations to take into account. The diameter growth of the crop trees is by far the best and simplest guide; unfortunately it indicates the status of only one component of the stand.

The heavier the thinnings the longer is the interval between them. Heavy, infrequent thinnings tend to reduce the total yield of a stand because of the long periods during which parts of the growing space remain unoccupied.

Scandinavian observations indicate that losses in production of gross cubic-volume may be expected if the interval between thinnings becomes longer than about 5 years and if the severity of thinnings is increased to correspond with the longer intervals (Braathe, 1957). This poses a dilemma for American forestry practice because, where thinnings are applied, the intervals are often rather long. The assumption that cubic-volume production is independent of stand density remains thoroughly valid only if thinnings are of no more than moderate severity and are started early with frequent repetition.

Nevertheless, a thinning regime that sacrifices some of the potential production of cubic volume can, through its effect on tree diameter, still increase the yield in terms of merchantable volume or value of wood. Almost any kind of thinning also augments the actual yield by enabling harvest of material that would otherwise be lost to natural suppression. In other words, the interval between thinnings must become very long indeed before the treatments cease to enhance the value of wood actually harvested from a stand.

The practice of repeating thinnings at equal intervals simplifies administration but has no other virtues. Actually young stands should be thinned more frequently than old because they close up more rapidly. For example, a rule sometimes followed in Denmark is that the number of years between thinnings should equal the age of the stand in decades. Another rule expressing the same idea is that of thinning when a certain fixed amount of growth in height, such as 10 or 20 feet, has taken place since the last thinning.

In North America it is rare that stands are thinned more frequently than every 5 years. However, if a stand can be thinned once at a profit there is seldom any good reason to allow more than 15 years to elapse before the next thinning.

Regulation of Stand Density

Thinning is fundamentally a technique for controlling the density of stands. Therefore, any well-conceived program of thinnings should be governed by some reasonably definite schedule indicating the density of the stand at all stages of its development. Such schedules are ultimately necessary to ensure the orderly development of final crops consisting of trees of the qualities, sizes, and volumes desired. They are also necessary for purposes of forest regulation to predict the yields that will be obtained in future years from intermediate and final cuttings. The development of such schedules is a complicated problem that has received the attention of generations of foresters and is likely to continue to do so. No one schedule would be optimum for all stands, even within a given forest type, because both economic and natural factors must be considered.

A thinning schedule must be based on some expression of the stage of development of the stand. The age of the stand is customarily used because it provides the only basis for determining the actual rate of growth. However, this leads to complications, at least in the derivations of thinning schedules, because stands on good sites go through about the same sequence of development faster than those on poor sites. If age is used as the sole criterion of stage of development, it is necessary to have a different thinning schedule for each site-quality class. However, if the range of sites is small, stand height can be used as a criterion of stand development in which both site quality and age are integrated.

Consideration of the details of any thinning schedule requires recognition of the fact that, at the time of each thinning, the trees of the stand are segregated into three categories. The first and most important group consists of the trees destined to form the final crop. The second comprises those trees that will be removed in subsequent thinnings but will be needed in the meantime to utilize the growing space that will eventually be occupied by the final crop. These two categories, which do not always have to be clearly distinguished, make up the growing stock left after each thinning. The final category consists of the surplus trees that are to be eliminated in the thinning.

Two fundamentally different modes of procedure can be distinguished, at least for purposes of discussion. In the first, the development of the *individual* crop tree is the most important consideration. At the time of each thinning, attention is concentrated on releasing the candidates for the final crop to such an extent that they will grow at the desired rate until the next thinning. Thinnings may be conducted among the intervening trees, especially if the crop trees are far apart, but this phase of the operation is relegated to secondary importance. No special consideration is given to maintaining any definite or uniform level of stocking on the average acre. According to this philosophy the yield of volume and value from the thinnings, although by no means unimportant, is of so little consequence compared with that of the final crop that it may be left to adjust itself automatically.

The "crop tree" approach is best adapted to situations where the primary objective is to produce saw logs. It is especially applicable in growing hardwoods for lumber, because the value of the product depends so much on the quality of the trees. Holsoe (1950) has shown how the growth of various species of hardwoods can be controlled by regulating the size of the crowns. The same general procedure can also be followed with conifers.

In the second, and more traditional, approach the main objective is to determine how much growing stock should be left after each thinning in order to give an optimum yield in terms of *volume per acre*. In theory, no effort is made to distinguish between the final crop trees and those that will be removed in subsequent thinnings. If this general approach is followed, it is necessary to exercise close control over the amount and distribution of the growing stock at the time of each thinning.

Actually it is rare that either approach is followed to the exclusion of the other. Even in cases where the final crop trees are the most important part of the total yield, it is usually advisable to formulate some schedule prescribing the average growing stock to be left on an acre after each thinning. The first approach evades the problem of securing efficient regulation of the density of whole stands. Since the second does not, it is now desirable to resume the discussion of the relationship between the density and growth of stands.

Attempts to develop basic thinning schedules. In spite of generations of attempts, it is still not possible to state precisely how dense any stand should be left after each of a series of thinnings in order to produce optimum growth in either volume or value.

Actually two separate problems are involved. The first is the basic one of elucidating the relationship between the density and stocking of thinned stands and their growth. The second is the development of sound scientific parameters of stand density for use in solving the first problem and the subsequent translation of them into simple parameters for applying the solution in routine thinning practice (Bickford, Baker and Wilson, 1957).

In the wisdom of hindsight it is possible to see that this development should have proceeded from the scientific construction of a biological basis for understanding the effect on growth of artificial reductions of stand density. Generations of effort have instead been devoted to empirical attempts to solve the problem by observational trial-and-error or mathematical short cuts, sophisticated and otherwise, that sometimes seem to involve little more than playing with numbers.

The current studies of the effect of stand density on the production of dry matter or total cubic volume that were reviewed in Chapter 2 presumably represent the appropriate kind of biological basis for further development. It was pointed out that the control of stand density is fundamentally a matter of controlling diameter growth by allocating varying amounts of aphotosynthetic area to the rather constant photosynthetic surface represented by the crown canopy. It is at least plausible to proceed from the tentative hypothesis that the smaller the amount of aphotosynthetic surface left in a thinned stand the thicker will be the layer in which a fixed amount of wood is annually deposited by the cambium of stems and branches of the stand. The idea that the total annual production is fixed is valid only if the stand continues full occupancy of the site and is not exceedingly crowded. It is assumed, in other words, that the smaller, within limits, the amount of aphotosynthetic area left per acre the greater will be the average diameter growth of the stems. If this relationship is to be usefully translated into quantitative terms, there must be some parameter of aphotosynthetic surface more readily evaluated than the total cambial area of stems and branches. If the assumptions are valid, there is no practical need to measure the photosynthetic surface because it is taken as constant and the chief problem is finding the most reliable and convenient index value for the cambial surface being nourished.

The demand for convenient parameters of stand density has led to the suggestion of a vast and confusing array. Among them are basal area, various relationships between either diameter or height and spacing, volume per acre, and functions of stand density based on some supposedly standard density such as that of "normal" stocking. The scientific investigations necessary to establish the nature of good thinning schedules are best conducted in terms of parameters like bole and crown surface area. Such parameters are too cumbersome for routine use in thinning practice, but once appropriate schedules have been developed it is no problem to translate them into more convenient units like basal area or even such simple expressions as numbers of trees per acre.

The most logical parameter, **bole surface area** per acre, was proposed by Lexen (1943). This measure is a close approximation of the cambial surface of the main stems of the trees, that is, of the most crucial component of the aphotosynthetic surface at which both respiration and accretion of wood occur. It does not include the cambial surface of the branches and roots and is, to this extent, an awkward compromise between mensurational convenience and biological perfection. However, except for unthrifty trees and those of great vigor with exceptionally large branches, the proportion of branch surface to bole surface and the amount of wood laid down for each unit of bole surface is probably about the same for all trees of a given pure, even-aged stand. If this be true, and the work of Satoo and Senda (1958) suggests that it is, the use of bole surface area per acre can be taken as a biologically sound measure of stand density for use in thinning.

Bole surface is hardly a convenient unit of measure for routine application in thinning, because it is a function of basal circumference, height, and taper of trees. However, in a uniform stand the different trees vary so little in taper that the **bole area equivalent,** which is the product of stand height and the sum of the circumferences of the trees, can be taken as an adequate index of the bole surface of the stand (Hiley and Lehtpere, 1955).

It is possible that this can be simplified even more in stands where all the trees are of nearly the same height. If both height and diameter are taken as constants, the sum of tree diameters per acre becomes an index of bole surface area, because the sum of the circumferences is merely the sum of the diameters multiplied by the constant π. It is significant that Cooper (1961) found that the mean annual increment of young ponderosa pine stands was better correlated with the sum of the diameters of the trees than with basal area per acre. Indexes of stand density based on bole surface area deserve more thoroughgoing tests than they have yet received.

The most common parameter of stand density is **basal area** per acre, which is a function of the sum of squares of the diameters of the trees. It came into use not strictly as a parameter of stand density but as an index of the cubic volume of a stand. Its biological significance is rather questionable because it is, in this sense, merely a measure of the cross-sectional area of physiologically dead stem tissue in a stand. Basal area can, however, be determined without measurements of height which are both laborious and subject to error. It is also fully as valid as any well-tested index of stand density and has the advantage of being simpler than most (Spurr, 1952).

The practical usefulness of basal area has been greatly enhanced by the introduction of the Bitterlich point-sampling technique. This enables quick measurement of basal area per acre, without laying out plots or measuring trees, by means of prisms or various angle-guages which may involve equipment no more complicated than a coin or one's thumb. The very similar, but less familiar technique of line-sampling (Grosenbaugh, 1958) can also be used to estimate the sum of the diameters per acre, the most important variable function of bole surface. Unless otherwise specified, subsequent discussion of stand density will involve basal area as the unit of measure because most experimentation and practice have been based upon it.

The practical results of empirical attempts to develop thinning schedules are embodied in European empirical yield tables (Oelkers, 1930–7; Sabroe, 1954; Wiedemann and Schober, 1957; Assmann, 1961) indicating the volume basal area, and other quantitative attributes of the trees cut and left in series of thinnings. These studies have only recently begun to produce any clear scientific basis for generalization about thinning procedure in either mathematical or biological terms. Many, but not all, of them describe rather conservative thinning aimed more at positive assurance of maximum cubic-volume production than at achievement of optimum diameter growth. However, they do convey the best available picture of the probable trend of stand density during series of thinnings based on the lessons of experience. It is, therefore, worth noting that these yield tables usually indicate that the basal area *remaining* after thinning should, during a series of thinnings, increase to a relatively constant or slowly rising level. Any theoretical scheme that departs widely from this pattern should probably be treated with skepticism.

Many of the mathematical approaches have been directed at developing measures of residual stand density (that is, the portion of the stand remaining after thinning), which, if held constant throughout the rotation, would automatically define a series of thinnings of uniform severity. Basal area is not the long-sought perfectly constant guiding index for thinning if only because it must increase from zero during the early life of any stand.

A number of the mathematical parameters which have been proposed are based directly or indirectly on normal yield tables. The most well-known example is stand density index proposed by Reineke (1933) and described by Mulloy (1944, 1946) and Spurr (1952). Parameters of this sort have been proposed chiefly as guiding constants and, if used as such, usually define series of thinnings in which basal area increases substantially with time. Since the results of empirical studies suggest that the basal area should not be allowed to increase much, if at all, during the middle and latter portions of the rotation, the use of guiding constants derived from normal yield tables is questionable.

The recommendations arising from mensurational studies have occasionally been expressed in certain "rules of thumb" regarding the proper spacing of the trees left after thinning. According to the widely advocated $D + x$ rule, the average spacing in feet should equal the average stand diameter D in inches plus a constant x. The values of x that have been suggested for various situations range from 1 to 8, the commonest value being 6. Rules of this form provide for a steady increase in basal area (Averell, 1945). Satisfactory results are not likely to be achieved with the $D + x$ rule unless the value of x is increased with age rather than held constant. Rules of the form Dx provide for a constant basal area (Davis, 1935); the value of the factor x for a basal area of 90 square feet per acre is, for example, 1.75, and for 150 square feet, 1.35.

Another way of regulating the spacing of trees left after thinning is to set the average spacing equal to a constant fraction of the height of the dominant trees. Wilson (1951) suggested that the spacing for tolerant species like spruce and fir be one-sixth of the height, and for intolerant trees like red and jack pine, one-fourth of the height. The spacing is thus governed by the height, which is the best possible index of the stage of development of the stand and also a characteristic which is not significantly affected by thinning itself. According to Wilson (1955), if the proper fraction of total height is chosen as the spacing, the resulting program of thinning closely follows some other schedules derived from empirical studies. This mode of definition of the severity of thinning treatments has the virtues of simplicity, objectivity, and independence of effects of thinning itself (Hummel, 1953). There is also evidence that it may be well correlated with bole surface area per acre in frequently thinned stands (Wilson, 1955), although the physiological significance of measuring stand density in terms of height is otherwise yet to be elucidated.

Once the details of a thinning program for a given situation have been decided upon by any line of attack, the kind of stand to be left after thinning can also be described simply in terms of the number of trees per acre to be left in thinnings made at specified ages or stand heights (Craib, 1947; Hiley, 1952; Penistan, 1961). The same information can also be converted to the approximate average spacing interval for the residual trees. Such simple measures of stand density are useful for conveying instructions to the uninitiated with regard to very specific kinds of uniform stands. The technique works best in plantations which are of absolutely even age and are much more uniform as to size and distribution of trees than natural stands. The specification of number of trees per acre or an average spacing value means practically nothing unless there is some additional means, direct or indirect, of evaluating and allowing for the average D.B.H. and height of the stand.

The density of a stand cannot be adequately measured in terms of cords, merchantable cubic volume, or board feet. These units do not include all the wood and their interpretation varies widely with different standards of utilization. Although the volume of wood yet to be produced by a stand is a phenomenon of both biological and economic significance, it is not directly controlled by the volume of wood, now physiologically dead, that has been produced in the past. There are better criteria for evaluating the productive ability of the trees that are left. The actual volume of trees removed from an acre has an important effect on harvesting costs but the volume that is left has little. Therefore, the percentage of volume that is removed in a thinning has less significance than the common usage of this mode of expression might suggest.

The more modern statistical and mathematical approach to the problem of regulating stand density has been followed chiefly with respect to loblolly and other southern pines. Among these efforts are those of MacKinney and Chaiken (1939), Chisman and Schumacher (1940), Deetlefs (1953, 1954), Warrack (1959), Schumacher and Coile (1960), Wahlenberg (1960), and Czarnowski (1961). Most of these methods are based on equations derived by statistical methods from observations of the relationships between growth and such parameters as number of trees and basal area per acre, average diameter and height of stands, live-crown ratios and other measures of crown dimensions, site quality and age, and indexes of stand density derived from mathematical hypotheses about the relationship between the average D.B.H. and number of trees per acre. The statistical approach is more objective than the others and will ultimately provide one of the best tools for building the long chain of relationships between the biological phenomena of stand density and the economic phenomenon of value of wood produced by a stand. The empirical equations so far developed by this approach tend to fall between the ends of this chain. Although somewhat conflicting, they are useful guides to practice for the species to which they apply. Their development has not, however, produced many of the broad generalizations that may ultimately be expected.

The practice of forestry, or any other applied science, must continue even while doubt remains about the exact nature of its scientific basis. So it is with thinning schedules. In order to illustrate the characteristics of a program for regulating stand density it is here arbitrarily assumed that the basal area left after a thinning should be increased gradually from middle age onward and that the objective is to obtain the greatest diameter growth possible without sacrifice of cubic-volume production. Such a program is illustrated graphically in Fig. 3-12.

During the series of thinnings depicted the basal area of the stand is periodically reduced and then allowed to increase in such fashion that it fluctuates between certain fairly definite limits. If growth of cubic volume is to be maintained at the highest possible level the basal area should be kept within the range for which growth is optimum and independent of stand density, that is, Density Type III in Fig. 2-4. Theoretically, the greatest diameter growth obtainable without sacrifice of production of cubic volume will result if the stands are periodically reduced to the lowest stocking possible in Langsaeter's Density Type III.

The lower limit is by far the most important of the two shown in Fig. 3-12 because it defines the density of the stand after each thinning. The length of time allowed to elapse between thinnings and the increase of basal area during that period are governed almost automatically by the extent to which the density of the stand is reduced at the beginning. In other words, the plan for controlling stand density throughout the rotation may be viewed largely in terms of the trend of the lower guiding limit defining the basal area left after each thinning. If thinnings are light and frequent, basal area will fluctuate within a narrower range than if they are heavy and infrequent.

The amount of basal area which should be reserved in the middle

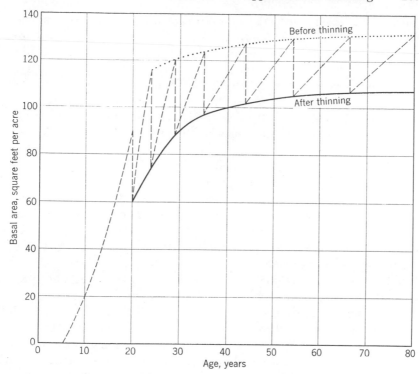

Fig. 3-12. A hypothetical example showing how basal area should vary during a series of thinnings. The solid line (————) indicates the lower guiding limit of basal area reserved after thinning. The dashed line (– – – –) shows the fluctuations in actual basal area. The dotted line (......) represents an approximation of the level to which basal area should be allowed to increase before thinnings are repeated. The interval of time elapsing between thinnings lengthens with age because the rate of growth in basal area declines as the trees grow larger. The arbitrary assumption is made that, in this case, the basal area left after each thinning should increase gradually from the middle of the rotation onward.

and later stages of the rotation varies widely, depending on the characteristics of the species, the site, and the objectives of management. If the objective is to maximize diameter growth without sacrifice of cubic volume growth the proper level will ordinarily be found somewhere between 50 and 175 square feet per acre. As was suggested in Fig. 2-5, the appropriate level is probably lower for hardwoods as a group than for conifers. That for shade-tolerant species will certainly be higher than for those of lower photosynthetic efficiency. While the evidence is far from conclusive, data from a variety of sources, including Wiedemann (1950–1) and Sabroe (1954), indicate that this level is in the range from 130 to 175 square feet of basal area per acre for conifers like the spruces, hemlocks, and true firs; from 60 for the least tolerant of the pines to about 125 for the most tolerant; and from as little as 40 square feet for some of the very intolerant pioneer hardwoods to no more than 100 for the most tolerant hardwoods like beech. Unfortunately there are no situations for which this lowest level of full occupancy of the site can be stated with any precision.

It is not clear whether the amount of basal area left, for a given species, should be greater on good sites than on poor. Assmann (1950) contended that it should while Mar:Møller (1947) claimed evidence that the same level of basal area was appropriate to all sites, at least for the tolerant species about which they were both concerned. Evidence from the rather intolerant hard pines indicates that more should be reserved on good sites than on poor.

If the pattern of residual stand density that gave maximum diameter growth without loss of cubic volume growth for a given species were known, it would provide a guide to thinning practice as valuable as it was once hoped that normal yield tables might be. However, while such a guide line would define logical thinning programs for some situations, it would merely provide a known point of departure for the formulation of thinning schedules designed to attain economic objectives other than those implicit in the "standard" case.

Development of economic thinning schedules. Much of the difficulty and confusion involved in developing definite and efficient thinning schedules has indeed come either from the failure to define the objectives clearly or, more basically, from the complexity of determining how to achieve the goals once they are set. The main objective of practically all thinning programs is to maximize the net yield of value from the stand. The fact that the main goal is an economic one automatically means that the best schedule for one owner is not the same as that for another, even though species, management objective, site and accessibility are the same.

Many of the thinning schedules developed in the past were predicated almost entirely on the objective of maximizing yield in cubic volume. The point that production of cubic volume is actually not much affected by variations in stand density was long obscured behind the cloud of experimental error arising from natural variation and the difficulties of precise measurements. In other words, it took a remarkably long time to find that the long-sought goal was really very easily attainable.

In the process it has become clear that for most purposes the logical objective is to keep reducing the stand density to the lowest level at which full occupancy is maintained. This should give the most rapid diameter growth that can be maintained without reduction in yield of cubic volume. The fear that rapid diameter growth might impair the quality of the wood now seems justified only in rather special cases. Rapid growth is sometimes undesirable for production of veneer from certain species and for that of strong timbers on poor sites. If timber is being grown for poles or other products in which it is desirable to restrict taper and branch diameter, there is a definite objection to heavy thinning; however, this is because of the distribution of diameter growth along the stem and among the branches rather than because of the rate itself.

If stands are being grown exclusively for pulpwood, the basic objective is to maximize the mean annual increment of tonnage in trees large enough for economical handling. This is distinctly not the same as seeking to maximize mean annual increment in terms of cord or cubic volume, an objective which now appears to rule much of the management of southern pines for pulpwood.

The view that pulpwood stands of loblolly pine should be grown on 35-year rotations and left unthinned is based mainly on the fact that normal yield tables (U. S. Forest Service, 1929) indicated that the mean annual increment in terms of cords of wood, 4 inches or larger in diameter, culminated at 35 years. This time of culmination is mainly the result of the fact that losses to suppression of utilizable volume become significant at this age (Mann, 1952). If thinnings are not made to salvage such losses before they occur, it might be logical to terminate the rotations at 35 years. However, any amount that is salvaged in thinning is credited to rather than subtracted from the actual yield and has the effect of making the logical rotation longer than it would be without thinning.

Since the weight per unit volume of wood increases as the trees become larger the rotation of highest mean annual increment is inevitably longer for tons than for cords. As has been shown by Kennedy (1961), the maximum yield of pulpwood tonnage from loblolly pine is likely to be obtained from thinned stands carried on rotations of about 50 years. It is significant that a pulpwood rotation of this length would be nearly as long as a saw-timber rotation; however, the details of thinning procedure for different product objectives are not necessarily the same even if the rotations are of similar length.

The effect of tree size on the cost of harvesting pulpwood is important enough to make it advantageous to reap the production in trees of reasonable size. It is, therefore, desirable to regulate stand density and length of rotation so as to obtain the best diameter growth attainable without reduction of yield. This suggests need not only for thinning but also for manipulating the timing of thinnings and the order in which diameter classes are removed so that the harvests are concentrated as much as possible in the ranges of diameter associated with lowest harvesting costs.

The greatest latitude for logical variation in thinning programs exists when the primary objective is production of saw timber. Here the basic objective is to maximize the yield in terms of lumber value, which is a complicated variable because not all board feet even within one tree are equally valuable. Tree diameter is such an important determinant of value that most thinning for saw-timber production should be the heaviest consistent with maintenance of full occupancy of the growing space. Clear justification can often be found, in fact, for reducing stand density still more and sacrificing some of the wood-producing potential of the site in order to secure rapid diameter growth. The ultimate limit on this course of action is ordinarily set by such characteristics as the excessive taper, large branches, coarse-grained wood, and short boles produced by trees in sparsely stocked stands. The economic optimum in saw-timber trees has less grace and beauty than the magnificent towering columns for which many untended stands of old-growth timber are famous.

First approximations of appropriate thinning schedules for saw-timber stands can be made by determining what schedule will maximize yield of board-foot volume. This procedure can be further refined by assessing this in terms of the part of the board-foot volume that is contained in those trees and logs that are of sufficient size to be handled at a *substantial* profit. For example, if 10 inches D.B.H. and top diameters of 6 inches represent the minima for profitable utilization, it may still prove best to follow the thinning schedule that will maximize the yield of board-foot volume in trees of 15 inches or larger D.B.H. and in logs that are 10 or more inches in diameter at the small end.

In saw-timber production the value of individual crop trees becomes so crucially important that the whole problem can often be approached simply by concentrating on the most promising trees and ensuring that they develop vigorous crowns and fine, clean boles. This approach differs from the more traditional attempt to secure optimum production of volume from each acre. The two approaches can be combined by setting up some attainable and optimum pattern of diameter growth for the crop trees, determining how much of the total basal area they will comprise at each stage of development, and then allocating the remainder to those trees that will be removed during the rotation (Heiberg and Haddock, 1955; Marsh, 1957; Staebler, 1960b). To do this one must know the rate at which a stand of Langsaeter's Density Type III (Fig. 2-4) will produce basal area at all ages.

Application of Principles

Although thinning schedules are most easily described in terms of single-product objectives, thinning is often associated with the kind of intensive and remunerative management that involves a variety of products. The empirical yield table prepared by Eyre and Zehngraff (1948) for red pine stands in Minnesota and presented in Table 3-2 depicts a thinning schedule for this kind of management. It also gives quantitative expression to some of the increases in yield of volume and value sought in thinning. Application of this schedule reportedly brings the total yield of the thinned stand to 9,730 cubic feet per acre, which is an increase of 84 per cent over the 5,300 cubic feet that might be harvested from a comparable unthinned stand.

Many important aspects of thinning practice are well illustrated by the famous thinning prescriptions of Craib (1947) for growing various American hard pines for saw timber in South Africa. The important effect of tree diameter on lumber values was clearly recognized so emphasis was placed on growing trees as rapidly as possible. The trees are planted at a wide spacing and artificial pruning rather than competition is depended upon to clear the boles and reduce the crowns. An effort is, in fact, made to prevent competition between trees by a program of thinnings so heavy that few trees ever lapse into the codominant position.

The thinning prescriptions are in terms of the number of trees cut and left at various ages for each species and site class. This mode of expression conveys an excessively spectacular idea of the severity of these thinnings. American pines grow very rapidly in many parts of the Southern Hemisphere so the time scale is compressed. The schedule for *Pinus patula* specifies reduction to 130 trees per acre at 18 years with these trees being harvested when they average 18 inches D.B.H. at 30 years. This is really more conservative than it sounds because the basal area reserved is actually of the order of 90 to 100 square feet per acre and the stands are not made to look like orchards. In fact, some of the thinning regimes applied to the same or similar hard pines in the southeastern United States may be even more severe.

Table 3-2.

Yield table for 1 acre of intensively managed red pine on an average site in Minnesota, showing stocking immediately after cutting and merchantable volume removed in preceding decade. The hypothetical sequence of operations consists of: precommercial thinning at 25 years, followed by commercial thinnings every 5 to 10 years until shelterwood cuttings commence at about 125 years. Data from Eyre and Zehngraff (1948).

| Age, yr. | Av. ht. Dominants, ft. | Growing Stock per Acre | | | Cut in Past Decade | | |
		Number of Trees	Basal Area, sq. ft.	Board ft.	Board ft.	+	Cords
20	19	1,500	70	—	—		—
30	31	1,100	95	—	—		—
40	43	830	110	1,500	500		5
50	52	620	118	4,200	1,300		6
60	60	470	122	7,800	1,400		5
70	67	350	122	11,000	1,800		4
80	72	270	121	14,000	2,000		3
90	77	220	119	16,000	2,500		2
100	80	180	117	16,700	3,300		2
110	83	150	113	16,300	4,000		2
120	85	120	105	14,700	5,000		2
130	87	50	52	8,100	9,600		5
140	88	Final removal cutting			9,600		5
Yield from thinnings					21,800 (53%)		31 (76%)
Yield from shelterwood cuttings					19,200 (47%)		10 (24%)
Total yield from intensively managed stand					41,000		41
Volume of comparable unthinned stand at 140 yr.					20,500		20

Estimate of stumpage values represented by growing stock and products removed in series of thinnings described above. The value of saw timber has been assumed to increase from $8 to $16 per 1,000 board feet during the rotation and that of pulpwood to vary between $0.75 and $2 per cord; these assumptions are based on data presented by Eyre and Zehngraff and represent prices of 1942 to 1945. All values rounded off to nearest dollar and neither discounted nor compounded.

Age, yr.	Value of Growing Stock, Saw Timber Only	Value of Products Removed in Previous Decade	Cumulative Value of Products Removed to Date
40	$ 12	$ 8	$ 8
50	34	16	24
60	70	18	42
70	110	24	66
80	154	26	92
90	192	33	125
100	217	46	171
110	228	59	230
120	220	78	308 *
130	130	161	469
140	—	161	630

Total value of unthinned stand would be $368 per acre at 140 years.

Increase in yield as a result of thinning: 42 per cent in value; 100 per cent in both board-foot and cord volume.

* Value of yield from all thinnings, 49 per cent of total.

As pointed out by Hiley (1948, 1959), Craib's thinning prescriptions were significant because they represented an abrupt and deliberately reasoned departure from the traditions of the more conservative kind of European thinning practice. In many parts of Europe wood is scarce and expensive while labor is (or was) cheap. Markets exist for wood of all sizes. The margins of profit from forestry are so wide that they sometimes breed complacency. Earlier experiences with overemphasis on the financial approach to forestry have also instilled caution. The tax system sometimes makes it advantageous to use heavy growing stocks as a refuge for capital. Insurmountable national timber deficits make it desirable to ensure maximum cubic-volume production. These considerations lend merit to the policy of establishing stands at high density and keeping them in that condition by rather light thinnings. This does not describe all European conditions or thinning practice but it does describe the kind that Craib found wanting in South Africa.

The immediate necessity was to supply softwood saw timber which would otherwise have to be imported. Markets for small trees were, at least at that time, poor. The only objection to seeking rapid diameter growth seemed to lie in the possibility that the wood produced might be excessively weak. However, through the work of Turnbull (1948) the question of the relationship between wood strength and growth rate was reopened. This led to the findings, earlier recounted, that wood strength is not controlled by growth rate. The active thinning programs that Craib proposed have since proceeded on a large scale being modified only to the extent that improved markets for pulpwood have tended to make it desirable to increase the initial stand density in order to increase the yield from thinnings. Pines intended for poles have been grown in separate stands of higher density in order to control stem taper.

The contrast between regimes of heavy thinning like that of Craib and the lighter thinnings of earlier tradition shows, not that one is right and the other wrong, but that stands of trees have a remarkable ability to respond to a wide range of variations in stand density. Economic conditions and objectives determine the way in which advantage is taken of this plasticity.

At one extreme there is the option of growing trees at low stand density with the goal of producing one clear log from a large-crowned tree on a short rotation. This approach is most logical for owners, such as individuals, whose economic outlook is necessarily short and who seek high returns from a limited investment in growing stock.

There may be a marked reduction in the total amount of wood produced and in annual dollar return per acre, but for those who must be in a hurry the sacrifice may be well justified.

Other owners, like the public, may be most concerned about the stability and quality of the regional timber supply or about maximizing the annual dollar return per acre with less anxiety about early returns or the amount invested in growing stock. For such owners it is most logical to develop trees of greater merchantable length and larger diameter on much longer rotations in stands of higher density subjected to more moderate thinnings.

Between the extremes just described it is possible to vary thinning regimes in many different ways in order to meet any set of attainable economic objectives. There is no purpose in trying to develop a standard thinning program that will fit all situations, even for a given species, because there is none.

Thinning in Less Intensive Practice

Much of the preceding discussion has, for simplicity, been based on the tacit assumption that thinnings are started fairly early and repeated at least several times during a rotation. This situation is still rather uncommon in North America where commercial thinnings tend to start late, if at all, and occur at rather long intervals. Such thinnings must be conducted on a modified basis and do not give results as favorable as the more intensive kind. Some of the modifications appropriate to the situation have already been considered.

The most common problem encountered in delayed thinning is that of dealing with stands that have become very crowded. They sometimes grow less rapidly in cubic volume than they would have had they not been thinned. This loss of growth may be offset by subsequent increase in growth or more often by increased growth of board-foot volume resulting from improved growth of the main crop trees. If not, the advantage of thinning is reduced to little more than forestalling losses from mortality and securing early income from the stand.

The sudden exposure of trees in tightly closed stands also increases the hazard of damage by wind and other agencies, especially if shallow-rooted trees are involved. Under such circumstances, it is best to make the first thinning light, repeating the treatment at frequent intervals with increasing severity until the density of the stand has been reduced to the desired level. During this process the strength and vigor of the trees may increase sufficiently to resist damage. Dominant trees are most likely to endure delayed thinning; the resistance of stands to delayed thinning is probably as much a function of the kind of trees left as it is of the number removed.

The first thinning in a stand is the most difficult from the financial standpoint; once the practice starts it rarely ceases. Therefore, the compromises that must be made as to the frequency of repetition of thinning are usually of smaller degree than those relating to initiation of thinnings. If subsequent thinnings must come very infrequently and the stands are reasonably windfirm, it is usually best to thin heavily. Unfavorable economic circumstances are more likely to be mitigated by the rapid diameter growth thus induced than they are to be aggravated by any resulting sacrifice of production of cubic volume.

The advantages of thinning are powerful enough to make it desirable for the American forester to devote energy and imagination to solving the problems that prevent or delay the initiation of thinnings. Success with thinning in North America depends heavily on the ability of foresters to find markets and uses for the products.

Woods labor is often unreceptive to any kind of partial cutting, especially those in which small trees are cut and large ones reserved. This situation is best attacked by training and equitable adjustments in piecework rates. It is always important to mark stands so that there is a place for every tree to fall and a reasonable amount of space in which to maneuver skidding equipment.

Outright investment in precommercial thinning can also provide the essential point of entry in converting a tightly closed and financially unrewarding stand into one in which a series of profitable thinnings can ultimately be made.

Thinning to Specified Density

In concluding this section it is perhaps well to point out that the practice of thinning can be conducted with reasonable confidence even though the exact schedule most appropriate to the situation is unknown (Fig. 3-13). The characteristics of the schedule which should ultimately be followed can indeed be determined only by experience with thinning.

In marking stands for thinnings on a routine basis it is not feasible to carry out the detailed measurements that would be necessary to ensure that any fixed amount of growing stock is left uniformly over the entire area. Occasional checks are sufficient to accomplish the purpose and these are expedited by the Bitterlich point-sampling

Fig. 3-13. A plantation of eastern white pine at Biltmore, North Carolina, at various stages during a series of five light, low thinnings. The plantation was established at very close spacing to check serious erosion and was first thinned at the twentieth year (Wahlenberg, 1955). Subsequent thinnings were made at intervals of about 6 years, reducing the basal area to approximately 100 square feet per acre each time. (*a*) 20 years—numbered trees being left in first thinning. (*b*) 26 years—freshly numbered trees being left in second thinning. (*c*) 32 years—just before third thinning. (*d*) 45 years—just after fifth thinning. (*Photographs by U. S. Forest Service.*)

techniques which obviate the necessity of laying out plots and measuring trees.

Unless one makes such periodic checks or has developed a very practiced eye the ordinary tendency is to mark too lightly. Much of the practical purpose of thinning schedules lies in the fact that they help overcome such timidity by providing an objective means of foreseeing the results. A thinning usually looks much more severe after the trees are marked than it does after they are cut; within a few years the rotting remains of the cut trees provide the only readily apparent evidence of any cutting.

Nobody's unguided intuition is perfect; neither is there any stand so uniform that it can be handled efficiently by blind adherence to any set method or schedule. Neither pure art nor exact science are separately equal to the strain of simultaneously balancing all the factors that affect the numerous choices involved in thinning.

Effect of Thinning on Forest Protection

Most thinning reduces losses to damaging agencies not only because of the salvage of anticipated losses but also because the vigor and strength of the trees is increased. This is especially true with respect to those numerous biotic enemies that characteristically attack weakened trees. However, the situation is not so simple as far as fire, atmospheric agencies, and some insects and fungi are concerned. This situation is perhaps clarified if a distinction is drawn between the **susceptibility** of stands to attack and the **vulnerability** to losses once attack has taken place. Thinning may temporarily predispose stands to attack by certain damaging agencies even while it gradually builds up the resistance of the trees enough to reduce the harmful effects of the same agencies.

It is only under exceptional circumstances that thinning increases susceptibility to attack by insects. Most of the difficulty comes from a few species of bark beetles; these tend to breed in logging debris and then move to live trees when the debris is no longer habitable (Schenk, Dosen, and Benjamin, 1957). The genus *Ips* and some species of *Dendroctonus* are perhaps the most troublesome, being capable of killing young conifers released in thinnings. Some damaging insects are also favored by the changes in microclimatic conditions induced by thinning; one of these is the poplar borer (*Saperda calcarata*) which attacks aspen (Ewan, 1960).

The damaging fungi that are called forth by thinning are also distinctly exceptional but can be very damaging when they attack. The most noteworthy of these are various root-rotting fungi, of which *Fomes annosus* is an outstanding example. This fungus is becoming increasingly serious in planted pines on the eastern seaboard of the United States, especially with species established on sites to which they are not adapted (Boyce, 1961). The cut surfaces of stumps are among the most favorable infection courts (Rishbeth, 1948). The first attacks often follow the first thinnings and the spread of the fungus is hastened by subsequent thinnings. Root-rots are so difficult to control that the only real solution is to shift to species that are resistant, usually by virtue of being better adapted to the sites.

Thinnings can also result in logging wounds on the residual trees. Such wounds provide infection courts for bark beetles, wood-rotting fungi, and other organisms like that which causes hypoxylon canker of aspen. The cure for such problems is obviously the reduction of logging injury.

A much more common kind of damage induced by thinning is that caused by wind and other atmospheric agencies. The tendency for tree stems and roots to grow in such manner as to become mechanically adapted to wind loads is enhanced by thinning. However, such adaptation develops too slowly to adjust the trees *promptly* to the sudden changes associated with thinning.

Building wind resistance in individual trees by thinning is such a slow process that it is ordinarily better to place primary reliance on the maintenance of smooth stand borders with curtains of foliage extending to the ground. If the permeability of the stand border is thus reduced a cushion of slow-moving air develops to windward and deflects much of the wind up over the stand. The creation of gaps must be avoided within the stand and especially along the edges because the force of the wind, which varies as the square of the velocity, is markedly increased when air is funneled into such gaps. If the stand border can be maintained as an adequate first line of defense against wind, thinnings can be conducted behind it with reasonable safety and can ultimately contribute to the resistance of the stand as a whole.

Resistance to damage by ice and snow differs in that it involves only vertically acting loads and depends more on the strength of upper portions of the stem. Thinning ultimately enhances resistance but also reduces the opportunity for heavily loaded crowns to lean on one another. The greatest risk comes from one-sided loads on leaning trees or those with asymmetrical crowns. Therefore, it helps to develop trees with strong, straight stems and symmetrical crowns;

this can be done by thinning more readily than by any other means. The weak and malformed trees that are most susceptible to such damage are the ones that would normally be removed in thinnings anyhow. There is no treatment that has much effect on the amount of ice breakage of terminal shoots and small branches; this kind of damage leads to stem crooks which may lead to unbalanced loading and more serious breakage in subsequent ice storms.

Thinning tends to expose the forest floor to desiccation and consequently causes a temporary increase in the risk that fires will start. It is difficult to dispose of the slash left by thinning, except in fire-resistant types where prescribed burning can be conducted. However, the amount of debris is small compared with that left by most kinds of reproduction cuttings. Furthermore, it is left in a shaded environment where it decomposes rapidly and rarely constitutes an intolerable fire hazard. In the long run it is better to reduce the potential amount of slash gradually in a series of thinnings, than to have all of it deposited on the ground during the period of reproduction cuttings.

Relation to Forest Uses Other than Timber Production

Thinning plays a role in the achievement of most purposes of management because it represents the primary means by which forest stands can be controlled and altered during the course of their development.

It increases the runoff of forested watersheds mainly by the temporary opening of the crown canopy which causes a reduction of interception of precipitation. More water reaches the soil, especially if it falls as snow, and less is lost by the direct evaporation of that which wets or clings to the branches. Goodell (1952) found that the yield of water might be increased by 15 to 20 per cent as a result of heavy thinnings in young lodgepole pine in Colorado. In most other situations the increase would be less. Regeneration cuttings cause a larger and less temporary increase in runoff, but they cannot be repeated as frequently as thinnings.

Thinnings are also useful in enhancing the development and controlling the composition of understory vegetation that may provide forage, browse and seeds for herbivorous animals, both wild and domestic. Tightly closed crown canopies usually keep this food supply above the reach of all animals but birds. The vegetation that is valuable from the standpoint of wildlife management and the grazing of domestic animals is sometimes the same as that which causes problems in the regeneration of species for timber production. Therefore, the understory vegetation must be manipulated with due regard for all the effects that it has on the economic use and overall ecological balance of the forest community. For example, attention must be given to the possibility that an understory layer ultimately harmful to reproduction and temporarily beneficial to wildlife may also lure browsing animals away from other stands actually being regenerated. The lesser vegetation is an integral part of the stand and should be regarded as something that can be usefully manipulated either for increase of benefits or reduction of harmful effects. No progress is made in this direction if it is looked upon only as an annoying impediment composed of plants unworthy of identification.

Thinning, like all forms of cutting, poses problems for intensive recreational use because slash is a far greater hazard and eyesore to the layman than it is to the forester. However, it is better to dispose of the slash than to refrain from thinning in areas of heavy recreational use. Trees must be vigorous if they are to endure the trampling of the soil by their admirers or the more active attacks of vandals. Reduction of the numbers of trees is inevitable and is better used as a means of stimulating the residual trees than as a last resort for protecting the public from injury by falling branches from dead trees.

Conclusion

Thinning represents the primary means by which the productivity of stands can be increased beyond the best that might be achieved under purely natural conditions. As a consequence, it is the one technique which, more than any other, distinguishes intensive silvicultural practice from extensive.

It is possible that the essential generalities about thinning have been buried in the flood of qualifications that must inevitably enter into any discussion. The most important fact to be noted is that the total cubic volume of wood which can be produced by a stand in a given length of time tends to be fixed and immutable. However, by skillful control of the growing stock the forester can marshal this production so as to capture the highest net return possible under the economic circumstances. The trees that are cut represent a salvageable surplus not needed to ensure full utilization of the growing space; they are, therefore, available for harvest. In the act of removing them it becomes possible to build more crown surface on selected individuals so that they will attain larger diameter, become more valuable, and be less vulnerable to damage.

The positive action of choosing the kind and number of trees to remain for future growth should be emphasized much more than the selection of trees to cut for immediate use.

REFERENCES

This list includes references for Chapters 2 and 3.

Adams, W. R., and G. L. Chapman. 1942. Crop tree measurements in thinning experiments. *J. Forestry* 40:493–498.

Alexander, R. R. 1960. Thinning lodgepole pine in the central Rocky Mountains. *J. Forestry* 58:99–104.

Anderson, E. A. 1951. Tracheid length variation in conifers as related to distance from pith. *J. Forestry* 49:38–42.

Assmann, E. 1950. Grundflächen- und Volumzuwachs der Rotbuche bei verschiedenen Durchforstungsgraden. *Forstwiss. Centralbl.* 69:256–286.

――――. 1961. *Waldertragskunde.* Bayerischer Landwirtschaftsverlag, Munich.

Averell, J. L. 1945. Rules of thumb for thinning loblolly pine. *J. Forestry* 43:649–651.

Baker, F. S. 1950. *Principles of silviculture.* McGraw-Hill, New York. Pp. 51–59, 71–74, 281–386.

Bamford, G. T., and S. Little. 1960. Effects of low thinning in Atlantic white-cedar stands. *NEFES Research Note* 104.

Bethel, J. S. 1940. Loblolly pine pulping qualities. *Paper Indus. and Paper World* 22:358–359.

Bickford, C. A., F. S. Baker, and F. G. Wilson. 1957. Stocking, normality, and measurement of stand density. *J. Forestry* 55:99–104.

Bormann, F. H., and B. F. Graham, Jr. 1959. The occurrence of natural root grafting in eastern white pine, *Pinus strobus* L., and its ecological implications. *Ecology* 40:677–691.

Boyce, J. S. 1961. *Forest pathology,* 3rd ed. McGraw-Hill, New York.

Braathe, P. 1957. *Thinnings in even-aged stands.* Faculty of Forestry, University of New Brunswick, Fredericton.

Bryant, B. S., Jr. 1951. The significance of specific gravity distribution with respect to tree form. *Univ. of Wash., Forestry Club Quarterly* 24(1):18–24.

Burger, H. 1929–1953. Holz, Blattmenge und Zuwachs. I–XIII. *Mitt. d. Schweizer. Anstalt f. d. forstliche Versuchswesen* 15:243–292, 19:21–72, 20:101–114, 21:307–348, 24:7–103, 25:211–279, 435–493, 26:419–468, 27:247–286, 28:109–156, 29:38–130.

Champion, H. G., and A. L. Griffith. 1948. *Manual of general silviculture for India,* rev. ed. Oxford University Press, London. Pp. 287–316.

Chapman, H. H. 1953. Effects of thinning on yields of forest-grown longleaf and loblolly pines at Urania, La. *J. Forestry* 51:16–26.

Chisman, H. H., and F. X. Schumacher. 1940. On the tree-area ratio and certain of its applications. *J. Forestry* 38:311–317.

Conover, D. F., and R. A. Ralston. 1959. Results of crop-tree thinning and pruning in northern hardwood saplings after nineteen years. *J. Forestry* 57:551–557.

Cooper, C. F. 1961. Equations for the description of past growth in even-aged stands of ponderosa pine. *Forest Sci.* 7:72–80.

Craib, I. J.   1947.   The silviculture of exotic conifers in South Africa.   *J. So. African Forestry Assoc.* No. 15:11–45.

Czarnowski, M. S.   1961.   Dynamics of even-aged forest stands.   *La. State Univ. Studies, Biol. Sci. Series* 4.

Davis, K.   1935.   A method of determining spacing in thinning.   *J. Forestry* 33:80–81.

Deen, J. L.   1933.   Some aspects of an early expression of dominance in white pine.   *Yale Univ. School of Forestry Bul.* 36.

Deetlefs, P. P. d. T.   1953.   Means of expressing and regulating density in forest stands.   *J. So. African Forestry Assoc.* 23:1–12.

———.   1954.   The relationship between stand density, crown size, and basal area growth in stands of *Pinus taeda* L. in the native habitat of this species.   *J. So. African Forestry Assoc.* 24:1–28.

Dosen, R. C., J. H. Stoeckeler, and F. G. Kilp.   1957.   Mechanized thinning in jack pine saplings.   *J. Forestry* 55:201–204.

Duff, G. H., and Norah J. Nolan.   Growth and morphogenesis in the Canadian forest species.
  1953.   I.   The controls of cambial and apical activity in *Pinus resinosa* Ait.   *Canadian J. Bot.* 31:471–513.
  1957.   II.   Specific increments and their relation to the quantity and activity of growth in *Pinus resinosa* Ait.   *Canadian J. Bot.* 35:527–572.

Ewan, H. G.   1960.   The poplar borer in relation to aspen stocking.   *LSFES Tech. Note* 580.

Eyre, F. H., and P. Zehngraff.   1948.   Red pine management in Minnesota.   *USDA Circ.* 778.

Fedkiw, J., and J. G. Yoho.   1960.   Economic models for thinning and reproducing even-aged stands.   *J. Forestry* 58:26–34.

Fleischer, H. O.   1949.   The suitability of second growth Douglas-fir logs for veneer.   *J. Forestry* 47:533–537.

Gaines, E. M., and E. S. Kotok.   1954.   Thinning ponderosa pine in the Southwest.   *RMFRES Sta. Paper* 17.

Gessel, S. P.   1959.   Forest soil fertility problems and research in the western United States.   *Proc., Soc. Am. Foresters Meeting,* 1958:177–180.

Gevorkiantz, S. R., P. O. Rudolf, and P. J. Zehngraff.   1943.   A tree classification for aspen, jack pine and second-growth red pine.   *J. Forestry* 41:268–274.

Goodell, B. C.   1952.   Watershed management-aspects of thinned young lodgepole pine.   *J. Forestry* 50:374–378.

Grosenbaugh, L. R.   1958.   Point-sampling and line-sampling: probability theory, geometric implications, synthesis.   SFES Occasional Paper 160.

Gruschow, G. F.   1949.   Results of a pre-commercial thinning in slash pine.   *Southern Lumberman* 179(2249):230–232.

Gruschow, G. F., and T. C. Evans.   1959.   The relation of cubic-foot volume growth to stand density in young slash pine stands.   *Forest Sci.* 5:49–55.

Guilkey, P. C.   1958.   Managing red pine for poles in Lower Michigan.   *LSFES Sta. Paper* 57.

Guillebaud, W. H., and F. C. Hummel.   1949.   A note on the movement of tree classes.   *Forestry* 23:1–14.

Hart, A. C.   1961.   Thinning balsam fir thickets with soil sterilants.   *NEFES Sta. Paper* 152.

Hawley, R. C. 1936. Observations on thinning and management of eastern white pine (*Pinus strobus* Linnaeus) in southern New Hampshire. *Yale Univ. School of Forestry Bul. 42.*

Heiberg, S. O., and P. G. Haddock. 1955. A method of thinning and forecast of yield in Douglas-fir. *J. Forestry* 53:10–17.

Heiberg, S. O., and D. P. White. 1951. Potassium deficiency of reforested pine and spruce stands in northern New York. *Soil Sci. Soc. Am., Proc.* 15: 369–376.

Hiley, W. E. 1948. Craib's thinning prescriptions for conifers in South Africa. *Quart. J. Forestry* 42:5–19.

———. 1952. Numerical thinning: with special reference to Japanese larch. *Forestry* 25:10–18.

———. 1959. Conifers: *South African methods of cultivation.* Faber and Faber, London.

Hiley, W. E., and R. Lehtpere. 1955. Thinning grades based on the thickness of annual rings. *Forestry* 28:17–32.

Holmsgaard, E. 1958. Comments on some German and Swedish thinning experiments in Norway spruce. *Forest Sci.* 4:54–60.

Holsoe, T. 1950. Profitable tree forms of yellowpoplar. *W. Va. AES Bul. 341.*

———. 1951. Yellowpoplar: reaction to crown release and other factors influencing growth. *W. Va. AES Bul. 344T.*

Hough, A. F., and R. F. Taylor. 1946. Response of Allegheny northern hardwoods to partial cutting. *J. Forestry* 44: 30–38.

Hummel, F. C. 1953. The definition of thinning treatments. *Proc., 11th Cong., Intl. Union Forest Research Org.,* Rome. Pp. 582–588.

Jackson, L. W. R. 1959. Loblolly pine tracheid length in relation to position in tree. *J. Forestry* 57:366–367.

Jacobs, M. R. 1939. A study of the effect of sway on trees. *Australia, Commonwealth Forestry Bur. Bul. 26.*

Kennedy, R. F. 1961. Thinning practices in sawlog rotation stands. *In:* A. B. Crow (Ed.), *Advances in southern pine management.* Louisiana State University Press, Baton Rouge. Pp. 61–67.

Kennedy, R. W., and J. M. Jaworsky. 1960. Variation in cellulose content of Douglas-fir. *Tappi* 43:25–27.

Labyak, L. F., and F. X. Schumacher. 1954. The contribution of its branches to the main-stem growth of loblolly pine. *J. Forestry* 52:333–337.

Langsaeter, A. 1941. Om tynning i enaldret gran- og furuskog. *Meddel. f. d. Norske Skogforsøksvesen* 8:131–216.

Larson, P. R. 1957. Effect of environment on the percentage of summerwood and specific gravity of slash pine. *Yale Univ. School of Forestry Bul. 63.*

———. 1960. A physiological consideration of the springwood summerwood transition in red pine. *Forest Sci.* 6:110–112.

Lexen, B. 1943. Bole area as an expression of growing stock. *J. Forestry* 41:883–885.

Løvengreen, J. A. 1949. Dependence of volume increment upon thinning grade and variations of the latter. *3rd World Forestry Congress (Helsinki), Bul.* 5:23–24.

Luther, T. F., and D. B. Cook. 1948. Commercial thinning in red pine plantations. *J. Forestry* 46:110–114.

Lynch, D. W. 1958. Effects of stocking on site measurement and yield of second-growth pondersoa pine in the Inland Empire. *IMFRES Res. Paper* 56.

McClay, T. A. 1955. The relation of growth to site and residual density in loblolly pine pulpwood stands. *SEFES Res. Note* 78.

McCulley, R. D. 1950. Management of natural slash pine stands in the flatwoods of south Georgia and north Florida. *USDA Circ.* 845.

Macdonald, J. A. B. 1961. The simple rules of the "Scottish eclectic" thinning method. *Oxford Univ. Forest Soc. J.* 5(9):6–11.

McKimmy, M. D. 1959. Factors related to variation of specific gravity in young-growth Douglas fir. *Oreg. Forest Products Res. Center Bul.* 8.

MacKinney, A. L., and L. E. Chaiken. 1939. Volume, yield, and growth of loblolly pine in the Mid-Atlantic Coastal Region. *SEFES Tech. Note* 33.

Mann, W. F., Jr. 1952. Response of loblolly pine to thinning. *J. Forestry* 50: 443–446.

Mar:Møller, C. 1946. Untersuchungen über Laubmenge, Stoffverlust und Stoffproduktion des Waldes. *Forstl. Forsøgsvaesen i Danmark* 17:1–287.

———. 1947. The effect of thinning, age, and site on foliage, increment, and loss of dry matter. *J. Forestry* 45:393–404.

———, and E. Holmsgaard. 1947. Staerk Hugst, svag Hugst og Hugst fra Toppen, et Forsøg i Rødgran. (Crown thinning, low thinning and selection thinning, an experiment in Norway spruce.) *Dansk Skovfor. Tidsskr.* 32:393–445. English summary.

Mar:Møller, C., et al. 1954. Thinning problems and practices in Denmark. *State Univ. N. Y., Coll. Forestry, Tech. Publ.* 76.

Mar:Møller, C., Müller, D., and J. Nielsen. 1954. Graphic presentation of dry matter production in European beech. *Forstl. Forsøgsvaesen i Danmark* 21:327–335.

Marsh, E. K. 1957. *Some preliminary results from O'Connor's correlated curve trend (C.C.T.) experiments on thinnings and espacements and their practical significance.* British Commonwealth Forestry Conference, 1957. Government Printer, Pretoria.

Meyer, W. H. 1942. Yield of even-aged stands of loblolly pine in northern Louisiana. *Yale Univ. School of Forestry Bul.* 51.

Mitchell, H. L., and P. R. Wheeler. 1960. Specific gravity—a measure of intrinsic wood quality. *Proc. Soc. Am. Foresters Meeting,* 1959:53–57.

Moss, V. D., and C. A. Wellner. 1953. Aiding blister rust control by silvicultural measures in the western white pine type. *USDA Circ.* 919.

Mulloy, G. A. 1944. Stand density vs. stand bole area and stand intensity indices in even-aged stands. *Forestry Chronicle* 20:167–170.

———. 1946. Rules of thumb in thinning. *J. Forestry* 44:735–737.

Myers, C. A. 1958. Thinning improves development of young stands of ponderosa pine in the Black Hills. *J. Forestry* 56:656–659.

Nelson, T. C., et. al. 1961. Merchantable cubic-foot volume growth in natural loblolly pine stands. *SEFES Sta. Paper* 127.

Oelkers, J. 1930–1937. *Waldbau.* Schaper, Hannover.

Ovington, J. D. 1956. The form, weights and productivity of tree species grown in close stands. *New Phytologist* 55:289–388.

———. 1957. Dry-matter production by *Pinus sylvestris* L. *Annals of Botany* 21 (n.s.):287–314.

Ovington, J. D., and W. H. Pearsall. 1956. Production ecology. II. Estimates of average production by trees. *Oikos* 7:202–205.

Ovington, J. D., and H. A. I. Madgwick. 1959. The growth and composition of natural stands of birch. 1. Dry-matter production. *Plant and Soil* 10:271–283.

Paul, B. H. 1930. The application of silviculture in controlling the specific gravity of wood. *USDA Tech. Bul.* 168.

———. 1946. Steps in the silvicultural control of wood quality. *J. Forestry* 44:953–958.

———. 1959. The effect of environmental factors on wood quality. *USFPL Rept.* 2170.

Penistan, M. J. 1961. Thinning practice. *Forestry* 33:149–173.

Reineke, L. H. 1933. Perfecting a stand-density index for even-aged forests. *J. Agr. Research* 46:627–638.

Reukema, D. L. 1961. Response of individual Douglas-fir trees to release. *PNWFRES Res. Note* 208.

Reynolds, R. R., W. E. Bond, and B. P. Kirkland. 1944. Financial aspects of selective cutting in the management of second-growth pine-hardwood forests west of the Mississippi River. *USDA Tech. Bul.* 861.

Rishbeth, J. 1948. *Fomes annosus* Fr. on pines in East Anglia. *Forestry* 22: 174–183.

Roe, E. I., and J. H. Stoeckeler. 1950. Thinning over-dense jack pine seedling stands in the Lake States. *J. Forestry* 48:861–865.

Sabroe, A. S. 1954. *Forestry in Denmark*, 3rd rev. ed. Danish Forestry Soc., Copenhagen.

Sakaguchi, K. 1961. (Studies in basic factors in thinning.) *Bul. Govt. Forest Exp. Sta.* (Tokyo) 131:1–95. (English summary:91–95.)

Satoo, T., R. Kunugi, and A. Kumekawa. 1956. (Materials for the studies of growth in stands. III. Amount of leaves and production of wood in an aspen (*Populus Davidiana*) second growth in Hokkaido.) *Bul. Tokyo Univ. Forests* No. 52:33–51. (English summary:51.)

———, and M. Senda. 1958. (Materials for the studies of growth in stands. IV. Amount of leaves and production of wood in a young plantation of *Chamaecyparis obtusa.*) *Bul. Tokyo Univ. Forests,* No. 54:71–100. (English summary:99–100.)

Schädelin, W. 1942. *Die Auslesedurchforstung als Erziehungsbetrieb höchster Wertleistung*, 3rd ed. Haupt, Berne.

Schantz-Hansen, T. 1952. The Cloquet red pine thinning plots. *Forestry* 50: 480–482.

Schenk, J. A., R. C. Dosen, and D. M. Benjamin. 1957. Noncommercial thinning of stagnated jack pine stands and losses attributable to bark beetles. *J. Forestry* 55:838–841.

Schumacher, F. X., and T. S. Coile. 1960. *Growth and yields of natural stands of the southern pines.* T. S. Coile, Inc., Durham, N. C.

Scott, D. R. M. 1955. Amount and chemical composition of the organic matter contributed by overstory and understory vegetation to forest soil. *Yale Univ. School of Forestry Bul.* 62.

Senda, M., and T. Satoo. 1956. (Materials for the study of growth in stands. II. White pine (*Pinus strobus*) stands of various densities in Hokkaido.) *Bul. Tokyo Univ. Forests,* No. 52:15–31. (English summary:29–31.)

Smithers, L. A. 1954. Thinning in red and white pine stands at Petawawa Forest Experiment Sta. *Canada, Forestry Branch, Silv. Research Note* 105.

Spurr, S. H. 1948. Row thinning. *Proc. Soc. Am. Foresters Meeting*, 1947: 370–377.

———. 1952. *Forest inventory.* Ronald Press, New York. Pp. 205–370.

Spurr, S. H., and Wen-yeu Hsiung. 1954. Growth rate and specific gravity in conifers. *J. Forestry* 52:191–200.

Spurr, S. H., and M. J. Hyvarinen. 1954. Wood fiber length as related to position in tree and growth. *Bot. Rev.* 29:561–575.

Staebler, G. R. 1956. Evidence of shock following thinning of young Douglas-fir. *J. Forestry* 54:339.

———. 1960a. Optimum levels of growing stock for managed stands. *Proc. Soc. Am. Foresters Meeting*, 1959:110–113.

———. 1960b. Theoretical derivation of numerical thinning schedules for Douglas-fir. *Forest Sci.* 6:98–109.

Stage, A. R. 1958. Growth of thinned ponderosa pine in western Montana. *J. Forestry* 56:757–760.

Takahara, S. 1954. (Influence of pruning on the growth of sugi and hinoki.) *Bul. Tokyo Univ. Forests*, No. 46:1–95. (English summary.)

Teeguarden, D. E., and D. T. Gordon. 1959. A precommercial thinning in ponderosa and Jeffrey pine. *J. Forestry* 57:900–904.

Turnbull, J. M. 1948. Some factors affecting wood density in pine stems. *Jour. So. African Forestry Assoc.* No. 16:22–43.

U. S. Forest Service. 1929. Volume, yield, and stand tables for second-growth southern pines. *USDA Misc. Pub.* 50.

Wahlenberg, W. G. 1952. Thinning yellow-poplar in second-growth upland hardwood stands. *J. Forestry* 50:671–676.

———. 1955. Six thinnings in a 56-year-old pure white pine plantation at Biltmore. *J. Forestry* 54:331–339.

———. 1960. *Loblolly pine, its use, ecology, regeneration, protection, growth and management.* Duke University, School of Forestry. Pp. 249–286, 321–332.

Warrack, G. 1952. Comparative observations of the changes in class in a thinned and natural stand of immature Douglas fir. *Forestry Chronicle* 28(2):46–56.

———. 1959. Forecast of yield in relation to thinning regimes in Douglas fir. *Brit. Columbia Forest Service Tech. Publ.* T51.

Webster, H. H. 1960. Timber management opportunities in Pennsylvania. *NEFES Sta. Paper* 137.

Wellwood, R. W. 1952. The effect of several variables on the specific gravity of second-growth Douglas-fir. *Forestry Chronicle* 28(3):34–42.

———. 1960. Specific gravity and tracheid length variations in second-growth western hemlock. *J. Forestry* 58:361–368.

Wenger, K. F., T. C. Evans, T. Lotti, R. W. Cooper, and E. V. Brender. 1958. The relation of growth to stand density in natural loblolly pine stands. *SEFES Sta. Paper* 97.

Wiedemann, E. 1950–51. *Ertragskundliche und waldbauliche Grundlagen der Forstwirtschaft.* J. D. Sauerländer, Frankfurt-a.-M.

Wiedemann, E., and R. Schober. 1957. *Ertragstafeln wichtiger Holzarten bei verschiedener Durchforstung.* Schaper, Hannover.

Wilson, F. G. 1951. Control of growing stock in even-aged stands of conifers. *J. Forestry* 49:692–695.

——. 1955. Evaluation of three thinnings at Star Lake. *Forest Sci.* 1:227–231.

Worthington, N. P., and G. R. Staebler. 1961. Commercial thinning of Douglas-fir in the Pacific Northwest. *USDA Tech. Bul.* 1230.

Yerkes, V. P. 1960. Effect of thinning on form of young-growth Douglas-fir trees. *PNWFRES Research Note* 194.

Ylinen, A. 1954. On the mechanical stem form theory of trees. *Proc. Finnish Acad. Sci. and Letters* 1953:105–129.

Zahner, R., and F. W. Whitmore. 1960. Early growth of radically thinned loblolly pine. *J. Forestry* 58:628–634.

Zasada, Z. A. 1952. Does it pay to thin young aspen? *J. Forestry* 50:747–748.

Zehngraff, P. 1950. Forestry in Denmark. *J. Forestry* 48:681–684.

Zobel, B. J., and R. L. McElwee. 1958. Variation of cellulose in loblolly pine. *Tappi* 41:167–170.

Zobel, B. J., C. Webb, and F. Henson. 1959. Core or juvenile wood of loblolly and slash pine trees. *Tappi* 42:345–356.

CHAPTER 4

Pruning

Trees must have branches and branches form knots which are the most common defects of wood grown in managed forests. Therefore, the control of the growth and elimination of branches is often nearly as important as that applied to the main stems.

Branches do not necessarily fall off when they cease to function, because their continued presence is not a crucial handicap to the survival of the tree. The knots formed by living branches are far less damaging than those left by dead branches, but it is nevertheless desirable to control their size. The main problem is dealing with branches that persist more than a few years after they die. In the managed forest one cannot wait out the centuries necessary to produce the kind of knot-free wood found in dwindling reserves of old-growth timber.

The elimination of branches by the physical and biotic agencies of the environment is called **natural** or **self-pruning**. Natural pruning takes place slowly during the life of the forest crop. In **artificial pruning** the removal of branches from chosen portions of stems is accomplished swiftly to increase the quality and value of the crop ultimately harvested.

Natural Pruning

The process of natural pruning consists of three steps: (1) killing and (2) shedding of the branch, followed by (3) occlusion or healing over of the branch stub. Clear wood is not produced until the branch stub and any bark or pitch pockets associated with it are completely walled over by solid wood. Natural pruning proceeds from the ground upward; no significant advantage is gained until virtually all branch stubs in the first log are covered.

The rate of dying of the lower branches is determined by the initial density of the stand and the vigor of the tree. As soon as the expanding crowns of adjacent trees close together the branches below the point of closure decline in vigor and ultimately succumb. Smith (1961) reported that the branches of Douglas-firs with vigorous crowns did not die as rapidly as measurements of only competitive influences would indicate they should. This is probably because the lower branches are nourished to some extent by those above and are able to survive longer on vigorous trees than they would if not so well supplied with carbohydrate.

These two influences also determine the diameters attained by the branches before they die, a factor influencing both the rate of shedding and the quality of the wood in the knotty core formed prior to completion of natural pruning. Where the production of lumber, with or without artificial pruning, is the major objective of management it is desirable to have the young stand dense enough that the lower branches do not grow larger than 1 to $1\frac{1}{2}$ inches in diameter.

Proper density is best secured by employing methods of regeneration which ensure establishment of four hundred to a thousand trees per acre rapidly enough to prevent any great variation in height of the young stand. Super-dominant trees develop large branches and prune slowly; trees that are in the lower crown classes from the start are likely to succumb before any advantage can be taken of their good natural pruning. If a stand is understocked when young it is rare that any amount of crowding later on will be effective either in reducing the size of branches or enhancing natural pruning (Tarbox and Reed, 1924; Grah, 1961). Branches live longer and grow larger on the middle and upper part of the bole than they do on the lower part because of the tendency for the amount of competition between crowns to decrease in the upper part of the canopy (Curtis, 1936; Rapraeger, 1939). Trees on poorer sites usually produce smaller branches and lumber of higher quality than those on better sites, although the clear internodes are longer on good sites (Cline and Fletcher, 1928; Paul, 1947a, 1947b).

The second and generally most crucial stage of the process of natural pruning is the shedding of the dead branches. As soon as the branch dies it is attacked by saprophytic fungi and insects that weaken the branch until it breaks of its own weight or is removed by forces exerted by other agencies, such as precipitation, wind, and the whipping action of subordinate trees. The activity of the fungi is the most important factor determining the rate of shedding. Paul (1938) found that the branches of the four species of pine common in the warm, humid climate of the South fell off in half the time required by those of red and white pine in the cooler and drier climate of the Lake States. He and Romell (1940) also noted that very small branches, which dry out readily, sometimes persist for unusually long periods. Otherwise, large, dead branches tend to be retained longer than small ones. Conditions that favor the retention of moisture in dead branches appear to hasten the rotting and shedding of branches. The loose, flaky bark of branches of the hard pines may retard desiccation sufficiently to account for the fact that these branches rot off more rapidly than those of smooth-barked species, like eastern white pine, which retain their dead branches almost indefinitely.

The so-called dry sap rots that hasten natural pruning are generally not caused by the same fungi that produce heart rot even though dead branches do provide important points of entry for heart-rotting fungi. Fortunately the interior of the living bole is usually partially sealed from the outside environment by deposits that form in the bases of the branches before, during, or after death. According to Mayer-Wegelin (1936), these deposits are composed of resins in conifers and tyloses or gums in hardwoods; they do not form to the same extent in all species and tend to be absent in the heartwood formed by large branches. Dead branches of highly resinous conifers, like the pines, are more effectively sealed from the rest of the tree than those of less resinous species like the spruces. Although these substances protect the bole from heart rot they sometimes have the unfortunate effect of hampering the growth of fungi in the branches and thus retard natural pruning.

The third step in the process of natural pruning is the occlusion of the short stub left by the dead branch. The speed of healing depends largely on the rate of diameter growth of the bole and the length of the stub; it is not greatly influenced by the diameter of the dead branch stub (Romell, 1940).

The knots produced while branches are still alive are known as **live,** or **intergrown** knots, usually being red in color. Those formed after the branches die are called **dead,** or **encased** knots; in conifers they often become **black** knots because of the deposition of resin in them after they are encased. As shown in Fig. 4-1, the annual rings formed around live, intergrown knots bend outward and appear to be continuous with the annual rings of the branches. Actually, the fibers of the bole and those of a living branch are continuous only on the lower surface of the branch base, so that only those from directly beneath lead upward through the bole into the branch (Paterson, 1938). Those at the sides sweep closely around the sides and top of the branch base and thence upward without actually being continuous with the fibers of the branch. This configuration is most readily observed by forcibly pulling a living branch out of the bole.

Annual rings around dead, encased knots bend inward and have no connection with those of the branches. Dead knots are serious defects in lumber because they are likely to fall out when they dry, especially if they are portions of branches which had long been dead and had started to decay when encased. In other words, live knots are almost always **tight** knots, but dead knots have a strong tendency to be **loose** knots. Boards with numerous loose knots are not included in the "knotty pine" lumber which is becoming increasingly popular and valuable. In some respects it is, therefore, better to have a branch remain alive than to have it die and stay on the tree. Fortunately, the base of a branch may go on living and growing slowly for a few years after the branch itself appears completely dead.

A branch increases in diameter as long as it lives. The resulting knot is thickest at the point where the branch joined the trunk when it died. The diameter of a live knot decreases rapidly in the direction of the pith so that the presence of a large branch on the outside of a log does not indicate knots of equal size in boards cut from the inside of the log.

Natural pruning can sometimes be deliberately accelerated by intentional manipulation of the density, form and composition of stands, although some sacrifice of diameter growth is almost always necessary. The simplest and most common method is to develop and maintain dense stocking in the main canopy. This keeps the lower branches small and causes them to die; however, it has little effect on the shedding of dead branches, and it causes slow healing of the scars.

If the dead branches rot off quickly under any conditions, as is the case with most hardwoods and some conifers, provision for high stand density may be all that is necessary. With most of the hardwoods it usually represents the best way because it not only enhances natural pruning but also tends to keep the boles from becoming crooked or forked. However, with any species, serious difficulties are likely to be encountered when natural pruning has been completed to the desired level and it becomes desirable to reduce stand density to accelerate the diameter growth of the clear boles. Crowding is a cumbersome way of achieving natural pruning but there are many circumstances in which it represents the only economical method.

In some instances the problem can also be solved by selection thinnings in which limby dominants are removed in favor of subordinate trees that show good natural pruning. This technique is useful if practiced in moderation but increases the time required to produce clear lumber.

Sometimes natural pruning can be stimulated in less cumbersome manner by developing a subordinate story of tolerant species just beneath the canopy of the main crop. Such an understory often maintains an environment beneath the canopy stable enough to induce the deterioration of dead branch stubs and, when the wind blows hard enough, the swaying trees of the understory will knock off the dead branches. Hopkins (1958) has, for example, shown that the best natural pruning of loblolly pine occurs if there are numerous hardwoods in the lower crown classes; those in the main canopy do not, however, stimulate the process. This suggests that there is little virtue in tolerating otherwise undesirable species in the main canopy solely to encourage natural pruning; such species may be very effective as a subordinate story but this is no reason to sacrifice any of the growing space of the main canopy to them.

Natural pruning is usually effective enough in hardwoods that no special measures are taken to induce it, although there are a few species, like pin and scarlet oak, that retain their dead branches so long that they are held in low repute. For most commercial conifers, particularly those of the North and West, rotations of at least 150 years are required to produce reasonable amounts of clear lumber, if reliance is placed on natural pruning. Even the southern pines, which sometimes start producing clear wood on the first log after 20 to 25 years (Paul, 1938), are often grown in stands so open that natural pruning is inadequate. Where silvicultural practice must be crude and extensive, natural pruning cannot be relied upon to produce substantial quantities of clear softwood lumber and veneer, except with unreasonably long rotations.

Objectives of Artificial Pruning

The most common and traditional purpose of artificial pruning is the production of clear material on rotations shorter than would be required with natural pruning. The necessary period of growth after treatment is rather long, so the practice ordinarily must be coupled with thinning to stimulate diameter growth. Pruning can also be done merely to prevent formation of loose knots, thus yielding lumber which is tight-knotted but not necessarily clear. This approach does not offer such rich rewards but involves a shorter waiting period.

Plantations are not likely to produce much clear lumber without pruning because the high cost of planting usually dictates initial stand density too low for satisfactory natural pruning; the same is true when sparse stocking develops in natural regeneration. It is rarely desirable, however, to attempt to improve very widely spaced trees by pruning large branches from them.

Artificial pruning is mandatory for production of clear lumber on acceptable rotations from such species as the spruces, the white pines, and Douglas-fir which characteristically retain their dead branches for decades. Significant advantage is gained by pruning these species because clear lumber can be laid down in portions of the bole that would otherwise yield only material of the lower categories of the common grades with large, loose knots.

Artificial pruning is fully as useful as a means of avoiding the production of the lower Common grades of softwood lumber characterized by loose or unsound knots. Lumber of these grades is rarely worth much more, and sometimes less, than the cost of producing it. A manufacturer can easily accumulate an unsalable surplus of such material as the by-product of better grades. Sometimes more than half the volume sawn from unpruned conifers 15 to 20 inches D.B.H. consists of such material, with the better tight-knotted lumber coming from the inner and upper portions of such trees. This is a matter of real concern in view of the commonly accepted view that most sawtimber trees in managed forests will be harvested when they reach this size (Rhodes, 1960). While some have taken the fatalistic view that the consumer might ultimately cease to discriminate between the nearly clear Select grades and the tight-knotted Number 1 and 2 Common grades, it seems unlikely the loose-knotted lumber of the lower Common grades will find equal favor.

Occasionally trees are pruned artificially to remove living branches infected with stem rusts and dwarf mistletoe. Pruning also improves access to stands during thinning operations and allows decomposition of slash to commence before the start of ordinary cuttings. Much of the pruning which has been carried out on this continent has been aimed primarily at improving the appearance of whole stands from an aesthetic viewpoint, an expensive objective rarely compatible with profitable timber production. All these advantages of pruning are subsidiary to the principal aim of improving timber quality.

Effect on the Tree

In spite of some opinion to the contrary, properly conducted pruning is not harmful to the tree. Careless pruning can, however, cause injury to the bole, leaving wounds extending through the bark into the cambium and even into the wood. Such injuries are generally caused by slovenly haste, use of improper tools, and pruning during the growing season when the bark is loose. Harmful effects can also result from pruning trees that are growing very slowly, removing large branches, eliminating too much of the live crown, or committing similar errors of judgment.

Defects. Bark and pitch pockets frequently form over the stubs of pruned branches, although their incidence can be held to a minimum by careful work and wise selection of trees to prune. This kind of defect is found at the end of the pruned stub where the callus, in healing over the cut surface, has caught and enclosed patches of bark and pitch instead of pushing them all outward (Fig. 4-1). Bark

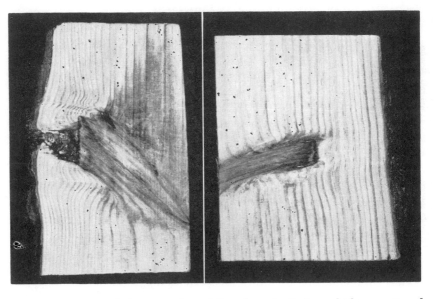

Fig. 4-1. Typical radial sections through branches of red pines which were pruned 14 years ago. The branch at *left* was alive and 0.9 inch in diameter when pruned; the stub was 0.7 inch long, and the tree lapsed into a codominant position after pruning. The pitch pocket which formed as a result of the slow growth and rather large size of the stub would not have occluded for several years. The branch at *right* was 0.5 inch in diameter and dead when pruned; the stub was 0.5 inch long. The tree remained in a dominant position and grew rapidly so that healing was virtually complete 7 years after pruning. Note that both calluses grew more rapidly from above than from below. (*Photographs by Yale University School of Forestry.*)

and pitch pockets occur most commonly in wounds that heal slowly on trees that are not growing well in diameter because of age or competition. The pruning of large branches, especially if they are dead or are on trees with thick bark, often results in the formation of pockets of pitch and bark. Under these circumstances the bark on the callus becomes very thick and is likely to be folded inward (Jacobs, 1938).

Computations of the diameter of the central knotty core in pruned trees must include an additional allowance for defects of this kind because they extend outward radially from the ends of the branch stubs. For most species, an allowance of 1 inch on each side of the core is ample. Even if no obvious pockets develop, the cut end of the branch stub and the callus tissue never grow together. The plane of separation thus created is the only one resulting from pruning itself; the old idea that pruning caused the formation of ordinary loose knots is without foundation.

Healing of wounds. The total time required for complete healing of a pruning scar depends on the rate of diameter growth of the portion of the bole next to the wound and the length of the branch stub (Romell, 1940). The diameter of the wound makes surprisingly little difference, although there is a tendency for the stubs that are left to be long if the branches are large (Nylinder, 1955). Ordinarily the length that the stub projects outward from the wood surface is controlled by and very nearly equal to the thickness of the bark on the stem.

Pruning scars heal most rapidly either at the sides or at the top. The lower part of the branch stub is usually the last to be covered (Fig. 4-1). Consequently, it is desirable to combat the natural tendency to make the pruning cuts that slant outward such that the lower part of the stub sticks out more than the upper. The most rapid callus formation results from the lateral proliferation of the cambium and parenchyma at the edges of the wound. The cambial cells are more likely to be parallel to the edges of the wound at the sides and top than at the bottom (Paterson, 1938).

Wounds created by removing live branches heal more rapidly than those formed by cutting off dead branches (Mayer-Wegelin, 1936). If the branches are alive, the cambial tissues form a cone around the base of the stem such that they bend outward. When the living wood is severed, the cambium and parenchyma at the edge of the wound are already in position for formation of a callus. Around dead branches, on the other hand, there is a minute circular cleft, beneath which the annual rings bend inward. The occlusion of dead branch stubs is much like the gradual submergence of a post set in a rising stream of water; unless special effort is made to wound living tissues by very close pruning, there is no true stimulation of callus formation over the dead branch stub. Actually the base of the branch tends to remain alive for several years after the rest of the branch is dead, so that a pruning wound made during that period heals in the same manner as one made in removing a branch with living foliage. In resinous species, live wounds are also covered with a protective coating of pitch more readily than those caused by cutting dead branches. The best time for removing a branch comes shortly before death or within several years thereafter.

The only important disadvantage of pruning dead branches is that the wounds heal more slowly than when live branches are removed. The growth of callus tissue over the stubs of dead branches can be stimulated by cutting into the cambium of the living branch collar so that the cuts are nearly flush with the bole (Curtis, 1936). The extra time required to do so is not, however, commonly worth the limited advantage gained (Adams and Schneller, 1939).

In judging the rate of healing of pruning scars from external appearances it should be remembered that the outer layers of bark were laid down many years ago because the bark grows outward from the cambium in the same manner that the wood grows inward. Therefore, the circular scars left on the bark by naturally or artificially pruned branches may persist even while several inches of clear wood are being laid down over the branch stub. The small grain distortions or dimples which may be formed in the clear wood after healing rarely constitute defects in the lumber.

Rot and discoloration of wood. Intelligently conducted pruning can reduce heart rot, but increases may result from recklessly exuberant pruning. The effect in either direction is easily exaggerated.

The cutting of dead branches or **dry pruning** is ordinarily beneficial in this respect. Projecting dead limbs, in spite of the fact that they are sealed to some extent by deposition of resins or gums in their bases, provide a natural means of entrance into the living tree for both insects and fungi. They also represent a pathway through which supplies of moisture and oxygen reach organisms inside the tree. The sooner they are removed and their stubs sealed with new wood, the better. Andrews (1954) showed that pruning of dead branches is an effective way of preventing western red rot in young ponderosa pines and of arresting infections that have already taken place. Ostrander and Foster (1957) contended that the remains of terminal shoots killed by the white pine weevil are a major source of entry for red rot in eastern white pine and advocated their elimination by pruning.

The removal of living branches, **live** or **green pruning,** is much more likely to cause rot in some groups of species than in others. It seems clear that the pruning of small living branches from resinous conifers like the pines and Douglas-fir is safe because the branches already contain some resin and the severing of the sapwood readily stimulates production of more. It is not, however, safe with these species or any others to prune branches that are larger than 1½ to 2 inches in diameter because they are likely to contain heartwood in which no protective substances form after pruning. Childs and Wright (1956) found that in Douglas-fir the greatest risk of fungal infection came from removing live limbs that were growing vigorously at points well above the base of the live crown. The removal of less vigorous limbs from the bottom of the crown was shown to involve no more risk than dry pruning. Most pruning done on this continent has been confined to these resinous species and it is not clear whether live pruning can be extended with equal safety to less resinous conifers or to hardwoods.

European evidence regarding the pruning of Norway spruce is, for example, highly contradictory. Mayer-Wegelin (1936) recommended that pruning of this species be delayed until branches had been dead for several years because no resin was deposited in the branch bases until they were dead and encased. Paterson (1938), however, contended that green pruning was actually safer than dry pruning because the cutting of living sapwood induces an artificial stimulation of resin production in spruce. Perhaps one can infer from this that the removal of recently dead spruce branches is more likely to lead to rot than the pruning of living ones or those that have been dead longer. Evidence about the relationship between pruning and rot in even less resinous conifers, such as hemlock or true fir, is very scanty.

Experience with green pruning of hardwoods has been limited. It has been found that small living branches can be safely removed from vigorous oaks (Roth, 1948) and northern hardwoods (Skilling, 1958); there is even some evidence that entry of rot through such branches is lessened by removing them before they die.

It is important to note that the rots that may appear beneath pruning wounds cease to develop when the wounds have occluded. Ordinarily they are limited to the knotty core that was laid down before healing was complete. These generalizations seem to hold good whether the fungi were already present in dead branches before pruning or became established after either green or dry pruning.

Fears about inducing rot by artificial pruning can usually be traced to unfortunate experiences with ill-advised pruning of excessively large branches, pruning of slow-growing trees, and the use of crude tools (Mayer-Wegelin, 1936; Romell, 1940). Difficulty with rots can ordinarily be avoided by confining pruning to relatively small branches that are dead or unthrifty but on vigorous trees.

The cause of the localized discolorations that sometimes occur in the wood around pruning wounds is poorly understood. Usually they do not yield wood-rotting fungi in laboratory cultures, although Childs and Wright (1956) expressed the opinion that those in Douglas-fir probably contained traces of incipient decay. It is also possible that they result from oxidation, desiccation, or obscure metabolic phenomena. In any event, they usually cease to enlarge when the wounds heal and rarely extend outside the knotty core.

Effect of live pruning on growth. If too many living branches are removed at once the crown surface may be so reduced as to cause serious retardation of growth in height and diameter.

The most critical factor affecting the destiny of a tree in competition with its neighbors is growth in height. Although the reductions in height growth caused by excessive green pruning are invariably small, their cumulative effect may be great enough to lead to the suppression of pruned trees by adjacent unpruned trees (Lückhoff, 1949). Therefore, growth in height is the best criterion of the allowable severity of green pruning.

Reductions of diameter growth from green pruning are proportionately of greater magnitude than those of height growth (Mar:Møller, 1960). As far as the survival of the tree is concerned they are of little importance. On the other hand, any reduction in diameter growth decreases both the rate of wound healing and that at which clear wood is produced. The diminution of diameter growth is not uniformly distributed over the bole, being greatest near the ground and becoming successively less marked with height in such a manner as to reduce the taper of the pruned log (Young and Kramer, 1952). Diameter growth either at the top of the pruned log or above in the green crown is not affected. Marts (1951) found that reductions from very drastic green pruning of longleaf pine are made chiefly at the expense of growth in early-wood and cause increases in wood density. In other words, the unfavorable effects of severe green pruning on growth in volume are mitigated to some extent by changes in taper and density that are ordinarily beneficial.

The unthrifty lower branches of a tree, which usually have unthrifty foliage or shade-leaves, lose more carbohydrate through respiration than they add from photosynthesis (Takahara, 1954). The removal of these branches does not reduce growth and may even increase it very slightly (Stein, 1955). Essentially parasitic branches of this kind are usually found below the point of contact between branches of adjoining trees in closed stands. A number of investigators have found that 25 to 30 per cent of the live crowns of a variety of conifers can be removed without reduction in height growth or serious decline in diameter growth (Barrett and Downs, 1943; Helmers, 1946; Boggess, 1950; Hallin, 1956; Slabaugh, 1957). In a detailed analysis of the growth of pruned loblolly pine, Labyak and Schumacher (1954) demonstrated that very little additional growth in total cubic volume resulted from leaving a live crown ratio of more than 50 per cent. Analysis of the findings of the other investigators likewise indicates that the live crown ratios of a variety of conifers can be reduced to approximately 50 per cent without reduction of diameter growth. Labyak and Schumacher also showed that the growth of cubic volume of clear wood was maximized by reducing the live crown ratio to about 40 per cent because the additional clear length compensated for the slight reduction in diameter growth. More detailed analysis would be required to determine the live crown ratio at which growth of clear wood in board-foot volume would be maximized.

Excessive green pruning may result in sunscalding of trees with smooth, thin bark. It can also lead to the development of epicormic branches on hardwoods as well as on those conifers, such as Douglas-fir, spruce, and true firs, which have numerous dormant buds.

Policies Followed in Pruning

Artificial pruning is more costly per tree than almost any other kind of silvicultural operation. The returns from it are long deferred, although not over an entire rotation. The funds available for stand improvement of any sort are usually limited so it is essential that they be expended to best advantage. Pruning can be highly profitable or extravagantly wasteful, depending on the judgment of the supervisor of the work. Some of the important considerations are discussed in the following paragraphs.

Choice of species. The limited resources usually available for pruning are best expended only on those species or individuals that do not prune well naturally but produce lumber or veneer that has well-recognized technical value if it is clear or free of loose knots.

There is little point in pruning trees that are likely to be used for framing timbers, rough construction, posts, poles, pulpwood or other products that command little or no premium if free from knots. Species or individual trees susceptible to serious mortality or decay from attacks of insects and fungi, including those attacks induced by pruning itself, should not be treated.

Choice of stand and site. If pruning is to be successful, the chosen trees must reach the desired diameter rapidly enough to ensure an adequate margin of profit on the investment. Therefore, pruning is best conducted on good sites and in stands that are sufficiently accessible to allow thinning. Thinning is necessary not only to promote the production of clear wood but also to ensure quick healing of wounds and the continued dominance of the pruned trees. It is unwise to invest in pruning stands that are subject to catastrophic losses from wind, fire, disease, or other damaging agencies.

Growth rate, size, and age of trees to be pruned. Pruning intended for production of clear lumber or veneer should be limited to trees that are already growing rapidly in diameter or can be made to do so promptly by thinning. This usually means pruning young, small trees, not necessarily because they are young and small but because such trees are most likely to be growing rapidly. The knotty cores will also be small and there will be ample time, even on a relatively short rotation, to develop thick shells of clear wood like that of the fine log shown in Fig. 4-2.

Large trees can be pruned if they are growing with unusual rapidity for their size. In fact, a given thickness of clear shell contains more board feet on a large tree than on a small one (Shaw and Staebler, 1952). However, it is also necessary to consider how much longer the tree is likely to be left. When all factors are taken into account, it is usually found best to confine the knotty core to a diameter somewhere between 4 and 12 inches; there is little use in trying to start production of clear lumber by pruning after the middle of a short rotation.

These restrictions can be relaxed somewhat if the objective is merely to ensure production of tight-knotted lumber by eliminating dead branches. This procedure differs mainly in that the clear shell desired is thinner but still important; the grade and value of tight-knotted lumber are substantially improved if the knots do not extend to the edges of the boards. It is still necessary to wait for growth to take place before harvest; the growth must also be rather rapid because the increase in value gained by treatment is smaller than when

Fig. 4-2. Cross section through a node of an eastern white pine which was green-pruned 42 years ago when 3½ inches in diameter. The average diameter growth of the tree was about 2.6 inches per decade in the period after pruning. The small wounds healed swiftly and almost perfectly. (*Photograph by Forest Products Laboratory, U. S. Forest Service.*)

clear wood is the goal. The sizes of trees pruned for this purpose would still be restricted by the desirability of avoiding trees that have already laid down wood that will yield loose-knotted lumber; when trees have reached this stage it is usually best to harvest them because their net value is fully as likely to decline as to increase with further growth.

At the other extreme, it is generally unwise to prune trees when they are so small and young that clear differentiation of crown classes has not yet taken place. The ideal time to start pruning comes immediately after an early initial thinning. If early thinnings cannot be made, pruning should either be delayed until the first thinning is imminent or limited to low pruning of trees that seem certain to remain vigorous. There are altogether too many instances in which money has been wasted by pruning trees that later suffered so severely from competition that they grew slowly or even died of suppression.

From another point of view, it is ordinarily best to delay pruning until the terminal shoots have grown to the height of the first log length thus avoiding the risk that forks or crooks may develop before this height is attained.

Bud pruning is a method of very early pruning developed in Russia. It is done by rubbing off the lateral buds or clipping off very young branches with the objective of producing logs with no knots whatsoever (Paul, 1946; Rowland, 1950). The technique has been tested on several species of pine, usually with results that were ultimately disappointing. Growth is ordinarily reduced, although the development of abnormally long needles on the vertical stems causes the reduction to be less serious than one might suppose (Bickerstaff, 1945; Marts, 1950; Fox, 1957). The main problem has usually been from the very serious effects of any kind of injury to the terminal shoots. The simplicity and cheapness of the actual operation is counterbalanced by the necessity of visiting the trees every year and the difficulty of pruning higher than one can reach. It is also necessary to prune more than the ordinary number of trees because of the high risk of damage and the tendency of untreated trees to outgrow the bud-pruned ones.

Very early pruning of a limited number of branches may also be justified if it will prevent the formation of forks and the kind of abnormally large branches or **ramicorns** that project at sharp acute angles from the bole and often become very persistent. These departures from normal branching habit are caused by injuries to the terminal shoots or buds and physiological factors that cause lateral branches to develop more rapidly than the terminal shoot. Such abnormal development is common when conifers form **lammas shoots** or extra whorls of branches late in the growing season. There are indications that the few large branches that persist on many hardwoods arise in this manner after damage to terminal buds. The stem crooks resulting from death of whole terminal shoots of conifers can be reduced by prompt removal of the dead leader and all but one of the laterals.

Very severe early green pruning may be used to slow down the growth of promising trees that might otherwise grow so much faster than their neighbors as to become coarsely branched wolf trees.

Number and charactristics of trees to be pruned. Only the best trees should be pruned and the work is ordinarily confined to those destined to form the final crop. Sometimes justification exists, however, for pruning trees that will be removed in thinnings late in the rotation; often these will be those pruned not for the production of clear lumber but to prevent formation of loose knots.

Selections of trees to prune are best made from the trees of largest diameter in the dominant crown class (Eversole, 1953), although thrifty codominants and slender dominants may be pruned if it is certain that they can be promoted to clearly dominant position by prompt thinning.

Accurate determination of the number of trees to prune on each acre depends on knowledge of the space that each will occupy at the end of the rotation. Ordinarily it should be anticipated that the crowns of the pruned trees will be allowed to expand rapidly under the influence of heavy, systematic thinnings. Costs are tremendously increased by the prevalent error of pruning more trees than can be carried through the rotation. Some losses will inevitably occur; allowance can be made for casualties by pruning a few more trees than will be necessary in the final crop.

The number of trees selected for one-log pruning is likely to fall between fifty and two hundred per acre if the objective is to obtain a final crop consisting of pruned trees. If it is hard to find trees that are of sufficient quality and vigor to prune, it is best to confine attention to the good trees without attempting to produce a full crop of pruned trees. It is usually logical to think in terms of rigid *minimum* specifications defining the characteristics of trees that are worth pruning and *maximum* numbers per acre.

Just before the first thinning it may occasionally be worth while to prune a larger number of trees to a height which can be reached conveniently from the ground. The main advantage of such treatment is that it facilitates thinning by improving access to stands with numerous low branches. The possibility of impromptu axe-pruning during the logging is thus forestalled; it is no more costly to prune the lower parts of the tree than to cut the same branches off after felling (Cook, 1951).

In all cases one should avoid pruning any of the outermost trees in a stand; these trees are generally of poor form and a curtain of foliage extending down to the ground is valuable in keeping destructive winds out of the rest of the stand.

The selection of the trees is the most crucial phase of pruning and the choices should be made by someone with a clear understanding of the way in which the pruned trees and the stand will grow and be treated in the future.

Height of pruning. Pruning should commence in youth when the lower branches start to die or when adequate differentiation into crown classes has taken place. The first operation usually consists in pruning off the branches that can be easily reached by a man standing on the ground. The pruning is then continued up the tree in steps at intervals of a few years until the desired length is freed of branches. In each operation the level of pruning is extended either to the topmost whorl of dead branches or into the lower portion of the living crown, depending on what policy is being followed with regard to green pruning. Under this plan, it will require two or three prunings to clear the trunk of branches to the ordinary height of 17 feet.

If one waits until the whole first log can be pruned at once, the lower part of the knotty core may become unnecessarily large. Jacobs (1938), Bull (1943), and Ralston and Lemien (1956) found that it took no longer to prune to a given height in two steps than in a single operation. The extra time required for pruning in two steps was found to be about equal to the greater resting time involved in the one-step method.

If the first log is pruned in several steps, the time interval between stages should be kept short enough that the knotty core at the top of the log does not become larger than at the bottom and thus defeat the purpose of pruning in steps.

Pruning becomes increasingly expensive as it is extended up the tree, because the diameter of the branches increases with height and also because the trees have to be climbed or pruned with tools mounted on long poles. At least a quarter and sometimes more than half of the board-foot volume of second-growth trees is laid down in the first 16-foot log. For these reasons it is customary to stop when the first log length is pruned. On the other hand, the branches on the next two logs become large and usually die thus leading to the production of substantial volumes of the loose-knotted grades of lumber. Consequently pruning the middle logs sometimes improves the ultimate grade recovery more than pruning the first log (Foster, 1957). Pruning at such high levels can be justified only on a very limited number of the best trees which must then be allowed to grow for a longer time than the remaining trees of more ordinary quality.

The lengths pruned should be adjusted to fit whatever log-lengths are likely to be most consistent with utilization practices at the time of harvest. If 16-foot logs are standard, as is most commonly the case, pruning should be extended to 17 feet to allow for trimming and the height of the stump. With some species and in some localities, almost any multiple of 2 feet from 8 feet on up would be acceptable, although 10- and 12-foot logs are often awkward to utilize efficiently. Veneer bolts are usually cut in 8½-foot lengths, a point significant because artificial pruning promises richer rewards for this kind of utilization than for any other (Lutz, 1958). The higher the pruning, the more careful should be the selection of the trees and the smaller the number per acre.

Choice of season. Live pruning should ordinarily be avoided during those parts of spring and summer when diameter growth is taking place. At such times the bark easily slips from the wood leaving serious wounds and the risk of fungal infection of the cut surfaces is at a maximum. Any part of the dormant season is satisfactory, although late winter and early spring appear preferable for conifers and late summer and autumn for hardwoods. If living tissues are not injured, there is no reason why the pruning of dead limbs cannot be done at any time of year.

Subsequent treatment. The thinning schedule must be closely linked with the pruning policy. Heavy thinnings are usually necessary to make a financial success of pruning. Conversely, artificial pruning will make possible heavier thinnings than would be justified if reliance were placed on natural pruning. If artificial pruning is to be employed, spacings in plantations can be wider, thereby effecting substantial savings in costs of establishment. It should be noted, however, that the cost of pruning large branches from trees planted more than 8 to 10 feet apart may equal or exceed the amount saved by planting fewer trees.

Adequate records should be kept of location of pruned stands, height of pruning, and age or diameter of trees at time of pruning; this information is eventually necessary for advantageous sale or efficient utilization of pruned trees. With species like the hard pines, which prune naturally at a moderately early age, it may be necessary to place permanent marks on the pruned crop trees as soon as it becomes difficult to distinguish between naturally pruned trees and those with much smaller knotty cores which have been pruned artificially.

Tools Employed in Forest Pruning

Good pruning requires that the cuts be made close to the tree trunk and flush with it, leaving no splinters of wood or broken stubs to interfere with callus formation. They should be made without tearing or loosening the bark around the branch stub.

The choice of tools depends on a number of factors, many of which are determined by differences between species. Among these are the inherent characteristics of bark and wood, size of branches, number of limbs per whorl and branch angle. There is a difference within a species between pruning dead and live limbs. Some tools are best suited to use only at certain heights above ground; others are effective at all heights. The skill and agility of the operator, as well as personal preference, play an important part in the selection of tools and techniques for pruning. Several types of hand pruning tools are shown in Fig. 4-3.

Hand and pole saws. The hand saws that are usually found most satisfactory are those that are curved with five to eight long, acute teeth per inch on the concave edge. Optimum lengths vary from 12 to 26 inches in more or less direct relationships with the sizes of branches. The blades must be rigid enough to prevent whipping and should cut mainly or exclusively on the pull stroke. A man standing on the ground can prune as high as 7 to 8 feet above ground with a hand saw. To prune higher with a hand saw he must use a ladder or somehow climb the tree.

The Meylan pruning saw is essentially a hand-saw blade mounted on a long axe handle. It is often better than the hand saw for pruning from the ground because it can reach to 9 or 10 feet. This greatly enhances the possibility of getting some clear material in utilizable length, especially for veneer bolts, from the relatively large number of trees that might be pruned in the comparatively inexpensive first stage of pruning. With the Meylan saw it is usually possible to remove the lowest branches without sticking one's face into them.

In removing branches more than 7 to 10 feet above ground it is possible to use a variety of kinds of saw blades mounted on light, but rigid poles of wood or aluminum alloy. Because it is awkward to prune branches that are relatively close to the ground with a long pole saw, it is necessary to use poles of different lengths for different zones of height. For example, a 7-foot pole is useful in the zone between

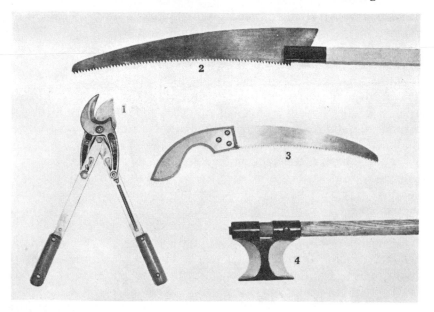

Fig. 4-3. Typical instruments used in pruning forest trees: (1) A pair of shears which has both blades sharpened and is designed for close pruning. (2) The blade of a pole saw. (3) A hand pruning saw. (4) The Rich pruning tool, typical of those which cut on impact. (*Photograph by Yale University School of Forestry.*)

7 and 12 feet; a 13-foot pole, in the zone between 12 and 17 feet. Pole saws are quite ineffective above the 20-foot level.

Hand and Meylan saws are safe, fast, and effective on branches of all sizes that can be removed without risk of fungal infection. They also enable closer pruning than is possible with other tools. All saws leave a cut surface rougher than those left by shears or tools cutting by impact. The difference is of no practical importance because healing progresses satisfactorily over either kind of surface.

Edged tools cutting by impact. Axes, brushhooks, hatchets, and similar cutting tools are dangerous to use for pruning and rarely give satisfactory results. The common outcome of axe-pruning is a high proportion of long or broken stubs, torn bark, and cuts into the bole. The time requirement is equal to or greater than that involved with a suitable saw (Bull, 1937). If a branch is so large that it can be removed more swiftly with an axe than a saw, it is generally too large to prune anyhow.

More satisfactory results can be obtained with impact cutting tools which consist essentially of chisels, pulling knives, or combinations of the two. These pruning irons are mounted on long poles and used exclusively for high pruning. They have straight, V-, or U-shaped blades that are pushed up underneath or pulled down over the branches. The tool, devised by Rich (1935) and shown in Fig. 4-3, is a combination of the two kinds of tools. Like all such pruning irons it is most effective on small branches found in trees in dense, naturally reproduced stands. It requires some skill and force to get close cuts with pruning irons.

Pruning shears. The conventional kinds of shears used in orchards or horticulture usually leave excessively long stubs or are otherwise unsatisfactory for purposes other than bud pruning. Special kinds of shears having two opposing and sharpened blades (Fig. 4-3) have been devised to make the close cuts required in forest pruning. However, even these are rarely used because they are expensive and useful only for pruning branches close to the ground. The use of shears might represent a promising avenue for the mechanization of pruning but appropriate equipment has yet to be devised.

Clubs. Dead branches of some species can be removed fairly swiftly and satisfactorily by knocking them off with clubs. Kachin (1940) described a special type of tool, known as the Hebo pruning club, for use on second-growth Douglas-fir. It consists of a handle shod with a steel ferrule at the striking end. It can be made in a large 33-inch size for use with two hands by a man on the ground or in a smaller 18-inch length for swinging with one hand. The smaller size is intended primarily for use in high pruning by men climbing the trees with climbing irons. A high proportion of the limbs are broken off inside the branch collar; wounds of this kind heal more rapidly than those made by other tools (Anderson, 1951). The Hebo club is not satisfactory for pruning thin-barked trees or those with tough branches.

Machines. Pruning could be done much more extensively and cheaply if the operation could be satisfactorily mechanized. The first machine in commercial production has a rotating spiral cutting head, like a spindle, which is opposed by a fixed guide in V-shaped arrangement and mounted on a 6- or 12-foot boom with the motor at the lower end.

Techniques of High Pruning

Low pruning can be done easily and swiftly from the ground with saws, shears or clubs, but the difficulty and cost increase rapidly as one prunes higher up the tree. High pruning can be done with pole saws, by climbing up a ladder and using a hand saw, or by climbing the tree itself and using a club or hand saw.

When limbs are small, the pole saw is faster than the hand saw operated from a ladder because more time is lost in moving the ladder than in shifting the pole saw. This is often true on rough or brushy terrain. However, the quality of high pruning done with hand saws is distinctly superior to that done with pole saws, especially if the branches are fairly large (Hawley and Clapp, 1935). Bull (1937) found that pole saws gave satisfactory results and were not unduly fatiguing if employed by men who had acquired the knack of using them and did not work with them too steadily. The choice depends on the circumstances.

The ladders in question should be as portable as possible and constructed of either a light, strong wood or a light metal alloy. The best types are tapered and have a curved, padded top rung that is concave toward the tree trunk as well as spikes projecting downward from the lower ends of the rails to keep the ladder from slipping. A different length of ladder is needed for each successive 5-foot increase in height of pruning and the lengths appropriate to each zone of height are the same as those for pole saws.

Another method of high pruning, the "Tarzan" method, involves climbing the tree to the desired height and then pruning one's way downward with a hand saw. This method is cheaper than pruning from a ladder but can be done only by relatively light, agile men. The main drawback is that the trees must be so large that the stems will not bend or break and there must be strong branches within easy reach of the ground.

It is also possible to climb the tree with climbing irons and a safety belt or by the techniques of rope work employed in tree surgery, pruning progressively upward or downward with hand saw or Hebo club. These are the only methods that can be used economically, safely, and effectively above a height of roughly 20 feet. The only pole-climbing irons safe enough for this operation are those that can be driven through the bark and into the wood. The significance of the damage caused by the spurs varies with the circumstances. It is of little consequence in instances where it amounts to no more than the formation of pitch pockets at the outer surface of the knotty core of conifers. Even this degree of damage can be avoided by using ropes or various kinds of "tree grippers" that can be substituted for climbing irons.

When pole saws or ladders are used the cost of high pruning increases rapidly with increasing height above ground. However, when the tree itself is climbed with climbing irons or similar devices it costs little more to prune 40 feet above ground than at 20 feet, except to the extent that the size and number of branches may differ.

Financial Aspects of Pruning

The comparison of ultimate values and present costs of pruning is somewhat simpler than with most silvicultural investments. Factors involved are: (1) initial cost, (2) mortality, (3) number of years remaining before harvest, (4) interest rate at which pruning cost is compounded, and (5) increase in value of product attributable exclusively to pruning (Smith, 1954, 1956). The computations are most useful if made so as to reveal the cost and return for each unit of volume of improved product resulting from treatment.

The time required for pruning varies widely, depending on the diameter and number, that is, the total cross-sectional area, of branches removed. Therefore, the cost of pruning depends largely on the initial spacing of the stand, its age, and the branching habit of the species. For example, Bramble, Cope, and Chisman (1949) found that it took three times as long to prune a red pine plantation initially spaced 10 by 10 feet as one spaced at 6-foot intervals. Cline and Fletcher (1928) found that it took almost four times as long to prune eastern white pines with a mean branch diameter of 1 inch as it did when this diameter averaged ¼ inch. McLintock (1952) showed that it took much longer to prune red spruce, which has numerous internodal branches, than eastern white pine, which usually puts out but one whorl of branches each year. He also found that the time required to prune red spruce depended directly on the number of branches per lineal foot.

Experience with American conifers has shown that it is possible to prune the first 16-foot logs of from four to eight trees per man-hour, although as many as twenty trees can be pruned in a man-hour under unusually favorable circumstances, as in young longleaf pine (Bull, 1937). The ordinary output has also been expressed as varying between 75 and 125 linear feet of bole per man-hour. The actual cost may range from 8 to 50 cents per tree.

The ultimate cost of pruning is the value of the initial cost adjusted to allow for mortality and, at least for analytical purposes, carried at compound interest until the time of harvest. The length of time necessary to achieve the desired thickness of clear shell depends entirely on the rate of growth. Most calculations indicate that pruning is profitable only if the average rate of diameter growth for the *entire* holding period exceeds 1.5 inches per decade (equivalent to 13.3 annual rings per radial inch). The practice is almost invariably found to be highly profitable if the average growth rate is 2.5 inches per decade (eight rings per inch) or better. At the time of pruning the trees should be growing much faster than the desired rate because of the inevitable deceleration of diameter growth. Therefore, it is distinctly advantageous to prune young, vigorous trees and forestall serious reductions in their diameter growth by thinning.

In the estimation of the value added by pruning, allowance must be made for the prospective effects of natural pruning and the relative proportions of tight- and loose-knotted wood that would be produced by unpruned trees. The increase in value is greatest with trees on which dead branches tend to persist. Theoretically, the increase in value due to pruning should accrue to stumpage because it costs no more, if as much, to manufacture products from clear logs as from rough ones. In practice, however, the owner who sells lumber or veneer from his own trees is far more likely to reap the reward from pruning than he who sells logs or stumpage. Therefore, the owner who plans to confine himself to selling logs or stumpage should not prune except in situations where a large margin of profit is assured; recognition of equitable log and tree grades would alter this situation.

Among the numerous published financial analyses of pruning are those of Burns and Nichols (1952), Finnis (1953), Bennett (1956), Campbell (1956), Ralston and Lemien (1956), and Fedkiw, Hopkins and Stout (1960). Such analyses generally show that artificial pruning is as lucrative as any kind of silvicultural investment, if performed intelligently and conservatively in combination with favorable conditions of growth, markets, and subsequent thinning. Returns as high as 8 to 12 per cent compound interest on the pruning investment are not uncommon under such circumstances.

The returns from artificial pruning are sometimes sufficient to offset the less attractive yields of the large investments occasionally necessary to establish a crop of trees. It is usually in connection with pruning that the forester becomes most keenly aware that most of the earning potential of a stand resides in that small fraction of the trees that are likely to be of both high vigor and outstanding quality.

Shearing and Pruning of Christmas Trees

Conifers being grown for use as Christmas trees often require special techniques of pruning to correct the effects of excessively rapid or asymmetrical growth and produce dense crowns of the proper shape.

The most common practice, referred to as **shearing,** is the clipping of both terminal and lateral shoots. The objective is to develop crowns which are narrow and globose at the bottom and conical in the middle and upper portions. Shearing is usually confined to the removal of part of the shoots of the current or most recent growing season. Buds formed just below the point of cutting must be depended upon for renewed elongation of the decapitated shoots. Species which have dormant buds throughout the length of each internode, like Norway spruce (Bramble, 1948), can be sheared at almost any season except early summer. Pines rarely have any dormant buds along the internodes and are best sheared when the shoots are actively elongating. This stimulates the prompt development of vigorous adventitious buds just below the cut ends (Bramble and Byrnes, 1953; Brown, 1960).

Excessively tall and rapidly grown trees can sometimes be converted into good Christmas trees in one operation simply by pruning off the lower three-quarters or more of the crown. The remaining tuft of crown at the top then grows much more slowly and may soon develop into a properly compact form without any shearing. This technique is successfully applied to fast-growing balsam firs of natural origin.

REFERENCES

Adams, W. R., and M. R. Schneller. 1939. Some physiological responses to close pruning of northern white pine. *Vt. AES Bul.* 444.

Anderson, E. A. 1951. Healing time for pruned Douglas-fir. *USFPL Rept.* R1907.

Andrews, S. R. 1954. Effect of pruning on western red rot in young ponderosa pine in the Southwest. *J. Forestry* 52:33–38.

Barrett, L. I., and A. A. Downs. 1943. Growth response of white pine in the southern Appalachians to green pruning. *J. Forestry* 41:507–510.

Bennett, F. A. 1956. Financial aspects of pruning planted slash pine. *SEFES Sta. Paper* 64.

Bickerstaff, A. 1945. Knot-free red pine by debudding. *Canada, Dominion Forest Service Silvicultural Res. Note* 76.

Boggess, W. R. 1950. The effect of repeated pruning on diameter and height growth of planted slash pine. *J. Forestry* 48:352–353.

Bramble, W. C. 1948. Effect of season of shearing upon the quality of Norway spruce Christmas trees. *J. Forestry* 46:820–822.

Bramble, W. C., H. N. Cope, and H. H. Chisman. 1949. Influence of spacing on growth of red pine in plantations. *J. Forestry* 47:726–732.

Bramble, W. C., and W. R. Byrnes. 1953. Effect of time of shearing upon adventitious bud formation and shoot growth of red pine grown for Christmas trees. *Penn. AES Prog. Rept.* 91.

Brown, J. H. 1960. Fall and winter pruning of pines in West Virginia. *W. Va. Univ. Exp. Sta. Current Rept.* 26.

Bull, H.   1937.   Tools and labor requirements for pruning longleaf pine.   *J. Forestry* 35:359–364.

———.   1943.   Pruning practices in open-grown longleaf pine.   *J. Forestry* 41: 174–179.

Burns, P. Y., and J. M. Nichols.   1952.   Oak pruning in the Missouri Ozarks.   *Mo. AES Bul.* 581.

Campbell, R. A.   1956.   Profits from pruning Appalachian white pine.   *SEFES Sta. Paper* 65.

Childs, T. W., and E. Wright.   1956.   Pruning and occurrence of heart rot in young Douglas-fir.   *PNWFRES Res. Note* 132.

Cline, A. C., and E. D. Fletcher.   1928.   *Pruning for profit*.   Mass. Forestry Assoc., Boston.

Cook, D. B.   1951.   Justifications for forest pruning in the Northeast.   *J. Forestry* 49:487–489.

Curtis, J. D.   1936.   A method of pruning dead branches.   *Forestry Chronicle* 12:291–299.

———.   1937.   An historical review of artificial forest pruning.   *Forestry Chronicle* 13:380–395.

Davis, K. P.   1936.   Test of pruning equipment and methods in western white pine.   *NRMFRES Applied Forestry Note* 76.

Eversole, K. R.   1953.   Better marking means cheaper pruning.   *PNWFRES Res. Note* 87.

Fedkiw, J., F. S. Hopkins, Jr., and N. J. Stout.   1960.   Economic aspects of growing high quality pine through pruning.   *Northeastern Logger* 8(10):16–19, 22–23, 39.

Finnis, J. M.   1953.   Experimental pruning of Douglas fir in British Columbia.   *Brit. Columbia Forest Service Res. Note* 24.

Foster, R. W.   1957.   A study of the growth and value of a high-quality eastern white pine tree.   *J. Forestry* 55:727–730.

Fox, H. W.   1957.   Bud-pruning red pine and eastern white pine in northern Illinois.   *J. Forestry* 55:359–363.

Grah, R. F.   1961.   Relationship between tree spacing, knot size, and log quality in young Douglas-fir stands.   *J. Forestry* 59:270–272.

Hallin, W. E.   1956.   Pruning ponderosa and Jeffrey pine.   *CFRES Forest Res. Note* 115.

Hawley, R. C., and R. T. Clapp.   1935.   Artificial pruning in coniferous plantations.   *Yale Univ. School of Forestry Bul.* 39.

Helmers, A. E.   1946.   Effect of pruning on growth of western white pine.   *J. Forestry* 44:673–676.

Hopkins, W. C.   1958.   Relationship of stand characteristics to quality of loblolly pine.   *La. AES Bul.* 517.

Jacobs, M. R.   1938.   Notes on pruning *Pinus radiata*, Part I.   Observations on features which influence pruning.   *Australia, Commonwealth Forestry Bur. Bul.* 23.

Kachin, T.   1940.   The Hebo pruning club.   *J. Forestry* 38:596–597.

Labyak, L. F., and F. X. Schumacher.   1954.   The contribution of its branches to the main-stem growth of loblolly pine.   *J. Forestry* 52:333–337.

Lückhoff, H. A.   1949.   The effect of live pruning on the growth of *Pinus patula, P. caribaea*, and *P. taeda*.   *J. So. African Forestry Assoc.* 18:25–55.

Lutz, J. F. 1958. Suitability of eastern white pine and red pine for veneer and plywood. *Proc. Soc. Am. Foresters Meeting,* 1957:113–117.

McLintock, T. F. 1952. Cost of pruning red spruce in natural stands. *J. Forestry* 50:485–486.

Mar:Møller, C. 1960. The influence of pruning on the growth of conifers. *Forestry* 33:37–53.

Marts, R. O. 1950. Wood quality of bud-pruned longleaf pine. *Southern Lumberman* 181(2273):197–199.

———. 1951. Influence of crown reduction on springwood and summerwood distribution in longleaf pine. *J. Forestry* 49:183–189.

Mayer-Wegelin, H. 1936. *Astung.* Schaper, Hannover.

Nylinder, P. 1955. Kvistningsundersökningar. I. Grönkvistning av ek. (Pruning investigations. I. Green pruning in oak.) *Meddel. f. Statens Skogsforskningsinstitut* 45(12):1–44. (English summary.)

Ostrander, M. D., and C. H. Foster. 1957. Weevil–red rot associations in eastern white pine. *NEFES Forest Res. Note* 68.

Paterson, A. 1938. The occlusion of pruning wounds in Norway spruce (*Picea excelsa*). *Annals Bot.* 2(n.s.):681–698.

Paul, B. H. 1938. Knots in second-growth pine and the desirability of pruning. *USDA Misc. Pub.* 307.

———. 1946. Tree pruning by annual removal of lateral buds. *J. Forestry* 44:499–501.

———. 1947a. Lumber grades vs. site quality of second-growth Douglas fir. *USFPL Rept.* R1688.

———. 1947b. Knots in second-growth Douglas fir. *USFPL Rept.* R1690.

Ralston, R. A., and W. Lemien. 1956. Pruning pine plantations in Michigan. *Mich. AES Circ. Bul.* 221.

Rapraeger, E. F. 1939. Development of branches and knots in western white pine. *J. Forestry* 37:239–245.

Rhodes, A. D. 1960. Putting quality back into white pine. (*Soc. Prot. N. H. Forests*) *Forest Notes* No. 66:3–7.

Rich, J. H. 1935. A new forest pruning tool. *J. Forestry* 33:1006–1007.

Romell, L-G. 1940. Kvistningsstudier å tall och gran. (Studies on pruning in pine and spruce.) *Meddel. f. Statens Skogsförsöksanstalt* 32(5):143–194. (English summary.)

Roth, E. R. 1948. Healing and defects following oak pruning. *J. Forestry* 46:500–504.

Rowland, C. A., Jr. 1950. Early results of bud-pruning in slash pine. *J. Forestry* 48:100–103.

Shaw, E. W., and G. R. Staebler. 1952. An analysis of investments in pruning. *J. Forestry* 50:819–823.

Skilling, D. D. 1958. Wound healing and defects following northern hardwood pruning. *J. Forestry* 56:19–22.

Slabaugh, P. E. 1957. Effects of live crown removal on the growth of red pine. *J. Forestry* 55:904–906.

Smith, J. H. G. 1954. The economics of pruning. *Forestry Chronicle* 30:197–214.

———. 1956. An example of the importance of change in form class to calculations of clear-wood growth. *Forestry Chronicle* 32:260–262.

Smith, J. H. G. 1961. Comments on "Relationship between tree spacing, knot size, and log quality in young Douglas-fir stands." *J. Forestry* 59:682–683.

Stein, W. I. 1955. Pruning to different heights in young Douglas-fir. *J. Forestry* 53:352–355.

Takahara, S. 1954. (Influence of pruning on the growth of sugi and hinoki.) *Bul. Tokyo Univ. Forests,* No. 46:1–95. (English summary.)

Tarbox, E. E., and P. M. Reed. 1924. Quality and growth of white pine as influenced by density, site, and associated species. *Harvard Forest Bul.* 7.

Young, H. E., and P. J. Kramer. 1952. The effect of pruning on the height and diameter growth of loblolly pine. *J. Forestry* 50:474–479.

CHAPTER 5

Release cuttings

Release cutting is the act of freeing a young stand of desirable trees, not past the sapling stage, from the competition of undesirable trees that threaten to suppress them. Distinction may be made between two kinds of releasing operations, **cleaning** or **liberation** cutting, which differ as to the ages and sizes of trees eliminated.

In the release of most young stands, the operation is, in effect, an uncovering of them through elimination of overtopping trees. The basic objective is to give the trees that are released enough light and growing space to grow adequately and develop into trees of the main canopy. Sometimes whole layers of overtopping trees are removed; sometimes they are merely interrupted over especially desirable small trees. The degree of release sought depends on the method and cost of release, the minimum amount of vacant growing space that must be created, and other considerations.

Release cuttings are most readily visualized in terms of freeing the crowns of existing desirable trees, but there are several additional considerations. The growing space in the soil may be fully as important as that in the crown, particularly on dry sites. Even when the crown of a tree is fully released its growth may still be hampered by competition for moisture and nutrients with the root systems of adjacent trees. Many techniques used for releasing stands are very effective in killing the tops of competing trees but do not prevent sprouting if the roots remain alive. Entirely new vegetation of aggressive competitors may claim new vacancies faster than the released trees can expand to fill them.

As with any of the numerous kinds of silvicultural treatment, release cuttings should be conducted with a clear understanding of the way in which all the vegetation of the site will develop after treatment. This is especially important with respect to the release of young stands. The very need for such operations indicates that the desirable trees command only a small fraction of the growing space so they must expand considerably to preclude recapture of the site by other species. If the work is conducted with little foresight and much wishful thinking, discouraging developments are likely.

Before the consideration of techniques of release cutting, it is first logical to examine the ways in which plants can be killed and the nature of the chemicals that are becoming increasingly useful for the purpose.

Lethal effects. The surest and most direct way to kill a plant is to tear it bodily out of the soil. This is still the most dependable way of dealing with perennial grasses and some other small plants that sprout profusely from the roots, although there are chemical techniques of killing such species. Quite sizable trees can be dealt with similarly by means of powerful machinery in preparing sites for regeneration (see Chapter 9).

Ordinary cutting merely decapitates the plant. It is completely effective against most conifers and other species that do not sprout, but is often worse than useless in controlling those that sprout profusely.

Girdling involves the removal or killing of a ring of bark around the tree so that the flow of carbohydrates through the phloem from the crown to the roots is blocked. The roots die if and when their food reserves are exhausted and the whole tree is thus killed. However, girdling is almost as effective as cutting in stimulating sprouting.

Fire usually kills trees by girdling and has the same effect on sprouting. It can be used as a tool for the control of stand composition, but in preparation for regeneration and not as a means of releasing new crops soon after they are established (see Chapter 9).

Most herbicides also have the effect of killing the phloem and thus girdling trees somewhere between the foliage and the roots. However, this is the minimum degree of damage associated with their successful use. They can, in addition, cause *direct* killing of the top of the tree, the buds from which sprouts arise and, if ultimate success is achieved, the roots.

Herbicides

The chemicals used for killing the weeds of the forest are, owing to their wide use in agriculture, most commonly called **herbicides.**

The term **silvicide** is widely used but semantically questionable since it means "forest-killer." Use of the word "poison" causes all kinds of problems with public and labor relations.

Among the comprehensive accounts of herbicides or their use in silviculture are those by Leopold (1955); Frear (1955); Dahms and James (1955); Walker (1956); Sampson and Schultz (1956); Sutton (1958); Woodford, Holly and McCready (1958); Arend and Roe (1961); Crafts (1961); Klingman (1961); and Kirch (1961).

Before taking up the use and methods of application of herbicides it is first important that one consider some of the physical and chemical characteristics of these compounds as well as their relationship to the physiology of plants. In practical application, one is primarily concerned with the physical properties that determine how these compounds enter plants and move after entry. Most compounds used for herbicides will kill the appropriate vital tissues once they get to them; the chief problem is to cause them to get there.

One group of auxin herbicides, the chlorophenoxy acids, which include 2,4,5-T, has come to be the most important and the basic principles of using herbicides have been developed mostly from learning about their behavior. Their mode of movement into and within plants can be altered to fit a variety of different patterns by changing their chemical structure, so they serve to illustrate the manner of movement of almost any herbicide.

The mobility of herbicides depends primarily on their degree of polarity, that is, on those electrical properties of their molecules which determine the nature of their attraction or repulsion for other substances. Highly polar compounds have a strong affinity for other polar compounds; for example, a salt that dissolves readily in water does so because both are polar compounds. Non-polar compounds have affinity for other non-polar compounds; for example, many familiar oils will partially dissolve the cutin of leaf surfaces and the suberin of bark because all of these substances are non-polar.

It is, for present purposes, not too much of an oversimplification to state that herbicides with polar molecules are water-soluble while the non-polar ones are oil-soluble. However, some of the most useful modifications of the chlorophenoxy-acid herbicides, while non-polar and oil-soluble, have certain chemical properties which moderately increase their degree of polarity. As a result they have a slight affinity for water; this makes them more readily emulsifiable so that they can be applied in mixtures of oil and water and will also move in the aqueous medium within the plant (Frear, 1955). Organic compounds with —OH groups and double-bonded oxygen atoms (=O) are some-what more polar than those, like simple, distinctly non-polar hydro-carbons, consisting entirely of carbon and hydrogen.

Polar herbicides are water-soluble and move readily with the normal translocation of sap once they are introduced into the xylem. Some, but not all, move in the phloem if they can gain entry to it. However, unless they can enter through incisions, stomata, or the unsuberized coverings of roots, it is difficult to get them to enter plants or even to stick to and spread over the non-polar cutin and suberin that cover most of the outer surfaces. In other words, the unaided penetration of water-soluble herbicides through intact surfaces of plants is poor but they move readily once they are inside.

Non-polar herbicides that are soluble in oil, but not in water, are rel-atively high in ability to adhere to and penetrate intact surfaces but do not necessarily move readily in the aqueous medium inside the plant. However, if the portions that have been built onto their molecules to make them non-polar are split off during their entry into the plant, the phytotoxic portion of the molecule, which is polar, may move rather freely inside the plant. Crafts (1960) demonstrated that the necessary splitting action could be accomplished by hydrolysis in the leaves so that the active portion of the herbicide molecule could move, leaving the non-polar portion behind. It is not known whether a similarly convenient splitting action takes place in non-polar, oil-soluble herbicides applied through wounds in the bark.

Auxin herbicides. The most promising group of herbicides is the ever-increasing number of compounds with molecular structures that resemble naturally occurring hormones sufficiently to enter and le-thally derange ordinary physiological processes. These "counterfeit hormones" act in exceedingly small quantities. The wholesale screen-ing that has shown these organic chemicals to be effective is far ahead of the physiological studies that will ultimately explain their effects and make them even more useful (Crafts, 1961).

The first of the chlorophenoxy acids was 2,4-dichlorophenoxyacetic acid, which was developed during World War II. More conveniently known as 2,4-D, it has the molecular structure

The three-dimensional shape of this molecule apparently resembles that of some unknown natural hormone, enzyme, or organic catalyst sufficiently to become attached to others. This presumably halts some part of the natural metabolism or shunts it onto some destructively unnatural pathway.

One of the most damaging of the known effects is the excessive and unproductive expenditure of carbohydrates through uncontrolled respiration (Leopold, 1955). Excessive proliferation of the cambium and other tissues induces mechanical crushing of some tissues, especially the phloem. Toxic substances may be produced by abnormal metabolism and there is also evidence that there may be interference with the vital role played by phosphorus and potassium compounds in the carbohydrate metabolism. Some of the cell proteins may also be broken down by hydrolysis. In other words, the chlorophenoxy acids derange not one but many physiological processes. It is perhaps somewhat more correct to state that they cause plant tissues to starve themselves to death than that they cause the plants to grow themselves to death, but neither statement covers all the physiological effects.

This particular compound is rendered more effective against many woody plants by substituting an additional chlorine atom for the hydrogen at the fifth numbered carbon in the benzene ring to produce 2,4,5-trichlorophenoxyacetic acid, or 2,4,5-T. A variety of other modifications of the molecule have been employed to produce varying patterns of susceptibility among species. For example, if a $-CH_3$ group is substituted for one hydrogen atom on the $-CH_2$ group, the result is silvex, 2-(2,4,5-trichlorophenoxy) propionic acid. This is fully as damaging to the oaks as the simpler compounds but significantly less damaging to cotton, a highly susceptible crop sometimes grown close to treated areas. It is possible that this compound and similarly modified ones may damage only those plants having enzymes capable of turning them into 2,4,5-T.

The pure acids so far discussed are insoluble powders which are too immobile to be of much use against plants. A variety of physical properties affecting mobility may be produced by substitutions for the single acidic hydrogen atom (enclosed in a box in the structural formula) of the acid. The remaining part of the molecule—the portion with the 6-carbon ring structure—has the phytotoxic effect, and it tends to remain an unbroken unit during its movement through the plant (Crafts, 1960).

Whatever is substituted for the hydrogen atom becomes what can be called the **carrier** portion of the molecule of the compound ultimately applied. This carrier segment determines the polarity, solubility, and volatility of the compound. It means little to state that 2,4,5-T was applied in a particular situation and not much more to indicate an unspecified ester of 2,4,5-T. Much of the confusion over the use of these compounds comes from lack of appreciation of the importance of the carrier effect.

When 2,4-D was first developed it was most logical to try the simplest approach first. This involved the sodium salt of the acid which did not prove to be sufficiently water-soluble. Attention soon turned to certain amines that are readily soluble in water. An important water-soluble form of 2,4-D and 2,4,5-T is the triethylamine, the carrier radical of which is

$$-NH(C_2H_5)_3$$

Use of water-soluble amines on woody plants was temporarily abandoned in the early 1950's because greater interest lay in compounds that would be more effective when sprayed on intact surfaces. However, they have come back into use because they are so readily translocated in the xylem if injected through the bark. Other amines that are soluble in oil are also being developed because they appear to be capable of good penetration through intact surfaces and rapid translocation thereafter; they also have a pattern of selectivity among species that is sometimes useful. In fact, even the pure acids can be rendered emulsifiable and can thus be employed when only highly susceptible species are to be killed.

The efforts to find compounds that would adhere to and penetrate the foliage more dependably led to the development of the esters, which are essentially non-polar. These compounds are ones in which various alcohols are substituted for the hydrogen atom on the acid radical. Their most significant characteristic is their solubility in the non-polar waxes or lipids, cutin and suberin, which cover leaves and bark.

It was soon found that improvements could be made upon the simple esters that were first used. Esters with less than 6 carbon atoms in the carrier segment of the molecule (Sutton, 1958) proved so volatile that their vapors could drift and damage susceptible agricultural crops. The highly volatile esters, which are now little used, are typified by the propyl ester, the carrier segment of which is

$$-CH_2CH_2CH_3$$

A molecule of this kind, very low in polarity owing to deficiency of —OH or =O groups, has insufficient ability to emulsify in water. Such small molecules also penetrate foliage so rapidly that they may kill the internal leaf tissues before they have allowed passage of enough herbicide to kill more permanent tissues elsewhere in the plant (Crafts, 1960).

Some of these difficulties have been reduced or overcome by the development of esters with longer carbon chains, higher molecular weight, and slightly greater polarity. The higher molecule weight reduces volatility and the risk of premature killing of the leaf parenchyma. The two esters that are now in most common use have these characteristics. They are the butoxy ethanol ester, the carrier segment of the molecule of which is

$$-CH_2CH_2-O-CH_2CH_2CH_2CH_3$$

and the propylene glycol butyl ether ester:

$$-CH_2CH(OH)CH_2O-CH_2CH_2CH_2CH_3$$

The increase in polarity enhances the capacity of these esters, while dissolved in oil, to become dispersed as emulsions in water. However, the mixtures are rendered much more readily emulsifiable if they are mixed with emulsifying agents and dissolved in oils with specific gravity close to that of water (Frear, 1955). The purpose is not only to substitute water for some of the oil in the sprays but also to create sprays that are less likely to drift. The emulsifying agents have molecules that are polar at one end, so that they have an affinity for water, and non-polar at the other, so that they also have an affinity for the esters, oils, and other non-polar materials. Other additives incorporated in the commercial stock solutions include materials that reduce surface tension of the liquids involved and thus cause them to spread over surfaces rather than to perch on them as spherical droplets.

The conventional emulsions are those in which oil solutions of the appropriate esters are dispersed as very fine and reasonably stable droplets within a matrix of water. This not only enables the substitution of cheap water for expensive oil in spray mixtures but also application in sprays of coarser droplets which are less subject to drifting. The "invert" emulsions (Kirch, Beatty, and Otten, 1958) that can be produced with the right combination of oils and additives are even less subject to drifting. In these, droplets of water are dispersed in a matrix of oil and the sprays have somewhat the same visibility, sticking qualities, consistency, and other properties as heavy cream. Theoretically invert emulsions are advantageous because the outer portions of the droplets, which first come in contact with the waxy treated surfaces, are composed of oil solutions of the active ingredients while the water, which is mainly a bulking agent, is inside the droplets.

The modifying additives that have been described are usually incorporated in the stock solutions by the manufacturers. The additives are often trade secrets so it is well to follow manufacturers' instructions carefully in adding diluents in the field and in providing whatever degree of agitation is necessary while the mixtures are being applied.

The cost of the various chlorophenoxy-acid compounds tends to vary with the size and complexity of the molecules. The amines are often cheaper than the esters and 2,4-D is cheaper than 2,4,5-T. It is partly for this reason that 2,4-D and 2,4,5-T are sometimes mixed.

While the cholorphenoxy acids are still the mainstays among auxin herbicides, others are continually being developed (Crafts, 1961). The substituted ureas are one of the newer groups. They are typified by fenuron, which is 3-phenyl-1,1-dimethylurea or

These compounds are water-soluble and have attracted attention chiefly because they can be applied to the soil and absorbed from it by the roots. They pass then to the xylem and move to the foliage in the transpiration stream but do not move in the phloem (Crafts, 1961). Their lethal effect is an interruption of the part of the photosynthetic process that evolves oxygen. This effect is so specific that the mammalian toxicity of the substituted ureas is much lower than that of the chlorophenoxy acids, which is itself negligible.

Monuron and diuron are quite similar to fenuron but less soluble and, therefore, probably less promising for silvicultural use. Substituted ureas remain effective in the soil until leached away. They do not appear to be especially selective and this reduces their usefulness for release work where it is desirable to kill some plants and not others. The substituted ureas are quite expensive in the quantities used if they are applied to the soil.

The use of amino triazole (3-amino-1,2,4-triazole)

$$
\begin{array}{ccc}
\text{H---N} & \text{-----} & \text{N} \\
| & & \| \\
\text{H---C} & & \text{C---NH}_2 \\
& \diagdown \diagup & \\
& \text{N} &
\end{array}
$$

is likewise not fully tested. It is also a water-soluble compound that deranges photosynthesis. It is rapidly and easily translocated throughout the plant after absorption by foliage or roots; moving in both xylem and phloem (Zimmerman, 1960).

Another group of water-soluble compounds that can be injected or used as foliage sprays are the polychlorinated benzoic acids of which 2,3,6-trichlorobenzoic acid

$$
\begin{array}{c}
\text{Cl} \\
\bigcirc \text{COOH} \\
\text{Cl} \quad \text{Cl}
\end{array}
$$

is the most active. It kills a number of species, including hickory, maple and some evergreens, that are resistant to other herbicides, although it is apparently exuded by the roots of treated trees and may move through the soil to kill adjacent untreated ones (Walker and Wiant, 1960). It is also available as an oil-soluble amine for use in basal spraying.

The most important grass killer is dalapon, or 2,2-dichloropropionic acid,

$$
\begin{array}{ccc}
\text{H} & \text{Cl} & \\
| & | & \\
\text{H---C} & \text{---C---} & \text{COOH} \\
| & | & \\
\text{H} & \text{Cl} & \\
\text{\scriptsize 1} & \text{\scriptsize 2} &
\end{array}
$$

This can be mixed or chemically combined with other herbicides to kill both grass and brush (Brown and Carvell, 1961). It is applied in water solution as a foliage spray.

The development of synthetic auxins is proceeding so rapidly that information on the subject goes out of date quickly. The manufacturers and the published proceedings of regional weed-control conferences are often the best sources of recent information on herbicides and their application. The literature of plant physiology provides the best guide to future uses of these remarkable compounds. Their application in silviculture lags behind that in agriculture.

Actually the use of such compounds chiefly for killing the weeds of the forest is rather unsophisticated in view of the more constructive purposes to which they might be applied (Leopold, 1955; Snow, 1959). It is within the realm of possibility that such materials might be used for controlling such important phenomena as seed production, dormancy, wood properties, root elongation, resistance to low temperature, height growth, and branch size. The traditional approach of silviculture has been essentially through manipulation of the external environment. To this has recently been added the approach of genetic manipulation. Both of these lines of attack tend to be slow, cumbersome, complicated, and imprecise. Although tampering with the physiology of trees will doubtless prove to have many pitfalls, it is probable that the effects will at least be promptly apparent.

Sodium arsenite. Some of the older herbicidal compounds have not been entirely displaced by the auxins. The most important of these is one of the oldest, sodium arsenite. Chemically it is a complex and variable mixture composed chiefly of Na_3AsO_3 and $NaAsO_2$ (Frear, 1955). This mixture of compounds is readily soluble in water if the solution is strongly alkaline, so it is actually applied in solutions containing sodium hydroxide. The arsenic is the poisonous element, acting as a simple heavy-metal poison which kills by shattering or "denaturing" and coagulating the long, convoluted protein chains in the cell nuclei of living tissues.

Sodium arsenite has always been viewed with skepticism because it has a far greater mammalian toxicity than any other herbicide used in silviculture. However, it can be purchased in forms, such as thick syrups applied from plastic squeeze-bottles (House, 1960), which are not subject to splashing and spillage, thus being moderately safe to handle. Nevertheless, it must be treated with extreme caution. The sodium hydroxide in the solutions, although far less lethal than the arsenic, can be very troublesome if it gets on the skin, especially in cuts, or into the eyes.

There is some risk that animals will be attracted by the salty taste of the solutions. While this has not really proven to be a serious danger (Webb, Rosasco, and Simkins, 1956), the nervous attitude of the public about poisons should be dealt with cautiously.

Sodium arsenite solutions are usually injected or applied to cut surfaces of wood so that they move directly into the sap stream. If applied in this manner, small amounts are quickly and dependably effective in killing the stems and crowns of trees without perplexing differences between species.

Ammate. A much safer water-soluble herbicide is Ammate or ammonium sulfamate, $NH_4SO_3NH_2$. It is so hygroscopic that the dry crystals will go into solution by absorbing moisture from the air after being deposited on cut surfaces. Upward translocation in the xylem is rapid and downward movement through the phloem, although slow, does occur (Carvell, 1955). Ammate is harmless to animals and gradually combines with water to form a residue of ammonium sulfate, which is a good nitrogen fertilizer. The toxic effect is a precipitation of the proteins of the protoplasm (Sampson and Schultz, 1956).

Although Ammate has usually been applied by introduction into the xylem it can also be used as a foliage spray. It is about equally effective against all species, although there are strange exceptions. It is quite unselective among species when used as a foliage spray. It also has the drawback of corroding metals in spray equipment very badly. However, the chief disadvantage is that, with any kind of application, it is effective only at high concentrations. It is, therefore, much more expensive to use than most other herbicides.

Ammate has found some favor in the control of vegetation adjacent to supplies of drinking water because it has no effect on the taste of the water. However, except for rather unusual circumstances, it is now largely superceded by herbicides that are fully as effective, almost as safe, and distinctly cheaper.

Expression of herbicidal concentrations. It is customary, whenever possible, to express the concentrations of herbicides applied as liquids in terms of the weight of active ingredient per unit of total volume. The amount applied in foliage spraying can also be conveniently expressed as weight of active ingredient per acre. When herbicides are applied to the stems of trees, it would theoretically be most logical to express the rate of application in terms of the weight of active ingredient applied per unit of circumference because the main objective is to kill a certain amount of cambium. However, this expression is more conveniently rendered into volume of material of specified concentration applied per inch of diameter. Each inch of diameter represents 3.14 inches of circumference; both diameter and volume are more easily gauged in the field than circumference and weight.

Amounts of chlorophenoxy-acid herbicides are expressed in terms of the weight of **acid equivalent,** which is the weight that the active ingredient would have if it were stripped of the carrier groups of the molecule and converted to the pure acid. The concentrations are conventionally expressed in terms of pounds of acid equivalent per gallon or hundred gallons of spray mixture. The expression "4 pounds a.h.g." means 4 pounds of acid equivalent per 100 gallons of spray mixture. The amounts applied in broadcast foliage spraying are commonly expressed in number of pounds of acid equivalent per acre.

The commercial stock solutions usually, but not invariably, contain 4 pounds of acid equivalent per gallon. The labels specify the amount and name of the herbicide (including the carrier segment of the molecule) but rarely the names of the additives and diluents which are stated only as amounts of "inert ingredients." One is not likely to gain worthwhile experience from the use of these compounds unless complete records are kept of the precise name of the herbicide, brand name, amount and kind of diluents added, and the time and weather conditions of application. It pays to heed the fine print on the can, as well as any other advice supplied by the manufacturer, at least until a substantial amount of independent experience has been gained.

The percentage of mortality induced by herbicidal application, like similar biological responses, does not increase in direct proportion to the amount applied. Instead it increases as the logarithm of the dosage such that the concentration of a spray may often have to be tripled to increase the mortality from 90 to 99.9 per cent. Unless the cost of the material is trivial in comparison with that of applying it, this means that it is economically wise to be content with mortality of 90 or 95 per cent and adjust the concentrations accordingly.

Knowledge of the mathematical dosage-response relationship can be used for determination of economical spray concentrations and rates of application (Carvell, 1956). Graphs of such biological relationships appear as sigmoid curves when plotted on arithmetic axes. These curves usually can be converted into straight lines if dosage is transformed to logarithms and mortality percentage to probits (Finney, 1952). If the application rates necessary to produce a variety of mortality percentages between roughly 20 and 90 per cent are then determined, the amount necessary to give a 95 per cent kill, or any other desired level less than 100 per cent, can be reliably established simply by extrapolation of the transformed straight-line relationship.

Before one becomes too concerned about determining the most economical dosage levels, it is first necessary to determine whether a particular herbicide or method of application will work. At this stage it is often premature to be greatly concerned about the prospective cost. Once a technique has been made to work, ways can usually be found to achieve substantial reductions in cost of application.

With the exception of sodium arsenite, none of the compounds mentioned in this chapter are known to present any major hazards to animals and man. None of the newer herbicides can be marketed until thorough tests have been made of their pattern of toxicity. However, the matter of protecting the general public and the consumer receives more attention than safeguarding the user. Consequently the precautions specified by the manufacturers should be rigorously observed. Beyond this, the need for direct contact with the chemicals should be reduced as much as possible, although this is usually to guard against unknown rather than known dangers. If they are used with informed respect there is no need for imaginary fears.

CLEANING

A **cleaning** is a cutting made in a stand, not past the sapling stage, in order to free the best trees from undesirable individuals of the same age which overtop them or are likely to do so. The need for cleaning arises in situations where the methods of cutting and site preparation employed during the regeneration period have created conditions favorable to undesirable as well as desirable plants.

The principal purpose is to regulate the composition of mixed stands to the advantage of the better species. Oftentimes the composition of the stand is radically changed as a result of these cuttings (Fig. 5-1). Cleanings are rarely essential in pure stands of reproduction, although they are sometimes carried out in order to remove trees of poorer form than those that are overtopped.

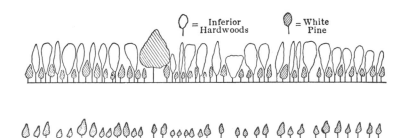

Fig. 5-1. A stand of eastern white pine before (*above*) and after (*below*) the removal of overtopping, inferior hardwoods in a cleaning. All trees overtopping the desirable ones must, in this instance, be removed because the young hardwoods grow so much faster than the pines. This treatment would best be accomplished by complete foliage spraying, although the large pine would have to be cut because it might otherwise develop into a limby wolf tree.

Weeding is a term that denotes the removal of all plants competing with the crop species, regardless of whether their crowns are above, beside, or below those of the desirable trees (Champion and Griffith, 1948).

Types of Vegetation Removed

If the cleaning is done by foliage spraying, the kind and amount of vegetation removed depends primarily on what is vulnerable to the chemicals used. If an appropriately selective chemical can be applied, most of the overtopping vegetation will be killed. The scattering of resistant individuals that is likely to remain may or may not have to be attacked by other means.

If the competing trees are treated individually as in anything involving cutting or basal spraying, it is important to remove no more than is necessary to accomplish the purpose. Otherwise the operations become unjustifiably expensive. There is no need to eliminate any plant that is not going to suppress, endanger, or hamper the growth of a distinctly desirable member of the new stand.

The plants removed include, in addition to overtopping trees of undesirable species, sprouts and other poorly formed specimens of desirable species that are competing with potential crop trees, climbing vines, overtopping shrubs, and sometimes rank herbaceous growth.

It is usually best not to succumb to the temptation to leave isolated individuals or small clumps of good trees that are substantially taller than those that are being released. It must be borne in mind that such isolated trees often develop into wide-spreading, branchy specimens which will suppress an inordinate number of better trees. Even if they develop satisfactory boles they are likely to become ready for harvest before the shorter surrounding trees and cause considerable damage when felled. If they are good specimens of species not really wanted on the site they may become a troublesome source of seed. On the other hand, if such trees come in large, densely stocked clumps it may be just as well to leave them to develop.

Cleanings are sometimes directed toward the complete elimination of the alternate hosts or favored food plants of dangerous pests of the main crop, such as species of *Ribes* in proximity to five-needled pines (Offord, Quick, and Moss, 1958). Diseased or insect-infested trees should also be removed if such action will really reduce the risk that desirable trees will be attacked.

Timing of Cleanings

Cleanings are the earliest kinds of operations that can be applied to new stands after establishment. They are best made as soon as the individuals that need help are threatened with injury. In tropical climates, cleanings may be needed during the first year; it may indeed be necessary to make several cleanings in a single year to control the luxuriant vegetation. In temperate climates, cleanings usually become desirable before the fifteenth year, although it is better to make them earlier. Cleaning by foliage spraying can be done at almost any age and the desirable vegetation is seldom benefited by delay.

If the cleaning involves treatment of individual plants, it is usually best to wait until the relationships between the competitors become reasonably predictable but not until the crowns of the crop trees have seriously declined in vigor. The best time often comes when the undesirable vegetation is slightly more than waist high. Very small stems are not very convenient to treat, but the difficulty and expense of treatment increases very rapidly after they attain 2 inches D.B.H. It is true that the cost, per acre, of treating overtopping trees from the ground decreases again when they attain sizes around 10 inches D.B.H., but by that time any overtopped trees that might once have been released in cleaning are likely to have disappeared.

The seedlings of most species make the best growth if they are released during the first growing season. There is often a perceptible difference in height between seedlings released at one and two months of age. Good reasons for intentional delay of cleaning are exceptional. Small seedlings of many species are protected by light shade but usually only during the first few weeks of life. Under unusual circumstances, shade may protect seedlings and saplings from frost or insects like the white pine weevil that attack exposed trees. Seedlings rooted in organic soils sometimes need protection from the sun. Occasionally a nurse crop may choke out harmful ground-cover plants like some of the ericaceous shrubs or, if of leguminous species or *Alnus,* may improve the supply of soil nitrogen on impoverished sites. It is sometimes advantageous to delay cleaning until the desirable trees have become sufficiently tall to remain free of overtopping sprouts or new seedlings long enough to commence rapid growth themselves.

It is occasionally argued that overtopped seedlings are likely to be killed or to suffer injury if they are released. Proven instances of such damage are scarce. If it is known to be likely, the release should be gradual rather than deliberately delayed. If trees have degenerated into poor physiological condition because they are overtopped, their health and ability to respond to release can only deteriorate from continued overtopping. Seedlings and small saplings ordinarily respond to release with surprising increases in the vigor of growth; it is the larger trees that have been overtopped for long periods that are most likely to succumb or increase in growth slowly.

Any benefits from the protection of overtopping vegetation are soon outweighed by serious reductions of growth. Continued suppression may cause the death of the better trees (Fig. 5-2). These effects are the result of either direct competition between the trees or the mechanical effect of the overtopping tree in whipping buds from the top branches and stems of the desirable trees (Spaeth, 1922).

The cleaning of a young stand need not be completed in a single operation. One cleaning sufficiently drastic to ensure permanent release may give the favored trees so much space that they develop poor form. In such cases it may be best to carry out several cleanings removing only enough at each time to allow the favored trees to recover a normal rate of growth and remain free until the next operation. However, the expense increases as the competing vegetation grows larger and each cleaning involves an extra cost of supervision and overhead.

A distinction should be drawn between repeated cleanings necessitated by sprouting of the treated vegetation and those needed because of the growth of competing trees left in previous cleanings. Before the introduction of chemicals capable of preventing sprouting, there was often no other alternative than to carry out numerous cleanings at short intervals (Lutz and Cline, 1947). This dismal situation often

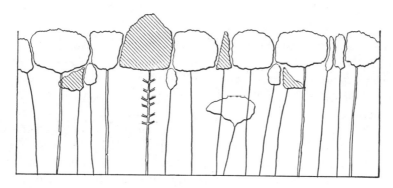

Fig. 5-2. The stand that would have developed after 40 years if that shown in Fig. 5-1 had not been cleaned. The only one of the pines (indicated by crosshatching) now in a dominant position is that which had a start over the hardwoods. The hardwoods have completed their early period of rapid growth and will produce a stand of far lower value and quality than the pure stand of pine which might have been created by cleaning.

discouraged attempts to control competition from sprouting species. Use of herbicides does not necessarily obviate the need for repetition of treatments but it does substantially reduce sprouting in many situations where it would be vigorous and inevitable after cleaning by cutting.

Extent of Release in Cleaning

With broadcast foliage spraying the extent to which the desirable vegetation is released is controlled only by the selectivity of the chemical applied. Some control is possible with hand-directed foliage spraying but it is usually neither possible nor necessary that it be very precise.

Where it is necessary or desirable to resort to comparatively expensive treatment of individual stems there is rarely any justification for bringing through more trees than can reach merchantable size. Ordinarily it is sufficient to release no more than 150 trees per acre. This number will usually be ample to provide trees for both the final crop and one thinning, as well as a margin for losses. The release of single trees at an average interval of 17 feet will give 150 trees per acre. The less desirable trees left in the process serve to fill out the stand and prevent the favored trees from developing into wolf trees.

In determining how much to remove around each favored tree, one must know the relative rates at which both desirable and undesirable trees grow in width of crown and height (Wahlenberg and Doolittle, 1950; Wenger, 1955). The most serious competition will come from the undesirable trees adjacent to the individual to be released. Trees that are farther away do not offer an immediate threat to the dominance of the favored tree but may eventually overtop it by the lateral expansion of their crowns. Therefore, it is usually best to think in terms of removing the trees that project upward into an inverted cone around the top of the tree to be favored (Fig. 5-3).

The magnitude of the angle represented by the cone should vary directly with the difference in rate of height growth between the released tree and its competitors as well as the extent to which the tree has been oppressed. If it is likely to grow at a rate equal to or faster than that of the weed trees, the imaginary cone can be narrow, such that only the trees currently overtopping it are removed. More often the disparity in growth which caused the unfavorable condition to develop is likely to continue; in such cases the angle must be fairly broad.

Trees that have been overtopped for a long time require more drastic release than those which are still vigorous. Jemison and Hepting

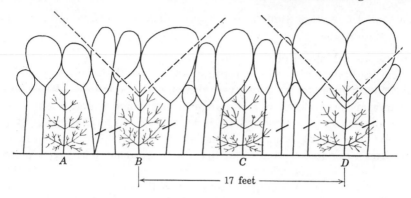

Fig. 5-3. An example of how the intensity of cleaning might be regulated in freeing a stand of conifers from overtopping hardwoods. The objective chosen here is to remove all hardwoods that project upward into an inverted cone with an apex which is 2 feet below the tops of the crop trees and has an angle of 90°. The trees to be removed are marked by dashes. Trees *B* and *D*, which are spaced to give a stand of about 150 conifers per acre, are the only trees deliberately released. Trees *A* and *C* are ignored. In a heavier cleaning the angle would be increased or the apex of the imaginary cone lowered. The extent of release would depend on the relative growth rates of the different species present and the amount of time that would be allowed to elapse before another cleaning.

(1949) found that small, overtopped hard pines in the southern Appalachians are generally more vigorous and require less release than taller and older trees in the same situation. They recommended that pines 2 to 5 feet tall be released by removing all hardwoods within 3 feet, but pines 6 feet or more in height should be freed of all hardwoods that stand within 6 feet and are more than two-thirds of the height of the pine. No useful purpose is served by releasing small-crowned trees that have been oppressed for a long time, especially if they are of distinctly intolerant species (Downs, 1946).

The kind of partial reduction of competing vegetation that has been described does not necessarily cause the released trees to grow at rates anywhere near as great as they might if all competition were eliminated. This is especially true if the site is dry or infertile and root competition remains serious. The main object of such treatment is merely to assist the released trees in surmounting their competitors by subsequent growth. The only justifications for not releasing more thoroughly are the higher cost, any beneficial effect of moderate competition on the ultimate form of the crop trees, and the possibility that the otherwise unwanted vegetation will resist the invasion of even more undesirable plants.

Cutting as a Method of Cleaning

The traditional method of cleaning was to cut the competing vegetation with hand tools. However, the chemical methods are usually cheaper and more likely to reduce sprouting, which is a problem with most of the species removed in cleaning. Therefore, cutting as a method of cleaning is mostly relegated to situations where there is too little work to be done to justify the equipment and preparation necessary to use herbicides.

Sprouting is, of course, rarely a problem if the species to be eliminated are conifers. It is possible that cleanings in mixed conifer stands of the kind described by Boyd (1959) in the western white pine type might be done fully as cheaply by cutting as by basal spraying. The selectivity of herbicides has not been improved to the point where foliage spraying could dependably be used to favor one conifer over another.

If cleaning is to be done by cutting of sprouting species, the only general way to reduce sprouting is to make the cuttings during the summer, especially during the period of most rapid growth. At that time the root reserves are at their lowest ebb and sprouting, while not prevented, is less vigorous than at other times (Buell, 1940; Stoeckeler, 1947).

The best tools for cleaning by hand cutting are those that can be held in one hand and have straight or concave cutting edges. The axe is a better tool for stems larger than 2 inches. Power-driven, brush-cutting saws are suitable for cleaning but many devices for applying herbicides are cheaper.

Foliage Spraying

In foliage spraying, herbicides are applied to the leaves with the expectation that they will be translocated from the leaves to the living tissues of more permanent parts of the plant. The branch surfaces almost invariably get sprayed in the process and it is probable that they too can serve as points of entry at least for oil-soluble herbicides. Because of their ability to penetrate into leaves, the oil-soluble chlorophenoxy acids are most commonly used for foliage spraying of woody plants. Therefore, unless otherwise indicated, the following discussion of foliage spraying will apply to the use of these materials.

The phloem is the pathway for translocation both upward and

downward from the leaves for carbohydrates and many herbicides. In fact, 2,4-D and other phenoxy acids will not move out of the leaves unless they are actively manufacturing and exporting sugars (Leonard and Crafts, 1956). When the leaves are expanding, spraying is quite ineffective because the sugars are then moving into the leaves. It is not clear whether the translocation of other herbicides from the leaves is also dependent on the movement of the sugars, but it is usually presumed that they are.

Even though the leaves are often killed by the herbicides this is actually an unwanted side-effect of treatment. The longer that killing of internal photosynthetic tissues can be postponed the greater will be the amount of herbicide that they allow to pass into the phloem (Crafts, 1960). Excessively rapid killing of the leaves is best avoided by using ester molecules of appropriate size and refraining from excessive dosages or the use of toxic oils as diluents.

Herbicides, whether oil- or water-soluble, enter the leaves most readily when they are turgid. Under such conditions the minute capillaries through the epidermis provide the most perfect water-filled passages to the interior of the leaf (Crafts, 1960).

The lethal effect of foliage spraying diminishes with increasing distance downward from the foliage. It is much more likely to kill the branch cambium than that of the main stems and more likely to kill the stems than the roots. As the herbicides move downward through the phloem they diminish in concentration because limited amounts are turned aside, often with some of the sugars, and deposited in the storage parenchyma of the rays or in the cambium and new tissues produced by it. Some is transferred from phloem to xylem and carried back upward (Radwan, Stocking, and Currier, 1960). Some may be immobilized by becoming attached to other structures and there is an additional effect of dilution as the materials move down the tapering stems.

Actively dividing meristematic tissues are much more vulnerable to the auxin herbicides (and probably the less subtle ones) than other living tissues. This is one of the reasons why the living conductive elements of the phloem can conduct herbicides without being killed even though the same concentrations turn aside and kill the adjacent cambium. *The killing of roots by chlorophenoxy acids does not take place when the root meristems are dormant and not actively dividing* even though an otherwise sufficient quantity of herbicides reaches the roots (Leonard and Crafts, 1956). The herbicide is instead deposited with the sugars in the relatively invulnerable and far less vital storage parenchyma of the roots; it may ultimately move out again when the meristems become active, causing delayed killing of the roots. It is very important to note that roots sometimes cease growth during normal periods of dryness in mid-summer or other dry periods even though photosynthesis may continue.

As a consequence of all the reasons stated, foliage spraying works best when the weather and soil conditions are most favorable for plant growth. Turgid leaves absorb the herbicide most rapidly; rapid photosynthesis stimulates movement out of the leaf and down the phloem; cambial tissues of stem and root are most vulnerable to herbicides when actively dividing. However, all of these considerations determine only the total amount of *initial* injury to the tissues of the plant. Trees growing on good sites can withstand more damage than those on poor sites. Ray (1959) observed in Arkansas that the same treatment that killed 80 per cent of the trees where the site index was 40, killed only 52 per cent at site index 90. It is possible that the most effective foliage spraying is that done at times of favorable growing conditions that are followed by drought. Treatment at times of unfavorable growing conditions is often unsuccessful.

Effective use of foliage spraying in releasing operations requires a high degree of selectivity because the desirable trees are likely to be sprayed with the undesirable. **Differential wetting** is usually the most important source of selectivity in herbicides. Broad-leaved species like hardwoods will usually retain more spray than narrow-leaved ones like conifers and grasses. It is for this reason as much as any other that foliage spraying is so useful for the common objective of releasing conifers from hardwood overstories. Any physical properties of the spray materials or the surfaces of the leaves that alter the amount of herbicide retained on the leaves also alter the pattern of selectivity among species.

Morphological selectivity results from differences between species in the location of vital meristems and the amount of root tissue relative to that of leaf surface. The high resistance of grasses results partly from the fact that their meristems are thoroughly ensheathed. However, woody plants probably do not differ much with respect to this kind of selectivity.

Biochemical selectivity depends on variations between species in the nature and activity of enzymatic systems. If a species is capable of inactivating an herbicidal auxin it will be resistant. White ash, which is not easy to kill by any method of applying chlorophenoxy acids, may well be such a species.   On the other hand, selectivity can be enhanced by using herbicidal molecules that can be broken down into active form only by the enzymes of a few species.   Silvex or 2-(2,4,5-trichlorophenoxy) propionic acid is presumably toxic to some oaks, and not to most other species, because these oaks can convert this herbicide to 2,4,5-T and the resistant ones cannot.   Certain phenoxybutyric acid compounds may have equally useful patterns of selectivity.   The detection of useful biochemical selectivity has so far depended entirely upon trial and error so developments along this line are as slow as they are promising.

Phenological selectivity is possible if there are times when desirable species are significantly less susceptible to damage than the undesirable.   Plants or parts of plants which are growing actively are much more susceptible to damage than those that are comparatively dormant.   The release of northern conifers from hardwoods by foliage spraying is, for example, safest late in the summer because the shoots of the conifers have then often formed buds, "hardened," and ceased growth (but not photosynthesis) while those of the hardwoods have not.   In putting this kind of selectivity to use, one should be guided as much by observation of the activity of the vegetation as by that of the calendar.

Finally there is some possibility of **selective placement** of the herbicides even with foliage spraying, although the ultimate expression of this kind of selectivity is reached with treatments of individual stems by other methods.   If spraying is done from the ground it can be directed at least to a limited extent.   If done from the air there is the possibility of using the undesirable overstory to protect the desirable understory that is to be released.

In foliage spraying distinction is made between high-volume sprays which are applied from the ground and low-volume sprays applied from air or ground.   In high-volume application low concentrations of herbicide are sprayed as rather coarse droplets in emulsions with amounts of water in the order of 30 to 130 gallons per acre.   In low-volume spraying only 5 to 10 gallons of spray are applied per acre but the concentrations are correspondingly greater.

A typical high-volume application would be one in which 2 pounds acid equivalent of an emulsifiable ester were applied on an acre in 30 to 50 gallons of water (Grano and Clark, 1958).   Foliage spraying with water-soluble herbicides like amino triazole or Ammate requires high-volume application.   This technique of foliage spraying is now usually reserved for situations where it is not feasible to spray from the air or to use mist-blowers; these are encountered when there is excessive danger from drifting, or when equipment for low-volume application is lacking.

In aerial spraying the size of the droplets is crucial only to the extent that it determines the amount of drift. Provided that the amount of herbicide adhering to the leaves remains the same, droplet size does not greatly affect the results obtained. It is possible to get uniform coverage even with rather coarse droplets and low volumes of spray because the material falls from above and is widely dispersed at the point of origin. When the materials have to be projected upward it is difficult to get similarly good coverage without using large volumes of spray or dispersing it into fine mists.

A typical aerial spraying designed to kill hardwoods and release pine in southwestern Louisiana (Peevy and Burns, 1959) involved the application on each acre of 2 pounds acid equivalent of the butoxy ethanol ester of 2,4,5-T in an emulsion consisting of 1.5 gallons of a diesel-oil solution of herbicide in 3.5 gallons of water.

Aerial spraying (Arend, 1959; Burns, 1961) can be done only when the wind is less than 5 miles per hour and preferably in the nearly calm conditions that sometimes prevail early in the morning. Excessive drifting not only endangers vegetation outside the area to be treated but also reduces the amount reaching the designated area. The hazard of drift can be reduced by spraying rather coarse droplets or using invert emulsions. Ordinarily the contractors who specialize in this kind of work can be depended upon to place the spray materials accurately enough for forestry purposes if the areas to be treated are well marked.

The boundaries of the areas to be sprayed must be marked so that they will be visible from low-flying aircraft. The pilot should be provided with a marked map but this alone is quite insufficient. Whenever possible the edges of treated areas should follow prominent features like ridges and roads, but there must be other markers as well. Flags or other markers placed on trees must project well above them to be visible. Smoke often drifts too much. Balloons are good and can be moved in protective cartons as necessary during the operation, although they may be damaged by oil in the sprays. The edges of the area can also be sharply designated several weeks in advance by applying some water-soluble herbicide like sodium arsenite in frills to the edge trees so that their dead foliage will be plainly visible. Unless the readily visible invert emulsions are used it is helpful to have men with flags or other markers moving along to designate the ends of treated swaths.

Aerial spraying is rarely feasible unless 500 acres or more can be laid out for treatment in a single project. The individual units treated must also be large; 10 acres is the absolute minimum and even this is very costly; ordinarily the economical minimum is approximately 50 acres. If foliage spraying is deemed desirable on smaller areas it is best to do it from the ground.

Costs are lower with fixed-wing aircraft than helicopters, but slow-flying helicopters can drive the spray down to the ground and may thus be cheaper in terms of the cost of producing a given effect, especially if there is understory vegetation to kill.

Low-volume spraying can be done from the ground as well as from the air and is a useful technique for small areas (MacConnell and Bond, 1961). The mist-blowers necessary for such application may be mounted on trucks or tractors. Light, power-driven, back-pack units are available and useful. The spray that they deliver is in droplets so fine that it resembles dense smoke or fog. The effectiveness of mist-blowers is limited to brush up to 20 to 40 feet tall. The amounts and concentrations of spray used are about the same as for aerial spraying.

With any kind of foliage spraying of saplings and seedlings done from the ground it is often desirable to wet the stems as well as the foliage. Stem-foliage spraying increases the chance of killing to the extent that the herbicide directly penetrates the bark. Aerial spraying with helicopters often has the same effect. Repetition of aerial spraying may be necessary to give resistant species double dosage or to deal with an undesirable understory remaining after the elimination of an overstory. If such an overstory consists of a moderate number of trees more than 4 inches D.B.H. it may be eliminated in advance by girdling or some other stem treatment thus exposing any remaining undesirable understory to aerial spraying.

The cost of a single aerial spraying, including materials, contracting of aircraft, and advance preparations, usually ranges from $5 to $12 per acre, although it would be higher for small areas. The cost of doing the work with back-pack mist-blowers from the ground is $6 to $15 per acre, depending on the height of the brush (House, 1960). The difference in the amount of area that can be covered in a season is, of course, tremendous.

Sometimes a single application is sufficient, but two at intervals of a year or more are often necessary. In a number of instances, a single foliage spraying followed by basal spraying or some other individual treatment of undesirable residuals is more efficient than repetition of foliage spraying.

Foliage spraying, including that done from the air, sometimes works well enough to prevent sprouting although the results are variable in this respect. If sprouting occurs when small seedlings are being released, some sort of additional treatment may be necessary.

The final result of any treatment employed to kill trees, whether it involves simple cutting, girdling, or the use of herbicides, cannot be assessed completely until 2 to 3 years afterwards. The killing of the tops may be evident in a few days or weeks, but sprouting may be initiated up to several years after treatment.

One of the disadvantages of foliage spraying is that it must be pre cisely timed and can be done only in a limited portion of the year. The details of timing are quite variable and depend on the phenology and seasonal pattern of susceptibility of the desirable and undesirable species (Arend, 1959). Treatment should be avoided, if possible, at any time when the shoots of the desirable trees are succulent. It is ideal if times can be found late in the growing season when the desirable species have formed buds and "hardened" while the undesirable species are more active and soil moisture conditions remain favorable.

The undesirable species ordinarily should be attacked after shoot elongation and the formation of new leaves is completed (Dahms, 1955). If herbicides are applied too early they may not move out of the expanding leaves and they will also tend to be moved too much toward the new shoots rather than downward. Late in the season the leaves become less permeable and the meristematic tissues may not be active enough to be killed. The low permeability of the leaves can be partially overcome by low-volume applications of esters in oil, which dissolves some of the cutin, but the plants are not necessarily physiologically susceptible.

If foliage spraying, or any other tree-killing technique, is applied early in the growing season after new shoots and leaves have formed, the risk of sprouting will be at its lowest. At this time of the season the carbohydrate reserves in roots and stems have been depleted to their lowest level for the formation of new tissues and less remains for the formation of sprouts than at other times (Woods, 1955). Fortunately this is also likely to be the time when carbohydrates and herbicides move downward most rapidly through the phloem. The direct killing by the herbicides is much more important than the low status of the root reserves in reduction of sprouting.

In the South most foliage spraying is done in June and early July; the results are poorer late in the summer, possibly because of the dwindling of soil moisture supplies. The repeated flushes of top growth in the southern pines make it difficult to find many times when they are not susceptible to injury, although the damage is usually slight and temporary. In parts of the West where the summers are dry, foliage spraying is also usually done in June and early July. There are exceptions to such generalizations and more will be found as experience increases. The troublesome vine maple of the Pacific Northwest is, for example, best attacked by aerial spraying immediately before and during the period in which the buds are opening rather than by true foliage spraying.

The great advantage of foliage spraying in general and aerial spraying in particular is that these techniques enable the conduct of cleanings on a grand scale. One hour of aerial spraying can accomplish as much as one man-year spent in brush-cutting done by a kind of labor that becomes ever more scarce and expensive.

Basal Spraying

This is a more selective, expensive, and reliable method of using herbicides to kill saplings and smaller woody plants in cleaning. Basal spraying involves application of herbicides, almost always esters of 2,4,5-T or 2,4-D in oil solution, to all the bark around the base of the stem. The main purposes are to girdle the plant and kill the dormant buds at the point of application. It is possible for enough of the herbicide to be translocated to the top through the xylem to produce a direct killing of the top. This effect helps, but it is not essential because effective girdling would usually cause the top to die ultimately.

Girdling takes place if sufficient spray is applied and if the bark is thin and permeable enough to allow the herbicide to penetrate to the cambium all around the tree. There is no advantage in having the ring of dead cambium and phloem wider than several inches in the vertical. It is commonly recommended that the spray be applied until the lowest foot of stem is thoroughly covered; this is only to ensure that enough runs down to kill the dormant buds beneath the bark as far down the root collar as possible. Sometimes application all around the root collar at the ground line is sufficient.

If the species is one that does sprout from the base of the stem and if sprouting is to be prevented, it is most important that the herbicide be applied to the bark that covers the dormant buds that produce the sprouts (Worley, Bramble, and Byrnes, 1957). The reason for this is that the downward movement of herbicides through the phloem below the point of application is not rapid or dependable. However, it does occur, at least in some species, during that period just after the completion of leaf expansion when downward translocation of sugars is most rapid (Bergeson and Lorenz, 1957; Shiue, Hossfeld, and Rees, 1958). The amounts that can move downward are easily depleted by "leakage" into the xylem where they are swept upward by the transpiration stream, which is far less sluggish than the downward movement in the phloem. In fact, polar compounds like monuron and amino triazole move into the xylem so easily that there is little opportunity for them to be moved downward; 2,4-D and 2,4,5-T, however, are more likely to be taken into the living conductive tissues of the phloem (Yamaguchi and Crafts, 1959). It is not clear why downward translocation should be so much poorer when herbicides are applied to the bark rather than to the foliage.

The result is that in basal spraying reliance is usually placed on having the herbicide run down the outside of the bark rather than having it move down internally. Killing of the roots is viewed as depending more on their being starved to death by girdling than on direct killing by the herbicide. The girdling accomplished by basal spraying is physiologically as perfect as any because the phloem and cambium are killed with a minimum of interruption of the xylem. Downward movement of carbohydrates is blocked yet their upward movement from the roots can proceed as long as the top remains alive.

Basal spraying is not recommended for trees any larger than 4 inches D.B.H. and works best on those that are 2 inches or less. Trees with smooth or thin bark are killed much more readily than those with thick, rough, or corky bark. The concentration of the sprays must be increased with increasing tree diameter, because bark thickness is so closely correlated with tree diameter. The effectiveness of basal spraying declines rapidly as soon as the basal bark becomes roughened. Where large undesirable trees are intermingled with smaller ones that can be dealt with by basal spraying, the larger ones can usually be killed by frilling them and applying the same spray used in basal treatment of the adjacent smaller ones.

One of the advantages of basal spraying is that it can usually be

done successfully at any time of the year. For this reason it is sometimes called "dormant" spraying, although this term is best reserved
to denote the timing rather than the technique of treatment. The
vigor of sprouting is least if treatment is done soon after the formation of leaves and new shoots has depleted carbohydrate reserves. In
practice, any real necessity for confining basal spraying to this time
of year seems limited to species like aspen, American beech, sassafras,
and black locust which sprout from the roots rather than the root
collar (Arend, 1953; Bramble et al., 1957). It will often be necessary
to attack the root suckers of these species with foliage spraying regardless of how the parent trees were killed. Most species can, however, be basally sprayed at any time except when the stems are wet or
when snow or some similar obstruction prevents effective application.
Worley, Bramble, and Byrnes (1957) actually found that the sprouting of bear oak, a troublesome shrubby species, was least after thorough basal spraying in midwinter, although the question of whether
the spray ran down to the ground was more important than the timing.

Basal spraying, when done during the dormant season, is the technique of using herbicides that is least likely to cause the appearance
of dead, brown foliage on the treated vegetation. This makes it a
good method to use where large amounts of dead foliage might cause
serious conflagrations of either fire or public indignation.

The selective kind of basal spraying done in silvicultural work is
usually carried out with low-pressure knapsack pumps. The nozzles
should be of such design that entire stems can be encircled with spray
quickly but without undue wastage of material. Oil solutions of
esters rather than oil-water emulsions are normally used. In general,
2,4,5-T, pure or in mixture with 2,4-D, is more effective on woody
plants than 2,4-D alone.

Spray concentrations ranging from 12 to 16 pounds acid equivalent
per hundred gallons are ordinarily recommended, although those as
low as 6 pounds are effective against small stems of susceptible species. It is better to use moderate concentrations in sufficient volume
to ensure that the solution gets all the way to the ground than to
apply high concentrations in sparing amounts.

The cost of basal spraying is highly variable and depends on the
size and number of stems to be killed as well as the concentration of
spray necessary to do the job. The order of magnitude of the cost
of the partial cleaning necessary to release an adequate number of
crop trees is $10 to $20 per acre; it may take 2 to 5 man-hours and 3
to 8 gallons of solution per acre. It is not much cheaper than clean-

ing by cutting but requires much less time and is far less likely to have to be repeated because of sprouting.

Basal spraying is costly enough that it is chiefly useful as a supplement to other techniques. It is very important as a means of eliminating small, undesirable woody plants that have not been killed in foliage spraying. It can also be used as a substitute for foliage spraying during the dormant season or in situations where the more expensive equipment necessary for foliage spraying is not available or economically justifiable. It is the best means of highly selective cleaning of stands of small saplings in situations where foliage spraying cannot be made sufficiently selective to accomplish the purpose.

Stump Spraying

Stumps of sprouting species can be kept from doing so by treating their surfaces in much the same manner as in basal spraying. If herbicides are placed on the cut surfaces within a few minutes of the cutting they may be drawn down into the outer xylem resulting in a kind of downward movement not obtained with basal spraying (Hay, 1956). However, if hours or days elapse before application, the cut surfaces become blocked by molds, air bubbles, and other obstructions so that there is no advantage in treating anything but the sides of the stumps. High concentrations of oil-soluble esters of phenoxy acids may be necessary if the bark is thick. Often it is just as well to wait and apply a much cheaper stem-foliage spray to the succulent sprouts soon after they appear. Stump spraying is not inherently superior to basal spraying. There is little reason to do it unless there is some real purpose in cutting the trees and preventing sprouting by immediate treatment.

Application of Herbicides to the Soil

Some water-soluble herbicides, notably fenuron, can be applied directly to the soil in pellets or other dry forms. The solutions produced by rain are taken up by the roots. These compounds have been used mostly to keep areas like firebreaks free of vegetation; they must be applied in large quantities for such purposes. Much of the active ingredient is lost not only to leaching but also to the tremendous absorptive capacity of the soil colloids. Furthermore, the root systems of trees are arranged in such irregular patterns that those of desirable trees are almost as likely to underlie the point of application as those of the undesirable. Sometimes these chemicals persist in the soil for periods that would be unduly long for silvicultural purposes. It is possible that they might be useful in light, random application for the precommercial thinning of excessively dense stands of natural re-production.

Application of Cleanings

In the era when cleaning could be done only by cutting, it was generally regarded as a practice that could be justified only where economic circumstances favored highly intensive silviculture. Herbicides have now made it feasible to contemplate cleaning by aerial spraying of natural stands in which no further silvicultural intervention could be justified until the time of the final harvest cuttings. Selective basal spraying still goes only with rather intensive practice.

The use of herbicides has made it possible to control composition on many of those inherently good sites where so many different species can grow that the better ones are mostly overwhelmed by the poor. In fact, there is a tendency to regard rather dry and inherently mediocre sites as "best" simply because certain conifers or other desirable species can be maintained on them without excessive hindrance by the undesirable. Now the sites that are "best" in this sense may be found higher on the scale of true biological site capacity.

It is, for example, now feasible to displace big-leaf maple and other poor hardwoods from moist, well-drained sites in the Coast Douglas-fir region, or, where desirable, red alder from the excellent sites of the Sitka spruce-western hemlock type. The best examples of this situation are found on millions of acres in the East that are now occupied by poor hardwoods but would yield much greater value if converted to conifers. This is not to imply that growing hardwoods is a futile business or that the very best sites can be put under complete control. The production of good hardwoods is rewarding on good sites; the markets for softwoods are not without limit and those for hardwood lumber of decent quality are excellent. In fact, selective cleaning in hardwood stands can be very worthwhile (Wahlenberg, 1950).

Improvements in composition could conceivably be made at almost any time in the life of a stand. However, if they are going to be made, it is usually best to make them as cleanings when the stands are young. When a stand is young it is much more plastic than it is after it has passed the sapling stage. If undesirable species dominate, the desirable, overtopped species will not only deteriorate in number, form, and vitality but will also become more irregularly distributed so that the opportunity to create a uniform, closed stand from them will diminish. Even though the lapse of time between the cleaning and the reaping of the benefits is long, the margin between the compounded cost of treatment and the value added by it is likely to be wider with early cleaning than with delayed improvement cutting. Artificial plantations represent a sufficiently high investment that cleaning should be carried out in them if necessary.

In general it is easier to conduct the kind of cleaning which accelerates plant succession than that which retards or reverses it. It is, for example, more difficult to free eastern white pine from the competition of red maple and various oaks than from pioneers like gray birch (Cline, 1929). On the other hand, there are cases where it is less necessary to release relatively tolerant species from the competition of pioneers than from undesirable tolerant species. Longwood (1951) found that little is gained by releasing sugar maple from the competition of the short-lived pin cherry. Oftentimes the main advantage to be gained from cleanings in hardwood stands is the elimination of large, vigorous clumps of sprouts.

The necessity for cleanings can be reduced by a concerted effort to conduct cuttings throughout the rotation so that undesirable vegetation does not become established. The simplest means of eliminating an undesirable species is to get rid of the seed source; cleaning represents the most difficult way.

It is not likely that operations aimed at the establishment of natural or artificial regeneration will often be conducted so perfectly that the composition of new stands will be controlled entirely by site preparation or skillful treatment during the previous rotation. Consequently it may be anticipated that there will always be plenty of situations in which cleaning is desirable. In many instances they will represent the most remunerative investments that can be made in silvicultural treatment. In other instances, alternative investments may seem more attractive but it should be noted that many of them require the kind of good stands that often can be made to exist only by cleaning.

LIBERATION CUTTING

Liberation cuttings are those made to free a young stand, not past the sapling stage, from the competition of older, overtopping individuals. They are made during the same period in the life of the main crop as cleanings, differing only with respect to the age of the trees removed. The trees that are cut or killed in place are either individuals that were left standing when the previous stand was harvested

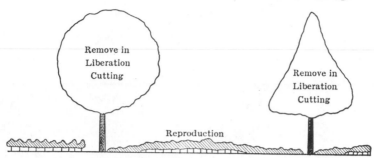

Fig. 5-4. A young stand of reproduction at the stage where a liberation cutting could be carried out to best advantage. The overtopping wolf trees have not yet caused any deformities or serious reductions of growth in the new crop.

or those which, for various other reasons, were present long before the natural or artificial establishment of the young trees (Fig. 5-4). Liberation cuttings are in many ways similar to the removal cuttings of the seed-tree and shelterwood methods of reproduction in which overstory trees are removed after the new crop is established. The trees involved, however, are usually undesirable specimens rather than ones left intentionally for seed or additional growth.

Trees that have developed with abundant growing space tend to become short and stocky wolf trees with little clear length and wide, spreading crowns. The shade and protection of these large trees soon cease to be beneficial and may cause the younger trees to die or be deformed (Fig. 5-5). Even if the young, overtopped trees do not succumb, they will grow slowly, be damaged by abrasion, or bend toward the light. Therefore, liberation cuttings should be made as early in the life of the young stand as possible. They can be conducted with most benefit and least damage to the new crop when the young trees are only a foot or two in height.

Methods of Liberation Cutting

The undesirable trees can be eliminated by cutting, girdling, or chemical treatment. Cutting is, of course, the most advantageous method if the trees can be utilized at a profit or at a loss no greater than the cost of killing them. After an operation of this kind it may be necessary to cut away any parts of tops that interfere with the young growth. In considering treatments that do not involve utilization of the trees, it is important to decide whether markets are likely to improve sufficiently to make them merchantable in the near

Fig. 5-5. The old post oak (*left of center*) was present when this 50-year-old stand of loblolly pine became established on an old field in North Carolina. The pine tree in the foreground and the trees in the right background have grown without interference from the wolf tree. An improvement cutting would be highly desirable in this stand, although it should have been conducted as a liberation cutting at least 40 years ago. (*Photograph by U. S. Forest Service.*)

future. Destruction of sound trees of saw-timber size and quality, merely because they are of currently unwanted species, has often proven to be a wasteful practice.

Cutting. The felling of large, undesirable trees without utilizing them is the most expensive form of liberation cutting. It may also result in far more damage to the young crop than would occur if the trees were killed and allowed to disintegrate in place. Therefore, such trees are felled, limbed, and left on the ground only where absolutely essential. This course of action is desirable where dead snags constitute a serious fire hazard. Cutting is also necessary along roads and in other situations where falling limbs and snags are likely to be a dangerous nuisance.

Girdling. The traditional method of killing trees without felling them is girdling. This involves severing the bark, cambium, and, sometimes, the sapwood in a ring extending entirely around the trunk of the tree. The materials already stored in the roots can still be carried up to the crown in the xylem, unless the sapwood has been interrupted. The roots die when the carbohydrates in them have been exhausted, a process that may take several years. If the sapwood is severed, the death of the crown is rendered more certain by the reduced flow of water, stored substances, and inorganic nutrients to it; the vigor of sprouting is, however, increased because the roots are not exhausted. The best time of year for girdling comes during the period of most active growth when the carbohydrate reserves of the roots are at their lowest ebb (Greth, 1957). Satisfactory results can usually be obtained without confining girdling to this period.

The basic requirement of girdling is complete severance of the cambial tissue. If any vertical strips of cambium are left intact, bridges of callus tissue are almost certain to form across the girdled ring. These bridges render the entire treatment ineffectual unless they are subsequently invaded by fungi. Even if the cambium is completely severed with a series of single incisions, callus tissue will often bridge over the gap. Therefore, it is desirable to cut out chips of bark and sapwood so that the cambium is actually removed in a visible ring rather than merely severed in a single cut. Trees that have deeply infolded bark around frost cracks or other deformities are almost impossible to kill by girdling. Mortality may also be reduced if the girdled trees are supported by substances transferred to them through root grafts by uninjured trees of the same species. For these reasons, girdling should not be expected to result in complete or immediate killing of all trees that are so treated.

The following methods of girdling are generally recognized (Westveld, 1942):

Notching, in which a notched ring is cut around the tree through the bark and ½ to 2 inches into the wood.

Single-hacking or **frilling,** in which a single line of overlapping axe cuts is made through the bark and into the wood.

Double-hacking, in which a line of chips is removed by striking two downward blows, the second being made about 3 inches above the other so that the chip may be thrown or pried out entirely.

Peeling or **stripping,** in which the bark is stripped off in a band at least 8 inches wide.

Axes are ordinarily used for girdling by the first three methods. Notches can also be cut rapidly with saws consisting of special chipper teeth mounted on flexible chains, resembling those of power saws, and drawn around the tree with two hands (Holekamp, 1958). A tree-girdling machine in common use is the "Little Beaver"; it has a cutting head that routs out a U-shaped groove and is powered through a flexible drive-shaft by a back-pack motor (Harrington, 1955). Peeling can be done with ordinary bark-spuds or axes.

The time required for girdling tends to vary directly with the circumference of the treated trees and, to a very limited extent, inversely with the number of trees per acre. Yocom (1952) determined that the man-hours necessary to girdle hardwoods in Alabama could be determined adequately by multiplying the sum of the diameters of the trees by 0.005 and the variable effect of number of trees per acre could be neglected.

Frill girdling, done by single-hacking, is the quickest and cheapest method but rarely gives satisfactory results. The cuts often heal over and it is difficult to detect unsevered strips because no chips are removed. However, when the frilling is used as a means of introducing herbicides it becomes one of the best alternatives to ordinary girdling. Double-hacking is by far the best method of girdling with the axe. It is easier than notching because all the strokes are downward; any slivers of inner bark that have been left are readily visible.

Peeling can be done cheaply and effectively but only during the spring and early summer when the bark strips easily. At other times it is not feasible because of the difficulty of removing the inner bark. It is the best technique from the standpoint of interrupting the phloem without halting the upward flow of stored substances from the roots.

Notching, on the other hand, usually causes the quickest kill of the top because it is the method that most completely severs the pathways of upward movement of water and nutrients. When done with machinery it is a cheap method. However, it is the most expensive, laborious, and dangerous way of girdling with the axe because there are so many upward strokes. Axe-notching is best reserved as a means of severing ingrown folds of bark that cannot be reached with double-hacking or peeling. The notches cut with machines are so narrow that it is sometimes necessary to cut two parallel grooves to kill a ring wide enough to prevent the formation of callus bridges.

Girdling is generally far less effective than herbicidal treatment in preventing sprouting. Therefore, if it is necessary to reduce sprouting of the treated trees, girdling is a suitable treatment only for species that do not sprout or for trees that are too large to sprout profusely. This generally means that girdling is as effective as applying herbicides for trees larger than 14 inches D.B.H. (Walker, 1956). However, some species sprout at larger sizes and it is often impossible to sever ingrown bark on large trees. Girdling can be quite effective on trees in the range from 4 to 10 inches, but chemical treatment is usually more satisfactory. Below 4 inches D.B.H., cutting is usually quicker than girdling and herbicidal treatments are superior to either. In other words, girdling is certainly satisfactory in many instances but is as good as chemical treatment only on large trees.

Herbicidal treatment. Liberation cutting can be accomplished by aerial spraying. The work can also be done by stump and basal spraying but the amounts of herbicide necessary on thick-barked trees usually make these techniques very costly. Trees larger than sapling size are killed most expeditiously by methods in which the herbicides are applied to incisions in the bark. This mode of application could also be used in cleaning, precommercial thinning, and improvement cutting but is most important as a means of liberation cutting.

Direct application of herbicides through incisions to the xylem, cambium, and living phloem overcomes most of the difficulties of getting the spray material to penetrate the bark. The water-soluble herbicides have their most important application in this mode of treatment, especially because they are physically available for movement in the xylem immediately after application. They also move farther laterally in the xylem than the oil-soluble herbicides (Carvell, 1959). Oil-soluble materials still have some advantages in this mode of application. They can penetrate and kill the uninterrupted bands of inner bark that are apt to be left in frill-girdling. They are less likely to be washed away by rain or exuding sap; this is an advantage if treatment is done at times when the herbicide cannot kill or move immediately and must persist at the point of application for extended periods.

Regardless of whether the incisions encircle the stem or are spaced at intervals around it, the most important objective is to girdle the tree by a combination of mechanical and chemical injury. The death of the top is rendered even more certain if enough herbicide is carried up through the xylem to kill all the cambium or foliage above the point of application. Downward movement to the roots is possible but very erratic; the cause of the small amount that does take place is still obscure (Kozlowski, 1961). Effects that directly or indirectly reduce sprouting are more common but equally difficult to explain.

Incisions that completely encircle the stem are the most effective in achieving girdling and killing of the tops. However, they require more labor than spaced incisions and have sometimes proven less effective in preventing sprouting (Campbell and Peevy, 1950). Nevertheless this method is more dependable and probably should be used if there is any doubt about the effectiveness of application in spaced cuts. Not only is the mechanical cutting reinforced by the herbicide at all points but any upward movement also takes place throughout the entire sheath of active xylem that underlies the cambium and not just in vertical bands.

Suitable continuous incisions can be made either as single-hacked frill girdles or as notches cut with the special girdling devices previously described. The application of herbicides to peeled girdles is usually done only for chemical debarking of pulpwood (Wilcox et al., 1956). There is little purpose in preparing the incisions by making notched or double-hacked girdles with an axe because the single-hacked girdles are usually sufficient.

The herbicides most commonly used on frilled or comparable girdles are esters of 2,4-D or 2,4,5-T in oil solution, ordinarily at concentrations of 8–16 pounds acid equivalent per hundred gallons, and applied with low-pressure knapsack sprayers, pump oil-cans and similar devices (Dahms and James, 1955; Walker, 1956). The use of water-soluble herbicides in frill girdles has not been tested as extensively but is basically superior (Crafts, 1961). Translocation in the xylem is much more rapid; the compounds are sometimes cheaper and they can be applied in concentrated form which reduces the volume of liquid that must be transported in the woods.

Application of herbicides in spaced incisions does not provide direct assurance that girdling will take place. However, if the ends of the incisions are no more than 2 to 3 inches apart there is sometimes enough dependable lateral movement of water-soluble herbicides to cause girdling (Carvell, 1959). It is also possible in many species for the conductive pathways along which herbicide moves upward from separate incisions to merge together higher in the stem (Greenidge, 1958; Rudinsky and Vité, 1959) and thus girdle the tree far above the ground. The crown itself is killed if enough herbicide is applied. The most tantalizing attributes of this technique are that it requires less labor than complete frilling and sometimes gives much better control of sprouting. It is a method which so far gives consistently good results only for certain species in particular localities and seasons (Leonard, 1956, 1957; Gibbs, 1959).

There are several methods of making the incisions and applying the herbicide to them. The best are those in which cutting and injection are done as nearly simultaneously as possible. This is especially advantageous if the tree is actively transpiring and the material injected is water-soluble. When the water columns in the xylem are broken by the cutting they pull away both upward and downward from the point of fracture and if the herbicidal solution is immediately available it will quickly move in both directions. However, this kind of force is spent in a matter of seconds and is always diminished by the air bubbles that are also drawn into the conductive elements. The same effect can probably be achieved with complete frilling; it has merely happened that simultaneous cutting and introduction of herbicide have usually been associated with treatment of spaced incisions.

Nearly simultaneous cutting and injection can be achieved with special tree-injectors or the combination of a hand-axe in one hand with a pump oil-can, plastic squeeze-bottle, or similar applicator in the other. The deeper the cutting into the xylem the better are the results (Leonard, 1957). Tree-injectors (Fig. 5-6) can be likened to huge hypo-

Fig. 5-6. A tree-injector being used to liberate a young stand of pitch pine in New Jersey. The valve of this injector is opened by pressing it against the stem of the tree above the incision; the chemical then squirts onto the blade and into the incision. (*Photograph by Cranco Co.*)

dermic needles, except that they have cutting edges rather than hollow needles and the herbicide runs down the surface of the blade rather than through a closed passage extending to the cutting edge. The long handle serves as the container for the herbicide which is released by a valve actuated by hand or other means. The tree-injectors are somewhat cumbersome but enable application of herbicide close to the root-collar, thus giving good control of sprouting.

Spaced incisions can also be made by chopping out notches or drilling holes in the bole or the upper surfaces of exposed roots. However, such large incisions are ordinarily necessary only for herbicides like Ammate that must be used in large quantities to be effective. Adequate amounts of most herbicides can be held in the incisions made by a single downward stroke of the blade of a hatchet, axe, or tree-injector. Transportation of herbicides should also be held to a minimum by using materials in the highest concentration and lowest weight or volume possible.

Even if herbicides cannot be applied within seconds after cutting into the xylem, they should be applied as soon as possible after preparation of the cut surface. The severed conductive elements soon become blocked by fungi, air bubbles, debris, wound gums, or resins. Application should proceed concurrently with the preparation of the incisions; delays of more than an hour or two greatly reduce the chance of successful killing. No mode of application is very successful when the cut xylem is exuding large quantities of sap.

Not all species are equally susceptible to killing by injection of herbicides and the differences do not follow any perfectly consistent pattern. As far as hardwoods are concerned, useful distinction can sometimes be drawn between the ring- and diffuse-porous. In ring-porous hardwoods, like oaks and hickories, most of the movement of sap takes place in the large vessels of the outermost annual ring; in the diffuse-porous, it occurs in a much thicker sheath of xylem composed of much smaller vessels (Wiant and Walker, 1961). This means that all of the conductive system of ring-porous hardwoods is readily accessible to this method of applying herbicides. In diffuse-porous species like the maples, beech, and sweet-gum, much deeper cutting would be required to ensure access to an equal amount of conductive capacity. In any event, the diffuse-porous species are sometimes rather difficult to kill and are the most likely to require such refinements as complete frilling, high dosages of introduced herbicides, and treatment in seasons of high vulnerability. Conifers are not especially difficult to kill with injected herbicides.

Actually, the downward pattern of movement of injected herbicides applied to cut surfaces is not understood any better than that associated with basal spraying. Some must move through the living phloem; otherwise it would be difficult to explain why dilute oil solutions of 2,4,5-T esters applied in frill girdles were found to control sprouting of post oak and sweet-gum in Texas better than concentrated solutions (Stephenson and Gibbs, 1959). Presumably the dilute solution would be less likely to block its own movement by rapid killing of the phloem.

"Back-flash" or root-graft transfer is one rather unpredictable and poorly explained phenomenon that sometimes occurs after the introduction of herbicides into the xylem. This takes place when the materials move downward so well that they are transferred through root grafts to the roots and xylem of adjacent untreated trees of the same species (Cook and Welch, 1957; Bormann and Graham, 1959; Stout, 1961). This is most unwelcome if the untreated trees that are killed were ones being released. On the other hand, it is a response that helps if the objective is to kill species that form root suckers (Rushmore, 1956). Probably the phenomenon is at least partly due to the fact that once the foliage of a treated tree is dead that of a neighboring healthy tree may exert a strong transpirational pull through the grafts and the herbicide merely moves in response to the forces placed on it. The same thing may explain why treated trees sometimes produce healthy basal sprouts that die a year or so later exhibiting symptoms of herbicidal injury (Leonard, 1957). It may also be of some significance that rapid upward movement through the xylem takes place only when transpiration is active and water movement within the tree may be quite erratic at night or in the dormant season.

With appropriate modification of dosages and techniques, herbicides can be successfully applied to cut surfaces at almost any time of year. However, as with other methods of application, the most complete killing and greatest reduction of sprouting is normally achieved with treatments made during the growing season. Ordinarily treatments made during the dormant season must be more thorough. Leonard (1957), for example, found that interior live oak in the Central Valley of California could be killed with application in spaced incisions during the winter rainy season but that herbicidal treatment of complete frills was necessary during the dry summers when the trees were more dormant. Until application in spaced incisions has been tested for the species, season, and site in question, it is probably best to rely on complete frill girdles.

A wide variety of herbicides are used in cut-surface applications. Oil solutions (or infrequently oil-water emulsions) of esters of 2,4,5-T, pure or in mixture with 2,4-D, are now in most common use. The water-soluble amines of 2,4,5-T and other chlorophenoxy acids are usually applied as undiluted concentrates at rates of ⅓ to 2 milliliters per inch of diameter.

Sodium arsenite solutions have been successfully used for decades in both complete frills and spaced incisions (Rushmore, 1958). They do not control sprouting very well but are as dependable as anything in killing the tops. Other water-soluble compounds, like the substituted ureas and amino triazole, are probably useful in this mode of application. Walker and Wiant (1960) obtained good results on hickories with 2,3,6-trichlorobenzoic acid applied in frill girdles.

The costs of these methods of applying herbicides vary widely but most often fall in the range between $4 and $10 per acre. The basic variable is the amount of bole circumference or diameter to be treated. Labor is usually a more important component of cost than materials and most of the labor is expended in preparing the incisions.

Application of Liberation Cuttings

Liberation cuttings are logically indicated in any situation where a young crop of potentially good trees is overtopped by older, distinctly less desirable trees. If the overtopped trees will respond vigorously and speedily form a new stand of good quality and stocking, there is no quicker or cheaper silvicultural means of making a silk purse out of a sow's ear.

It is usually cheaper to conduct liberation cuttings in old stands where the trees to be killed are relatively few, large in size, and less likely to sprout than in younger stands with more numerous, smaller trees. This is not a reason for delaying treatment of the younger stands in order to reduce the cost because the overtopped, desirable trees will grow little in the interim even if they are not suppressed to the point of death. However, other things being equal, it is ordinarily best to assign highest priority to liberation cuttings in which large trees are eliminated because the costs per acre tend to be lower and the opportunity to make profitable utilization of some of the trees greater. The time between liberation cutting and the reaping of the benefits is sometimes shortest if the trees that are released are rather large, although it is entirely possible for young and vigorous seedlings that have been released to overtake much older saplings that have been overtopped so long that their crowns have become very small.

In the application of liberation cuttings, care should be taken not to create situations in which high shade is replaced by more detrimental crown competition in the stratum occupied by the desirable seedlings or saplings. This can happen if the trees that are eliminated sprout profusely or if fast-growing weed species become established after treatment.

Liberation cuttings may be applied to advantage in almost any forest type, especially in situations where poor management or market restrictions have left stands with an overburden of cull trees. They have been widely employed in releasing conifers from hardwoods in eastern forests, especially in freeing pines from oaks (Fig. 5-7). Mann (1951) cited a typical liberation cutting designed to free loblolly and shortleaf pine seedlings from an overstory of hardwood saplings and trees. This cutting required 2 man-hours per acre and increased growth sufficiently that all compounded costs of treatment could be

Fig. 5-7. Stand of loblolly and shortleaf pine, Kisatchie National Forest, Louisiana, approximately 5 years after liberation by the girdling of an overstory of oak. Most of the young pines were small seedlings at the time of release. (*Photograph by U. S. Forest Service.*)

paid off in a thinning conducted 10 years later. The results of a long-term trial in New Hampshire have shown that the production of red spruce can be increased from 2 cords per acre in 40 years to 23 cords merely by killing overstory hardwoods (Westveld, 1937).

The desirability of liberation cutting is not confined to situations where the objective is to free conifers from hardwood competition. Liberation cuttings represent one of the most expeditious methods of restoring culled forests of old-growth hardwoods to productivity (MacLean, 1949; Jensen and Wilson, 1951). They also offer a means of improving the composition of mixed coniferous stands in the West and elsewhere.

Release Cutting and Public Psychology

The application of herbicides to the control of stand composition has finally placed the forester in the position where the conversion of forest types can be accomplished quickly and on a large scale.

The public speedily develops a fond attachment for whatever vegetation it becomes accustomed to seeing. Unless forcefully informed, most people are not aware that degenerate forests were ever any handsomer or more useful than those in view, nor is it apparent to them that seemingly destructive measures will achieve improvements. A large and influential body of public opinion views application of chemicals to the forest with consternation. Neither the ownership of the land nor the virtue of the treatments makes much difference.

Uninformed criticism is usually the most vitriolic; it can be quieted provided that the truth is heard amid the uproar. The most valid criticisms ordinarily revolve around the important effect of vegetation on wildlife; generalizations about this relationship are dangerous and all should give way to precise knowledge about particular situations. However, it can be said that the kind of forest that is best from the standpoint of timber production is not likely to be optimum for wildlife management, although it may well be superior to the unmanaged forest. Furthermore, the kind of vegetation that favors one kind of animal will inevitably depress the population of some other, so choices must be made in the management of both wildlife and timber.

To proceed from the general to the particular, it may be noted that release cutting often has a temporarily beneficial effect for many kinds of animals. Like many other silvicultural operations it brings the crown canopy back closer to the ground where it provides improved cover for some animals and browse or herbiage for others. On occasion the vigorous sprouting otherwise viewed as a sign of frustration may be deliberately sought as a source of browse. However, such sprouts do not produce oak mast and similar foods for wildlife. The oaks are more often the object of attack in release cutting than any other group of trees, yet their acorns are very important in the nutrition of many animals (Reid and Goodrum, 1958). This is merely a single example of the kind of situation in which management for timber and that for wildlife can conflict. Such relationships must be recognized and management decisions made in the light of full knowledge of them.

REFERENCES

Arend, J. L. 1953. Scrub aspen control with basal sprays. *LSFES Tech. Note* 401.

————. 1959. Airplane application of herbicides for releasing conifers. *J. Forestry* 57:738, 740, 742, 744–745, 747–749.

————, and E. I. Roe. 1961. Releasing conifers in the Lake States with chemicals. *USDA Agr. Handbook* 185.

Bergeson, E. D., and R. W. Lorenz. 1957. Seasonal effectiveness of 2,4,5-T basal sprays for eradicating ribes in white pine blister rust control in Illinois. *J. Forestry* 55:17–19.

Bormann, F. H., and B. F. Graham, Jr. 1959. The occurrence of natural root grafting in eastern white pine, *Pinus strobus* L., and its ecological implications. *Ecology* 40:677–691.

Boyd, R. J. 1959. Cleaning to favor western white pine—its effects upon composition, growth, and potential values. *J. Forestry* 57:333–336.

Bramble, W. C., et al. 1958. Variation in development of low plant cover following chemical brush control. *Proc. Soc. Am. Foresters Meeting, 1957:* 67–71.

Brown, J. H., and K. L. Carvell. 1961. Radapon for effective control of grass around planted seedlings. *Down to Earth* 16(4)

Buell, J. H. 1940. Effect of season of cutting on sprouting of dogwood. *J. Forestry* 38:649–650.

Burns, P. Y. 1961. Use of aircraft for foliar applications of herbicides in southern forests. *In:* R. W. McDermid (Ed.), *The use of chemicals in southern forests.* Louisiana State University Press, Baton Rouge. Pp. 84–100.

Campbell, R. S., and F. A. Peevy. 1950. Chemical control of undesirable southern hardwoods. *J. Range Management* 3:118–124.

Carvell, K. L. 1955. Translocation of Ammate. *Forest Sci.* 1:41–43.

————. 1956. The use of chemicals in controlling forest stand composition in the Duke Forest. *J. Forestry* 54:525–530.

————. 1959. Comparison of Veon 245 and Esteron 245 for killing cull oaks. *Down to Earth* 15(3):14–15.

Champion, H. G., and A. L. Griffith. 1948. *Manual of general silviculture for India.* Oxford University Press, London. Revised edition. Pp. 284–321.

Cline, A. C. 1929. *Forest weeding with special reference to young natural stands in central New England.* Massachusetts Forestry Association, Boston.

Cook, D. B., and D. S. Welch. 1957. Backflash damage to residual stands inci-
dent to chemi-peeling. *J. Forestry* 55:265–267.

Crafts, A. S. 1960. Evidence for hydrolysis of esters of 2,4-D during absorption
by plants. *Weeds* 8:19–25.

———. 1961. *The chemistry and mode of action of herbicides.* Interscience, New
York.

Currier, H. B., and C. D. Dybing. 1959. Foliar penetration of herbicides—
review and present status. *Weeds* 7:195–213.

Dahms, W. G. 1955. Chemical brush control on central Oregon ponderosa pine
lands. *PNWFRES Research Note* 109.

Dahms, W. G., and G. A. James. 1955. Brush control on forest lands.
PNWFRES Research Paper 13.

Downs, A. A. 1946. Response to release of sugar maple, white oak, and yellow-
poplar. *J. Forestry* 44:22–27.

Finney, D. J. 1952. *Probit analysis.* Cambridge University Press.

Frear, D. E. H. 1955. *Chemistry of the pesticides,* 3rd ed. Van Nostrand, New
York.

Gibbs, C. B. 1959. Amines of 2,4-D hold promise for hardwood control. *Down
to Earth* 15(3):6.

Grano, C. X., and R. H. Clark. 1958. Tractor-mounted spray for controlling
small hardwoods. *Southern Lumberman* 196(2445):28.

Greenidge, K. N. H. 1958. Rates and patterns of moisture movement in trees.
In: K. V. Thimann (Ed.), *The physiology of forest trees.* Ronald Press,
New York. Pp. 19–41.

Greth, J. W. 1957. Ax girdling kills large cull hardwoods. *CSFES Sta. Note*
107.

Harrington, T. A. 1955. More power to girdling. *Forest Farmer* 14(8):12,
16–17.

Hay, J. R. 1956. Translocation of herbicides in marabú. *Weeds* 4:218–226,
349–356.

Holekamp, J. A. 1958. Brady tree girdler. *Am. Pulpwood Assoc. Equipment
Handbook, Release* 330.

House, W. P. 1960. Some comments on chemical weeding. (*Soc. Prot. N. H.
Forests*) *Forest Notes* 66:31–32; 67:23–25.

Jemison, G. M., and G. H. Hepting. 1949. Timber stand improvement in the
southern Appalachian region. *USDA Misc. Pub.* 693.

Jensen, V. S., and R. W. Wilson, Jr. 1951. Mowing of northern hardwood reproduction not profitable. *NEFES Northeastern Research Note* 3.

Kirch, J. H. 1961. Foliar applications of chemicals to weed tree species. *In:*
R. W. McDermid (Ed.), *The use of chemicals in southern forests.* Louisiana
State University Press, Baton Rouge. Pp. 73–83.

———, R. H. Beatty, and R. J. Otten. 1958. Invert emulsions—a new type of
formulation. *Hormolog* 2(1):15.

Klingman, G. C. 1961. *Weed control: as a science.* Edited by L. J. Noordhoff.
Wiley, New York.

Kozlowski, T. T. 1961. The movement of water in trees. *Forest Sci.* 7:177–192.

Kramer, P. J., and T. T. Kozlowski. 1960. *Physiology of trees.* McGraw-Hill,
New York.

Leopold, A. C. 1955. *Auxins and plant growth.* University of California Press,
Berkeley.

Leonard, O. A. 1956. Effect on blue oak (*Quercus douglasii*) of 2,4-D and 2,4,5-T concentrates applied to cuts in trunks. *J. Range Management* 9: 15–19.

———. 1957. Effect of phenoxy herbicide concentrates applied to cuts of sprouting tree species. *Weeds* 5:291–303.

Leonard, O. A., and A. S. Crafts. 1956. Translocation of herbicides. III. Uptake and distribution of radioactive 2,4-D by brush species. *Hilgardia* 26: 366–415.

Longwood, F. R. 1951. Why release young maple from pin cherry? *LSFES Tech. Note* 360.

Lutz, R. J., and A. C. Cline. 1947. Results of the first thirty years of experimentation in silviculture in the Harvard Forest, 1908–1938. I. The conversion of stands of old-field origin by various methods by cutting and subsequent cultural treatments. *Harvard Forest Bul.* 23.

MacLean, D. W. 1949. Improvement cutting in tolerant hardwoods. *Canada, Dominion Forest Service Silvicultural Research Note* 95.

MacConnell, W. P., and R. S. Bond. 1961. Application of herbicides with mist blowers: a promising method for releasing conifers. *J. Forestry* 59:427–432.

Mann, W. F., Jr. 1951. Profits from release of loblolly and shortleaf pine seedlings. *J. Forestry* 49:250–253.

Offord, H. R., C. R. Quick, and V. D. Moss. 1958. Blister rust control aided by the use of chemicals for killing ribes. *J. Forestry* 56:12–18.

Peevy, F. A., and P. Y. Burns. 1959. Effectiveness of aerial application of herbicides for hardwood control in Louisiana. *Weeds* 7:463–469.

Radwan, M. A., C. R. Stocking, and H. B. Currier. 1960. Histoautoradiographic studies of herbicidal translocation. *Weeds* 8:657–665.

Ray, H. C. 1959. Aerial chemical reduction of hardwood brush as a range improvement practice in Arkansas. *Proc. Soc. Am. Foresters Meeting, 1958:* 201–205.

Reid, V. H., and P. D. Goodrum. 1958. The effect of hardwood removal on wildlife. *Proc. Soc. Am. Foresters Meeting, 1957:*141–147.

Rudinsky, J. A., and J. P. Vité. 1959. Certain ecological and phylogenetic aspects of the pattern of water conduction in conifers. *Forest Sci.* 5:259–266.

Rudolf, P. O., and R. F. Watt. 1956. Chemical control of brush and trees in the Lake States. *LSFES Sta. Paper* 41.

Rushmore, F. M. 1956. Beech root sprouts can be damaged by sodium arsenite treatment of parent tree. *NEFES Research Note* 57.

———. 1958. Sodium arsenite in spaced ax cuts: an effective stand-improvement technique. *J. Forestry* 56:195–200.

Sampson, A. W., and A. M. Schultz. 1956. Control of brush and undesirable trees. *Unasylva* 10:19–29, 117–129, 166–182.

Shiue, C.-J., R. L. Hossfeld, and L. W. Rees. 1958. Absorption and translocation of 2,4,5-trichlorophenoxyacetic acid derivatives in quaking aspen. *Forest Sci.* 4:319–324.

Snow, A. G., Jr. 1959. Hormones and growth regulators can be useful to foresters. *NEFES Sta. Paper* 130.

Spaeth, J. N. 1922. Notes on release of white pine in the Harvard Forest, Petersham, Mass. *J. Forestry* 20:117–121.

Stephenson, G. K., and C. B. Gibbs. 1959. Selective control of cull hardwoods in east Texas. *SFES Occ. Paper* 175.

Stoeckeler, J. H. 1947. When is plantation release most effective? *J. Forestry* 45:265–271.

Stout, B. B. 1961. Season influences the amount of backflash in a red pine plantation. *J. Forestry* 59:897–898.

Sutton, R. F. 1958. Chemical herbicides and their uses in the silviculture of forests of eastern Canada. *Canada, Forestry Branch, Tech. Note* 68.

Wahlenberg, W. G. 1950. A long-term test: a quarter century of forest regrowth in a cut-over and cleaned Appalachian cove. *Southern Lumberman* 181(2272):183–187.

Wahlenberg, W. G., and W. T. Doolittle. 1950. Reclaiming Appalachian brush lands for economic forest production. *J. Forestry* 48:170–174.

Walker, L. C. 1956. Controlling undesirable hardwoods. *Ga. Forest Research Council Rept.* 3.

———. 1959. Brush control in the Georgia Piedmont. *J. Range Management* 12:16–18.

Walker, L. C., and H. V. Wiant, Jr. 1959. Silvicide screening. *Ga. Forest Research Council Prog. Rept.*

———. 1960. Effects of chlorobenzoic acids on *Carya* spp. *Ga. Agr. Research* 2(1):10, 12.

Webb, W. L., E. M. Rosasco, S. V. R. Simkins. 1956. Effect of chemical debarking on forest wildlife. *State Univ. N. Y. Coll. Forestry Bul.* 77. Pp. 35–41.

Wenger, K. F. 1955. Growth and prospective development of hardwoods and loblolly pine seedlings on clearcut areas. *SEFES Sta. Paper* 55.

Westveld, M. 1937. Increasing growth and yield of young spruce pulpwood stands by girdling hardwoods. *USDA Circ.* 431.

———. 1942. Some effects of incomplete girdling of northern hardwoods. *J. Forestry* 40:42–44.

Wiant, H. V., Jr., and L. C. Walker. 1961. Variable response of diffuse- and ring-porous species to girdling. *J. Forestry* 59:676–677.

Wilcox, H., et al. 1956. Chemical debarking of some pulpwood species. *State Univ. N. Y. Coll. Forestry Bul.* 77. Pp. 1–34.

Woodford, E. K., K. Holly, and C. C. McCready. 1958. Herbicides. *Annual Rev. Plant Physiology* 9:311–358.

Woods, F. W. 1955. Control of woody weeds: some physiological aspects. *SFES Occ. Paper* 143.

Worley, D. P., W. C. Bramble, and W. R. Byrnes. 1957. Investigations of the use of 2,4,5-T esters as a basal spray in the control of bear oak. *Weeds* 5:121–132.

Yamaguchi, S., and A. S. Crafts. 1959. Comparative studies with labeled herbicides on woody plants. *Hilgardia* 29:171–204.

Yocom, H. A. 1952. Estimating the time needed for girdling hardwoods. *J. Forestry* 50:484.

Zimmerman, M. 1960. Transport in the xylem. *Annual Rev. Plant Physiology* 11:167–190.

CHAPTER 6

The control of cutting
and its use for improvement
and salvage

IMPROVEMENT CUTTINGS

Improvement cuttings are made in stands *past the sapling stage* for the purpose of improving composition and quality by removing trees of undesirable species, form, or condition from the main canopy. The unsatisfactory conditions corrected by improvement cuttings are generally those that might have been avoided if cleanings and liberation cuttings had been made earlier in the life of the stands.

The most fundamental characteristic of improvement cuttings, aside from the fact that they are delayed until the main crop is past the sapling stage, is the elimination of poor trees in favor of the good. The stems removed include: (1) inferior species, (2) crooked, leaning, extremely limby, or otherwise badly formed trees, (3) overmature individuals, and (4) trees seriously injured by biotic or atmospheric agencies. It is important to note that these inferior trees are removed only when such action will encourage the growth of desirable subordinate trees. The objective in operations of this kind should be to find and encourage the good trees rather than merely to look for undesirable trees to eliminate. Another point to be borne in mind is that trees are not worthy of release unless they are sufficiently healthy to resume rapid growth.

Improvement cuttings may be applied in stands of almost any combination of species and age classes. Those applied to even-aged stands are nearly identical with selection thinnings; in both kinds of cutting, dominant trees are removed to favor better trees in the subordinate crown classes. If the species removed from an even-aged aggregation are essentially the same as those favored, the operation may be regarded as selection thinning and as improvement cutting if they differ. Improvement cuttings are more easily recognized when applied to stands of irregular age distribution. A cutting designed to free good trees, which have grown beyond the sapling stage, from the competition of *older,* undesirable trees is clearly an improvement cutting, provided that there is no definite effort to make way for new reproduction.

Improvement cuttings are often conducted simultaneously with true thinnings or reproduction cuttings. It should be understood that improvement cuttings are strictly preliminary operations designed only to set the stage for systematic thinnings and reproduction cuttings. They are not carried out continuously throughout a rotation and should not be regarded as permanent substitutes for the standard methods of cutting.

In spite of the difficulty of defining improvement cuttings, the situations in which they are needed are easily recognized in the field (Fig. 6-1) and their application rarely requires much skill. It is much easier to choose the trees to be removed in improvement cuttings than those to be cut in any thinnings or reproduction cuttings that are carried on concurrently.

The trees designated for elimination in improvement cuttings may be harvested in conventional fashion or merely killed and left standing. If they can be converted into useful products at a cost no greater than that of killing them, it is usually desirable to do so. The trees involved are generally of sufficient size to be suitable for cordwood or saw logs. However, they are not necessarily of good enough quality and may be either too scattered for efficient utilization or too numerous for the markets to absorb. If there is no economically sound prospect of utilizing trees, they can be killed by the techniques described in the discussion of liberation cuttings (Chapter 5).

The importance of improvement cuttings should not be gauged by the amount of space here devoted to their discussion. They represent one of the most common forms of cutting employed in silvicultural practice on this continent. Because of the lack of skillful treatment in the past, there are millions of acres of American forests that will require improvement cuttings before they can be placed under efficient management. During recent years, improvement cuttings have been

Fig. 6-1. A stand of bottomland hardwoods in Mississippi with defective trees, the remnants of an age class older than the main stand, marked to be killed or harvested for fuelwood in an improvement cutting. (*Photograph by U. S. Forest Service.*)

conducted on a large scale in eastern forests, where there are such vast areas of cutover lands. In many localities they are at present so nearly synonymous with sound silvicultural practice that the possibility that any other kind of cutting might become advisable is sometimes overlooked.

Timing and Severity of Improvement Cuttings

An improvement cutting is, almost by definition, an operation that might have been conducted to greater advantage earlier in the life of the stand. The longer undesirable dominant trees remain in a stand the greater is the harm to the better individuals and the smaller is the prospect of correcting the condition. Therefore, it is desirable that improvement cuttings be performed at the earliest opportunity and extended as rapidly as possible over all stands which require them. No useful purpose is served by restricting the volume annually removed in improvement cuttings with the idea of achieving a sustained yield of low-grade material (Minckler, 1951).

The most important factors governing the rate at which improvement cuttings can be extended over a given property are (1) the volume of low-grade material which can be absorbed by the market and (2) the funds annually available for investment in those kinds of improvement cutting which do not return an immediate profit. Improvement cuttings are often delayed until the trees to be removed have grown large enough to be harvested profitably. The wisdom of this policy depends on the value of the increment of the large, undesirable trees relative to that of the smaller and better trees that might otherwise occupy the growing space.

Improvement cuttings should generally precede harvest cuttings by at least 10 years so that full benefit can be obtained from the release of the better trees.

One improvement cutting may be sufficient to put the stand into condition for thinning or reproduction cutting. On the other hand, there may be so many undesirable dominants that their simultaneous removal would create large vacancies in the growing space. In such situations it may be necessary to carry out two or three improvement cuttings at intervals in order to obtain the desired result. If improvement cuttings are light and repeated several times, they often give better results than a single cutting sufficiently drastic to eliminate all the poor trees at once. Light cuttings are not only less likely to result in creation of vacancies in the stand but they also enable the coverage of more area for each unit of low-grade material removed or for each dollar invested. Each improvement cutting in such a series should, however, be heavy enough to provide at least temporary release to that number of desirable trees eventually required to form a reasonably well-stocked stand.

If a stand contains only a few trees that are likely to increase in value through added increment, it is better to start the establishment of a new stand by natural or artificial regeneration than to extend the rotation by means of improvement cuttings. If natural reproduction is to be sought in such instances, the best source of seed may well be the very same poorly formed, dominant trees of desirable species that would be removed in improvement cuttings; their elimination in preliminary improvement cuttings might thus delay establishment of a new stand.

It is conceivable that the tendency to discriminate against fast-growing wolf trees in improvement cuttings might ultimately favor a progeny of inherently slow growth in height. There do not actually seem to be any grounds for believing that ordinary improvement cutting involves either the intensity or repetition of selections necessary to effect significant changes in the genetic constitution of natural populations. However, clarification of the situation waits upon improved knowledge of the pattern of hereditary variation within species; it is probable that some species resist change more than others.

In true improvement cuttings the basic objective is to release pre-existing trees rather than to make way for reproduction. In practice it will often be found expedient to create some gaps larger than can be filled by the expansion of the crowns of the remaining trees. Where this is done the action, whatever it be called, should be viewed as reproduction cutting and conducted in such manner as to ensure that the vacancies will be promptly restocked with desirable regeneration.

Application in Even-aged Stands

An improvement cutting applied in an even-aged stand is fundamentally a cleaning delayed until after the desirable trees have passed the sapling stage. The delay is usually the result of neglect, although it may aso be dictated by a desire to wait until the unwanted trees can be removed at a profit. Regardless of the reason for the delay, an improvement cutting is unlikely to result in the development of a stand as good as that which might have been produced if cleanings had been conducted earlier.

The application of improvement cuttings to even-aged stands is usually a matter of dealing with mixtures of desirable and undesirable species. In fact, most previously untreated stands containing more than one species could be improved by such cuttings. Stands of this kind may originate after fires, clearcutting, windstorms, or other disturbances sufficiently drastic to eliminate the pre-existing stand. Plantations that have been neglected for a long time often reach the stage where improvement cuttings must be carried out to free them of undesirable volunteer species.

In the eastern forests, valuable conifers have a discouraging tendency to grow more slowly in youth than the less valuable hardwoods. Stands consisting entirely of mixed hardwoods may also become dominated by trees of poor form or undesirable species. In both cases, hardwoods originating from stump sprouts are the worst offenders, although pioneer species like gray birch and aspen are less serious only by virtue of the fact that they are relatively short-lived. Improvement cuttings are less frequently needed in even-aged mixtures of conifers mainly because the various species usually do not differ greatly in value.

Application in Irregular Stands

Improvement cuttings are most widely applied in poor stands that are so irregular in the distribution of age and size classes that immediate application of any standard method of thinning or reproduction cutting is out of the question. Operations of this kind are essentially delayed liberation cuttings. They may be conducted in pure or mixed stands for the purpose of improving composition from the standpoint of both quality and species.

Improvement cuttings are almost always needed in building up depleted forests that have a long history of neglect or mismanagement. Ordinarily the undesirable trees are remnants of previous stands and are consequently older and larger than the more desirable trees (Fig. 6-1). The better trees are usually those that originated after the cuttings or other disturbances that led to the development of unsatisfactory conditions. Good, subordinate trees must be present in adequate numbers and be capable of response to release if rehabilitation by improvement cutting is to be a success.

The practice of "high-grading" forests by removing only the biggest and best stems almost invariably leads to the development of irregular stands that are partially or entirely dominated by undesirable trees. The purpose of improvement cuttings in these stands is to remove the overburden of defective material in order to set the stage for productive management. An irregular, defective stand can also be created by fire and other damaging agencies, if they do not cause sufficient injury to destroy the entire stand. Irregular stands in need of improvement cuttings may develop on vacant areas, such as abandoned fields, burned-over lands, or old clearcut areas, if the initial stocking is very sparse. In such cases the first trees to appear often develop into wolf trees but eventually provide a source of seed for the establishment of dense clumps of good trees in the spaces that were not stocked originally.

Improvement cuttings in irregular stands bear a superficial, and sometimes misleading, resemblance to the cuttings of the selection method of reproduction that are designed to develop and maintain uneven-aged stands (Chapter 14). Both tend to involve the removal of the largest and oldest trees. However, in the selection method there is a definite intention of securing reproduction and maintaining a variety of age classes in the stand. Even if some new growth is established after improvement cuttings, one is not necessarily committed to a permanent policy of uneven-aged management. The improvement cuttings might, of course, be used to set the stage for such management, but they can also be part of a plan aimed at the creation of even-aged stands. Actually the removal of an overburden of old, defective trees usually decreases rather than increases the range of age and diameter classes present in a stand. Attempts to control the volume removed in improvement cutting according to the methods of regulation associated with the selection system are usually premature. If there is a large volume of defective material, such practice is likely to delay the rehabilitation of the stand and add unnecessarily to the burden of management computations.

It is especially desirable to take advantage of every opportunity to conduct thinnings in clumps of good trees simultaneously with improvement cuttings in irregular stands. The combination of the two operations frequently increases the volume harvested sufficiently to enable their application in stands where neither operation would be financially feasible if done separately.

Improvement cuttings are commonly necessary in the culled stands of hardwoods which are so prevalent in the East and South. The standards of utilization for hardwood lumber are more exacting than those that ordinarily apply to softwoods. Old-growth hardwood stands are notorious for their high proportion of cull resulting from heart rots. Sound defects, especially knots and related deformities, are even more common owing to the deliquescent habit of branching exhibited by most hardwood species. The presence in intimate mixture of a large number of species with widely varying utility has also contributed to the prevalence of highly selective forms of cutting.

The existence of such stringent standards for high-quality lumber and the difficulty of producing timber without defects make it essential that poor hardwoods be eliminated in improvement cuttings whenever possible. In marking stands for such cuttings it is important to recognize that the outward signs of serious defects may be such things as inconspicuous distortions of the bark or small seams and bulges as well as the more obvious crooks, forks, and large branches (Lockard, Putnam, and Carpenter, 1950). It must be anticipated that at least some of the hardwoods released by improvement cuttings will form epicormic branches (see Chapter 15).

In many stands all or part of the material to be eliminated in improvement cuttings cannot be utilized profitably and the undesirable trees are girdled or poisoned. The investment required for such treatment is usually of the order of several dollars per acre and, at least on good sites, is likely to be returned by increased growth of high-quality material in approximately a decade.

Improvement cutting is almost invariably the first operation required in managing the degraded bottomland hardwood forests of the South (Fig. 6-1; Putnam, Furnival, and McKnight, 1960). The same is commonly true of cutover stands in both the northern and central hardwood types (MacLean, 1949; Wahlenberg, 1953; Minckler, 1955). The irregular stands of hardwoods that sometimes develop on abandoned fields in the absence of a source of coniferous seed usually require improvement cuttings in the preliminary stages of management.

Irregular, mixed stands of hardwoods and conifers are usually the places where investments in improvement cutting are likely to prove most profitable (see Fig. 5-5). The growth of such valuable species as red spruce, eastern white pine, and loblolly pine is frequently hampered by hardwoods left standing when the mixtures were culled over for the best of the softwoods. The situation is especially serious where the hardwoods are representatives of late successional stages and encroach steadily on the more valuable conifers.

The need for improvement cuttings in pure coniferous stands is most often encountered in those that consist of two age classes. The trees of the older class are usually those that either were left as unmerchantable in a previous cutting or were once the only trees of a sparse stand which originally developed on a vacant area. The older, defective trees are likely to be the parents and competitors of a denser, subordinate age class of superior form. This condition is especially prevalent in stands that have developed on abandoned fields in the East, although it is by no means uncommon in culled or second-growth stands of conifers in western forests. The sparse and irregular stocking of stands of the interior ponderosa pine type is, for example, highly conducive to the development of conditions that can be corrected only by improvement cutting. Wolf trees often appear in these forests even in the absence of human disturbance; improvement cuttings designed to eliminate such trees are an important step in putting such stands under management (Pearson, 1950).

SALVAGE CUTTINGS

Salvage cuttings are made for the primary purpose of removing trees that have been or are in imminent danger of being killed or damaged by injurious agencies other than competition between trees.

The kind of salvage cutting easiest to visualize is that aimed at capturing the highly perishable values in trees that are seriously damaged, dying, or already dead. A more sophisticated variant, sometimes called **presalvage cutting,** is that designed to anticipate damage by removing highly vulnerable trees.   **Sanitation cuttings** involve the elimination of trees that have been attacked or appear in imminent danger of attack by dangerous insects and fungi in order to prevent these pests from spreading to other trees.   Such cuttings are not necessarily confined to the removal of merchantable trees.

The removal of dead or dying trees from the subordinate crown classes constitutes thinning rather than salvage cutting, regardless of the nature of the agency ultimately responsible for mortality.   The initiating cause of death of such trees is competition, and the agency that finally eliminates them is usually one of natural selection rather than a potential source of damage to the main stand.

Economic Role of Salvage Cutting

The recovery of timber values that might otherwise be lost is one important and expeditious silvicultural means of securing yields greater than those available from the unmanaged forest.

Damage to forests from fungi, insects, fire, wind, and other agencies occurs almost continuously.   A silvicultural rotation covers such a long period that losses of this kind are almost inevitable.   Although the forester can reduce the resulting losses, he is almost never able to prevent them.

The objective of salvage cuttings, as the name indicates, is to utilize the injured trees with the idea of minimizing the financial loss.   They are not conducted unless the material taken out will at least pay for the expense of the operation, except in cases where real justification exists for true sanitation cuttings.

Even when the damaged material can be salvaged at a profit, the injuries that made the operation necessary ordinarily result in a loss of production.   This is true especially when the damage occurs in the first half of the rotation.   The loss is caused partly by deterioration of the injured trees before being salvaged, partly by reduction in stocking, and partly by the necessity of cutting the injured trees before they have reached optimum size.   However, if the salvaged trees are parts of overmature stands that are not increasing in value, there is a subsequent gain of production to the extent that the vacancies are claimed by younger and more vigorous trees of desirable species.

The immediate financial loss depends largely on the extent and distribution of damage.   If trees die sporadically and at widely scattered places in a stand, they may become a total loss because of the impracticability of harvesting them.   The immediate loss is likely to be at a minimum if mortality is moderate and closely concentrated in time and space. When catastrophic losses have occurred over a wide area, the returns from salvage cutting are often reduced by the necessity of selling the products on a glutted market. The costs of logging are generally higher in salvage cutting than in operations where the trees to be removed have been chosen by intention rather than by accident.

Simple Salvage Cuttings

Ordinarily it is no problem to select the trees to be taken out in salvage cuttings. Sometimes, however, the mortality caused by the attack of a damaging agency does not take place immediately. This is particularly true where surface fires have occurred because the main cause of mortality is the girdling that results from killing of cambial tissues. As with other kinds of girdling, the top of the tree may remain alive until the stored materials in the roots are exhausted. It is usually a year or more before the majority of the mortality has occurred (Stickel, 1935). By this time, those trees which were killed immediately have often deteriorated seriously. It is, therefore, advantageous to have some means of anticipating mortality before it has actually occurred. The predictions must be based on outward evidence of injury to the crown, roots, or stem.

The severity of a salvage cutting depends entirely on the proportion of the stand occupied by the damaged trees. If isolated trees remain undamaged it is best to harvest them if they are likely to succumb eventually or if it will become difficult to remove them after they are surrounded by young saplings. Occasionally they can be left for seed trees or for further growth, but only if such action is clearly justified.

Regeneration after salvage cuttings is often a difficult problem, especially if the residual stand is too young or too poorly distributed to provide a reliable source of seed. It is commonly necessary to resort to artificial regeneration. Unfortunately, prompt salvage cutting is frequently premature from the standpoint of obtaining natural reproduction because the damaged trees may bear large crops of seed before they die. As a consquence, the forester may be faced with the alternatives of serious loss through deterioration of damaged timber or heavy expense for planting. This dilemma can sometimes be solved by the temporary reservation of some of the less damaged trees as a source of seed (McConkey and Gedney, 1951).

Salvage cuttings should normally be completed as soon as possible after mortality or injury has occurred. Dead trees generally start to deteriorate rapidly during the first growing season after death, so it is usually advisable to get the trees out of the woods before insects and fungi have become active in the spring.

Unfortunately there are many situations in which the amount of salvageable material is so great that it cannot be removed within a few months or a year, even if all other operations are suspended. Under such conditions it is highly desirable to know how long the dead or damaged trees are likely to remain sufficiently sound to be worth salvaging. Entomological and pathological investigations have made this information available for a number of different species (Boyce, 1961). With this type of knowledge it is possible to conduct large salvage operations in a systematic and efficient manner.

The amount of time allowable varies widely depending on the circumstances. The sapwood of virtually all species is highly perishable but the heartwood of the most durable may remain sound for many years. Ordinarily dead trees of small diameter become valueless long before large trees. Deterioration usually proceeds more rapidly on good sites than on poor. Differences in the rate of decay of various species are also significant. The basic objective should be to schedule salvage operations in different places in such order that the value of timber saved will be at a maximum. This does not necessarily mean that the most valuable material should be salvaged first.

The harvesting of damaged timber is often more difficult and expensive than cutting in undamaged stands. This is especially true if large groups of trees have been broken off or uprooted by wind. In conducting salvage operations it is important to remember that the money lost through inefficient logging can easily exceed the potential values wasted through decay of unsalvaged timber. The extremes of both haste and procrastination should, therefore, be studiously avoided in salvage cutting.

It must be anticipated that salvage cuttings will be necessary from time to time in any forest. In stands that are extraordinarily susceptible to injury, the time and place of harvesting operations may be dictated largely by damaging agencies. It is also a good policy to expect some mortality after even the most well-conducted partial cuttings. If full advantage is to be taken of opportunities for salvage of merchantable material, it is essential that all parts of a forest be made accessible by a good system of roads. Boldt and Salminen (1956), for example, described a situation in Upper Michigan in which the pre-existence of a road system enabled the prompt salvage, after a small tornado, of values worth about $1000 for each mile of a network of minor roads serving 125 acres per mile.

Presalvage Cutting

Most methods of cutting are guided to some extent by the intent of harvesting trees that are especially vulnerable to loss. In some North American forests, however, this objective becomes the paramount guiding principle during the early stages of management. Necessity for this approach is often encountered in regions where there are extensive areas of old-growth stands that have been subjected to little or no cutting. Under these circumstances, most common in parts of Canada and the West, neither the markets nor the objective of establishing an orderly sustained yield will permit the rapid replacement of deteriorating stands with young and more resistant ones. One of the symptoms of this embarassment of riches is the need for a race between salvage cuttings and the inroads of damaging agencies (McMahon, 1961). In such contests, the forester is often hobbled by the inadequacy and expense of access to the stands.

Wherever possible, it becomes very desirable not only to harvest merchantable trees that are already killed or damaged but also through presalvage cuttings to anticipate losses that are likely to occur before definite steps can be taken to replace the stands. Of course, once access is gained to forests of this kind, the forthright replacement of the most decrepit stands should be vigorously prosecuted by means of true reproduction cuttings. The temptation to deal first with the closed stands that have not yet started to break up should be restrained and attention turned as much as possible to those that are already deteriorating. The purest kind of presalvage cuttings are applicable to an intermediate category of stands which cannot be scheduled for early replacement but are already subject to significant losses of scattered trees.

The same approach is desirable in stands, young or old, in which attacks by damaging agencies are so chronic that silviculture is ruled by them. Usually more complete command of the situation can ultimately be taken by shifting to species or age classes less vulnerable to damage. Sometimes there is no better solution than the indefinite continuation of regularly scheduled salvage cuttings as the basic program of silviculture. One of the most outstanding examples of this distressing state of affairs is to be found in those badly eroded areas of the Piedmont Plateau where shortleaf pine is badly affected by the littleleaf disease and replaceable only with species that also have disadvantages (Campbell and Copeland, 1954).

The rational conduct of presalvage cuttings depends on the identification of those trees that are likely to be lost and the estimation of the length of time that they may be expected to endure. This is a more difficult problem than determining how soon obviously damaged trees will die or how rapidly dead trees will deteriorate.

If the main source of anticipated damage is wind, ice, or other climatic agency, the mechanical structure of the trees and their position within the stand are the important criteria. Trees with asymmetrical crowns or previous injury from frozen precipitation are prone to additional damage fom this source. In managed forests losses to fire are usually kept in check by normal means of fire control or by true salvage cutting when these fail. However, the removal of trees that have been chipped for naval stores is an example of presalvage cutting done in anticipation of the serious damage such trees might suffer in event of fire or beetle outbreaks.

When biotic agencies or physiological factors such as those related to site factors are the causes of anticipated losses, the vegetative vigor of the trees is usually the criterion employed in presalvage cutting. Trees of relatively high vigor are less vulnerable if attacked because they are likely to endure the amount of loss of vital tissues that would kill trees of low vigor. The relatively abundant pitch flow from trees of good vigor even actively resists attack by *Dendroctonus* bark beetles which dictate more presalvage cutting than any other damaging agency. The presalvage of trees of low vigor is rendered all the more logical because they grow little in volume or value.

A number of tree classifications have been developed for the guidance of presalvage cutting. One of the best-known examples of such a classification is that developed by Keen for the interior ponderosa pine type of California and the Northwest (Miller and Keen, 1960). Vulnerability to loss from bark beetles is so closely correlated with growth rate and the various stages of the life cycle of ponderosa pine that this classification is suitable for selecting trees for cutting even where risk of beetle attack is not the main consideration.

Keen's classification (Fig. 6-2) is based on the two major factors of age and crown vigor. There are four age classes and four vigor classes within each age class, making a total of sixteen classes. The four age classes are termed: 1—young, 2—immature, 3—mature, and 4—overmature; they should be thought of as grouped by relative maturity rather than by any definite ranges of age. Actual age limits for the groups vary in different parts of the ponderosa pine region. Color and type of bark, total height, shape of top, characteristics of branches, and diameter are the chief external indications of maturity. The four crown vigor classes are: A—full vigor, B—good to fair vigor, C—

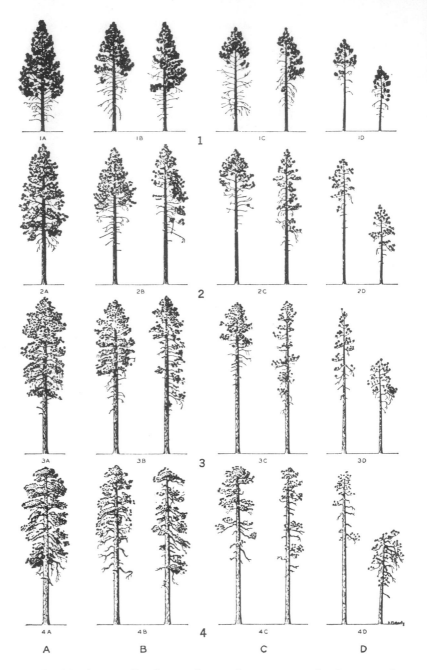

Fig. 6-2. Keen's tree classification for ponderosa pine. The four age classes range from 1, the youngest, to 4, the oldest; the four crown vigor classes, from A, the most vigorous, to D, the poorest. (*Sketch by U. S. Forest Service.*)

fair to poor vigor, and *D*—very poor vigor. The size of the crown (length, width, and circumference), its density, and the shape of its top indicate the crown vigor and consequently the inherent capacity of the tree to grow and endure exposure to beetles.

Keen's classification was originally designed to provide a means of evaluating the risk that trees left after selection cutting would be attacked by beetles during a cutting cycle of approximately 30 years. The possibility of making light cuttings at much more frequent intervals. has necessitated introduction of another classification designed for use in determining which trees are in imminent danger of death (Salman and Bongberg, 1942). The most important criteria are the condition of the needles, the number of dead twigs in the crown, and the health of the top of the crown, although allowances are also made for obvious signs of injury from beetles and other agencies. The most recent modification of this classification and its use have been described by Sowder (1951), Whiteside (1951), and Hallin (1959).

Keen's tree classification has been modified by Hornibrook (1939) for use in the Black Hills and by Thomson (1940) for the Southwest. Classifications that are similar in general purpose to those developed for ponderosa pine have been applied in other forest types.

Presalvage cuttings based on a similar classification can be used as a means of arresting losses in overmature stands of the western white pine type (Wellner and Boyd, 1960). This forest type provides an excellent illustration of the situation in which it is desirable to keep the salvage cuttings as light as possible with the deliberate intention of restricting the establishment of reproduction. In this instance, cuttings would have to be far heavier than those necessary for salvage to provide the amount of light necessary for establishment of western white pine. Heavy salvage cuttings would merely make way for the less desirable shade tolerant species. When any form of salvage cutting is carried to the point that reproduction is likely to appear it is most important to commence looking upon the operation as reproduction cutting and modify procedures enough to secure desirable reproduction.

Sanitation Cuttings

These differ from other forms of salvage cuttings only to the extent that they are combined with or represent precautions to reduce the spread of damaging organisms to the residual stand. Sanitation cuttings may also be undertaken in anticipation of attack in attempts to forestall the establishment of damaging organisms entirely. They can be and usually are combined with salvage or presalvage cuttings; any cutting is a sanitation cutting to whatever extent it eliminates trees that are present or prospective sources of infection for insects or fungi that might attack other trees.

Sanitation cuttings are not effective and not worth conducting unless the characteristics of the stands and the organisms are such that the removal of susceptible trees will actually interrupt the life cycle of the organisms sufficiently to reduce their spread to other trees. The elimination of *Ribes* shrubs from stands of five-needled pines is an effective form of sanitation cutting although other terms could be applied to the operation. However, the removal of such pines already infected with the blister-rust fungus is not effective sanitation cutting because the spores that carry the fungus from pine to *Ribes* can travel such tremendous distances that no practical advantage is gained. The cutting of infected pines would, however, constitute useful salvage cutting, although direct attack on the fungus with the antibiotic, cycloheximide, might save the trees and thus be even more advantageous (Moss, Viche, and Klomparens, 1960).

The light partial cuttings often applied to deal with *Dendroctonus* beetles in ponderosa pine in the western interior are termed "sanitation-salvage cuttings" because they reduce the number of the very kind of feeble trees which sustain the beetle population.

It should not be tacitly assumed that the vigor of trees is the sole criterion of their susceptibility to attack, even though it may be a good indicator of their capacity to endure damage. Some economic pests of the forest, notably insects, multiply most rapidly on vigorous hosts just as grazing animals prefer forage from healthy plants. Fortunately the vast majority of insects attracted to thrifty trees are well-adapted parasites that do not endanger their own existence by killing their hosts; these insects rarely become cause for concern and may even escape notice. However, there are some important exceptions. In other instances, the presence of certain especially attractive species, regardless of their vigor, may determine whether a stand is threatened by pests that can harm more than one species.

The spruce budworm, one of the most dangerous insects of the North American forest, is an excellent example of an insect which is not merely a predator of the weak and also has a marked preference among species (Morris, 1958). The most typical form of this versatile insect is the scourge of the eastern portion of the spruce-fir forests, where massive outbreaks develop at intervals of several decades. It is poorly named because its early instars are heavily dependent on balsam fir and only the later instars feed very successfully on spruce.

The trees that are most susceptible to attack, but not especially high in vulnerability to loss, are large balsam firs with spire-shaped crowns. These bear abundant staminate flower buds which are highly nutritious for young budworms. Susceptibility to attack is determined more by the proportion of mature balsam fir in whole forests than by the characteristics of individual trees or stands. It can be reduced to a limited extent under present extensive management by replacing large tracts of mature forests with an intermingled arrangement of stands in which the susceptible mature stands are diluted among younger and less susceptible stands. Vulnerability to the losses that are likely to occur after a stand is attacked can be somewhat reduced by presalvage of firs and spruces with low live-crown ratios.

There are many other defoliating insects which are governed more by the species competition of the forest than by the vigor of the trees. However, the wholesale changes in stand composition often necessary to reduce their depredations involve so many other considerations and procedures that they are not looked upon as sanitation cuttings. A sanitation cutting is usually thought of as an operation in which a few trees are cut in a stand almost exclusively with the object of safeguarding the much larger number that remain.

Sometimes sanitation cuttings must be associated with special measures to provide additional assurance that the damaging organisms will not spread to the residual stand. If the pests are exclusively parasitic on living tissues, it is sufficient to kill the infested trees and leave them in the woods. Occasionally special measures are desirable to accelerate the killing. Treatment of girdled trees with sodium arsenite is, for example, employed to hasten the death and desiccation of trees in spot infections of the oak-wilt fungus (Ohman, Anderson, and French, 1959).

If the insects or fungi involved are capable of multiplying as saprophytes in dead material, it may be desirable to utilize the wood at a loss. This approach can be used to increased advantage against bark beetles if "trap" logs or trees left temporarily to attract them are hauled to the mill or log pond before the emergence of the entrapped brood. However, it may still be necessary to burn the slash that remains or to treat the stumps with insecticides.

If utilization is out of the question, it may be advantageous to carry out treatments designed to restrict the activity of the pests. Sometimes this can be done in connection with slash burning. Bark beetles can also be controlled by insecticides or by stripping the bark from felled trees. Occasionally it helps to shift the logs to spots that are either too exposed or too shaded for the particular insect or fungus to flourish. The most troublesome organisms are certain fungi, especially some of those causing heart rots, which produce conks on fallen trees. If trees infected with such fungi must be left in the woods, there is little which can be done to prevent the formation of new fruiting bodies. However, if the trees are felled, the distance over which the spores are disseminated is reduced and the accelerated disintegration of the wood hastens the end of the period of danger (Hepting and Roth, 1950).

There are some agencies of damage against which sanitation cuttings are, for practical purposes, so ineffective as to be useless. Fungi that inhabit the soil and damage the roots of trees are not likely to be halted even by sanitation cuttings that are carried to the extent of removing the stumps. Some organisms spread so rapidly or over such long distances that sanitation cutting may be a meaningless gesture as far as the effective protection of the stand is concerned. It is for reasons of this sort that simple salvage cutting is more common than sanitation cutting.

Sometimes the salvage of entire stands may be looked upon as a desirable measure of sanitation even if the damaged stands by themselves are not worth the effort. Stands that have been badly damaged by fire, wind or similar agencies frequently support the development of large populations of bark beetles which can cause serious injury to adjacent stands. The expense of salvaging such foci of infection may be amply rewarded by reduction of losses in adjacent stands.

In any kind of salvage or sanitation cutting in which the effects of insects or fungi are involved, there is no substitute for a thorough understanding of the life histories of the organisms involved. The details of procedure useful in dealing with one kind of injury may be hopelessly ineffective or needlessly intensive as a means of reducing losses from other seemingly similar agencies of destruction.

CONTROL OF CUTTING

The problems of administering cutting operations are not any more closely related to improvement and salvage cuttings than they are to other kinds of intermediate or reproduction cutting. It is not logical, however, to postpone their consideration further. The success of even the soundest ideas and most adroit procedures of silviculture usually depends on the proper execution of the harvesting operations that are ordinarily used to carry them into effect. Cutting is the chief tool by which the forest is controlled; this is true even when the main objectives are the management of resources other than timber, such as water, forage, or wildlife.

The most important problems are encountered in the application of the numerous kinds of partial cutting that are so commonly essential to the efficient use of the capacity of the forest to produce wood and other benefits. These problems are changed in kind but not in magnitude when whole stands are cut in single operations.

The felling and removal of the trees is often conducted by a logging operator who may have bought the timber or contracted to log it. The labor is often performed by employees who are paid according to the volume of material which they handle. The interests of both parties lie in harvesting the timber as efficiently as possible; there is little economic incentive for them to pay much attention to the preservation of growing stock, advance reproduction, or source of seed to be left on the area. Under the circumstances, it is essential that the forester devise means of controlling the operation to the extent of preventing the cutting or destruction of those trees, both large and small, that must remain to ensure continuity of production.

From the silvicultural standpoint it is best to have the forester direct the harvesting operations. The prevalent practice of placing the removal of the timber in the hands of purchasers or contractors, whose primary interest is in cheap logging, is not ideal. All operations connected with the removal of wood and timber from the forest, at least up to the point of delivery at the sides of forest roads, can be conducted to silvicultural advantage by the forest officers. The general principle of unified control of all woods operations is applicable to any forest, although the degree of integration ultimately possible is bound to be restricted when the owner confines himself to selling stumpage.

There are two methods of specifying which trees to cut and which to leave: (1) control through inspection alone and (2) control through the marking of the trees, which also involves inspection.

Control through Inspection

Definite instructions as to the type of cutting desired can be given to the man in charge of logging the area, and his work can be controlled by inspection of the operations. The simplest instructions consist of nothing more than designation of the diameter limits or species to which the cutting is to be confined, although this practice is seldom compatible with efficient silviculture. Better results can be achieved by laying out more definite rules for cutting or by marking a small plot typical of the whole stand to demonstrate the type of cutting desired.

Control by inspection works best when the personnel doing the cutting understand which trees to cut and have no reason, economic or otherwise, to depart from the instructions. Inspections must be frequent and careful, particularly at the beginning of each operation.

Although it is usually cheaper, inspection is less effective than control through marking of the trees. It is used chiefly when marking is simply not feasible, although it does also have a place when cutters are properly trained and capable of applying the simpler silvicultural operations according to generalized instructions.

Control through Marking the Trees

A close degree of control can be maintained by designating either the individual trees that are to be cut or those that are to be left. The operator is responsible only for the work of removing the designated trees with due care for those left standing; the selection of the trees is entirely within the province of the forester. Marking is far superior to inspection as a method of control because an exact designation by individual trees is substituted for verbal or written instructions. It is the method most commonly used, except where the silvicultural practice is of low intensity. Inspection is necessary under the marking method to ensure that cuttings are properly executed, but success is not so dependent upon the close, frequent inspections necessary under the first method.

Ordinarily the trees to be cut are marked, because they are normally less numerous than those to be left. However, if the majority of the trees are to be cut, it is better to mark those that are to be left; this should be done without wounding the living portion of their bark. It becomes desirable to mark the trees to be left if they are ones designated for pruning or for reservation in very heavy thinnings and in those kinds of reproduction cutting in which only a few trees are left. This has the incidental advantage of focusing the attention of the timber marker on the residual growing stock. However, the cost of marking is great enough that it is always best to put the marks on whichever category of trees is in the minority. Where an area is to be cut clear, it is sufficient to mark the boundaries of the area to be so treated.

The marks placed upon the trees should be readily visible, difficult to counterfeit, and durable enough to last through the period of the projected cutting.   In selecting tools for doing the marking, the ease, rapidity, and expense of the work are important considerations. Among the implements used are axes, timber scribes, and paint guns.

Usually two marks are placed on each tree, one at a height where it is easily visible and another on a root swelling or so low on the trunk as to appear on the side of the cut stump.   The mark on the stump enables one to determine whether the felling has been conducted according to the marking.   The lower mark may be omitted when the felling crews can be depended upon to adhere to the marking.

Various schemes involving numbers and shapes of marks can be devised to stipulate such things as the direction in which a tree is to be felled, the product for which it is to be prepared, whether it is to be felled or killed, how high it should be pruned, or whether its utilization is at the discretion of the logger.   Occasionally it may be desirable to put distinctive marks, as permanent as possible, on crop trees to expedite consistent treatment in marking for subsequent cuttings.   Any such special marking schemes should be so devised as to eliminate the possibility of misinterpretation.   The colors of paint chosen for marking trees and for such other purposes as designating property boundaries should follow some standard system.

Marking axes and timber scribes are used mainly where the amount of timber to be marked is too small to justify the advance preparations and transportation of materials necessary for the use of paint guns.   Axes are also useful where much of the timber is likely to be rotten because they can be used to "sound" the trees to detect rot. Marking axes are usually fitted with special dies so that distinctive initials can be stamped on the blazes.

Paints and paint guns that function with a minimum of trouble and preparation are now available, so it is usually expeditious to use them instead of cutting tools.   The chief cost of marking has come to be that of time rather than of materials.   The use of paint guns substantially reduces the time spent in making the marks and obviates the necessity of walking right up to each tree.   No wounds are left and the tools are safer than axes or scribes.   The only real problems lie in the cost and bother of procuring, transporting, and handling the paint.

The best way to mark a stand is to proceed back and forth across it systematically, completing one long, narrow strip on each trip.   The marks should be placed so as to face the next unmarked strip, unless they are used to designate the direction of felling.   After some practice, the task can be carried out swiftly with little lost motion.   If the strips are sufficiently narrow, one may even be able to mark one strip and simultaneously note the characteristics of the back sides of trees to be considered on the next strip. Sometimes it is necessary to tally the trees that are to be cut and, less often, those which are to be left.

In stands with any important component of deciduous species, marking can be done much more rapidly after the leaves have fallen than in the summer, because the visibility is much better. Where it is extraordinarily important that marking be based upon the vigor or other characteristics of the tops of the trees, it may be necessary to have markers work in pairs with one man marking and the other observing the tops from a distance. Ordinarily it is most efficient if each marker works individually or if there are two or three markers and one tallyman.

The cost of timber marking is usually figured as a cost per unit of product designated for removal. It varies over a wide range depending upon the size of the timber, the measurements taken during the process, the amount cut per acre, topography, density of undergrowth, time required for travel to and from the job, cost of materials used, and the rate of pay of the personnel doing the work. It may be as little as 5 cents per thousand board feet where patches of large old-growth timber are being designated for clearcutting. On the other hand, the cost of marking small pulpwood trees is usually 25 to 75 cents per cord, a major portion of the stumpage value.

The cost of timber marking in stands managed on economic rotations is far from negligible and must be assessed in terms of the value of the benefits produced. The immediate benefits are the only ones properly charged against the cost of marking the timber that is removed. These values lie in such things as the information gathered about the quantity and quality of material being cut and the important opportunity to lay out efficient patterns for felling and extraction of the trees.

The essentially silvicultural benefits come mainly from increases in *future* production gained by exercise of discrimination among individual trees and conscious creation of vacancies suitable for establishment of reproduction. The cost of these benefits is more logically charged against the acre than against the volume removed. The production of value per acre can usually be estimated, at least as to order of magnitude; the question of whether marking is worth the expense is most likely to come into question when this production is small. Justification rarely exists for deciding that all stands will or will not be marked. The seemingly costly marking of trees of low value in a young stand may actually yield much more future benefit than marking in an old stand of valuable trees.

The gathering of data by the timber markers is often an operation fully as time consuming as the marking itself and one which is seldom essential to future benefits. This usually involves tallying the trees that are to be cut and less frequently those that are left as well. The question of whether such data are going to be used to significant advantage should be closely scrutinized (Bromley, 1951). If they are to be gathered, attempts should be made to do so by efficient schemes of sampling that will yield the essential information at the lowest posible cost (Putnam, Furnival, and McKnight, 1960).

Good stands that are growing well and producing trees of substantial size can be marked at reasonable costs. The most worrisome problems come with small trees and poor, slow-growing stands on difficult terrain. Marking can usually be justified where saw-timber production is one of the goals, but if management is exclusively for pulpwood the question of whether to mark should be examined carefully (McLintock, 1948; Lundgren, 1959).

Guidance of Timber Markers

The professional forester who has attained a position of responsibility and acquired some experience is likely to have become too expensive a man for routine timber marking. Although, at this point, he may cease to do much of any timber marking himself he becomes more than ever concerned about how it is done. He becomes an instructor and supervisor of timber marking, and, instead of marking a stand himself, he may now be able to do no more than inspect it briefly and direct how it shall be marked. This state of affairs is a powerful argument in favor of trying to develop reasonably homogeneous stands, thus avoiding needlessly complicated schemes of silviculture. Even-aged stands are much more expeditiously handled than uneven-aged and the actual expense of marking them is also lower because the timber to be removed is more concentrated in space.

If a forester is going to be effective as a supervisor of timber markers, he must have some proficiency of his own but, above all, he must have a clear idea of his objectives for each kind of stand. These must be developed in the light of the thoroughest possible understanding of local economic conditions, logging practice, and the ecology of all species in the stand (Martin, 1945). It is then necessary to convey these ideas to his staff in such manner that they can be depended upon to apply their independent judgment to the attainment of the objectives.

Good judgment about timber marking is not developed without years of experience in a given locality. The best test of the wisdom of a particular marking project comes a number of years afterwards when the vegetation has adjusted itself to the conditions created by the cutting. The pressures of forest administration are so great that it is too easy to concentrate on marking for this year's cutting and forget to go back to inspect the results of the cutting of several years ago. It is also easy to become so obsessed with the imaginary virtues of an established marking policy as to be blind to any shortcomings that may be manifest in the results of its past application. The forester should take advantage of every opportunity to improve his skill by marking timber for cutting and then observing the results as dispassionately as possible.

Successful marking is so firmly grounded on a knowledge of local conditions, both natural and economic, that it may seem thoroughly unsusceptible of standardization. Nevertheless certain generalizations can be made regarding the proper marking practice for each forest type within a given region having reasonably uniform conditions. These generalizations, which are termed **marking rules,** are most helpful in orienting beginners. Demonstration and test plots may be used for training inexperienced men in marking timber.

Many organizations with a large and continually shifting personnel entrusted with the management of large holdings, have found marking rules valuable in standardizing practice among individuals and for various areas of the same forest type. On the other hand, arbitrary insistence on conformity to marking rules, can eventually inhibit rather than encourage the development of skill and good judgment on the part of the individual. The extent to which this is true depends upon the intelligence of the personnel, the accuracy of the rules, and the manner in which they are enforced. There must be some sort of continuity in the treatment of individual stands and the success of the management plan for a whole forest may depend on the characteristics of the trees that are cut and left in each harvesting operation.

The simplest kind of marking rules are instructions describing the kinds of trees to be cut or to be fostered as candidates for the final crop. Tree classifications are useful in conveying the necessary information and ensuring consistency of treatment. However, such classifications should be carefully devised to accentuate the decisive differences between trees. Furthermore, their application should not be so automatic that the marking simply becomes a mechanical task of assigning trees to arbitrary categories.

Good examples of tree classifications, other than those developed for ponderosa pine, are those of Taylor (1939) for lodgepole pine; Roe (1948) for western larch and Douglas-fir in Montana; and de-Grace (1950) for white and Engelmann spruce. The only general one is the crown classification described in connection with thinning. Certain others are discussed in Chapter 14 on the selection system, a reproduction method in which tree classifications are especially important.

When silvicultural policies have become sufficiently well developed, it becomes logical to supplement or replace marking rules based on individual trees with schedules for the intermediate and reproduction cuttings to be applied throughout whole rotations in particular kinds of stands. The schedule of treatments proposed by Eyre and Zehngraff (1948) for intensive management of red pine in Minnesota (Table 3-2) provides an excellent example.

Control of Waste and Destruction in Logging

A certain amount of waste and destruction of timber is inevitable in any logging operation. Such losses should be held to a minimum because they reduce both present and future yields from the area.

The waste and destruction may be classified as follows:

1. Material left in the tops through failure to utilize the trunk up to the minimum merchantable top diameter.

2. Material left in unnecessarily high stumps.

3. Material left in partially unmerchantable trees, including windfalls and dead trees, through failure to utilize the merchantable portions of such trees.

4. Destruction of residual growing stock.

5. Damage to the soil as a result of log transportation.

Waste of presently merchantable material, as described under the first three categories, is evidence of inefficiency in logging. Merely as a matter of good business, the logging operator may be expected to avoid these losses, as soon as they come to his attention, without necessarily considering silvicultural practice. Close utilization of material in tops and partially unmerchantable trees has an indirect silvicultural benefit because of the reduction of inflammable material and the removal of trees that might harbor destructive insects and fungi.

In judging whether material is being wasted in high stumps, big tops, and partially defective trees, careful consideration must be given to prevailing standards of merchantability. The conditions that govern logging practice and market requirements vary widely even within short distances. The same standards of merchantability are not necessarily applicable to two different logging operations proceeding simultaneously in one forest. The terrain and the type of equipment used may have an important effect on the costs of logging even though all other conditions are comparable.

Destruction of residual growing stock is of more vital silvicultural importance than the other kinds of waste because it reduces future yields. Most of the damage to the residual stand comes from the cutting, breakage, or crushing of trees that impede the felling and removal of the trees designated for cutting. The wounding of standing trees during felling and skidding is another important source of injury, especially because of the wood-rotting fungi that often invade exposed wood (Wright and Isaac, 1956). Young trees are also cut for skids, corduroy roads, and other uses incidental to the harvesting operation. Supplies of such material can often be secured, with little if any added cost, from inferior species, tops, or cull material.

The greatest destruction of growing stock is likely to occur in stands of irregular form, where trees of various ages from small seedlings on up are intermingled. Greatest damage is likely to occur to large seedlings and small saplings that are tall enough to impede operations but not durable enough to resist breakage (Westveld, 1931). Seedlings less than 2 feet in height are comparatively supple and are, therefore, more likely to escape destruction. Heavy cutting causes more damage than light (Lynch, 1953).

It is difficult to lay down any general rule regarding the extent of damage which can be accepted without endangering future production in partially cut stands. Although losses are usually expressed in terms of the percentage of stems destroyed or injured, the most significant point is their distribution. For example, if each milacre in need of reproduction has one seedling the area may be fully stocked even though 70 per cent of the total number were destroyed. On the other hand, a loss of 10 per cent of the total might be so concentrated as to leave large openings entirely without trees.

Damage from felling can be reduced by refraining from dropping trees upon advance regeneration or against trees that are to be left standing. If damage to young growth cannot be entirely avoided, the trees should be felled in such a pattern that the damage will be well distributed and have the effect of thinning the residual stand. Much difficulty can be forestalled by giving attention to the matter at the time of marking as well as during the operation itself.

In marking timber, it is important to consider each tree not only

from the standpoint of its productive potentialities but also with regard to the problems that might be encountered in felling it or one of
its neighbors. *No tree should be marked for cutting unless a way
can be seen, or created, to fell it without inconvenience or excessive
damage to the residual stand.* It may then be necessary to supervise
the operation closely or train the felling crews to ensure that they follow the plan embodied in the pattern of marking. Even then some
unanticipated losses may occur. In such cases, provision should be
made for salvaging any unmarked trees that are seriously damaged
in the course of logging.

Little additional damage is likely to occur during limbing and bucking of felled trees, if the crews refrain from swamping out any young
trees that do not actually impede the operation or constitute a source
of danger to personnel. In logging heavy timber it is sometimes advantageous to finish the operation in two stages, removing the logs
produced in the first stage before cutting the remaining marked trees
(Sias, 1953). This practice has the favorable effect of avoiding congestion and confusion, thereby reducing damage to the residual stand,
breakage of felled trees, and the amount of labor required for both
limbing and bucking.

Destruction caused by the transportation of logs and other products
is a major source of injury to the residual stand. This damage may
occur not only during skidding but also from construction of roads
and landings. Investigations on steep and very steep terrain in stands
of old growth in Idaho (Haupt, 1960; Moessner, 1960) indicate that in
heavy cuttings as much as 15 to 25 per cent of the soil may be bared
by haul roads and skid trails. The area that is rather permanently
removed from production by haul roads varies significantly depending
on the kind of skidding equipment used; it is very high if most of the
movement of logs within the cutting area is done after logs are loaded
onto trucks. The disturbance of the soil on tractor skid trails is mostly
temporary and so much less serious than that on haul roads for trucks
that it is desirable to accomplish as much movement of logs as economically possible with tractors. Because of this it may be desirable
to use heavy, powerful tractors rather than lighter ones; while they
damage skid trails more, their use does not necessitate putting so
much area into even more destructive truck roads. Mitchell and
Trimble (1959) found that in logging smaller timber on steep terrain
in West Virginia the proportion of ground surface disturbed could be
held to 5 per cent or less.

The only significant risk of damage to the soil in harvesting operations is that which results from log transportation. Cutting itself rarely causes erosion or any other form of damage to the soil. Removal of the unincorporated organic matter, if not too extensive, may even be beneficial through its effect in preparing the ground for the establishment of light-seeded species. However, deep gouging and rutting of the mineral soil can lead to serious erosion, especially on steep slopes, fine-textured soils, and in dry regions where revegetation is slow. This kind of damage is associated primarily with the use of heavy, powerful skidding equipment and the excavation required in construction of roads and similar improvements. The most serious effect of such damage to the soil lies in the siltation of streams rather than in extensive and permanent reduction of the productivity of the site.

Erosion along roads and skid trails can be reduced by locating them so as to avoid steep grades and places where extensive cutting and filling will be necessary. On steep slopes, skid trails that converge downward should be avoided as much as possible. The location of roads close to and parallel with streams increases siltation. Proper attention to drainage of roads not only reduces erosion but prolongs their usefulness. This applies not only to roads in current use but also those that are not used between logging operations. If the drainage systems of temporarily abandoned roads cannot be cleared of debris periodically, they should be opened enough at the end of each period of use that they will function without attention.

It is frequently advantageous to suspend log transportation during periods when roads are muddy because the risk of creating conditions favorable to erosion is then at a maximum. Precautions of this kind often have the effect of reducing logging costs by preventing the damage and delay that occur when equipment gets stuck in the mud. Some readily accessible stands should be reserved for cutting in muddy weather.

Greatest destruction occurs when cable skidding is done with powerful, stationary machinery. Any method of skidding, such as the high-lead system, in which the timber from an area is drawn to a central point by immobile equipment is compatible only with clearcutting. Even those trees that are unmerchantable are usually knocked over when the cables are shifted. This type of equipment can be used economically only where there are large volumes of big timber concentrated in relatively uniform stands, as in old-growth Douglas-fir. It is probable that such equipment will rarely be employed in the second-growth stands of the future, except on ground that is too steep or too soft for tractor logging. Even then it will not be necessary to use skidders that are so powerful or so difficult to move because the timber will be of much smaller size.

Direct skidding of logs with horses or mules, particularly where the timber is small enough to be handled by one animal, rarely causes serious damage to reproduction and young growth. Trimble (1942) found that less than 20 per cent of the spruce and fir reproduction in pulpwood stands in the Northeast was destroyed by horse logging. Even in that forest type, however, damage can be reduced by drawing the wood out in long lengths prior to bucking. Otherwise much reproduction is destroyed when large loads of wood bucked at the stump are extracted over a closely spaced network of trails. On saw-log operations, however, damage is usually increased by skidding in tree lengths prior to bucking, regardless of the type of power used.

Tractors are now in much more general use than animals and stationary skidding equipment. They are more damaging than animals but far less so than cable skidders. The extent of damage caused by tractor skidding depends on the size and power of the equipment. Heavy tractor-arch units, such as are necessary for handling big timber, have a wide turning radius and may be very destructive. Equipment of this kind can also break out wide swaths through the stand and dig deeply into the mineral soil (Garrison and Rummell, 1951; Steinbrenner and Gessel, 1956).

Ordinarily the damage caused by tractor logging may be kept within acceptable limits if the operation is carefully planned in advance and conducted under close supervision. If certain practices, discussed in the next paragraph, are followed, the damage under any type of tractor logging can be held to a reasonable amount (Weidman, 1936; Cosens, 1952; Morris, 1955).

Main tractor roads should be laid out before cutting. They should be as straight as possible and yet avoid clumps of young growth. Tractors should not be driven across from one road to another. Trees should not be felled parallel with the roads because this necessitates turning the logs. If the trees are felled in a herringbone pattern with respect to the roads, they can be pulled out with a minimum of turning. Tractors should, if possible, be turned in openings and then backed to the load. Sometimes the necessity of swinging tractors around through young growth can be avoided by using models fitted with winches and short cables; logs can be drawn out of clumps of advance reproduction without driving a tractor in to get them. In any case, logs should be pulled out endwise and not pivoted around trees or clumps of young growth. It may even help to leave a few high stumps as buffers at strategic points where many logs are turned adjacent to residual timber. Two logs should not be hooked together at the same bucking cut and then pulled out sidewise.

In the last analysis, genuine cooperation on the part of the felling and skidding crews is essential if logging damage is to be kept at a minimum. No silvicultural operation, regardless of how well it is conceived, can be any better than the way in which it is applied in the woods.

REFERENCES

Boldt, C. E., and W. A. Salminen. 1956. Permanent logging roads facilitate economic timber salvage. *LSFES Tech. Note* 450.

Boyce, J. S. 1961. *Forest pathology,* 3rd ed. McGraw-Hill, New York.

Bromley, W. S. 1951. An economical method of marking timber. *J. Forestry* 49:518–519.

Campbell, W. A., and P. Spaulding. 1942. Stand improvement cutting of northern hardwoods in relation to diseases in the Northeast. *Alleg. FES Occasional Paper* 5.

Campbell, W. A., and O. L. Copeland, Jr. 1954. Littleleaf disease of shortleaf and loblolly pines. *USDA Circ.* 940.

Cosens, R. D. 1952. Reducing logging damage. *CFRES Forest Research Note* 82.

deGrace, L. A. 1950. Management of spruce on the east slope of the Canadian Rockies. *Canada, Forestry Branch Silvicultural Research Note* 97.

Deitschman, G. H., and D. E. Herrick. 1957. Logging injury in Central States upland hardwoods. *J. Forestry* 55:273–277.

Eyre, F. H., and P. Zehngraff. 1948. Red pine management in Minnesota. *USDA Circ.* 778.

Garrison, G. A., and R. S. Rummell. 1951. First-year effects of logging on ponderosa pine forest range lands of Oregon and Washington. *J. Forestry* 49:708–713.

Hallin, W. E. 1959. The application of unit area control in the management of ponderosa-Jeffrey pine at Blacks Mountain Experimental Forest. *USDA Tech. Bul.* 1191.

Haupt, H. F. 1960. Variation in areal disturbance produced by harvesting methods in ponderosa pine. *J. Forestry* 58:634–639.

Hepting, G. H., and E. R. Roth. 1950. The fruiting of heart-rot fungi on felled trees. *J. Forestry* 48(8):332–333.

Hornibrook, E. M. 1939. A modified tree classification for use in growth studies and timber marking in Black Hills ponderosa pine. *J. Forestry* 37:483–488.

Jemison, G. M., and G. H. Hepting. 1949. Timber stand improvement in the southern Appalachian region. *USDA Misc. Pub.* 693.

Lockard, C. R., J. A. Putnam, and R. D. Carpenter. 1950. Log defects in southern hardwoods. *USDA Agr. Handbook* 4.

Lundgren, A. L.   1959.   Costs of marking black spruce for cutting in northern Minnesota. *LSFES Tech. Note* 546.

Lynch, D. W.   1953.   Logging damage increases under heavy cutting of second-growth ponderosa pine. *NRMFRES Res. Note* 121.

McConkey, T. W., and D. R. Gedney.   1951.   A guide for salvaging white pine injured by forest fires. *NEFES Northeastern Research Note* 11.

MacLean, D. W.   1949.   Improvement cutting in tolerant hardwoods. *Canada, Dominion Forest Service Silvicultural Research Note* 95.

McLintock, T. F.   1948.   Cost of timber marking in pulpwood stands. *J. Forestry* 46:763–764.

McMahon, R. O.   1961.   The economic significance of mortality in old-growth Douglas-fir management. *PNWFRES Res. Paper* 37.

Martin, R.   1945.   Timber marking for second-cycle cutting in northern Wisconsin. *J. Forestry* 43:655–657.

Miller, J. M., and F. P. Keen.   1960.   Biology and control of the western pine beetle. *USDA Misc. Pub.* 800.

Minckler, L. S.   1951.   Annual cuttings unsound in unmanaged woodlots. *J. Forestry* 49:649.

Mitchell, W. C., and G. R. Trimble, Jr.   1959.   How much land is needed for the logging transport system? *J. Forestry* 57:10–12.

Moessner, K. E.   1960.   Estimating the area in logging roads by dot sampling on aerial photos. *IMFRES Research Note* 77.

Morris, B. W.   1955.   An example of tree-length skidding as a silvicultural tool. *J. Forestry* 53:666–667.

Morris, R. F.   1958.   A review of the important insects affecting the spruce-fir forest in the Maritime Provinces. *Forestry Chron.* 34:159–189.

Moss, V. D., H. J. Viche, and W. Klomparens.   1960.   Antibiotic treatment of western white pine infected with blister rust. *J. Forestry* 58:691–695.

Ohman, J. H., N. A. Anderson, and D. W. French.   1959.   Comparison of dry and chemical girdling to prevent sporulation of the oak wilt fungus. *J. Forestry* 57:503–506.

Pearson, G. A.   1950.   Management of ponderosa pine in the Southwest. *USDA Agr. Monograph* 6.

Putnam, J. A., C. M. Furnival, and J. S. McKnight.   1960.   Management and inventory of southern hardwoods. *USDA Agr. Hbk.* 181.

Roe, A. L.   1948.   A preliminary classification of tree vigor for western larch and Douglas-fir trees in western Montana. *NRMFRES Research Note* 66.

Salman, K. A., and J. W. Bongberg.   1942.   Logging high-risk trees to control insects in the pine stands of northeastern California. *J. Forestry* 40:533–539.

Sias, R. C.   1953.   Two-stage falling in an overmature stand. *J. Forestry* 51:288–290.

Smyth, A. V.   1959.   The Douglas-fir bark beetle epidemic on the Millicoma Forest: methods used for control and salvage. *J. Forestry* 57:278–280.

Sowder, J. E.   1951.   A sanitation-salvage cutting in ponderosa pine at the Pringle Falls Experimental Forest. *PNWFRES Research Paper* 2.

Steinbrenner, E. C., and S. P. Gessel.   1956.   Effect of tractor logging on soils and regeneration in the Douglas-fir region of southwestern Washington. *Proc. Soc. Am. Foresters Meeting*, 1955: 77–80.

Stickel, P. W.   1935.   Forest fire damage studies in the Northeast. II. First-year mortality in burned-over oak stands. *J. Forestry* 33:595–598.

Taylor, R. F.   1939.   The application of a tree classification in marking lodge-pole pine for selection cutting.   *J. Forestry* 37:777–782.

––––.   1946.   A comparison of silvicultural marking and cutting practice rules in a northern hardwood stand.   *J. Forestry* 44:41–46.

Thomson, W. G.   1940.   A growth rate classification of southwestern ponderosa pine.   *J. Forestry* 38:547–553.

Trimble, G. R.   1942.   Logging damage in partial cutting of spruce-fir stands. *NEFES Tech. Note* 51.

Wahlenberg, W. G.   1953.   Three methods of rehabilitation for depleted Appalachian hardwood stands.   *J. Forestry* 51:874–880.

Weidman, R. H.   1936.   Timber growing and logging practice in ponderosa pine in the Northwest.   *USDA Tech. Bul.* 511.

Wellner, C. A., and R. J. Boyd.   1960.   Partial cuttings in mature stands of the western white pine type.   *Proc. Soc. Am. Foresters Meeting,* 1959:27–32.

Westveld, M.   1931.   Reproduction on pulpwood lands in the Northeast.   *USDA Tech. Bul.* 223.

Whiteside, J. M.   1951.   The western pine beetle.   *USDA Circ.* 864.

Wright, E., and L. A. Isaac.   1956.   Decay following logging injury to western hemlock, Sitka spruce, and true firs.   *USDA Tech. Bul.* 1148.

PART II
REGENERATION

CHAPTER 7

Planting

The time ultimately comes in the life of every stand when it must be reproduced. Intermediate cuttings may greatly enhance the value of a crop of trees, but they are not absolutely necessary. On the other hand, continuity of forest production is simply not possible without periodic replacement of stands.

Artificial reproduction is that obtained by **planting** young trees or applying seed, which is termed **seeding** or **direct seeding**. **Natural regeneration** is obtained either from seedlings originating by natural seeding or from sprouts and other plants representing vegetative reproduction.

The most dangerous stages in the life of a tree come when it exists only as an embryo in a seed or when it is a tender young seedling. In nature the greatest mortality comes even before germination; that which takes place during the first few weeks after germination is usually far greater than that throughout all the remaining life of a stand. Planted trees are not exposed to the rigors of the site to be restocked until they have successfully passed the critical stages of germination and early development. These trees are sometimes wild stock procured elsewhere in the forest, but it is usually most economical to rear them in the protected environment of nurseries.

Most forest planting in North America involves the conifers, especially the pines, spruces, and Douglas-fir, because the prospects of successful establishment and high financial yield are greater with conifers than with hardwoods. Therefore, the material in this chapter will apply to the conifers, unless otherwise stated. More detailed information on artificial regeneration will be found in books like those of Toumey and Korstian (1942) and Wakeley (1954).

GENETIC CONSIDERATIONS

Artificial regeneration offers vastly greater opportunity than natural seeding to modify the genetic constitution of stands. If intelligently used, this power can be of substantial benefit. If used in ignorance, the results can be almost disastrous.

Artificial regeneration always involves choices, deliberate or otherwise, of genetic material, and these can be made with varying degrees of refinement. The decision to plant a particular species is essentially a genetic choice and automatically becomes even more so because the trees that are actually planted inevitably come from a minute segment of the whole natural population of the species. Efforts are now usually made to control at least the locality of origin of seed. It is becoming increasingly common to attempt to take advantage of the genetic material represented by the best members of local strains. Beyond this lie efforts to employ artificial breeding and hybridization to create genetic combinations that would not be likely to develop in nature. Reference should be made to publications like those of Lindquist (1948), Larsen (1956), Wright, Bingham and Dorman (1958) and Mergen (1959) for more complete information on forest genetics.

From the genetic standpoint, the best that can be said of an outstandingly good tree found in the wild population is that it represents a good **phenotype**. This is another way of saying that the effects of its environment *and* its genetic constitution have produced an outward appearance that happens to be good. If such a tree were highly rated by an objective scoring system, it might be called a **plus** tree. According to the same parlance and procedure, a whole stand with good phenotypic characteristics would be rated as a plus stand.

If the sexually or vegetatively reproduced progeny of good phenotypes display the same good characteristics in comparison with others when grown under uniform environmental conditions, this is evidence that the parents are good **genotypes**. Such findings suggest, in other words, that the good characteristics were conferred upon the parents by their genetic constitution and not solely by favorable environment. The evidence is stronger if the tests were made on sexually propagated progeny, because this indicates that the parents not only have good genetic traits but are also capable of transmitting them. Trees or stands thus proven to be genetically superior are termed **elite**.

If natural or artificial selections are made in favor of a certain characteristic and repeated over many successive generations it is possible that nearly all of the favored progeny ultimately produced will become **pure** or **homozygous** with respect to the characteristic. If two trees are homozygous for resistance to some insect and are interbred, all of their offspring will be resistant. If one carried genes responsible for both resistance and susceptibility, it would be **heterozygous** with respect to this character and the progeny would vary in resistance.

The pressures of selection are such that natural populations of trees tend to become homozygous and resistant to artificial alteration with respect to characteristics crucial to their survival. The less crucial characteristics which are most susceptible to improvement by artificial selection are, unfortunately, likely to be controlled by genetic patterns that remain heterozygous. Until individuals can be developed that are reasonably homozygous with respect to these characteristics, the interbreeding of carefully chosen forest trees is not likely to produce a high proportion of trees with the desirable genetically controlled characteristics sought. The pure-line breeding common in annual crop plants is greatly simplified by the opportunity to make careful selections every year.

Although it is a case of making a virtue of necessity, successful breeding of improved strains of forest trees is not dependent on the ability to produce pure lines. Crops of forest trees are started with many more individuals than are necessary for the final crop, so selections in favor of the desired qualities can be made in the process of thinning. If the desired characteristic is rapid growth in height, the selections will take place automatically. In fact, if all the individuals were exactly similar, thinning would be essential to prevent stagnation. Therefore, seed producers that will yield a progeny with a moderate proportion of the kind of phenotypes sought are fully as useful as a pure strain would be. A mixture of genotypes in the progeny also provides an important safeguard against the disasters that might result if the genotypes for which the progeny was originally selected proved to be vulnerable to some source of damage that was not foreseen. This is especially important because it takes so long to determine whether a promising genotype of a tree species is really reliable.

The longevity of trees which makes their genetic improvement such a slow process also has the desirable effect of enabling the semipermanent maintenance of parent trees that are proven sources of desirable progeny. While it is almost impossible to develop the pure lines used in breeding annual plants, the problem of maintaining good genotypes is comparatively simple. Vegetative propagation provides the only quick and certain way of transmitting the germ plasm of a good genotype to new individuals and increasing their numbers. This is feasible for forest planting only with trees such as poplars that will root from cuttings planted in the field (Schreiner, 1959). However, techniques of vegetative propagation are practically indispensable in the intensive work necessary for proper testing of the genotypic characteristics of promising phenotypes, controlled breeding, and the establishment of seed orchards (Nienstaedt et al., 1958).

The most reliable plant breeding can be done with characteristics that are controlled by single genes. Only slow and uncertain progress can be made with improvements in characteristics controlled by the combination of a number of genes.

The application of genetics to the improvement of a species is not something achieved by half-measures. Very discriminating selections of phenotypes with the desired characteristics must first be made in the forest. Tests must then be made under controlled, uniform conditions to determine whether they are good genotypes; these are best done by vegetative propagation of cuttings or scions from the chosen trees. Those which seem likely to be good genotypes can then be crossed with others to determine whether the sexually reproduced progeny include an adequately high proportion of good phenotypes. If they do, they can then be established in seed orchards to serve as a source of seed for the production of superior planting stock. This is a slow process, especially if done step by step, but it can be accelerated by starting many of the steps simultaneously and subsequently eliminating trees that are later found to have been derived from genotypes poorer than those sought.

It is important to determine the normal relationship between such characteristics and environmental forces so that individuals that depart from this pattern in a desirable direction can be detected. A superior individual is most obvious when surrounded by more ordinary trees and there is less chance that its superiority is the result of a favorable environment. However, a whole stand with many superior trees is much more likely to have genotypes homozygous for the desirable characteristics. In other words, the isolated individual is more likely to be heterozygous and to carry undesirable genes than trees in a whole stand of desirable individuals. This particular difference bears no relation to the valid point that the progeny arising from natural pollination of the isolated individuals might be of undesirable male parentage.

Careful distinction should be drawn between the different degrees of control and improvement of genetic characteristics that are sought. The most conservative objective is merely to assure that the new stands are at least as good as the natural population of the species in the locality. This can be done by restricting the collection of seed to the locality; it seems like a simple step but the problems of procuring seed in quantity are so great that it is often a struggle to adhere even to this restriction.

The next step is to try to take advantage of the best phenotypes or genotypes in the natural population of the locality. Individuals or stands of plus and elite trees can be used as sources of seed for planting, although it is ultimately most convenient if cuttings or scions from them are established in special seed orchards.

The advisability of further and more artificial genetic refinements depends upon the degree of faith placed in the virtues of the natural population. The position can be taken that the natural genotypes have met the test of survival in the locality for at least thousands of years and are thus highly dependable in meeting the rigors of the future. According to this viewpoint, one would be content with the natural genotypes that carried the characteristics most suitable from the economic standpoint. However, it is also possible to point to situations in which local populations do not have the most satisfactory strains. Natural adaptations that enhance survival often reduce the economic value of trees, although the ability to survive is no small economic advantage by itself. There is clear justification for ignoring the natural population in breeding trees to resist introduced pests like the chestnut-blight fungus, to endure the unnatural site conditions encountered on strip-mine banks, or to cope with other problems induced by man.

There is always the risk that genotypes selected for a few desirable characteristics will later prove highly undesirable because of characteristics that were not appreciated at the time of selection. In order to hedge against disaster it is often desirable to establish seed orchards composed of a number of interbreeding genotypes, all of good quality but different, in order to increase the possibility that the progeny will include genotypes that can adapt to a variety of sites and endure unexpected difficulties.

Experimentation in the genetic improvement of forest trees has progressed to a level even more sophisticated than attempts to use the best genotypes of the natural population. Artificially induced cross-pollination makes possible the creation of genotypes that could not have developed in nature (Duffield and Snyder, 1958). These include not only interspecific hybrids but combinations of different geographic races of a single species. Some interspecific hybrids exhibit hybrid vigor in the sense that they grow substantially faster than either parent; they may also have other unusually desirable characteristics. The same is true of polyploids arising from failures of mitotic divisions that result in genotypes with multiples of the normal chromosome numbers; these may arise through natural accidents or artificial treatments. The possible benefits and risks of mistakes resulting from the use of such genetic aberrants are great.

It is not clear how much effect, if any, thinnings or other partial cuttings, such as those aimed at natural reseeding, have on the genetic constitution of the ultimate natural progeny. It is well known that substantial genetic variation exists in nature, although some species are much more variable than others. It is quite another matter to determine the degree to which the good genotypes present are homozygous or heterozygous with respect to the characteristics involved. Probably the greater the variability the more heterozygous are the various genotypes and the more resistant the progeny to alteration by any sort of selectivity. Furthermore, the degree of selectivity that is possible in such partial cuttings is exceedingly low from the standpoint of the tree breeder.

Repeated high-grading, especially if continued for centuries, is distinctly dysgenic in the sense that it deteriorates the natural population. Lindquist (1948) observed such effects in the forests of the more populous parts of Sweden. Furthermore, excellent trees represent rare combinations of desirable genetic traits; such combinations can be irretrievably lost in high-grading. Natural selection automatically eliminates the most undesirable. The harm that can be done by dysgenic cutting is, therefore, greater than the benefits to be gained by eugenic cutting.

Choice of Species

The most important decision made in artificial regeneration is the selection of the species used in each new stand. The species chosen should first of all be adapted to the site, that is, to the climate, soil, and biotic environment (Anderson, 1950). The species selected from those suited to the site should be the ones that promise the best net returns. The factors considered in this choice are (1) costs of establishment and management, (2) losses to injurious agencies, (3) rate of growth, and (4) usefulness and value of the products. Native species already thriving in the locality are the safest choices, and every effort should be made to use the best-adapted strains that are to be found.

Introduced species and strains, as well as hybrids and strains developed by artificial breeding, should be used with caution until their superiority to the best of the indigenous strains has been demonstrated in trials extending over all or most of a rotation. Planting, when coupled with attempts to introduce genetically superior material, offers opportunity to improve upon the trees that might be obtained from natural regeneration. At the same time, however, it can lead to serious mistakes that are simply impossible to commit if regeneration can be obtained only from indigenous genetic strains already on the site.

The success of introductions is governed exclusively by natural factors; political boundaries and similarities of human culture are of no significance. The red spruce of the North Carolina mountains is, for example, as foreign to the coastal plain of that state as the Aleppo pine of Algeria. The race of ponderosa pine which grows in the California Sierras (Weidman, 1939) has no more place than sugar pine in the Black Hills of South Dakota (Fig. 7-1). Any introduced

Fig. 7-1. Foliage characteristics of two distinct races of ponderosa pine. *Left:* Open, plumelike arrangement of long, slender needles of North Plateau race from eastern Oregon. *Right:* Compact, brushlike arrangement of short, thick needles typical of race found east of the Continental Divide from Colorado northward. The needles shown on the right are more resistant to frost and winter injury than those on the left (Weidman, 1939). (*Photographs by U. S. Forest Service.*)

species or strain should come from a locality with climate and soils closely similar to those of the home region. The climatic criteria are: (1) both mean and extreme temperatures, (2) length of growing season, (3) amount, distribution, and effectiveness of precipitation, and (4) latitude (which controls day-length and is associated with some of the other factors).

The most successful introductions have generally involved moving species to the same latitude and position on the continent that they occupied in the native habitat because this is most likely to provide similarity of climate. For example, many conifers of the western coasts of North America have been remarkably successful at the same latitudes in western Europe. The forest economy of many countries in the Southern Hemisphere is heavily dependent on pines introduced from localities of comparable climate in the southern United States, California, and Mexico. It should be noted, however, that the famous Monterey pine has not done well everywhere in the Southern Hemisphere or even in Florida (Scheer, 1959); it has thrived only in places with the same climatic pattern as the California coast.

Dramatic movements of species across major geographic barriers have been more successful than seemingly modest extensions of their natural ranges. If the new regions are climatically similar to the indigenous, the results are sometimes very favorable. The intercontinental movements mentioned in the previous paragraph have placed the species where they were adapted to grow but had been prevented from doing so only by the intervening oceans and inhospitable land surfaces. On the other hand, extensions of the natural ranges of some American conifers by distances of 100 miles or less have sometimes proven highly unsuccessful. This has been true of the southward extension of the range of red pine and the northward movement of loblolly and slash pine as well as of coast redwood.

It is imperative that introduced plants be transported in the form of seed rather than seedlings so that the risk of spreading parasitic insects and fungi will be kept at a minimum. If the pests of the species can be left behind, the introduced species may be more satisfactory in the new habitat than it was in the old (Moulds, 1957).

SEED COLLECTION AND TREATMENT

Harvesting of Seed

The large investments involved in artificial regeneration make it highly desirable to start with good seed. This applies not only to genetic considerations but also to the germinative capacity of the seed.

The germinative capacity of the seed depends on many factors, but mostly on the extent of successful pollination between trees. Self-fertilization of female flowers or strobili by pollen from the same tree often results in a high proportion of infertile seeds; there are many natural factors and circumstances that tend to prevent self-pollination. There must be substantial numbers of trees of the same species nearby if sufficient cross-pollination is to occur.

In general, large seeds have higher germinating power and produce larger seedlings than do small seeds. Investigations of the genus *Pinus* have shown that the size of young seedlings is closely related to the size of the seeds but that the size of the seeds does not reflect genetic differences (Spurr, 1944; Righter, 1945; Hough, 1952; Langdon, 1958). The effect of these initial differences in seed weight on the size of seedlings usually disappears after several years, provided that the large seedlings do not compete with the small. Both seeds and seedlings can be safely selected or graded on the basis of size to secure the cultural advantages of large size and high initial vigor without affecting the proportion of good genotypes. However, once the very small are eliminated, it is rare that any significant advantage is gained by further discrimination.

The most serious difficulties from unwise selection of genetic material can be avoided by attention to the **provenance** or geographical origin of the seed. Unless better sources are known, a definite effort should be made to obtain seed from trees of native stock growing as close as possible to the planting site. It is, for example, the goal of the U. S. Forest Service (1948) to use stock produced from seed collected within 100 miles horizontally and 1000 feet vertically of the point where it is to be used. When seed is purchased the seller should be required to state the provenance, altitude, date of collection, and capacity to germinate as well as whatever more detailed information he can be compelled or induced to provide. Regardless of how the seeds are obtained, as precise records as possible should be kept of the genetic origin of the stock used in each plantation, for only in this way will it be possible to gain future advantage from experience with trees of different origins.

Most of the problems of getting good seed arise from the difficulties of seed collection. The work is arduous, especially if the cones or fruits must be gathered from standing trees. Furthermore, the period during which seed of most species can be collected is short; crops worth harvesting are likely to be produced only during good seed years.

The best seed producers are dominant trees. Those of middle age usually produce the most abundant crops of seed with the lowest proportion of sterile seeds. However, it is easier to collect from young trees and there is no reason to avoid them unless an excessively high percentage of their seed is found to be infertile. Unfortunately, it is simpler to collect seed from short, deep-crowned trees of poor form than from tall, straight, well-pruned ones. Poor form in the parent does not necessarily indicate that the progeny will be undesirable, but it does increase the possibility. Therefore, it is advisable to confine collection of seed to the best trees available, preferably those adjacent to other good trees.

A representative sample of seeds from each tree, regardless of age, should be tested in the field before effort is expended on gathering cones from it. Such testing is done by cutting the seeds in cross section to determine how many of them are hollow or "blind." Operations can be expedited by locating stands with large crops of fertile seeds a few weeks before the seeds mature.

The proper time for collecting cones is just after they have matured, but before they commence to open and shed their seeds. The length of the period in which collections can be made varies considerably with species. The most critical problem is to determine when the seeds are mature. The time-honored method is to cut the cones open and inspect the seed to appraise its degree of hardness. With some species, collections may begin when the stored substances in the seed are no longer milky. Oftentimes the date of maturity can be predicted in a given locality from germination tests of seeds gathered at different times in former years. Usually cones commence to dry out rapidly as soon as they are ready for harvesting. The most dependable methods of judging maturity are based on this phenomenon.

The cones of many species, particularly the hard pines, are best collected when their specific gravity has decreased to about 0.85. The average specific gravity of a sample of cones is most easily determined by finding out what proportion of them will float in such liquids as S.A.E. 20 lubricating oil (sp. gr. 0.88), mixtures of equal parts of kerosene and linseed oil (sp. gr. 0.86), or other oils (Fowells, 1949; Wakeley, 1954). Changes in color are also associated with desiccation, although they are more difficult to define and evaluate.

The cones or fruits can be cut from the trees by means of long poles equipped with hooked blades. The simplest method is to collect from trees felled when the seeds have just matured. Discrimination should be exercised in gathering cones that have been cut down or stored by squirrels because these animals often cut the cones long before the seeds are mature. Silen (1958) found that Douglas-fir cones could be gathered several weeks before they were mature and would ripen satisfactorily if stored in moist peat moss at ordinary temperatures.

The best practices for collecting or applying any subsequent treatment to the seed of forest trees vary widely with species. It is desirable to consult the *Woody-Plant Seed Manual* (U. S. Forest Service, 1948) for the details of treatment of any species.

Actually the collection of large quantities of seeds from the wild forest is as inefficient as it is difficult to control from the genetic standpoint. It is far better to set aside or establish stands of good genotypes and manage them intensively and exclusively for the production of seed. In the initial stages of efforts in forest genetics, the first step is the reservation and culture of **seed production** areas. These are simply stands of good quality, chosen on the basis of phenotypic characteristics, that are very heavily thinned not only to stimulate seed production but also to eliminate poor phenotypes (Rudolf, 1959).

The term, **seed orchard,** is restricted to stands established for seed production and composed of trees known to be of good genotypes on the basis of tests of their progeny (Zobel et al., 1958; Southern Forest Tree Improvement Committee, 1960). They must be isolated from contaminating sources of pollen by distances of several hundred feet. They are usually established by vegetative propagation from the chosen genotypes. In order to maintain a moderately variable gene pool in the progeny, it is desirable to include at least fifteen genotypes or clones in each orchard. A **clone** is the vegetatively reproduced progeny of a single genotype. In order to ensure cross-pollination, the trees in a seed orchard should be so arranged that trees of the same clone do not stand adjacent to one another. Seed orchards may be started before the completion of progeny testing, but any unsatisfactory genotypes should be eliminated as they are detected.

Any area used exclusively for seed production is treated like a fruit orchard. The trees should be wide-spaced and pruned in such manner that the crowns remain close to the ground. If the trees are of good genotypes, the fact that they bear no resemblance to forest-grown trees is of absolutely no consequence to the genetically or environmentally controlled characteristics of their progeny. The trees produce a crop of very high value and can be fertilized, irrigated, cultivated, and sprayed with fungicides or insecticides as necessary to stimulate seed production (Hoekstra, Merkel, and Powers, 1961).

These treatments have the important additional effect of reducing the extreme fluctuations of seed production encountered in wild stands.

Extraction of Seed

The methods of extracting seeds depend on the nature of the fruit. The cones of most softwoods and the dry fruits of some hardwoods will shed their seeds if dried in open air or in kilns. However, the seeds of the closed-cone pines can be extracted only in kilns. The seeds of trees with fleshy or pulpy fruits may be removed by macerating or crushing them in special machines (Engstrom and Stoeckeler, 1941). Seeds borne in pods or husks can be extracted by threshing.

The cones of many softwoods can be opened merely by spreading them out in trays in open sheds or in direct sunlight, although this method is less satisfactory than heating them in kilns. The cones of many species must, however, be air-cured for about two weeks in this manner before they are placed in kilns. If they are too moist when kiln-dried they have a tendency to become "case-hardened" on the outside, which makes them very difficult to open by any means. The simplest type of kiln is operated entirely by convection. Such kilns consist of little more than rooms in which the cones are spread out in layered trays; they are heated from below, and the heated air rises up through the cones and goes out by way of ventilated slots in the top. The danger of uneven heating is so great that the process must be carried on slowly at relatively low temperatures.

Greater efficiency is obtained in forced-air kilns which are ventilated by means of fans and operated at temperatures of 115° to 170°F. Provision is usually made for close control over temperature and humidity in kilns of this kind (Rietz, 1941). Definite schedules of drying are followed just as in drying lumber in similar kilns. Equipment has also been developed for extracting seeds by heating the cones directly with infrared lamps (Lanquist, 1959).

Regardless of how the cones are opened it is desirable to shake the seeds out as soon as possible. This is usually done in cone tumblers which consist of rotating cylindrical screens.

After extraction the seeds of most species must be de-winged and then cleaned of waste material. This is usually done with special equipment designed to rub off the wings, screen out the coarse debris, and blow out the fine or light particles of waste. It is also possible to agitate the seeds on special tables designed to separate them according to specific gravity and eliminate those that are blind or empty (Switzer, 1959). These treatments reduce the volume of useless material that must be stored and processed; they also facilitate testing and sowing, ultimately making it possible to increase the uniformity of nursery seedbeds.   However, all such treatments should be as gentle as possible because each seed is a living plant likely to be killed by rough handling.

Seed Storage

The infrequency of seed crops makes it advantageous to have some means of storing seeds for several years without loss of viability.   Fortunately the seeds of most commercial species can be stored for periods of 3 to 10 years and sometimes longer if held at low temperature and low moisture content in sealed containers (Holmes and Buszewicz, 1958).   The proper moisture content varies from 4 to 12 per cent, depending on the species, and the temperatures should be below 41°F, preferably in the range from 0° to 32°F (Allen, 1957).   These conditions are readily available in most commercial cold-storage plants.   It is important to dry the seed uniformly and to prevent fluctuations in moisture content during storage.   Under these conditions respiration continues at the low level necessary to keep the embryos alive and only small amounts of the stored carbohydrates are converted into carbon dioxide in the process (Crocker, 1948).   Proper storage facilities are essential to the maintenance of stocks of seeds with high germinative capacity and good genetic qualities.   Without them the nurseryman is forced to obtain seed wherever he can get it.

Large nutlike seeds, such as those of oak and walnut, must be stored in moist, cool sand or peat moss; they cannot be stored longer than a single winter under any conditions.   The storage of moist or dry seeds of any commercial species in heated rooms should be avoided.

Treatment of Seeds to Hasten Germination

The seeds of a number of species often germinate slowly or fail to germinate at all after sowing (Crocker, 1948; Crocker and Barton, 1953).   There are two main causes of this phenomenon, which is referred to as **dormancy.**   The first is called **internal dormancy,** a condition ordinarily resulting from incomplete digestion of the fats, proteins, and other complex insoluble substances stored in the seed.   Before germination can occur these materials must be broken down into simpler organic substances, such as sugars and amino acids, that can be translocated to the embryo.   The essential conditions are created by storing the seed in cool, moist substances just as it would be in the natural forest floor. Moist peat moss or sand at temperatures somewhat above freezing is the best medium for this treatment, which is called **stratification.** The enzymes which catalyze the breakdown of the complex stored substances are capable of functioning in a cool, moist environment, but those which cause the rapid respiration necessary to release energy for growth of the embryo are not. Consequently the stored substances eventually used by the embryo are mobilized without being converted into carbon dioxide by useless respiration. The seeds of many conifers develop internal dormancy to some extent.

The stratification of seed in mixtures with other materials is a time-consuming procedure and also has the disadvantage of exposing the seeds to mold. With some species it is fully as effective and much simpler to soak the seeds at 41°F for 1 or 2 weeks (Rudolf, 1950b). Good results have also been obtained with some species by soaking the seeds briefly in water and then refrigerating them in polyethylene bags (Hosner, Dickson, and Kahler, 1959; Malac, 1960); these have the virtue of being impermeable to water but permeable to carbon dioxide and oxygen so that they permit gas exchange without loss of water. Seed disinfectants should be used to prevent molding during stratification. The most convenient way to avoid difficulty is to sow seed in the fall after all danger of premature germination of any nondormant seed is past. If sowing must be delayed until spring, stratification is often desirable.

The second cause of imperfect germination is **seed-coat dormancy.** This occurs in seeds that have protective coverings so impervious that either oxygen or moisture is excluded from the embryo. This kind of dormancy can be broken by mechanical abrasion or chemical softening or etching of the seed coat. The first kind of treatment is referred to as **scarification** and may be accomplished by grinding the seeds in mixture with coarse, sharp sand or in machines equipped with disks or cylinders of abrasive paper. Chemical treatment is usually done by soaking the seeds in concentrated sulfuric acid (Stoeckeler and Jones, 1957). Black locust is one species that can be treated effectively by either method. Some species, notably basswood, have both kinds of dormancy and require stratification after treatment of the seed coat. It is probable that seed-coat dormancy is broken in nature by the grinding of seeds in the gizzards of birds or by the gradual decay of seed coats by fungi. It is most common in hardwoods with hard seed coats and rare in conifers. The natural function of both forms of dormancy is the prevention of premature germination.

Seed Testing. Before the amount of seed to be sown on a given area can be calculated, the **germinative energy** of each lot must be known. This value is the percentage of seeds in a well-mixed sample which will germinate under optimum conditions during the period of most active germination (Fig. 7-2). This period extends through the first 7 to 35 days following the start of the test. Little advantage is gained by determining the total percentage of seeds potentially capable of germinating, that is, the **germinative capacity.** Only those seeds that germinate quickly are likely to produce seedlings vigorous enough to survive competition in the open.

Germination tests can be made in a variety of ways (Baldwin and Holmes, 1954; Grano, 1958). The most convenient method is to determine how many seeds will actually germinate during a given period in the greenhouse or laboratory. The germination medium may be acidic sand or peat moss in flats, or absorbent paper in special germinators. In either case the seeds are kept moist (but not submerged in water) at temperatures that are either maintained at 86°F continuously or allowed to drop to 68°F at night. Results may sometimes

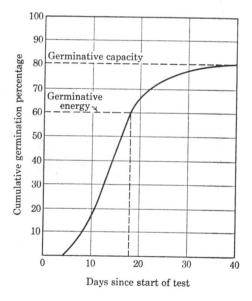

Fig. 7-2. Cumulative germination curve showing relationship between germinative energy and germinative capacity. In this example, only those seeds which had sprouted by the time, 18 days after the start of the test, when the rate of germination started to decline should be regarded as capable of germination in the nursery.

be obtained with less delay through the treating of the seeds with hydrogen peroxide (Ching and Parker, 1958). The cutting test by which sound seeds may be distinguished from blind seeds gives results that are far too high; it is valuable only for making quick estimates when seed is being collected.

The germination percentage as determined in greenhouse tests is inevitably higher than the survival that can be obtained when the seed is actually sown in nurseries. The discrepancy between germinative energy and field germination tends to increase with decreasing germinative energy. The actual proportion of the germinating seeds that produce living seedlings at the time of lifting from the seedbed is the **tree** or **survival percentage**. Although this is the most desirable criterion of all, it cannot be predicted without relating it to germinative energy over a period of years at each nursery.

It may also be desirable to determine the **purity** of each lot of seed. This is expressed as the percentage, by weight, of clean, whole seeds, true to species, in an unbiased sample consisting of both seeds and impurities.

Average values for various characteristics of seeds of many species have been compiled by the U. S. Forest Service (1948).

NURSERY OPERATIONS

The production of forest planting stock in nurseries is an operation more closely related to agronomy or horticulture than to silviculture. Cheap and efficient production can be achieved only in large nurseries with an output running into millions of trees per year. Success hinges on the accurate application of a highly specialized technique, requiring constant vigilance and variation in its application. The problems of nursery management are essentially local; proper methods can be worked out only by experimentation at each nursery. The employment of skilled specialists capable of efficient management can be justified only when the output of the nursery is large. Where only a small amount of planting is to be done it is usually better to buy the planting stock than to start a nursery.

Forest planting stock is almost invariably grown from seed, although vegetative propagation from rooted cuttings is a useful technique of perpetuating valuable strains for special purposes.

Location and Establishment of Nurseries

The most important consideration in growing forest planting stock is the selection of a suitable location for the nursery. More problems have been created in nursery management by poor judgment in this matter than by any subsequent errors. Nurseries should be located on level or gently sloping ground suitable for agriculture. The best soils are sandy loams free of stones and moderately well drained. They should be inherently fertile and also acidic, with a pH between 5.0 and 5.5, particularly if conifers are to be grown. The nursery should be located on a site where the soil thaws slightly earlier than the areas to be planted, thus guaranteeing that the stock can be lifted as soon as needed for planting. The site should also have reasonably good air drainage so as to reduce the risk of injury to the stock from extreme temperatures. The soils and vegetation should be carefully investigated to determine whether problems with insects, fungi, nematodes, or weeds are likely to be serious; recently cultivated land is often undesirable from this standpoint.

Shipping costs may be held to a minimum if the nursery is located near the center of the locality it is to serve. It must also be readily accessible to main highways, electric power, and a source of seasonal labor. There must be an abundant supply of clear water, of as low alkalinity as possible, and ample space for the conduct of operations. It is poor economy to locate a nursery in a situation that does not meet most of these requirements.

Rapid increases in the cost of labor have forced a degree of mechanization and simplification of nursery operations once scarcely contemplated.

Fertilization and Management of Nursery Soils

The problems of managing nursery soils are more critical than those of most agricultural soils because of the very large investment and value represented by an acre of tree seedlings. The delicately balanced nutrient cycle of the forest does not exist in forest nurseries. Large quantities of inorganic nutrients are removed in the tops and roots of each crop of seedlings; adhering soil colloids are also lost. In fact, tree seedlings exhaust the soil more rapidly than many agricultural crops. Therefore, fertility can be maintained only by proper application of both organic matter and inorganic fertilizers. Ordinarily, it cannot be maintained solely by using composts and other organic materials because of the expense and practical difficulties encountered in obtaining and handling the large volumes of material that would be necessary.

Attention must also be given to preventing deterioration of the physical properties of the soil. The main purpose of applying organic matter and plowing in cover crops is to protect the structure and water-holding capacity of the soil. It is also desirable to protect the soil surface as continuously as possible with seedlings, cover crops, or mulches. If the nursery is on sloping ground subject to erosion, it is necessary to construct low terraces.

The problems of treating nursery soils must be worked out by careful and skillful study at each nursery. The pitfalls are many and usually invisible to the uninitiated. A fuller appreciation of this topic may be gained from such references as those of Wakeley (1954), Stoeckeler and Jones (1957), Wilde (1958), May (1958), and Stoeckeler (1960).

Preparation and Sowing of Seedbeds

The standard width of seedbeds is 4 feet; they are customarily separated by paths 15 to 24 inches wide. They should be as long as possible so that mechanical equipment can be used on them with a minimum of turning. These long strips may, however, be divided into standard 12-foot units if necessary to facilitate hand sowing, treatment, control of operations, or record keeping.

Relatively deep plowing and thorough harrowing are necessary to permit proper root development. If drainage is impeded to any extent, the beds should be slightly elevated and convex in cross section; otherwise they should be flat. In either case the form and lateral spacing of seedbeds can be created with rotatillers or specially constructed scraping devices known as seedbed shapers. The surfaces of the seedbeds should be pulverized by raking or other means just before sowing so that the seed will be in contact with loosened, moist soil.

There are two general methods of sowing. In **broadcast** sowing the seeds are distributed uniformly over the seedbed; in **drill** sowing they are arranged in parallel, uniformly spaced bands that run the length of the beds and are as narrow as possible. Broadcast sowing produces uniform stands of seedlings which close together in one season and then tend to protect themselves against damaging agencies and competition from weeds; in theory it gives the best seedlings because lateral development is uniform in all directions (Pein, 1953). Broadcast seeding is done by hand or with machinery. The main disadvantage of this method is that the bed cannot be weeded with mechanical cultivators, although the introduction of weed-killing sprays has largely overcome this drawback.

Drill sowing is almost invariably carried out with equipment that sows the seed at any rate desired, covers it to the proper depth, and rolls the beds, all in one operation. The drills are usually 4 to 8 inches apart, although much wider spacings are used for certain hard-

woods. Weeding between the rows can be done with cultivators or
sprays.

The amount of seed to be sown should be calculated for each lot of
seed from the data on germinative energy and other characteristics.
The general formula employed is:

$$W = \frac{A \times S}{C \times P \times G \times L}$$

in which W = pounds of seed, A = square feet of area to be broadcast
with seed *or* linear feet of drill, S = number of seedlings desired per
square *or* linear foot, C = number of seeds per pound of absolutely
clean seeds at the moisture content of sowing, P = purity of sowing
lot expressed as a decimal, G = germinative energy expressed as a
decimal, and L = the estimated survival per cent expressed as a decimal.

Much difficulty in subsequent treatments and inventories can be
avoided by mixing the seed thoroughly so as to maintain uniformity
among seedbeds. Allowances should be made for reductions in production from irregularly distributed, catastrophic losses; however, this
should be done by sowing a larger area at the optimum rate, rather
than by increasing the amount of seed sown on a fixed area.

The desirable density of seedbeds varies from 10 to 100 seedlings
per square foot, depending on the size of seedlings of the species involved. For most conifers the optimum density varies from 25 to 60
per square foot. As many as 200 per square foot may be grown if the
seedlings are to be transplanted in the nursery before being sent into
the field. The costs of treatments of seedbeds are logically viewed
as costs per square foot of bed. Therefore, the aim should be to obtain the level of density that will yield the greatest number, per square
foot, of seedlings larger than whatever size is set as a minimum standard (Shoulders, 1960). If the seedlings come up too densely after
broadcast sowing the seedbeds can be thinned by means of devices
fitted with whirling hammer knives or minute jets of burning gas
designed to kill seedlings along very narrow, parallel lines.

After the seed is sown it is pressed into the soil with rollers. The
depth of sowing should be one to four times the diameter of the seed;
deeper sowing is necessary in sandy soils than in those with a high
clay content. With broadcast sowing, it is often necessary to add a
covering of clean sand after rolling.

After sowing is completed the seedbeds may be covered with straw
or long strips of burlap until germination commences. If the seed is

sown in the fall and there is danger of frost heaving, a covering of straw is necessary. Seedlings must be mulched in similar fashion during subsequent winters if there is danger of loss from frost heaving.

The seedbeds should be protected from birds and rodents during the germination period. Wire screens are effective but expensive. It is often cheaper to poison the rodents and shoot or scare away the birds. One of the best ways is the direct application to the seeds of various poisons and repellants, some of which also happen to be good insecticides and seed disinfectants.

Control of Weeds

One of the largest sources of expense in nurseries is weeding, which is necessary several times a season. The costs of weeding are greatly reduced by the use of petroleum sprays. The light oils used contain 14 to 25 per cent xylene or similar aromatic hydrocarbons. This treatment cannot be employed without thorough experimentation by the user. Dosages must be carefully regulated to allow for differences in the resistance of various species and age classes of tree seedlings. Very uniform application with power equipment is necessary to prevent localized overdoses. Application must be avoided when temperatures are high, and consideration must be given to variable influences of soil moisture and weather conditions (LaCroix and Guard, 1958). The spraying is best done when the weed seedlings are just emerging rather than after they have become readily apparent to casual observation. Unfortunately these sprays cannot be used in weeding hardwoods and certain conifers.

If petroleum sprays cannot be used, seedbeds that have been sown broadcast must be laboriously weeded by hand. With drill sowing much of the weeding can be done mechanically. Hand and mechanical weeding actually damage seedlings enough that spraying is superior.

Regardless of the method of weeding every effort should be made to reduce the amount of weed seeds in the nursery. Prompt weeding will eliminate weeds before they bear seed. Manure should be composted for long periods, and only mulches relatively free of weed seeds should be used. The cover crops, which should be grown on seedbeds that are being left fallow, must be dense enough to suppress growth of weeds. As a last resort, seedbeds may be treated with soil fumigants and other chemicals, prior to sowing.

Where seedlings are left in broadcast-sown seedbeds more than one year, relatively little weeding is necessary after the first year, because the density of the seedlings is so planned that they close together during the first growing season.

Watering and Shading of Seedbeds

It is generally necessary to water seedbeds, at least during the first growing season. This can be done by means of semipermanent, overhead sprinkling systems, although the portable sprinklers used in agriculture can also be employed. The schedule of irrigation varies with fluctuations in soil moisture and the stage of development of the seedlings. Excessive watering is costly and may result in loss of nutrients through leaching. There is evidence that the ability of seedlings to resist drought after planting is increased if they are watered only moderately in the nursery (Wakeley, 1954). Reduction or cessation of irrigation in late summer accelerates the hardening of the seedlings before frost. However, water should not be deliberately withheld to the point of preventing normal growth. In general, it is better to apply a given amount of water in relatively large and infrequent applications than to distribute it in a large number of small doses. Evaporational losses are reduced by watering during the cooler parts of the day.

Seedlings of the northern conifers must often be grown under partial shade for the several months that elapse before they pass out of the succulent stage. This is done by putting various kinds of portable screens about a foot above the seedbeds. These screens should be removed as soon as danger of heat injury is past because full light is required for satisfactory growth. The danger of heat injury can sometimes be avoided more economically by watering the seedbeds lightly in sunny weather; such watering should commence as soon as the temperature of the soil surface reaches 120°F. There is no truth in the belief that conifer seedlings are seriously harmed by watering them when the sun is shining.

Protection Against Insects and Fungi

Protection of nursery seedbeds demands constant vigilance, quick action, and accurate knowledge of the pests. Most, but not all, of them can be controlled by the use of standard insecticides and fungicides applied at certain critical stages in the life cycles of the pests. Every forest nursery is certain to have dangerous insects and fungi, characteristic of the locality, which the nurseryman must learn to recognize and be prepared to combat on short notice. Particular attention should be given to the eradication of the alternate hosts of any stem rusts that may threaten conifers grown in the nursery.

Damping-off of young, succulent seedlings is one disease of almost universal occurrence. It is caused by a wide variety of weakly parasitic fungi that ordinarily infest organic debris. The means of control vary with the different groups of fungi. However, they tend to be most serious in soils with a pH higher than 5.5. Therefore, it is desirable to avoid the use of lime, fertilizers with basic reaction, or even alkaline sands and peats. Covering seed with clean, relatively sterile sand tends to reduce damping-off. The fungi ordinarily develop most rapidly in moist, shaded conditions and very dense seedbeds. Difficulties are reduced by any procedure, such as fall sowing, that favors prompt germination and produces relatively sturdy seedlings. A variety of organic fungicides applied to the seed are highly effective and the same materials can be sprayed on the soil to halt the spread of established infections. Sometimes it is necessary to acidify the soil with sulfuric acid or various sulfates and, in extreme cases, to sterilize the soil with the same fumigants and other chemicals used against weed seeds.

Detailed information about the pests and disorders of nursery stock may be found in treatises like those of Davis, Wright, and Hartley (1942), Craighead (1950), and Keen (1952), as well as in textbooks on entomology and pathology and manuals of nursery practice.

Lifting, Transplanting, and Pruning of Nursery Stock

Although seedlings may be dug out of seedbeds with spading forks it is more economical to use special machines where large quantities are involved. These devices consist essentially of metal blades that are drawn under the beds to loosen the soil and sever the longer roots of the seedlings. Men follow the lifter and carefully pull the loosened seedlings from the soil. It is important to note that even the most expert job of pulling seedlings still leaves some of the root tissue behind in the soil and that all the problems associated with the exposure of the roots start with lifting. It is significant that Schubert and Lanquist (1959) found that the survival of nursery stock was increased by spraying it with a water mist while it passed through a mobile piece of equipment designed to enable the packing of the nursery stock to be done immediately after lifting.

When there is need for stock sturdier than that which can be grown in the seedbeds, the seedlings are dug up and replanted in wide-spaced rows elsewhere in the nursery. This process is known as transplanting; trees produced by this method are called **transplants** to distinguish them from **seedlings** grown in the original seedbeds. Transplanting has the effect of making the root systems more compact with a larger number of fine lateral roots than found in seedlings; the tops of transplants are also bushier and sturdier than those of trees grown in crowded seedbeds. This rearrangement takes place if the plants are left to grow in the transplant beds for one or, less commonly, two years.

Hand transplanting can be done by inserting seedlings in notches along portable **transplant boards** in such manner that the roots hang down and can be placed against the vertical walls of shallow trenches before the soil is packed against them. However, the only way that forest planting stock can be transplanted at anything approaching reasonable cost is with modified agricultural transplanting machines. With such machines the seedlings are usually strung in spaced pockets on revolving disks which set the plants down into trenches where they are tamped in place by packing wheels.

Seedlings should be sheltered from sun and wind during transplanting. The operation is best performed in spring, when root growth is at a maximum; fall transplanting is inadvisable if there is risk of frost heaving. Transplant beds rarely need shading or watering. The interval between transplant rows should be absolutely uniform so as to facilitate mechanical cultivation.

Transplanting is so expensive that it has come to be general practice to grow seedlings at wide spacings in seedbeds so that they will become sturdy enough without transplanting. The use of petroleum sprays for weeding has done much to make this policy feasible. It is widely held that the survival of transplants in the field is not sufficiently superior to justify the cost of producing them, except where planting sites are very dry or brushy.

Root pruning is also a substitute for transplanting, although stock is most often sent into the field without either kind of treatment. Root pruning is usually done with thin, horizontal blades drawn under the beds at depths of 4 to 6 inches. The seedlings are then left to grow for another year.

The purposes of root pruning and transplanting are to reduce the over-all dimensions of the root systems without reducing their absorptive surface. It is not done because there is any advantage in having plants with small root systems. In fact, one of the main difficulties with even the best bare-rooted planting stock is that it ordinarily leaves the nursery with the root systems greatly reduced and badly damaged and the ability of the tops to respire and transpire scarcely diminished. Another way of bringing the tops into better balance with the roots is to prune the tops. This can be done by going over the seedbeds with mowing or shearing devices and clipping off the tops of the terminal shoots. If this is done when the shoots are succulent and actively growing, most conifers will promptly form new buds capable of developing into symmetrical, normal-appearing tops. This rather tricky process is usually resorted to only when the stock must be left in the nursery for another year and might otherwise become too large.

Sometimes it is desirable to trim the roots of lifted seedlings to eliminate long, stringy roots which are difficult to plant properly. This should not be considered unless the vertical lengths of the roots exceed the anticipated depth of the planting holes.

Grading of Nursery Stock

The primary classification of nursery stock depends on its age and treatment. These two characteristics are designated by two figures, the first showing the number of years through which the plants grew as seedlings, and the second the number of years they were grown as transplants. For example, "1-0" indicates a 1-year-old seedling which has not been transplanted; "2-1" designates a 3-year-old transplant grown 2 years as a seedling and 1 year as a transplant.

Before nursery stock is shipped into the field it should be culled over for the purpose of eliminating trees that will not survive after planting. It is always essential to remove plants infested with virulent insects or fungi, those which have been badly damaged in handling, and those with distinctly poor roots. Investigations of southern pines (Wakeley, 1954; Silker, 1960) and white spruce (Mullin, 1959) have shown that further segregation is an uncertain proposition. The main difficulty is that the remaining seedlings can be graded only on the basis of external appearance, although the important criteria are the internal physiological qualities. If the stock is to be planted by machine, it may be desirable to sort it into grades of uniform size to facilitate the work. However, uniformity of size is best achieved by uniformity of treatment in the seedbeds, or by separating the seeds into different classes of size and sowing them in separate beds.

It is generally unwise to attempt planting of conifers that have a basal stem diameter or caliper less than $5/64$ of an inch or a ratio, by weight, of top to root greater than 4 to 1. Standards for hardwood species vary widely but most of them should have a stem caliper greater than $6/64$ of an inch and be at least 8 inches tall.

The culling, grading, and counting of large volumes of stock is usually done on moving conveyer belts under shelter. This kind of handling of the stock should be done quickly, with a minimum of handling, and under such conditions that the drying of the roots is reduced as much as possible. It is possible to set up rapid means of counting seedlings individually or to develop procedures in which the numbers of trees ready for bundling are determined by weight on the basis of carefully drawn samples that are both weighed and counted.

Transportation and Storage of Nursery Stock

The use of bare-rooted stock is customary in forest planting on this continent. Balled stock, that is, trees transported with the original soil around the roots, is exceedingly expensive and is used in forestry only under special conditions. It is commonly employed in the tropics where the seedlings of many species become too large to plant several weeks after germination and so must be planted while still actively growing. Balled stock or that planted in pots of disintegrating materials is also used in very hot or dry climates (Goor, 1955; Parry, 1956).

If bare-rooted stock is to remain viable, respiration and transpiration must be held to a minimum during transit. It is for this reason that success usually depends on doing both lifting and planting during periods when the trees are dormant or nearly so. The crucial test is the ability of the roots to renew rapid growth after planting. Bare-rooted stock quickly loses this capacity if water and carbohydrates are squandered in transit because the tops are growing too actively or because the plants become too warm or dry.

Planting stock is usually shipped as bundles of plants wrapped in such manner as to keep the roots moist but with sufficient provision for ventilation to avoid heating from fungal activity. The traditional practice is to construct bales consisting of two tight bundles of trees arranged so that the tops are open to the air at each end with the roots of opposite facing bundles in close contact with each other. The roots are then protected with sphagnum moss or similar material, and the whole bales are wrapped in water-proof paper and burlap. However, polyethylene film is used increasingly (Mullin, 1958); because of its impermeability to water and permeability to carbon dioxide it can even be used to seal up the plants entirely without the inclusion of moss or other moist material (Duffield and Eide, 1959).

The most satisfactory way to store nursery stock, whether for a few days or over winter, is under refrigeration at temperatures slightly above the freezing point. The stock is stored after bundling; sometimes it remains in better condition if wrapped in polyethylene film.

Leafless hardwoods endure storage better than conifers. Storage of this sort is most commonly done to hold the stock dormant for a few weeks until planting sites in localities colder than the nursery become ready for planting. Seedlings lifted in the fall are stored over winter to plant on sites that become ready for planting in the spring before stock can be lifted in the nursery. Short-term storage is also useful in evening out the flow of operations during the brief shipping season. If facilities for refrigeration are lacking, stock can be kept for a few days in cool sheds or cellars. However, it is best to reduce the lapse of time between lifting and planting as much as possible.

Nursery Records

Efficient management of nurseries requires the maintenance of complete maps, records, inventories, and accounts of costs. It should be possible to determine the history of each seedbed in detail so that present developments can be interpreted in terms of past treatments. Occasional inventories must be made of the amount of stock in various stages of growth by random sampling of the beds (Mullin, Morrison, and Schweitzer, 1955). Records of the history of each lot of stock, from seed to packing shed, are indispensable for improvements in practice; whenever possible these histories should be extended to the plantations in the field. The annual schedule of operations should be carefully planned with particular reference to the unavoidable peak of activity in the spring. Olive and Umland (1952) described a system of cost accounting which they found useful in the management of nurseries.

Cost of Nursery Stock

The true costs (including public subsidies) of producing planting stock, vary widely and depend on costs of labor as well as the technique and efficiency of production. The southern pines, for example, are usually planted as 1-0 stock, which can be produced for approximately $5 per 1000. Northern conifers, which are usually planted as 3-0 seedlings, can be produced for roughly $8 to $12 per 1000 in large nurseries and for about $20 per 1000 in small operations. Transplants usually cost $18 to $30 per 1000.

FIELD PLANTING

Planting constitutes one of the most costly investments that can be made in the production of a forest crop. The success of a whole rotation is often determined by the soundness of decisions made at the time of planting. The act of establishing a plantation almost invariably commits the forester to subsequent operations designed to protect the investment. Errors made at the time of planting generally increase the amount of treatment necessary later on, and they are not often entirely corrected in the process. It is significant that mistakes in planting have been singled out as the most serious technical blunders committed during the formative period of American forest practice (Zon, 1951).

The only insuperable drawback of planting is the inevitable damage to the roots of the trees. This causes semipermanent malformations of the root systems which predispose the planted trees to root rots and other disorders the full importance of which is quite obscure (Gruschow, 1959). Most of the other difficulties are theoretically correctable.

Selection of Planting Stock

After the species to be planted has been chosen, the next decision concerns the size and age of stock. Actually latitude for choice exists only for species of slow juvenile growth. Some species grow so rapidly that nothing larger than 1-0 seedlings can be planted efficiently. The basic criterion of judgment is the total cost per established tree, which includes the expense of planting others that failed to survive.

The initial survival of planted trees depends chiefly on the ability of their root systems to re-establish contact with the soil promptly. This ability is primarily a function of the physiological condition of the plants; their size and other externally visible characteristics are actually important to survival only to whatever extent they reflect physiological condition. The ability of bare-rooted stock to regenerate roots can be controlled by the conditions of growth in the nursery, the care given to trees after lifting, and above all by the season of lifting and planting.

Costs of growing and planting nursery stock rise with increased age and size. Although size is not necessarily a good criterion of physiological condition, survival is often better with the larger kinds of planting stock. Plants with tops shorter than 4 inches are very unlikely to survive and those taller than 1 foot usually can be moved only as balled stock; the choice thus lies in the range from 4 to 12 inches.

Large and vigorous trees usually have abundant stores of carbohydrates which may be drawn upon while they are becoming established. Their more extensive root systems enable them to establish contact with a greater volume of soil than can smaller trees. On the other hand, their larger foliage area causes them to require more water and carbohydrates than the smaller trees, so these advantages are not entirely uncompensated. The comparatively great depth of the root system of a large plant is likely to ensure contact with the relatively stable moisture supply of the deeper soil layers. The thick bark and dense foliage of a large plant tends to afford protection against heat injury, a source of mortality that is sometimes fully as important as drought (Maguire, 1955). Deep-rooted plants are also less subject to frost heaving. Trees with very short tops may be so easily covered with fallen leaves, eroding soil, or other debris as to be unsuitable in some situations. Large planted trees are better adapted to competition with grass or low shrubs than smaller trees, although this advantage is of little consequence if the competing vegetation is tall. Small stock is, however, easier to plant and less liable to injury in handling.

The choice of size of planting stock usually lies between transplants and seedlings, although root-pruned seedlings sometimes represent an intermediate category. The rate of juvenile growth of the species is an important consideration. There has never been much question that the fast-grown 1-0 seedlings of the southern pines and many hardwoods could be planted at a cost per established tree lower than that of larger stock. At the other extreme, species like the spruces, which have very slow juvenile growth, usually give best results if planted as 2-2 transplants.

With species like the northern and western pines as well as Douglas-fir the decision must be based on the character of the planting site. Although the rate of survival of transplants is better than that of seedlings on most sites, 2-1 transplants cost three to five times as much as 2-0 seedlings (Rudolf, 1950a). Therefore, it is highly desirable to confine the use of transplants to situations where the survival of planted seedlings is very poor. These places are to be found on very dry soils, steep southerly or westerly slopes, and areas with heavy grass or brush competition. Situations of this kind are more common in regions of relatively dry climate, such as California, the interior of the West, and the Lake Region, than in coastal sections. The use of 2-0 Douglas-fir, often root-pruned, is more or less standard in the Pacific Northwest (Kummel, Rindt, and Munger, 1944). In the Northeast most conifers are planted as 3-0 seedlings and transplants are no longer used to any great extent.

The increasingly widespread use of seedlings has come about as much from improvements in methods of growing seedlings as from the desire to avoid the heavy costs of labor involved in transplanting. By using oil sprays for weeding it is economical to grow vigorous seedlings in seedbeds with a low density of stocking. As a consequence, the 2-0 and 3-0 seedlings that can be produced at present are larger and more vigorous than those that were held in low regard several decades ago. The practice of root-pruning makes it possible to duplicate some of the characteristics of transplants in seedling stock.

Natural seedlings, or **wildlings,** found in the forest are rarely as desirable as nursery-grown seedlings. It is usually expensive to collect them, and they often lack the vigor and good root systems needed in planting stock.

Density of Plantations

One of the advantages of artificial over natural reproduction lies in the closer control of the number and distribution of trees on each acre. The stocking of new plantations is most commonly thought of in terms of the spacing of individual trees. The optimum spacing is that which will produce the greatest volume of product in the size, form, and quality of trees required. The trees must be planted densely enough to allow a closed canopy in time to ensure the development of stems of acceptable form.

Several factors enter into the choice of the spacing interval. Trees in stands with wide spacing grow more rapidly than those planted on a narrower spacing. At any given age, they are larger in diameter and have greater taper, thicker branches, and crowns that are both deeper and wider than trees in densely stocked plantations (Adams and Chapman, 1942; Bramble, Cope, and Chisman, 1949; Eversole, 1955). These characteristics give wide-spaced trees the *appearance* of being somewhat shorter than those of densely stocked stands. Actually, most studies have indicated that growth in height is not significantly altered by spacing, at least within the range of density ordinarily chosen. There is a tendency for height growth to be reduced in exceedingly dense stands or in truly isolated trees.

In theory, the greatest *cubic* volume of wood is produced in those plantations that are just dense enough to achieve full occupancy of the site as early as possible without being so closely spaced that they suffer diminution of height growth. As spacings are widened beyond this optimum, production of cubic volume is lost because all stands remain understocked until the crowns or root systems close. *After* full stocking has been attained, production of total cubic volume tends to be the same regardless of what the initial spacing may have been. In other words, the difference in total production resulting from variations in spacing depends on the length of time that the new stand took to achieve full occupancy of the site. Therefore, the gross production of wood by stands planted at close spacing is usually greater than that of those planted at wide spacing (Satoo, Nakamura, and Senda, 1955).

Actually the objective is to achieve optimum yield of utilizable wood and not to maximize gross production in terms of *total* cubic volume or tonnage. All units of economic yield, such as cords, board feet, merchantable cubic feet, or utilizable tonnage, involve various minimum diameter limits. The greater the minimum diameter limit, the wider should be the spacing interval. In other words, an owner who desires the greatest yield in pulpwood larger than 8 inches should employ a wider spacing than one who sets a minimum top diameter of 5 inches. The ideal number of trees to plant on an acre is precisely the number that can be grown to the smallest size that can be utilized profitably. Under the economic conditions found in North America it is often necessary to plant more in order to ensure that the crop trees do not become wolf trees.

The question of whether early thinnings can be made profitably has an important bearing on the spacing. If they cannot be made, it is undesirable to have the stands close any earlier than is essential for the development of acceptable form. If early thinnings for small products are profitable, then it is advantageous to employ a narrow spacing in order to boost the yield from thinnings as high as possible. Consequently the owner who wishes to produce both saw logs and pulpwood should plant more trees per acre than he who plans on producing only saw logs.

Very wide spacing leads to the development of large branches and strongly tapered, poorly formed boles. Some of these disadvantages can be overcome by artificial pruning, the expense of which may be more than offset by the saving in planting costs. However, it must be borne in mind that the time required for pruning increases rapidly with the size of the branches. If a plantation does not close in early life the danger of invasion by competing vegetation is substantially increased. The risk of damage by fire, erosion, some insects, and certain other injurious agencies decreases abruptly when plantations close.

Choice of spacing depends to some extent on the characteristics of the species. Wide-crowned trees like loblolly pine should be planted on a wider spacing than those like longleaf pine, which has a relatively narrow crown (Ware and Stahelin, 1948). Hardwoods are best planted very close together in order to encourage the development of straight boles.

The primary advantage of wide spacing is the lower cost per acre of nursery stock and planting. The number of trees required for planting an acre varies inversely as the square of the average spacing interval. For example, an 8-by-8-foot spacing requires 681 trees per acre; 6-by-6, 1210; and 4-by-4, 2722.

The spacing of plantations is not something which should be regarded as rigid for each species or locality. The opportunity to vary initial spacing of plantations provides fully as important a means of manipulating the development of stands as the related technique of thinning. The spacing should be determined for each situation and based on such considerations as site, growth habit of the species, expected survival, product objectives, future silvicultural treatment, and the kind of logging equipment likely to be used in future cuttings. In most situations, the average spacing interval will not be closer than 6 feet nor wider than 10 feet. Planting for erosion control, where quick closure is desired, may be as close as 3-by-3 feet. For very small products like Christmas trees a 4-foot interval is often employed.

There is no reason why the trees have to be planted in squares provided that the distribution is reasonably even. Where trees are planted with machines or in furrows created by plowing, it is cheaper to set the trees at 5-foot intervals in the rows with a distance of 10 feet between rows than to plant approximately the same number at a spacing of 7-by-7 feet. This arrangement also has the advantage of leaving avenues for extracting the products of thinnings. The rectangular arrangement does lead to the development of crowns that are ellipsoidal in horizontal cross section, but this is not a serious drawback.

Regularity of spacing should not be pursued to the exclusion of other considerations. Deviations from the spacing pattern are fully justified if patches of poor soil or competing vegetation can be avoided or if trees can be placed on the shady sides of obstacles like stumps or logs. The effect of natural obstacles and mortality among the planted trees always reduces the initial stocking below the figure theoretically indicated by a given interval of spacing and should be taken into account in planning operations.

Mixed Plantations

Planting provides an excellent opportunity to control the composition of the new stand. The establishment of planted mixtures of species is entirely feasible and sometimes has important advantages. The arrangement and subsequent treatment of mixed plantations require forethought and skill. These considerations, as well as the relative merits of pure and mixed stands, are described in Chapter 16.

Season of Planting

Success in planting bare-rooted trees depends on putting the trees in the soil during or immediately before periods of active root elongation (Stone and Schubert, 1959). Trees are usually so adapted that such periods come at the times of year when both the temperature and moisture content of the soil are at favorable levels. The period of most rapid growth of roots occurs in the spring, usually just before the buds break dormancy. This is also the period when, in most climates, the soil moisture is most certain to be adequate and when the plants are emerging from a clearly defined condition of dormancy. Therefore, stock planted early in the spring can make contact with the soil more swiftly than at any other time.

If soil moisture is adequate, there is usually another period of moderately active root growth in the fall so that trees that have hardened and formed buds can then be planted with fair success. Planting during the period of active top growth in late spring and summer is inadvisable because of the rapid transpiration and respiration of young tissues and the prevalence of hot, dry weather; root growth is slow during the summer at least on sites that tend to become dry at that time (Stevens, 1931; Turner, 1936). The seasonal pattern of root growth is not the same in all species. For example, Baldwin (1938) found that fall planting was successful for white pine and spruces but not for red and Scotch pine in New Hampshire.

Planting cannot be carried out during freezing weather because the bare roots of the stock are easily killed if frozen. Insecurely established trees are also highly susceptible to winter injury; this kind of damage is caused by unseasonably warm winds which dry out the foliage of conifers rooted in frozen soil. The impossibility of planting in snow-covered or frozen soil obviously precludes winter planting in many regions.

In the Gulf States, planting is confined to the mild winter, although operations must be suspended during freezing weather; the tops are dormant but root growth continues during December and January which are the best months for planting (Wakeley, 1954). In the

North and West, early spring is clearly the best season, although planting of some species can be resumed on certain sites in the fall as soon as the soil becomes thoroughly moistened.

One of the disadvantages of fall planting is that the trees do not have long to establish contact with the soil and are subsequently susceptible to frost heaving and winter injury. The risk of frost heaving is reduced if the soil is sandy or covered by an undisturbed mat of grass or other low vegetation. A deep, persistent cover of snow reduces both frost heaving and winter injury.

There is also evidence that conifers continue to store carbohydrates in the nursery until the beginning of winter. Therefore, trees lifted in spring have more stored materials than those lifted in fall.

Fall planting is advantageous only to the extent that it enables better distribution of the seasonal work load in the nursery and in the field.

Site Preparation

Successful planting often depends on such measures as the reduction of competing vegetation, the removal of physical obstacles to planting, and the drainage of water toward or away from the planted trees (see Chapters 5 and 10). The control of competing vegetation is especially important because many planting sites are already crowded with undesirable plants. Unless a distinct vacancy is found or created in the growing space it is very difficult for a planted tree to survive or grow satisfactorily. Even a cover of grass offers much more serious competition than might be inferred from its low stature.

In the era before the availability of herbicides and powerful land-clearing equipment, only minimal measures were possible. Many plantings failed; more started slowly as the trees struggled upward through masses of competing vegetation. This situation need no longer be endured, although drastic measures do not always provide the optimum balance between cost and benefit. It is, in any event, more economical to attack the problems *before* planting than to attempt corrective action after the planted trees are in the way.

When special measures for site preparation cannot be used, the more expensive method of hand **scalping** at the time of planting may be employed if necessary. This involves scraping away undesirable vegetation from spots one or two feet square around the places where the trees are to be planted. It is moderately effective in thick grass or very low brush and is best done with the same grub hoes used in planting.

Methods of Planting

The methods of planting trees in the field are numerous, varying widely in the technique and the tools used. All, however, are designed to set the plants in such a way as to ensure a high rate of survival at reasonable cost under different local conditions.

Successful planting depends on the ability of the roots of the planted trees to regain contact with the soil so that the uptake of water and nutrients can resume. The first essential is that the roots be placed in soil in which water is immediately available; the moisture content must be well above wilting coefficient and the soil temperature must be sufficiently far above the freezing point that water can move readily. Moist mineral soil is by far the most dependable source; organic materials are not reliable unless they are peats and mucks situated so that they remain close to saturation without being deficient in oxygen.

When bare-rooted stock is lifted from the nursery virtually all of the mycorrhizal mycelia and root hairs that constitute the main absorptive portion of the roots are destroyed. Until these unicellular strands resume proliferation the plant has no means of absorbing water that is not immediately adjacent to the existing roots. Fortunately suberized roots can absorb water directly (Kramer and Kozlowski, 1960), thus providing planted trees with an immediate, but limited, supply of water. Presumably this is one of the reasons why it is so essential that the soil be solidly packed around the roots of planted trees.

Until the main absorbing network redevelops the planted tree has only slightly more ability to capture moisture than a cut flower in water. The development of new root hairs depends on the elongation of root tips, many of which are broken off during lifting. New root tips must form before any major portion of the permanent and readily visible part of the root system can extend itself in the soil. The root system of a planted tree elongates rapidly only during rather limited periods when the normal physiological rhythm of growth is directed toward this process. It is, furthermore, reasonable to suppose that such elongation of the roots will not become very active until photosynthesis becomes vigorous again. Since this is not likely to occur until resumption of active absorption of water and nutrients, any complete dependence on elongation of root tips and on absorption by root hairs would seem to jeopardize survival of planted trees.

Mycorrhizal mycelia are probably much more effective than root hairs in re-establishing early contact with the soil. The fungi that are involved need only a supply of reserve foods from the plant and the proper conditions of moisture and temperature to resume growth; consequently they are not dependent on the resumption of full activity by the whole plant. It is significant that most tree species normally enter into mycorrhizal relationships and very often do not survive planting unless the appropriate fungi were present in the nursery and caused the formation of mycorrhizae on the roots of the planting stock (Wright, 1957). There are numerous instances in which the planting of exotic species has become spectacularly successful, after earlier failures, as soon as the proper fungi were introduced in the nurseries.

The ability of the absorptive system to redevelop is diminished more than appearances would suggest because so many bare roots die between lifting and planting. The roots closest to the root collar appear to be more likely to survive than those farther from the stem.

Trees should ordinarily be planted at the same depth they occupied in the nursery with the roots spread out in a manner as natural as possible. The roots should also be arranged so that none of them turn upward.

When the roots are longer than can be conveniently planted, the lower portions may be pruned. Every precaution should be taken to ensure that the roots of the planting stock remain visibly moist at all stages of handling. Soil, as moist and fresh as available, should be firmly packed around the roots. The holes in which the trees are planted should be filled completely, leaving no air spaces. Litter or other organic debris should not be used for filling the holes unless the soil itself is organic. The trees should be planted firmly enough to resist a gentle tug with thumb and forefinger.

Trees are usually planted with stems erect and roots spread out in a vertical plane. It is not necessary that the stems be absolutely erect because they straighten up shortly after planting. However, substantial deviation from the vertical has the effect of reducing the depth of the roots. It has sometimes been recommended that trees, particularly seedlings, be deliberately planted in an oblique plane rather than vertically (Moulopoulos, 1947). It is claimed that this technique enables the soil to be packed more firmly around the roots and that the trees, if slanted toward the south, shield their own bases from the sun.

The placement of the roots in a vertical or nearly vertical plane is distinctly unnatural and may be disadvantageous. It is least desirable in species like the spruces which have roots that characteristically grow in a horizontal plane. There are methods of planting by hand which make it possible to arrange the roots of such species laterally rather than horizontally; they are often used in Europe (British Forestry Commission, 1958) and it is probable that more attention should be given to their use on this continent. Any sort of placement of the root systems in planting is unnatural. Some roots almost always die after they have grown a while and they are replaced by new roots arranged in positions better adapted to the soil. However, many abnormalities of arrangement persist indefinitely.

The methods of planting bare-rooted trees have been divided by Toumey and Korstian (1942) into two general categories. In the **compression methods** a hole is made for the plant by pushing the soil aside with a sharp instrument driven into the ground; after the tree is inserted the soil is pressed back around its roots. In the **dug-hole methods** the soil is actually removed and piled at one side to be packed in around the roots after the tree is placed in the hole. An excellent account of most of the tools and the details of their use has been prepared by Rudolf (1950a).

Several types of heavy dibbles or planting bars, one of which is shown in Fig. 7-3, have been developed for use in planting relatively small seedlings in sandy soils. All operations involved in the use of this tool follow the principle of the compression method, as shown in Fig. 7-4. The technique is known as the **bar-slit method.** In this kind of planting one must be careful to shake the roots of the tree down so that they lie vertically and then hold them in this position while the slit is closed. This is the fastest method of planting trees

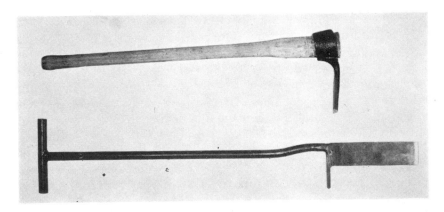

Fig. 7-3. Two types of tools commonly used for planting trees. The upper tool is an ordinary grub hoe; the lower, a planting bar designed for planting by the compression method. (*Photograph by Yale University School of Forestry.*)

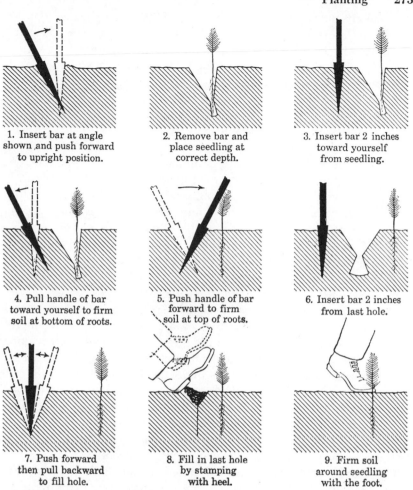

1. Insert bar at angle
shown and push forward
to upright position.

2. Remove bar and
place seedling at
correct depth.

3. Insert bar 2 inches
toward yourself
from seedling.

4. Pull handle of bar
toward yourself to firm
soil at bottom of roots.

5. Push handle of bar
forward to firm
soil at top of roots.

6. Insert bar 2 inches
from last hole.

7. Push forward
then pull backward
to fill hole.

8. Fill in last hole
by stamping
with heel.

9. Firm soil
around seedling
with the foot.

Fig. 7-4. Steps in the use of the bar-slit method of planting seedlings in sandy soil. (*Sketch by U. S. Forest Service.*)

by hand; according to Rudolf, an experienced crew can set out an average of 1500 trees per man-day with planting bars.

On soils that are stony or have such a high clay content that they become compact under true compression, a modified compression method can be employed. Grub hoes (Fig. 7-3) are used for this method, which is called the **grub-hoe-slit** or **mattock-slit method** (Lynch, 1952). This technique differs from the true compression method only in that the soil is partially lifted from the hole rather than merely pushed aside. An average of 700 trees per man-day can be planted by this method. One advantage of the grub hoe is that it can be used for scalping whereas planting bars cannot.

Where unrooted cuttings or seedlings with a single stiff root are to be planted, a tool made from a round bar of uniform diameter is cheap and efficient, particularly in heavy soils. Maisenhelder (1951) has described such a bar, either $\frac{1}{4}$ or $\frac{1}{2}$ inch in diameter, for planting cuttings and seedlings of cottonwood.

The main drawback of the compression method is the difficulty of being certain that the holes are completely closed or that the roots of the seedlings are free of U-shaped bends. These problems can be partially avoided by refraining from working the blades of the tools back and forth after driving them into the soil. The holes created as a result of this error are shaped like hourglasses in vertical cross section; it is difficult to work the roots past the constriction and impossible to be certain that the lowest part of the hole is closed. Even the grub-hoe modification of the compression method may be difficult to apply in soils that are very stony or cohesive.

The dug-hole methods must be used where the compression methods fail to give good results. Grub hoes are usually employed in this method, sometimes with one man digging the holes and another doing the planting. The holes are made sufficiently wide and deep to accommodate the roots of the trees. The mineral soil is piled beside the hole separate from leaves, sod, and other debris to facilitate planting and to ensure the use of clean soil next to the roots. The trees are planted entirely by hand immediately after the holes are dug so that the exposed soil will not become desiccated. There are several different methods of shaping the holes and planting the trees.

The simplest dug-hole method is called the **side-hole method** (Fig. 7-5). One side of the hole is left smooth and vertical; the roots are spread out against this wall and packed firmly in place by hand with a thin layer of fresh, loose soil. The rest of the mineral soil is then scraped into the hole and trodden down with the heel. Usually the area around the hole is scalped before the hole is dug so that the tree will not be immediately adjacent to competing vegetation. The side-hole method can be used to ensure satisfactory planting under any conditions. The only technical disadvantage is the fact that the roots are placed in a vertical plane. However, it is not a rapid method because it ordinarily takes a man-day to plant about 600 trees (Rudolf, 1950a).

The best technique for ensuring good placement of roots in three

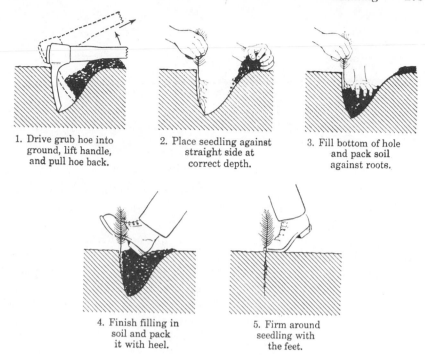

1. Drive grub hoe into
   ground, lift handle,
   and pull hoe back.

2. Place seedling against
   straight side at
   correct depth.

3. Fill bottom of hole
   and pack soil
   against roots.

4. Finish filling in
   soil and pack
   it with heel.

5. Firm around
   seedling with
   the feet.

Fig. 7-5. The side-hole method of planting. (*Sketch adapted from one by U. S. Forest Service.*)

dimensions is the **center-hole method.** This involves placing the tree in the middle of the hole then sifting and packing the loose soil between the various strands of roots, without forcing them into either a vertical or horizontal plane. Only about 200 trees can be planted in a man-day by this method.

The same general effect can be produced more swiftly by the so-called **wedge method.** The objective of this procedure is to create a hole with a ridge in the middle such that a vertical cross section would resemble the letter W (Fig. 7-6). Half of the roots of the tree are spread out on each sloping surface and tamped down in that position. Rudolf (1950a) described how the holes could be made with several strokes of a grub hoe and stated that 500 trees per man-day could be planted by this method. This procedure is well adapted to the planting of species like the spruces which have distinctly horizontal root systems.

Perfectly horizontal placement of roots can be achieved by such

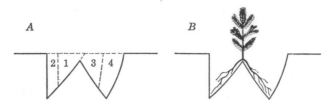

Fig. 7-6. The wedge method of planting as described by Rudolf (1950a). *A* shows the sequence in which soil is removed by four strokes of a grub hoe to create the hole. *B* shows the tree ready to be tamped in place.

techniques as making T-shaped incisions in turf with spades, turning up the resulting flaps, spreading out the roots of the tree, and then tamping the flaps back over them.

Planting is often done after the preliminary furrowing of areas covered with grass sod or peaty materials (Shipman, 1958). It may take some experimentation to determine the best position to plant the trees after such treatment. The competing vegetation is killed not only in the furrow but also beneath the overturned sod. Some of the top soil and other superficial layers rich in nutrients are likely to have been removed from the troughs and concentrated beneath the ridges at the sides. The best compromise between freedom from competition and availability of good soil conditions is often obtained by planting the trees along the lines where the ridges and troughs intersect. The summits of the ridges are favorable only where the soil is very poorly drained and would possibly not have supported tree growth without the furrowing. The bottoms of the furrows may be most favorable in dry, deep soils, especially where plows with double moldboards have been used to turn the competing vegetation off to the side in both directions.

Although they have rarely been applied in America, a variety of techniques have been developed in Mediterranean countries to increase the survival of trees in dry climates (Goor, 1955). These include the planting of trees in various kinds of basins and terraces designed to catch surface runoff and the practice of putting stones around the trees (Rotty, 1958) to shade the stems, redistribute water from rains, and to restrict evaporation from the soil. These treatments increase the amount of hand labor but greatly improve the survival of planted trees in climates like those of the American Southwest.

Most forest planting is done with various planting machines which operate on the principle of the compression method. These machines

Fig. 7-7. The essential parts of a tree-planting machine. The round cutting disk or coulter at right cuts through roots and sod ahead of the split plowshare or trencher. The trees are put down in the slit made by the trencher between the two wings or guides at its back end. They are then tamped in place by two rubber-tired wheels mounted at the rear of the machine. (*Photograph by Louisiana Forestry Commission.*)

cut a narrow trench through the ground by means of a specially designed plowshare (Fig. 7-7). The trees are placed in the slot just behind this trencher and the soil is pressed firmly back into place by two wheels which are mounted close together at the rear of the machine. Some of these machines are designed for use on slopes, brushy ground, or soils which are encumbered with roots and stones; many such sites are unfortunately too difficult to be planted with machinery.

Planting machines have been used most extensively on level, open areas of sandy soils in the South and the Lake Region. They can plant from 5000 to 15,000 trees per day, depending on site conditions, and represent by far the most economical method of planting large areas. Various brush-clearing devices or plows are often fitted onto the tractors that draw the planting machines so that site preparation and planting are accomplished simultaneously. Except where the soil is rocky or full of other impediments, the quality of planting done by machines is at least as good as that done by hand by ordinary labor. Even if machine planting cost as much per tree as hand planting, which it does not, it would still be the better method simply because

Fig. 7.8. A wheeled tractor fitted with a lug bar being used to facilitate hand planting by the side-hole method on an abandoned field in New Hampshire. (*Photograph by U. S. Forest Service.*)

so many more acres can be planted in short periods when the work can be done.

Hand planting can, however, be greatly expedited if the planting holes are dug by machines. There has been some experimentation with motor-driven soil augers for this purpose. So far the greatest success has been with the use of various special lugs attached to the tracks or wheels of tractors (Powell, 1948; Anderson, 1957). As the tractors move along the lugs leave holes behind as they are lifted out of the ground; a crew follows planting trees by the side-hole method (Fig. 7-8).

Care of Planting Stock in the Field

If it becomes necessary to store planting stock after it is received from the nursery, it is better to store it in the original bundles in cool places, as previously described, than to store it in the field. As an emergency measure, it can also be heeled in on the planting site and taken out as needed. **Heeling-in** consists of storing planting stock in a trench dug in moist soil with a smooth, vertical or slanting side as deep as the roots of the trees are long. The plants are put in this trench in a relatively thin layer and covered with soil up to the root collars. Protection from sun and wind is essential. Ordinarily a day's supply of planting stock, if kept shaded and moist while on the planting site, will be damaged less in the original bundles than if heeled in.

The trees can be carried in pails, baskets, bags, or trays by the planting crews. It is essential that the roots of the planting stock remain moist until planted. Moss, a puddle of wet mud, or other material for keeping the roots moist is often placed in the container.

Protection of New Plantations

Plantations are fully as subject to damage from biotic and atmospheric agencies as natural stands in the same stage of development. It is an open question whether they are more subject to injury. Losses in artificially regenerated stands represent greater wastage of direct investment than comparable damage in stands that have been reproduced naturally. The large investment in plantations requires a correspondingly heavy outlay for protection which should be regarded as part of the cost of artificial regeneration (Boyce, 1954).

Wild animals are an important cause of damage to plantations. Although there are no certain measures of control, it is generally best to attack the problem by indirect means. Rodents tend to prefer dense cover and can sometimes be discouraged by eliminating brush before planting. Temporary reductions of the rodent population may be achieved by distributing poisons on the planting area or applying them directly to the stems of the trees. Progress in the development of effective repellants for use against larger animals has been slow, but some compounds now on the market are occasionally satisfactory (Duncan and Whitaker, 1959). Another solution is to avoid planting in places or during years of high population of the most damaging animals. The use of fences against wild animals is common in Europe but usually far too costly under American conditions.

Damage by domestic grazing animals may be controlled by proper herding or fencing, depending on the custom of the locality. Sometimes livestock can be lured away from planted areas by putting out salt elsewhere.

One of the most important causes of plantation failure is the competition of woody vegetation. All too often plantations are established and then left to fend for themselves. Even those made in open areas can be overwhelmed by fast-growing vegetation that may seed in after planting. The costs of releasing plantations can be reduced by avoiding the temptation to plant up brushy areas or spots adjacent to clumps of existing trees. The underplanting of trees beneath brush or existing stands of trees involves a definite commitment to carry out subsequent release cuttings. This procedure should not be undertaken without due consideration for the possibility that labor and funds may not be available for release cutting when needed.

The holes created in new plantations by scattered losses can sometimes be remedied by subsequent planting, or, **refilling.** Replacement of losses should not be undertaken unless the ultimate value of the plantation is distinctly threatened by understocking. Refilling should be carried out before the surviving trees commence to grow rapidly in height. Since most losses occur during the first growing season, the ideal time for refilling comes a year after the original planting. It is usually a waste of effort to refill a plantation more than several years old because the original survivors will retain their initial advantage in competition. Relatively large stock should be used in refilling, and it should be planted in such manner as to avoid the cause of previous failure.

Cost of Planting

The cost of planting varies widely, depending on such factors as cost of labor, planting stock, equipment, site preparation, and treatment subsequent to planting. At one extreme are the open areas on the South Atlantic Coastal Plain which can be restocked with 1-0 seedlings planted by machine at costs of less than $15 per acre. At the other extreme, and in the same locality, are situations in which so much site preparation is necessary that costs as high as $60 per acre are not only common but expended on large areas. In the North and West, where older and more expensive planting stock must be used, costs of planting, exclusive of site preparation, are seldom less than $20 per acre and, where hand planting is involved, are often around $40 per acre.

There is obviously considerable latitude for judgment in the application of a technique with such variable costs, especially when the benefits are so long delayed. Planting is such a soul-satisfying operation that its economic analysis is often overlooked. On the other hand, there are situations where it is arbitrarily viewed as impractical and consequently not even considered when it might actually be the key to success. The most important considerations, among the many that normally affect intensity of silvicultural practice, are the inherent site quality and the existing vegetation.

Planting Sites

Distinction should be drawn between planting for the production of profitable crops and the reforestation of degraded areas to prevent erosion and similar sources of injury to adjacent lands. Where the goal is production of wood crops, operation should commence on the areas that can be planted most profitably. If the objective is protection of the soil, the first areas treated should be those that are the source of greatest damage.

The most profitable places for planting are good sites free of competing vegetation. The schedule of priorities for planting open areas can be based on the characteristics of the soils. Various methods for predicting site index from the semipermanent properties of soils and other measurable site factors have been widely used (Coile, 1952). The pre-existing vegetation often serves as a good indicator of site quality. Where conversion from one forest type to another is contemplated, the site index of the existing tree species may provide a simple integrated expression of the site factors useful in predicting the site index of the desired species (Foster, 1959). The approach to site classification proposed by Hills and Pierpoint (1960) provides a good framework for consideration of all the site factors that might be taken into account. This general line of approach is useful not only in determining the site quality for a given species but also in choosing the proper species (Anderson, 1950).

In general, the areas most in need of reforestation from the standpoint of protecting the land are also likely to be free of woody vegetation. It is rare that a good case can be made for planting areas already clothed with dense brush or forest for the sole purpose of protecting soil or watersheds. Consequently open areas have first priority for planting, regardless of the purpose, and the remaining areas may be judged almost entirely on the basis of the profits to be derived from wood production after planting. Ordinarily the next areas to be planted will be those stocked with shrubs or plants that cannot produce useful products. Next in line come areas now supporting stands which are capable of producing merchantable material but which could be used for growing more valuable species. Finally there are the areas now stocked with good stands which could be improved still further or regenerated more expeditiously by planting than by natural means.

Application of Planting

For many decades forest planting in North America was used almost exclusively as a means of reforesting abandoned agricultural lands, burns, and other open areas where dependence could not be placed on natural regeneration. This essential first task is yet far from complete and there are still many localities in which this is still almost the only objective of planting.

Forest planting is cheap in the South, and more is done there than in all other regions put together. Most of the wholesale planting of pine in the South is still concentrated on the extensive open, grassy areas that have been created there. However, the second phase, the use of site preparation and planting to convert large areas of poor hardwoods to pine stands, is now well underway. The third phase, the use of planting to replace good stands of pine with pine, is more often planned and talked of than applied.

There is no reason to suppose that these "phases" should follow one another on any rigid basis. In the Douglas-fir Region, planting is employed chiefly in reforesting old burns and in expediting harvesting and regeneration of old-growth areas where it is difficult to compromise between efficient logging and dependable natural regeneration. Planting is seldom employed there for type conversion and may prove to be less useful for regeneration of second-growth stands than it is for replacement of old-growth. In the northeastern quarter of the United States and adjacent Canada, planting is still used primarily for reforestation of old fields and for Christmas tree production. It is becoming increasingly important in type conversion where poor hardwoods, such as the extensive stands of off-site aspen in the Lake Region, now abound. However, natural regeneration of good stands is usually viewed as sufficiently dependable that the substitution of planting will remain uncommon until this attitude changes, if it ever does.

Owing to their rapid growth and the relative ease with which they can be planted conifers are likely to remain far more important than the hardwoods in planting. In the regions where hardwoods occur naturally, most of the areas to be reforested are abandoned agricultural lands covered with grass and other herbaceous growth. Planted hardwoods do not thrive on these sites (Lane and McComb, 1948). Sometimes the best way to create hardwood stands on sod is to plant conifers and then await the natural establishment of a deciduous understory (DenUyl, 1951). If the soil is not too heavy for such use of planted conifers, this procedure may be desirable merely to forestall the development of the stands of poorly formed trees that often appear when hardwood species slowly recolonize grassy areas. The sequence of one rotation of mediocre conifers followed by one of hardwoods of seedling origin is infinitely superior to that of one rotation of wolf trees succeeded by hardwoods of sprout origin.

Hardwood plantations can make satisfactory growth on barren areas created by erosion, recent cultivation, site preparation, or the deposition of overburden from open-pit mining. They will also grow well on cutover lands and brushy areas that are free of grass, provided that the competition of shrubs and coppice shoots is kept under control.

The methods of planting for control of erosion and related objectives sometimes differ considerably from those of ordinary planting. Much attention has been given to the problems of revegetating banks of overburden left behind in strip-mining (Limstrom, 1960). Accounts of the techniques of stabilizing gullies in the Piedmont Region of the South were presented by Meginnis (1933) and Broadfoot (1951). The planting of shelterbelts in the Great Plains was described by George (1948) and by Read (1958).

REFERENCES

Adams, W. R., and G. L. Chapman. 1942. Competition in some coniferous plantations. *Vt. AES Bul.* 489.

Allen, G. S. 1957. Storage behavior of conifer seeds in sealed containers held at 0°F, 32°F, and room temperature. *J. Forestry* 55:278–281.

Anderson, K. 1957. An improved device for planting tree seedlings. *J. Forestry* 55:215–216.

Anderson, M. L. 1950. *The selection of tree species: An ecological basis of site classification for conditions found in Great Britain and Ireland.* Oliver and Boyd, Edinburgh.

Baldwin, H. I. 1938. Comparison of spring and fall planting. *N. H. Forestry and Recreation Dept., Fox Forest Note* 8.

————. 1942. *Forest tree seed.* Chronica Botanica, Waltham, Mass.

Baldwin, H. I., and G. D. Holmes. 1955. Handling forest tree seed. *FAO Forestry Development Paper* 4.

Boyce, J. S. 1954. Forest plantation protection against diseases and insect pests. *FAO Forestry Development Paper* 3.

Bramble, W. C., H. N. Cope, and H. H. Chisman. 1949. Influence of spacing on growth of red pine in plantations. *J. Forestry* 47:726–732.

British Forestry Commission. 1958. Forestry practice. *Forestry Commission Bul.* 14.

Broadfoot, W. M. 1951. Forest planting sites in north Mississippi and west Tennessee. *SFES Occasional Paper* 120.

Ching, T. M., and M. C. Parker. 1958. Hydrogen peroxide for rapid viability tests of some coniferous tree seeds. *Forest Sci.* 4:128–134.

Coile, T. S. 1952. Soil and the growth of forests. *Advances in Agronomy* 4:329–398.

Craighead, F. C. 1950. Insect enemies of eastern forests. *USDA Misc. Pub.* 657.

Crocker, W. 1948. *Growth of plants; Twenty years' research at Boyce Thomson Institute.* Reinhold, New York. Pp. 28–138.

Crocker, W., and L. V. Barton. 1953. *Physiology of seeds.* Chronica Botanica, Waltham, Mass.

Davis, W. C., E. Wright, and C. Hartley. 1942. Diseases of forest-tree nursery stock. *U. S. Civilian Conservation Corps, Forestry Pub. 9.*

DenUyl, D. 1951. From field to forest—a 50-year record. *J. Forestry* 49: 698–704.

Duffield, J. W., and E. B. Snyder. 1958. Benefits from hybridizing American forest tree species. *J. Forestry* 56:809–815.

Duffield, J. W., and R. P. Eide. 1959. Polyethylene bag packaging of conifer planting stock in the Pacific Northwest. *J. Forestry* 57:578–579.

Duncan, D. A., and L. B. Whitaker. 1959. Cattle repellents for planted pines. *USFS Tree Planters' Note* 36:9–12.

Engstrom, H. E., and J. H. Stoeckeler. 1941. Nursery practice for trees and shrubs suitable for planting on the prairie-plains. *USDA Misc. Pub.* 434.

Eversole, K. R. 1955. Spacing tests in a Douglas-fir plantation. *Forest Sci.* 1:14–18.

Foster, R. W. 1959. Relation between site indexes of eastern white pine and red maple. *Forest Sci.* 5:279–291.

Fowells, H. A. 1949. An index of ripeness for sugar pine seed. *CFRES Forest Research Note* 64.

George, E. J. 1948. Spacing distances for windbreak trees on the northern Great Plains. *USDA Circ.* 770.

Goor, A. Y. 1955. Tree planting practices for arid areas. *FAO Forestry Development Paper* 6.

Grano, C. X. 1958. Tetrazolium chloride to test loblolly pine seed viability. *Forest Sci.* 4:50–53.

Gruschow, G. F. 1959. Observations on root systems of planted loblolly pine. *J. Forestry* 57:894–896.

Hawley, R. C., and H. J. Lutz. 1943. Establishment, development, and management of conifer plantations in the Eli Whitney Forest, New Haven, Connecticut. *Yale Univ. School of Forestry Bul.* 53.

Hills, G. A., and G. Pierpoint. 1960. Forest site evaluation in Ontario. *Ont. Dept. Lands and Forests Research Rept.* 42.

Hoekstra, P. E., E. P. Merkel, and H. R. Powers, Jr. 1961. Production of seeds of forest trees. *In: Seeds. USDA Yearbook of Agr.* 1961. Pp. 227–232.

Holmes, G. D., and G. Buszewicz. 1958. The storage of seed of temperate forest tree species. *Forestry Abst.* 19:313–322, 455–476.

Hosner, J. F., R. K. Dickson, and L. Kahler. 1959. Storing loblolly pine seed in polyethylene bags for stratification. *J. Forestry* 57:495–496.

Hough, A. F. 1952. Relationships of red pine seed source, seed weight, seedling weight, and height growth in Kane Test Plantation. *NEFES Paper* 50.

Keen, F. P. 1952. Insect enemies of western forests. *USDA Misc. Pub.* 273 (rev.).

Kramer, P. J., and T. T. Kozlowski. 1960. *Physiology of trees.* McGraw-Hill, New York.

Kummel, J. F., C. A. Rindt, and T. T. Munger. 1944. *Forest planting in the Douglas-fir region.* United States Forest Service, Portland, Ore.

LaCroix, J. D., and A. T. Guard. 1958. Controlled environmental conditions influencing the effects of petroleum naphtha on slash pine seedlings. *J. Forestry* 56:348–349.

Lane, R. D., and A. L. McComb. 1948. Wilting and soil moisture depletion by tree seedlings and grass. *J. Forestry* 46:344–349.

Langdon, O. G. 1958. Cone and seed size of south Florida slash pine and their effects on seedling size and survival. *J. Forestry* 56:122–127.

Lanquist, K. B. 1959. Portable automatic cone kiln. *USFS Tree Planters' Note* 35:10–14.

Larsen, C. S. 1956. *Genetics in silviculture.* Transl. by M. L. Anderson. Oliver and Boyd, Edinburgh.

Limstrom, G. A. 1960. Forestation of strip-mined land in the Central States. *USDA Agr. Handbook* 166.

Lindquist, B. 1948. *Genetics in Swedish forestry practice.* Chronica Botanica, Waltham, Mass.

Lynch, D. W. 1952. Forest tree planting in the Inland Empire. *NRMFRES Misc. Pub.* 5.

Maguire, W. P. 1955. Radiation, surface temperature, and seedling survival. *Forest Sci.* 1:277–285.

Maisenhelder, L. C. 1951. Planting and growing cottonwood on bottomlands. *Miss. AES Bul.* 485.

Malac, B. F. 1960. More on stratification of pine seed in polyethylene bags. *USFS Tree Planters' Note* 42:7–9.

May, J. T. 1958. Soil management in southern pine nurseries. *Mich. State AES, Proc. First No. Am. Forest Soils Conf.*:141–146.

Meginnis, H. G. 1933. Using soil-binding plants to reclaim gullies in the South. *USDA Farmers' Bul.* 1697.

Mergen, F. 1959. Forest tree breeding research. *Unasylva* 13:81–88, 129–137.

Moulds, F. R. 1957. Exotics can succeed in forestry as in agriculture. *J. Forestry* 55:563–566.

Moulopoulos, C. 1947. High summer temperatures and reforestation technique in hot and dry countries. *J. Forestry* 45:884–893.

Mullin, R. E. 1958. An experiment with wrapping materials for bales of nursery stock. *Ont. Dept. Lands and Forests Research Rept.* 37.

———. 1959. An experiment on culling and grading of white spruce nursery stock. Part A. The percentage of cull. *Ont. Dept. Lands and Forests Research Rept.* 38.

Mullin, R. E., L. M. Morrison, and T. T. Schweitzer. 1955. Inventory of nursery stock. *Ont. Dept. Lands and Forests Research Rept.* 33.

Nienstaedt, H., et al. 1958. Vegetative propagation in forest genetics research and practice. *J. Forestry* 56:826–839.

Olive, C. L., Jr., and C. B. Umland. 1952. Cost accounting in TVA nurseries. *J. Forestry* 50:831–833.

Parry, M. S. 1956. Tree planting practices in tropical Africa. *FAO Forestry Development Paper* 8.

Pein, E. 1953. *Forstsamen-Gewinnung und Forstpflanzen-Ansucht in den USA und in Deutschland.* Schaper, Hannover. (English chapter summaries.)

Powell, G. M. 1948. A tree planting spade for a crawler tractor. *J. Forestry* 46:278–281.

Read, R. A. 1958. The Great Plains Shelterbelt in 1954. *Nebr. AES Bul.* 441.

Rietz, R. C. 1941. Kiln design and development of schedules for extracting seed from cones. *USDA Tech. Bul.* 773.

Righter, F. I. 1945. *Pinus:* The relationship of seed size and seedling size to inherent vigor. *J. Forestry* 43:131–137.

Rotty, R. 1958. Three rocks—for better planting survival. *USFS Tree Planters' Note* 33:3–5.

Rudolf, P. O. 1950a. Forest plantations in the Lake States. *USDA Tech. Bul.* 1010.

———. 1950b. Cold soaking—a short-cut substitute for stratification? *J. Forestry* 48:31–32.

———. 1959. Seed production areas in the Lake States. *LSFES Sta. Paper* 73.

Satoo, T., K. Nakamura, and M. Senda. 1955. (Materials for the studies of growth in stands. I. Young stands of Japanese red pine of various density.) *Bul. Tokyo Univ. Forests* No. 48:65–90. (English summary: 89–90.)

Scheer, R. L. 1959. Comparison of pine species on Florida sandhills. *J. Forestry* 57:416–419.

Schreiner, E. J. 1959. Production of poplar timber in Europe and its significance and application in the United States. *USDA Agr. Handbook* 150.

Schubert, G. H., and K. B. Lanquist. 1959. Mist sprayer improves seedling harvester. *USFS Tree Planters' Note* 38:19–20.

Shipman, R. D. 1958. Planting pine in the Carolina Sandhills. *SEFES Sta. Paper* 96.

Shoulders, E. 1960. Seedbed density influences production and survival of loblolly and slash pine nursery stock. *USFS Tree Planters' Note* 42:19–21.

Silen, R. R. 1958. Artificial ripening of Douglas-fir cones. *J. Forestry* 56: 410–413.

Silker, T. H. 1960. Economic considerations of growing and grading southern pine nursery stock. *USFS Tree Planters' Note* 42:13–18.

Southern Forest Tree Improvement Committee. 1960. *Minimum standards for progeny-testing southern forest trees for seed-certification purposes.* Southern Forest Experiment Station, New Orleans.

Spurr, S. H. 1944. Effect of seed weight and seed origin on the early development of eastern white pine. *J. Arnold Arboretum* 25:467–480.

Stevens, C. L. 1931. Root growth of white pine (*Pinus strobus* L.). *Yale Univ. School of Forestry Bul.* 32.

Stoeckeler, J. H. 1960. Soil fertility in forest nurseries. *Advances in Agronomy* 12:128–170.

———, and G. W. Jones. 1957. Forest nursery practice in the Lake States. *USDA Agr. Handbook* 110.

Stone, E. C., and G. H. Schubert. 1959. The physiological condition of ponderosa pine (*Pinus ponderosa* Laws.) planting stock as it affects survival after cold storage. *J. Forestry* 57:837–841.

Switzer, G. L. 1959. The effect of specific gravity separation on some common indices on loblolly pine seed quality. *J. Forestry* 57:497–499.

Toumey, J. W., and C. F. Korstian. 1942. *Seeding and planting in the practice of forestry,* 3rd ed. Wiley, New York.

Turner, L. M. 1936. Root growth of seedlings of *Pinus echinata* and *Pinus taeda. J. Agr. Research* 53:145–149.

U. S. Forest Service. 1948. Woody-plant seed manual. *USDA Misc. Pub.* 654.

Wakeley, P. C. 1954. Planting the southern pines. *USDA Agr. Monograph* 18.

Ware, L. M., and R. Stahelin. 1948. Growth of southern pine plantations at various spacings. *J. Forestry* 46:267–274.

Weetman, G. F. 1958. Forest seeding and planting techniques and equipment. *Pulp and Paper Res. Inst. of Canada, Tech. Rept.* 74.

Weidman, R. H. 1939. Evidences of racial influence in a 25-year test of ponderosa pine. *J. Agr. Research* 59:855–887.

Wilde, S. A. 1958. *Forest soils.* Ronald Press, New York.

Wright, E. 1957. Importance of mycorrhizae to ponderosa pine seedlings. *Forest Sci.* 3:275–280.

Wright, J. W., R. T. Bingham, and K. W. Dorman. 1958. Genetic variation within geographic ecotypes of forest trees and its role in tree improvement. *J. Forestry* 56:803–808.

Zobel, B. J., et al. 1958. Seed orchards—their concept and management. *J. Forestry* 56:815–825.

Zon, R. 1951. Forestry mistakes and what they have taught us. *J. Forestry* 49:179–183.

CHAPTER 8

Regeneration from seed

The regeneration of most North American forests still depends on harnessing the remarkable capacity of forest communities to maintain themselves by natural seeding. The fact that natural revegetation usually proceeds rapidly after disturbance does not mean that economically desirable kinds of trees will always appear or that they will do so at the convenience of the forester. The attainment of natural regeneration after cutting is easy only if there is no great concern about the kind of trees that become established or when they do so. If the goal is to get prompt regeneration of some specific kind, the operation often demands more skillful attention than planting; in fact, it may tax the technical ability of the forester more than any other kind of silvicultural operation.

Although most natural regeneration is obtained from seed, there are some species, mostly hardwoods, which can be reproduced by natural vegetative propagation (see Chapter 15). Natural and artificial regeneration from seed differ only in the origin of the seed supply. Many of the basic problems are the same so it is logical to consider them together.

When regeneration is obtained from seed both the seeds and the infant seedlings are exposed to all the vicissitudes of the natural forest. The mortality of both seed and seedlings is tremendous, although it diminishes rapidly with increasing age and is determined by environmental factors that are at least partially controllable.

ECOLOGICAL REQUIREMENTS
OF NATURAL REGENERATION

Adjustment of Growing Space and Microenvironment

Successful regeneration of any sort, natural or artificial, can occur only if a sufficient amount of growing space becomes available for the establishment and subsequent growth of the new trees. It is easy to ensure that the appropriate vacancies are created in the potential crown space by cutting or other means. It is not so simple to be sure that an adequate volume of soil space is rendered vacant and available for new growth.

It is possible to make quite severe partial cuttings that create no real vacancies in the soil. If intraspecific root grafts exist, the root systems of the trees that were cut may simply be added immediately to those of adjacent uncut trees of the same species. Even more commonly the roots of adjacent trees expand into the vacancies in the soil more rapidly than the roots of newly established trees can claim them. Lesser vegetation, definitely including grasses, will sometimes occupy the soil space so completely as to exclude tree seedlings. The most spectacular and best-known examples of such phenomena exist in the rather arid ponderosa pine forests (Pearson, 1923, 1942). However, examples of the same sort of thing are not difficult to find in more humid climates.

Although it is easy to determine whether adequate vacancies have been made in the crown space, there are often strong temptations to refrain from making them. Consequently it is common to find places where natural regeneration is inadequate, stunted, perishing, or absent in excessively small gaps left in partial cuttings that were supposedly intended to make way for it.

The shapes and sizes of vacancies that can be created in the growing space to make room for the establishment of regeneration are limited only by whatever requirements exist for a supply of seed. Such vacancies do not have to be created all at once but can be enlarged in a series of operations; this sequence is often necessary for species that can become established only under some sort of shelter yet will not commence rapid growth without release.

The natural vegetation of any forest regions is usually capable of claiming any kind of vacancy that might be created in the growing space by purely natural disturbances. Scarcely any kind of natural **ecological niche** goes uncolonized if it is remotely favorable for plant growth. Evolution has produced lichens that can grow on bare rocks and even plants which are adapted to grow in rotten knot-holes of standing trees. It is through this versatility that forest vegetation is able to approach full occupancy of the growing space.

No tree species is adapted to grow in all the different kinds of vacancies that might be created; in fact, a certain degree of specialization exists (Hutnik, 1952). Some are adapted to colonize barren areas left after severe fires or other drastic disturbances that leave the site completely exposed. Pioneer hardwoods, like some of the birches, aspen, and cottonwood, typify this group. At the other extreme are the numerous species that are so tolerant of shade that they are capable of becoming established in the very limited amount of growing space that sometimes becomes available beneath closed stands. There are a very large number of intermediate categories such as those which can become established in exposed areas beneath very temporary herbaceous plants.

Some species have such a narrow range of adaptability that they are capable of becoming established only in rather specific kinds of ecological niches. Others are much more adaptable and can cope with a variety of site conditions. The different kinds of ecological niches also vary in receptivity. Some offer conditions so inhospitable to plants that only a few very durable species can become established in them. Others are so favorable that many species can appear and are likely to do so in riotous profusion.

From the supply of species available in a particular situation those few that are economically desirable are chosen as building materials for the main stand. Attention then logically turns to the identification of the kinds of environmental conditions to which these species are adapted. In the conduct of cuttings intended to make way for natural regeneration, attempts are then made to create the appropriate conditions over an adequate proportion of the area where new trees are desired. *The ideal objective is to create vacancies that are not merely favorable to the desired species but are more favorable to the desired species than to any others.*

As far as initial establishment is concerned, a surprisingly small number of suitable ecological niches may suffice. The small tree enduring the most crucial stage of its existence lives in a minute world several inches in diameter. The establishment of 1000 desirable trees per acre theoretically requires only that number of suitable spots rather evenly distributed over the acre; these might not occupy as much as one thousandth of the total area. Of course, this presumes a supply of seed sufficient to ensure that one germinable seed of desirable species lands on each spot and survives the seedling stage. Furthermore, the outcome also would depend on the characteristics of whatever other vegetation became established on the other 99.9 per cent of the area. The desirable species can be rescued by release cuttings if necessary, but it is better to devise ways of discouraging the establishment of fast-growing, undesirable vegetation in the first place.

This basic approach to the development of methods of regeneration cutting is obviously more easily described than applied. The vegetation of any forest community is subjected to many different kinds of disturbances and reacts in an almost infinite variety of patterns. There is really no large body of knowledge regarding the relationship between the microenvironment and natural regeneration. Most of the existing information logically defines the most favorable kinds of seedbeds and sizes of openings.

The identification of ideal kinds of ecological niches or microenvironments need not wait upon formal research. When a forester finds clumps of the kind of natural reproduction desired, the examination necessary to determine why the environment was so favorable will usually suggest ways in which the appropriate conditions can be created in cutting.

The environmental characteristics of the spots in question are mainly effects of the microclimate and soil. To the extent that these effects can be controlled they are governed largely by the arrangement of any vegetation that is already present and whatever treatment has been applied to the forest floor. The most important factors are the kind and degree of both shading and root competition (Shirley, 1945). The less vegetation left on the site the greater will be the amount of light, soil moisture, and nutrients available to the regeneration.

On the other hand, exposure of the ground surface increases the risk of damage to seedlings from extremes of temperature. The air within several inches of the surface is held virtually motionless because of friction (Geiger, 1957). Radiant energy enters and leaves this stratum freely but the transport of heated air into and out of it depends mostly on wind-induced turbulence and is very sluggish. The vertical movement of heated air, as well as of water vapor and carbon dioxide, results very largely from the chaotic movement of "clumps" of gas molecules in little swirls and eddies embedded in successively larger swirls and eddies. The net effect is to move heat, water, carbon dioxide, and various materials from strata where they are present in abundance to those where they are less abundant. This **turbulent** transfer is vastly more efficient in air than monomolecular processes like heat conduction (from the collisions of single molecules) and diffusion of gases (from the movement of single molecules). The rate at which it proceeds depends on the extent to which the wind penetrates the thin stratum above the surface.

If direct sunlight reaches the ground, the surface becomes remarkably hot and the air is strongly heated from below. The question of whether lethal temperatures (122°F and higher) are attained depends upon the rate at which heat is transferred downward by conduction in the soil and upward by turbulent transfer. If the ventilation is poor, as in a small opening surrounded by trees, unprotected succulent seedlings are swiftly killed by heat injury even though they may be well supplied with water. The heating effect is accentuated if the ground is covered by litter which insulates the mineral soil and restricts downward conduction of heat.

At night the net flow of heat is reversed. Surfaces are cooled by radiation to the sky and the heat losses are replaced only by upward conduction of heat from the soil and downward movement of warm air by turbulent transfer. If the air is initially cool and dry (dewpoint below 32°F), succulent shoots are likely to be damaged by frost. The cooling is also slowed by re-radiation of heat back to the surface from any surrounding trees that block the outgoing radiation. Frost damage is most severe in the centers of openings where there is the least return of heat by re-radiation. Heat injury, however, is most likely along the sunlit northern edge of a forest opening and virtually impossible along the shaded southern margin.

In very small openings, the development of extremes of surface temperature is impeded by side shade; in large openings, the wind causes enough turbulent transfer of heat to restrict the diurnal range of surface temperature. There is evidence that the greatest extremes of temperature occur when the diameter of an opening is 1½ times the height of the surrounding trees (Geiger, 1957). Presumably this is the situation in which the combined effect of side shade and ventilation is the least.

Microclimatic differences between spots can also be systematized in terms of the distinction shown in Fig. 8-1 between conditions found (1) in unshaded, *open* areas, (2) in the side shade and partial protection of uncut timber along the *edges* of openings, and (3) under *full* shade. The edge zone is exposed to the scattered, diffuse light from the sky but not to any harmful effects of direct sunlight. Although the total amount of light is distinctly reduced, diffuse radiation is

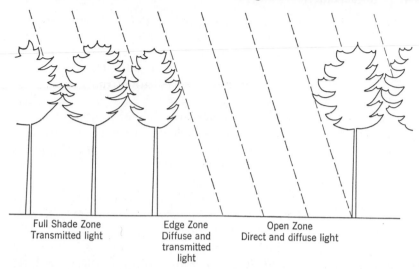

Full Shade Zone
Transmitted light

Edge Zone
Diffuse and
transmitted
light

Open Zone
Direct and diffuse light

Fig. 8-1. The zonation of solar radiation that controls most of the alterable microclimatic factors significant in natural regeneration.

relatively rich in the blue wave lengths most effective in photosynthesis. This transitional zone extends, for practical purposes, not only for a fluctuating distance outward from the edge of an uncut stand but also a short distance inward beneath standing trees. The illumination under full, overhead shade consists mainly of whatever direct sunlight penetrates through interstices in the crowns and the filtered light, rich only in the photosynthetically useless green and infrared wave lengths that are transmitted through the foliage. The differences between these zones correspond roughly to differences in degree of root competition, except that sunlit edges of openings are subject to nearly full light and undiminished root competition.

Some species are adapted to one part of the spectrum of conditions illustrated in Fig. 8-1, some to another; some parts of the spectrum are favorable to many species, others to but few. The benefits of shelter can be important but should not be overemphasized. All tree species ultimately arrive at the stage where they grow best if free of shade and root competition; in fact, some do so on the day of germination.

The other basic factor affecting regeneration from seed is the physical nature of the forest floor. The most important kind of physical difference is that between bare mineral soil and surfaces composed of litter or other unincorporated organic matter. Mineral soil is a much more stable moisture source and comes in closer contact with small seeds than does litter. Under direct sunlight surfaces composed of litter become hotter than those of mineral soil. The thickness of litter determines the crucial distance that seedling roots must penetrate before they reach mineral soil. There are kinds of organic seedbed materials, living and dead, other than ordinary litter. On sites and in regions where decomposition is slow, rotten wood may be a common and favorable kind of seedbed (Place, 1955). Living mosses can be very unfavorable or very favorable depending on whether they or newly germinated seedlings grow faster in height.

In other words, the effect of the microenvironment on regeneration is controlled by (1) amount of overhead cover, (2) proximity to competing vegetation, and (3) physical characteristics of the seedbed. Once the most favorable combination of these conditions is identified, it becomes much easier to determine what kinds of cutting or treatments of the vegetation and forest floor should be applied to secure natural regeneration.

The next step is ensuring that established individuals have or are given sufficient space to grow satisfactorily. This is especially true if the species actually requires some shelter from taller vegetation to become established. The conditions for successful establishment are not necessarily the same as those required for rapid growth (Fraser, 1959). There are many species, mostly relatively tolerant of shade, that are adapted to respond to a sequence of changing environmental conditions rather than a single set. In fact, the ability to become established under shade and then to respond to release after long suppression is often a characteristic of more dependable survival value for a species than capacity for sudden colonization of large exposed areas after catastrophes.

The objective of treatments aimed at natural regeneration is to tip the environmental balance in favor of the kind of new crop desired. The environmental effects are bound to consist of both favorable and unfavorable influences; the objective is to make the good outweigh the bad. Most environmental influences are fixed by the regional climate, the major characteristics of the soil, and similarly immutable factors. Attention must, therefore, center on the changes that can be made in the microclimate, pre-existing vegetation, and alterable characteristics of the soil and forest floor.

Unwanted vegetation is not wished away simply by single-minded consideration of the desirable species. Where possible, the measures employed should create conditions that are not only favorable to the good species but also detrimental to the undesirable. For example, Schubert (1956) found that in clearcut openings the desirable sugar pine grew much faster than the prolific and less desirable white fir because, in the frost pockets thus created, the fir was much more susceptible than the pine to frost damage and deer browsing.

All too often both good and poor species are favored by nearly the same ecological conditions. If a seed source of both is present, it is practically impossible to create environmental conditions that are favorable to the spruces and not equally favorable to the true firs, which are often less desirable. The white pines require somewhat the same conditions that encourage species of the genus *Ribes* which are the alternate hosts of the blister-rust fungus (Haig, Davis, and Weidman, 1941).

Excessively drastic cuttings may result in the establishment of fast-growing pioneer vegetation which will overtop desirable trees of a later stage in succession. Protection of reproduction of early or intermediate successional stages from weed species of later stages is especially difficult. Although these problems may sometimes be overcome by judicious cuttings it is often necessary either to eliminate the undesirable seed source before cutting or to reduce the competing vegetation after the new stand is regenerated. Delay or failure in restocking of cutover areas by desirable species usually results in the invasion of weed species; natural reproduction should, therefore, be secured promptly as well as abundantly. Provision for a plentiful supply of seed will ensure success in many, but certainly not all, instances. Unless some unfavorable factor dominates the situation, the greater the number of seeds the more certainly will an adequate number of them lodge in favorable spots and develop properly.

Essential Steps in Natural Regeneration

Successful natural reproduction depends on the completion of a long sequence of events (Baker, 1950; Wenger and Trousdell, 1957); failure of any single link in the chain is fatal.

Seed supply. The first and most obvious prerequisite is an adequate supply of seed. No tree or group of trees is a dependable source unless it is sufficiently old and vigorous to produce seed. Such seed bearers should, furthermore, be located so that wind or other agencies will ensure pollination and properly distribute the seeds over the area to be regenerated. Regardless of how carefully the seed bearers are chosen and fostered, it must be remembered that most species do not produce every year the abundant crops of seed which are necessary for satisfactory regeneration.   This characteristic makes it difficult to carry out reproduction cuttings with equal chance of success each year.   The limited crops of seed which are produced almost every year give rise to little or no reproduction. The origin of many stands can be traced to unusually good "seed years" that were followed by satisfactory conditions for germination and establishment of seedlings.

Good seed years do not occur at regular intervals.   If there are any real cycles of seed production they are very complicated; at least they have yet to be detected or explained.   The first essential is an ill-defined state of physiological readiness for flowering.   Even after flowers or strobili appear, it is common for adverse weather or infestations of insects and fungi to intervene and prevent pollination or maturation of flowers and fruit.   In general, the more favorable the conditions of soil and climate for plant growth, the more frequent are good crops of seed.

In spite of remarkable adaptations for dispersal over long distances, the seeds of only a few species are distributed in adequate numbers beyond a distance a few times the height of the seed bearers. With many wind-disseminated species, particularly most of the conifers, seeding is not uniform in all directions because dispersal is most effective when dry winds are blowing.   With species disseminated by birds, mammals, gravity, or flowing water, it is important that the forester proceed with a clear understanding of the factors involved.

Both before and after the seeds fall from the trees they are likely to be eaten by insects, birds, and rodents.   Although these predators of seeds are held in check by natural controls that may be strengthened by direct or indirect artificial measures, the most practical means of combating the menace is to ensure that the supply of seed is sufficient both to feed the predators and to regenerate the forest.   Sometimes the most important predators are also the most effective agents of dissemination; if it were not for squirrels and other rodents the heavy seeds of oak, hickory, and walnut would not be carried farther than gravity would take them.

Germination.   Successful germination depends largely on the rainfall and the nature of the spot where the seeds are deposited.   Moisture is the most critical and variable factor.   The embryos in excessively dry seeds either die or remain dormant; if the seedbed is too wet the seeds will rot without germinating or they will suffer from deficiency of oxygen.   The kinds of dormancy encountered in artificial seeding control the timing of germination. Processes that break dormancy are normally completed in seedbeds that are otherwise favorable for development of the seedling, and are rarely critical in *natural regeneration*.

In general, the seeds of wind-disseminated species germinate best on or slightly beneath the surfaces of seedbeds that tend to remain moist; bare mineral soil is usually the best seedbed for such species. Seedbeds of horizontally oriented materials, such as coniferous litter, tend to be unfavorable because they inhibit penetration of seeds into moist substrata; vertically arranged materials, like grass, are less resistant (Osborne and Harper, 1937). Large seeds, such as oak acorns, usually do not germinate unless buried beneath litter or mineral soil, because they must be completely surrounded by a moist medium if they are to survive (Korstian, 1927). Delays in germination are dangerous because they lengthen the period of exposure to birds and rodents. Losses from germination failure, which are usually caused initially by desiccation of seedbeds, are frequently more serious than losses of germinated seedlings (Smith, 1951).

Early survival. New seedlings are most vulnerable during the first few weeks of their existence, while their stems are still green and succulent (Smith, 1958). Heat injury resulting from extremely high temperatures on surfaces exposed to direct solar radiation takes a heavy toll, particularly among conifers. Tender seedlings in shaded situations are subject to damping-off caused by a wide variety of weakly parasitic fungi that are normally saprophytic and incapable of attacking larger seedlings. Cutworms and other insect larvae are particularly active during this period; most of the species involved are omnivorous feeders which will eat anything green and succulent. The better known forest insects and fungi generally attack trees that have passed the succulent stage. Seedlings that germinate late and remain succulent in the fall are commonly killed by frost. The dangerous succulent period ends when the outer cortical tissues of the stem become dry and straw colored, a process referred to as "hardening." Thereafter the attrition of various damaging agencies continues, but the period of catastrophic losses is generally at an end.

Drought is distinctly different from heat injury and is as likely to take place after the succulent stage as during it. It will not occur if seedling roots extend themselves rapidly enough to maintain contact with portions of the soil where water is available. This is most important where the seasonal distribution of precipitation and the rate of evaporation cause the soil to dry from the surface downward during the course of the growing season.   Here the seedling must manufacture enough carbohydrate to enable the roots to grow downward faster than the deepening of the stratum in which water is unavailable. This is one reason why shaded seedlings are more likely to die of drought than those growing in the open (Haig, 1936, Kozlowski, 1949).

DIRECT SEEDING

Success in natural regeneration usually depends on whether a very small proportion of a large quantity of seed lands in favorable spots and is overlooked by all the animals that feed on seeds.   This random process could ordinarily be duplicated artificially only by broadcast distribution of hundreds of thousands of seeds per acre; it would be much more costly and not often as successful as planting.   In establishing stands by direct seeding, the odds against success must be reduced by (1) control of seed-eating animals and (2) distinctly favorable conditions of site and seedbed.   Artificial means are now at hand for providing this combination of effects.   Ordinarily success also depends on whether there is sufficient rain after sowing to keep the uppermost layer of soil adequately moistened throughout the period of germination and the succulent stage.

Control of Seed-Eating Animals

Almost any site that supports a forest or is capable of doing so also supports a large population of small mammals and is also combed over periodically by birds seeking food (Smith and Aldous, 1947). These seed predators are rarely obvious to casual inspection, especially during the middle of the day.   However, superficial digging in the litter and soil often reveals so many rodent tunnels that one is led to wonder how any seeds would go uneaten.   These populations vary widely in time and space; variations between seasons and between years are large and not impossible to predict.   In general, areas of rather barren soil support lower populations of small mammals than those covered with trees, brush, grass or litter; they also offer less shelter to seed-eating birds.   In direct seeding it is well to take advantage of and even to create times and places of low animal population, but dependable results usually require more direct measures to ward off these animals.

Site preparation to reduce the amount of cover over the soil is very important in improving germination and survival of seedlings but is not especially effective in controlling the seed predators. Screens and traps are amply effective but so expensive that they are really useful only for various investigative purposes. Rodents have a good sense of smell and are rarely outwitted by covering the seeds. Even the wholesale poisoning of rodents on regeneration areas is a rather inefficient and questionable technique, although it can be made to work. If the population of seed predators is reduced this merely creates an ecological vacuum; breeding or reinvasion can restore the population even during the period that seeds remain edible (Hooven, 1958).

During the early 1950's direct seeding was brought to the realm of practicality by the introduction of chemicals that effectively repelled small rodents, shrews, and birds (Spencer, 1956, 1959; Woods et al., 1959). These compounds, even though some are highly poisonous, act as repellants because the animals either reject them or soon learn to do so. The compounds are also either nonpoisonous to the seeds or can be applied so that they are not. This means that the rodent population of the seeded area tends to become "educated" not to feed on the seeds; the existence of a population of "educated" predators forestalls invasion by the less learned. The first compounds, tetramethylene disulpho *tetramine*, a rodent repellant, and Morkit, a bird repellant containing anthraquinone, became commercially unavailable after their effectiveness was demonstrated (Spencer, 1959). Fortunately it was found that other available chemicals were suitable.

The compound now most widely used against rodents is endrin (hexachloroepoxy-octahydroendo, endodimethano naphthalene), originally developed as an insecticide; it kills some of the rodents but repels many of them and is only slightly phytotoxic (Dimock, 1957). It is usually applied to the seed at the rate of 1 or 2 pounds of 50 per cent wettable endrin powder per 100 pounds of seed. Two chemicals are available that repel but do not kill birds (Mann and Derr, 1961). One of these is Arasan (thiram or tetramethyl thiram disulfide); it was developed as a fungicide for seed treatment and is thus beneficial in reducing damping off and other difficulties with fungi; it is sometimes effective by itself as a rodent repellant. The recommended rate of application is 7.5 pounds of active thiram per 100 pounds of seed. Sublimed synthetic anthraquinone is less irritating to the skin and mucous membranes and should be substituted for Arasan if sowing is to be done by hand. The recommended rate of application is 15 pounds per 100 pounds of seed.

The seeds are first coated with special latex or asphalt adhesives and then, within 1 or 2 minutes, mixed with the repellant chemicals in a rotating drum (Mann and Derr, 1961). A small amount of aluminum powder may then be added to make the seeds flow more easily. Arasan is irritating and endrin is distinctly poisonous, so neither should be used without protective clothing to prevent inhalation of dusts and contact with the skin. Workers using endrin should wear rubber gloves and bathe at the end of the day because this compound can be absorbed through the skin.

The small seeds of species like western red-cedar and Engelmann spruce are less subject to rodent predation than large seeds, such as those of the pines (Schopmeyer and Helmers, 1947). However, the repellants, while not yet perfected for use on all species, are cheap enough that there is no reason to do without them in direct seeding.

Effect and Modification of Site Factors

Success in direct seeding also depends on rendering the microsite as favorable as possible and ensuring prompt germination. The seeds should be placed in contact with mineral soil and, if possible, covered to the greatest depth consistent with successful germination. Moisture must be almost continuously available at or close to the surface of the mineral soil until the seedling roots have penetrated to a stable moisture supply. The amount of water several inches below the surface that might support the damaged root system of a newly planted tree is not necessarily enough. Consequently there are some climates and soils that are too dry for successful direct seeding.

The most favorable soils are those well supplied with moisture because of their topographic position, although poor aeration in excessively wet spots can also cause failure. Stoeckeler and Sump (1940), for example, found that spot seeding of jack pine on sandy soils was successful only if the water table lay within 2 to 5 feet of the surface. They determined that the presence of the high water table was decisive largely because it prevented surface temperatures from rising to the lethal range. Moist but well-drained soils that are supplied with water by seepage from higher ground are also very favorable. Soils of extremely coarse or extremely fine texture are less favorable than those of loamy texture.

As far as the germination and initial establishment of seedlings is concerned, a light cover of vegetation over bare mineral soil is almost ideal. It allows the seeds to come in contact with the mineral soil yet it shields the surface from direct sunlight thus reducing heat injury and direct evaporation from the soil. Although desiccation of most of the soil layer results from removal of water by plants, that of the surface and about the first half inch of soil is caused more by direct evaporation than by transpiration. Therefore, the vegetation that restricts the supply of water to a well-rooted seedling can actually increase the amount of water available during germination and the crucial days thereafter.

One excellent cover is a season's growth of grass that has sprouted after the elimination of any accumulation of dead grass and other litter by fire. This kind of cover, called a "one-year rough," is, except for the competition it ultimately causes, favorable for seeding of longleaf pine; it hinders birds and shields the seedlings, which germinate in the fall, from frost. Herbaceous weeds over bare mineral soil are also beneficial. In fact, in the Pacific Northwest direct seeding of conifers is sometimes facilitated by a preliminary seeding with wild mustard to provide such cover on burned areas (McKell and Finnis, 1957). This adroit use of short-lived cover crops has given good results in other instances and seems worthy of further development.

The shade of woody plants is beneficial in the early stages, but its ultimate effect depends on the extent to which it competes with established seedlings for light, water, and nutrients. The best shade is that cast by dead materials, such as stumps, logs, or light slash.

Very low cover may impede foraging by birds but almost all the other effects of cover are likely to favor seed predators. Vegetative cover tends to reduce mechanical erosion of repellant materials from seeds. Sometimes this makes it possible to sow in the fall and allow stratificiation to proceed naturally. The sowing of open areas often must be restricted to the period immediately before germination because the repellant coatings deteriorate too much if exposed.

On most sites, the outcome of direct seeding still depends on the vagaries of rainfall. The careful selection and preparation of sites can only mitigate the baneful effect of one or two rainless weeks during the period of germination and initial development. If climatic records indicate that failures ought to be anticipated, for example, in 1 year out of every 4, the true cost of each successful operation should be regarded as increased by 25 per cent. There are regions where the rainfall is so undependable that direct seeding may have to be restricted to sites where the soils remain moist during drought periods.

The chances of success are significantly increased if the seed is treated so that it will be capable of prompt and vigorous germination. This shortens the period of exposure to predators as well as that during which unfavorable weather can be critical. The same seed of mediocre quality that germinates well in the nursery may fail under the more rigorous conditions of the wild. Therefore, fresh seed is distinctly preferable to that which has been in cold storage for several years. If the seed is dormant and cannot be after-ripened naturally by fall sowing, it must be stratified. Such stratification must precede treatment with repellants and sowing should follow within a day or two because stratified seed is very perishable. Finally results are greatly improved if the seed is buried at optimum depth on favorable microsites.

Relative Merits of Direct Seeding and Planting

There is much more risk of poor survival with direct seeding than with planting. New seedlings that germinate and grow in the field have scant protection from the numerous lethal agencies that can be controlled in the nursery. Trees established by direct seeding grow no more rapidly than natural seedlings, so they suffer more from competing vegetation. Furthermore, there is no opportunity to shorten rotations as there is in planting.

Direct seeding is inherently cheaper than planting because it involves less labor and equipment; investments in nurseries and the overhead charges involved in their operation are avoided. Large areas can be seeded more quickly, on shorter notice, and with fewer organizational problems. The only preliminary step is seed collection, although such large quantities are required that the normal problems of procurement are aggravated. It will be years, if ever, before seed of demonstrably superior genetic quality will be abundant enough to permit its use in direct seeding.

The roots of trees established by seeding develop naturally and are not subject to the deformities that are suspected of making planted trees susceptible to windthrow and root rot. Species that develop taproots or distinctly shallow, lateral root systems grow best if their roots develop naturally.

Direct seeding is possible on soils where planting machines cannot be used because of stones, stumps, or other obstructions, *but only if the sites are otherwise favorable.*

If dense stocking is desirable, it is more economically secured by direct seeding than by planting. However, the risk of localized understocking and overstocking is far greater. Stands established by direct seeding are likely to require more subsequent treatment, such as refilling, release cutting, and precommercial thinning, than planted stands.

Direct seeding can often be conducted over longer periods than planting and during colder or wetter weather. The main limitations on timing are those imposed by excessively dry weather and any need for minimizing the period of exposure to seed-eating animals or for avoiding unseasonable germination. Since germination often occurs after older seedlings have broken dormancy, the best time for direct seeding may actually come shortly after the regular spring planting season thus enabling continuation of activity even where planting is the standard method of artificial regeneration.

Broadcast Seeding

The simplest type of direct seeding consists of scattering seeds uniformly over the area to be restocked. This is likely to be a waste of seed unless mineral soil has been exposed over most of the area. Such complete preparation is most likely to be associated with accidental or intentional burning severe enough to reduce the unincorporated organic matter. Mechanical site preparation for broadcast seeding is justified mainly as a means of removing vegetation that will ultimately compete with the new crop after it is established.

Broadcast sowing is very rapid and is most often used when there is necessity of covering large areas quickly. Its most serious drawback is the lack of any provision for covering the seeds. For this reason it is best done during moist weather.

The seeding rates vary considerably depending on the favorability of site and anticipated weather. Recommendations ordinarily call for 10,000 to 25,000 viable seeds per acre, provided that these seeds are treated with appropriate repellants; however, the seeding rate should be carefully adjusted from year to year on the basis of quantitative observations of the results of previous seeding projects.

Most broadcast seeding is done from the air. The use of aircraft is usually feasible only if several hundred acres or more can be done in a single project. Uniformity of seeding is possible only if the distributing equipment is closely calibrated and if moving flagmen are stationed on the ground. Fixed-wing aircraft do a faster and cheaper job than helicopters, but are best adapted to seeding over gentle terrain where the areas to be seeded are also large and uniform. Helicopters are most suitable if the terrain is rugged or if the areas to be seeded are intermingled with those on which seeding is unnecessary or unlikely to succeed. Helicopters can also fly in moist weather that is good for direct seeding but hazardous for the operation of fixed-wing aircraft. The cost of aerial seeding is rarely more than $1 per acre, exclusive of the cost of seed and site preparation.

Broadcast seeding can also be done on the ground at rates up to 20 acres per man-day with crank-operated "cyclone" seeders like those used for sowing grain crops. The cost is about the same as for aerial seeding but it takes much longer to cover a given tract.

Strip and Spot Seeding

Failure in direct seeding is least likely if the seeds are sown in spots or strips that are specially prepared or selected. The sowing itself is inherently more expensive than broadcast seeding but distinctly cheaper than planting. Strip and spot sowing are more economical of seed than broadcast sowing and can be done successfully in a much wider range of times and places.

If the terrain is suitable and there is no necessity for attempting to eliminate all the vegetation that will ultimately compete with the new crop, the mechanical preparation of the soil is most efficiently accomplished by furrowing or disking in strips. Although the seed is sometimes broadcast on the strips, it is usually much better to take full advantage of the preparatory work and apply the seeds so that they are covered with soil or pressed into it.

Where tractor-drawn equipment has been used to prepare strips it is usually logical that the seed be sown with specially modified grain drills also drawn by tractors (Mann and Derr, 1961). The preliminary plowing or disking can be done as a separate operation or combined with the sowing. The soil to which the seed is to be applied should first be compacted either by the tracks of the tractor or by a roller. The next part of the apparatus is a drill modified to deliver one seed at a time. After the seed is deposited another roller presses it into the soil. The seed can also be covered with other devices such as dragging chains (Schubert, Buck, and Evanko, 1960). Tractor-drawn seeders can cover 20 to 60 acres per day on gentle terrain in the South and the cost, including the seed, is roughly half that of planting seedlings by machine.

In preparing the strips attention should be given to preventing difficulties with standing water or erosive effects. If the drainage is so poor that even temporary pools of water are likely to form, it is desirable to create ridges on which to plant the seed. Anything that will allow flowing water to move the seed sideways should be avoided because this effect can kill seedlings that have not taken root firmly. Movement of soil or debris may also bury the seeds too deeply. Unless definite ridges are desirable, devices that scrape or chop up the surface are superior to plows that make furrows.

Spot seeding is limited to operations which are too small to justify use of tractors or where steep terrain and obstructions prevent their use. The spots are prepared with hand tools or merely by kicking the debris to the side.

It is difficult to arrive at the proper relationship between the spacing of seed-spots and the number of seeds applied to each. If one seed is sown on each spot, many spots must be prepared and seeded to allow for all the failures; if enough are sown on each spot to ensure that each has one established seedling, some spots will be choked with seedlings. The ordinary compromise is that of sowing several seeds each on spots spaced at intervals closer than would be used in conventional planting; it must then be anticipated that the stocking of the stand will be erratic and that it might become desirable to thin overcrowded spots and patches (Foiles, 1961).

The seeds can be placed by hand, although the repellants that should be used are poisonous enough to dictate use of rubberized gloves. Various special seeding devices resembling corn planters are much more convenient (Mann and Derr, 1961); they require less contact with the seed and enable the sowing of up to 5 acres per man-day. The only other tools especially designed for spot seeding are the dibbles used for planting acorns and other large nuts. These are bars shaped to punch holes into the soil obliquely so that the seeds can be planted on their sides (Toumey and Korstian, 1942).

Application of Direct Seeding

Broadcast seeding from the air is employed to an increasing extent in the more humid portions of the Pacific Northwest as a means of reforesting recent burns and as a supplement to or replacement for natural seeding after the clearcutting and broadcast burning of old-growth stands.

Both aerial and ground seeding are coming into wide use in the large-scale reforestation and type conversion programs underway in the South (Woods et al., 1959). This is especially true where the objective is to reforest large areas with pines at rates of speed that cannot be achieved by planting (Mann and Burkhalter, 1961). Direct seeding is also used in a more limited role on wet sites and places where planting machines cannot go.

The most important use of direct seeding in the South is for the establishment of longleaf pine (Fig. 8-2; Derr and Mann, 1959). The stemless, tap-rooted seedlings are nearly impossible to plant successfully because the buds are so likely to become buried or excessively exposed by the slightest erosion around them. The discouraging

Fig. 8-2. A stand of longleaf pine in Louisiana established by direct seeding on disked strips. The seedlings are in the middle of the fourth growing season and have been sprayed once with a fungicide for control of brown-spot disease. (*Photograph by U. S. Forest Service.*)

tendency of the seedlings to linger in the grass for years without growing in height has also led to the common practice of reforesting extensive areas of old longleaf lands with planted slash and loblolly pine. Direct seeding of longleaf pine is much more successful than planting; it can be done by broadcast seeding, preferably on one-year roughs, or by drill sowing on prepared strips. In fact, the reduction of grass competition on prepared strips sometimes causes speedy emergence from the grass stage.

Heavy-seeded hardwoods, such as oak, walnut, and hickory, have large taproots that are easily damaged in planting. The best artificial regeneration of these species is obtained by direct seeding, although the control of rodents is still a serious problem. Screens and other physical barriers are usually necessary; the use of repellants on large nuts has yet to be perfected.

Some species with very small seeds, such as redwood (Fritz, 1950) and western red-cedar (Schopmeyer and Helmers, 1947), can be reproduced more readily by direct seeding than by planting.

Fair success has been obtained in the Lake Region with jack pine as well as with red and bur oak (Rudolf, 1950). The direct seeding of black locust on spoil banks is reasonably successful provided that the slopes are not too extreme and the soil is at least slightly favorable (Brown and Tryon, 1960). Even before the development of satisfactory animal repellants, there were enough examples of successful direct seeding to warrant regarding it as useful, although limited in application (McQuilkin, 1949).

In general, however, direct seeding is now employed only where it is desirable to reforest large areas quickly, on unusual sites that are difficult to plant but are otherwise favorable, and for rather peculiar species that are difficult to plant successfully. Now that ways are being found to overcome the most serious difficulties, it is logical to suppose that the advantage of low cost will cause wider and more versatile application of direct seeding, especially in those regions where rainfall is ample and planting is expensive.

RELATIVE MERITS OF PLANTING
AND NATURAL REGENERATION

In methods of natural reproduction from seed, skillful treatment, which is not necessarily cheap, is substituted for the heavy expenditure of effort required by planting. Natural regeneration from sprouts is usually simple. Direct seeding is, for purposes of comparison, more like natural regeneration than planting.

The major disadvantages of planting are: (1) the relatively high initial cost; (2) the opportunity to make mistakes in fitting species and strains to the environment; and (3) the damage and deformation of root systems inevitably resulting from use of bare-rooted planting stock. The significant advantages are: (a) close control over the arrangement, composition, and genetic qualities of new stands; (b) shortening of period of establishment; (c) avoidance of dangers to which seed and new seedlings are exposed in the field; and (d) freedom from restrictions on harvesting techniques.

Planting, *if properly done*, creates stands that can be treated more efficiently and yield greater volumes and values than naturally regenerated stands. It is significant that it usually takes a whole rotation to determine whether wise decisions were made at the time of planting. The returns from planting are also delayed as long as those from any silvicultural investments. Analysis frequently shows that investments in the improvement of established natural stands are rewarded more handsomely and quickly. Artificial regeneration is a highly seasonal operation that usually requires increasingly specialized facilities and availability of temporary employees.

Natural reproduction is generally cheaper, or at least requires less direct cash outlay, than artificial reproduction. On many forest areas natural reproduction can be secured for practically nothing or at a fraction of the expenditure required to reforest artificially. The stand finally produced from cheaply obtained natural reproduction may or may not compare favorably in composition or density to one created artificially. There are, on the other hand, some instances in which natural regeneration costs more than artificial reproduction. Increased costs of logging, unsalvageable losses in residual stands, expenses for seedbed preparation and other essential operations may cause initial expenditures for natural regeneration to be greater than those for planting.

The choice between natural and artificial regeneration is not, of itself, a decision between even- and uneven-aged management, pure or mixed stands, late or early successional stages, and adherence to or departure from the pattern of development that would take place in nature. It is no coincidence that planted stands are most often pure, even-aged, and not entirely in harmony with plant succession, but naturally reproduced stands can be made to display the same characteristics. The causes of success or failure are fully as likely to be found in these other considerations as they are in whether regeneration is artificial or natural.

REFERENCES

(Other references on the ecology of natural regeneration will be found in Chapters 9–16.)

Baker, F. S. 1950. *Principles of silviculture.* McGraw-Hill, New York. Pp. 182–280.

Brown, J. H., and E. H. Tryon. 1960. Establishment of seeded black locust on spoil banks. *W. Va. AES Bul.* 440.

Derr, H. J., and W. F. Mann, Jr. 1959. Guidelines for direct-seeding longleaf pine. *SFES Occasional Paper* 171.

Dimock, E. J., II. 1957. A comparison of two rodent repellants in broadcast seeding Douglas-fir. *PNWFRES Research Paper* 20.

Foiles, M. W. 1961. Effects of thinning seed spots on growth of three conifers in the Inland Empire. *J. Forestry* 59:501–503.

Fraser, J. W. 1959. The effect of sunlight on the germination and early growth of jack pine and red pine. *Canada, Forestry Branch, Forest Research Div. Tech. Note* 71.

Fritz, E. 1950. Spot-wise direct seeding for redwood. *J. Forestry* 48:334–338.

Geiger, R. 1957. *The climate near the ground.* Translated from German by M. N. Steward and others. Harvard University Press, Cambridge. Revised.

Haig, I. T. 1936. Factors controlling initial establishment of western white pine and associated species. *Yale Univ., School of Forestry Bul.* 41.

———, K. P. Davis, and R. H. Weidman. 1941. Natural regeneration in the western white pine type. *USDA Tech. Bul.* 767.

Hooven, E. F. 1958. Deer mouse and reforestation in the Tillamook Burn. *Oreg. Forest Lands Research Center, Research Note* 37.

Hosner, J. F., and L. S. Minckler. 1960. Hardwood reproduction in the river bottoms of southern Illinois. *Forest Sci.* 6:67–77.

Hutnik, R. J. 1952. Reproduction on windfalls in a northern hardwood stand. *J. Forestry* 50:693–694.

Korstian, C. F. 1927. Factors controlling germination and early survival in oaks. *Yale Univ. School of Forestry Bul.* 19.

Kozlowski, T. T. 1949. Light and water in relation to growth and competition of Piedmont forest tree species. *Ecological Monographs* 19:207–231.

Lavender, D. P. 1959. Effect of ground cover on seedling germination and survival. *Oreg. Forest Lands Research Center, Research Note* 38.

McKell, C. M., and J. M. Finnis. 1957. Control of soil moisture depletion through use of 2,4-D on a mustard nurse crop during Douglas-fir seedling establishment. *Forest Sci.* 3:329–335.

McQuilkin, W. E. 1949. Direct seeding of trees. *In:* Trees, USDA *Yearbook of Agr.* 1949. Pp. 136–146.

Mann, W. F., Jr., and H. D. Burkhalter. 1961. The South's largest successful direct-seeding. *J. Forestry* 59:83–87.

Mann, W. F., Jr., and H. J. Derr. 1961. Guidelines for direct-seeding loblolly pine. *SFES Occasional Paper* 188.

Muelder, D. W. 1959. Contribution to a better understanding of the process of natural reproduction in California. *Proc. Soc. Am. Foresters Meeting,* 1958:148–150.

Osborne, J. G., and V. L. Harper. 1937. The effect of seedbed preparation on first-year establishment of longleaf and slash pine. *J. Forestry* 35:63–68.

Pearson, G. A. 1923. Natural reproduction of western yellow pine in the Southwest. *USDA Bul.* 1105.

———. 1942. Herbaceous vegetation a factor in natural regeneration of ponderosa pine in the Southwest. *Ecological Monographs* 12:315–338.

Place, I. C. M. 1955. The influence of seed-bed conditions on the regeneration of spruce and fir. *Canada, Forestry Branch Bul.* 117.

Rudolf, P. O. 1950. Forest plantations in the Lake States. *USDA Tech. Bul.* 1010.

Schopmeyer, C. S., and A. E. Helmers. 1947. Seeding as a means of reforestation in the Northern Rocky Mountain Region. *USDA Circ.* 772.

Schubert, G. H. 1956. Early survival and growth of sugar pine and white fir in clear-cut openings. *CFRES Forest Research Note* 117.

Schubert, G. H., J. M. Buck, and A. B. Evanko. 1960. Rangeland drill used in reforestation in California. *PSWFRES Misc. Paper* 42.

Shirley, H. L. 1945. Reproduction of upland conifers in the Lake States as affected by root competition and light. *Am. Midland Naturalist* 33:537–612.

Smith, C. F., and S. E. Aldous. 1947. The influence of mammals and birds in retarding artificial and natural reseeding of coniferous forests in the United States. *J. Forestry* 45:361–369.

Smith, D. M. 1951. The influence of seedbed conditions on the regeneration of eastern white pine. *Conn. AES Bul.* 545.

Smith, F. H. 1958. Anatomical development of the hypocotyl of Douglas-Fir. *Forest Sci.* 4:61–70.

Spencer, D. A. 1956. The effects of rodents on reforestation. *Proc. Soc. Am. Foresters Meeting*, 1955:125–128.

———. 1959. Prevention of mammal damage in forest management. *Proc. Soc. Am. Foresters Meeting*, 1958:183–185.

Stoeckeler, J. H., and A. W. Sump. 1940. Successful direct seeding of northern conifers on shallow-water-table areas. *J. Forestry* 38:572–577.

Toumey, J. W., and C. F. Korstian. 1942. *Seeding and planting in the practice of forestry*, 3rd ed. Wiley, New York.

Vanselow, K. 1949. *Theorie und Praxis der natürlichen Verjüngung im Wirtschaftswald*, 2nd ed. Neumann, Berlin.

Wenger, K. F., and K. B. Trousdell. 1957. Natural regeneration of loblolly pine in the South Atlantic Coastal Plain. *USDA Production Research Rept.* 13.

Woods, F. W., et al. 1959. *Direct seeding in the South—1959, a symposium.* Duke University, School of Forestry, Durham, N. C.

CHAPTER 9

Preparation and treatment of the site

In considering the regeneration of stands, emphasis is traditionally and logically placed on the pattern by which the pre-existing stand is removed. Most of the remaining chapters of this book are, in fact, devoted to these patterns of cutting. Such emphasis on harvest cutting should not obscure the fact that regeneration may also depend on accessory measures to dispose of debris, reduce the competition of unharvested vegetation, and prepare the soil for the new trees. It is almost as logical to prepare the ground for forest crops as to prepare it for agricultural crops. The only real differences are that there is less readiness to invest in forestry, and most forest species are much better adapted to conditions found in nature.

Acceptable regeneration can often be obtained without deliberate site preparation, but it is important to distinguish between total absence of such treatment and the unintentional kinds resulting from logging and slash disposal or prescribed burning undertaken for fuel reduction. This is not to say that the effects of logging, slash disposal, and prescribed burning always facilitate regeneration. If reliance is being placed on established advance regeneration, it may be logical that the harvesting of the previous crop be accomplished with as little disturbance as possible. The risk of harm to the soil must also be considered.

Site preparation, whether deliberate or unintentional, may be more crucial in the establishment of regeneration than the method of reproduction cutting. Many species can be reproduced by several different methods of cutting but by only one general program of site preparation dictated by the characteristics of the species and the site.

The various techniques of site preparation have both harmful and beneficial effects as well as overlapping objectives. Some of them are not primarily intended to facilitate the growing of crops of trees. The objectives include the control of competing vegetation, the modification of forest floor and mineral soil, the control of damaging agencies, the improvement of forage production, and the removal of impediments to logging and other operations. Most of the treatments are applied during the period of establishment, but some are started well in advance of harvest cutting or applied occasionally throughout the rotation.

The more important of the various treatments, other than those covered in previous chapters, may be imperfectly divided into the following categories:

1. Disposal of logging slash
2. Treatment of the forest floor and competing vegetation:
   a. prescribed burning
   b. mechanical treatment
3. Treatment of the mineral soil
   a. fertilization
   b. drainage and irrigation

SLASH DISPOSAL

Effects of Slash

The appearance of debris left by harvesting operations is so offensive that it is not easy to be entirely objective about determining the extent of disposal. Slash can be simultaneously harmful and beneficial; its treatment can be very expensive and the resulting benefits are mostly rather indirect. Consequently, the problems created by the presence of slash must be thought of as an integrated whole in terms of their effect on the productivity, utility, and safety of specific stands.

Slash in relation to forest fires. Most slash disposal is still applied primarily to reduce the potential fuel for forest fires (Davis, 1959; Fahnestock, 1960). Slash is a fire hazard mainly because it represents an unusually large volume of fuel distributed in such a way that it is a dangerous impediment in the construction of fire lines. The foliage and wood of living trees do not ordinarily burn in forest fires. Therefore, the debris left after trees are cut represents potential fuel which would not be present in an undisturbed forest.

The greatest menace exists during the short period in which the foliage and small branchlets remain on the slash; they are readily ignited and burn rapidly. The larger materials are not easily kindled and do not normally burn rapidly, although they give off large quantities of heat. However, when conditions are favorable to very hot fires the size of the units of fuel is no longer a factor limiting the rate at which a fire will spread. Therefore, during bad fire weather, fires can burn rapidly in large concentrations of slash and may "blow up" into well-nigh uncontrollable conflagrations. The main objective of slash disposal for fire control is the prevention of such catastrophes.

Fires on cutover areas almost invariably start and spread in the litter of the old forest floor. An area can be rendered temporarily fireproof through the elimination of this blanket of fuel, but the effect lasts only until the first crop of herbaceous vegetation dries out. Therefore, no method of treating the potential fuels of forest fires is a substitute for a good system of fire control. The prevalence of fires on heavily cutover areas is the result, not of the presence of slash, but of the desiccation of the exposed forest floor.

Policies of slash disposal have been heavily influenced by the popular misconception that the danger of bad fires on cutover lands can be eliminated by destruction of logging debris. Actually the menace of slash can be diminished not only through reduction of its amount but also through any measures that break up its continuity, protect it from sun and wind, or decrease the risk of ignition.

Effect of slash on reproduction. In addition to being a hazard and impediment in fire control, logging debris often hinders the establishment of reproduction. This harmful influence is caused principally by the heavy shade and injurious mechanical effect of the dense concentrations of slash which are bound to be deposited on parts of the cutover area. In such places advance regeneration is buried or crushed and the establishment of new seedlings is prevented by the shade. Slash composed of green branches is more detrimental than that of dead branches because of the heavier shade.

The magnitude of the harmful effect depends on the proportion of the area covered as well as the thickness and density of the slash. Thick, dense layers of slash, until broken up by decay, prevent the establishment of reproduction. Sometimes the first plants to appear on the sites of old slash piles are undesirable grasses, herbs, and shrubs which may usurp the area for long periods. Thin, loose layers of slash, on the other hand, may be of real benefit to young seedlings by protecting them from extremes of temperature, desiccation, grazing animals, and the competition of intolerant vegetation.

The amount of slash left after cutting obviously varies with the proportion of the stand removed and the extent to which the trees felled are utilized. After light, partial cuttings the areas of dense slash may be so small and so well scattered that satisfactory reproduction is not impeded. Furthermore, partial cuttings usually create microclimatic conditions more favorable to rapid decomposition of debris than do clearcuttings.

Many factors determine the amount and kind of slash disposal, if any, needed to favor reproduction in any given situation. For example, a cutover area can have a large volume of slash but so many well-distributed spots favorable to reproduction that no treatment would be necessary for this particular purpose. In fact, as far as reproduction itself is concerned, most problems ordinarily arise from the larger aggregations of slash covering rather small proportions of cutover areas. On many occasions, the lopping of some of the slash to release advance reproduction that has been bent over may be more useful than actual destruction of any slash.

The method of slash disposal often determines the composition of the new crop arising on the treated areas. Where fire is used it is almost inevitable that intolerant, pioneer vegetation will colonize the burned spots. The question of whether this is desirable depends entirely on the nature of the invading vegetation in contrast to that which would otherwise appear. Any form of slash burning is certain to cause some damage to advance regeneration. Sometimes the seeds present on the slash or in the forest floor represent the most dependable source of regeneration.

The use of fire for slash disposal often simulates the effects of the destructive fires that have led to the re-establishment of certain subclimax types under natural conditions. For example, in the coast Douglas-fir and western white pine types, the practice of broadcast burning after clearcutting produces conditions comparable to those under which pure stands of these species originated in nature. Unfortunately, the heavy concentrations of logging debris make these fires more intense than those in the undisturbed forest and, therefore, not entirely beneficial to reproduction. On the other hand, burning of the slash of northern hardwoods, although rarely necessary for purposes of fire protection, might represent a means of securing satisfactory reproduction of paper birch.

Slash disposal has received far more attention as a means of fire protection than as a method of stimulating reproduction. This attitude has sometimes led to the application of methods of slash disposal which are not compatible with the renewal of the forest. The modifications of practice beneficial to reproduction lie in the direction of partial, rather than complete, disposal of slash.

Slash in relation to the soil. The presence of decaying slash is generally beneficial to the physical properties of the forest soil, but it has a tendency to cause a temporary deterioration of the chemical properties. A cover of slash holds the litter in place and tends to shield bare soil from erosion and frost heaving. However, the haphazard deposition of slash over actively eroding surfaces is not as effective as casual consideration might indicate. Slash also tends to conserve the moisture in the soil and decelerate the rate at which snow melts. As it decays it also tends to build up the amount of organic matter incorporated in the mineral soil, thus improving its physical properties.

On the other hand, the inorganic nutrients in the slash remain unavailable to the new crop until they have been released by decay. Substantial amounts of nitrogen are bound away in the bodies of the microorganisms responsible for the final stages of decay. These effects may be detrimental on infertile soils or in climates where thick layers of organic matter normally accumulate beneath the forest.

The influence of slash burning on the soil is quite naturally opposite to that of leaving the slash (Burns, 1952). The possibility of physical damage to the soil by erosion is increased, especially on steep slopes and on relatively compact soils with a high content of clay and silt. Hot fires in thick accumulations of slash cause localized physical deterioration of the superficial layers of mineral soil. Accumulations of charcoal increase the risk of damage to reproduction by heat injury. Improvements in the chemical properties are tempo rary and largely associated with the quick release of the nutrients stored in the slash. This temporary increase in the supply of nutrients stimulates the fixation of atmospheric nitrogen by soil microorganisms. However, the increase in pH sometimes promotes the development of the fungi that cause damping-off of seedlings (Tarrant, 1956).

In general, slash disposal by burning tends to harm fine-textured soils or those on steep slopes. It does not harm, and may even improve, coarse-textured soils or those which are encumbered with thick accumulations of unincorporated humus.

Slash in relation to insects and fungi. The insects and fungi that feed on logging debris are more beneficial than harmful because they are primarily responsible for the disintegration and decay of unburned slash. The vast majority of them are scavengers or saprophytes which do not attack living trees.

The few species of bark beetles and heart-rotting fungi which can spread from slash to living trees are mostly found in the cull logs, stumps, and large branches that are rarely eliminated in conventional slash disposal. The injurious fungi that proliferate in large pieces of slash are, for example, those which had already infected the living trees (Boyce, 1961). Some of them may produce fruiting bodies more abundantly after cutting than in living trees. The treatment of slash to control insects and fungi is, therefore, best accomplished by such measures as close utilization, application of insecticides, and indirect methods of combating the proliferation and spread of harmful organisms. Ordinary slash-burning does not necessarily have any effect on the situation and may even aggravate it by killing unmerchantable, standing trees.

The most important aspect of the influence of insects and fungi on slash is the rate at which they bring about disintegration. It may take anywhere from several years to several decades for slash to decompose enough to cease being a significant detriment. It is necessary to know how much time is required because this has an important bearing not only on the question of whether or how to treat the slash but also on the planning of subsequent operations.

Hardwood slash, for example, tends to remain moist and decays so rapidly that special measures of disposal are rarely necessary. Spaulding and Hansbrough (1944) found that slash of species with coarse branches decays more rapidly than slash of species, such as the spruces, that have many fine twigs. They also noted that decay was rapid when there was a proper balance of oxygen and moisture in the wood but was very slow on sites that were extremely wet or dry. The shaded conditions that prevail after partial cuttings are especially favorable to decomposition of slash.

Slash in relation to harvesting operations. Efficiency in log transportation depends to a large extent on the success with which the slash is concentrated during felling. The interests of both logging and silviculture are usually best reconciled by concentrating the slash in a large number of small, compact piles or in long narrow strips. The consolidation of slash into a few very large piles is as detrimental to silvicultural purposes as the diffuse scattering of debris is to efficient transportation of logs. There are occasions when the slash from one cutting may remain long enough to be a serious impediment to subsequent operations.

The amount and size of logging debris naturally depend on the extent to which felled trees are utilized. Large, untrimmed tops left on the ground are especially detrimental. They cover a large amount of space and have loosely arranged twigs and foliage which enable fires to travel rapidly. Increased intensity of utilization reduces the amount of large debris; moreover, it almost automatically ensures that the fine fuels, although not reduced in volume, are left more compact and closer to the ground so that they burn more slowly.

Slash in relation to aesthetics and wildlife. In the eyes of the layman, logging debris is not only unsightly but also an intolerable menace to public safety. Therefore, it is desirable to dispose of slash or refrain from cutting in recreational areas and along public ways. Laws in many states require that slash be disposed of within specified distances of highways, railroads, habitations, and adjoining properties.

Slash should not be deposited in waterways because in decomposing it may reduce the oxygen content of the water below the level required by many species of gamefish. Drastic cutting along the margins of small streams may also increase the temperature of the water too much for the maintenance of a desirable population of fish. On the other hand, slash often provides excellent cover for birds and small mammals, a point sometimes useful in convincing the public of the disadvantages of needless slash disposal.

Methods and Application of Slash Disposal

Safe and efficient burning of slash depends on a good knowledge of the control and behavior of fire in the forest. More complete accounts of the procedures may be found in the literature of fire control. Attention is here confined to those aspects that impinge on silvicultural practice.

Tremendous advances in fire control have caused slash disposal to be one part of American forestry practice that has become less important with the passage of time. Fires that once might have become large are now more likely to be controlled when small, so the chance that fire will spread to any particular cutover area is much smaller than formerly.

Study of the problems involved have also shown that slash itself is not as great a menace as once supposed. Modern utilization of felled timber is usually much closer. Cutting is, in general, lighter than before; partial cutting is more common and clearcut areas are smaller; these factors tend to reduce the amount of slash that is on the ground at any one time as well as the sizes and degree of exposure of the concentrations. Finally the cost of labor has risen so much that the advantages of slash disposal are now, in many localities, no longer worth the price.

As a consequence slash is now treated mostly where it can be destroyed by cheap broadcast burning or in regions with long, severe fire seasons where some hazard reduction is essential. Efforts are often limited to eliminating slash in narrow bands along routes of travel or at intervals across cutover areas in order to break up large concentrations and to provide places for fire-line construction in event of need.

Slash disposal has been and remains much more important in the West than in any other part of North America because of the long, rainless summers. In fact, some sort of slash disposal is required by law, although specific release from the requirement is possible where circumstances warrant. In the northern coniferous forests of the Lake States and Canada limited kinds of slash disposal are sometimes desirable. In the southern pine forests slash rots so quickly that it rarely requires treatment and the basic purpose is often more effectively accomplished by prescribed burning of the forest floor anyhow. In the eastern hardwood forests and in the Northeast slash also rots quickly enough that disposal is required only along roads and in similar places.

Broadcast burning. In broadcast burning, the slash on clearcut areas is burned as it lies within prepared fire lines. Practically all the remaining vegetation, except for that of sprouting species, is destroyed. This precludes reliance on advance reproduction but eliminates much of any undesirable vegetation that is present (Morris, 1958). The extent of exposure of mineral soil is actually rather variable depending on the moisture content of the forest floor at time of burning. Usually an ample amount of mineral soil is exposed; the areas where fires burn with such sustained heat as to damage the physical properties of the soil are rarely large enough to be of much significance. The sites are left in reasonably good condition for hand planting, direct seeding, or natural seeding from adjacent stands.

Broadcast burning is associated mainly with the clearcutting of old-growth stands in the West, especially the coast Douglas-fir (Munger and Matthews, 1941) and western white pine types (Fig. 9-1). It can also be applied on areas where scattered seed trees have been reserved provided that fuel is removed from beneath the trees. Where broadcast burning is applied the whole program of silvicultural practice is restricted to a few rather narrow pathways, especially if the supply of seed for natural reproduction is crucial. It is, for example,

Fig. 9-1. Broadcast burning in preparation for planting after the clearcutting of an overmature stand of the western white pine type, Deception Creek Experimental Forest, Idaho. Note the large volume of defective grand fir and western hemlock which had to be felled before the burning. If this had been left standing, the resulting dead snags might have become ignited in wildfires and spread burning embers far and wide. (*Photograph by U. S. Forest Service.*)

important to modify the timing and extent of broadcast burning so as to avoid destruction of seed that has already fallen. Broadcast burning is more compatible with artificial than with natural regeneration, especially if the treated areas are large.

Spot burning. Sometimes the main advantages of broadcast burning can be achieved merely by burning on part of the slash-covered area. Spot burning is a modification of broadcast burning in which slash is burned in patches with dangerous concentrations. It can be employed only where there is little risk that the fire will spread. The only favorable conditions for spot burning occur where patches of slash dense enough to burn without piling are interspersed with areas relatively free of slash. Spot burning is regarded as a more desirable practice than broadcast burning after partial cuttings in the fire-resistant redwood type (Fritz, 1951). It has also been recommended in the Douglas-fir region as a substitute for broadcast burning in situations where treatment must be carried out in the autumn after a good crop of seed has fallen (Silen, 1952).

Burning of piled slash. Slash disposal associated with partial cutting usually involves the burning of piled slash. Where much of this sort of work is necessary it is now ordinarily done by pushing the slash into piles with bulldozers or similar equipment for subsequent burning (Harris, 1958). Use of such equipment has the important incidental advantage of reducing the competing vegetation and exposing the mineral soil on the treated areas. This effect makes an important contribution to the success of natural regeneration or planting where competition from brush is a serious problem after partial cuttings as in the mixed conifer types of the Sierra Nevada (Gordon and Cosens, 1952; Fig. 9-2).

The older methods of hand piling have little silvicultural effect other than freeing advance regeneration and exposing some mineral

Fig. 9-2. Dense, 6-year-old natural regeneration of ponderosa pine resulting from very intensive site preparation at Blacks Mountain Experimental Forest on the eastern slope of the Sierra Nevada. Most of the slash was piled mechanically in windrows along the edge of the opening, which was created in a group-selection cutting. During the next good seed-year the area was disk-plowed and the rodent population was reduced by poisoning. (*Photograph by U. S. Forest Service.*)

soil. As far as the techniques are concerned, distinction is drawn between **progressive burning** in which the slash is laid on piles as the burning progresses and **piling and burning** in which the piles are constructed well in advance of the time when it becomes safe enough to burn them. Hand piling has become so expensive that it is done only where a very limited amount of slash disposal is necessary.

The only region where any large amount of piling and burning has ever been done is the West and there it is now done largely with bulldozers fitted with modified blades. Mechanical piling is well adapted to the rather open forests of the interior ponderosa pine type, provided that the terrain is not too steep or rocky. The opportunity to dispose of large material in which bark beetles might breed represents a highly important advantage as far as management of ponderosa pine is concerned. Mechanical piling has also been used after clearcutting in the lodgepole pine type, and it leads to fully as good fuel reduction and to better reproduction than broadcast burning, which has been common practice in the past (LeBarron, 1952).

Lopping and scattering of slash. Some of the objectives of slash disposal can sometimes be accomplished without burning. The fire hazard can be reduced somewhat simply by lopping the tops so that the severed branches lie closer to the ground. This is especially advantageous in freeing saplings and seedlings of advance growth that have been bent over by falling tree tops. A limited amount of this kind of work often obviates the necessity for planting or waiting for new natural reproduction and forestalls subsequent difficulties with malformed dominant trees. The release of bent trees should be done as promptly as possible; they straighten up much better at the beginning of the growing season than if they are not given an opportunity to do so until growth has been going on for several weeks.

Although lopping is one of the cheaper forms of slash disposal, anything that involves scattering or moving slash can be rather expensive. Lopped slash is sometimes scattered in instances where any sort of burning would destroy too much advance reproduction. The deliberate scattering of slash provides an artificial means of seed dispersal for closed-cone conifers like jack pine.

It is also possible to break up concentrations of slash or eliminate it in strips along routes of travel simply by moving it. None of these techniques of redistributing slash reduce the total amount of fuel. However, they are often more compatible with silvicultural objectives than methods involving burning, especially in situations where the risk of wild fire is not very great.

Direct control of bark beetles in slash. If the hazard of outbreaks of bark beetles is serious and the utilization cannot be close enough to eliminate the felled material in which they breed, it may be most expedient to spray the slash with insecticides (Jackson, 1960). The best time for spraying the bark comes just before the normal time of egg laying. Other techniques of direct control are mentioned in the section on salvage cutting (Chapter 6).

Chipping of slash. Portable chipping devices are used to a limited extent where slash disposal is absolutely essential and the equally expensive method of hand piling and burning is the only other solution. Chipping is in many respects an ideal solution because no burning is necessary. However, the high cost greatly curtails its use, except in rare instances when profitable use can be made of the chipped debris.

TREATMENT OF THE FOREST FLOOR AND COMPETING VEGETATION

It has already been stated that the establishment and development of a new forest crop can take place only if sufficient growing space is made available by harvesting or killing all or part of the preceding crop. Similarly, any sort of regeneration from seed is affected by the condition of the seedbed. Such basic requirements cannot always be met by judicious adjustment of the pattern of cutting, by intentional or unintentional disturbance in logging, or by treatments of undesirable vegetation that are delayed until after the reproduction is established. Deliberate measures like prescribed burning and mechanical site preparation are sometimes necessary to create the appropriate environmental conditions for natural or artificial reproduction.

Seedbed Preparation

The preparation of seedbeds ordinarily involves treatment of the **forest floor,** which is the layer of unincorporated organic matter which lies on top of the mineral soil and is composed of fallen leaves, twigs, and other plant remains in various stages of decomposition. This material does not make a good seedbed for most small-seeded species, especially if it is exposed to desiccation and heating by the sun or is too thick for speedy root penetration. Bare mineral soil is generally a much more favorable seedbed; the only important exceptions exist with heavy-seeded species, such as oaks or walnuts, which germinate best if the seeds are buried an inch or more beneath the surface of the litter.

There are two general methods of eliminating or reducing the dead organic material of the forest floor. One of these is **prescribed burning;** the second is **scarification** which consists in removing the forest floor or mixing it with the mineral soil by mechanical action. Both methods have harmful as well as beneficial effects that must be understood if they are to be applied successfully. Scarification is the more effective and expensive method of the two, and it can be applied in situations where prescribed burning cannot.

The effects of the various methods of scarification depend on the action of the equipment used. In considering these techniques for exposing the mineral soil, distinction should be made between devices that plow or mix the soil and those that merely scrape off the forest floor. Plowing overturns the normal profile, thereby burying the unincorporated organic matter beneath the mineral soil. Unless the soil is plowed so deeply that infertile subsoil is brought to the surface its effect is more favorable than that of scraping. If the forest floor is scraped away, the inorganic nutrients which it contains are removed. The harm is only temporary if the materials are moved only a short distance to the side. On the other hand, the damage to the soil may be even more serious and permanent if substantial amounts of mineral soil are scraped off with the unincorporated organic matter.

The unfavorable effect of complete removal of the forest floor was observed by LeBarron (1944) who found that, although it enhanced regeneration of jack pine and black spruce, it caused the seedlings to grow poorly and show signs of nutrient deficiency. It is reasonable to assume that scraping causes more damage to the soil than fire because it is at least as harmful to the physical properties and removes inorganic nutrients which would be left behind by burning. Plowing, on the other hand, should be less deleterious than burning because the organic materials are left to decompose in the mineral soil where they are ultimately beneficial to the physical properties.

Burning of the forest floor rarely has any significantly harmful effect on ordinary kinds of soil (Burns, 1952; Vlamis, Biswell, and Schultz, 1955; Fuller, Shannon, and Burgess, 1955; Lotti, Klawitter, and Le-Grande, 1960). Soils composed entirely of organic materials constitute the only clear exceptions; such soils, which occur on rocky ledges and in swamps or peat bogs, can be completely destroyed by fire.

The only nutrient element that is definitely lost to the atmosphere during burning is nitrogen. However, the sudden release of calcium and other elements to the mineral soil usually stimulates the nitrogen-fixing organisms of the soil enough that the losses of nitrogen are quickly replaced.   There is actually little opportunity for loss of nutrients through leaching.   Any nutrient ions moving downward through the soil are usually taken up by the roots of plants or absorbed on the surfaces of both organic and mineral colloids.   It is possible for nutrients to be lost from the ashes by surface flow over sloping, impervious soils.   Even the organic matter content of the mineral soil is sometimes increased by burning.   Such increases may be caused by the accelerated incorporation of organic materials that are disintegrated but not carbonized by burning.   However, it should be noted that most studies of the effect of fire on the soil have involved flat terrain and sandy soils of highly stable physical properties.   Harmful effects would be most likely on sloping terrain and fine-textured soils where the effect of fire has not been investigated as much.

Competing Vegetation

The harvesting of trees inevitably leaves some vacant growing space, at least temporarily.   Even after a very heavy cutting, however, there may be more serious competition, existing or potential, from unwanted vegetation than might be inferred from outward appearances or the severity of the cutting.   Unless the markets are good, there is certain to be a residue of trees that were not worth cutting.   There may also be low vegetation consisting of grasses, herbaceous plants, shrubs, or advance growth of undesirable arborescent species.   If no vegetation shows above ground, there may still be root stocks of sprouting species.   Finally, if little or no vegetation remains and if the site is reasonably favorable for plants, the way is open for invasion by whole armies of plants.

The most serious problems arise when the competing vegetation has existed for many years and is not worth harvesting at all.   The low shrubs of brushfields and the grasses or other herbaceous growth of "open" lands do not cast as much shade as a closed forest but can cause even more root competition as far as seedlings are concerned. Consequently, pre-existing vegetation is most likely to have to be controlled when it is so worthless that artificial regeneration is necessary.

Grass is the common kind of competing vegetation encountered in the planting of abandoned agricultural lands and as part of the natural vegetation of the ponderosa and longleaf pine types.   Evidence is rapidly accumulating that it represents a more serious problem than is often appreciated.   It is now clear that competition with grass is the chief reason why longleaf pine seedlings linger for years in the so-called grass stage during which they fail to grow in height (Shipman, 1958; Bruce, 1959). The elimination of grass competition by plowing or herbicides may solve the very difficult problem of reforesting the old longleaf pine sites with this species rather than other pines that are not clearly adapted to grow there. It is probable that the presence of grass is at least partly responsible for the phenomenon of "check" in planted spruce, a condition of very slow initial growth that may last for a decade or more.

Although a cover of grass reduces frost heaving and frost damage to trees nestled down beneath the grass, it tends to increase frost damage to young trees projecting above it. On cold, frosty nights the mat of grass so effectively insulates the soil that it prevents heat from moving upward to replace that lost by the radiational cooling of the upper surfaces of the vegetation. This phenomenon and ordinary competitive effects (Merz and Finn, 1955) are responsible for the baneful effect of grass on planted hardwoods. There is even evidence that grasses produce unidentified chemical substances that inhibit the growth of trees (Schreiner, 1945). The fact that conifers often succeed in competition with grass is no sign that they are unaffected by it.

In the past, it has often been impractical to provide young trees with anything approaching complete freedom from competition. Herbicides and heavy mechanical equipment have now provided the power to kill the roots of competing vegetation. The spectacular increases in seedling growth that can be attained by such treatment have been observed in a wide variety of species and regions.

Techniques of Treatment

Prescribed burning and mechanical site preparation are techniques in which both the forest floor and competing vegetation can be treated simultaneously. Before considering these two methods in detail, attention is called to other means of accomplishing the objectives.

Some scarification of the mineral soil and reduction of competing vegetation is accomplished during logging and any disposal of slash that is undertaken. Although the resulting disturbance is often adequate it seldom exposes any substantial amount of mineral soil or eradicates much sprouting vegetation. Logging does not result in very complete scarification unless there is a deliberate attempt to skid almost every log over a different pathway on snow-free ground. The one kind of slash disposal most likely to achieve complete site preparation is that in which the slash is piled with bulldozers equipped with root rakes or similar equipment. Broadcast burning often eliminates most of the unincorporated organic matter, but does not necessarily reduce sprouting vegetation very much. Practically all the other methods of logging or slash disposal have limited and erratic effects.

There is no silvicultural treatment other than those mentioned that significantly interrupts the continuity of the forest floor, but there are a number of ways of attacking the competing vegetation. Most of these, such as cutting, girdling, and chemical treatment were considered in Chapter 5. Cutting and girdling are, like fire, entirely adequate for species that do not sprout but rather frustrating to employ against those that do. Herbicides have yet to be perfected to the point where they are successful against all kinds of sprouting vegetation but, from the standpoint of cost and effectiveness, have great potentialities. The expensive methods of mechanical site preparation have the most nearly certain effectiveness, except in the increasing number of situations where the chemical methods can be made to give dependable results.

Grazing and browsing animals are sometimes appropriately selective in their feeding habits to cause moderate and temporary reduction of competing vegetation. Most of the grasses and other plants upon which they feed are capable of sprouting. Feeding that is heavy enough to reduce the competing vegetation substantially is often associated with effects harmful to tree seedlings. Nevertheless regulated herds of domestic animals can sometimes be used to control undesirable vegetation without suffering from malnutrition.

Prescribed Burning

Fire, like cutting, can be used both constructively and destructively in handling the forest. The practice of using regulated fires to reduce or eliminate the unincorporated organic matter of the forest floor or low, undesirable vegetation is called **prescribed** or **controlled burning**. The burning is conducted under such conditions that the size and intensity of the fires are no greater than necessary to achieve some clearly defined purpose of timber production, reduction of fire hazard, wildlife management, or improvement of grazing.

These particular terms, the first of which is preferred, have been coined to distinguish the use of fire as a silvicultural tool from its application for purposes bearing little relationship to the maintenance of productive forests. Very similar types of burning have been traditionally employed in many localities, especially in the South, to keep the forest open enough for grazing or other uses.

For purposes of this discussion, prescribed burning is regarded as involving fires that are set to burn through fuels that naturally occur on the forest floor, usually under existing stands. The burning of slash involves hotter fires and much heavier concentrations of fuel so that it is a kind of treatment easily recognizable as being in a class by itself. However, it could be and often is regarded as a form of prescribed burning.

The role of fire in nature and silviculture. As has already been pointed out, the formative processes in the development of forest stands are disturbances that kill trees and make way for new ones. The characteristics of all stands are determined by the kind, frequency, and magnitude of disturbances that have affected the sites in the past. Climax communities are, in this sense, results of long series of small, light disturbances while pioneer stages are the product of catastrophe. Fire is one of the most common kinds of natural disturbance and many species, including some of the most valuable of the North American forest, represent natural adaptations of the vegetation to fire (Ahlgren and Ahlgren, 1960). Some are adapted to reproduce after severe fires with effects akin to those of broadcast burning and others to much gentler disturbances like those of prescribed burning. These species may be divided into several categories depending on the nature of their adaptation to fire.

The closed-cone pines constitute the first group. They are best exemplified by jack pine and include lodgepole, Monterey, bishop, and sand pine. In these species regeneration occurs naturally after a crown fire has killed the old crop, exposed the mineral soil, and opened the cones. The second group is composed of species like the cherries and a number of undesirable shrubs, including certain species of *Ribes*, that have hard-coated seeds capable of surviving for long periods in the forest floor and springing up after fires (Quick, 1956). The third group consists of the large number of species that can reproduce from stump sprouts or root suckers; this group is composed mainly of broad-leaved trees and shrubs but also includes a few conifers. The fourth category consists of light-seeded species that thrive on seedbeds of bare mineral soil exposed by fire but are not outstandingly resistant to fire.

The fourth group includes many valuable species such as the birches, Douglas-fir, eastern and western white pine, the spruces, sweet-gum, and yellow-poplar. Regeneration of these species after fires comes from seeds already present on the old trees or from those subsequently produced by trees that happened to survive because of their size or location. Those that are true pioneers form all or part of the main canopy almost from the time of their establishment. Those that are rather tolerant of shade are likely to become established simultaneously with faster growing pioneer species and remain underneath until the death of the pioneers, which are usually short-lived. In other words, this fourth group is a heterogeneous one including a wide range of species that do not all respond to fire in exactly the same way.

In all four categories mentioned the species involved are primarily adapted to regeneration after catastrophic fires that destroy most of the trees of one generation and prepare the way for another. It would be absurd to duplicate these conflagrations because of both the waste and the danger to public safety which would result. Under present practice, the effects of these fires are simulated only where fire is used for slash disposal, particularly that done by broadcast burning. There is the possibility that prescribed burning may prove useful for accomplishing certain objectives in the management of these species. At present, however, the usual practice is to simulate the effects of fire by means other than burning.

Finally there is a fifth category of species which have sufficiently fire-resistant bark to withstand burning at intervals throughout most of a single generation. This group consists of certain hard pines, notably those of the South. The most outstanding is longleaf pine, which thrives only as a result of periodic fires. The others are loblolly, pitch, shortleaf, slash, and ponderosa pine; there is a strong possibility that red pine also belongs in this group. Occasional surface fires were beneficial to the maintenance of these species in the original forest because they arrested natural succession, exposed favorable seedbeds, and prevented more destructive fires. Up to the present time prescribed burning has been extensively applied only to this group of fire-resistant trees. It has been practiced on a large scale mainly on the Atlantic Coastal Plain from New Jersey southward (Crow, 1955); its use in the ponderosa pine types of the West is increasing.

There is no reason why a species should have but one means of adaptation to fire. Critical examination will reveal that a number of species could be fitted into several of the categories just mentioned. Pitch pine, a species that grows on sites where it is constantly bedeviled by fire, is an outstanding example of such a species. It develops the thick, fire-resistant bark characteristic of trees of the fifth group. Its cones have some tendency to be serotinous, like the pines of the first category. Seedlings and saplings killed by fire sprout from the base, like species of the third group mentioned (Little and Somes, 1956); older trees defoliated by fire usually sprout new crowns. Like all the species of the fifth category it could be regarded as a particularly well-adapted member of the fourth.

It should not be inferred that any of these species are regenerated only after fire or similar devastation in the original forest. Regardless of the extent to which any one of them was favored by fire, it would be naive to suppose that the use of fire was mandatory in its silvicultural treatment and could not be simulated by other means. The question of whether prescribed burning should be used in the silviculture of a species naturally adapted to fire depends on whether the wastage and danger associated with natural fires can be eliminated. It must be anticipated that the applicability of prescribed burning will also vary with the circumstances prevailing in each stand.

Purposes and effects of prescribed burning. When properly applied in appropriate situations, prescribed burning represents an expeditious means of accomplishing a number of objectives.

1. The most common objective of prescribed burning is still **fuel reduction.** In many respects it is a more satisfactory method than conventional slash disposal because it eliminates most of the readily inflammable fuels rather than just the debris left from logging. It is, however, important to note that prescribed burning does not render any area fireproof, except temporarily, and is, therefore, no substitute for a well-developed system of fire control.

The most important effect of prescribed burning in fuel reduction is the interruption of the horizontal and sometimes the vertical continuity of inflammable materials. The interruption of any vertical curtain of fuel is especially significant in the slash pine type of the Southeast and the oak-pine type of southern New Jersey. Areas of slash pine which have not been burned for a decade or more develop a tall understory of various inflammable shrubs that become draped with fallen pine needles (Bickford and Newcomb, 1947). In fuels of this kind surface fires can rapidly develop into disastrous crown fires because there is a ready path for the flames to follow from the ground up into the crowns. In the oak-pine type of New Jersey the presence of a shrubby understory tends to create the same dangerous condition (Little, Allen, and Moore, 1948). In each of these regions, successful silviculture depends heavily on the prevention of crown fires and it has been shown that prescribed burning is the only dependable means of forestalling them.

2. Prescribed burning is also effective in **preparation of seedbeds** for regeneration of wind-disseminated species like the pines which

become established most readily on bare mineral soil. This effect is also beneficial in hampering reproduction of the heavy-seeded oaks that would displace many of the pines in the course of natural succession.

3. Prescribed burning is also a means of achieving **control of competing vegetation.** This often has the effect of arresting natural succession by killing understories representing stages later than the one desired. However, where the aim is to prevent invasion by hardwoods, as in stands of southern pines, burning must be done fairly often because only the seedlings are likely to be killed by fire; saplings will resprout and larger trees may only be scarred. Roots of perennial grasses are killed by prescribed burning only where there are large units of fuel, such as fallen snags or large chunks of wood, that ignite and burn for a long enough period to heat the soil in depth (Weaver, 1951). Both in nature and in practice, surface fires must occur quite frequently if they are to be very effective in keeping brush and other understory vegetation in check. Fire is really a rather cumbersome tool for the accomplishment of this purpose and it is now fortunate that it can now be supplemented or replaced by herbicides.

Beyond these three main purposes of controlled burning, there are several others which have been clearly established only in the case of longleaf pine and, to a limited extent, slash pine; these are as follows:

4. The **improvement of grazing,** for which fire has been used traditionally, may be obtained by prescribed burning in the longleaf and longleaf-slash pine types (Wahlenberg, Greene, and Reed, 1939; Lemon, 1946). These forests have a characteristic understory of grass which can be enhanced in amount and quality by periodic removal of the litter and dead grass. Although annual burning might be best for production of forage, it is incompatible with the perpetuation of any tree species, even longleaf pine. Grass can also be maintained by repeated burning beneath stands of other southern pines, but the grass is of poor quality and can exist only at the expense of timber production.

5. The herbaceous legumes and possibly other food plants which become established after burning are valuable for the **management of wildlife.** Stoddard (1935) has found that prescribed burning maintains a good supply of food for the bobwhite quail in the Southeast.

6. The most decisive influence of prescribed burning on the silviculture of longleaf pine is control of the fungus (*Scirrhia acicola*)

causing the defoliating brown-spot disease (Siggers, 1944). If the infected needles are not burned off periodically, the seedlings will often fail to emerge from the protracted grass stage and eventually succumb.

There is probably no kind of silvicultural practice which has produced more violent disagreement among American foresters than prescribed burning. These differences of opinion have quite naturally involved the effects of burning on the forest and all aspects of its management.

The most significant objection is based on psychological grounds. The reduction of losses from man-caused fires remains one of the most important problems of American forestry. It is not easy to reconcile the deliberate burning of forests with all the efforts being made to prevent accidental and incendiary fires and to educate the public about their harmful effects. However, prescribed burning has its greatest usefulness, and is indeed used the most, in those very regions where difficulties with fire are the greatest, simply because valuable species that are naturally well adapted to fire are most likely to occur there. In many respects the use of fire in slash disposal and prescribed burning is actually a concession to the inevitable in localities where fires are discouragingly common and fuel reduction almost essential.

It has already been indicated that only exceptional kinds of soils are harmed by fire and that prescribed burning is useful only in forest types where natural fires are common. If burning had any seriously harmful effects on the soils involved, they would probably already be ruined. Successful programs of prescribed burning generally have the effect of making fires either less severe or less frequent than they were before the initiation of comprehensive programs of fire control and silvicultural management. The harmful effects of fire are much more likely to take the form of obvious and long-enduring effects on the vegetation than of subtle damage to the soil (Lutz, 1956).

The effects of prescribed burning on standing timber depend on the size of the trees and the extent to which their stems and crowns are heated by the fires (Hare, 1961). Except for longleaf pine, there is no American species that can withstand controlled burning until rough, thickened bark has developed on the lower parts of the stems; the main portion of the crown canopy must also be well above the height of the flames.

The extent of injury to any part of the tree depends on whether the living tissues are heated above the lethal threshold of 122°F and how long such a temperature is maintained. Therefore, any factor that hastens the transport of heated air out of the forest reduces the danger of damage. On level terrain it is, for this reason, better to conduct prescribed burning when there is a gentle breeze than in calm weather; however, on pronounced slopes sufficient updrafts develop to allow burning when there is no wind (Biswell, 1958).

The initial temperature of the living tissues is also important in determining the highest temperature that they attain. The risk of injury is lowest when burning is done in the winter because it takes such a large amount of heat to raise the tissues to lethal temperatures. Head-fires, which travel with the wind, are often less damaging than back-fires, which burn against the wind, because the heat is carried upward more rapidly and high temperatures are not as long sustained close to the ground. However, head-fires are more likely to spread to the crowns and should thus be avoided where the crowns are likely to be damaged.

Such evidence as is available indicates that the light surface fires used in prescribed burning cause slight reductions both in diameter growth of saplings and in height growth of trees up to pole size, at least in slash pine (McCulley, 1950). These effects probably exist in longleaf pine as well, but they are generally more than compensated for by control of the brown-spot fungus (Bruce, 1951). Any loss in growth from prescribed burning in southern pines is likely to be insignificant compared with the consequences of avoiding the use of fire when there is some good reason for employing it.

Prescribed burning is applicable only in stands composed of trees that have reached fire-resistant size. It is not easily used in uneven-aged stands because it damages reproduction. The only way in which controlled burning can be applied in uneven-aged stands is to handle them by the group-selection method with a cycle of cutting and burning no shorter than the time required for reproduction to appear and develop resistance to fire (Chapman, 1942).

The surest way to avoid damage to the forest from prescribed burning is to conduct it under the right conditions according to carefully developed plans. Like all silvicultural operations, it is not an end in itself but a means of achieving some well-defined goal of management.

Methods of prescribed burning. The customary plan of action in conducting a prescribed burn is to isolate the area to be treated by means of plowed lines wide enough to contain the fire. Since the construction of these lines is costly, every reasonable advantage should be taken of pre-existing barriers such as roads and swamps. The whole operation should be carefully mapped out with special regard for the selected conditions of wind and weather under which the burning is to be conducted (Hills, 1957; Davis, 1959). The fire lines should be plowed out in advance according to this plan, but not so early that they are covered over with fallen leaves before the burning is done.

The most common practice is to use back-fires (Fig. 9-3). Flanking or "quartering" fires, which are set in lines parallel to the wind, spread more rapidly, but are somewhat more likely to scorch the foliage of saplings or taller trees. Head-fires can be used when the forest floor is too moist to be burned by back-fires, thus increasing the number of days when treatment can be conducted. They are in some respects safer than back-fires because they are more likely to go out than to escape from control if the wind shifts unexpectedly. The heat from them is carried away rapidly so that they are less likely to produce fire scars on the stems of trees than are back-fires. If head-fires can be used safely, they are cheaper than back-fires because they can cover an acre much more rapidly.

Fig. 9-3. Prescribed fire backing into the wind beneath a stand of slash pine. (*Photograph by U. S. Forest Service.*)

The area to be treated should be subdivided into units no larger than can be burned in a period of about 10 hours, although several units may be burned simultaneously. It is unwise to let a fire run for a longer period because of the possibility of unforeseen changes in wind and weather.

The most important consideration is selection of the time of burning. Careful attention must be given to weather forecasts and measurements of fire danger. The wind should be steady both as to speed and direction. The moisture content of both fuel and soil is significant not only from the standpoint of safety but also as a means of determining whether the forest floor is sufficiently inflammable for economical treatment.

The burning should obviously be planned and conducted by personnel experienced in control of wildfires. This policy is desirable not only for the sake of safety but also to provide the men with an opportunity to increase their knowledge of fire behavior. The size of the force and the amount of fire equipment at hand should be large enough to deal with any fires that escape.

The costs of prescribed burning depend on the size and shape of the units burned, the inflammability of the fuels, the length of fire line that has to be constructed, and the size of the crew. On the Atlantic Coastal Plain the cost of burning units larger than 25 acres is about 50 cents per acre (Lotti, Klawitter, and LeGrande, 1960), with the cost of fire lines being the chief variable. Higher costs may result when there is a heavy accumulation of fuel or so little that the fires must be relighted occasionally. The costs of burning small tracts, areas with irregular boundaries, or narrow strips along roads are inordinately high. However, if large areas can be treated in one operation, several burnings can be done for the cost of one broadcast spraying with herbicides. If the undesirable vegetation is small, such a series of burns may be almost as effective in controlling the vegetation and also reduces the amount of fuel very substantially.

Application of prescribed burning. The details of prescribed burning vary according to the species and objectives of treatment, the most important variable being the schedule of burning.

The unraveling of the ecological relationship between fire and longleaf pine represents one of the most interesting developments in American silviculture (Chapman, 1926; Wahlenberg, 1946; Bruce and Nelson, 1957). It has been established that this valuable species is not only adapted to fire but must also be subjected to periodic winter burning if it is to grow in dense, thrifty stands. The best procedure for obtaining reproduction is to burn the seedbed in the winter preceding seed fall so that there will be one season's growth of grass to protect the seeds and tender young seedlings. The seedlings germinate in the autumn and do not become fire-resistant until the following summer. This explains why the traditional practice of *annual* burning for forage production, to say nothing of clearcutting and the depredations of hogs, did so much to convert cutover longleaf lands to grassy plains.

The seedlings fail to grow in height for at least several years and sometimes for as many as a dozen years while a long taproot is developing. During this grass stage they are highly resistant to fire but their development and survival is seriously handicapped by the brown-spot disease (Siggers, 1944) and competition from grass. When infection by brown spot approaches a dangerous level, usually after the third growing season, it is necessary to conduct another burning. Although it has been customary to use back-fires for this purpose, head-fires are less damaging to the seedlings because they do not create such high temperatures at ground level (Byram, 1958). The infected needles are burned off in the fire thereby reducing the production of spores sufficiently to allow at least a year without serious fungal defoliation. However, the burning may prove futile if there are any untreated areas nearby because spores can spread in rapidly from the side by rain splash and reinfect seedlings on the burned areas. Therefore, the treated areas must be large, preferably 200 acres or more. The burning is continued, if necessary, at intervals of about 3 years until the seedlings finally start to emerge from the grass.

As soon as fairly large numbers of seedlings have started to grow in height, burning should be suspended until they become about 4 feet tall because they tend to lack fire resistance during this period. Fortunately this period is not long and damage from the brown-spot disease decreases rapidly as the seedlings develop crowns above the 2-foot levels (Siggers, 1944). After the trees are more than 4 feet high, prescribed burning is conducted as often as necessary to prevent accumulation of fuel, improve production of forage, or keep undesirable shrubs and scrub oaks in check. The interval between burns during the remainder of the rotation should be 3 years or somewhat longer.

The use of prescribed burning in the management of slash pine is primarily a means of reducing the fire hazard and, as is sometimes the case with longleaf pine, of facilitating the gathering of naval stores. Slash pine is not sufficiently resistant for controlled burning until at least 12 to 15 feet in height and 10 years old (McCulley, 1950). The

Fig. 9-4. The upper photograph shows an untreated 45-year-old stand of lob-lolly pine with a dense hardwood understory at the Santee Experimental Forest on the South Carolina coastal plain.   The lower photograph was taken on the same spot 6 years later, just after the second of two partial cuttings and after four prescribed burning operations.   (*Photograph by U. S. Forest Service.*)

interval between burns should be determined on the basis of the ac-cumulation of fuel beneath the stands; it will usually be from 5 to 10 years.   If the stands are being turpentined, burning can be conducted if the litter is raked from the trees that are being worked.   The main purpose of prescribed burning is to forestall the tendency of slash pine stands to develop an inflammable understory of gallberry and other shrubs draped with fallen needles. The disastrous fires that develop in this kind of fuel represent the most serious threat to the culture of slash pine.

The outstanding objective of prescribed burning in the loblolly-shortleaf pine type is control of hardwoods that are so well adapted to growth in the shade (Kozlowski, 1949) that they are a constant threat to the perpetuation of pine (Fig. 9-4). Prescribed burning is also very useful in seedbed preparation (Fig. 9-5) and fuel reduction. Pines that are free to grow become resistant to winter fires at an age of about 10 years or when they are 3 inches in diameter at 1 foot above ground (Chapman, 1942). A series of winter fires, if repeated at intervals of 5 to 10 years, will keep the hardwoods in check because those less than 1 or 2 inches D.B.H. are killed back to the ground. However, the actual preparation of sites for regeneration usually requires summer burning.

Fig. 9-5. A stand in the same place and treated similarly to that shown in Fig. 9-4, but after an additional 5 years, with dense natural reproduction of pine replacing the original hardwood understory. The treatment here consisted of one winter fire followed by three successive annual summer burnings. (*Photograph by U. S. Forest Service.*)

Several summer fires are capable of killing the root stocks of small gums, oaks, and other hardwoods that invade middle-aged stands (Lotti, Klawitter, and LeGrande, 1960). Summer fires are also much more effective than winter fires in exposing mineral soil (Ferguson, 1958) and involve no risk of destroying any seeds that have fallen. Rather sizeable hardwoods can also be dealt with by combinations of prescribed burning and broadcast spraying of herbicides. The burning kills back the hardwoods and the succulent sprouts from them are then killed by spraying early in the next growing season. This tends to exhaust the supply of dormant buds before the new sprouts can produce any more. Prescribed burning in this forest type has been done mostly on the flat terrain and sandy soils of the coastal plain and is more difficult to apply on the Piedmont Plateau.

In the pitch-shortleaf pine forests of southern New Jersey prescribed burning plays the same role in control of hardwoods and seedbed preparation that it does in the loblolly-shortleaf type; it also aids in the prevention of disastrous crown fires as in the slash pine type (Little and Somes, 1961). The pines become resistant to fire when they attain a D.B.H. of 2 inches, which usually occurs at an age of 20 years. Thereafter burning at intervals of 4 or 5 years is necessary for fuel reduction and control of hardwoods. Repeated crown fires have reduced the forests of this locality to degraded stands of oak and pine sprouts. Prescribed burning, by reducing the danger of such conflagrations, offers the only economical means of ensuring their replacement by productive stands of pine originating from seed.

The observations of Weaver (1951, 1955, 1959) and Cooper (1960) in the typically uneven-aged stands of the interior ponderosa pine type have demonstrated that fire had a role in the original forest similar to that which it played in the southern pines. It occurred at intervals frequent enough to restrict the amount of inflammable debris; reproduction was often abundant on the barren places created by the burning of such debris. On the best sites, fire prevented invasion by the relatively tolerant and less valuable Douglas-fir and true firs. There are also indications that light surface fires improve forage production and reduce the danger of serious fires. Weaver also found that fire occasionally prevented the stagnation of dense groups of saplings by thinning out the trees of the lower crown classes. However, subsequent trials (Morris and Mowat, 1958; Lindenmuth, 1960) have indicated that fires severe enough to accomplish any thinning seem to kill more potential crop trees than they release. The other points made in favor of prescribed burning by Weaver seem valid enough; there remain only the problems commonly encountered in using fire in uneven-aged stands where old resistant trees are intermingled with groups of seedlings and saplings that are not resistant.

It is clear that fire had some effect, not yet well defined, in the maintenance of sugar and ponderosa pine in the mixed conifer forests of the western slope of the Sierra Nevada (Mason, 1955; Burcham, 1960; Wagener, 1961). These forests are as difficult to reproduce as they are magnificent. However, the situation is complicated by the presence of a number of shrubby species that are favored as much by burning as are the pines. Most of the recent investigations of the use of fire in these forests have been the outgrowth of prescribed burning designed to eliminate woody vegetation and improve grazing in the foothills (Biswell, 1958). However, satisfactory fuel reduction and control of brush has been achieved under established stands of ponderosa pine. Further developments probably await more complete understanding of the ecology of the wide variety of trees and shrubs found in these forests.

Many of the better forests of moist, cool, northern climates, especially the birch and coniferous types, owe their origin to the effects of fire (Ahlgren, 1959). However, most of the fires involved were of the catastrophic kind that occurred at long intervals rather than the light, frequent fires duplicated by prescribed burning. Therefore, prescribed burning, as distinct from broadcast burning of slash, is likely to have a more limited place in the management of these forests than in regions where fires have been more frequent.

Experimentation in Ontario has indicated that hot fires burning in slash and natural fuels can be used to open the cones on standing jack pines for seeding cutover areas or replacing poor orchard-like stands (Chrosciewicz, 1959).

There is a significant pattern in the development of the application of prescribed burning in those localities where it is used. When management is started in a forest type that owes its better characteristics to repeated burning, it is most logical to attempt to conduct silviculture by methods that do not include prescribed burning. If this line of action produces a satisfactory result, there is no reason for resorting to the use of fire, which is at best a treacherous tool.

There are, nevertheless, some instances where such exclusion of fire created situations in which the problems multiplied progressively. The essential conditions for reproduction of the desirable trees were created less frequently, and the understories filled up with arborescent or shrubby species that were adapted to the new conditions and were often of little value. As fuels accumulated, wildfires that formerly caused little damage showed an increasing tendency to develop into conflagrations; oftentimes this development proceeded more rapidly than fire control could be improved to meet it. Frequently the point was reached where undesirable, sprouting vegetation could no longer be eliminated by fire and had to be left or attacked by more laborious methods. It is possible that this pattern of events will be recognized in regions well beyond the boundaries of the Atlantic Coastal Plain and the range of ponderosa pine.

Mechanical Treatment

The mechanical methods of site preparation may include a number of different and distinct processes which are described in the following paragraph. Sometimes only one of these processes is accomplished; several of them can be done simultaneously; all of them are sometimes done as parts of one treatment.

The **reduction of undesirable vegetation** can be done by uprooting large woody plants, chopping up smaller plants, or plowing under grasses and other herbaceous growth. The objective of this step is usually to disrupt the roots of the undesirable plants enough to kill them. Of course, mechanical equipment can be used simply to cut or break off the stems of woody plants, especially those that are incapable of sprouting. It is entirely possible that one might attempt to eliminate only the woody vegetation and leave any grasses or other low plants alone, especially if their competition is not likely to be significant and excludes more troublesome plants.

Practically all site preparation involves some **redistribution of dead vegetation.** This may range from concentrating uprooted trees into high windrows to the gentle scarification of thin litter beneath otherwise undisturbed vegetation. With large debris the objective is partly to remove obstacles to subsequent operations. It may also be desirable to hasten the destruction of debris; this can be done not only with fire but also by pushing it into compact piles or working it into the mineral soil so it will rot more quickly. With the gentler kinds of treatment there may be no objective other than **exposure of mineral soil.** Any method of mechanical site preparation exposes some of the mineral soil, often in the process of doing something more difficult.

If the site is subject to extremes of moisture conditions, activities occasionally include **reshaping** the soil surface. This usually is done by some sort of plowing or scraping to create low ridges in wet places or shallow trenches in dry situations.

If previous operations have left the ground too uneven, **smoothing**

Fig. 9-6. A bulldozer and two rolling brush cutters being used to destroy a cover of poor oak and grass preparatory to planting pine on a dry, sandy site on the Southeastern Coastal Plain. The two water-filled drums are hitched at an angle to one another and to the direction of travel to impart a shearing action to the sharp blades. (*Photograph by Caterpillar Tractor Co.*)

of the surface may be desirable. This is often necessary if large trees have been uprooted and the area is to be planted with machines. The smoothing is usually done with harrows and it does not necessarily destroy any ridges and trenches that were deliberately created previously. Some smoothing may be desirable simply to facilitate future logging operations or other use of the stands.

There is, of course, a wide range in the kind and size of equipment used to perform these processes. The choice depends on the objectives and the amount of physical work needed to achieve them. The lighter kinds of work can be done with hand tools, although American labor costs are so high that the work is usually done with tractor-powered devices. Some of the equipment is very large and powerful, especially if large trees are to be uprooted. Scarification alone requires the least power and can often be done by dragging various types of harrows, rakes, or special devices (Vanselow, 1949) over the ground with horses or light tractors. Single- or double-moldboard plows, including those designed for constructing fire lines, can be used for furrowing.

Most efforts at site preparation are directed mainly at the destruction of competing vegetation. Vegetation of sapling size or smaller can be broken up and worked into the soil with heavy disk plows or rolling brush choppers (Fig. 9-6; Hopkins and Anderson, 1960). If the vegetation is chopped up and worked into the soil, it is often desirable to apply two treatments, the second following after there has been some opportunity for sprouting to take place (Woods, 1959).

Bulldozers or similar devices (Fig. 9-7; Edminster and Ryerson, 1960) can be used against vegetation of any size from small brush to large trees. However, they must be fitted with special toothed blades or "root rakes" (Fig. 9-8) if they are to be very effective in uprooting anything without scraping away too much topsoil. The uprooting of large areas of sizeable trees is sometimes done by using powerful tractors to drag battleship anchor chains over the ground. The huge links of these chains pinch around the bases of the trees

Fig. 9-7. Clearing of oak on a dry upland site with a Rome "K-G" blade. The sharpened blade is set at an angle so that it can be used to shear off the trees at or below the ground line; the upper bar pushes the trees over as they are being severed. The "stinger" at one end of the blade is shown splitting the stem of a large tree so that it can be cut off or pushed over in two passes of the machine. (*Photograph by Caterpillar Tractor Co.*)

Fig. 9-8. A brush rake clearing a brush field for planting, Eldorado National Forest, California. (*Photograph by U. S. Forest Service.*)

and remain engaged until the trees are pulled over. Ordinarily pairs of tractors are used to drag one chain. The uprooted trees must then be pushed into windrows with bulldozers.

Mechanical control of competing vegetation is used chiefly in situations where prescribed burning is unsafe or ineffective and herbicides have not proven sufficiently effective. The use of bulldozers for such work is necessary if the piling of slash or the removal of large obstacles to machine planting is one of the subsidiary objectives of the treatment.

The most thorough and intensive application of this kind of site preparation is conducted on the Atlantic Coastal Plain for the conversion of degenerate hardwood stands to pine by planting (Wackerman and Chaiken, 1958). Although prescribed burning is very useful in the pine forests of this region it is seldom a safe or effective means of destroying hardwood stands. In fact, many of the poor stands in question have sprouted up as a result of fires (Fig. 9-6); the chief effect of fire would be more sprouting. Furthermore, pure hardwood leaf litter is usually either too moist to burn or so dry that it easily burns out of control. Some sites are also too wet to burn effectively.

So far the use of herbicides has not been perfected to the point where they are widely regarded as an acceptable substitute.

Mechanical site preparation of the kinds described is usually a preliminary to planting.   If there has been any substantial overturning or upheaval of the mineral soil, it is necessary to delay planting for several months to allow the soil to settle.   Otherwise there is risk that many of the roots of the seedlings will be planted in air pockets and die of drought.   The smoothing of areas with heavy harrows is often aimed chiefly at making it possible to plant with machines.   Although the competing vegetation is greatly reduced by such drastic treatment there are usually some sprouting rootstocks left in the soil.

In all treatments of this sort it is desirable to avoid the horizontal movement of organic materials and topsoil as much as possible.   The churning or overturning of these materials in place is distinctly preferable to any sort of scraping action (Grelen, 1959).   The importance of these considerations depends on the vertical distribution of the nutrient capital of the site and that of the physical properties of the mineral soil (Wilhite, 1961).   Ordinarily, but not invariably, most of the nutrient capital is contained in the living and dead organic materials and the first few inches of topsoil.   If the soil consists of a thin layer of sandy soil over an impervious substratum, any sort of scraping can severely reduce the available root space.   The bulldozer is an instrument of last resort that is capable of damaging the soil more than fire or any other tool yet devised.   It should not be anticipated that all of the harmful effects will appear early in the life of the new forest crop.

The costs of complete mechanical treatment of an area vary from about $10 to $50 per acre and probably depend mostly on the volume of debris that is being moved.   With very heavy equipment, the cost often depends mostly on how much of the depreciation is charged against the operation.   Efforts to reduce costs by restricting activities to the clearing of narrow lanes through the undesirable vegetation do not always prove effective.

It is reasonable to suppose that the use of herbicides will ultimately be perfected to the point where the use of heavy equipment can be restricted to situations where there is compelling necessity to eliminate the obstruction or fire hazard represented by the undesirable vegetation.   Scarification will probably be used increasingly as an aid to natural regeneration of light-seeded species.   In many situations where fire cannot be used, scarification is one of the most expeditious means of increasing the effectiveness of a natural source of seed.

It is important to note, however, that excessively thorough exposure of mineral soil may lead to the establishment of very dense reproduction of desirable species that will require precommercial thinning or of an overwhelming growth of fast-growing weeds that will have to be treated subsequently.

TREATMENT OF THE MINERAL SOIL

Ordinarily exposure of the mineral soil is the most that need be done in the way of seedbed preparation for reproduction. Even this may actually be detrimental for some heavy-seeded species. In some instances the surface of the mineral soil may be too compact for easy penetration by the roots of germinating seedlings. This is most likely if the soil has a high clay content and has been subjected to heavy grazing, erosion, or severe burning. The condition can be remedied by mechanical loosening of the soil but the effect is so temporary that such treatments are rarely applied. The best way of dealing with soil compaction is to prevent if from occurring in the first place. The only permanent means of rehabilitation is the maintenance of an undisturbed forest floor over a period long enough to enable the soil fauna and plant roots to rework the soil thoroughly.

Fertilization, drainage, and irrigation are intensive treatments of the soil aimed more at improvement of site quality than at preparation for regeneration. The proper conduct of these treatments depends so heavily on knowledge of the complex chemical properties of soils and their moisture relationships that it is logical to refer to works on forest soils and other accounts, such as those of White and Leaf (1956), Arneman (1960), and Willis et al. (1961), for more complete information.

Fertilization

Few forest soils provide an optimum supply of the nutrient elements essential for the growth of trees. Sometimes marked deficiencies may exist because of improper land management in the past or merely because of inherently low natural fertility of the site. The correction of such deficiencies by fertilization is, at least in North America, still in the experimental stage so it is difficult to be very specific about the results.

It is almost always possible to produce significant increases in growth by the application of nitrogen fertilizers (Gessel, 1959). Unfortunately this important element is rather expensive and the price of the increased amount of wood is rarely great enough to pay for the cost of treatment. Furthermore, nitrogen is the one important nutrient element that can be lost to the atmosphere; it is not clear how long the increased growth resulting from its use can be sustained without further applications.

Fertilization with elements of mineral origin, such as potassium, phosphorus, and calcium, rarely produces such marked response as nitrogen fertilizers but the effects are more enduring because these elements are much more likely to be retained in the nutrient cycle of the forest. So long as the foliage and litter are not removed from the site, the harvesting of wood has little effect on the nutrient capital. There are a number of instances in which substantial benefit has been gained at moderate cost by application of potassium and phosphorus. It should be noted, however, that outstanding responses to the more common fertilizer elements have been obtained mostly on sites that are so poor that their intensive treatment is still a dubious proposition. It is conceivable that there are some soils where application of very small quantities of trace elements, such as zinc, boron, and copper, might yield substantial benefits. Such instances are known in the forests of Australia, a continent famous for a variety of unusual nutrient deficiencies, but are either less common or not so frequently detected in America.

The long history of experimentation with fertilizers in agriculture is sufficient to indicate that there are substantial differences in the nutrient status of different soils and the requirements of different species. Therefore, it is not reasonable to suppose that either the details or the feasibility of forest fertilization can be established without a large number of very localized trials; most of these still lie in the future.

Most fertilization has so far been done in connection with planting, especially that done for erosion control or similar special purposes on depleted soils. It is possible that fertilization may prove to be a necessary and economical kind of corrective action to remedy the drawbacks of the drastic kinds of mechanical site preparation described in the previous section. It has been established that broadcast fertilization of planting sites is best deferred until the planted trees have outgrown any undesirable vegetation that might respond more vigorously than the new crop. This difficulty can be avoided by applying slowly soluble fertilizers in the holes where the trees are planted.

There is evidence that fertilization might be used to increase the amount and frequency of seed production not only of seed orchards but also of individual trees being used as sources of natural regeneration (Steinbrenner, Duffield, and Campbell, 1960).

Drainage and Irrigation

Correction of the extremes of soil moisture is somewhat unusual in American forestry because it is expensive and there are vast areas where adequate growth can be obtained without such treatment. The most common kinds of effort in this direction involve various kinds of plowing in preparation for planting rather than the creation of spectacular systems of ditches. With modern plows it is not difficult to create furrows carefully designed to cause water to collect in spots where trees are to be planted or to throw up ridges on which trees can grow in soils that would otherwise be poorly aerated.

A more intensive and expensive kind of plowing is commonly employed in preparing moist and degraded sites in western Europe for planting. Much of the large-scale reforestation that has been undertaken in Britain during recent decades has necessitated deep plowing to break the hardpans and drain the moss layers that developed after ancient deforestation and centuries of grazing.

During recent years some major drainage projects have been undertaken in order to grow pine on coastal swamps in the Southeast (Maki, 1960). The drainage canals are sometimes large enough that the fill from them is used as the foundation for the network of extraction roads designed to serve the drained areas (Miller and Maki, 1957). Unless there are already natural stands of pond pine such as exist in many of the North Carolina swamps, mechanical site preparation is also necessary for the subsequent planting of pines. Such efforts are very expensive and are usually undertaken to assure supplies of pulpwood to particular mills. The ultimate outcome of these projects is yet to be determined, but they are doubtless the most ambitious yet undertaken in American silviculture.

There are as yet no important instances in which forest crops have been grown under irrigation on this continent. However, there are a few places in the Mediterranean countries and the Middle East where wood is in such short supply that hybrid poplar and other species are grown on irrigated lands.

REFERENCES

Ahlgren, C. E. 1959. Some effects of fire on forest reproduction in northeastern Minnesota. *J. Forestry* 57:194–200.

Ahlgren, I. F., and C. E. Ahlgren. 1960. Ecological effects of forest fires. *Bot. Rev.* 26:483–533.

Arneman, H. F.   1960.   Fertilization of forest trees.   *Advances in Agronomy* 12:171–195.

Bickford, C. A., and L. S. Newcomb.   1947.   Prescribed burning in the Florida flatwoods.   *Fire Control Notes* 8(1):17–23.

Biswell, H. H.   1958.   Prescribed burning in Georgia and California compared. *J. Range Management* 11:293–297.

Boyce, J. S.   1961.   *Forest pathology*, 3rd ed.   McGraw-Hill, New York.

Bruce, D.   1951.   Fire, site and longleaf height growth.   *J. Forestry* 49:25–28.

———.   1959.   Effect of low competition on longleaf pine seedling growth. *Proc. Soc. Am. Foresters Meeting*, 1958: 151–153.

Bruce, D., and R. M. Nelson.   1957.   Use and effects of fire in southern forests: abstracts of publications by the Southern and Southeastern Forest Experiment Stations, 1921–55.   *Fire Control Notes* 18:67–96.

Burcham, L. T.   1960.   Planned burning as a management practice for California wild lands.   *Proc. Soc. Am. Foresters Meeting*, 1959:180–185.

Burns, P. Y.   1952.   Effect of fire on forest soils in the pine barren region of New Jersey.   *Yale Univ. School of Forestry Bul.* 57.

Byram, G. M.   1958.   Some basic thermal processes controlling the effects of fire on living vegetation.   *SEFES Research Note 114.*

Chapman, H. H.   1926.   Factors determining natural reproduction of longleaf pine on cut-over lands in La Salle Parish, Louisiana.   *Yale Univ. School of Forestry Bul.* 16.

———.   1942.   Management of loblolly pine in the pine-hardwood region in Arkansas and in Louisiana west of the Mississippi River.   *Yale Univ. School of Forestry Bul.* 49.

Chrosciewicz, Z.   1959.   Controlled burning experiments on jack pine sites. *Canada, Forestry Branch, Forest Research Div. Tech. Note* 72.

Cooper, C. F.   1960.   Changes in vegetation, structure and growth of southwestern pine forests since white settlement.   *Ecological Monographs* 30: 129–164.

Crow, A. B. (Ed.).   1955.   Modern forest fire management in the South. *Proc., Fourth Annual Forestry Symposium, La. State Univ.*

Davis, K. P.   1959.   *Forest fire: control and use.*   McGraw-Hill, New York.

Edminster, T. W., and G. E. Ryerson.   1960.   Machines for clearing land.   *In:* Power to produce.   *USDA Yearbook of Agr.* 1960.   Pp. 103–106.

Fahnestock, G. R.   1960.   Logging slash flammability.   *IMFRES Research Paper* 58.

Ferguson, E. R.   1958.   Age of rough (ground cover) affects shortleaf pine establishment and survival.   *J. Forestry* 56:422–423.

Fritz, E.   1951.   Some principles governing the growing of redwood crops.   *J. Forestry* 49:263–266.

Fuller, W. H., S. Shannon, and P. S. Burgess.   1955.   Effect of burning on certain forest soils of northern Arizona.   *Forest Sci.* 1:44–50.

Gessel, S. P.   1959.   Forest soil fertility problems and research in the western United States.   *Proc. Soc. Am. Foresters Meeting*, 1958:177–180.

Gordon, D. T., and R. D. Cosens.   1952.   Slash disposal and site preparation in converting old-growth sugar pine-fir forests to regulated stands.   *CFRES Forest Research Note* 81.

Grelen, H. E.   1959.   Mechanical preparation of pine planting sites in Florida sandhills.   *Weeds* 7:184–188.

Hare, R. C. 1961. Heat effects on living plants. *SFES Occasional Paper* 183.

Harris, H. K. 1958. Slash disposal by dozer, Northern Rocky Mountains. *Fire Control Notes* 19:144–154.

Hills, J. T. 1957. Prescribed burning techniques in loblolly and longleaf pine on the Francis Marion National Forest. *Fire Control Notes* 18(3):112–113.

Hopkins, H. G., and L. N. Anderson. 1960. The Marden brush cutter for slash disposal and ground preparation. *J. Forestry* 58:377–379.

Jackson, W. L. 1960. A trial of direct control of pine engraver beetles on a small logging unit. *PSWFRES Misc. Paper* 44.

Kozlowski, T. T. 1949. Light and water in relation to growth and competition of Piedmont forest tree species. *Ecological Monographs* 19:207–231.

LeBarron, R. K. 1944. Influence of controllable environmental conditions on regeneration of jack pine and black spruce. *J. Agr. Research* 68:97–119.

———. 1952. Silvicultural practices for lodgepole pine in Montana. *NRMFRES Sta. Paper* 33.

Lemon, P. C. 1946. Prescribed burning in relation to grazing in the longleaf-slash pine type. *J. Forestry* 44:115–117.

Lindenmuth, A. W., Jr. 1960. A survey of effects of intentional burning on fuels and timber stands of ponderosa pine in Arizona. *RMFRES Sta. Paper* 54.

Little, S., J. P. Allen, and E. B. Moore. 1948. Controlled burning as a dual-purpose tool of forest management in New Jersey's pine region. *J. Forestry* 46:810–819.

Little, S., and H. A. Somes. 1956. Buds enable pitch and shortleaf pines to recover from injury. *NEFES Sta. Paper* 81.

———. 1961. Prescribed burning in the pine regions of southern New Jersey and Eastern Shore Maryland—a summary of present knowledge. *NEFES Sta. Paper* 151.

Lotti, T., R. A. Klawitter, and W. P. LeGrande. 1960. Prescribed burning for understory control in loblolly pine stands of the coastal plain. *SEFES Sta. Paper* 116.

Lutz, H. J. 1956. Ecological effects of forest fires in the interior of Alaska. *USDA Tech. Bul.* 1133.

McCulley, R. D. 1950. Management of natural slash pine stands in the flatwoods of south Georgia and north Florida. *USDA Circ.* 845.

Maki, T. E. 1960. Improving site quality by wet-land drainage. *In:* P. Y. Burns (Ed.), *Southern forest soils.* Louisiana State University Press, Baton Rouge. Pp. 106–114.

Mason, H. L. 1955. Do we want sugar pine? *Sierra Club Bul.* 40(8):40–44.

Merz, R. W., and R. F. Finn. 1955. Yellow-poplar responds to preplanting ground treatment. *CSFES Tech. Paper* 150.

Miller, W. D., and T. E. Maki. 1957. Planting pines in pocosins. *J. Forestry* 55:659–663.

Morris, W. G. 1958. Influences of slash burning on regeneration, other plant cover, and fire hazard in the Douglas-fir region. *PNWFRES Research Paper* 29.

———, and E. L. Mowat. 1958. Some effects of thinning a ponderosa pine thicket with a prescribed fire. *J. Forestry* 56:203–209.

Munger, T. T., and D. N. Matthews. 1941. Slash disposal and forest management after clear cutting in the Douglas-fir region. *USDA Circ.* 586.

Quick, C. R.   1956.   Viable seeds from the duff and soil of sugar pine forests. *Forest Sci.* 2:36–42.

Schreiner, E. J.   1945.   How sod affects establishment of hybrid poplar plantations. *J. Forestry* 43:412–427.

Shipman, R. D.   1958.   Planting pine in the Carolina Sandhills. *SEFES Sta. Paper* 96.

Siggers, P. V.   1944.   The brown spot needle blight of pine seedlings. *USDA Tech. Bul.* 870.

Silen, R. R.   1952.   Timing of slash burning with the seed crop—a case history. *PNWFRES Research Note* 81.

Spaulding, P., and J. R. Hansbrough.   1944.   Decay of logging slash in the Northeast. *USDA Tech. Bul.* 876.

Steinbrenner, E. C., J. W. Duffield, and R. K. Campbell.   1960.   Increased cone production of young Douglas-fir following nitrogen and phosphorus fertilization. *J. Forestry* 58:105–110.

Stoddard, H. L.   1935.   *Use of fire on southeastern game lands.* Cooperative Quail Study Association, Thomasville, Ga.

Tarrant, R. F.   1956.   Effects of slash burning on some soils of the Douglas-fir region. *Soil Sci. Soc. Am. Proc.* 20:408–411.

Vanselow, K.   1949.   *Theorie und Praxis der natürlichen Verjüngung im Wirtschaftswald.* 2nd ed. Neumann, Berlin.

Vlamis, J., H. H. Biswell, and A. M. Schultz.   1955.   Effects of prescribed burning on soil fertility in second growth ponderosa pine. *J. Forestry* 53:905–909.

Wackerman, A. E., and L. E. Chaiken (Ed.)   1958.   Evaluation of forest rehabilitation programs.   *Proc., Third Conf. on Southern Industrial Forest Management, Duke Univ. School of Forestry.*

Wagener, W. W.   1961.   Past fire incidence in Sierra Nevada forests. *J. Forestry* 59:739–748.

Wahlenberg, W. G.   1946.   *Longleaf pine.* Charles L. Pack Forestry Foundation, Washington.

———, S. W. Greene, and H. R. Reed.   1939.   Effects of fire and cattle grazing on longleaf pine lands as studied at McNeill, Mississippi. *USDA Tech. Bul.* 683.

Weaver, H.   1951.   Fire as an ecological factor in the southwestern ponderosa pine forests. *J. Forestry* 49:93–98.

———.   1955.   Fire as an enemy, friend, and tool in forest management. *J. Forestry* 53:499–504.

———.   1959.   Ecological changes in the ponderosa pine forest of the Warm Springs Indian Reservation in Oregon. *J. Forestry* 57:15–20.

White, D. P., and A. L. Leaf.   1956.   Forest fertilization. *(N. Y.) State Univ. Col. Forestry Tech. Publ.* 81.

Wilhite, L. P.   1961.   Recent advances in site preparation techniques. *In:* A. B. Crow (Ed.), *Advances in southern pine management.* Louisiana State University Press, Baton Rouge. Pp. 26–33.

Willis, W. H., et al.   1961.   Forest fertilization. *In:* R. W. McDermid (Ed.), *The use of chemicals in southern forests.* Louisiana State University Press, Baton Rouge. Pp. 3–62.

Woods, F. W.   1959.   Converting scrub oak sandhills to pine forests in Florida. *J. Forestry* 57:117–119.

PART III

SILVICULTURAL SYSTEMS

CHAPTER 10

Development of
silvicultural systems
and methods of reproduction

A **reproduction method** is a procedure by which a stand is established or renewed; the process is accomplished during the regeneration period by means of artificial or natural reproduction. The various methods include the removal of the old stand, the establishment of a new one, and any supplementary treatments of vegetation, slash, or soil that are applied to create and maintain conditions favorable to the start and early growth of reproduction. Any procedure, intentional or otherwise, that leads to the development of a new stand of trees is identifiable as a method of reproduction.

The term **silvicultural system** is more comprehensive and designates a planned program of silvicultural treatment during the whole life of a stand; it includes not only the reproduction cuttings but any intermediate cuttings. The reproduction methods employed have such a decisive influence on the form and treatment of the stand that the name of the method is commonly applied to the silvicultural system; the shelterwood system, for example, leads to reproduction by means of the shelterwood method of cutting.

A refined and intensive silvicultural system consists of a number of steps conducted in logical sequence. In an application of the shelterwood system there might, for example, be some early cleanings in established reproduction, followed by pruning and a sequence of free, crown, and low thinnings, all leading to the series of partial cuttings that are designed to establish natural reproduction under the old stand and are characteristic of the shelterwood method. A less intensive application of the same system might involve nothing more than final harvest cutting in two stages.

In the consideration of silvicultural systems and reproduction methods, heavy and perhaps undue emphasis is placed on the effect of spatial patterns of cutting on the establishment of regeneration. As was indicated in Chapters 7, 8, and 9, this effect is important but not necessarily decisive in regeneration. The greatest significance of the pattern of cutting lies in its influence on a whole complex of biological, physical, and economic considerations, such as logging problems, efficiency of use of the growth capacity of the site, and protection of the stand. The development of a silvicultural system is controlled fully as much by these considerations as by the vital objective of establishing new crops.

Classification of Reproduction Methods

Many different methods of reproduction have been developed, but they can all be reduced on analysis to a few standard methods that denote distinctly different principles. The details of applying the same reproduction method vary widely as they are altered for each species, forest region, and objective of management. Some variants are simpler than others, but no single, detailed procedure is the standard for each general method. As with many classifications, there is a wide range of variation in each category and some borderline cases may not clearly fit any pigeonhole.

The following list of six general reproduction methods has been judiciously simplified and represents the classification that has been most widely accepted on this continent. Each method might be further subdivided, and each will be more fully defined and discussed in subsequent chapters.

High-forest methods—producing stands originating from seed.
Even-aged Stands:
    Clearcutting method—removal of the entire stand in one cutting with reproduction obtained artificially or by natural seeding from adjacent stands or from trees cut in the clearing operation (Chapter 11).
    Seed-tree method—removal of the mature timber in one cutting, except for a small number of seed trees left singly or in small groups (Chapter 12).
    Shelterwood method—removal of the mature timber in a series of cuttings, which extend over a relatively short portion of the

rotation, by means of which the establishment of essentially even-aged reproduction under the partial shelter of seed trees is encouraged (Chapter 13).

Uneven-aged Stands:

Selection method—removal of the mature timber, usually the oldest or largest trees, either as single scattered individuals or in small groups at relatively short intervals, repeated indefinitely, by means of which the continuous establishment of reproduction is encouraged and an uneven-aged stand is maintained (Chapter 14).

Coppice-forest methods—producing stands originating primarily from vegetative regeneration (Chapter 15).

Coppice method—any type of cutting in which dependence is placed mainly on vegetative reproduction.

Coppice-with-standards method—production of coppice and high forest on the same area with the trees of seedling origin being carried through much longer rotations than those of vegetative origin.

A number of more complicated classifications exist, although they do not differ in principle from that just presented. Some of the most complete are in the German literature and have been reviewed by Spurr (1956). Troup (1952) described and classified silvicultural systems as applied throughout the world. It is significant that European authorities disagree considerably about the interpretation and details of classification. This demonstrates that even in the relatively simple forests of that continent silviculture is a flexible art that has been varied so widely to fit different conditions that the methods defy precise classification.

Any classification of methods of reproduction is merely a device for systematizing description of the wide variety of procedures which have been used in practice. Development of methods effective in specific situations comes first in both time and importance; the classification of these methods comes afterwards. No classification should ever be interpreted as a complete set of rigid prescriptions for all the methods of reproduction cutting which might be employed.

The adoption of a simple scheme for use on this continent does not indicate that American silviculture is relatively simple. Actually the forests of this continent are vastly more complex than those of Europe, and it is logical to anticipate that American silviculture will become quite complicated.

The Basis of Distinction between Reproduction Methods

The classification of reproduction methods is usually based on (1) mode of origin of regeneration as well as on arrangement of cuttings in (2) time and (3) space. The first distinction is the relatively simple one which may be drawn between high-forest methods involving regeneration from seed and those for coppice forests reproduced vegetatively from sprouts, root suckers, or layered branches.

As far as arrangement of cuttings in time is concerned, the most important distinction is between (1) methods in which reproduction cuttings extend throughout the rotation leading to the creation of uneven-aged stands and (2) methods for the maintenance of even-aged stands in which regeneration cuttings are concentrated at the end of each rotation. The methods for even-aged stands, however, also differ according to the number of cuttings which are required to replace one stand with another.

The complexity of many classifications results from recognition of the almost infinite variations that can be created in the horizontal, geometric pattern of cutting areas. Each general method can be applied so that openings and uncut timber are left either in uniform distribution or in concentrated strips, groups, wedges, and the like. In the general classification used here, simplicity has been achieved largely by restricting the amount of attention given to modifications involving differences in spatial arrangement.

Although the various reproduction methods are normally thought of as involving natural regeneration, artificial regeneration may be substituted wholly or partially in any of the methods. Reproduction arising from artificial seeding or planting is regarded as having originated from seed.

The ultimate distinction between reproduction methods is the form of forest produced. The size, shape, and position of the areas cut over, as well as the proportion of the timber removed determine the arrangement of age classes, which is in turn the chief factor governing forest form. Each reproduction method, when systematically applied, produces a characteristic stand structure by which it can be recognized.

Certain methods result, for example, in the maintenance of even-aged stands whereas others produce stands with varying numbers and proportions of identifiable age classes. The distribution of age classes in the managed stand depends upon the length of the reproduction period. Reproduction may be continuously in the process of establishment during this period, and the trees of the new crop may vary in age by as many years as the reproduction period is long. Where reproduction is starting throughout the life of the stand an essentially all-aged stand is likely to result. If regeneration is established by cutting at infrequent intervals, the stand will have as many age classes as there are cuttings during the rotation.

Where the regeneration period is reduced to one year, as it may be in the coppice method or where a clearcut area is planted, the stand is absolutely even-aged. Most even-aged stands, however, contain trees of more than one age because the reproduction period can rarely be restricted to a single year. A stand may be considered even-aged for purposes of management if the difference in age between the oldest and youngest trees does not exceed 20 per cent of the length of the rotation. The age of trees which grew from small "advance reproduction" developing under larger trees is generally best dated from time of release; seedlings of some species can respond to release after decades of such suppression.

Even-aged stands tend to be uniform in height and are characterized by intimate competition between trees of approximately the same size. The lowermost branches die continuously as a result of shading, and the trees develop relatively short, narrow crowns. Uneven-aged stands are distinctly irregular in height with great variation in size of trees. Competition between age classes is unequal; the smaller, younger trees tend to grow slowly because they are suppressed by the larger, older trees which grow quite rapidly. However, these characteristic differences from the even-aged form are most pronounced along the margins of the small even-aged groups that must inevitably make up most of an uneven-aged stand; within these groups, particularly if they are young or large in area, essentially even-aged conditions prevail.

The method of reproduction being employed in a given stand may not be evident to the casual observer. The identification and definition of a method of cutting depend fully as much on the results actually obtained, the intent of the treatment, and the nature of subsequent operations as they do on the pattern according to which the trees are removed. A reproduction cutting is a reproduction cutting only to the extent that it leads to the establishment of a new crop. If something intended as a thinning results in the establishment of vigorous reproduction it is best regarded as having been a shelterwood cutting; however, if the residual stand is then allowed to suppress the reproduction to the point of elimination, the initial cutting was indeed a thinning. A partial cutting aimed at starting the development of an uneven-aged stand is selection cutting only if subsequent operations are sufficiently consistent with the first to result in the ultimate creation of such a stand.

Identification of the silvicultural system is also complicated because it may be changed during the course of a rotation or because different parts of the same stand are reproduced by different methods. If the reproduction method originally contemplated is one that involves a sequence of partial cuttings, there is often latitude for changing to methods that are found more satisfactory during the sequence. Variation in procedure within a stand is most likely to be dictated by differences of site, accessibility, or the condition of the stand itself. Such changes of method in time and within stands are likely to be common when a forest is, like most American forests, being brought under management for the first time. In fact, it is by means of such changes that the procedures are perfected and the pattern of stands molded into arrangements that are rational from the standpoint of site variations and economic management.

A cutting does not have to be planned by a forester or involve any thought whatever about the future to be recognizable as a kind of intermediate or reproduction cutting. It matters not how indiscriminately the trees are removed or how haphazardly the new growth develops. Of course, it is not necessarily easy to categorize cuttings that involve no future plans and the act of doing so may be purely an intellectual exercise; the point is that the use of standard cutting techniques as defined in silvicultural terminology is not merely a fancy refinement limited to intensive forestry.

One of the most important reasons why methods of reproduction and silvicultural systems are classified and recognized is that the act of doing so indirectly forces planning for the future care, development, and replacement of stands. The deliberate decision to employ a particular method of reproduction is in itself an act of planning without which the management of stands easily becomes a kind of rudderless drifting, governed more by current market demands than by any intentions about the future.

FORMULATING SILVICULTURAL SYSTEMS

Logical programs for the long-term management of particular stands or kinds of stands are not devised by making judicious selections from classifications and schematic descriptions of silvicultural systems. This book, for example, and in spite of certain superficial resemblances, is not a cookbook from which such choices can be made and applied. A good silvicultural system is not chosen but formulated as a solution to a specific set of circumstances. Moreover, it is also subject to evolutionary development as circumstances change and knowledge of them improves. The history of the management of red pine in northern Minnesota, as described by Eyre and Zehngraff (1948), is an excellent example of such an evolutionary process showing how a refined application of the shelterwood system gradually developed from initial attempts involving the seed-tree method.

The formulation of a silvicultural system should start with an analysis of the natural and economic factors that are likely to affect the growing timber crop. The solution is then devised to go as far as possible in capitalizing on the opportunities and conquering the difficulties found to exist.

When the important act of inventing the solution has proceeded far enough the less important step of attaching a name to it can be taken. The standard terminology should be used to the extent of its limited capacity for providing information in terms meaningful to all foresters and then supplemented with the additional, detailed information that is usually necessary.

If one starts over again with freshly invented terms, like "unit area control" and "selective cutting," and eschews the standard terms, the result is confusion that sometimes seems to increase rather than decrease with the amount of explanation. However, the validity of the plan is more important than the name. The procedure which some California foresters call "unit area control" represents a rational approach, born of thorough analysis, to the silviculture of the conifer forests of the Sierra Nevada (Hallin, 1954, 1959; Davis, 1959). It is perhaps beside the point that it is difficult for outlanders to determine whether this term is a synonym for "group-selection system" or another word for "silviculture." Possibly a term like "Dunning's group-selection system," named after the chief originator of the scheme, might convey more information without adding to the already excessive confusion of silvicultural terminology.

If silvicultural systems are not chosen ready-made from a manual, it is logical to examine the various considerations that enter into their construction and evolutionary development. In the first place, a rational silvicultural system for a particular stand should fit logically into the overall management plan for the forest of which the stand is a part. Secondly, it should represent the best possible amalgam of attempts to satisfy all of the following major objectives, each of which will be discussed in detail in the remainder of this chapter and also referred to in subsequent chapters. These basic objectives are as follows:

1. Harmony with goals and characteristics of ownership
2. Provision for reproduction
3. Efficient use of growing space and site productivity
4. Control of damaging agencies
5. Provision for sustained yield
6. Optimum use of forest capital
7. Concentration and efficient arrangement of operations

These objectives are fully as likely to conflict as to harmonize with one another. It is for this reason that the procedures followed in applying systems with the same name vary widely depending on the relative importance attached to different objectives. It is also why close examination of the details of the various techniques applied in forestry seems to reveal so many contradictory purposes. Many of the contradictions are partially resolved in the development of management plans for the whole forest. The purpose here is only to consider the ways in which silvicultural systems are affected by these conflicting objectives and can also be adapted to resolve some of them.

A major portion of the problem is actually solved merely by categorizing the various objectives of forestry and becoming aware that they represent forces pulling the forester in different directions. Analysis will demonstrate that single-minded concentration on any one of these objectives, unless it be recognition of the owner's desires, can ultimately lead to ridiculous results. The best solution obviously lies in finding the most appropriate blend of partial fulfillments of all significant objectives. The test of suitability of a solution is normally made in economic terms, although the testing is more of an intuitive art than an exact financial analysis.

Harmony with Goals and Characteristics of Ownership

Choice among all the alternatives of silvicultural treatment is greatly simplified by clarification of the objectives of ownership. This logical first step automatically eliminates many of the possible alternatives. It also forces recognition of the fact that it would not necessarily be in the interest of two different owners to manage the same stand in the same way. On this continent laws about silvicultural practice are minimal or absent, so silviculture on different ownerships should be the same only to the extent that natural and economic conditions are similar. There is no justification for an American forester to embark in arrogant wisdom on any "standard" procedure for the growing of a particular species regardless of whether the technique fits the owner's purposes.

The objectives of ownership clearly dictate the relative amount of attention paid to management for timber, wildlife, forage, water, recreation, or other products and benefits that the forest may provide. On publicly owned land managed for multiple use the silviculture logically differs from that on similar land that might be owned by a lumber company for the purpose of growing saw timber; this would in turn differ from a paper company's silviculture for pulpwood production. If an owner is most interested in wildlife or in preserving some old-growth timber purely for aesthetic purposes and is made fully aware of all the consequences of his aims, the forester should modify the silviculture accordingly. In fact, the forester's occupational bias in favor of efficient timber production is, on occasion, more of a liability than an asset.

Analysis of the objectives of ownership will normally define the kind of vegetation to be maintained, the kind of trees that are to be grown, and the amount of time, money and care that can be devoted to the process. The intensity of practice is determined by the amount of money that the owner is willing and able to place in long-term silvicultural investments as well as by the interest return required on such investments. If long-term investments cannot be made, the silvicultural treatment must be limited to those things which can be done in the process of harvesting merchantable timber. Where the owner is an individual and the future of the enterprise seems limited to his life expectancy, attention may well be restricted to securing maximum benefits through his lifetime; techniques of manipulating the existing growing stock would probably take precedence over securing new reproduction.

Provision for Reproduction

Continuity of any forestry enterprise ultimately and absolutely depends on replacing old trees with new. The process of regenerating stands can only rarely be accomplished without resolute sacrifice of some other objectives.

To establish any kind of reproduction it is necessary to reduce the competition from the old vegetation enough to provide sufficient growing space for the new. This often requires the cutting of some trees before they are mature and the reservation of others beyond the point of maturity as a source of seed or shelter for the new crop. The efficiency of harvesting operations is also reduced whenever trees that might be cut profitably are left to provide for reproduction as well as when trees are harvested at a loss to make way for reproduction.

The period during which reproduction is established can also be one in which full occupancy of the site is lost and the stand exposed to sources of injury that could be avoided if the stand did not have to be reproduced. Loss of full occupancy of the growing space can result from delays in the establishment of natural reproduction. Even if a stand is replanted the day after a clearcutting, some years elapse before the new trees expand enough to reoccupy the site fully. The environmental conditions necessary for reproduction may call forth a whole suite of damaging insects and other injurious agencies not found in older forests. Among other things, the risk and hazard of fire are usually greatest during the reproduction period.

Even if advance reproduction of desirable species appears without effort, it must often be released in a manner and at a time not ideal from other standpoints. The whole situation is a good argument for undertaking to reproduce stands no more often than necessary and for going about it with sufficiently single-minded purpose that it is accomplished in a short, well-defined period. If one awaits the appearance of natural reproduction as the unearned by-product of the attainment of other purposes at various vaguely defined times during the rotation, he usually does not get good reproduction and finds himself conducting expensive and cumbersome treatments to remedy the deficiency.

The act of reproducing a stand from seed must be anticipated throughout the rotation and it is primarily to emphasize this point that has become traditional to name the silvicultural system in terms of the method of reproduction contemplated. The classification of the methods of reproducing stands from seed serves as a convenient framework for consideration of the relationship between silvicultural systems and the ecological factors involved in securing natural reproduction.

The various high-forest methods represent a complete gradational series of different degrees of exposure of the forest floor to solar radiation and atmospheric agencies. They also differ with regard to the degree of root competition and the supply of seed from the residual stand left in the cutting area. The manner in which certain critical factors are altered by various kinds of reproduction cuttings are depicted in generalized and imprecise fashion in Fig. 10-1. This illustrates the concept that the effects of the various methods cover the

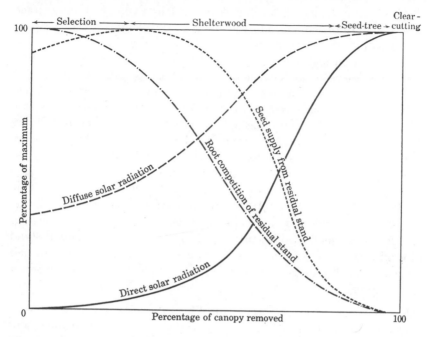

Fig. 10-1. A generalized representation of the effects of the initial cuttings of various methods of reproduction, when applied uniformly over an area in a humid, temperate climate, on several factors usually critical in the establishment of natural reproduction.

widest possible range of environmental responses to cutting. The graph is not intended to indicate all critical environmental factors nor does it apply to all conditions of climate and soil. Influences of the kind shown are subject to silvicultural control, within limits.

The clearcutting method, at one extreme, increases exposure of the site to the maximum and decreases root competition to the minimum. However, the supply of seed must come from adjacent stands, unless it has already been provided by the trees removed. In the seed-tree method a supply of seed is produced on the area, although the remaining trees do not appreciably modify the environment. The outstanding feature of the shelterwood method, as the name implies, is the shelter provided by the residual stand, particularly against direct solar radiation. The vigor of the remaining trees, that is, the "shelterwood," may be improved sufficiently to increase the supply of seed to the maximum. Once reproduction has become established, the shelterwood is removed, leaving an essentially even-aged stand freed from competition with the residual stand; this essential characteristic of the shelterwood method is not indicated in Fig. 10-1.

The selection method is represented as involving very light cuttings that do not create an environment significantly different from that found in undisturbed stands. Actually the primary distinguishing feature of the selection method is the creation of an uneven-aged stand, which may also be accomplished by removing the trees in patches large enough to produce conditions similar to those resulting from use of the clearcutting or shelterwood method. Similarly the shelterwood method includes modifications in which small clearcuttings are made in strips or patches with much of the shelter coming from the side shade of adjacent trees. If the residual stand is removed rapidly enough to produce a new, relatively even-aged stand, such cuttings are classed as shelterwood cuttings. If removal of the residual stand proceeds very gradually and results in a stand classed as uneven-aged for purposes of management, the cuttings should be regarded as selection cuttings.

Efficient Use of Growing Space and Site Productivity

One of the first steps in putting a whole forest under management is usually to assure the establishment of desirable vegetation on all vacant areas capable of supporting it. Useful vegetation should be growing on all suitable areas if only to provide a broader base over which to spread the various fixed expenses. Subsequent steps for increasing the efficiency of use of the forest proceed toward the ideal objective of full and continuous occupancy of all growing space by the trees or other plants that will make best use of each spot. This process logically proceeds until arrival at the point of diminishing returns halts the addition of further refinements.

Even a stand which has no obvious gaps does not maintain full occupancy of the growing space or use it with equal efficiency throughout its life. The times when it does not are most likely to come when it is young and when it is old. As was described in Chapter 2, the biological productivity of a stand is highest at some period intermediate between youth and middle age. Optimum economic productivity is achieved somewhat later because of the effect of tree size on the utility of wood. However, in almost any terms, the annual productivity increases rapidly with age during youth and declines gradually with the onset of old age.

The decline in production in the later stages is caused mostly by decreasing biological efficiency, although the attrition of damaging agencies and possibly other factors that are not well understood cause the trees to lose full command of the site. It is comparatively simple to avoid the inefficiencies of old age simply by commencing the replacement of mature stands at the right time.

The inefficiencies of youth are more nearly inevitable and difficult to mitigate. A young stand does not arrive at the peak of biological efficiency until the roots and live crowns of the trees have expanded both horizontally and vertically to occupy all the space that they are capable of claiming. The presence and vigor of shrubs and other accessory vegetation is often an indicator of the extent to which such stands fall short of full occupancy. The most serious loss of potential production occurs during any interval of time that elapses between the removal of the previous crop and the establishment of a new one. This kind of loss can be overcome by prompt regeneration and constitutes one of the strongest arguments for planting.

Prompt regeneration, regardless of how it is obtained, does not overcome the loss of potential production endured while the new crop gains full occupancy. The way to overcome this source of inefficiency is to establish the new crop before the old is cut and then gradually remove the old crop as the new one claims increasing growing space in building full command of the site. This way is not always feasible but is actually a more nearly ideal solution to this particular problem than clearcutting and *then* planting.

It is distinctly less than ideal to obtain early and full occupancy of the site with new stands so dense that precommercial thinning would be beneficial. A utopian degree of efficiency would be achieved if the new stand arrived at full occupancy with just that number of trees that could ultimately be used profitably without any growing space having been wasted during the transition from the old stand to the new.

During the rotation increased efficiency in the use of growing space can be sought by application of intermediate cuttings, including thinning and techniques of adjusting stand composition. It is by such measures that silvicultural treatment usually makes its principal contribution to increasing the yield over that naturally available without treatment.

Stands that approach the ideal of efficiency in utilizing the growing space are not likely to be uniform and simple in composition by species and age classes. Site conditions are rarely so uniform that a single species will make best use of all parts of a large tract. The use of many forms of the shelterwood and selection systems enables maintenance of nearly full occupancy of the site during the reproduction period but involves at least some departure from the uniformity of perfectly even-aged stands.

Mixed stands are complicated yet, if they include tolerant species of high photosynthetic efficiency, are likely to make more efficient use of site productivity than most kinds of simple, pure stands. Pure, even-aged stands, unless the species is of very high photosynthetic efficiency, have a tendency to lose complete command of the growing space at middle age and allow the entry of understory species that are sometimes undesirable. The kind of simplicity and uniformity of stands that helps maintain efficiency in harvesting, administration, and other operations is thus not entirely compatible with the most efficient use of growing space.

Many silvicultural systems, especially those that involve cutting a number of times during a rotation, contain important provisions for some reduction of the enormous loss and waste that hobbles forestry enterprises. There are not only the obvious losses from damaging agencies and natural suppression but also subtle losses of growth from excessive competition of poor trees with better ones. In addition to these losses is the waste which constantly burdens harvesting and manufacturing operations. It is only natural to attempt to reduce this loss and waste by such measures as frequent cutting, thinning, salvage cutting, and integration of harvesting operations for multiple-product utilization.

Nevertheless, like all worthy motives, this objective can become a fetish if pursued too far. The cost of reducing waste and loss as well as that of capturing more complete occupancy of the site must always be weighed against the cost of the additional effort involved. The point of diminishing returns is reached long before the staff has hastened hither and yon through the forest planting up every vacant square rod, salvaging every dying tree, thinning every stand, and utilizing every crooked top log.

Control of Damaging Agencies

Any successful silvicultural system is modified by the objective of creating stands with adequate resistance to insects, fungi, fire, or other injurious biotic and physical agencies. The management of some forest types is indeed governed by this consideration. The modifications are mostly specific steps taken against specific damaging agencies and cannot be safely based on generalities intended to apply to all forests. Appropriate procedures cannot be developed without detailed knowledge of the behavior of the damaging agencies.

Most of the generalizations about the damaging agencies of the forest are more nearly true than false, but they cannot be accepted as a basis for silvicultural procedure without being scrutinized for applicability in each instance. Among these are the view that vigorous, fast-growing trees are more resistant than less thrifty, slow-growing ones; that mixed stands are safer than pure; that uneven-aged stands are more resistant than even-aged; and that close duplication of natural conditions will safeguard against most difficulties. Exceptions are numerous.

The stem rusts of conifers and the white pine weevil are, for example, more serious pests of vigorous trees than of the less thrifty. There are some insects and fungi that alternate between different host species and are thus most dangerous in mixed stands containing the appropriate hosts. Pure stands of spruce are much less susceptible to the spruce budworm than are mixtures of spruce and the highly susceptible balsam fir. In uneven-aged stands there is excellent opportunity for infection of young age classes from older trees by pathogens like dwarf-mistletoe which attack trees of all ages, thus enabling an infestation to remain established in a stand indefinitely. Highly artificial stands of well-tested exotics from faraway continents are sometimes less subject to damage than in the native habitat.

Consideration of biotic enemies best starts from recognition of the fact that the trees of any kind of forest represent a source of food to a wide variety of organisms. Owing to the availability of food, organisms ranging from minute viruses to large herbivorous mammals have evolved that are adapted to feed upon the forest. These organisms are so dependent upon the vegetation that changes in the forest cause changes in the populations of dependent organisms. Changing the forest does not get rid of parasites; it merely exchanges one group of parasites for a new set which may be more or less harmful and difficult to handle.

Fortunately, only a very few of the dependent organisms are harmful. In a sense, the parasite that kills its host and thus its supply of food is a poorly adapted one. This is why introduced parasites often cause much more economic loss than the native ones. The well-adapted parasites sometimes cause so little damage that they go almost unnoticed. However, there are also some of these that can cause substantial economic damage without threatening the life of the tree. For example, the heart-rots which attack the nonliving wood inside a tree can ruin the utilizable wood without significantly harming the vital processes of the tree. Need for modifying silvicultural systems to reduce losses to biotic enemies can normally be confined to those few which can cause serious economic loss; the vast majority which merely feed on the trees without economic damage can, from this standpoint, be ignored.

The silvicultural approach to reducing losses to damaging agencies is mainly one of avoiding the conditions, environmental or otherwise, that are conducive to damage. The direct measures, including such steps as salvage of damaged trees, suppression of going fires, and use of insecticides, must be resorted to when silvicultural measures have proven ineffective or, more often, were not applied.

Examples of control of damage by modification of silvicultural systems are many and varied. Among these are such things as the application of various forms of selection and salvage cutting to the control of *Dendroctonus* bark beetles of ponderosa pine. So long as old-growth timber of this species remains in places like northeastern California and eastern Oregon, its management will consist of a race to cut trees of low vigor before the beetles kill them. With species, such as aspen and balsam fir, that are seriously threatened by heart-rot the objective of terminating the rotation before trees become old and highly susceptible is a ruling consideration.

In many parts of the Atlantic Coastal Plain stands of various species of hard pines are so constantly threatened by fire that prescribed burning becomes essential for fuel reduction and this usually necessitates some form of even-aged management. Damage by deer and other mammals is of increasing concern in American forestry; while the measures of control are yet to be perfected, they are more likely to consist of silvicultural manipulation of the vegetation than of such direct measures as hunting.

The pattern of any sort of cutting is sometimes adjusted to avoid wind damage to residual trees; gaps and weak places in stand borders are, for example, often the places where serious blowdowns start. The shelterwood system is often used for eastern white pine partly because white pine weevils prefer to lay their eggs on pine leaders exposed to direct sunlight; the partial shade of a shelterwood tends to protect pine saplings from the serious deformities caused by this insect.

There are so many different kinds of modifications aimed at reduction of specific kinds of damage that it is hard to detect any general or consistent way in which they conflict with other objectives. However, these measures usually complicate harvesting and other operations. The indirect silvicultural measures of control are often the slowest to take effect but the most enduring (Graham, 1959). The direct control measures, most strikingly typified by the use of insecticides, have their most powerful effect when immediate reduction of losses is imperative but usually do not correct the characteristics of the vegetation that make damage possible.

Provision for Sustained Yield

One of the objectives of forestry that is usually taken for granted is that of making the forest the source of an indefinitely sustained and uniform flow of wood and other benefits. There is hardly any objective more ancient and honorable, but it is not so sacred that either the idea of sustained yield or the traditional methods of securing are above skeptical scrutiny. Actually, planning for sustained yield is almost entirely part of forest management because the forest and not the stand is the logical unit for this kind of planning. However, the requirements of a sustained-yield program can dictate modifications of the silvicultural treatment of individual stands that would seem to make no sense whatever without an understanding of the reasons for them.

Over the centuries there has been nothing that has come closer to putting silvicultural practice in a straitjacket than attempts to develop sustained yield by simple, arbitrary procedures. Modern techniques for this purpose are much less restrictive and increasingly effective; they are also far easier to accommodate to other objectives than are the traditions lingering from the days when silviculture could not be so flexible. The idea of the silvicultural system itself emerged mainly as a device to ensure that the cutting practices followed in stands would be orderly enough to fit into the old, simple plans for sustained-yield management for whole forests. In fact, the reputation of the silvicultural system as a highly rigid procedure comes more from the requirements of this ancient kind of management than from any that have directly to do with growing stands of trees.

The first planned forestry in the western world appears to have developed in western Europe late in the Middle Ages (Knuchel, 1953). The main objective was to guarantee the perpetual supply of indispensable fuel from sprouting hardwoods. Transportation was so primitive that the forest area tributary to a community was rigidly circumscribed. Sustained yield was achieved by what has come to be called the **area method of regulation** of the cut. This consists basically of dividing the total forest area into as many equally productive units as there are years in the planned rotation and harvesting one unit each year (Fig. 10-2). Such management under the coppice system worked very well, because there is no kind of reproduction more certain or prompt than that which comes from stump sprouts. It was almost equally successful in growing conifers by clearcutting and planting, a system that imitated agriculture and represented the next step toward more efficient forestry. With such a scheme reproduction was also reasonably sure and could be obtained without delay.

If sustained yield were the only objective or if the coppice system and that of clearcutting and planting were the only silvicultural systems, there would be no need of any other methods of regulating the cut to secure sustained yield. However, this regimented kind of forestry with its fixed rotations and annual cutting areas does not provide adequate latitude for all the kinds of silviculture in which partial cutting is necessary for the attainment of other objectives. The method of regulating the cut by area can be applied without great difficulty so long as the stands remain essentially even-aged, that is, if partial cutting is limited to procedures such as thinning and most kinds of shelterwood cutting. However, this method becomes almost impossible to apply if stands depart significantly from the even-aged condition.

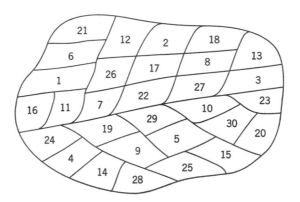

Fig. 10-2. Schematic diagram of a forest divided into thirty equally productive stands so that the cut can be regulated by area to provide a sustained yield under purely even-aged management on a 30-year rotation. The numbers indicate the sequence of cutting according to an arrangement designed to avoid having contiguous areas under regeneration. Note that stand boundaries conform to the terrain of a typical stream drainage rather than any arbitrary pattern.

It may be necessary to work with the uneven-aged condition simply because the particular stands involved happen to be uneven-aged when placed under management. In other instances, the ecological requirements for natural regeneration, wildlife and watershed management, or protection of the forest necessitate diversity of age classes within stands. Efficient use of growing stock requires recognition of the fact that not all the trees of a stand are of the same age or even of the same size when the best time comes to cut them; this point tends to argue for some departure from the even-aged condition.

The area method is not applicable to those unhappy situations in which severe economic limitations dictate "high-grading," the kind of partial cutting in which only the biggest and best trees can be cut. This kind of cutting may have to be applied to even-aged as well as uneven-aged stands. While it is hardly an efficient kind of silviculture, it is one in which sustained-yield management is possible and at the same time both difficult and crucial. Careful scrutiny is necessary to ensure that the rate of removal of large trees is kept in balance with the ability of the smaller trees of the residual stands to supply a flow of large trees of adequate quality in the future.

European foresters became aware of the desirability of occasional departures in the direction of uneven-aged management about a century ago (Knuchel, 1953). By that time, the concept of achieving sustained yield through regulation of the cut by area was firmly entrenched not only in the tradition of forestry but also in the laws regulating forestry. Consequently, the idea of introducing more latitude into silviculture could not then be adopted without substantial concessions to the objective of sustained yield and the traditional technique of ensuring it. The method of regulating the cut by volume and probably the concept of the silvicultural system were fruits of these concessions.

In the **volume method of regulation** of the cut the basic procedure is to determine the allowable annual or periodic cut in terms of volume of wood with due regard for the rate of growth, current and potential, and for the volume of growing stock, existing and desired (Davis, 1954). Ideally this means that if one could ever determine and create the appropriate volume of growing stock made up of the proper distribution of sizes and kinds of trees he could depend upon having it yield annually a certain well-defined volume of growth available for cutting. If this could be done, the length of the rotation and the amount of area exposed by cutting each year would not have to be known.

This means of defining the growing stock is basically nothing more than a sophisticated expression of the area method of regulation. Instead of working directly with the idea of cutting equal areas each year under a definite rotation, one determines the distribution of number of trees with respect to D.B.H. that would prevail in the forest at hand if it were composed of a series of even-aged stands with each age class, from age 1 to that of rotation age minus 1, represented by an equal area. The resulting diameter distribution defines the growing stock that should be left after each year's cutting if sustained yield is to be assured; the allowable annual cut is whatever volume this growing stock will yield in annual growth. The process of determining the appropriate growing stock and the allowable annual cut will be discussed in more detail and more critically in Chapter 14 on the selection method.

It is easy to get the impression that the volume method frees the forester of the tyranny of the area method only to condemn him to the hard labor of creating and maintaining balanced uneven-aged stands by the selection system. It is true that this technique can be used to make a single stand into a self-contained unit of sustained yield. However, there is seldom any point in going to this extreme because the stand itself rarely needs to be a sustained-yield unit.

The main virtue of the volume method is that it frees the forester of the rigid restraints of either extreme. It enables him to make a sustained-yield unit out of a forest composed of almost any combination of patterns of even-aged, two-aged, balanced uneven-aged, and irregularly uneven-aged stands that might be desirable to satisfy other objectives. If it is most feasible to keep certain kinds of stands in the even-aged condition, it is still possible to have others elsewhere in the forest in an irregularly uneven-aged status without disrupting a sustained-yield program. The chief requirement is that all the stands of the whole sustained-yield unit in combination conform to the appropriate distribution of diameter classes. Although it calls for skillful forest management, this approach is better than trying to fit the forest into a highly arbitrary pattern merely to simplify the bookkeeping. Usually it also enables conversion of an existing growing stock into a properly distributed one much faster than would be the case if each stand had to be made perfectly even-aged or uneven-aged and balanced.

Many of the rigid ideas about regulation of the cut have been handed down from bygone times when transportation was poor, and sustained yield was more of a crucial necessity than now. The techniques of both area and volume regulation were so crudely developed that the stands had to be uniform if the techniques were to work at all. The age distribution and basic program of management had to be sufficiently simple and sharply defined to be clearly comprehensible to anyone concerned with regulating the cut. The silvicultural system was the vehicle of terminology by which this information was conveyed.

In a sense, the silvicultural system, once established, was looked upon as a binding contract between silviculture and forest management. This viewpoint still finds expression in the idea that there is some sort of requirement that a whole forest should be handled according to a single silvicultural system. The same tradition likewise makes it easy to conclude that stands must be reproduced at the end of the planned rotation regardless of market conditions or any other consideration. It also leads to the idea that it is mandatory that stands should be either distinctly even-aged or definitely balanced and uneven-aged and cannot be anything in between. There are plenty of good reasons for imposing some degree of uniformity and homogeneity on forest stands, but these are more likely to involve the objectives of increasing the efficiency of logging and other operations in the stands than just that of assuring sustained yield.

Developments much more recent than the volume method of regulation have also contributed to the partial liberation of forestry techniques from the restraints of the ancient rigid patterns of sustained-yield management. The application of electronic computers and improved techniques of forest inventory to forest management have, since about 1950, significantly improved the efficiency of the volume method and other means of analyzing the growing stock and growth of forests. Furthermore, analysis of the economics of forestry has become more sophisticated and given basis to certain skepticism about the need for perfection in sustained-yield management.

Modern experience shows that market fluctuations make it neither possible nor desirable to maintain a constant growing stock and annual cut. The minor fluctuations are smoothed by assessing the situation in terms of decades or other periods longer than one year, but the major fluctuations induced by wars, depressions, and technological changes cannot be buffered in this fashion. The result is that perfection is something ultimately approached but not achieved.

Efforts to attain sustained yield, even if not pursued to the bitter limit, often require modifications of silvicultural procedure within stands which make sense only when the management of the whole forest is considered. The greater the discrepancy between the proper distribution of age classes and that which exists on the whole forest, the wider is the departure of silvicultural procedure from that otherwise most logical for the particular stand.

This situation is readily apparent in America because real forest management has only recently started and with forests that rarely have any real semblance of the distribution of age classes necessary for sustained yield. Forests that have not been subject to much cutting or severe natural catastrophe have a plethora of overmature stands and a paucity of any age classes younger than the ultimate rotation age. If heavy cutting has been concentrated in a brief period during the past, almost all the stands will be of one age class dating from the time of the cutting. Even where the inheritance consists of uneven-aged stands of natural or accidental origin it is usually found that some age classes are deficient and others present in surplus.

Much of the management of old-growth Douglas-fir in the Pacific Northwest revolves around problems of this kind. Management might, for example, start with a large virgin forest consisting almost exclusively of stands that originated after a single massive fire that occurred 375 years ago. If one wished to convert this to a sustained-yield forest on a 100-year rotation the simplest way would be to clearcut 1 per cent of the area annually for the next century. One could accelerate this process, among other ways, by cutting over the old-growth more rapidly and by planning to cut some of the first new stands before they reached 100 years. However, it is still necessary to leave substantial acreages of old timber standing for decades without any real increase in value. If one considered only the silviculture of the individual stand, it would seem witless not to replace all the old timber with young vigorous stands immediately.

It is not uncommon in the East to find whole forest regions in which practically all the forests consist of middle-aged stands left from heavy cuttings of decades past. The forest manager may find that he has neither timber of mature size nor stands of seedlings and saplings. A period may elapse in which he is limited mainly to various kinds of intermediate cuttings which yield income but do nothing to correct the distribution of age classes. The first stands that reach the condition where they can be harvested and replaced may be removed long before they are mature, just to get some new age classes started. Later some of the stands with which he started may be held well beyond the logical rotation age in order to have something to cut when the missing younger age classes would have been coming to maturity.

Almost any sort of adjustment of age-class distribution is likely to involve holding some stands beyond rotation age and, at other times, cutting some before they become mature.

The same kind of manipulations may be made in more detail with particular diameter classes. Consider, for example, the case of a forest being managed with the intention of growing the crop trees to 20 to 24 inches D.B.H. There is an over-all surplus of trees in the range from 17 to 20 inches compensated by deficiencies in all diameter classes below 15 inches. If trees smaller than 10 inches D.B.H. are unmerchantable, adjustments must be made mainly by the cutting of trees that are larger than 10 inches. The surplus diameter classes should be picked over very carefully with several definite objectives in mind. In general, the *best* trees should be reserved in sufficient quantity not only to replace the trees larger than 20 inches that are harvested but also to provide an adequate volume to compensate for part of the present deficiency of trees now less than 15 inches. The removals from the surplus diameter classes should, to the greatest extent possible, come from the poorest members and provide for the early establishment of new reproduction in order to accelerate recruitment of new age classes.

While the surplus diameter classes are winnowed quite rigorously the deficient diameter classes receive an indulgent treatment that might seem inconsistent. In these classes it even becomes desirable to try to make good trees out of poor ones. While one would be unlikely to release a 19-inch codominant in these circumstances, it would be logical to cut an 18-inch dominant to promote two adjacent 12-inch codominants to the dominant position. It might be justifiable to release and prune a 10-inch tree with a 25 per cent live-crown ratio if one could be sure that it would ultimately recover and develop into a good tree. This would not be the most logical way to grow good trees if one could start from the beginning with seedlings, but there is the necessity of creating a good 12-inch tree in 15 years rather than in several decades.

The adjustments are by no means always made with partial cuttings. In the example at hand, one might carry out the seemingly reckless and premature harvest of a fairly good stand with trees mostly in the 17- to 20-inch range even while he was carefully nursing a rather poor adjacent stand in which most of the trees were 8 to 15 inches.

Because of its honored status, the objectives of sustained yield has been hard for American foresters to keep in proper perspective. Fortunately, the various arbitrary procedures by which the sustained yield is sought loom larger in abstract thought about forest management than they do in actual practice. One does not often see either pure and simple applications of the area method or real attempts to develop perfectly balanced uneven-aged stands. The more flexible procedures just described are normally those employed.

On the other hand, there are situations where the goal of perfection is so far off that there is a subconscious tendency to ignore the whole problem and allow the age distribution of forests to wander where it will while other objectives are actively pursued. While there is much to be said for avoiding heavy-handed tampering with the age distribution of good and productive forests already in existence, it is dangerous to ignore imbalances. The consequences of such imbalances must be foreseen; definite decisions must be made about whether to attempt adjustments and, if so, how silvicultural procedures must be modified to accomplish the changes.

Optimum Use of Forest Capital

A good growing stock has a high stumpage value and the money that could be realized from its liquidation represents a substantial investment. When stumpage was plentiful and cheap, the major investments in American forest enterprises were usually those tied up in manufacturing and harvesting equipment. The supply of stumpage, once purchased, was usually thought of strictly as a stockpile and not as the kind of capital investment from which return in the form of wood growth might be expected.

This situation has changed as the supply of wild stumpage has dwindled, as the value of stumpage has soared, and as it has become necessary to develop forest management for sustained yield. The value of the growing stock necessary for the sustained support of a set of harvesting and manufacturing equipment now usually exceeds the value of the equipment, sometimes by a substantial margin. It may, for example, take a growing stock with a liquidation value of $80,000,000 to support the perpetual operation of a $5,000,000 investment in lumber manufacturing and harvesting equipment. Formerly the all-important goal was to obtain a good return on the investment in equipment; now the shoe is on the other foot, and it becomes increasingly logical to view the equipment as a major weapon in the battle to ensure an adequate return on the investment in growing stock.

Unfortunately, the rate of return represented by the annual production of stumpage value by a forest growing stock is rarely very high. An annual yield of $4,000,000 in stumpage value from an $80,-000,000 investment in growing stock would be respectable enough, yet would represent only 5 per cent interest on the investment. Were it not for the possibility of boosting this return by profit on value added through subsequent manufacture, many investors would not be interested in retaining much money in forest growing stock. Obviously the investment in growing stock must be kept from getting too large and, at the same time, the value represented by its growth and yield must be increased as much as possible.

There are many ways of viewing and attacking this problem, which is basically one of forest management and economics. Attention is here limited to a few of the ways in which its solution may affect the silvicultural treatment of stands and the contributions which such treatment can make to the solution.

The main silvicultural approach to the problem is typified by, but not limited to, the effect of thinning. The removal of trees of positive stumpage value in thinning definitely reduces the investment tied up in standing trees. Properly conducted thinnings have the simultaneous effect of increasing the rate of value production of the stand over what it would have been without thinning. In all of the technique of forestry, there is probably no more powerful contribution that can be made to the crucial problem of increasing the rate of interest on forest capital. Part of the increase comes from making good trees grow in size and value at a greater rate; part comes simply from the more passive effect of eliminating trees that are poor investments in favor of those that will yield good returns.

This same general approach is used to detect those stands which cease to return enough interest to remain as parts of the growing stock and should be replaced by new stands that will be better investments. Silvicultural techniques are modified most, however, when partial cutting is indicated.

The idea of regarding the individual tree as the basic unit of production is appropriate because the trees in a given stand are not exactly the same and do not grow at the same rate. They might do so in stands with the spacing of orchards but not in forest stands. Even in the finest stands most of the capacity to produce value is concentrated in a limited number of trees, usually the biggest and best. As a result, the trees of even the most uniform stands do not all reach the optimum time for cutting simultaneously.

Variation among the economic potentialities of trees is best understood and handled by application of the concept of **financial maturity**

(Duerr, Fedkiw, and Guttenberg, 1956). In this approach the value that a tree would have if it were harvested now is treated as an investment and the prospective increase in value of the tree as the anticipated income on that investment. If the tree will not return an acceptable rate of compound interest on the investment which it represents, it is regarded as being at or past the point of financial maturity and should be cut. If it will increase in value at a rate equal to or greater than the acceptable rate, it is not yet financially mature and would best be left to grow.

The values employed are either stumpage values or conversion surplus, which is the difference between the sale value of the end product and all the direct costs of converting the trees into the end product. The use of stumpage value is most appropriate if the owner merely produces stumpage; conversion surplus, if he also engages in the harvesting and manufacturing. In either case, it is important that the predicted increases in value allow not only for increase in volume but also for change in quality.

The rate of compound interest demanded on the investments represented by the trees depends on the owner and will not be the same for all kinds of owners. The most logical rate is that which the owner might realistically obtain from some alternative investment that he has an opportunity to make. Ordinarily it will range from 4 to 6 per cent and the realistic alternative investments lie elsewhere in the forest enterprise involved. The time period of the investment is usually taken as extending from the time of one cutting in a stand to the next.

This approach can also be used to choose between two trees that are competing for the same growing space; in such instances, the tree that will return the highest rate of interest is the one to leave. The concept is not limited to use in partial cutting; if a stand is to be reproduced by clearcutting it is logical to terminate the rotation when the rate of return on the investment represented by the whole stand falls below the acceptable rate.

This kind of analysis usually reveals in financial terms that fast-growing trees of high quality are more promising growing stock than those that are slower in growth or poorer in quality. The feeble 25-year-old intermediate that has just become merchantable for pulpwood may have the same degree of financial maturity as the 30-inch veteran which has finally started to decrease in growth after 120 years. By means of such analysis it is often possible to restrain the subconscious tendency to carry most trees of a stand too long and to cut the few best ones too soon.

This concept places so much emphasis on the variation between individual trees that it is altogether too easy to jump to the conclusion that it can be applied only by means of the single-tree selection system. If the stands are uneven-aged or irregular a pure application of this approach will normally lead to some form of uneven-aged management (Duerr, Fedkiw, and Guttenberg, 1956). If the stands are even-aged, a series of thinnings leading to shelterwood cutting, all under even-aged management, would represent almost perfect application of the idea (Fedkiw and Yoho, 1960). In most overmature stands this approach would dictate a prompt clearcutting. If a perfectly balanced, uneven-aged stand of good quality already existed and were handled solely on the basis of financial maturity, the cuttings might automatically maintain the distribution of diameter classes appropriate to sustained-yield management of the stand. However, the distributions of age and diameter developed by such cutting are essentially an image of those that existed initially, although this image would gradually be blurred in random fashion by the effects of the differences in vigor and quality among the trees cut and left in successive harvests.

Cuttings based on financial maturity may thus have some effect in broadening the distribution of age classes but are distinctly different from the systematic manipulations necessary to create and maintain sustained-yield units. *The objectives of securing sustained yield and optimum use of growing capital are distinctly separate and usually conflict with one another.* The fact that they may coincide in ideally balanced, uneven-aged stands is the exception rather than the rule.

The concept of financial maturity is such a powerful analytical tool that it is prudent to call attention to its inherent shortcomings and to the errors that are often made in its application.

In the first place, the concept does not take into account any investments other than those represented by the as yet unrealized value of standing timber. There is no accounting for the value of or carrying charges on land, roads, manufacturing facilities, or any of the other investments that make up the whole enterprise (Worrell, 1953). No consideration is given to any of the actual cash investments that may have been made in the past treatment of the trees in question.

Rigid adherence to the principle of financial maturity can conflict with management objectives other than sustained yield. The tendency toward single-minded concentration on individual trees often results in failure to leave enough vacant growing space or to meet the other ecological requirements for reproduction. Even when financial maturity is a good guide to partial cutting throughout the rest of the rotation it is often best to depart from it during the relatively brief interval in which the establishment of reproduction must become the ruling objective. In using the financial-maturity concept it is very difficult, although not impossible, to compare the prospective returns from continued growth of existing trees with those from the new trees that might replace them.

To the extent that cuttings guided by financial maturity lead to the creation of irregular stands they may complicate and reduce the efficiency of logging and other operations involving the stands.

Attention should also be called to some of the pitfalls which, although not inherent in the approach, can often beset its application. It is based heavily on predictions of future growth and economic conditions and thus can be no better than these predictions. For example, its rigid application to the management of ponderosa pine in the Pacific Northwest proved somewhat disenchanting, largely because elaborate predictions of future lumber prices made in the 1930's proved so hopelessly wrong in the 1940's. The complexity of calculations for so many different kinds of trees often leads to use of the simplifying and highly erroneous assumption that all trees of a particular diameter and species are the same.

This approach is, of course, most useful as a guide to timber marking. It is only natural that the essential predictions of future growth are influenced by observations of increment borings or bark characteristics, both of which indicate growth rates of the recent past. The important consideration, however, is future rate of growth, especially if this is likely to be increased by the effects of partial cutting. Similarly, it is necessary to anticipate correctly the changes that will take place in the quality of the tree because this may affect value as much as growth in volume. These kinds of predictions involve more than mere extrapolation; there is nothing better than a clear understanding of what is likely to happen after a cutting, even if it can be used only intuitively.

The procedures followed in analysis of financial maturity provide no very tangible means of calculating the prospective interest return on trees or stands that are so young or poor that they have no current value. Future production ultimately depends on the way this part of the growing stock is handled. Care must be taken that proper numbers of good, young trees continually renew the merchantable portion of the growing stock and that encroachment of the poorer trees on the growing space is combatted. These two objectives, like that of regeneration, are all too easily overlooked in the single-minded concern over merchantable growing stock implicit in the concept of financial maturity.

Pursuit of the objective of optimum use of existing growing stock easily becomes a means of rationalizing evasion of other crucial problems. This is especially true in stands in which only a fraction of the trees are of merchantable size or quality. Such trees are then gradually cut in the hope, often desperate and sometimes vain, that smaller or poorer residual trees will develop into good ones for subsequent harvests. If the likelihood of getting desirable reproduction is in doubt, the issue is sometimes evaded by prolonging the rotation and trying to bring all of the existing trees to good size. If such evasions are necessary they should be honestly recognized and corrections for their consequences made in management plans and cutting budgets; meanwhile basic solutions should be sought for the causes of the situation. It is too much to expect that the best course of silvicultural action will always be found to follow the path of least resistance.

The rather aimless procedure just described often occurs during the period when forests or stands are being placed under management. At such times it is often difficult to determine what kind of forest to create or, even if a goal has been decided upon, it may still take time to invent means of getting there. In complicated situations this period may extend over several decades, during which time it may be very difficult for even the professional onlooker to determine what is going on. The greatest danger in such procedures is that they may be complacently accepted as permanent solutions.

In summary, it is well to reiterate that forestry enterprises must rely heavily on obtaining adequate returns from the forest capital. This depends ultimately on obtaining good growth in both size and quality from trees comprising a growing stock that is not allowed to build up to the point where it becomes a large amount of capital yielding low returns. The concept of financial maturity is a useful guide in modifying silvicultural practice to make best use of the growing stock, even though it is subject to errors in application. It usually constitutes a powerful argument *for* partial cutting and *against* those radical or deliberate changes in the age distribution of existing forests that would necessitate cutting financially immature trees.

Concentration and Efficient Arrangement of Operations

In the previous pages attention has been devoted to a number of considerations which tend to argue more against than in favor of developing uniform stands. It has, for example, been pointed out that the objective of sustained yield is hardly cause by itself for inflicting the uniformity of the pure, even-aged stand on silviculture. In general, highly flexible procedures of cutting and arrangement of stands enable the closest approach to optimum use of both growing stock and growing space, and in lesser degree to the successful regeneration of the forest and its protection against damaging agencies. These objectives are, however, not always best attained by creating or maintaining irregular stands and there are other important reasons for resisting the temptation to do so. Most of these involve the point that all sorts of operations can become very complicated and expensive in a stand or forest composed of a minutely divided mosaic of age classes or species.

The harvesting of timber crops is usually the most expensive operation conducted in the forest; it is thus important to arrange stands so that costs, per unit of volume harvested, will be kept at the lowest level consistent with other objectives. Transportation is the component of logging costs most affected by the arrangement of stands. If the merchantable age classes or species are scattered rather than concentrated in a contiguous unit, the gross area which must be covered to harvest a given volume of timber in a single operation is correspondingly increased. This is especially true if terrain is difficult, if roads must be built or improved for each operation, or if the cost of shifting heavy equipment from one operation to another is high. If the heterogeneity of the stands dictates handling a broader range of sizes, qualities, and species of trees than is possible with a single set of machinery or a single procedure there is the additional cost of having a wider variety of equipment or of trying to handle material with equipment not suited to the purpose. The cost of supervision also tends to increase the more scattered and complicated the operation.

In general, those costs of logging that are affected by the volume removed per gross acre are the ones that are increased by heterogeneity of stands or the scattering of small stands. The ideal stand from this viewpoint would be the largest even-aged, pure stand that could be harvested during the period that would normally elapse before the equipment would have to be removed for overhaul, change of season, or other cause not related to stand characteristics.

In considering the relationship between silviculture and logging costs, it is crucial to distinguish between the foregoing category of costs and those most strongly affected by tree size. These generally involve handling and processing operations other than transportation. For example, the costs of felling, bucking, loading, and manufacturing material from forty 20-inch trees are not significantly different if they come from one acre or from 10 acres of gross stand area. The larger the trees, the lower are these handling costs per unit of volume, at least up to the point where the trees are too large to be handled by the chosen kind of equipment.

If absolutely the only objective were to minimize transportation costs that depend on the volume of cut per gross acre, the solution would be to cut everything worth the cost of harvesting and processing. If, on the other hand, it were to minimize handling costs that depend on tree size, only the larger trees would be cut.

The question at hand, however, also involves planning for the production of material for future harvests. Not only does this mean that a host of other objectives must be considered but also that the plan covers a series of harvests rather than just one. In principle, it is no more difficult to accelerate the rate at which trees grow to good size in uniform stands than it is in heterogeneous ones. In other words, problems involving tree size can be solved in either kind of stand but those involving transportation can best be solved with uniform stands. It is, therefore, ordinarily better from the standpoint of a long-term program of harvests to work toward increasing the uniformity of stands and to resist tendencies toward the haphazard mixture of age classes and species.

Another cogent argument for uniform stands is the point that the forest industries are hamstrung at all stages of harvesting and manufacture by the tremendous variability of raw wood. This necessitates repeated sorting and complicates all handling operations; some of this extra work is avoided in the processing of competitive materials that are more homogeneous. To cite merely one example, the variability in size of trees dictates that logging equipment be made versatile at the expense of being completely efficient. Any silvicultural steps that can be taken to reduce variability are advantageous, although there are inherent biological limits to the uniformity that can be achieved. Variation in diameter as well as in other characteristics is bound to appear in any stand that fully occupies the site for any length of time and in stands where competitive effects are used to develop good stem form. However, it is certainly possible to improve upon the heterogeneity often found in nature.

Many methods of partial cutting, especially thinning, can be applied so as to enable the systematic removal of various relatively uniform categories of trees at successive intervals, with a high proportion of the volume being harvested from favorable ranges of diameter. The main objective should be to obtain the widest possible margin between the costs of logging and the value of the material harvested during a series of harvests. This goal is not likely to be achieved if the sole consideration is minimizing the cost of each separate harvest without regard for those that will follow. Silvicultural measures to create trees of good size and quality, preferably in stands of high volume per acre, contribute fully as much.

Most other operations are facilitated by systematic arrangement of uniform stands. Silvicultural operations like pruning, release cutting, and site preparation can become very complicated and expensive in heterogeneous stands. Such blanket operations as prescribed burning and application of chemicals from the air are prohibitively expensive or impossible unless large areas can be treated as solid units. Timber marking is very time-consuming and expensive in heterogeneous stands, a situation aggravated by the fact that the more complicated the stand the more expensive the talent required for the marking.

Administrative and supervisory activities of all sorts are difficult in heterogeneous stands and forests. While uniformity of stands may not be mandatory for sustained-yield management, it is at least helpful. It is much easier to keep track of uniform stands and to detect the places where protective measures and silvicultural treatments are necessary.

Heterogeneity of stands and forests is a characteristic which should not be encouraged or endured without good reason or because of vague naturalistic doctrines not known to apply to the circumstances. There are, of course, important arguments for heterogeneity; the logic for them is outlined in the preceding sections and in some subsequent chapters. However, none of them are reasons for purely haphazard or random scattering of species and age classes, except in situations where the forest is inherited in such condition and there seems no real cause for alteration.

There are strong natural tendencies for stands to become heterogeneous. The important decisions, therefore, relate to determining the degree of heterogeneity that is to be tolerated and whether to try to make stands more heterogeneous or more uniform.

Where it is desirable to create new stand boundaries and variations within stands they should coincide with such features as changes in site, variations in accessibility, and barriers to damaging agencies, all adjusted as much as possible to follow such pre-existing differences in arrangement of species and age classes as occur at or near logical dividing lines.

Resolution of Conflicting Objectives

It should now be apparent that there is no inherent harmony among the various major objectives sought in managing forests. Such harmony can be made to exist only by weighing the various objectives individually and inventing silvicultural systems that represent analytical compromises within forest management plans created by the same kind of procedure.

The disharmony that has been deliberately painted in tones of sharp contrast is most evident if one considers all forestry in general. Fortunately these conflicting objectives need be resolved only for particular forests or stands. Analysis of each situation will usually reveal a few ruling considerations; the necessity of giving first attention to these will simplify and govern the solutions.

The process starts with a consideration of the goals of the forest owner. Each of the remaining objectives must then receive some attention; it would almost invariably be a mistake to pursue any single one to the bitter limit. The analytical process generally works downward from the forest to the stand, but not without the formation of some preliminary idea of the range of treatments and results that is silviculturally feasible. Some immutable and absolutely restrictive natural factors are bound to exist and these must be recognized early in the process. However, the remaining latitude of silvicultural possibilities is likely to be broad enough that further efforts to narrow the range down in the direction of the optimum silvicultural system may be based on analysis of the economic effect of all factors, natural and otherwise.

In the chapters that follow there are some examples not only of methods of reproduction but also of some particular silvicultural systems and the reasoning underlying their development. All of them are best regarded merely as very generalized and sketchy examples chosen mainly to illustrate specific points. Published accounts of complete silvicultural systems that have been developed and applied are few and usually generalized to the extent of referring to certain forest types in large regions rather than to specific forest properties. In application, silvicultural systems include a myriad of additional variations designed to accommodate differences in objectives of ownership, accessibility, site quality, and all the other factors that make every stand different from all others. The complete silvicultural system is usually a plan that exists in the mind of the forest manager and it is more important that it be there than nonexistent.

The Silvicultural System as a Working Hypothesis

The practice of silviculture must be conducted in the absence of complete knowledge about the immutable natural and changing economic factors that affect each stand. Furthermore most of the treatments cannot be properly evaluated until many years after their application. Decisive action cannot await absolute proof of validity nor can it be evaded indefinitely by fence-straddling.

The forester must, therefore, proceed as far as possible on the basis of proven fact and then complete his plans in the light of the most analytical opinions he can form. This necessity of substituting opinion for fact is a treacherous undertaking, especially because opinions to which one is committed by his actions easily become mistaken for facts. The soundest basis for action derived from a mixture of proven fact and unproven opinion is the *working hypothesis,* which is not truth but the best estimate of truth formed by analyzing all available information. It is not allowed to become a *ruling doctrine* but is, instead, constantly tested against new information and modified accordingly. It is not embraced so wholeheartedly that it cannot be discarded and replaced. One must always be ready to admit, at least to himself, that an earlier decision was wrong and correct his procedures accordingly.

The silvicultural system is logically based on a working hypothesis and is altered as it becomes necessary to change the hypothesis. Lest they become ruling doctrines, existing procedures should be constantly examined to determine whether they have outlived their time or become inconsistent with new information. It is, for example, logical to consider whether silvicultural practices developed in the era of railroad logging remain valid for tractor logging. Similarly, it is well to question whether thinning policies should not be altered when it is found that the rate of diameter growth does not, as was once believed, control the properties of wood.

Radical changes and excessive fluctuations in policy lead to lost motion. If the silvicultural system of the moment has been kept in conformity to the circumstances by repeated small modifications, radical departures are unlikely to be necessary. It is also necessary to avoid the petulant temptation to discard tested procedures in favor of those that are radically different and untested because of problems of the moment. If once promising plantations become riddled with root rots, one should not necessarily swear off planting. Neither should the lapse of 9 years between good seed crops cause a wholesale shift to artificial regeneration. Sudden, extreme reactions are almost sure to breed their kind at an early age.

Forestry is almost unique in the extent to which the actions of the present govern those of future generations of practitioners. Any treatment that is applied to a stand now is likely to restrict the choices available in subsequent treatment. In a sense, the forester conducting a treatment in a stand is entering into a pact of mutual understanding with his successors about that stand. He is entitled to expect that they will honor his objectives by giving them the benefit of all doubts, but not to the extent of slavish adherence to original plans. His successors are committed to correcting his mistakes by making changes and modifications in the procedure at the proper times. It must be recognized that the period of regeneration is about the only one during which major changes can be made in the handling of a stand. The period of intermediate cutting is one of modification rather than change. The stands that a forester inherits from the past he must treat as best he can; those that he starts anew provide him the best places to inflict his own ideas on the future.

REFERENCES

Barrett, J. W. (Ed.). 1962. *Regional silviculture of the United States*. Ronald Press, New York.

Davis, K. P. 1954. *American forest management*. McGraw-Hill, New York.

———. 1959. Comments on "What is unit area control?". *J. Forestry* 57:517–518.

Duerr, W. A., J. Fedkiw, and S. Guttenberg. 1950. Financial maturity: a guide to profitable timber growing. *USDA Tech. Bul.* 1146.

Eyre, F. H., and P. Zehngraff. 1948. Red pine management in Minnesota. *USDA Circ.* 778.

Fedkiw, J., and J. G. Yoho. 1960. Economic models for thinning and reproducing even-aged stands. *J. Forestry* 58:26–34.

Graham, S. A. 1959. Control of insects through silvicultural practices. *J. Forestry* 57:281–283.

Hallin, W. E. 1954. Unit area control—its development and application. *CFRES Misc. Paper* 16.

———. 1959. The application of unit area control in the management of ponderosa-Jeffrey pine at Black Mountain Experimental Forest. *USDA Tech. Bul.* 1191.

Knuchel, H. 1953. *Planning and control in the managed forest.* Translated from German by M. L. Anderson. Oliver and Boyd, Edinburgh.

Spurr, S. H. 1956. German silvicultural systems. *Forest Sci.* 2:75–80.

Troup, R. S. 1952. *Silvicultural systems,* 2nd ed. Edited by E. W. Jones. Oxford Univ. Press, London.

Wellner, C. A., and R. J. Boyd. 1960. Partial cuttings in mature stands of the western white pine type. *Proc. Soc. Am. Foresters Meeting,* 1959:27–32.

Westveld, R. H. 1949. *Applied silviculture in the United States,* 2nd ed. Wiley, New York.

Worrell, A. C. 1953. Financial maturity: a questionable concept in forest management. *J. Forestry* 51:711–714.

CHAPTER 11

The clearcutting method

In the clearcutting method the area is cut clear in the literal sense of the word; virtually all the trees, large or small, in the stand are removed in the process. This is the meaning of "clearcutting" in its narrowest sense and in its usage as a technical term of silviculture. However, it is also loosely applied to any type of cutting in which all the merchantable timber is cut and all trees that cannot be utilized profitably are left. This broader usage of the term is technically incorrect but is so common that it is sometimes prudent to speak of clearcutting in the silvicultural sense as "complete clearcutting."

The other kinds of clearcutting are most logically thought of as representing other methods of cutting. If a substantial number of trees are left because they are of small size, inferior species, or poor quality, the cutting is best regarded as either selection thinning or a very crude application of the selection method. If the trees remaining are saplings or seedlings representing advance reproduction, the cuttings should be thought of as variants of the shelterwood method. If regeneration arises primarily from sprouts, the coppice method of cutting is clearly involved, regardless of how completely the old stand is removed. The true clearcutting method lays bare the area treated and leads to the establishment of an even-aged high forest.

Reproduction is secured after the cutting either artificially, by seeding or planting, or naturally, from seed borne either by trees outside the area cleared or by the trees felled in the cutting.

Form of Forest Produced

Complete clearcutting is most simply applied to stands, whether even- or uneven-aged, in which practically all the trees are merchantable, although this is not by itself a reason why such stands should be cut clear. The new stand originating on a clearcut area is even-aged, irrespective of whether the timber before the cutting was ir-regular or even-aged. In almost all stands of merchantable timber, no matter how even-aged in form, there will be occasional trees below merchantable size, cull trees, or individuals of unsalable species which remain standing after a clearcutting. If such trees are not knocked down in logging or are not likely to succumb to wind or exposure, it may be necessary to fell or kill them (Brender, 1961). The de-sirability of doing so depends on how much such residuals will impede the new crop.

Applicability of Clearcutting

The clearcutting method is logically applied, in preference to those involving partial cutting, when residual trees are not worthy of re-tention for further increase in value, source of seed, protection of the new crop, or other useful purposes.

This method and the closely related seed-tree method are applicable *only* with species that are capable of establishment in conditions of full exposure and can be depended upon to develop satisfactorily in simple, even-aged aggregations. If they are found to do so in nature, it may be presumed that they will in managed forests. There are, in fact, some intolerant pioneer species that *require* the exposure created by clearcutting or very heavy partial cutting.

Clearly justifiable application of clearcutting is also found in the harvesting of stands that are thoroughly mature or overmature. Clear-cutting should also be seriously considered if the methods of partial cutting would be substantially more costly or if this method provides the most expeditious means of replacing a poor stand with a good one. If such conditions exist and the desirable species is ecologically adaptable to the conditions created, clearcutting may be distinctly superior to any other method of regeneration.

The points that have been mentioned so far apply nearly equally both to the intensive method of clearcutting with artificial regenera-tion and to that involving natural regeneration, which is more diffi-cult yet is often associated with extensive silviculture. Even though artificial regeneration can be and occasionally is used to remedy fail-ures of natural regeneration after clearcutting, it is useful to consider the two procedures separately.

CLEARCUTTING WITH ARTIFICIAL REPRODUCTION

In this, the simplest of all methods of regeneration, the stand is cut clear and reproduced by seeding or planting. The size and pattern of cutting areas are not limited by the necessity of reserving a source of seed but are instead adjusted to create efficient arrangements of stands conforming to differences in site factors.

If the new crop is planted, there is no need to modify procedures to protect the seedlings from the hazards of the natural environment that are by-passed in the nursery. The equipment and techniques used in logging and site preparation are quite unrestricted. Composition and arrangement of the new stand are under close control; opportunity exists for the introduction of superior genetic strains and species of trees.

The technique of reproducing stands by clearcutting with seeding or planting is simply described but is distinctly not a silvicultural system that is shorn of refinements or is easy and inexpensive to apply. It is instead one of the most intensive methods of silvicultural practice; the establishment of the new crop requires substantial amounts of attention, work, and expense. It is seldom logical to assume that such heavy initial investments will be most richly rewarded if the stands receive no other treatment until the time arrives for a final, highly mechanized clearcutting. It is significant that in Europe, where this method has long represented the most common procedure, thinnings and other intermediate cuttings have been developed to a high degree of complexity and the reproduction method is the only part of the program that is simple in concept.

The very nature of the development of stands of trees is such that real efficiency in the use of growing space and the production of wood cannot be achieved without partial cutting at some point in the rotation. If the trees are spaced so wide that they develop equally during a short rotation and arrive simultaneously at the logical time for clearcutting, full occupancy of growing space is not achieved until late in the rotation. If full occupancy is gained early then some of the production is wasted unless some trees are removed in partial cuttings made in anticipation of losses. With the clearcutting method these partial cuttings are simply restricted to the period of intermediate cuttings.

Clearcutting with artificial regeneration usually involves the planting of nursery stock. It also affords an opportunity for the most thoroughgoing kind of site preparation because there is no need of avoiding damage to large or small residual trees. It is more likely than any other method to necessitate some sort of slash disposal because so much debris is deposited on the ground at once. The various preparatory treatments are likely to include control of undesirable vegetation by the use of fire, herbicides, or mechanical equipment. It is usually most expeditious to control existing vegetation before planting, even though continuing efforts are likely to be needed against undesirable vegetation reinvading before the planted trees fully claim the site. All of these accessory measures, many of which are crucial to success, have been covered in previous chapters.

One of the most important virtues of this method is the opportunity to avoid the delay in establishment of regeneration that frequently results if one depends on natural reseeding. There is an additional gain of time if the planting stock is already 1 or more years of age. Delay in replanting is dangerous because of the risk of invasion by undesirable vegetation. In spite of this factor, there are instances in which it may be desirable to wait several years before planting; if this be necessary, it is logical to delay some of the preparatory measures as well. The most common need for delay is caused by insects like the pales weevil (*Hylobius pales*) that breed in freshly cut stumps or tops and feed on the thin bark of young seedlings. This particular insect may cause such damage for 2 or 3 years after the cutting of some of the northern and southern pines. It can be combatted either by treating the planted trees with insecticides or by delaying planting until the stumps have ceased to supply food.

When existing stands are being regenerated artificially, the clearcutting method is generally used, although seeding or planting may be used to supplement or replace natural reproduction in any of the other methods of cutting.

Application of Clearcutting with Artificial Regeneration

The most important application of clearcutting with planting or seeding that is currently envisioned in North America involves the growing of southern pines with short rotations on the southern coastal plains. So far this approach has been applied mainly in the conversion of poor stands of hardwoods and grossly understocked stands of pine to well-stocked stands of slash or loblolly pine by planting. Thorough site preparation is often involved mainly because of the importance of eliminating competing vegetation and making way for machine planting. It is hoped that planting stock of genetic strains superior to any obtainable from natural regeneration will soon become available. The replacement of good stands of pine by such measures is still mostly something planned for the future, because it will not be until the 1970's that many stands now managed on this basis become old enough to cut.

This kind of silvicultural system is in the initial stages mostly on lands owned by pulp and paper companies. The most common plan is basically that of a 30-year rotation with a thirtieth of the forest being cut clear in large units and replanted each year. This is area regulation as strict and simple as any employed in the more traditional kind of European forestry. In some instances no thinning is contemplated, although the difficulties involved in thinning such stands are so small that foresters are unlikely to cast aside the advantages that can be gained.

The objectives are to simplify forest administration to the utmost and achieve those efficiencies that can be gained by conducting harvesting and silvicultural treatments as single operations over large areas. Emphasis is thus placed on solving the mechanical problems that have been faced in the past with far less attention to natural and economic problems likely to be posed in the future.

There is no large part of the continent where *both* climate and terrain are as favorable to such intensive practice as the southern coastal plain. It is, therefore, likely that this general pattern will be used widely, although probably not in the degree of simplicity in which it is described. The doubts that have materialized about some of the details will produce modifications and variations in technique, although not necessarily in the basic principle (Chaiken, 1960). There is need, however, for fitting the species and treatments more closely to the site conditions which are far less uniform than the grandiose simplicity of the management plans would suggest.

In any particular locality, there is a tendency to practice **monoculture,** that is, to rely exclusively on single species, ordinarily slash or loblolly pine. It is obviously desirable to diversify the risks by using the widest possible variety of species. Most of the southern pines do not form satisfactory mixtures, so this can be done chiefly by interspersal of moderate-sized even-aged stands of different species and age classes. The most serious barrier to diversification has been the difficulty of planting the indigenous longleaf pine and getting the seedlings to initiate height growth. It now seems probable that these difficulties can be overcome by direct seeding or use of site preparation to control competition from grass. The increasing preva-

lence of fusiform rust and *Fomes annosus* root rot in slash and loblolly pine is, in some localities, reason enough for diversification of
species.

There has been a powerful temptation to extend the planting of
slash and loblolly pine outside their natural ranges and to move them
over short distances onto soils where they are not clearly adaptable.
Damage from ice and snow sets distinct limits on the northward extension of these species. The most subtle questions revolve around
the question of how far slash pine can be safely extended onto the
deep dry sands that once supported longleaf pine. Slash pine was,
in nature, almost totally restricted to swamps by the frequent fires on
dry sites. Now that fires have been brought under reasonable control it is clear that major extensions are feasible but question remains
as to how the species will react to diseases on different kinds of well-
drained soils.

It is not easy to foretell the changes that are likely to take place
in a scheme of management not yet in full operation. Departures
from the basic idea of growing southern pines in pure, even-aged
stands are, however, likely to be uncommon. If the existence of such
stands of these species was of itself invitation to calamity, this would
have become obvious in the existing natural stands of this sort.

One of the purposes of this short-rotation management is allegedly
that of maximizing the production of pulpwood, which has been
viewed as the sole objective of management. As was pointed out in
Chapter 3, the 30-year rotation is too short to maximize *tonnage* production in loblolly pine, although it may not be far from appropriate
for slash pine. Some increase and variation in rotation lengths seem
likely even if tonnage production of pulpwood remains the sole objective. This objective is economically justifiable only if pulpwood is
in short supply and if the forest is viewed solely as a source of cheap
raw material for the pulp mill. As the total investment in land and
silvicultural treatment increases relative to that in manufacturing facilities, this viewpoint becomes less tenable. Provided that pulp requirements can still be met, it becomes logical to seek higher returns
on the forestry investments by growing not only pulpwood but also
products of higher stumpage value. This would necessitate methods
that involve greater discrimination among trees during the rotation.

The detailed modifications that have been considered so far would
not necessarily require departure from the basic scheme of artificial
regeneration after clearcutting. When the time comes to reproduce
uniform stands, the advantages of natural regeneration, still under

even-aged systems, may be found greater than may now seem apparent. Trousdell (1959), for example, found that the site preparation necessary for replacement of clearcut pine stands by machine planting was not a simple undertaking and that it sometimes involved the liquidation of adequate natural regeneration already established. He also pointed out that the root systems of planted trees often had serious deformities; it is probable that such malformations are unusually susceptible to attack by root rots.

It is noteworthy that the rather artificial kind of silviculture envisioned and the allegedly greedy economic philosophy behind it have sometimes caused bitter experiences in Europe and fallen into evil repute in some circles (Plochmann, 1960). It would be naive to suppose that the routine of clearcutting and planting will not run afoul of nature at some times and places. However, it is unlikely that all the problems will arise everywhere; each problem is separate and can usually be dealt with by separate modifications where necessary; many of them can be anticipated and avoided by vigilant observation and careful analysis of each situation. Reasons exist for considerable variation in the silviculture of the southern pines; in fact, almost every silvicultural system has been successfully applied to their management somewhere.

This method is used in old-growth stands in the Douglas-fir region of the Pacific Northwest primarily to ensure prompt regeneration without the extra logging costs or risks of loss involved in leaving large, valuable trees as sources of seed. The logging equipment now used in harvesting such large timber is more mobile than that once necessary, but is still heavy and expensive to move from one small clearcut area to another. The steep terrain also makes logging roads very costly. If clearcutting with natural regeneration is used, a large amount of valuable standing timber must be left exposed to wind around the perimeters of clearcut areas. Consequently the economies that can be achieved by clearcutting very large areas at once are often much greater than the cost of artificial seeding and even of planting, which is expensive in this region.

Actually the practices following are far from stereotyped. Stands are often cut clear in such patterns as to provide for natural reseeding and then either planted or seeded from helicopters if natural regeneration does not appear in a year or two. Sometimes the clearcut areas are kept small to reduce the risks involved in broadcast burning of slash even though planting or direct seeding is used to ensure prompt regeneration. In other instances, reliance is placed on natural restocking within several hundred feet of a seed source and the centers of the clearcut areas are planted.

Clearcutting with planting or seeding is of general applicability in situations where the previous stand is not a desirable or dependable source of seed. It appears, for example, to provide the only means of restoring those conifer forests of the Lake Region that have, on millions of acres, been displaced by poor-quality aspen after destructive cutting and fire (Shirley, 1941; Rudolf, 1950). Similar conversions of forest type have already been alluded to in connection with the culture of southern pines. There are, in fact, such large areas where the rehabilitation of forests depends on this kind of effort that it will long remain one of the most important applications of clearcutting and artificial regeneration. The crucial step is the "clearcutting" of existing undesirable vegetation. On the whole, it is easier to replace pioneer species with ones of a later successional stage than to reverse the natural succession; however, the availability of herbicides and heavy mechanical equipment for site preparation provides far greater freedom of action than was possible when such work could be done only by cutting.

This general method can, of course, also be used for conversion of forest types after the harvesting of merchantable stands if it is necessary to replace them with ones of more desirable species. It is thoroughly applicable to the regeneration of stands of good species where no change of composition is desired. If the new crop is planted rather than seeded, it may even provide a means of using the clearcutting method to reproduce some species which will not germinate or survive the seedling stage on open areas.

Stands of good species that have not been subjected to thinnings or improvement cuttings may reach maturity so densely stocked that even the dominant trees are too slender to withstand wind after partial cutting. It is also possible for all of the trees to be of such poor quality that none are worth retaining for additional growth. Under such circumstances it is logical to consider whether clearcutting with planting might be more successful or economical than partial cutting aimed at natural regeneration. The answer will depend, among many things, on whether a planted crop will develop satisfactorily and on the cost of planting.

One interesting application of clearcutting and planting is in the regeneration of decadent, overmature stands of the western white pine type of the northern Rocky Mountains. The old-growth stands are almost never pure, the white pine being vastly outnumbered by more tolerant conifers of lower value, such as western hemlock, western red-cedar, and several true firs. Most of these associated species become highly defective from heart rot at a relatively early age and remain alive to encumber the stands with large volumes of useless material.

In nature, stands of western white pine were regenerated almost exclusively after catastrophic fires in otherwise undisturbed stands. It has been customary on national forests to clearcut the most defective overmature stands, eliminate the slash by broadcast burning, and replant (Davis and Klehm, 1939), as shown in Fig. 11-1. This treatment reduces the fire hazard by eliminating the slash and puts the land into productive condition without the uncertainties of natural regeneration. The menace of blister rust is so great that it has sometimes been found necessary to carry out two broadcast burns to eliminate the *Ribes* (Wellner, 1946). The defective residual stand is not felled after logging but is killed by light, broadcast burning which

Fig. 11-1. Clearcutting with artificial regeneration of western white pine, Coeur D'Alene National Forest, Idaho. An overmature stand of white pine and western hemlock was felled and the area was planted after a broadcast burn. Only about 20 per cent of the hemlocks were sufficiently sound to be removed and utilized. The picture on the left shows the site after burning; that on the right, the same place 10 years after planting. (*Photographs by U S. Forest Service.*)

reduces the logging debris and stimulates the germination of *Ribes* seed stored in the forest floor. After several years have elapsed, the dead trees of the old residual stand are felled and the area is burned again with a hot fire which kills the young *Ribes* and any remaining stored seeds. The area is then planted; control of blister rust must be subsequently maintained. It should be emphasized that the technique is applicable only in the most defective stands. In other situations, it is better to regenerate western white pine by shelterwood cuttings.

The method of clearcutting with artificial regeneration is technically applicable to the management of almost any kind of forest. It stands in sharp contrast to the seemingly closely related method of clearcutting with natural regeneration which is of much more limited application and gives satisfactory results only under favorable conditions.

It is logical to anticipate that the system of clearcutting and planting will be applied increasingly wherever silviculture becomes more intensive. This tendency is already apparent in the management of coastal Douglas-fir as well as slash and loblolly pine. This development has not occurred because these species are difficult to reproduce naturally; actually natural reseeding is as effective with these species as with any. The main reason is instead that in intensive management it is often cheaper to plant than suffer the loss of several years of wood production.

It is not especially relevant that there are some countries overseas where this system is such a standard procedure that methods of natural regeneration are occasionally regarded as useless curiosities. These are usually places where labor is cheap and wood is costly. Since the opposite economic relationship prevails in North America, application of the system is unlikely to become universal or remotely approach becoming so.

CLEARCUTTING WITH NATURAL REGENERATION

In this method dependence is placed on establishment of regeneration from natural seeding of the clearcut area. This reproduction should, for best results, start immediately but it is usually delayed until there is a good seed crop coupled with weather conditions favorable to the germination and survival of seedlings. Excessively slow regeneration, in addition to increasing the risk of invasion by undesirable vegetation, may result in the development of somewhat irregular stands in which the first trees to appear become wolf trees. The sources from which the seed may come are enumerated in the following paragraphs.

Seed from adjacent stands. Seed of this origin is disseminated by wind over the cleared area, most thickly close to the parent trees on the borders of the clearing, and in decreasing amount toward the center. Reproduction arising from such seeding is likely to be too dense near the source of seed and sparse or absent at greater distances, as shown in Fig. 11-2. Douglas-fir, loblolly pine, birches, and a number of other American species can be successfully reproduced by seeding of this kind.

Seed from the trees harvested. With almost any species, a substantial amount of seed may come from the trees removed in clearcutting, provided that the cutting is made during a good seed year. The seeds may still be on the trees at the time of cutting, or they may have fallen recently. With most species the only seed from the cut trees which is useful for regeneration is that produced in the current year. Certain softwoods, however, have stored seed in **serotinous** cones that open gradually over a period of years, as is true of black spruce, or which rarely open to any extent except under the influence of high temperatures. The most prominent species in the latter group are jack and lodgepole pine; some other less important hard pines that also reproduce in nature after crown fires have this characteristic.

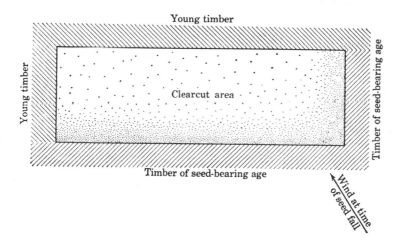

Fig. 11-2. Clearcutting the whole stand, with reproduction secured by seed disseminated from seed trees located outside the cut stand. The density of the reproduction 5 years after the cutting is indicated by the dots.

Seed stored in serotinous cones remains viable for many years, but special measures are often necessary to secure the release of this vast quantity of seed after cutting.

Regeneration arising from seed produced by the trees removed in clearcutting is uniform and complete if the conditions created by the cutting are subsequently favorable. For this reason it is distinctly advantageous to carry out any method of regeneration cutting when abundant crops of ripe seed are on the trees or have recently fallen.

Seed stored in the forest floor. Appreciable numbers of seeds of a *few* species may remain viable in the humus layers beneath uncut stands for periods longer than one year. The best example is Atlantic white-cedar, the seeds of which are stored in large quantities in the cold and poorly aerated peats on which this species grows; the period of storage extends for at least 2 years, but it may be appreciably longer (Little, 1950). There is no evidence of storage of this sort in other commercial species. On the other hand, the hard-coated seeds of some undesirable shrubs and small trees, notably those of *Ribes*, may be stored in the litter for decades. At one time it was held that seeds of Douglas-fir were stored in the duff for many years and clearcutting could, therefore, be applied without any real necessity for restricting the sizes of cutting areas. This theory was conclusively disproven by Isaac (1943) who found that the seeds of neither Douglas-fir nor its associates remained viable in the forest floor to any significant extent for more than 1 year.

Conditions Essential to Success of the Method

Satisfactory natural regeneration after a clearcutting depends, first, on the distribution of an abundant supply of seed over the entire area and, second, on the existence of conditions favorable to the germination of the seed and the development of the seedlings.

The method involves sudden and complete exposure of the ground which creates a very rigorous environment for the new crop. The supply of water in the mineral soil is, however, usually increased because the combined effects of decreased root competition and reduced interception of precipitation more than compensate for the increased evaporation. The solar energy needed for photosynthesis is unrestricted. Although such conditions tend to hamper the establishment of seedlings of most species, they are usually highly favorable to the growth of established plants.

In order to secure a new crop, the species being reproduced must be fully adapted to these difficult conditions. This drawback of the clearcutting method can, on appropriate occasions, be turned into an advantage in favoring some species which are both hardy and desirable over those which are neither desirable nor capable of enduring the extreme conditions created.

Where surrounding trees are the only source of seed, the clearing must be sufficiently small (usually long and narrow) to allow for adequate dissemination to all points. Safe widths for clearings to be stocked by wind-disseminated seed are likely to range, depending on species, from *one to five times the height of the adjacent timber* from which seed will be obtained. Direction of the wind at the time of seed dispersal should be known, and the clearing should be so located that its long axis is at right angles to this direction.

Most dissemination occurs during dry, sunny weather when the winds are brisk and gusty. The most effective winds are frequently those that blow out of the dry interior regions of continents; they are not necessarily of the same direction as the so-called "prevailing winds." In rugged terrain, it is best to have the long axes of the openings run at right angles to the contour lines because the winds responsible for dispersal of seeds are usually altered in direction so that they blow up or down valleys. Where other considerations dictate that the clearings be oriented in a manner less favorable from the standpoint of seed dispersal, the dimensions of the openings should be correspondingly reduced.

Heavy-seeded species, depending principally upon gravity for dissemination, will not furnish sufficient seed from trees outside the clearing. When seed in the forest floor or on the trees to be cut can be reliably depended upon, the weight of the seeds and the dimensions of the clearing become less important.

Allowances must be made for the substantial losses that occur after dissemination, especially from rodents. The effectiveness of natural seed crops can be increased by the poisoning of rodents on cutover areas. These difficulties are best avoided by providing seed sources adequate to shower areas to be regenerated with tens, if not hundreds, of thousands of seeds per acre. The effectiveness of the seed supply can be increased by improving the condition of the seedbeds.

After an adequate dispersal of seed over the clearing is provided for, favorable conditions for germination and early growth of seedlings of the desired species must be established and maintained for a few years. In the clearcutting method, these conditions are fixed largely by the characteristics of the opening created, and only a limited amount of control is possible after cutting. In this respect the slope and aspect of the terrain are more important than the size of the clearcut area. Ordinarily reproduction after clearcutting is best on sloping terrain oriented so that the effects of sun and wind are somewhat reduced; south-facing slopes are almost invariably difficult to regenerate by this method.

Environmental conditions are actually far from uniform even on extensive clearcut areas. Isaac (1943) showed that Douglas-fir seedlings survive and grow best in the "dead shade" of the stumps, large pieces of logging debris, and dead vegetation found on clearcut areas; survival is poor on completely exposed surfaces and beneath dense shade or the living shade of shrubs. Success consequently depends on the frequency with which such favorable spots are created during cutting or by special treatment thereafter. The more abundant the seed supply, the greater is the likelihood that seeds will reach these spots in adequate numbers.

Arrangement of the Clearcut Areas

In the simplest mode of application the clearcutting method involves removal of all the timber on the area chosen for creation of a new even-aged stand. The trees removed from one or more such areas will make up the annual cut of a forest managed entirely under the clearcutting system. If cuttings are to be made annually and continuously, the forest should eventually contain at least as many stands as there are years in the rotation (Fig. 10-2). These stands should be kept relatively small or at least narrow in one dimension. Stands cut in consecutive years should be scattered throughout the forest and so arranged that timber of seed-bearing age is adjacent on one or more sides and recently cutover stands are not contiguous.

Modifications of the Method

Modifications in application of the method may consist of: (1) variations in the size and shape of clearcut areas, (2) use of supplementary measures to prepare the site or distribute cone-bearing slash, and (3) arrangements by which individual stands are clearcut in strips or patches with a period longer than one year being taken to remove the whole stand.

The maximum size of openings and the minimum amount of supplementary work performed are set by the ecological characteristics of the species to be reproduced. Further refinements lead in the direction of artificial regeneration or the substitution of one of the methods that involves partial cutting.

The type of modification which involves gradual removal of the stand in strips or patches during a small fraction of the rotation enables use of the clearcutting method in a stand which, if cut as a single unit, would leave an opening too large to be restocked by seed from adjacent stands. This problem may arise where an extensive even-aged stand is deteriorating rapidly and must be salvaged within a few years. In other instances, harvesting operations may involve the construction of facilities that must be amortized by continuous use over a period of several years or more. If clearcutting is the method to be used in these situations, the arrangement of cutting areas in strips or patches and temporary reservation of intervening timber as a source of seed are the best solution.

Three separate kinds of arrangement may be distinguished in this variant of the clearcutting method. They are referred to as clearcutting in (1) alternate strips, (2) progressive strips, and (3) patches.

Clearcutting in alternate strips. Under this arrangement the stand is divided into a series of strips as shown in Fig. 11-3. The first strip is cut clear, the next left standing, the third cut, and so on throughout the stand. A few years later, after reproduction is established, the timber on the uncut strips is removed. The second cutting must follow within a few years after the first if the even-aged character of the stand is to be preserved. One-fifth of the length of the rotation is the period of time theoretically allowable. There is no necessity that either the first or the second cutting be accomplished in a single year.

The timber on the uncut strips furnishes all or part of the seed for stocking the cut strips and, to some extent, protects the cutover area and the new crop. To perform these functions to best advantage the uncut strips must be relatively close together and at right angles to the wind direction at time of seed dispersal. The width of the cut strips depends on the distance of effective seed dispersal; ordinarily it should not exceed five times the height of the stand.

When the strips of timber left at the time of the first cutting are removed, natural reproduction on these areas cannot be secured in the same way as on the strips first cut. No belts of timber are left to furnish seed. Either the seed must come from the trees that are cut, or else artificial reproduction must be used. If a seed year can be selected as the time for making the second cutting, successful regeneration may be secured. In the many cases where cutting cannot be delayed until a seed year, some method other than clearcutting may be adopted to reproduce the residual strips. The seed-tree method or the shelterwood method may be used for this purpose, although they involve two or more cuttings to remove the timber and thus lengthen the total period of regeneration.

In some cases, natural reproduction may be established under the

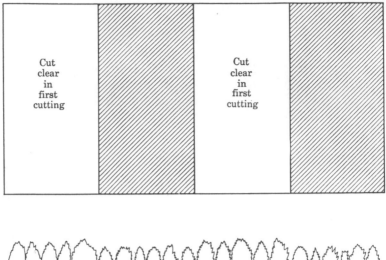

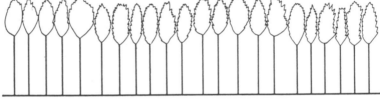

Fig. 11-3. The arrangement of the strips within a pine stand reproduced by clearcutting in alternate strips 80 feet wide. The upper sketch shows the horizontal arrangement of the two sets of strips. The lower sketch shows a vertical profile of the new stand 50 years after the first cutting and 45 years after the second. The older trees are about 80 feet tall, whereas the younger have an average height of 75 feet; this difference would be of little significance in practice.

uncut strips if they are narrow enough to admit light from the side. The same effect may be achieved by starting shelterwood cuttings in the residual strips at the time of the first cutting.

There is no reason why half the stand must be clearcut in the first operation; actually the proportion may vary from 30 to 70 per cent. In view of the greater difficulty of securing regeneration on the strips cut in the second operation, it is ordinarily better to remove more than half the stand in the first cutting. However, there are several reasons for not making the uncut strips too narrow. They must be wide enough to provide sufficient seed and to be windfirm in storms. Furthermore, they must contain enough timber to make the second operation practicable as a logging proposition. In general the strips left should be at least as wide as the height of the timber. Some wind-fall must be anticipated along the borders of the cleared area, al-though this can be reduced by locating the cutting boundaries in places where the timber is relatively windfirm.

Clearcutting in progressive strips. In this modification of the method three or more operations are required to remove the entire stand. In the simplest application, strip cuttings are made at short intervals of time starting at one side of the stand and advancing pro-gressively across to the other side. If an even-aged stand is to be created by this method, the entire series of cuttings must be finished within a period of 10 to 20 years, depending on the length of the rotation.

In large stands this simple form of progression is impractical, since the entire stand cannot be cut over in a short enough time to pro-duce even-aged timber without making the individual strips too wide for satisfactory reproduction. In overcoming this difficulty, several cutting sections are laid out as shown in Fig. 11-4, and operations proceed simultaneously in each cutting section. Clearcut strips suf-ficiently narrow to ensure adequate seed dispersal are made across each cutting section, and the process is repeated until the entire area is clearcut. The reserved strips of each cutting section furnish seed and protection to seedlings. Each successive cutting should be carried out as soon as reproduction is established on the adjacent strip cut previously.

In regenerating the last strip of each cutting section, one encounters the same problems faced when clearcutting in alternate strips. How-

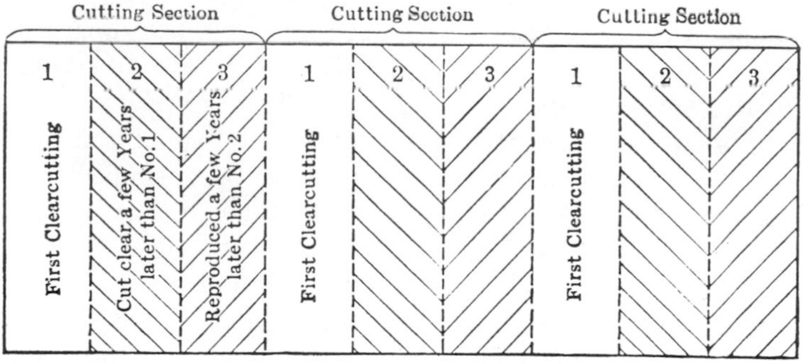

Fig. 11-4. Clearcutting a single stand in progressive strips, using three cutting sections. The last strip (Number 3) in each section may be reproduced by a method other than clearcutting.

ever, the proportion of the area which may have to be artificially seeded or planted is reduced by the very nature of the progressive arrangement and may be decreased still further by making the last uncut strip relatively narrow.

If the winds responsible for damage to standing timber and those that disperse the seed come from roughly the same direction, it is advantageous to advance the successive cutting strips toward the windward, that is, against the direction of the winds involved. The cutting thus progresses so that the rather unstable and suddenly exposed trees beside the clearcut strips are on the leeward edges of the strips of standing timber. In this scheme of arrangement it is highly desirable that the windward edge of the last strip that is cut be composed of trees that are unusually windfirm.

Clearcutting in patches. On rugged and irregular terrain or in even-aged stands which lack uniformity, the regular arrangement of cutting areas employed in the strip methods is impractical. Some of the advantages of these methods may be retained, however, if the stand is removed in a series of clearcuttings made in patches.

In the first cutting, portions of the stand are selected which for some reason should be cut before the rest of the stand. In succeeding operations, these patches are enlarged or new patches are created elsewhere in the stand. The first areas to be cut may be ones with injured or overmature trees, places where previous disturbances have allowed the establishment of advance regeneration, or soils where the trees are shallow-rooted and subject to windfall if exposed by cutting of adjacent areas.

The advantage of these modifications of the clearcutting method is that they enable this method to be employed in regenerating even-aged stands which cannot be reproduced by natural seeding if all the timber is removed in a single cutting. The desirability of recognizing them as distinct methods of cutting rather than as series of unrelated clearcuttings of separate stands lies in the fact that, if conducted as outlined above, each leads to establishment of a single, relatively homogeneous stand. With the passage of time, the groups of new trees on each strip or patch tend to approach the same size and become indistinguishable. The difficulties of administering a forest consisting of a patchwork of minute stands are thus avoided.

The systematic arrangement of the strip methods is also useful in ensuring that seed-bearing timber is adjacent to cutover areas for as long a period as possible. The primary advantages lie in simplicity of administration, which is very important in the remote forests to which these methods of cutting are adapted. In such places the stand, as delimited on type maps for purposes of management, must be large and it may be desirable to concentrate the regeneration cuttings into a short period at the end of each rotation.

Fundamentally there is no reason why tracts of timber could not be cut in a series of strip or patch cuttings with longer intervals between operations. Each strip or patch might then be recognized as an individual stand or as part of a stand with a number of distinct age classes. The scheme of cutting in strips and patches is also followed in connection with the seed-tree, shelterwood, and selection methods. If the uncut areas are exceedingly small and widely spaced, the technique is regarded as a variant of the seed-tree method. If the cuttings are narrower than one-half the height of the uncut trees, the side shade is great enough that the operations are clearly best regarded as modifications of the shelterwood or selection methods.

Advantages and Disadvantages of the Clearcutting Method

Most of the advantages of the method of clearcutting with natural regeneration involve the fact that all operations are concentrated in time and space. Logging, administrative work, and silvicultural operations can proceed with a high degree of simplicity and efficiency. The equipment and methods of logging can be chosen without regard to protecting residual trees within the cutting area. Such measures of site preparation as slash disposal and exposure of mineral soil are often more essential than with the shelterwood or selection methods, but are not obstructed by any residual stand.

No trees are left on the cutting area where they may be lost to wind and other atmospheric agencies, although the risk of losing exposed trees in adjacent stands is increased.

Timber marking is limited to defining the boundaries of areas to be cut clear. The method also lends itself to the simple technique of regulation of the cut by area.

The outstanding disadvantage of the method is that regeneration is usually staked on one throw of the dice, often against heavy odds. The only remedy for failure is artificial regeneration. Any source of seed provided by the previous stand is available but once. Unless the cutting areas are so narrow as to offset many of the advantages of concentrating operations, the possibilities of adequate dispersal of seed from adjacent timber are uncertain. If the desired species does not claim the large amount of vacant growing space promptly, undesirable vegetation is almost certain to do so. Clearcutting is ordinarily an invitation to colonization by the light-seeded pioneer species of the locality. The prospect of success is good if the desired species is the most aggressive of these; otherwise the result may be either disaster or a substantial amount of release cutting.

All parts of the new stand pass simultaneously through the various stages of development and the hazards attendant on each stage. The seedlings are exposed not only to the benefits of full sunlight and minimal root competition but also to the direct and indirect consequences of extremes of temperature. A stand which is completely open initially and eventually closes passes through almost the entire spectrum of microclimatic conditions. This increases, for example, the likelihood that the stand will pass through a stage in which it provides a favorable environment for some insect pest. The risk and hazard of fire are bound to be high at some stage. Special measures necessary to protect against any source of damage are, however, likely to be necessary only during short and easily recognizable periods.

Neither clearcutting nor any other method of cutting is, of itself, likely to cause serious damage to ordinary kinds of soil (Lutz and Chandler, 1946). Accelerated decomposition of humus layers sometimes follows clearcutting and may be beneficial to both chemical and physical properties of the soil. In swampy places, the reduction in transpiration caused by removal of trees may result in an undesirable elevation of the water table.

Clearcutting tends to reduce protection against erosion, landslides, and rapid runoff of water. The risk of this kind of damage is greatest with cutting on steep slopes; this poses a serious dilemma because these are the very kind of sites where exclusive concern for logging problems would dictate use of the clearcutting method. It should be noted, however, that any difficulties with soil erosion and flash floods are caused more by disruption of the soil, which can be controlled to some extent, than by cutting itself. On the other hand, when it is desirable to increase the yield of water from a forest area, significant but temporary advantages may be secured from the reduction of interception of precipitation resulting from clearcutting (Colman, 1953; Goodell, 1959).

Clearcutting is aesthetically the least desirable of the four high-forest methods, chiefly because of the monotonous regularity of arrangement of age classes and the devastated appearance of recently cutover areas.

The disadvantages of clearcutting have frequently been exaggerated, largely because the silvicultural method has been so commonly confused with the old-style clearing of the forest without any consideration for reproduction.

One criticism frequently leveled at the clearcutting method is that it leads to the development of a young stand from which no merchantable material may be extracted for a long period of time. The same is held to be true of the seed-tree and shelterwood methods which also lead to the development of even-aged stands. Although this objection is valid for each individual stand, it does not necessarily apply to a forest composed of even-aged stands. Under proper management, a forest operated under any system designed to maintain even-aged stands has essentially the same number of trees in each class of age or diameter as it would if it consisted of a single all-aged stand. The only difference is that each age class is segregated into one or more stands in which intermediate and regeneration cuttings may be executed at appropriate times.

Application of the Clearcutting Method

This method, as one of natural reproduction, is best adapted for use with species that can reproduce in nature after fire or other drastic disturbance. These species are almost invariably light seeded and wind disseminated; they usually represent early or intermediate stages in succession and tend to occur in pure stands. These characteristics apply to a wide variety of species; loblolly pine, the coast form of Douglas-fir, jack pine, lodgepole pine, and paper birch are examples of important species which unquestionably fit in this category.

The kind of natural disturbance most nearly duplicated by clearcutting is extensive windfall followed by fire, a sequence of events which may well have terminated the existence of many old-growth forests in the past. Actually the more common natural cataclysm that the forester attempts to simulate by clearcutting is fire alone.

There are several important differences between the effects of clearcutting and those of fire in standing timber. As shown in Fig. 11-5, fires in otherwise undisturbed stands often do not destroy the entire supply of seed on the area affected. Scattered trees or patches of them may remain alive temporarily or indefinitely; seeds on the trees, particularly those in serotinous cones, may be showered over the area immediately after the fire. With clearcutting the seed source does not remain on the area affected. Like all forms of cutting, clearcutting removes much of whatever meager protection might be provided by standing dead trees. Finally, special measures of site preparation are necessary to duplicate the effect of fire in exposing the mineral soil.

Fig. 11-5. Excellent natural regeneration of Douglas-fir 11 years after the Yacolt Burn of 1902 on the Gifford Pinchot National Forest in southwestern Washington. The seed came from scattered living trees like those in the background. A second fire at this stage would kill the reproduction and the old residual trees, allowing the area to revert to brush. (*Photograph by U. S. Forest Service.*)

The clearcutting method may also be used for any species, regardless of successional position, which is capable of effective dissemination and survival under the conditions created. The fact that a species is tolerant of shade does not necessarily mean that it is intolerant of exposure, although this is frequently true. When species representative of later stages in succession enter into the restocking of a clearcut area, they are most apt to come from advance reproduction present before cutting. Although it is desirable to regard restocking from advance growth as characteristic of the shelterwood method, areas that have been cut clear often become restocked by combinations of advance growth and new seedlings. Such cuttings are shelterwood cuttings to the extent that reproduction comes from advance growth and clearcuttings to the extent that reproduction comes from seed germinating after cuttings. There is little purpose in trying to split hairs, but it is important to distinguish between the two sources of regeneration.

Stands of old-growth timber commonly contain much advance growth in the openings that inevitably develop in the course of time. The trees are of great size and, if sound, are usually always merchantable; few if any are worthy of retention for further growth, and most defective trees should not be allowed to remain standing. The cumbersome equipment required to harvest such timber is better adapted to clearcutting than to any other method.

All these factors in combination tend to make the clearcutting method well suited to the regeneration of old-growth stands, provided that the ecological requirements of the desirable species are not violated. This general method of dealing with old growth has been used successfully in a wide variety of forest types located on good soils in regions of favorable climate; in many of these types, however, more reliance is placed on advance growth than on new regeneration.

The most outstanding application of the clearcutting method in North America is in the old-growth Douglas-fir forests of the Pacific Northwest. Other reproduction methods are usually not adaptable to the difficult problems of harvesting the large timber in these stands and replacing them with vigorous young stands. Under entirely natural conditions the Douglas-fir stands of this coastal region were regenerated after lightning fires (Fig. 11-5). The seed supply came from large scattered trees which survived the fires, a condition that approximated the result of seed-tree cuttings. In the absence of fire, the even-aged stands of Douglas-fir tended, after a century or more, to disintegrate slowly and to be replaced by more tolerant western hemlock, western red-cedar, and true fir (Munger, 1940); Douglas-fir does not replace itself under these conditions because it does not regenerate under heavy shade. Most of the old-growth stands are several centuries in age and consist of varying numbers of large, fine Douglas-firs, which are remnants of the original stand, and a heavy understory of the more tolerant species. With the exception of the red-cedar, which tends to become stag-headed on release, many of the understory trees, the hemlocks and true firs, have by this time become quite old and far more defective than the ancient Douglas-fir. In other words, most of these stands contain little timber worthy of retention even where tractor logging could be used to conduct partial cuttings.

Advantage is taken of the great height of the timber, which may exceed 200 feet, in obtaining reproduction after clearcutting. Isaac (1943) found that seed dispersal from uncut timber is satisfactory, although not necessarily prompt or abundant, up to a quarter-mile in any direction. The various high-lead and sky-line skidding devices commonly used for logging the old-growth timber cannot be operated effectively unless substantial areas are cut clear from single settings. From the standpoint of efficiency in logging, the clearcut patches must be at least 15 acres in size and preferably much larger. Where real attempts are being made to obtain adequate natural regeneration, the sizes normally range from 40 to 160 acres; early restocking of larger clearcuttings almost invariably depends on artificial regeneration (Cornelius, et al., 1959).

Where the high-lead system of skidding is used, most of the defective or otherwise unmerchantable trees are knocked down, thus completing the clearcutting. The large volume of slash created may constitute an intolerable fire hazard, and the law usually requires some form of slash disposal. This is often accomplished by broadcast burning, although permission may sometimes be obtained for various kinds of partial disposal. Broadcast burning eliminates advance regeneration of more tolerant species and also reduces the thickness of the forest floor. This treatment is not entirely beneficial, however, particularly on southerly slopes, because excessive exposure may cause erosion and may create conditions too extreme for adequate regeneration. Isaac (1938) found that satisfactory survival of Douglas-fir seedlings is obtained mainly in places shielded from the sun by non-living materials. It is, therefore, not desirable to reduce the amount of debris too drastically. For this reason it appears best to carry out broadcast burning when the weather does not favor hot fires. This is especially desirable if a good crop of seeds has just been shed by the trees being harvested.

Actually the correlation between the sizes of clearcut patches and success of natural regeneration is rather low (Lavender, Bergman, and Calvin, 1956), because it affects only the dispersal of seed. Equally important are such variables as seed production, competing vegetation, rainfall distribution, and the effects which slash disposal, slope, and aspect have on the microclimate. After excellent seed years, satisfactory restocking may occur on cutover areas that seem most unpromising; during the long intervals between good seed crops, no combination of treatments gives really satisfactory natural regeneration. Treatments that have given good results in western Washington are likely to prove far too heavy-handed in southwestern Oregon where the rainless summers are longer. Actually there is an increasing tendency to reduce the degree of uncertainty by direct seeding or planting, sometimes as standard procedure and sometimes if efforts to get natural regeneration fail.

Standing timber reserved for seed should remain until the cutover areas have restocked. The natural stands that followed large fires were usually nearly pure Douglas-fir, probably because this was the species slowest to succumb and thus most likely to bear seed after fire. However, if the stands left for seed after clearcutting are ones in which associated species have increased, the new stands are likely to contain more of the associates in mixture with the Douglas-fir. In view of the risk of losing sizable patches of Douglas-fir to root rot caused by *Poria weirii* and because of other considerations, this development is not undesirable.

Removal of the whole stand may be accomplished in two or more operations. If some of the uncut timber can be left for long periods, the individual clearcut areas may be regarded as separate stands. In any event, the arrangement of cutting areas should be carefully planned and integrated with the transportation network (Ruth and Silen, 1950; Silen, 1955).

As far as the patterns of clearcutting are concerned, the only one that ever gained even brief acceptance as a regional stereotype is the well-known arrangement in so-called staggered settings. This sometimes represents rather systematic application of the alternate or progressive system of clearcutting in strips. While these schemes were frequently found to be the most logical, it soon became apparent that there was no arrangement that was optimum for the entire region any more than there was an optimum size for the cutting areas.

The variations currently applied represent attempts to solve particular problems or combinations of them. One line of attack has been to substitute artificial for natural regeneration in order to restrict the costs of logging. This has been most common where the cost of rapid extension of roads to small, widely scattered clearcut patches is regarded as an excessive capital investment better spread over a longer period. In other instances, emphasis has shifted to the important economies involved in prompt salvage of rapidly deteriorating portions of stands. When this becomes a dominant objective, the condition of various stands or parts of stands governs the arrangement of clearcuttings more than any preconceived pattern, and investments in roads are made at a deliberately accelerated rate.

One of the most serious problems involved is the damage caused by winds, usually southwesterly, to timber left standing adjacent to the clearcut areas (Gratkowski, 1956). The corners of the clearcuttings are most vulnerable because the speed of the wind is accelerated as it is funneled into such constrictions. The problem is most serious with small staggered settings because of the high ratio of perimeter to area of clearcutting. The losses are reduced somewhat by placing the edges of clearcut areas where the timber is exceptionally wind-firm, as along minor ridges. Salvage of windthrown timber can be expedited by locating roads along the contour at the top and bottom edges of cutting areas so that the corners are readily accessible. A more drastic modification of policy is to shift to progressive-strip cutting on a large scale, with the clearcutting of whole drainages advancing approximately from northeast to southwest to the extent that terrain allows (Ruth and Yoder, 1953). It is significant that the very sharp and steep ridges common in this region induce complicated aerodynamic effects that cause the worst wind damage to occur on lee slopes. In regions of gentler topography and more rounded ridges such damage is most likely to occur on the windward exposures where simple logic would lead one to expect to find it.

Some of the variations lead outside the clearcutting method. State laws in Washington and Oregon requiring the reservation of 5 per cent of the standing volume for a source of seed have sometimes led to the reservation of scattered culls as seed trees. While this is often a subminimal measure for obtaining natural regeneration, 5 per cent of the volume reserved in this manner is, because of its more even distribution, more effective than the same small amount left in concentrated blocks or strips (Bever, 1954). Shelterwood cutting, because of the protection it affords against heat injury, is sometimes successful on hot, south-facing slopes in southwestern Oregon where even planting after clearcutting often fails.

It is likely that the methods of regeneration cutting employed in the coast Douglas-fir region will ultimately come to cover almost the entire range of possibilities. Clearcutting has been dictated largely by the exigencies of harvesting very large timber on steep terrain. It is really remarkable that such large-scale clearcutting and broadcast burning has been at all consistent with natural regeneration. As attention shifts to the regeneration of smaller timber grown on much shorter rotations, both logging and silvicultural practice will become more flexible. However, many of the slopes are so steep and difficult of access that clearcutting will probably remain common.

The same kind of clearcutting of large areas has given good results in the natural regeneration of old-growth coastal forests of western hemlock and Sitka spruce from Oregon to southeastern Alaska (Fig. 11-6; Andersen, 1956). Seed dispersal is effective to distances of a quarter-mile or more and, since slash disposal is rarely necessary

Fig. 11-6. Natural regeneration of western hemlock and Sitka spruce resulting from clearcutting of old growth, Tongass National Forest, Alaska. The new crop is derived partly from wind-dispersed seed and partly from advance reproduction. (*Photograph by U. S. Forest Service.*)

because of the moist climate, there is often ample advance regeneration to supplement that established after cutting (James and Gregory, 1959). The greatest difficulties actually come from invasion of shrubs and red alder, the only truly arborescent American alder.

Successful natural regeneration of loblolly and some other southern pines depends more upon control of hardwoods and exposure of mineral soil than on the arrangement of the seed source. Clearcutting in alternate or progressive strips can, for example, be used with loblolly pine (Pomeroy and Korstian, 1949). The cut strips may be 150 to 200 feet wide if bordered on the windward side by seed-bearing timber. One abundant seed crop is sufficient to establish at least a thousand seedlings per acre. A high proportion of the seeds carried beyond 300 feet are light and infertile. Few seeds are dispersed more than 100 feet against the normal direction of warm, dry winds.

On the basis of experience with favorable conditions on the South

Carolina coastal plain, Lotti (1961) concluded that systematic programs of thinning and prescribed burning would enable natural regeneration of loblolly pine by clearcutting throughout almost all months of practically any year. The development of good seedbearers by thinning provides ample crops of seed almost annually, assuming that litter and understory hardwoods are sufficiently reduced by prescribed burning. For harvests between April 1, the time of germination, and about August 1, when the seedlings harden, he recommended the reservation of seed trees to allow for losses from logging damage to succulent seedlings. During the remainder of the year either the newly fallen seeds or the hardened first-year seedlings are regarded as a source of regeneration sufficient to allow clearcutting.

The species of pines that have serotinous cones are the one important group that are generally more satisfactorily reproduced by clearcutting than by any other method. If the cones are truly serotinous the seed crops of many years are stored in the crowns of the trees and there is no necessity of reserving standing trees. The main problems are to get the cones to open and to expose enough mineral soil. In fact, if all the cones on standing trees remain tightly closed, the act of reserving any timber strictly for a seed source may be futile. Since it is rarely possible to duplicate the severe crown fires that bring these stands into being in nature, the effects of the fires must be simulated by other means.

Reasonably successful techniques for this purpose have been developed for jack pine in the Lake Region (Eyre and LeBarron, 1944) and sand pine in Florida (Cooper, Schopmeyer, and McGregor, 1959). The lodgepole pine of the Rocky Mountains is quite variable in the extent to which it exhibits the closed-cone habit (Crossley, 1956; Tackle, 1959) and must be handled accordingly.

The first prerequisite is exposure of mineral soil which is a far better seedbed than undisturbed litter. Since means of using prescribed burning for this purpose have not been successfully perfected, it is usually done by some sort of mechanical scarification. If most of the cones are tightly closed, it is then necessary that cones or cone-bearing slash be scattered fairly uniformly over the area in such manner that a sufficient number of cones lie exposed to the sun and within a foot of the ground. Within this zone of sluggish air movement it is possible for temperatures to increase to about 120°F, which is the melting point of the resin that seals the cone scales. The necessity of such high surface temperatures poses a dilemma because they cause heat injury to the seedlings. Consequently it is necessary that some of the seeds fall into small spots shaded by debris.

It would be ideal if the scarification could be accomplished before clearcutting, but it is usually more expeditious to do it afterwards or by appropriate modifications of skidding procedures. The most common procedure is to disk the areas after cutting and then lop and scatter the slash; if these steps are reversed the cones are likely to be buried unopened (Cayford, 1958). However, successful results can occasionally be obtained if the slash is bunched with bulldozers equipped with toothed blades if enough cones are broken off and deposited on scarified soil during the process. If slash burning is necessary it must be limited to part of the slash that has been bunched into concentrated areas; broadcast burning or complete slash disposal destroys too much seed.

These species display some regional variation in the degree to which the closed-cone habit is manifest. In localities or stands in which the cones do not remain closed at all, the practices just described are neither necessary nor even desirable. If the cones do not remain closed at all, it is necessary to employ some sort of partial cutting or to clearcut in narrow strips with dependence on seeding from the side. Such variations are especially common in the management of lodgepole pine; Lexen (1949), for example, found that clearcut strips less than 180 feet wide were most appropriate. If some of the cones open and some do not, there is ample opportunity to compromise between the two approaches. Variations in cutting practice, degree of scarification, and slash treatment can be employed to reduce the risk of getting excessively dense natural regeneration that is likely to stagnate. However, if all the cones are truly serotinous, definite efforts must be made to open them and the difficulties are compensated only by the fact that the size, shape, and arrangement of clearcut areas can be governed entirely by considerations other than seed dispersal.

An important incidental advantage of clearcutting in the management of lodgepole pine is that it provides one of the surest means of eradicating infestations of the common parasitic seed plant, dwarf-mistletoe. Since the seeds of the pathogen must come from living trees, it is necessary only to prevent slow reinfestation from adjoining stands adjacent to the clearcut areas (Hawksworth, 1958). With partial cutting, the mistletoe is very likely to spread from the old stand to the new unless great care is taken to cut all the infected trees of the previous crop.

The seeds of serotinous conifers rarely exhibit dormancy so there is little natural control over the season of germination. Therefore, it is necessary to time the release of seed so that the seedlings will germinate at the proper season. With jack and lodgepole pine, the seeds must germinate before summer so that the seedlings will harden before the first frost. With sand pine in Florida, however, it is best to schedule scarification and slash treatment such that seedlings commence development during late fall or early winter when rainfall is adequate to prevent drought and the risk of heat injury is lowest. It is indeed remarkable how much careful effort is necessary to obtain natural regeneration of these species which are adapted to reproduce themselves so easily and abundantly after catastrophic fires.

The use of true clearcutting for the regeneration of shade-tolerant species is best illustrated by its application in the Engelmann spruce types of the Rocky Mountains (LeBarron and Jemison, 1953; Horton, 1959). Success depends mostly on the degree of scarification accomplished in site preparation. One of the basic objectives is to increase the proportion of spruce relative to that of alpine fir which usually predominates in the advance reproduction. Although the techniques have yet to be perfected, this kind of heavy cutting coupled with site preparation appears to be one of the few ways of encouraging spruces over true firs in the regeneration of the intimate mixtures in which the two genera often grow.

Among the eastern hardwoods there are a few species that regenerate well in the full light provided by clearcutting. One of them, paper birch, requires absolutely bare mineral soil and full light (Nash, Duda, and Gray, 1951); the primary requirement is complete clearcutting followed by scarification or burning. However, precise means of accomplishing this without unduly encouraging regeneration of the undesirable gray birch or aspen remain obscure.

REFERENCES

Andersen, H. E. 1956. Clearcutting as a silvicultural system in converting old forests to new in southeast Alaska. *Proc. Soc. Am. Foresters Meeting,* 1955: 59–61.

Bever, D. N. 1954. Evaluation of factors affecting natural reproduction of forest trees in central western Oregon. *Oreg. State Board of Forestry, Research Bul.* 3.

Brender, E. V. 1961. Residual saplings in clearcut and planted stands. *Ga. Forest Research Paper* 4.

Cayford, J. H. 1958. Scarifying for jack pine regeneration in Manitoba. *Canada, Forestry Branch, Forest Research Div. Tech. Note* 66.

Chaiken, L. E., et al. 1960. Possible consequences of southern pine monocultures. *Proc., Fourth Conf. on Southern Industrial Forest Management, Duke Univ. School of Forestry.* Pp. 11–42.

Colman, E. A. 1953. *Vegetation and watershed management.* Ronald Press, New York.

Cooper, R. W., C. S. Schopmeyer, and W. H. D. McGregor. 1959. Sand pine regeneration on the Ocala National Forest. *USDA Production Research Rept.* 30.

Cornelius, R., et al. 1959. Economic logging layout. *Pacific Logging Congress, Loggers Handbook* 19 (II):22–34.

Crossley, D. I. 1956. Effect of crown cover and slash density on the release of seed from slash-borne lodgepole pine cones. *Canada, Forestry Branch, Forest Research Div. Tech. Note* 41.

Davis, K. P., and K. A. Klehm. 1939. Controlled burning in the western white pine type. *J. Forestry* 37:399–407.

Eyre, F. H., and R. K. LeBarron. 1944. Management of jack pine stands in the Lake States. *USDA Tech. Bul.* 863.

Goodell, B. C. 1959. Watershed studies at Fraser, Colorado. *Proc. Soc. Am. Foresters Meeting,* 1958:42–45.

Gratkowski, H. J. 1956. Windthrow around staggered settings in old-growth Douglas-fir. *Forest Sci.* 2:60–74.

Hawksworth, F. G. 1958. Rate of spread and intensification of dwarfmistletoe in young lodgepole pine stands. *J. Forestry* 56:404–407.

Horton, K. W. 1959. Characteristics of subalpine spruce in Alberta. *Canada, Forestry Branch, Forest Research Div. Tech. Note* 76.

Isaac, L. A. 1938. Factors affecting establishment of Douglas fir seedlings. *USDA Circ.* 486.

———. 1943. *Reproductive habits of Douglas-fir.* Charles L. Pack Forestry Foundation, Washington.

James, G. A., and R. A. Gregory. 1959. Natural stocking of a mile-square clear cutting in southeast Alaska. *Alaska Forest Research Center, Sta. Paper* 12.

Lavender, D. P., M. H. Bergman, and L. D. Calvin. 1956. Natural regeneration on staggered settings. *Oreg. State Board of Forestry, Research Bul.* 10.

LeBarron, R. K., and G. M. Jemison. 1953. Ecology and silviculture of the Engelmann spruce-alpine fir type. *J. Forestry* 51:349–355.

Lexen, B. 1949. Alternate clear-strip cutting in the lodgepole pine type. *RMFRES Sta. Paper* 1.

Little, S., Jr. 1950. Ecology and silviculture of whitecedar and associated hardwoods in southern New Jersey. *Yale Univ. School of Forestry Bul.* 56.

Lotti, T. 1961. The case for natural regeneration. *In* A. B. Crow (Ed.), *Advances in southern pine management.* Louisiana State University Press, Baton Rouge. Pp. 16–25.

Lutz, H. J., and R. F. Chandler, Jr. 1946. *Forest soils.* Wiley, New York. Pp. 478–479.

Munger, T. T. 1940. The cycle from Douglas fir to hemlock. *Ecology* 21:451–459.

Nash, R. W., E. J. Duda, and N. H. Gray. 1951. Studies on extensive dying, regeneration, and management of birch. *Maine Forest Service Bul.* 15.

Plochmann, R. 1960. The struggle for mixed forests. *Am. Forests* 66(8):12–15, 55–56, 58, 60.

Pomeroy, K. B., and C. F. Korstian. 1949. Further results on loblolly pine seed production and dispersal. *J. Forestry* 47:968–970.

Rudolf, P. O. 1950. Forest plantations in the Lake States. *USDA Tech. Bul.* 1010.

Ruth, R. H., and R. R. Silen. 1950. Suggestions for getting more forestry in the logging plan. *PNWFRES Research Note* 72.

Ruth, R. H., and R. A. Yoder. 1953. Reducing wind damage in the forests of the Oregon Coast Range. *PNWFRES Research Paper* 7.

Shirley, H. L. 1941. Restoring conifers to aspen lands in the Lake States. *USDA Tech. Bul.* 763.

Silen, R. R. 1955. More efficient road patterns for a Douglas-fir drainage. *Timberman* 56(6):82, 85–86, 88.

Tackle, D. 1959. Silvics of lodgepole pine. *IMFRES Misc. Publ.* 19.

Trousdell, K. B. 1959. Site treatment reduces need for planting at loblolly harvest time. *SEFES Sta. Paper* 102.

Wellner, C. A. 1946. Recent trends in silvicultural practice on national forests in the western white pine type. *J. Forestry* 44:942–944.

CHAPTER 12

The seed-tree method

In this method the area is cut clear except for certain trees, called **seed trees,** left standing singly or in groups for the purpose of furnishing seed to restock the cleared area naturally. Only a small proportion of the original stand is left. After a new crop is established these seed trees may be removed in a second cutting or left indefinitely.

In some classifications the seed-tree method has been included under either the clearcutting or the shelterwood method. The retention of some trees on the cutover area, together with the fact that the seed supply is furnished by them rather than by adjacent trees or those cut down, warrants the distinction from clearcutting. The few, scattered trees left in seed-tree cuttings do not protect the site to any significant extent nor is their potential increase in value an important consideration. The method, therefore, lacks some of the most distinctive characteristics of shelterwood cutting.

Form of Forest Produced

As is the case with clearcutting, the seed-tree method is most readily applicable to even-aged stands in which all the trees are of merchantable size. Of course, the stands to be replaced can also be uneven-aged and any trees that are unmerchantable can be destroyed if necessary. However, this method of natural regeneration differs from most kinds of clearcutting in that there are no restrictions on the size and arrangement of cutting areas because adjacent stands are not depended upon as sources of seed. The stands of a forest managed under the seed-tree system may be as large as desirable from the standpoint of management.

Use of this method results in the production of even-aged stands, except insofar as remaining seed trees constitute an upper story above the new crop. Under exceptional circumstances seed trees may remain throughout the rotation.

Details of the Method

In the simplest form of this method the seed trees are left isolated and fairly uniformly distributed after most of the stand has been removed, as shown in Fig. 12-1. If conditions are satisfactory, natural reproduction springs up under and around the seed trees in sufficient quantity to form a new stand.

Characteristics of seed trees. The seed trees must be chosen with care, since they are the source of a seed supply which is apt to be limited. Windfirmness is a primary consideration. The isolated position of the trees and the suddenness with which the protection of the rest of the stand is removed make them particularly susceptible to windthrow.

The most windfirm trees are those which have grown with relatively little competition on deep soils and have stocky, tapering boles with correspondingly well-developed root systems. Such trees also have wide, deep crowns and relatively large live crown ratios. Trees with short, narrow crowns are, in spite of the smaller area on which wind may act, very susceptible to breakage and uprooting because they have weak roots and slender boles without much taper. The height of the seed tree is also of importance because the force of the wind increases rapidly with distance above ground; short trees are less susceptible to damage than tall trees with the same proportional development of crown. Trees that have wide, horizontal openings between branches are more likely to stand against wind than those with compact crowns (Curtis, 1943). The seed-tree method should not be used with characteristically shallow-rooted species, like the spruces, or with species that have wood of low strength, like eastern white pine. It is not applicable to any species growing on moist or thin soils where the rooting stratum is shallow.

The seed trees must be old enough to produce abundant fertile seed; the age at which seed bearing begins in closed stands is the safest criterion. Early and abundant production of seed may be encouraged by proper thinning or even by fertilization of the soil around the chosen trees. Rather young loblolly pines have, for example, been stimulated to develop into effective seed producers by special thinnings in which all stems within 20 feet were cut at least 3 years before the seeds are needed (Wenger and Trousdell, 1957). Seed trees should also be selected from among the dominants and better co-

Fig. 12-1. Two winter views of the same spot in a 95-year-old stand of lob-lolly pine at the Bigwoods Experimental Forest, North Carolina, immediately before and after a cutting in which eight seed trees were reserved on each acre. The larger hardwoods were killed with herbicides and prescribed burning was done in the late summer to kill small hardwoods, dispose of slash, and prepare the seedbed. (*Photograph by U. S. Forest Service.*)

dominants. Such trees are stronger and usually produce more and better seed than trees of the lower crown classes. In forest trees, good vegetative development is best viewed not as a deterrent but as a prerequisite for dependable seed production. The seed-producing ability of good trees is often substantially and quickly enhanced by their release in seed-tree cuttings (Allen and Trousdell, 1961). In fact, a few good seed trees sometimes produce as much seed per acre as the entire stand before cutting.

It has been demonstrated that, among loblolly pines of otherwise satisfactory vegetative vigor, the most fruitful trees are those that have been the best cone producers in the past (Pomeroy, 1949). The best seed trees usually have at least fifty old or fifty ripe cones in each crown, unless there have been several poor seed years, in which case the best are those with at least a few ripe cones.

The kind of trees used for seed trees depends to some extent on the intensity of silviculture practiced. If a second cutting can be made within a few years to utilize the seed trees, there is little reason not to pick fine, healthy dominants, presumably containing valuable timber. When the seed trees must be abandoned after they have served their purpose, individuals of lower commercial value may have to be chosen. In stands that are distinctly even-aged, the reservation of the smaller trees is likely to be a futile gesture. However, in uneven-aged stands, it may be possible to find relatively small trees that are sufficiently sturdy and vigorous to serve as seed trees.

The seed-tree method theoretically provides an opportunity for more rigorous selection of the parents of the new crop than is attainable with any other method of natural regeneration. As long as the patterns of inheritance of the characteristics of tree species remain obscure, it is most rational to assume that undesirable characteristics are heritable and to attempt to confine choices to the best phenotypes.

If there is some compelling reason why the most valuable trees cannot be reserved for seed, it is wise to grasp every opportunity to evade the problem. In general, the most important way that this can be done is to select trees which have developed imperfectly because of strong and obvious environmental influences that are likely to have operated at random. Trees that have developed poor form because of lack of competition would be logical choices in such circumstances. Trees that have become poor because of apparent susceptibility to damaging agencies that operate in immature stands should be rejected. On the other hand, there is probably no reason to avoid trees damaged by any heart rots that characteristically infect trees only when they are older than the normal rotation age.

Under any circumstances, the problem of making selections is complicated by the fact that the hereditary characteristics that make a tree high in quality, vigor, and resistance to injury are not necessarily combined with those that govern seed production. All too commonly the best seed producers are trees of high vigor and low quality. If the phenotypic selections involved cannot be rigorous, it is probably advantageous to reserve a relatively large number of seed trees and thus increase the size of the gene pool represented in the progeny.

Number and distribution of seed trees. After the kind of seed trees has been determined the number per acre must be fixed. The principal factors are: (1) the amount of viable seed produced per tree, (2) the probable proportion of seed trees which will survive, (3) the percentage of the seed which will finally produce established seedlings, and (4) the distance to which seed can be dispersed in sufficient quantity to ensure full stocking. The very nature of the method requires that it be applied only to species that are wind disseminated.

As a general rule, in species with relatively light seeds, satisfactory dissemination can be counted upon for distances from the tree at least equal to and sometimes two to five times its height. The amount of viable seed produced per tree usually is the limiting factor in determining the number of trees to leave rather than the maximum distance of dissemination. With large individuals of a decidedly light-seeded species, two trees per acre may be enough. The same species in small-sized second-growth timber may require ten seed trees per acre. A relatively large number may likewise be necessary to ensure uniform distribution if the distance of dissemination is short, regardless of how prolifically seeds are produced. The number of seed trees required is relatively high where conditions are somewhat unfavorable for germination and establishment of seedlings.

The number and distribution of seed trees influence the pollination of female flowers and stroboli and, therefore, the number of viable seeds produced. A few species, like white ash and cottonwood, are actually dioecious; both male and female trees of these species must be left regardless of the method of regeneration employed. Furthermore, the male and female flowers of the same tree rarely become mature simultaneously. The possibility of self-fertilization is also reduced by the tendency for female flowers to develop at the top of the tree, above the male flowers; the wind is not often turbulent enough to cause much pollen to rise straight upward. Self-fertilization usually results in the production of a high proportion of inviable seeds. The concentration of pollen grains also decreases rapidly with distance from the source because of atmospheric turbulence (Wright,

1953); therefore, the proportion of fertile seeds probably decreases as seed trees become more widely separated.

It may, therefore, be assumed that isolated seed trees produce a lower percentage of *viable* seeds than they would if adjacent to other trees of the same species. Furthermore, since *total* seed production is usually increased by releasing trees from competition, it is clear that the fruitfulness of trees in closed stands is not a good criterion of the kind and number of isolated seed trees required to restock a cut-over area.

The proper number of seed trees to leave per acre cannot be settled without knowledge of seed production and the early development of reproduction for the species and locality in question. First, an arbitrary standard must be set indicating the minimum number of safely established seedlings that constitute a satisfactorily stocked stand. For example, this minimum might be placed at a thousand trees per acre at the fourth year. The next step is to determine, after allowing for losses of seed before germination and of seedlings thereafter, the amount of seed per acre needed to secure established reproduction of the prescribed density. When the total requirement of seed is known the number of trees required per acre may be calculated, provided that the seed production of the trees can be predicted.

Seed production ranges from nothing in years of failure to large crops at more or less regular intervals. If there is any tendency toward *regular* periodicity of good seed crops it is so obscured by disrupting influences that it has so far failed to provide a basis for reliable predictions. Garman (1955), however, found evidence that good seed production of Douglas-fir in British Columbia was correlated with low seed production in the previous year and low precipitation during the spring. He postulated that high precipitation during the spring might damage the flowers and hamper pollination, although this explanation remains in doubt because Silen and Krueger (1962) found that rainy weather did not interfere with pollination in Washington and Oregon.

Wenger (1957), on the other hand, found that the amount of seed produced by loblolly pine in Virginia bore a direct and positive relationship to the amount of precipitation during the three spring months, somewhat more than 2 calendar years in advance of seed fall, when the cone buds are formed. However, this relationship was modified by a measurable tendency for seed production to be depressed by an amount proportional to the size of the seed crop 2 years earlier.

Wenger's observations suggest that cone production is enhanced by favorable growing conditions at the time the cone buds are initiated. Both his observations and those of Garman indicate that the presence of a good crop of maturing cones inhibits the development of the cone buds that would yield seed 1 year later in Douglas-fir and 2 years later in loblolly pine. The difference in timing is merely the result of the fact that the cones of virtually all of the pines take 2 years to mature. The inhibitory effect may result from depletion of some unknown essential factor the supply of which must be replenished before a large crop of cones can again be produced. There is also evidence to suggest that the supply of cones and fruit exists in balance with the population of insects that feed upon them. The failure of a single seed crop may reduce the population of seed insects enough to allow the maturation of a better seed crop in some subsequent year.

With the possible exception of loblolly pine, it is still rarely feasible to predict the size of seed crops more than a few months in advance. A seed crop usually must be very close to maturity before its magnitude can safely be used as a basis for regulating the number of seed trees. If a satisfactory seed crop were then in prospect, the seed from the entire stand would soon be available and the number of trees reserved might not be particularly relevant.

In practice, it is probably best to reserve enough trees to restock the area in a single, moderately good seed year. Excellent crops are too infrequent to be depended upon, and meager crops are usually consumed by rodents or birds. It is unwise to reduce the number of seed trees to the point where the product of several good seed years will be necessary.

Even among trees known to be seed bearers the actual production of seed varies with size, crown class, and vigor. Within trees of the dominant and codominant crown classes, seed production is most readily correlated with D.B.H., probably because measurements of this parameter are less subject to error than those of crown size (Wenger and Trousdell, 1957). Once trees have reached seed-bearing age it is rare that any decline of seed production with advancing age is of much significance, provided that the trees remain healthy.

If it is not going to be feasible to salvage the seed trees after they have served their purpose, it becomes logical to attempt to reserve the smallest merchantable volume that will provide the requisite amount of seed per acre. The best way to do this is to determine which diameter classes of trees of the upper crown classes produce the largest amount of seed per unit of merchantable volume of product value and then leave such trees in the required numbers. This approach is really a rather desperate measure that should be reserved for cases of real rather than imaginary necessity.

The usual number of seed trees varies from two to ten per acre. If more than ten are left the residual trees cover a considerable part of the area and begin to resemble a shelterwood. Few if any species are capable of restocking an area thoroughly if less than one seed tree per acre is retained.

An attempt should be made to secure a uniform distribution of seed trees over all parts of the cutover area. However, it is more important to select the proper individuals than to attain an absolutely even spacing. Where the topography is uneven it will generally be best to leave a majority of the trees on the higher ground in order that the distance of dissemination may be as great as possible. If the soil is not too thin, such trees have frequently developed a fair degree of windfirmness from long exposure.

Cultural operations. Just as in the clearcutting method, provision for an adequate seed supply is not sufficient; favorable conditions for the establishment of a new crop must be created and maintained until success is assured. It is generally mandatory that some sort of site preparation be carried out to ensure that the ratio of established seedlings to seeds is as high as possible. As in the case of clearcutting, failure to apply the seed-tree method successfully may often be traced to neglect of this requirement. In most instances satisfactory regeneration can be expected only during the period that the effects of site preparation endure.

Observations of natural regeneration from loblolly pine seed trees in Virginia (Wenger and Trousdell, 1957) provide an excellent example of the importance of site preparation in the application of this method (Fig. 12-1). An average of only 9 sound seeds was required to establish one seedling on mineral soil exposed by logging or disking; 15 seeds were necessary on a burned surface; where litter or slash were undisturbed, over 40 seeds. The number required varied considerably with moisture conditions such that as many as 30 seeds were sometimes necessary to yield one first-year seedling on prepared seedbeds; such an upper limit could not be determined for the untreated seedbeds because there were instances of complete failure.

Removal of seed trees. When enough seedlings have become established to make a full stand, the purpose for which the seed trees were left is accomplished. If it will pay financially, they may then be removed, leaving the new crop to develop unhampered. A certain amount of damage to the reproduction is inevitable during this operation. If the new crop is adequate for a fully stocked stand, this damage is not serious; in fact, excessively dense clumps of reproduction may be crudely thinned by felling or skidding the boles of the trees across them. The seed trees should ordinarily be removed as soon as possible because seedlings become less limber and more susceptible to breakage as they grow larger.

If a second cutting is not feasible, the seed trees are allowed to grow. Some may live to be cut when the new crop is harvested and furnish material of exceptional size and quality. Many will succumb to the ravages of insects, fungi, lightning, and wind. Trees grown in closed stands and then suddenly isolated suffer through changed site conditions and are apt to be weakened, suffer sunscald, or become stag-headed.

If satisfactory regeneration does not develop after the occurrence of one, or at most two, good seed crops, two courses of action are open. Measures of site preparation may be repeated or intensified. More commonly it will be necessary to fill the unstocked spaces by planting.

Modifications of the Method

Group seed-tree method. One of the common variations is to leave the seed trees in groups, strips, or rows instead of scattered singly over the area. The concentration of seed trees on restricted areas makes it somewhat easier to protect them during the initial cutting and also to salvage them when they have served their purpose. It is possible that pollination is also improved, although this hypothesis has never been tested. However, the distribution of seed over the area to be restocked cannot be as uniform as under the scattered seed-tree method unless a larger proportion of the stand is reserved. If the volume reserved is the same, the distances between groups or strips will be longer on the average than those between single seed trees and may be so great as to prevent dissemination of seed over the entire area. When seed trees are left in strips or groups it may be difficult to obtain regeneration on the ground beneath them after they are removed; this problem can usually be avoided by making shelterwood cuttings in these concentrations of trees at the time they are reserved.

The trees that are left in such arrangements are not any more resistant to wind and other damaging agencies than comparable trees left entirely isolated. A clump must be rather sizeable before the trees lend one another any mutual protection or support. In general, the vulnerability of seed trees is best regarded as being primarily a function of their individual characteristics. On the other hand, the concentration of seed trees into groups and strips can reduce the amount of disruption of the soil around the reserved trees. Wenger and Trousdell (1957) found that this sort of damage caused a number of different kinds of mechanical and physiological injury and was probably the most readily controllable source of early mortality of seed trees of loblolly pine. In other words, it is not only important to select the trees carefully but also to avoid injury to them and the soil around them during logging.

Reserve seed-tree method. Sometimes seed trees are reserved not only to provide seed for regeneration but also with the deliberate intention of obtaining further increment from them. In this modification of the method the trees are selected both for seeding capacity and for ability to grow satisfactorily through all or part of a second rotation. The two purposes cannot be combined in overmature stands or with trees that have any tendency to deteriorate after sudden exposure. Ordinarily the vigor and potential quality of the chosen trees should be as high as possible. The reserved trees form the discontinuous upper story of a two-storied stand.

It is inevitable that retention of the seed trees will hamper or even preclude the growth of younger trees beneath them. The importance of the effect can be assessed by comparing the increase of value of the seed trees with the value of the loss of potential growth of the suppressed trees. A more crucial consideration is the risk of loss of the scattered overstory trees (Little and Mohr, 1957). Because they project above the surrounding trees they are greatly exposed to lightning. Trousdell (1955) found that in southeastern Virginia the annual losses to lightning occurred at the rate of two trees per 100 acres, regardless of how many trees were reserved. This rate is perhaps close to the national average, although somewhat greater losses would have to be anticipated in regions where thunderstorms are more frequent. It is at least high enough to suggest caution in use of the reserve seed-tree method. The best way to reduce the losses would be to salvage lightning-struck trees that are not shattered. An increase in the number reserved would reduce the percentage, but not the number, that were struck.

This general procedure is occasionally useful where it is desirable to grow pulpwood or some similar product on a rotation shorter than that required for the trees to reach seed-bearing age. This dilemma can be solved without artificial regeneration by retaining an adequate number of seed trees for a period somewhat longer than two rotations. In this way the *potential* seed bearers reserved at the end of one rotation would be available for regenerating the area at the end of the next rotation and would be cut as soon as they had served their purpose. If the basic rotation were 30 years, the trees retained when they were 30 years old would not actually serve as seed trees until they were 60 years old and would be removed at an age of about 65 years.

Reserve seed trees are infrequently left standing to provide seed if regeneration that is already established or is expected from other sources is lost to fire. There is no point in reserving such **fire seed trees** unless they are likely to survive the fires and function effectively thereafter.

Usually the costs of intensified fire control and of replanting that percentage of the cutover area likely to be burned are less than the values that might be abandoned in fire seed trees left on the entire cutover area. The general principle is merely one that should be considered before any stand not yet at seed-bearing age is irrevocably separated from a source of seed.

Advantages and Disadvantages of the Seed-Tree Method

This method is so similar to clearcutting that it has essentially the same advantages and disadvantages (see Chapter 11).

The presence of seed trees does not interfere significantly with any operations except the use of fire and certain kinds of cable-skidding equipment. One important difference is that there is a source of seed on every acre so no reliance need be placed on adjacent stands. Very large areas can, therefore, be cut over in single operations.

The other unique attributes of the method are governed by the characteristics of the seed trees. Theoretically there is no method of natural regeneration that provides opportunity for such rigorous control of the species and phenotypic characteristics of the seed source. The supply of seed is also more uniformly distributed and abundant than when adjacent stands are used as sources of seed. On the other hand, there is no method of cutting that exposes the seed source to greater risk of premature destruction.

Application of the Method

The seed-tree method may be used for most of the species that can be reproduced by the clearcutting method. There is, however, little purpose in using it for regenerating stands of closed-cone pines if standing trees are not really an effective source of seed.

The seed-tree method has a common natural counterpart in the situation, already illustrated in Fig. 11-5, in which fire, alone or preceded by blowdown, has killed all but the most resistant trees in the stand. Many valuable, light-seeded species are naturally adapted to regenerating after such catastrophes. In one way or another, the forester attempts to duplicate or improve upon this situation when regenerating the species involved. The essential requirements are that a satisfactory source of seed be reserved and that the effects of these natural fires in preparing the seedbed be simulated at least in part. The clearcutting, seed-tree, and shelterwood methods may all be modified to satisfy these requirements.

The seed-tree method is a sound technique under the right conditions but has acquired a bad reputation because too much has been expected of it. It has been applied too frequently as a half-hearted compromise between indiscriminate clearcutting and proper silvicultural practice. Various states have, for example, enacted laws requiring the reservation of specified numbers of seed trees during logging operations. Usually these laws do not require the reservation of enough trees or else they contemplate use of the seed-tree method for species not adapted to it. Silviculture by legislative prescription is a poor substitute for determination on the part of forest owners to keep their lands productive.

Many of the failures of the seed-tree method have been associated with its application under extensive practice. The causes are not inherent in the intensity of practice but are the result of problems often encountered in such practice. If the seed trees cannot be salvaged when they have served their purpose or been damaged, there is a strong tendency to reserve trees of inadequate quality and vigor in insufficient numbers. This causes delays or failures of restocking and increases the risk of invasion by undesirable vegetation. The control of such vegetation and initial preparation of the site are likely to be overlooked because of shortage of funds for the outright investments involved.

There has also been a tendency to reduce the number of seed trees below a truly effective minimum. Baker (1950) has shown that the numbers of seed trees prescribed for many species are sufficient for satisfactory restocking only after several good seed years have occurred. Some of the species involved simply do not bear enough seed to allow use of the seed-tree method, and others are not ecologically adapted to it.

The natural regeneration of longleaf pine, although difficult, is most readily accomplished by the seed-tree method, or closely related modifications of the shelterwood method. This species, which once covered millions of acres of dry, sandy soils in the South, is not easy to grow under management. It has been eliminated from vast areas by clearcutting, annual burning, and other depredations (Wahlenberg, 1946). Loblolly and slash pine have invaded many of these dry sites or been planted there.

Although longleaf pine has winged seeds, they are so large and heavy that they are not dispersed effectively beyond a distance of about 100 feet (Boyer, 1958). Most of the sites are so dry that root competition prevents seedlings from surviving more than several years within about 30 feet of older trees (Chapman and Bulchis, 1940). If the seeds were dispersed over longer distances, this root competition could be avoided by use of the method of clearcutting with seeding from the side.

Under the circumstances, several alternatives present themselves as possible courses of action. One of these is the recently perfected technique of direct seeding which could follow clearcutting. Another would be to clearcut immediately after seeds had fallen from the trees. Unfortunately this approach is usually too risky because the seedlings are likely to be lost to frost or fire during the first winter after the autumn in which they germinate; hogs may also destroy the new crop even after it has reached the sapling stage.

One common solution has been to reserve no more than four seed trees per acre and attempt to increase the effectiveness of this scanty seed source by using fire to prepare the seedbed (Chapman, 1926). Unless the seed trees can be removed almost immediately after establishment of regeneration, a larger number would be undesirable because the root competition of four seed trees is often sufficient to preclude regeneration on about one-quarter of an acre. However, it should be noted that this approach had its genesis in the days of railroad logging when seed trees became inaccessible once reserved. The difficulties with root competition and seed supply can often be avoided by leaving more seed trees, sometimes enough to constitute a shelterwood, and then removing all or part of them when reproduction has started (Smith, 1955).

The seedlings become resistant to fire during their first summer. The seedbed is prepared by burning in the winter or spring preceding seed fall; the cones take two years to mature so that seed crops can be predicted fairly reliably a year in advance. This burn allows the characteristic grassy understory one season to develop sufficiently to shield the seeds from birds. However, the needle litter, which prevents the seeds from penetrating to mineral soil (Osborne and Harper, 1937), is temporarily eliminated.

Controlled burning is also carried out occasionally during the protracted seedling stage in order to burn off needles infected with the brown-spot fungus and thus keep the disease in check. Efficiency in burning and satisfactory control of brown spot are best attained by treating large areas simultaneously. Furthermore, hogs from the open range must be excluded and the cost per acre of fencing large areas is lower than that of small tracts. It is, therefore, desirable that individual even-aged stands of longleaf pine be at least 40 acres in area. This factor is another which makes it more satisfactory to extend seed-tree cuttings over large areas than to clearcut in small areas and depend on seeding from the side.

The seed-tree method has been used very successfully in loblolly pine (Wahlenberg, 1960) and also appears to be satisfactory for slash pine (McCulley, 1950) and shortleaf pine (Liming, 1945; Dale, 1958). The seeding distances of these species are far greater than those of longleaf pine, so that there is more latitude for use of different reproduction methods and modifications of them. Investigations of seed-tree requirements of loblolly pine (Wenger and Trousdell, 1957) have provided means of adjusting the number of seed trees for variations in annual seed production, tree diameter, and seedbed conditions. They concluded, for example, that five seed trees per acre, 18 inches D.B.H., would be sufficient to restock 60 per cent of the milacres with year-old seedlings after a good seed year. After a mediocre seed year, nine trees of the same size would be required. They also stated that the number of seed trees could be reduced to two-thirds of the indicated number if prescribed burning was used for site preparation and to one-third if the seedbeds were disked. However, they specified that at least three seed trees should be left on each acre under any conditions in order to provide adequate cross-pollination.

Most of the investigations of seed production by loblolly pine, including that just discussed, have been carried out in the favorable conditions of the Atlantic Coastal Plain. Further inland, on the Piedmont Plateau, seed production is substantially poorer. Under these conditions it is more desirable to reserve sufficient seed trees to constitute a shelterwood (Brender, 1958).

All the southern pines are relatively windfirm, and seed trees chosen from the dominant and codominant classes respond well to exposure. Ordinarily they grow sufficiently well to yield a good income during the period that they are retained; the terrain is favorable to their salvage. Therefore, there is no reason to regard seed trees of southern pine as an outright investment made purely in the interest of restocking the stand. The only reasons for limiting the number of southern pine seed trees are: (1) to reduce root competition on dry sites; (2) to prevent overstocking, as may prove to be the case with slash pine; and (3) to concentrate on production of pulpwood, giving over as little area as necessary to growth of trees large enough to act as seed bearers.

Among broadleaved species, yellow-poplar is an example of a tree known to be adapted for regeneration by the seed-tree method (Carvell and Korstian, 1955; Engle, 1960). Its seeds are readily disseminated by wind, and good seed crops may be expected almost annually (McCarthy, 1933). The seedlings develop adequately only in full light on bare surfaces of the moist, well-drained soil of good sites; therefore, heavy cutting and scarification are essential. The flowers of yellow-poplar are unusual in that they are pollinated by insects; the low viability of the seed is apparently due to the high frequency of self-fertilization (Carpenter and Guard, 1950). It would appear from this that best results might be obtained from paired, adjacent seed trees, although large, isolated trees are usually effective in giving rise to some reproduction. Only a few seed trees are required; even in stands cut at 40 years of age no more than five per acre are necessary.

The application of the seed-tree method in regenerating coast Douglas-fir has been limited because of the high risk of wind damage and the difficulty of preserving scattered seed trees when logging is done with cable skidding devices. Consequently the method has been most successful on deep, dry soils where isolated trees are relatively windfirm (Taylor, 1951). Furthermore, increasing diversification of logging machinery has introduced more opportunity for departure from complete clearcutting than was formerly available. Garman (1951, 1955) found that two or three seed trees per acre, even if defective as a result of heart rot, provided a larger supply of seed and more uniformly distributed regeneration than patch clearcutting.

One of the most interesting and instructive accounts of the seed-tree method involves its application in old-growth stands of red pine on Indian lands now included in the Chippewa National Forest. Slash was piled and burned after cutting, and 5 to 10 per cent of the volume was retained in seed trees. This pioneer silvicultural effort proved moderately successful, but subsequent investigation showed that most of the red pine reproduction actually came from advance regeneration (Eyre and Zehngraff, 1948). Where advance regeneration was absent the areas were often invaded by jack pine. With red pine neither the abundance nor the distance of dispersal of seed is sufficient to justify use of the seed-tree method. Fortunately it has now become practicable to use the shelterwood method in this locality.

This case illustrates how regeneration from seed trees may be supplemented by that from other sources. There is no fundamental reason why advantage should not be taken of advance growth, seed from cut trees, or that from adjacent stands in application of the seed-tree method. Supplementary reproduction of this sort may indeed result in success where regeneration from seed trees would be ineffective. It should also be noted in this connection that casual observation of good reproduction on areas with seed trees may lead to dangerous exaggeration of the effectiveness of the seed trees involved.

The seed-tree method seems destined to become less prominent in American silviculture with the passage of time. Because of the introduction of flexible techniques of logging there are many localities where trees left as a source of seed are easily salvaged after they have served their purpose. Under these conditions it is advantageous to leave an ample number of trees for seed rather than the minimum number implicit in the seed-tree method. Therefore, the seed-tree method is gradually being displaced by shelterwood cutting as a method of natural regeneration. Nevertheless, there will remain situations in which this method of cutting, applied with caution and supplemented by appropriate measures of site preparation, will prove to be superior to other methods.

REFERENCES

Allen, P. H., and K. B. Trousdell. 1961. Loblolly pine seed production in the Virginia-North Carolina coastal plain. *J. Forestry* 59:187–190.
Baker, F. S. 1950. *Principles of silviculture.* McGraw-Hill, New York. Pp. 182–217.
Boyer, W. D. 1958. Longleaf pine seed dispersal in south Alabama. *J. Forestry* 56:265–268.
Brender, E. V. 1958. A 10-year record of pine seed production on the Hitchiti Experimental Forest. *J. Forestry* 56:408–410.
Carpenter, I. W., and A. T. Guard. 1950. Some effects of cross-pollination on seed production and hybrid vigor of tuliptree. *J. Forestry* 48:852–855.
Carvell, K. L., and C. F. Korstian. 1955. Production and dissemination of yellow-poplar seed. *J. Forestry* 53:169–170.

Chapman, H. H. 1926. Factors determining natural reproduction of longleaf pine on cut-over lands in La Salle Parish, Louisiana. *Yale Univ. School of Forestry Bul.* 16.

———, and R. Bulchis. 1940. Increased growth of longleaf pine seed trees at Urania, La., after release cutting. *J. Forestry* 38:722–726.

Curtis, J. D. 1943. Some observations on wind damage. *J. Forestry* 41:877–882.

Dale, M. E. 1958. Ground treatment and seed supply influence establishment of shortleaf pine reproduction. *CSFES Sta. Note* 119.

Engle, L. G. 1960. Yellow-poplar seedfall pattern. *CSFES Sta. Note* 143.

Eyre, F. H., and P. Zehngraff. 1948. Red pine management in Minnesota. *USDA Circ.* 778.

Garman, E. H. 1951. Seed production by conifers in the coastal region of British Columbia, relating to dissemination and regeneration. *Brit. Columbia Forest Service Tech. Publ.* T35.

———. 1955. Regeneration problems and their silvicultural significance in the coast forests of British Columbia. *Brit. Columbia Forest Service Tech. Publ.* T41.

Liming, F. G. 1945. Natural regeneration of shortleaf pine in the Missouri Ozarks. *J. Forestry* 43:339–345.

Little, S., and J. J. Mohr. 1957. Growth and mortality of residual loblolly pines after a seed-tree cutting. *NEFES Forest Research Note* 75.

McCarthy, E. F. 1933. Yellow poplar characteristics, growth, and management. *USDA Tech. Bul.* 356.

McCulley, R. D. 1950. Management of natural slash pine stands in the flatwoods of south Georgia and north Florida. *USDA Circ.* 845.

Osborne, J. G., and V. L. Harper. 1937. The effect of seedbed preparation on first-year establishment of longleaf and slash pine. *J. Forestry* 35:63–68.

Pomeroy, K. B. 1949. Loblolly pine seed trees: selection, fruitfulness, and mortality. *SEFES Sta. Paper* 5.

Siggins, H. W. 1933. Distribution and rate of fall of conifer seeds. *J. Agr. Research* 47:119–128.

Silen, R. R., and K. W. Krueger. 1962. Does rainy weather influence seed set of Douglas-fir? *J. Forestry* 60:242–244.

Smith, L. F. 1955. Development of longleaf pine seedlings near large trees. *J. Forestry* 53:289–290.

Taylor, D. R. 1951. Forestry in old-growth in the Douglas-fir region. *J. Forestry* 49:35–38.

Trousdell, K. B. 1955. Loblolly pine seed tree mortality. *SEFES Sta. Paper* 61.

Wahlenberg, W. G. 1946. *Longleaf pine, its use, ecology, regeneration, protection, growth, and management.* Charles L. Pack Forestry Foundation, Washington.

———. 1960. *Loblolly pine, its use, ecology, regeneration, protection, growth and management.* Duke University, School of Forestry, Durham, N. C.

Wenger, K. F. 1957. Annual variation in the seed crops of loblolly pine. *J. Forestry* 55:567–569.

———, and K. B. Trousdell. 1957. Natural regeneration of loblolly pine in the South Atlantic Coastal Plain. *USDA Production Research Rept.* 13.

Wright, J. W. 1953. Pollen-dispersion studies: some practical applications. *J. Forestry* 51:114–118.

CHAPTER 13

The shelterwood method

The shelterwood method involves the gradual removal of the entire stand in a series of partial cuttings which extend over a fraction of the rotation. The cuttings usually resemble heavy thinnings, and, under intensive practice, regeneration by the shelterwood method logically follows a series of thinnings. Natural reproduction starts under the protection of the older stand and is finally released when it becomes desirable to give the new crop full use of the growing space. The most fundamental characteristic of the shelterwood method is the establishment of a new crop before completion of the preceding rotation.

Within the framework of the shelterwood method, it is possible to achieve wide variation in the relative degrees of shelter and exposure both in space and time. Adjustments can be made to meet the environmental requirements of almost all species except those that are exceedingly intolerant of shade or root competition. The shelterwood method is also employed partly or even primarily as a means of increasing the efficiency of use of the growing stock. Space is made available for reproduction by cutting trees that are no longer capable of much further increase in value; those that are left may be chosen not only as a source of seed or protection for the new stand but also for their capacity to increase in value at an attractive rate. These two sets of objectives are readily combined because the trees of greatest vigor and highest quality are likely to be those that will provide the most seed and also grow most rapidly in value. In other words that are perhaps more forceful than elegant, the best trees grow best and a policy of cutting the worst first has much to recommend it.

Form of Forest Produced

The shelterwood method includes all the forms of partial cutting, except seed-tree cutting, in which essentially even-aged stands are created or maintained. Although it is most readily adaptable to the regeneration of even-aged stands, it can be used to convert stands of irregular and uneven age distribution to even-aged form, especially where merchantable age classes predominate. The irregular shelterwood system is a variant of the method useful for situations where it is desirable to keep stands in the twilight zone between the truly even-aged condition and the uneven-aged form maintained by deliberate application of the selection method.

The shelterwood method is a logical further development of the seed-tree method in which sufficiently large numbers of seed trees are retained to protect the site as well as to provide seed. A series of shelterwood cuttings is usually completed in a period of no more than one-fifth of the rotation. Regeneration periods as long as 40 to 60 years may sometimes be used in stands that are managed on long rotations or are composed of species with widely differing rates of growth. With a regeneration period of such length, the individual trees of the new stand will have a relatively wide range of age, although the stand remains more nearly even-aged than otherwise and is managed as such.

Details of the Method

In the shelterwood method, as its name implies, reproduction is secured under the shelter of a portion of the old stand. The first cuttings create vacancies in the growing space of the stand in which the new crop can become established. Besides furnishing seed, the old stand affords protection to the young seedlings. A time finally arrives when this shelter becomes a hindrance rather than a benefit to the growth of the seedlings. It is then necessary to remove the remainder of the old stand, giving the new stand possession of the area and opportunity to develop in even-aged form.

The whole process is usually accomplished within a relatively short period. Where adequate advance reproduction has become established entirely as a result of the natural opening-up of old stands, a single cutting may be sufficient. Normally, however, the shelterwood method requires a minimum of two cuttings. Under intensive practice, several cuttings are made in the gradual process of simultaneously freeing the reproduction and removing the mature stand. Regardless of the number of cuttings, the largest, most vigorous, and best-formed individuals of desirable species are retained until the final cutting. In this way the best trees of the stand are left to provide seed for the new crop; meanwhile they continue to lay down wood of high quality at a rapid rate. Trees of the poorer categories are gradually removed in successive cuttings with the least desirable usually being cut first.

The sequence of operations may involve three different kinds of cutting applied in the following order:

1. **Preparatory cuttings,** which prepare for reproduction.
2. **Seed cuttings,** which assist in establishment of the reproduction.
3. **Removal cuttings,** which free the established seedlings.

The detailed application of the method under intensive practice can best be presented by taking up each of these cuttings in turn.

Preparatory cuttings. If natural reproduction is to start under the old stand a supply of seed must be available and site conditions must be favorable for germination of seed and establishment of seedlings. It is sometimes necessary to carry out preparatory cuttings to encourage the development of thrifty seed bearers or to accelerate the decomposition of unfavorable humus layers.

Such cuttings are primarily useful in improving conditions for the eventual germination and establishment of seedlings. If the unincorporated humus layers are excessively thick, their decomposition may be hastened by opening the canopy to admit more solar radiation and precipitation to the forest floor. This need be considered only with tightly closed stands in regions of cool or dry climate favorable to the development of thick humus layers.

When stands are so dense that the prospective seed bearers have short, narrow crowns and do not produce seed in abundance, preparatory cutting may be necessary to allow the enlargement of the crowns which is conducive to seed production. The cutting may also assist in developing windfirm trees which can safely be left isolated in the later cuttings.

Preparatory cutting involves objectives additional to those of low thinning but differs little otherwise. Most of the trees that are cut come from the lower crown classes. In principle, openings are made in the main canopy only to the extent necessary to permit the development of vigorous seed bearers. In practice, there is no reason why undesirable or defective trees of the dominant and codominant classes cannot also be removed. However, efforts should be made to avoid creating the kind of environment that will favor the establishment of undesirable species more shade-tolerant than those ultimately desired. If such species are likely to invade after light cutting and the objective is solely to develop the seed bearers, the preparatory cutting is logically confined to removing a few competitors of the chosen trees.

In the majority of cases no preparatory cuttings are necessary, particularly where their purpose has been largely accomplished by systematic thinnings prior to the reproduction period. In fact, reproduction of some species may become established as a result of thinnings or even in the absence of cutting. The various active measures of site preparation are usually more expeditious than preparatory cutting as a means of reducing the accumulation of humus and controlling undesirable vegetation beneath the old stands. For these reasons the seed cutting is generally the first step in shelterwood cutting and the preparatory cutting is necessary mainly where the vigor or seed production of the stand must be increased before the more drastic seed cutting. Operations to control undesirable vegetation are very likely to be desirable and are most easily conducted immediately before the seed cutting so that they will not be impeded by slash.

Seed cutting. The purpose of the seed cutting is to open up enough vacant growing space in a single operation to allow the establishment of regeneration.

The seed cutting should be carried out during a year in which the desirable species bear seed in abundance. Otherwise undesirable vegetation may become established after the cutting. The best time of year for this cutting comes after the seed has matured and before it germinates. The desirability of executing cuttings to make way for regeneration during good seed years is not peculiar to the shelterwood method. A similar policy would be at least equally appropriate in stands managed under other methods of reproduction.

With the shelterwood system it is more nearly practicable to confine true regeneration cuttings to good seed years than with any other. In all other methods, with the possible exception of the selection system, an annual harvest of trees of the best quality is possible only if true regeneration cuttings are carried out somewhere in the forest every year. In the shelterwood method, the trees removed in the seed cutting, which is the true reproduction cutting of the method, are not the best trees in the stand. During years of poor seed production, timber of high quality may be harvested by removal cuttings in those stands where regeneration has already become established as a result of previous seed cuttings.

In any method of natural regeneration it is desirable to attempt to concentrate true reproduction cuttings in periods when good seed crops are in prospect or have recently fallen. When seed production is poor the problem is best evaded by emphasis on intermediate cuttings and the harvesting of timber in places where regeneration already exists. The shelterwood method provides a systematic means, under even-aged management, for reconciling the need for a steady flow of products with the natural tendency for reproduction to become established at erratic and infrequent intervals.

The trees removed in the seed cuttings are the least desirable remaining in the stand. They include any remaining intermediate and overtopped trees as well as all or part of the codominants (Fig. 13-1). It is particularly important that trees of undesirable species be cut (or killed) regardless of crown class. Any trees too poor to retain for further growth should be removed, although the temptation to eliminate all coarse, branchy dominants should be restrained if these are the only good seed-bearers.

The seed cutting is best confined to a single operation so that the new crop will be reasonably uniform in age and size. In this way the severity of the cutting can also be adjusted so as to create a range of environmental conditions which is restricted as closely as possible to that which is optimum for germination and establishment of the species desired. A series of seed cuttings of ever-increasing severity might involve the reservation of a shelterwood that was at first too dense and later too thin to provide the proper environment.

Where moisture deficiencies are likely to limit regeneration, an excessively dense overwood may cause too much root competition and interception of precipitation. If heat injury to succulent young seedlings is the primary difficulty, the seed cutting should be regulated so as to increase the amount of diffuse light admitted from the sky as much as possible without allowing much direct sunlight to reach the forest floor.

The appropriate density of the overwood can be determined only by observation and experimentation. It will differ within wide limits depending on the requirements of the species sought and the site factors; it may also be as important to make conditions unfavorable to undesirable species as to create those favorable to the desirable. If the species that appear are more shade-tolerant than those desired, it is usually necessary to increase the severity of the seed cutting. If, for example, the existing species to be reproduced is pine and some more tolerant species invades after shelterwood cutting, it is probably a sign that the cutting was not heavy enough or site preparation was inadequate.

Fig. 13-1. An even-aged hardwood stand, predominantly of various oaks, in the Eli Whitney Forest, Connecticut, being reproduced by the uniform-shelterwood method. The first picture shows the stand after earlier thinning and salvage of blight-killed chestnut have accomplished the purposes of seed cutting. The second picture, taken 8 years after the first, shows the dominant red oaks left after the first of two removal cuttings. The mixed hardwood reproduction, which is leafless and invisible in the second picture, is well established and ready to make rapid growth. (*Photograph by Yale University School of Forestry.*)

Wellner (1948) found that the basal area or sum of the diameters of the reserved stand provides a satisfactory index of the amount of light admitted by an overwood. By means of such indexes experience gained in one stand may be used in regulating seed cuttings in other stands. In terms of volume, the amount removed should be from 25 to 75 per cent of the total. Inasmuch as the subsequent removal cuttings are likely to result in damage to reproduction, it is advantageous to take off as much of the old stand as possible in the seed cutting.

It is not necessary that the distribution of reserved trees be absolutely uniform. An uneven distribution may occasionally be favorable to the seedlings in their competition with the older trees for soil moisture. In the seed cutting advantage is taken of all groups of advance growth which may have started naturally or as an unintentional result of preparatory cuttings or thinnings. Over such groups the cutting is heavy and may remove all the old timber. In fact it is possible to find stands in which reproduction has started so well after thinnings that neither preparatory nor seed cuttings are needed. Here the first reproduction cutting will be a removal cutting.

If satisfactory regeneration does not become established as a result of the seed crop present at the time of seed cutting or from seed produced in the next few years, two courses of action are available. The inadequate natural reproduction may be supplemented by planting, or measures of site preparation may be applied during a subsequent seed year. If good reproduction is secured without delay, 3 to 10 years usually elapse before the stand is ready for the first removal cutting.

Removal cuttings. Removal cuttings have, in varying degrees, the objectives of gradually uncovering the new crop and of making best use of the potentialities of the remnants of the old crop to increase in value. There may be one or, in intensive management, several removal cuttings, the last of which is called the **final cutting.** The ideal objective of this process is to proceed so that the new crop fills the growing space as fast as the old crop is caused to relinquish it. Although perfect achievement of this goal is impossible, the procedure enables regeneration to be accomplished without reducing total wood production as far below the capacity of the site as would be the case if a new crop of seedlings, natural or planted, were left to regain full occupancy alone.

The largest and most vigorous trees usually have the greatest capacity to increase in value and so are the ones most logically reserved

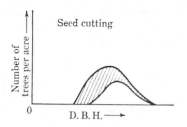
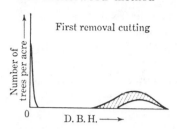

Fig. 13-2. Diameter distribution curves showing (by cross-hatching) the relative numbers of trees of different diameters removed in a typical seed cutting and the first of two removal cuttings. In the seed cutting (*left*) the smaller and less desirable trees, representing about a third of the volume, are cut. In this example, the first removal cutting (*right*) takes place after the trees left in the seed cutting have increased substantially in diameter and after some of the reproduction resulting from that cutting has grown to measurable D.B.H. The trees reserved in the first removal cutting are the biggest and best in the stand; they will all be harvested in the second and final removal cutting.

until the final cutting (Fig. 13-2) unless they happen to be ones that interfere unduly with the new crop.

After the reproduction is established it is watched for signs of unthriftiness. If the young trees develop unhealthy foliage, bend aside toward the light, or fail to maintain a satisfactory rate of growth in height, the competition of the overwood should be eliminated or reduced. The condition of the reproduction is unlikely to be uniform throughout the entire stand. Some patches may need release while others continue to require protection or a source of seed for additional reproduction. Therefore, the removal cuttings are not made evenly over the whole area. A group may be cut clear in one place, and a few trees thinned out in other places; elsewhere there may be no need for cutting.

It is important to distinguish between the conditions suitable for the establishment of regeneration and those that are necessary for it to initiate and maintain satisfactory growth in height. If the regeneration consists of a mixture of species, and if the desirable species are not especially tolerant of shade and competition, it is necessary to release the established reproduction in order to increase the likelihood that the desirable species will grow as fast or faster in height as the undesirable. There are many intolerant species which tend to increase in height growth with each added increment of light up to full sunlight whereas the tolerant species often attain maximum height growth at some intermediate light intensity. The survival of the in-

tolerant species usually depends on their ability to outgrow their competitors but they must have sufficient growing space before they can
exhibit this potentiality. In other words, the fact that it may be easy
to get a good stand of desirable seedlings under some sort of cover
should not obscure the necessity of releasing them in such manner
that they not only grow rapidly in height but also grow more rapidly
than any undesirable competitors. If, on the other hand, the desirable
species are more shade-tolerant than the undesirable species and if
the same relative effects of light on height growth that have been
described prevail in the situation involved, it may be desirable to retain some sort of overhead cover until the desirable tolerants have
overtopped the undesirable intolerants.

The intervals between removal cuttings and the periods over which
they are extended are highly variable; except for the necessity of fostering the development of the new crop there is little reason why
their timing cannot be fitted to any management considerations. If
the new crop is to be even-aged, the period of removal cuttings should
not exceed 20 per cent of the length of the rotation.

The removal cuttings are almost certain to cause some injury to
the young stand. This can be reduced, but not eliminated, by care
and planning in the felling and skidding operations. The least injury
is likely to result if the overwood is harvested while the seedlings are
still flexible. Greatest difficulties result when it is necessary to fell
trees with broad crowns into stands of saplings. The damage usually
appears more serious than it really is and it is sometimes even a benefit in disguise. Shelterwood cutting often leads to the development
of grossly overstocked patches of reproduction that look handsome
when young but are apt to stagnate in the sapling stage. These
clumps can be crudely thinned by the skidding or felling of trees
across them. In fact, it is usually best to direct the inevitable logging
damage toward the densest parts of the new stand or those that are
entirely unstocked and away from the sparsely stocked portions.

Modifications of the Method

The patterns in which shelterwood cuttings are arranged in time and
space are subject to wide variation. Modifications involving the arrangement of cuttings by area are as follows:

1. **Uniform method**—application uniformly over the entire stand.
2. **Strip-shelterwood method**—application in strips.
3. **Group-shelterwood method**—application in groups or patches.

The details already described relate particularly to the uniform method, although in the strip and group modifications the same principles are applied in cuttings that do not extend over the entire stand in any one year. Another kind of modification, in which some of the trees of the overwood are retained long after the seed cutting, is referred to as the **irregular shelterwood method.**

Strip-shelterwood method. In this modification the stand is cut in strips that are advanced gradually across the area. At any given time cutting is concentrated in certain strips and the rest of the stand remains temporarily untouched.

Starting on one side of the stand, a seed cutting is conducted on the first strip. After a few years a removal cutting is made on the first strip, and the adjoining strip is given a seed cutting. A few years later the first strip is subjected to a final cutting, the second strip to a removal cutting, and a third strip to a seed cutting. In this manner (Fig. 13-3), the series of cuttings progresses strip by strip across the stand. It may be necessary to divide a large stand into cutting sections, as shown in Fig. 13-3, if the whole stand is to be even-aged in the next rotation.

The strip-shelterwood method can be applied in a variety of other ways. In the simplest application, the only kind of cutting involved would be clearcutting in very narrow strips so that the side shade of the trees on the adjacent strip of uncut timber takes the place of

Cutting section A				Cutting section B			
1	2	3	4	1	2	3	4
Seed cutting in 1954 Removal " " 1959 Final " " 1964	Seed cutting in 1959 Removal " " 1964 Final " " 1969	Seed cutting in 1964 Removal " " 1969 Final " " 1974	Seed cutting in 1969 Removal " " 1974 Final " " 1979	Cuttings made in same arrangement and time as in cutting section A			

Fig. 13-3. Diagram of a stand reproduced in two cutting sections by the strip-shelterwood method. The period of regeneration is about 25 years in length, and the stand is kept in even-aged form. A preparatory cutting is unnecessary in most cases and hence is omitted from the diagram.

the protection of an overwood. In this modification the strips would be no wider than half the height of the mature timber.

The most intensive application, developed by Wagner (1923) for regenerating Norway spruce in southern Germany, involves cutting in strips so that there is a gradual transition from clearcutting to light preparatory cutting across a strip about 100 feet wide. Within this strip may be found examples of preparatory, seed, removal, and final cutting, but each on such a narrow zone and so intimately associated with the other as to be scarcely distinguishable. This strip is advanced slowly across the stand, at a rate of 6 to 25 feet per year, just as fast as the reproduction becomes established and capable of being released.

It is not necessary that the strips be straight. An irregular or undulating line may even be advantageous in exposing a longer frontage for regeneration and thus hastening the advance of the strip.

The strip-shelterwood method has several advantages over the uniform method. The risk of windfall in the residual stand is reduced because part of the stand is kept intact as a windbreak and a relatively small number of trees is left isolated at any one time. If the strips are advanced from north to south in the direction of the sun, the full canopy of each uncut strip effectively shields a narrow strip of the forest floor from the desiccating and heating effect of the direct rays of the sun without excluding much diffuse radiation from the sky (Fig. 8-1). Damage to reproduction from the removal of mature timber can be kept at a minimum, because it may be possible to remove the mature timber through the uncut strips rather than always over the area being reproduced, as must be done in the uniform application.

The initial location, orientation, and direction of progress of the strips must receive careful consideration in all strip methods. If protection of the regeneration is the critical factor, the strips should be advanced toward the south or southwest, that is, toward the midday or afternoon sun. If protection of the reserved trees from wind is most important, the strips should be advanced toward the direction from which the most dangerous winds are likely to come.

The topography will influence the arrangement of the strips. On slopes the strips are best advanced from the top downward, thus allowing the timber to be taken out downhill and not through the area being reproduced. The strips may also run from the top to the bottom of the slope and advance along the sidehill, provided that the necessary protection can be secured by so doing. Troup (1952) presented an excellent account of the manner in which strip-shelterwood cuttings are arranged to solve various problems of logging and silviculture in Europe.

Group-shelterwood method. Patches of advance regeneration arising from thinnings or from natural disturbances commonly develop in even-aged stands. Where this condition is prominent, shelterwood cuttings can be made, not uniformly over the area, but entirely with reference to the special requirements of each group of advance reproduction. These clumps of regeneration are enlarged by the removal of all or most of the trees above them and initiating preparatory or seed cuttings around them. The holes created in the canopy are gradually enlarged to keep pace with the establishment of reproduction, in the same fashion that strips are advanced through the stand in the strip-shelterwood method. The gaps may be expanded uniformly in all directions as shown in Fig. 13-4, or, if desirable, they

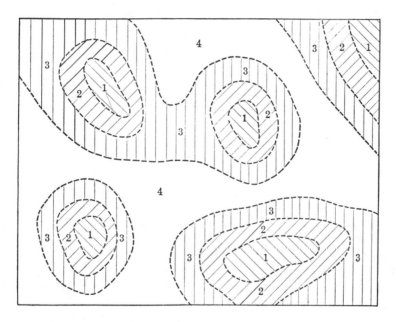

Kind of Cutting	Areas Marked:-			
	1	2	3	4
Preparatory and Seed Cutting combined	Received Cuttings in Years as follows:-			
		1960	1965	1970
Removal Cutting		1965	1970	1975
Final Cutting	1960	1970	1975	1980

Fig. 13-4. Arrangement of cuttings in a stand reproduced by the group-shelterwood method. Advance reproduction was present before the cutting on areas marked "1."

may be extended chiefly along their southern margins in order to avoid exposing young seedlings to direct sunlight. If the stand does not contain enough clumps of advance reproduction to furnish sufficient starting points for the first cutting, they may be created arbitrarily by making small openings or conducting seed cuttings in small patches.

After the groups of advance growth are well established and somewhat enlarged, it often may be better to remove the rest of the stand gradually in the form of an advancing strip than to widen each group until they all merge. In this way logging injury to reproduction may be reduced by avoiding the necessity of transporting timber through areas under regeneration.

The group-shelterwood method is more favorable to tolerant than to intolerant species because the cuttings tend to follow rather than guide the development of natural reproduction. It is also unsuitable for species sensitive to injury by frost because the small gaps tend to act as frost pockets. Logging and administration of operations are sometimes difficult because of the unsystematic distribution of the cutting areas. For these reasons the group-shelterwood method is generally less satisfactory than the strip and uniform methods and is most useful where advance regeneration is so well established as to dictate the pattern of shelterwood cuttings.

Irregular shelterwood method. This modification is characterized by a relatively long regeneration period during which some of the trees of the overwood are retained to complete growth to optimum size and quality. The trees reserved may be the best and most vigorous of the dominants, as in typical shelterwood cuttings. They may also be trees of the lower crown classes that have grown slowly in the past but are capable of rapid growth if released. In either case, the reserved trees tend to hamper the development of regeneration beneath them so that the new stand will have a distribution of ages broader than that of truly even-aged stands.

The irregular shelterwood method stands in an intermediate position between the methods of even- and uneven-aged management. It involves the maintenance of two age classes through all (Fig. 13-5) or at least more than 20 per cent of the rotation. Partial cuttings made with the deliberate intention of developing or permanently maintaining at least three age classes are arbitrarily distinguished as representing uneven-aged management under the selection system.

The irregular shelterwood method is like the reserve seed-tree method except that more trees are retained and not all of them need

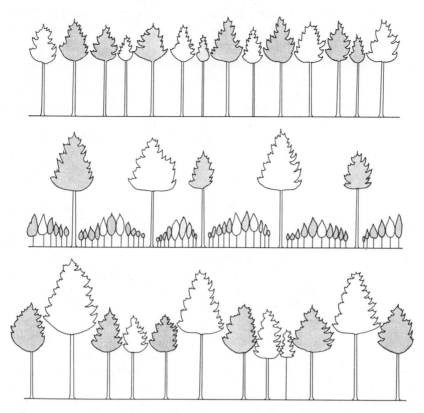

Fig. 13-5. A stand of a moderately tolerant conifer at three stages in the application of the irregular shelterwood system. Each sketch shows the stand before a cutting in which the trees with the dark crowns are reserved. The *upper* sketch shows the initial even-aged condition just before trees still capable of increase in value are reserved in a seed cutting. The *middle* sketch shows the stand one-third of the way through the next rotation and ready for the *second* of two removal cuttings. A few merchantable trees are thinned from the new stand and three original trees are left to grow until the end of the second rotation. The tree on the left illustrates the use of the method to grow a few trees to great size and value; the main justification for leaving small-crowned trees like the two on the right would be to remedy a deficiency, on the forest as a whole, of good stems in their diameter class. The *lower* sketch shows the stand after additional thinnings, at the end of the second rotation, and ready for seed cutting as well as for the harvest of the three original trees. These three trees could have been cut earlier; there is no necessity that they be carried through two whole rotations.

act as seed bearers.   The main objective is to allow trees of poten- tially high quality to grow until they reach optimum value.   Treat- ment of this kind is warranted only when most of the trees of a stand reach optimum value long before the few found worthy of retention. This situation is actually rather commonly encountered, although its existence is not of itself sufficient reason for embarking on the irregu- lar shelterwood system.   The same general objective is commonly sought in all shelterwood cutting, except in this case it is pursued so long that reproduction tends to suffer as a result.   This course of action is, therefore, justified only if the increment of valuable wood obtained is worth more than the potential growth of the younger trees that would be oppressed by the reserved trees or destroyed during the process of harvesting them.

Reproduction is secured in the same manner as in regular shelter- wood cuttings; the only difference is that the removal cuttings are extended over all or part of the new rotation.   The trees most suitable for retention are ordinarily those that have always been dominants because they are the ones most likely to grow rapidly and to be suf- ficiently healthy to endure the vicissitudes of long life.   However, if regeneration is already established or if other trees can serve as seed bearers, it may be feasible to reserve some former codominants with small crowns and clean boles if they really have the capacity to en- dure, develop larger crowns, and soon commence the rapid growth of wood of high quality.   Codominants are not likely to do this unless they are of at least moderately tolerant species.

The irregular shelterwood method is also used sometimes for man- aging essentially even-aged stands composed of different species which are naturally segregated into different strata in the crown canopy. These stratified mixtures will be considered separately in Chapter 16. The present chapter deals chiefly with the most common kinds of stands in which each age class forms a single stratum in the crown canopy.

Modifications for application in extensive silviculture.   The discus- sion of the shelterwood method has up to this point related primarily to its intensive application.   This method, because it involves several cuttings on the same area within a relatively short period, is best suited to conditions allowing intensive management.   Such manage- ment can be conducted if there are markets for trees of low value or funds to invest in killing them.   There must also be permanent roads affording easy access to all parts of the forest.

However, the shelterwood method is so well adapted to the reproductive requirements of many important species that it is applied in modified form under circumstances where only extensive silviculture can be practiced. These modifications consist of: (1) reducing the total number of cuttings, (2) lengthening the period between cuttings, and (3) omitting refinements for securing complete restocking.

Under extensive application no preparatory cuttings or thinnings are made. The natural opening-up of the stand as a result of old age or accidental factors is relied upon instead to produce conditions favorable to the start of reproduction. Sometimes cuttings are deferred until considerable advance reproduction is already established under the original stand so that even the seed cutting can be omitted.

The advance growth so released may be of a later successional stage than the overwood. This procedure is particularly useful where it enables a pioneer species, such as jack pine, to be replaced by a more valuable and less intolerant species, such as red pine (Robertson, 1945).

Best results are obtained with advance regeneration that has become established rather recently at moderately close, uniform spacing. The quality of advance reproduction and its rate of response after release decline the longer it is suppressed (Vaartaja, 1951). If the live crowns of such trees have been seriously reduced, they may even become overtopped by new seedlings or younger advance growth. Large, straight, thrifty saplings are, however, usually satisfactory (Hallin, 1959). A distinctly undesirable kind of advance growth is that consisting of thrifty, scattered individuals that develop into wolf trees after release and preclude the growth of smaller trees of better quality. It is sometimes desirable to eliminate such excessively vigorous components of advance regeneration, those that are already malformed, and any that are so unthrifty as to grow only well enough to hamper the development of smaller trees of greater potential vigor.

If advance reproduction is already well established throughout the old stand and no worthwhile purpose is served by retaining any trees for future growth, all the old stand may be taken off in a single removal cutting. Such cuttings are usually termed "clearcuttings," although from the silvicultural standpoint they are best regarded as crude shelterwood cuttings because the new crop has been started under shelter. This procedure is often satisfactory for rehabilitating degenerate old-growth stands. The drawbacks of this "one-cut" shelterwood method are the complete absence of control over the nature of the reproduction and the heavy losses of volume sustained while the advance regeneration is becoming established. It is a technique that has a definite place in regenerating certain kinds of culled or virgin old growth, but it is less likely to succeed on the short rotations contemplated in commercial forestry.

If advance reproduction is incomplete or if part of the old stand is capable of further growth, the timber is removed in two or three cuttings. This procedure is called the two- or three-cut shelterwood method. The purposes of the first cutting are the partial uncovering of advance reproduction and the establishment of reproduction on areas not yet stocked. The trees removed should, insofar as possible, include those of species not desired in the new stand and individuals that would be cut in preparatory and seed cuttings under more intensive practice. An adequate number of vigorous, windfirm seed-bearers should be retained to ensure restocking, although some of the reserved trees may be healthy individuals not yet large enough for convenient utilization, as in the irregular shelterwood method. The residual stand is then removed in one or two cuttings in a period 10 to 50 years after the initial operation.

Special measures to prepare the site for reproduction, eliminate competing vegetation, and control the composition or density of the regeneration are usually omitted in extensive application of the shelterwood method.

Advantages and Disadvantages of the Shelterwood Method

Reproduction is generally more certain and complete than with the clearcutting and seed-tree methods because of the more abundant source of seed and the protection against damaging agencies provided by the overwood. The fact that the main harvest cuttings follow rather than precede the establishment of reproduction is an important safeguard. The best trees are retained until after regeneration is established and may, therefore, be cut in poor seed years. With other methods, a sustained annual harvest of large timber is practically impossible unless true reproduction cuttings are made in poor seed years.

The average length of the rotation may be shortened because one even-aged crop starts before the preceding one is harvested. The growing space is more fully utilized during the regeneration period than with other methods of reproducing even-aged high forests so there is less loss of potential wood production. The accelerated increment of the overwood after seed cuttings also enables trees of large diameter to be produced more rapidly than in closed stands.

The shelterwood method usually provides the best means of applying the concept of financial maturity to even-aged stands. Efficient use may thus be made of the capacity of the better trees of the growing stock to increase in value without sacrificing the advantages of concentration of operations associated with even-aged management. The method calls for greater technical skill than the clearcutting or seed-tree methods, but the operations are more systematic and simpler to administer than those under the selection system. The different steps are separate and distinct in time; the state and progress of regeneration are always readily visible (Trevor, 1938).

The large number of residual trees and any reproduction are not only apt to be damaged in logging but they also impede harvesting and site preparation. Slash disposal is, however, less necessary than with methods involving heavier cutting; each cutting leaves less debris; the shaded conditions stimulate decomposition and reduce danger of fire. The presence of shade often eliminates need for exposing mineral soil.

The shelterwood method can be applied intensively only if there are markets for trees of small size or poor quality, unless such trees can be killed rather than harvested. The cost of logging is greater than when virtually all the trees are cut in a single operation. The otherwise sound principle of cutting the poor trees before the best can make the first cuttings of the shelterwood sequence financially unattractive, especially if the cost of making the stands accessible is high. Some of these difficulties are partially evaded in the modifications associated with extensive practice. They can be largely overcome once the forest is well served with roads and so organized that both seed and removal cuttings can be carried on simultaneously in different places.

The method is superior to all others except the selection method with respect to protection of the site and aesthetic considerations.

Application of the Shelterwood Method

The wide latitude possible for variation in the arrangement and severity of cutting under the shelterwood method make it adaptable to any but extremely intolerant species. These same factors also make it applicable in extensive as well as intensive practice.

In following the shelterwood method, the forester attempts to duplicate the natural processes that lead to the disintegration of old stands and their replacement by new growth arising under the shelter of an overwood. In nature, even-aged stands eventually open up slowly under the influence of insects, fungi, wind, and other damaging agencies. In this way they are gradually replaced by irregularly uneven-aged stands in which intolerant species are usually less abundant than in the previous stand (Jones, 1945). This process does not necessarily lead to the development of essentially all-aged stands, as has often been contended. In the shelterwood method removal of the old stand is accelerated enough to cause it to be replaced by an even-aged crop, which may contain a high proportion of relatively intolerant species; this situation is occasionally duplicated in nature by the effects of light surface fires.

Although the shelterwood method may be applied to a wide variety of species, it is most useful in reproducing those that require protection during the initial stages of development as well as a large supply of seed. Many of these species have been described as "tolerant in youth but intolerant after reaching the sapling stage," an observation that is significant in determining their silvicultural treatment.

It is regarded as the best basic method for both eastern and western white pine as well as red pine. It has also been used with success for reproducing loblolly, shortleaf, and pitch pines. There is evidence that it may be superior to the seed-tree method for regenerating longleaf pine, provided that the overwood is removed before the new trees are more than 2 years old (Croker, 1956). The even-aged stands of ponderosa pine in the Black Hills of South Dakota, where summer rains make natural regeneration more abundant than in other parts of the range of the species, are well adapted to shelterwood cutting.

The shelterwood method is particularly well adapted to eastern white pine (Fig. 13-6; Horton and Bedell, 1960). This species regenerates very poorly in direct sunlight because of reductions in germination caused by desiccation and the serious losses of succulent seedlings from heat injury (Smith, 1951). Scarification of the forest floor is effective in reducing these losses only on moist sites where the mineral soil does not become too dry. Occasionally seedlings may be shielded by a low, thin cover of grass, herbaceous vegetation, dead slash, or certain mosses, but the most dependable protection comes from the overwood left in shelterwood cuttings. If the shade is too dense the seedlings will be overwhelmed by more tolerant hardwoods or conifers (Scott, 1958). On dry sandy soils in eastern Ontario, Atkins (1957) found that the undesirable balsam fir became established under white pine stands if the light intensity was less than about 25 per cent of full sunlight.

Once established, the seedlings must be deliberately exposed to more light if they are to grow vigorously. However, it is still desirable to retain partial shade in order to prevent excessive damage by the white pine weevil. This insect feeds only on the stems of the

Fig. 13-6. A 74-year-old stand of eastern white pine in the Pack Demonstration Forest, at Warrensburg, New York, being regenerated by the shelterwood method. The seed cutting was carried out 12 years previously. (*Photograph by State University College of Forestry, New York.*)

terminal shoots; if these shoots are killed they are replaced by one or more lateral branches which straighten up satisfactorily only if one assumes dominance and the stand density is very great. These deformities cause by far the most serious difficulties in growing eastern white pine; except in the coldest parts of the range the problem is of far more consequence than the blister rust. The female weevils prefer to lay their eggs under warm, dry conditions and tend to avoid leaders that are protected from direct sunlight (Belyea and Sullivan, 1956; Sullivan, 1959). Therefore, it is desirable to maintain the partial shade of an overwood until the reproduction has developed into saplings with the desired length of straight stem. The optimum level of light intensity appears to be about 50 per cent because this offers sufficient protection from the weevil; the height growth, but not that in diameter and volume, is nearly as good as it would be in full sunlight (Logan, 1959). The protection period is so long that the irregular shelterwood method, with its long regeneration period, may prove more satisfactory than modifications which do not provide for such a long period of shading. This is also consistent with the usefulness of the concept of financial maturity in managing this species, the individuals of which vary widely in quality (Northeastern Forest Experiment Station, 1959).

The shelterwood method is equally desirable for regenerating mature stands of the western white pine type, although damage by weevils is not a factor. This species also requires protection from direct sunlight during the period of establishment, after which the young crop should be fully exposed (Haig, Davis, and Weidman, 1941). Another advantage of shelterwood cutting in this type is that it tends to reduce the population of *Ribes* by encouraging the stored seeds to germinate under shade too heavy to allow these shrubs to survive or add to the supply of seed (Moss and Wellner, 1953). Cuttings which remove 25 to 60 per cent of the merchantable volume and leave an even canopy are sufficient to achieve this purpose and promote regeneration of white pine as well (Wellner, 1946). The first cutting should be light and aimed at the removal of trees of poor vigor, low quality, and undesirable species. This kind of cutting is not the sole solution to the blister-rust problem because the need for subsequent control is not entirely eliminated. The method is also as favorable to reproduction of shade-enduring western hemlock and other less desirable species as it is to white pine. Therefore, cultural operations may be necessary to keep the white pine in a dominant position.

One of the best accounts of intensive application of the shelterwood method in North America is that by Eyre and Zehngraff (1948) describing the evolution of silvicultural management of red pine in Minnesota. The point of departure was the seed-tree method which was found wanting largely because of the inadequacy of the seed supply. As market conditions improved, it became obvious that the shelterwood system had important advantages in enabling good regeneration, reducing the danger of invasion by brush, and allowing retention of the best trees for growth to optimum size and quality.

Under conditions favorable to intensive practice, these writers recommended rotations of 140 years with cuttings commencing before the stands are 40 years old and being repeated at intervals of 5 to 10 years thereafter. Up to an age of 80 years these cuttings should consist of thinnings to anticipate mortality among the lower crown classes and improvement cuttings to eliminate trees of poor form. Any jack pines present in the stands should be cut during the same period because they cannot be depended upon to survive longer. Between the ages of 80 and 120 years, red pines, chiefly codominants suitable for poles or piling, are removed in thinnings designed to free the dominants; these thinnings thus serve as preparatory cuttings. It is recommended that the seed cutting be made at about age 125 with half of the crown canopy and basal area being removed. The overwood is again reduced by half at 130 years to release reproduction established during the preceding decade. If adequate regeneration is not yet established by then the area should be either planted or disked during the midsummer of a good seed year. The final removal cutting is made at 140 years if adequate reproduction has been obtained. The numerical schedule for this silvicultural system is given in Table 3-2. The same results could be obtained on a much shorter rotation in less rigorous climates, although the same general procedure might well be followed. Where conditions do not favor intensive silviculture, Eyre and Zehngraff recommended use of the two-cut shelterwood method, with no more than 20 years elapsing between the seed and final removal cuttings.

The same general principles can be followed for reproducing a wide variety of light-seeded species, regardless of tolerance or successional position. The only requirement is that the desirable species involved be adapted to germination and survival under the partial shade and root competition of an overwood. The shelterwood method is probably not applicable to very intolerant pioneer species like paper birch or the true poplars that require a seedbed of mineral soil exposed to full light. Neither is it applicable to species like jack pine in which the closed-cone habit is so well developed that the seeds are released only by crown fires or when the cones are lying on the soil in direct sunlight. On the other hand, with species like lodgepole pine, in which the cones are only partially serotinous, partial shade has been found advantageous in reducing the danger of overstocking (Bates, Hilton, and Krueger, 1929).   The usefulness of the method is also limited on sites so dry that seedlings will not survive in wide zones around overstory trees.   Otherwise, the requirements of almost any species can be met by appropriate regulation of the density and arrangement of the overwood, supplemented on occasion by measures to prepare the site and eliminate competing vegetation.

The application of the shelterwood method to tolerant conifers is exemplified by its superiority over other methods in the regeneration of eastern hemlock and the Rocky Mountain form of Douglas-fir. These two trees are essentially similar in their silvical habits.   Eastern hemlock develops best form in dense, even-aged stands that may be created by a series of light shelterwood cuttings (Foster and Kirkland, 1949).   The first cuttings should be in the nature of preparatory cuttings in order to stimulate decomposition of the thick humus layers characteristic of hemlock stands.   These light cuttings inhibit the invasion of blackberries, raspberries, pin cherry, and other undesirable pioneers, which are the only species capable of colonizing hemlock litter that is exposed to direct sunlight.   A comparison of the different reproduction methods carried out in Colorado by Roeser (1924) showed that a two-cut shelterwood system provided the densest and most vigorous reproduction of the mountain form of Douglas-fir.

The shelterwood method is also well adapted to the management of heavy-seeded species, notably oaks.   These species bear so few seeds which are dispersed over such short distances by rodents and gravity that the seed bearers must be numerous and closely spaced for adequate regeneration.   Investigations by Korstian (1927), Wood (1938), and Downs and McQuilkin (1944) have shown that oak acorns must be buried beneath litter and protected from desiccation by a forest canopy if they are to germinate.   Although these conditions might be provided by selection cuttings removing single trees, oak seedlings tend to grow slowly and develop into trees that lean toward the light when established in small openings.   Therefore, it is desirable that they grow in even-aged stands.

Regeneration of oak, in contrast to that of most light-seeded species, tends to appear gradually as advance growth that slowly accumulates under stands after they have reached middle age (Scholz, 1952). Several good acorn crops occurring over a period of a decade or more are necessary (Gysel, 1957). Thinnings and light seed cuttings stimulate the establishment of seedlings (Carvell and Tryon, 1961).   The tops of the seedlings characteristically grow up and die back repeatedly while the large taproots remain alive and continually increase in size (Leffelman and Hawley, 1925). Once this peculiar advance reproduction becomes dense enough it may be released to develop into a stand of whatever form is desired. At least 50 per cent of the basal area of the overwood must be removed for satisfactory growth of seedlings (Kuenzel and McGuire, 1942).

The choice of the method employed for handling oak stands really has little to do with reproduction. Most of the new crop of oak is actually obtained as advance growth beneath stands that are either undisturbed or have been subjected to light seed cuttings designed chiefly to eliminate undesirable species (Tryon and Finn, 1949). The main advantage of removing the overwood in a series of cuttings, as shown in Fig. 13-1, rather than all at once, is the added increment of clear wood obtained by holding the best dominant trees. Those of the lower crown classes should not be retained for this purpose because they are likely to develop epicormic branches. Where only extensive practice is possible, the whole stand may be removed in a single cutting anytime after adequate advance growth has become established.

Advance reproduction plays an important role in the regeneration of most American hardwoods. The only important exceptions among the more desirable species are very intolerant ones like yellow-poplar and the birches. With most species, however, the best policy appears to be to wait for advance regeneration to develop naturally or to hasten it by means of light shelterwood cuttings. Once established the advance growth can be freed to develop in dense even-aged stands or as well-stocked clumps in uneven-aged stands, as described under the group-selection method. In most instances cuttings designed to release advance growth of hardwoods should be heavy. Many of the more valuable species are not extremely tolerant of shade and must outgrow their competitors if they are to survive. Rapid growth in height is important for all the species because it is usually difficult to secure straight stems. The faster a tree grows in height the fewer are the injuries that can occur during the development of each segment of stem length. It is, for example, important that the young trees be given an opportunity to elevate their crowns quickly through the stratum in which deer can browse the terminal shoots.

Hardwood stands often become cluttered with trees that are too poor or small to be merchantable at the time of reproduction cuttings. This leads to a tendency to reserve them in the desperate hope that growth or improved markets will make it profitable to harvest them later. Such trees frequently suppress the reproduction and prevent the development of new and better stands.   The best way to break this bottleneck is to kill the offending trees.

Damage to small seedlings during cuttings is of little consequence for most hardwood species because the **seedling sprouts** which grow from stumps 2 inches in diameter or less are fully as good as true seedlings.   Seedling sprouts may, in fact, grow more rapidly and develop better form than true seedlings.   It has occasionally been recommended that advance growth of hardwoods be mowed back at the time of cutting in order to obtain an even stand of vigorous seedling sprouts (Tryon and Finn, 1949).   Investigations by Leffelman and Hawley (1925) as well as by Jensen and Wilson (1951) indicated that the improvements resulting from complete mowing are insufficient to justify the expense, although it may be desirable to cut back individual stems of undesirable characteristics.

The possibility of depending on advance growth for regeneration of hardwoods offers wide latitude in the kinds of cutting which may be used to rehabilitate defective stands of old growth under both extensive and intensive practice.   Jemison (1946) found that good results can be achieved in the Appalachians either by eliminating the entire overwood in a single cutting or by removing all large trees except those good enough to be retained for further growth.   Curtis and Rushmore (1958) obtained better success with the development of reproduction of yellow birch and sugar maple by shelterwood cutting than with light selection cutting or clearcutting.   The main problem in such stands is to dispose of enough poor trees to admit adequate light while retaining enough good trees to provide supplemental seeding and continuing growth of good saw timber.

Among the many forest types in which advance growth plays an indispensable role in regeneration are those composed of various species of spruce, growing in pure stands or, more commonly, in mixture with true firs.   Where such stands are managed for the production of pulpwood on an extensive basis, the cuttings usually involve the removal of all trees large enough for that purpose.   This kind of treatment is most logically regarded as "one-cut" shelterwood cutting because success depends on the amount of advance reproduction present and the degree of care exercised in protecting it during logging (Fig. 13-7).   If true firs are present, they tend to increase in abundance at the expense of the spruce, a development which is not altogether desirable because the fast-growing firs are so susceptible to the spruce budworm and early infection by heart rots.   In spite of such imperfections, the reproduction is usually ample and sometimes overabundant.

Fig. 13-7. A stand of balsam fir and red spruce in northern Maine 20 years after a single cutting that removed all merchantable pulpwood. The regeneration, in which fir predominates, came entirely from advance growth present at the time of cutting. The birch snags succumbed to exposure after being left in the cutting. (*Photograph by U. S. Forest Service.*)

This technique is more likely to succeed in stands that have commenced to open up from loss of scattered firs than it is in most stands of second growth (Westveld, 1931; Long, 1947). Advance growth of spruce is seriously deficient in most stands at the end of an ordinary pulpwood rotation. The development of good advance growth of spruce and fir under purely natural conditions is actually the result of serious losses of utilizable material that might be salvaged if the stands were readily accessible. In the more accessible stands it is gradually becoming feasible to shift to somewhat more intensive management involving various kinds of partial cutting; some of these are considered in Chapter 16. Methods like uniform shelterwood cutting would not be very appropriate for most mixtures of spruce and fir because they would involve the harvesting of the trees of the lower canopy strata before any significant advantage was taken of their good capacity for growth after release. However, the simpler kinds of shelterwood cutting are effective in handling pure, even-aged stands of spruce which form a single canopy layer.

It is noteworthy that the regeneration of most of the important forest types of the northeastern United States and eastern Canada depends on some kind of advance regeneration. This situation has its advantages and is not confined to the locality mentioned. Excessive familiarity with it can lead to certain erroneous conclusions. It is sometimes assumed that there is really no other kind of natural regeneration and that the composition of the advance growth, being taken as the true manifestation of the capabilities of the site, inexorably determines the composition of the next stand. These fallacies easily lead to a kind of drifting silviculture in which one accepts whatever species appear as a result of natural succession or of the kind of cutting that is financially most expedient at the moment.

Distinction should be drawn between extensive application of the shelterwood method based on unearned advance regeneration and the more intensive applications in which such regeneration is established by deliberate measures. In remote stands of old growth already stocked with acceptable advance growth, most factors usually favor extensive application. Second-growth stands, which are thriftier, more regular, and made up of smaller trees than old-growth timber, offer better opportunities for intensive management under the shelterwood method. As the regeneration of such stands becomes a more pressing problem, this method will become an increasingly important silvicultural technique.

REFERENCES

Atkins, E. S. 1957. Light measurement in a study of white pine reproduction. *Canada, Forestry Branch, Forest Research Div. Tech. Note* 60.

Bates, C. G., H. C. Hilton, and T. Krueger. 1929. Experiments in the silvicultural control of natural reproduction of lodgepole pine in the central Rocky Mountains. *J. Agr. Research* 38:229–243.

Belyea, R. M., and C. R. Sullivan. 1956. The white pine weevil: a review of current knowledge. *Forestry Chronicle* 32:58–67.

Carvell, K. L., and E. H. Tryon. 1961. The effect of environmental factors on the abundance of oak regeneration beneath mature oak stands. *Forest Sci.* 7:98–105.

Croker, T. C., Jr. 1956. Can the shelterwood method successfully regenerate longleaf pine? *J. Forestry* 54:258–260.

Curtis, R. O., and F. M. Rushmore. 1958. Some effects of stand density and deer browsing on reproduction in an Adirondack hardwood stand. *J. Forestry* 56:116–121.

Downs, A. A., and W. E. McQuilkin. 1944. Seed production of southern Appalachian oaks. *J. Forestry* 42:913–920.

Eyre, F. H., and P. Zehngraff. 1948. Red pine management in Minnesota. *USDA Circ.* 778.

Foster, C. H., and B. P. Kirkland. 1949. *The Charles Lathrop Pack Demonstration Forest, Warrensburg, N. Y. Results of twenty years of intensive forest management.* Charles L. Pack Forestry Foundation, Washington.

Gysel, L. W. 1957. Acorn production on good, medium, and poor oak sites in southern Michigan. *J. Forestry* 55:570–574.

Haig, I. T., K. P. Davis, and R. II. Weidman. 1941. Natural regeneration in the western white pine type. *USDA Tech. Bul.* 767.

Hallin, W. E. 1959. Release of sugar pine seedlings and saplings by harvest cutting. *PNWFRES Research Note* 179.

Horton, K. W., and G. H. D. Bedell. 1960. White and red pine, ecology, silviculture, and management. *Canada, Forestry Branch Bul.* 124.

Jemison, G. M. 1946. Rehabilitation of defective Appalachian hardwood stands. *J. Forestry* 44:944–948.

Jensen, V. S., and R. W. Wilson, Jr. 1951. Mowing of northern hardwood reproduction not profitable. *NEFES Northeastern Research Note* 3.

Jones, E. W. 1945. The structure and reproduction of the virgin forest of the north temperate zone. *New Phytologist* 44:130–148.

Korstian, C. F. 1927. Factors controlling germination and early survival in oaks. *Yale Univ. School of Forestry Bul.* 19.

Kuenzel, J. G., and J. R. McGuire. 1942. Response of chestnut oak reproduction to clear and partial cutting of overstory. *J. Forestry* 40:238–243.

Leffelman, L. J., and R. C. Hawley. 1925. Studies of Connecticut hardwoods: The treatment of advance growth arising as a result of thinnings and shelterwood cuttings. *Yale Univ. School of Forestry Bul.* 15.

Logan, K. T. 1959. Some effects of light on growth of white pine seedlings. *Canada, Forestry Branch, Forest Research Div. Tech. Note* 82.

Long, H. D. 1947. *The prevention of regeneration failures of pulpwood species.* Pulp and Paper Research Institute of Canada, Montreal.

Moss, V. D., and C. A. Wellner. 1953. Aiding blister rust control by silvicultural measures in the western white pine type. *USDA Circ.* 919.

Northeastern Forest Experiment Station. 1959. What's known about managing eastern white pine. *USDA Production Research Rept.* 38.

Robertson, W. M. 1945. Succession cutting in pine. *Canada, Dominion Forest Service, Silvicultural Research Note* 74.

Roeser, J., Jr. 1924. A study of Douglas fir reproduction under various cutting methods. *J. Agr. Research* 28:1233–1242.

Scholz, H. F. 1952. Age variability of northern red oak in the upper Mississippi woodlands. *J. Forestry* 50:518–521.

Scott, D. R. M. 1958. Forest ecology, as related to white pine silviculture in central Ontario. *Proc. Soc. Am. Foresters Meeting,* 1957:72–74.

Smith, D. M. 1951. The influence of seedbed conditions on the regeneration of eastern white pine. *Conn. AES Bul.* 545.

Sullivan, C. R. 1959. The effect of light and temperature on the behaviour of adults of the white pine weevil, *Pissodes strobi* Peck. *Canadian Entomologist* 91:213–232.

Trevor, G. 1938. Silvicultural systems. *Manual of Indian silviculture, Part II.* Oxford University Press, London. Pp. 307–318.

Troup, R. S. 1952. *Silvicultural systems,* 2nd ed. Edited by E. W. Jones. Oxford University Press, London. Pp. 28–108.

Tryon, H. H., and R. F. Finn. 1949. Twenty-year progress report, 1928–1948. *Black Rock Forest Bul.* 14.

Vaartaja, O.   1951.   Alikasvosasemasta vapautettujen männyn taimistojen toipumisesta ja merkityksestä metsänhoidossa.   (On the recovery of released pine advance growth and its silvicultural significance.)   *Acta Forestalia Fennica* 58 (3):1–133.   (English summary.)

Wagner, C.   1923.   *Der Blendersaumschlag und sein System,* 3rd ed.   Laupp, Tübingen.

Wellner, C. A.   1946.   Recent trends in silvicultural practice on national forests in the western white pine type.   *J. Forestry* 44:942–944.

———.   1948.   Light intensity related to stand density in mature stands of the western white pine type.   *J. Forestry* 46:16–19.

Westveld, M.   1931.   Reproduction on pulpwood lands in the Northeast.   *USDA Tech. Bull.* 223.

Wood, O. M.   1938.   Seedling reproduction of oak in southern New Jersey.   *Ecology* 19:276–293.

CHAPTER 14

The selection method

The term, **selection system,** is applied to any silvicultural program aimed at the creation or maintenance of uneven-aged stands; the **selection method** is employed for the regeneration of such stands. An uneven-aged stand contains at least three well-defined age classes.

There is no silvicultural system that is subject to a wider variety of interpretations. As was described in Chapter 10, there are a number of conflicting objectives that must be taken into account in the treatment of forests. The disharmony is so great in connection with the selection system that the system itself becomes almost incomprehensible unless the definitions are further qualified. The two qualifications applied in this chapter are not universally accepted nor are they the only ones possible, but they seem realistic and consistent.

The first qualification is that the constituent even-aged aggregations involved in this interpretation of the selection method are small. The second is that regulation of the cut by volume within a stand is *not* regarded as an essential characteristic of the selection method.

The need for a restricted definition arises from the fact that there is not, in the strictest sense of the term, any such thing as an uneven-aged stand. Even when a single large tree dies it is replaced, not by one new tree, but by many which appear nearly simultaneously. This is true even if the new trees are from advance regeneration. The uneven-aged stand is an artificial entity required for the comprehension of what might otherwise be a chaos of little "stands." The question of how large an even-aged aggregation must be to represent an individual stand depends entirely on the purpose for which one happens to be looking at the forest at the moment. If he is concerned about silviculture or harvesting, he may see many little even-aged stands; if he is concerned about such large-scale concepts as sustained yield, he can scarcely afford to consider small units.

In the essentially ecological viewpoint of silviculture, it is best to set an ecological definition on the minimum size of an even-aged stand as a simplifying assumption for this chapter. This is taken as the size of the largest opening entirely under the influence of adjacent mature timber. It is presumed that the opening of critical size would be that which, at the very center, exhibited the same temperature regime as any larger opening. Such an opening is probably about twice as wide as the height of the mature trees, but this is really a guess based on sketchy information.

It is traditional to assume that uneven-aged stands should be made into sustained-yield units and that the selection system is, therefore, practically synonymous with regulation of the cut by volume (Meyer et al., 1961). This view is difficult to reconcile with all the other considerations that must enter into both silviculture and forest management. The idea is born of attempts to make the stand, which is essentially a silvicultural unit, large enough to be a satisfactory unit of record keeping for sustained-yield management. Many such attempts envision the creation of intricately constructed, homogeneous, uneven-aged stands of very large sizes by silvicultural procedures which are usually unsound on both ecological and economic grounds. The procedures that would be involved are described later in this chapter in spite of the present writer's doubts about their feasibility.

The best way to resolve this particular conflict between silviculture and sustained-yield management is simply to recognize that each line of endeavor is best viewed on a different map scale. The stand is essential to silvicultural considerations but is too small in size and too changeable in its boundaries to be useful for record keeping (Davis, 1954). If a stand is not a sustained-yield unit there is rarely need to have much quantitative information about it. From the statistical standpoint, it takes almost as much effort to keep accurate records on a small tract as it does on a large one. It is no longer necessary to combine the mapping of stands with timber inventory work. The stand maps can be made from aerial photographs; in fact, the photographs themselves often make good stand maps with little further modification. Meanwhile, the continuing development of small-sample techniques and other improvements in mensurational work make sustained-yield management an ever more versatile procedure.

Silvicultural adjustments represent the only way that sustained yield can be achieved.   There are, however, so many different ways of making such adjustments and keeping track of the results that there is now little reason why the choice and conduct of silvicultural systems should be governed by attempts to facilitate the bookkeeping of sustained yield.   There are plenty of sound economic reasons for simplifying or otherwise altering stands, but these are more likely to involve operations in the woods than those which go on in the office.

Basic Procedure
In the selection method of reproduction, the mature timber is removed either as single scattered trees or in small groups at relatively short intervals; such cuttings are repeated indefinitely with the deliberate purpose and effect of creating or maintaining an uneven-aged stand.   This process depends on the establishment of reproduction at intervals and making it free to grow so that the continuing recruitment of new age classes is achieved.   The method is usually associated with natural reproduction but there is no reason why planting or artificial seeding could not be used.   True reproduction cutting is typically accomplished by cutting the oldest or largest trees.   The seed and any protection necessary for natural reproduction come from the trees that remain around the openings.

Intermediate cuttings may be made among the younger trees at the same time that the older or larger trees are removed.   Each immature even-aged aggregation is treated essentially as if it were a stand by itself.   Within the whole uneven-aged stand the periods of regeneration and intermediate cutting may thus extend through the entire rotation and be indistinguishable from one another.

Form of Stand Produced
The creation and perpetuation of uneven-aged stands is the most fundamental characteristic of the selection method.   The only essential requirement is that there be at least three successful reproduction cuttings during the equivalent of one rotation.   It should not be inferred that either the cuttings or the resulting age classes need be equally spaced in time.   Neither the development of the uneven-aged condition nor that of any specified distribution of age classes is an end in itself.   There must be an objective in having such a condition, and there is no reason to have any more age classes than are necessary.

The ordinary reason for maintaining most uneven-aged stands is merely the fact that they were inherited in that condition and cannot be rendered even-aged without cutting too many young trees prematurely.   It may also be that the desirable species reproduce and grow best or are least likely to suffer damage in the environment of an uneven-aged stand. Such purposes can be served without necessarily having the age classes spaced at equal intervals of time.

The only objective served by having evenly spaced age classes is that of making the stand a self-contained unit of sustained yield which will provide harvests of equal volumes of wood at regular intervals. It is better to mold the whole forest into a single sustained-yield unit composed of various combinations of even- and uneven-aged stands than to attempt to accomplish the purpose within stands. The procedures are basically the same whether they are applied to whole forests or to individual stands. The only reason for considering them here is that they become an integral part of the silvicultural treatment of stands from which sustained yield is sought.

Balanced Uneven-Aged Stands

A stand that is an ideal sustained-yield unit is **all-aged,** containing trees of every age class from 1-year seedlings to veterans of rotation age, with each class occupying an equal area. Since it requires at least a dozen 1-inch trees to cover the space eventually occupied by a single mature véteran, the diameter distribution approximates the smooth, "J-shaped" curve shown in Fig. 14-1A. Actually this kind of diameter distribution is more essential to sustained yield than the all-aged condition, although one cannot be obtained without the other. The term "uneven-aged" does not mean that every single 1-year age class is represented. The appropriate diameter distribution may exist if three, or preferably more, 20-year age classes are arranged so that they make up a single stand with a J-shaped distribution curve, as shown in Fig. 14-1B. A stand of this kind may be referred to as a **balanced uneven-aged stand,** although it can be treated as essentially all-aged. Stands that have several age classes but do not approximate the all-aged form are best designated **irregular uneven-aged stands** (Fig. 14-1D).

The configuration of the proper J-shaped curve is, according to the hypothesis of de Liocourt, convertible to a straight line if the logarithms of the numbers of trees are plotted over the arithmetical diameters (Meyer et al., 1961; Sammi, 1961). The slope of the straight lines involved is not the same for stands of all species. It is governed by the interdependent factors of (1) rate of diameter growth of the trees at different ages or sizes, (2) the varying amounts of growing space needed by trees if they are to increase in diameter at such rates, and (3) the largest diameter to which the final crop trees are to be grown.

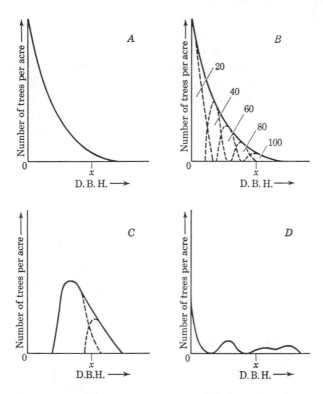

Fig. 14-1. Several types of diameter distributions found in uneven-aged stands. *A* shows the distribution curve of an all-aged stand of 1 acre containing sufficient trees in each diameter class to produce an unvarying number of trees of optimum size (of diameter *x* or larger) at rotation age. *B* indicates how a balanced uneven-aged stand of the same diameter distribution may be composed of five age classes, each occupying an equal area, with a 100-year rotation. *C* represents a stand with two closely spaced age classes and no advance reproduction. Uncritically supervised selection cuttings in stands of this kind will produce abnormally high yields of timber until all existing trees reach optimum size; thereafter they will yield nothing until the new growth reaches merchantable size. It is difficult to create the balanced distribution in such stands in one rotation period, especially if the smaller trees do not respond to release after selection cuttings. *D* shows one of the many kinds of irregular uneven-aged distributions which may be found in virgin stands. This one contains four well-distributed age classes, one of which is well beyond optimum age for a commercial rotation. Such a stand could be gradually converted to the balanced form provided that the intermediate age classes did not deteriorate after partial cutting.

The straight-line logarithmic relationships do not appear to allow for enough trees in the seedling and sapling sizes.

One can sometimes make another approximation of the proper distribution of diameters by deducing it from yield tables for even-aged stands of the same species growing under comparable schedules for regulation of stand density on similar sites. The procedure is to determine how many trees there would be in each diameter class in a whole series of 1-acre even-aged stands covering the desired range of age. The resulting figures are taken as indicating the appropriate distribution of diameters in a balanced selection stand of as many acres as there were age classes used in the computations. In other words, a balanced uneven-aged *stand* would have as many trees in each diameter class as a balanced (or "normal") *forest* that was composed of even-aged stands, covered an equal area, and contained the same age classes.

There are indications, however, that a balanced uneven-aged stand actually has somewhat fewer small trees and more big ones than a comparable even-aged forest (Bourne, 1951; Walker, 1956). This results from the fact that areas laid bare by the removal of the oldest trees are reoccupied partly by new reproduction and partly by the expanding crowns of adjacent groups of intermediate age. Therefore, the area covered by each small even-aged group tends to increase as it grows older. In the process each group tends to be subjected to decreasing competition with the passage of time because it is gradually allowed to expand into parts of areas vacated by older groups. Consequently trees in the well-managed selection stand tend to accelerate in growth during middle age, which is the reverse of the situation in an even-aged stand. The magnitude of this effect is greatest where each age group is reduced to one tree at maturity because the total perimeter per acre of boundaries between little even-aged groups is at a maximum. If the even-aged aggregations were large, this particular effect would be correspondingly small.

If the species are sufficiently tolerant that advance reproduction can become established and make any significant growth under older trees, a similar kind of increase of efficiency of diameter distribution and utilization of growing space will result. This phenomenon also reduces the amount of growing space that need be taken from large trees and allocated exclusively to seedlings and saplings. This is the same effect that was discussed at greater length in connection with the shelterwood method; the opportunity to use it depends more on the ecological characteristics of the species than on whether the stand is even- or uneven-aged.

Both of the effects described in the two paragraphs above theoretically enable the creation of a growing stock capable of providing a sustained yield and consisting of more large trees and fewer small ones than would be the case in a whole "balanced" forest of large, simple even-aged stands. As was noted in connection with thinning, a cubic foot of wood laid down on large trees is of greater utility and value than the same volume added to several small ones. This is especially important if trees are being grown for saw timber, because the yield is measured in board feet; furthermore, wide boards are worth more than narrow ones.

Each of the phenomena, but especially that in which young trees start under old, also reduce the length of time that area is allocated to the small trees that do not fully occupy the soil and have not yet become tall enough to support all the foliage that can be produced. To the extent that more complete utilization of growing space is thus attained, the total production of wood is at least theoretically increased.

The measurement of growth is so frustrating that the magnitude of these effects, if they exist, has never been precisely determined. Evidence gathered by Burger (1942) in Switzerland did not indicate that total production of wood was significantly affected by the distribution of age classes within stands. However, it is possible that a comparison in terms of board-foot volume might have produced a different result. Walker (1956) concluded from observations of oak stands in Pennsylvania that uneven-aged stands actually grew less in cubic- and board-foot volume than comparable even-aged stands. He pointed out, however, that the growth of the uneven-aged stand might be more valuable because of the higher proportion of large trees on which the wood was laid.

As was pointed out in Chapter 2, trees that are large and old do not have the physiological capacity to use a given unit of growing space as efficiently as smaller and younger trees. This effect must to some extent offset the advantage gained by allocating space to old trees at the expense of younger ones.

Until it can be shown that the diameter distribution of intimate mixtures of age classes does make such stands substantially more efficient than forests of even-aged stands in the production of volume or value, it seems most logical to proceed on the assumption that the differences are small.

In a balanced uneven-aged stand there is theoretically a stable equilibrium between growth, harvested yield (assuming no loss through unsalvaged mortality), and reproduction. Growth remains constant from decade to decade, and, if a volume equal to decennial growth is removed by cutting an appropriate number of the largest trees during each decade, the reproduction developing on the area exposed should be just sufficient to maintain the balance. It should be noted that this ideal condition may be approached but is almost never achieved, at least in a single stand.

The balanced uneven-aged form is rarely found even in virgin stands. It has been observed in some stands of old-growth timber representing late successional stages, such as mixtures of eastern hemlock, sugar maple, and beech in Pennsylvania (Hough and Forbes, 1943; Meyer and Stevenson, 1943). Virgin stands of relatively intolerant species, like eastern white pine, tend to be even-aged. Most virgin stands, regardless of successional status, have an irregular distribution of age and diameter classes, exemplified by Fig. 14-1D, in which certain young or middle-aged categories may be lacking. A balanced uneven-aged stand can come into existence naturally only if an originally even-aged stand is gradually replaced as a result of a long series of minor catastrophes occurring at regular intervals. This sequence of events is purely fortuitous, because both the severity and the frequency of the attacks of damaging agencies are ordinarily irregular. Therefore, the balanced selection stand is best regarded as something that can exist only if created by careful silvicultural treatment over a long period.

Table 14-1 shows the tentative diameter distributions and other data that embody a silvicultural system recommended for the uneven-aged management of southern bottomland hardwoods. Reference may be made to comparable distributions for northern hardwoods (Meyer, 1952; Eyre and Zillgitt, 1953; Gilbert and Jenson, 1958) and loblolly pine (Reynolds, 1959). Diameter distributions of this sort are usually based on a combination of mensurational data, theoretical considerations, and experience with selection cuttings. A perfect diameter distribution would be one that was found to remain stable throughout an entire rotation, except for fluctuations due to the periodic cuttings. It would probably take several rotations of trial and error to achieve and prove the existence of this state of perfection. Management can proceed effectively enough even if the conformity to such provisional guides is only approximate. However, the actual diameter distributions must be watched for the development of obvious imbalances so that appropriate adjustments can be made.

In theory, the oldest age class in a balanced all-aged stand is cut each year, the next oldest in the following year, and so on indefinitely. Ideally, the reproduction springs up in the openings immediately after

Table 14-1.   Diameter distribution of trees cut and left on an average acre of good site at the end of each 10-year cutting cycle in an intensively managed stand of southern bottomland hardwoods (Putnam, Furnival, and McKnight, 1960)

D.B.H., (in.)	Trees Left after Cutting			Trees Cut		
	Number of Trees	Basal Area (sq. ft.)	Bd.-ft. Volume (Doyle Rule)	Number of Trees	Basal Area (sq. ft.)	Bd.-ft. Volume (Doyle Rule)
2	26.0	0.58		22.0	0.48	
4	17.2	1.50		12.8	1.11	
6	10.5	2.07		5.3	1.03	
8	8.2	2.86		4.0	1.41	
10	7.0	3.82		2.0	1.10	
12	6.5	5.10		.1	.08	
Total	75.4	15.93		46.2	5.21	
14	6.0	6.41	312	—	—	—
16	5.3	7.40	503	.40	.56	38
18	4.3	7.60	632	1.30	2.30	191
20	3.2	6.98	688	2.10	4.58	451
22	2.3	6.07	678	2.00	5.28	590
24	1.6	5.03	524	1.60	5.03	724
26	1.1	4.06	561	1.20	4.42	609
28	.8	3.42	524	.80	3.42	524
30	.45	2.21	369	.65	3.19	533
32	.27	1.51	272	.53	2.96	532
34	.11	.69	139	.34	2.14	408
36	.04	.28	57	.23	1.63	335
38	.02	.16	28	.10	.79	163
40	—	—	—	.04	.35	76
42	—	—	—	.02	.19	37
Total	25.49	51.82	5287	11.31	36.84	5211
All trees	100.89	67.75	5287	57.51	42.05	5211

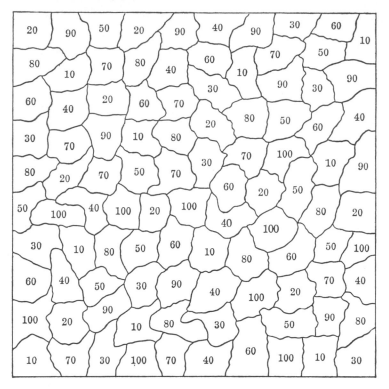

Fig. 14-2. A 1-acre portion of an ideal single-tree selection stand managed on a rotation of 100 years under a 10-year cutting cycle. Ten age classes are represented, each occupying approximately one-tenth of the area. The numbers indicate the ages of the individual groups of trees.

cuttings. By the time every age class in an all-aged stand has been cut over once, the seedlings started on the area occupied by the age class that was cut first will have matured. Thus in a truly all-aged stand an old age class, consisting of scattered, single trees, ripe for cutting, will be available each year. The volume of this age class will be equivalent to the annual growth of the whole stand. Each age class should occupy its proper percentage of the area. For example, if there are 100 age classes, each class should have 1 per cent of the crown space allotted to it; then if 1 per cent of the area, in this instance, is annually cleared of trees, only the trees belonging to the oldest age class will be removed. Since the trees making up the oldest age class are single, scattered individuals, it is necessary to work through the whole stand to find and harvest them each year. If the whole forest were managed as a single all-aged stand, operations would have to cover the entire forest annually.

In practice, considerations of both logging and silviculture necessitate certain changes in this theoretical procedure. The annual working of the whole area to secure a small cut per acre makes logging expensive. Therefore, a definite **cutting cycle** or period between cuttings is established. Under this scheme the entire forest is not cut over each year, but is divided into as many portions as there are years in the cutting cycle (Figs. 14-2 and 14-3). All selection cuttings made in a given year are restricted to one of these areas and no further harvest cuttings are carried out there until the next cutting cycle. The volume removed from any one of these portions is theoretically equal to the growth during one cutting cycle. Cuttings in successive years progress from one area to another and finally, after the cutting cycle is ended, return to the first area. The interval between cuts on a given area determines the length of the cutting cycle, which may vary from several years to several decades under American practice.

Creation of balanced uneven-aged stands. It has been necessary to dwell at some length on the principles involved in maintaining the

Stand 1 contains age classes: 1, 11, 21, 31, 41, 51, 61, 71, 81, and 91	*Stand 2* contains age classes: 2, 12, 22, 32, 42, 52, 62, 72, 82, and 92	*Stand 3* contains age classes: 3, 13, 23, 33, 43, 53, 63, 73, 83, and 93	*Stand 4* contains age classes: 4, 14, 24, 34, 44, 54, 64, 74, 84, and 94	*Stand 5* contains age classes: 5, 15, 25, 35, 45, 55, 65, 75, 85, and 95
Stand 6 contains age classes: 6, 16, 26, 36, 46, 56, 66, 76, 86, and 96	*Stand 7* contains age classes: 7, 17, 27, 37, 47, 57, 67, 77, 87, and 97	*Stand 8* contains age classes: 8, 18, 28, 38, 48, 58, 68, 78, 88, and 98	*Stand 9* contains age classes: 9, 19, 29, 39, 49, 59, 69, 79, 89, and 99	*Stand 10* contains age classes: 10, 20, 30, 40, 50, 60, 70, 80, 90, and 100

Fig. 14-3. Diagram of a selection forest managed on a rotation of 100 years with a cutting cycle of 10 years. The forest contains ten stands, one of which is cut through each year, thus giving equal annual cuts. Each stand contains ten age classes, and together the age classes in the ten stands form a continuous series of ages from 1 to 100 years.

balanced distribution of age and diameter classes in stands that have already been brought to this condition. However, such stands exist far more often in print than in nature so the procedure for creating reasonable approximations of them is really more important.

Theoretically an absolutely even-aged stand can be replaced by a balanced uneven-aged stand during the period of one rotation. If the new stand is to have five age classes with a rotation of 100 years, all that is necessary is to conduct cuttings leading to the establishment of reproduction on one-fifth of the area at 20-year intervals. This necessarily means that some parts of the stand must be cut before or after the age of economic maturity. The disadvantages of such awkward timing of the harvests can sometimes be mitigated if any parts of the stand that mature early are replaced first and those that continue to increase in value longest are cut last. The conversion will be successful only to the extent that the cuttings are appropriately timed and heavy enough to lead to the establishment of the age classes and species of reproduction desired. It is usually a fallacy to pretend that the large trees of essentially even-aged stands are older than the small ones and to attempt to make the conversion by successive cuttings of dominants.

The creation of balanced uneven-aged stands can be carried out more rapidly and easily in stands that already contain several age classes in irregular distribution. It will still be necessary to make the sacrifice represented by cutting some trees earlier or later than might otherwise be desirable. Sometimes small, relatively old trees of the lower crown classes can be substituted for nonexistent dominants of the same size and younger age, thus inventing "age" classes that might otherwise take decades to grow from seedlings. This short-cut is useful to the extent that the trees involved can withstand exposure and return to full vigor. However, it is a procedure that sometimes becomes so attractive that it is indulged in to the exclusion of the creation of the new age classes of seedlings that must be continually recruited and made free to grow if the balanced distribution of age classes is to be completely developed.

The readjustment of the age-class distribution of a stand is likely to be accomplished with least sacrifice of other objectives if it is prosecuted slowly. Several rotations might well be required to transform essentially even-aged stands to the balanced uneven-aged form; it is logical to wonder whether silvicultural policies would remain stable over such a long period.

Procedures and precautions necessary for sustained yield. If the stand is to be treated as a sustained-yield unit and the whole forest consists of similarly treated stands, any errors that lead to the over-cutting of stands may endanger the continuity of operations on the whole property.

The basic procedures of regulating the cut are the same whether the sustained-yield unit is 100 acres or 100,000. The main essential is to develop a **normal** distribution of age classes, that is, an arrangement in which all classes, from the youngest to those of rotation age, are represented by equal areas. If, as under even-aged management, the areas and ages of all stands can be readily determined, this can be done by area regulation. Under complete uneven-aged management the areas of individual age classes are so small and scattered that the allowable cut must be determined in relation to the annual (or decennial) growth of the stand. This depends, in turn, on knowing and regulating the distribution of numbers, volumes, or basal areas of trees of different diameter classes.

Under either kind of management, an attempt is made to arrive at an average distribution of diameters which will coincide with the appropriate J-shaped curve (Fig. 14-1A). Once this perfect balance is secured the total annual cut of the forest can be equal to the annual growth without endangering future yields. If there is a surplus of trees of mature size, the annual harvest may actually exceed the growth until the balanced distribution is created. If there is a deficiency of trees of optimum size, the annual cut must be less than the growth so long as this condition prevails. *A surplus in one part of the diameter distribution can exist only if there is a compensating deficiency in another.*

The degree of precision of regulation of the cut necessary for the maintenance or creation of any real approximation of a balanced, uneven-aged stand cannot be achieved without making an inventory of the stand before marking it for cutting. Usually this involves determining the distribution of diameter classes by basal area or numbers of trees per acre. The prospective cut is then allocated among the various diameter classes on the basis of a comparison between the actual distribution and that which is assumed to represent the balanced condition.

The use of volume regulation for sustained yield is not a technique that works in the absence of an understanding of the numerous sources of error. The risk of error is greatest when individual unbalanced stands are being converted to the proper distribution of age and diameter classes.

The most important source of error is the temptation to regard stands as balanced and uneven-aged when they are not. A stand can have a diameter distribution that plots as a J-shaped curve on arithmetic axes or even as a straight line logarithmically and still be far from balanced. Regardless of what may be said about the validity of those specific straight-line logarithmic relationships that are recommended, it is clear that not just any such relationship is satisfactory.

An even more reprehensible error, not uncommon, is that of treating even-aged stands as if they were balanced and uneven-aged. This folly ordinarily starts with the lazy assumption that stands are uneven-aged if they merely exhibit a broad *range* of diameter classes. It is especially easy to be deluded in mixed, even-aged stands composed of species that develop at different rates. A balanced uneven-aged stand simply cannot have a canopy that is smooth on top or open at any level beneath nor can the trees of pole size out-number the saplings. These characteristics are associated more with even-aged stands, which have a strong tendency to remain even-aged regardless of treatment.

The practice of ignoring small trees in timber inventories leads to misapprehensions about the diameter distribution of uneven-aged stands, especially if the proper distribution is not well known. If no real account is made of small trees and almost anything that looks like a J-shaped diameter distribution of larger trees is accepted, it becomes all too easy to ignore the necessity of continuing recruitment of seedlings and saplings. The greatest danger of misapprehension exists with such distributions as those shown in Fig. 14-1, *C* and *D*.

If several species are present, there is a strong tendency for the more tolerant ones to predominate in the reproduction, thus endangering the sustained yield of any desirable intolerant species present in the larger diameter classes. The tendency can be combatted only by attempting to make the cuttings heavy enough to provide the proper environmental conditions for the desired species of reproduction and, if necessary, by release cutting. Advance reproduction has many desirable attributes but begins to make a positive contribution to sustained yield only when it is made open to the sky and becomes free to grow.

As its name implies, the volume method of regulation is often applied such that the estimates of growth and growing stock are made largely in terms of volume. Although most of this discussion has involved reference to the distribution of *numbers of trees* per acre with respect to D.B.H., the actual application often involves distribution of volume with respect to D.B.H. The distribution of basal area can also be used and is not as subject to the errors possible when volume is used.

The measurement of the volume of trees and stands is inherently subject to error; the risk of error is compounded by the necessity of estimating growth from the difference between two sets of fallible volume estimates.   Careful allowances must also be made for the components of (1) growth on trees present at beginning and end of period, (2) unsalvaged mortality during the period, (3) volume harvested during the period, and (4) "ingrowth" (Gilbert, 1954).   Ingrowth takes place when trees pass some arbitrary minimum diameter and are counted for the first time; its contribution to growth can be large because the trees suddenly acquire a substantial volume that was really laid down mostly before the start of the measurement period. In the typical unbalanced stand, the magnitude of these components fluctuates markedly from period to period.

There is even more opportunity for error if volume estimates are made in board feet rather than cubic feet.   The ingrowth, a component always difficult to assess properly, is usually very large when measured in board feet.   The board-foot volume of a tree increases so rapidly with diameter that small fluctuations in the diameter distribution cause remarkable differences in the apparent growth.   This phenomenon is accentuated by the use of misleading log rules; with the Doyle Rule, for example, there are overestimates of growth in diameter classes less than 22 inches.

The assumption that the allowable annual cut is equal to the annual growth is valid only if the distribution of diameter classes is balanced.   If a stand is overstocked with older age classes and deficient in the younger ones, the annual growth is greater than that of a balanced stand; annual harvests conducted at an equivalent rate are greater than can be indefinitely sustained.   The best way to guard against this dangerous kind of error is to check the estimates against the mean annual increment of even-aged stands of the same composition, managed with comparable intensity on similar sites with rotations of the same length.

It is usually necessary for purposes that are basically economic to know the volume of the growing stock and its growth in terms of merchantable units of volume (Wahlenberg, 1956).   These quantities are in one way or another based on measurements of tree diameter, basal area, and cubic volume; they can be determined after the computations involved in regulating the cut as readily as they could have if used in the regulatory calculations.   It is, for example, useful to know that in uneven-aged stands of northern hardwoods in Upper Michigan the reservation of 4000 to 7000 board feet per acre will, with a 15-year cutting cycle, give best growth and highest compound interest on investment in growing stock (Eyre and Zillgitt, 1953). However, the characteristics of this growing stock are more easily and reliably regulated in terms of the distribution of numbers of trees or basal area than of board-foot volume with respect to diameter.

Once the appropriate distribution of age classes has been converted to a diameter distribution and created in a stand, it is necessary to consider the small but crucial changes that will be made in the diameter distribution at the time of each cutting. Selection cuttings in such

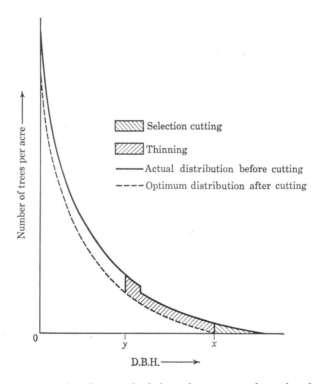

Fig. 14-4. Diameter distribution of a balanced uneven-aged stand under intensive management, indicating the number of trees of different diameter classes theoretically removed in a single cutting. All trees larger than diameter x, which has been set as the index of rotation age, are removed. The trees of smaller diameter may also be reduced in number by thinning, provided that they are larger than the tree of lowest diameter (y) which can be profitably utilized. Under extensive practice there would have been no cutting of trees less than diameter x and most of those represented above as being cut in thinnings would have been lost through natural suppression.

stands involve successive harvests of the *largest* trees in a stand; the age of these trees relative to that of their neighbors is actually a secondary consideration.

A diameter limit (point x in Fig. 14-4) is established as an indication of age, with the understanding that trees below this size are in general to be reserved and those above cut. This diameter limit should be regarded as a flexible guide rather than as a rigid dividing line. Depending on their silvicultural condition, especially capacity for further increase in value, a few trees above the limit should be left and some below the limit should be removed.

Under intensive practice, true thinning may be conducted simultaneously with the harvest cutting. Such thinning must be carefully distinguished from the harvest of the oldest trees and should take place in clumps of trees too young for harvest cutting. The methods of thinning followed are the same as those employed in even-aged stands. Unlike the harvest cuttings, the thinnings should not remove the largest trees in the various clumps, unless they are of undesirable form or species. The primary objective of the thinnings should be to anticipate the inevitable reduction of numbers denoted by the steep slope of the "J-shaped" curve (Fig. 14-4), so as to salvage prospective mortality and allow the remaining trees space for more rapid growth.

Irregular Uneven-Aged Stands

The only real objective of the balanced arrangement is that of making the stand a sustained-yield unit. There is no need to apply the regulatory procedures that have just been discussed to a stand unless it must provide a sustained yield. Usually the whole forest rather than the stand is the unit from which sustained yield is necessary. The objective can be attained far more easily and quickly by integrating many stands in such manner that the deficiencies of essential age or diameter classes in some stands are compensated by the surpluses in others. In this way a balanced condition can be obtained for the forest without attempting thorough readjustment of any individual stands.

If an entire forest ownership consists of one stand of about 20 acres or less and is required to produce a sustained yield, it would probably be essential to develop a balanced uneven-aged stand. While such small ownerships are numerous, it is seldom realistic to assume that the individuals likely to own such tracts are in an economic position to have any serious interest in developing perfect sustained yield.

There are numerous valid reasons other than sustained yield for deliberate maintenance of uneven-aged stands. These other objectives can be achieved without the balanced arrangement. Long-continued application of the concept of financial maturity in efforts to extract optimum value from the growing stock is very likely to cause the development of uneven-aged stands. If this concept is the best key to intelligent management of an uneven-aged stand, it is as logical to use the selection system as it would be to employ the shelterwood system under similar circumstances in an even-aged stand. However, the sequences of cutting necessary for sustained yield and those guided by the concept of financial maturity are usually compatible only in uneven-aged stands that are already balanced and composed of good trees. If the diameter distribution is unbalanced, it can be brought into balance only by cutting some trees long before or long after they are financially mature.

The maintenance of some sort of uneven-aged arrangement may be desirable in some instances only because it ensures a permanent seed source in the stand, creates an environment required for reproduction of certain species, or makes the whole stand more resistant to damaging agencies. There may even be no other reason than ensuring the continued representation of some large, handsome trees in stands of recreational significance. Requirements of this sort may necessitate uneven-aged stands but not necessarily balanced ones. In fact, forthright attempts to create the balanced condition easily conflict with the attainment of other important objectives of stand management.

The detailed timber inventories and other computational work necessary to develop and maintain balanced uneven-aged stands require much attention from highly trained personnel who often have more productive things to do with their time.

In other words, adoption of the selection system does not necessitate development of the balanced arrangement. It is feasible to maintain an unbalanced uneven-aged stand indefinitely and reap any benefits, other than sustained yield, that may be induced by the uneven-aged arrangement. The distribution of age and diameter classes can be allowed to fluctuate almost at random, except to the extent that the cutting or reservation of particular classes must be adjusted to balance the books of sustained yield for the whole forest. In this kind of management, the allowable cut and its approximate distribution among diameter classes are determined for the entire forest and then harvests are made in various stands on the basis of other considerations, silvicultural and otherwise, until the scheduled volume and kinds of trees are cut.

Modifications of the Method

Single-tree selection method.   In this form of the method each little even-aged component of the uneven-aged stand occupies the space created by the removal of a single mature individual or exceedingly small clumps consisting of several such trees (Fig. 14-5).   The development of reproduction in the very small, scattered openings thus created is the main characteristic of the method.   The species most likely to be perpetuated are those that are very tolerant, although the opening left by the removal of even a single large tree will, if site conditions are otherwise favorable, allow the establishment of a few trees representing early successional stages.   The species com-

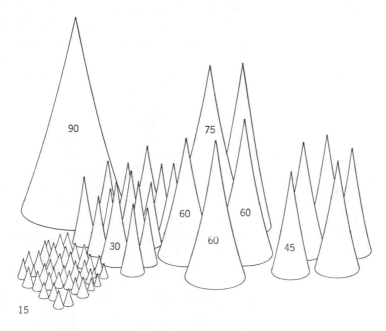

Fig. 14-5.   Schematic oblique view of a ¼-acre segments of a balanced uneven-aged stand being managed by the single-tree selection system on a 90-year rotation with a 15-year cutting cycle.   Each tree is represented by a cone extending to the ground; the numbers indicate ages.   Each age group occupies about ½₄ acre.   The 90-year-old tree is now ready to be replaced by numerous seedlings while the numbers of trees in the middle-aged groups are appropriately reduced by thinning.

position of the reproduction depends as much on the competitive influence of adjacent trees and the way that they are subsequently treated as it does on the size of the holes initially created.

The space left by the removal of each mature tree must be filled by numerous seedlings which are reduced to roughly a dozen saplings as the clump develops. The number of trees is gradually reduced either by thinning or through natural competition until but one tree is left at the end of the rotation for each that was initially cut.

The single-tree selection method has been regarded as the ultimate ideal by some advocates of the naturalistic doctrine of silviculture. The basis for this contention is the theory that climax stands eventually become balanced and develop into the same form created by the single-tree selection method. Actually there is no evidence to indicate that this delicately balanced state is commonly reached in nature or that any clearly decisive advantage is secured by creating it.

The only good examples of intensive management under the single-tree selection method are to be found in the mixed forests of fir, spruce, and beech in some of the high terrain of Central and Western Europe. The success of the selection system in these localities is often the result of the high quality of the European silver fir which tends to predominate in the stands and cannot be reproduced in distinctly even-aged stands (Knuchel, 1953; Köstler, 1956). Unlike most true firs, this tolerant species can be grown on a long rotation without serious loss from decay. The irregular shelterwood method is actually employed fully as often as methods designed to maintain truly uneven-aged stands.

The popularity of the single-tree selection method has arisen at least partly from the desire to emulate this fine and renowned example of skillful silviculture. This imitation may represent an attempt to expand a rather special kind of regional silviculture into a method suitable for all forests that are not pure and even-aged. In any event, efforts to copy the method have not met with equal success in other parts of Europe or elsewhere. It has, for example, failed as a means of regenerating and managing Norway spruce in Scandinavia. However, true single-tree selection cutting has not been tested long enough in any American forest type composed of tolerant species to determine the real extent of its applicability.

Logging under the single-tree selection method is both difficult and expensive, especially if the cuttings are made frequently and lightly with the precautions necessary to protect young growth.

Really successful applications of this method involve intensive silvicultural practice.   On the other hand, it is used in crude fashion, with very erratic results, in situations where only large trees can be utilized profitably.   Certain aspects of this and other applications of the selection method under extensive practice will be discussed in a subsequent section.

Group-selection method.   This modification of the selection method is more readily adapted to a wide variety of conditions than any other because the ecological requirements of most species can be met within its framework.   The sizes of the even-aged aggregations vary from those created by the removal of two or more mature trees up to those which are twice as wide as the mature trees.   This kind of cutting has real ecological significance because such openings are neither well ventilated nor very effectively shielded from sun and frost by the adjacent trees.   Consequently they are subject to a wide diurnal range of temperature which some species can endure better than others.   Geiger (1957) found that this effect was most accentuated in Norway spruce stands when the width of openings was one-and-a-half times the height of the surrounding timber.

Methods of cutting that create larger even-aged aggregations are sometimes called group-selection cutting.   The only real reason for doing so is the desire to avoid recognizing the "groups" as stands in mapping or other administrative operations.   It seems better to handle this semantic dilemma by regarding the stands as uneven-aged with **large** groups than to include, under the classification of selection cutting, operations that sometimes involve the clearcutting of a dozen acres.

There is no reason why all the mature trees of a group must be cut at a single time.   If desirable because of the ecological requirements for reproduction, need for application of the financial-maturity concept, or some other valid consideration, the groups can be reproduced by small-scale applications of the shelterwood and seed-tree methods. The group-selection method is not one procedure but a category including many variations that could be separated only with difficulty and by the use of complicated terminology.

The type of uneven-aged stand that might be created by clearcutting small groups will be illustrated in Fig. 16-2; this is a sample of only one of the many variations possible under this system and is more complicated than most.

The group-selection method has certain definite advantages over single-tree selection cutting.   Harvesting of the older trees can be carried out somewhat more cheaply and with less damage to the residual stand. There is greater latitude for creating the kind of environmental conditions necessary for reproduction. The trees develop in clearly defined even-aged aggregations; this is of substantial advantage in developing good form in many species, especially in hardwoods. This modification is also more readily applied to stands which have become uneven-aged through natural processes because such stands are more likely to contain even-aged groups of mature trees than a mixture of age classes by single trees. Furthermore, the openings created are large enough that the progress of regeneration and the growth of younger age classes are more readily apparent.

It is important to consider the significance of the effects involved in having trees growing on the edges of even-aged aggregations. The total perimeter of such edges is, of course, at a maximum with the single-tree selection method. The effects are both beneficial and harmful but vary according to the circumstances. Influences on reproduction are beneficial to the extent that side-shade protects young seedlings. However, the competition of the older trees is detrimental if competition for soil moisture and nutrients is serious. The roots of the older trees are not only capable of spreading out into the newly created openings, they may even do so automatically if they are already attached to the roots of the cut trees through intraspecific root grafts. On the other hand, this lateral expansion of the roots and crowns of older trees along the edges of groups is precisely the same effect that makes it possible to allocate more area to the growth of large trees than is the case with forests of even-aged stands.

The juxtaposition of different age classes provides an opportunity to release the young trees along each edge once each rotation when the older adjoining groups are harvested. This takes the place of one heavy thinning and is of some advantage when ordinary thinning must be long delayed or is not feasible. The effects of this phenomenon on the form of the edge trees vary considerably depending on the species and circumstances. The development of large branches is forestalled as long as there are larger trees at the side but the effect is reversed when the larger trees are removed. Distinctly phototropic species, such as most of the hardwoods, do not fare well because of the tendency of the stems to bend outward toward the light or to become crooked if the terminal shoots are battered by the crowns of taller trees. This is not so true of distinctly geotropic species like conifers which tend to grow straight under all circumstances. In climates subject to wet, clinging snows, any trees growing beside taller conifers are likely to be broken or ruined when accumulations of snow suddenly slide off the higher crowns.

Many species of wildlife profit from the combination of environmental conditions existing along the boundaries between very young groups and older trees. Several different kinds of protective cover are available in close proximity to the variety of food plants that may be fostered by the broad spectrum of microclimatic conditions existing between the edges and the centers of the young groups.

In the application of the group-selection method it is logical to weigh the relative advantages and disadvantages of growing trees along the edges of groups. If the advantages outweigh the disadvantages, an effort may be made to increase the length of group perimeter per acre by creating smaller groups.

There is no necessity that the individual groups in one stand be uniform in size, shape, or arrangement, nor is it necessary that one age class be represented by a single group. In fact, if proper advantage is taken of the existence of groups of different ages when an irregularly uneven-aged stand is placed under management, such regularity is unlikely. A systematic arrangement of individual groups would be convenient but is usually almost impossible to secure. If the total area occupied by different age classes can be determined with a fair degree of accuracy, the cut under the group-selection method can be regulated by area as well as by volume.

Strip-selection method. In both the single-tree and group-selection methods, the timber of the oldest age class is scattered through the stand and must often be extracted across areas under regeneration. The attendant difficulties of logging and administration may be alleviated by bringing all the trees of each class together in a separate part of the stand. This is best done by the strip-selection method in which each age class is concentrated in a long, narrow strip. The adjoining age classes on the two sides are respectively younger and older than the strip between. A complete series of age classes from reproduction to mature timber may thus be formed in consecutive order. This kind of arrangement is similar to the strip-shelterwood method, except that it has the objective of securing a complete range of age classes across the whole series of strips.

This arrangement enables the transportation of logs through the next strip to be harvested. There is ample opportunity to obtain reproduction under an overwood as in the shelterwood method. Successive cuttings should progress toward the south or against the direction of the most dangerous winds, as in the strip-shelterwood method. If protection against wind is desired, the strip-selection method has the additional advantage of creating a stand that is streamlined so that the main force of strong winds is diverted up and over the stand

(Fig. 14-6). This pattern of cutting is often used for natural regeneration of Norway spruce in central Europe (Troup, 1952; Köstler, 1956).

The same general arrangement was proposed by Anderson (1960) as a means of increasing the amount and duration of storage of snow in drifts on southerly slopes in the Sierra Nevada where the yield of water is a major consideration. If the strips are made parallel to the contour and are advanced downslope and southward, the drifts tend to accumulate along the southern margins of the openings because of eddying effects that decrease the speed of the southwesterly storm winds in the lee of the tall timber. The melting of such drifts is decelerated not only because of their depth but also because of the shade. The duration of melting can be extended even longer if the strips are L-shaped with a short extension of the strip running upslope at a right angle with the main contour-strip. This increases the amount of air that is cooled by nocturnal radiation and can flow down to chill the drifts along the contour. The successive, parallel strips would have to advance diagonally rather than at a right angle to the long axis of the strips.

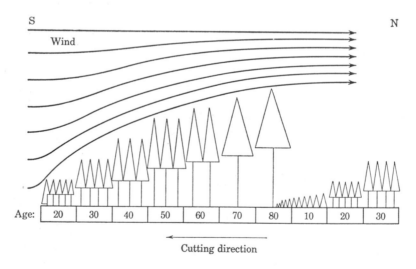

Fig. 14-6. Cross section along a north-south axis through a portion of a stand reproduced by the strip-selection method and managed on an 80-year rotation with a cutting cycle of 10 years. By this means the stand is streamlined against southerly winds and regeneration is protected from the direct rays of the sun. Cutting progresses from north to south; the 80-year-old strip is about to be cut clear.

The oustanding drawback of the strip-selection arrangement is the difficulty of creating it. The sequence of age classes is highly artificial and radically different from any likely to be found in nature.

The continuous forest or "Dauerwald." The concept of the "continuous forest" involves the intensive management of uneven-aged stands without systematic programs of silvicultural treatment or adjustment of the arrangement of diameter or age classes (Troup, 1952). It was developed early in the present century by a few German foresters more or less as a reaction against all policies of strict regimentation of stands for management purposes. No definite rotation age is recognized and no special plans are made for securing reproduction. All efforts are concentrated on tending the individual trees which are provided ample room for growth by frequent cuttings. They are retained just as long as their growth is satisfactory and they do not interfere with better trees. Inevitably the time comes when each tree should be harvested and any measures to replace it with natural regeneration are likely to be limited to the control of undesirable vegetation.

The one guiding principle recognizable in the idea of the Dauerwald is that of harvesting trees according to the concept of financial maturity, even though adherence to this principle may be entirely intuitive. In any event, it is this part of the idea that has been most vigorously espoused by such American foresters as Reynolds (1959).

The lack of attention to reproduction that is associated with this scheme would hardly seem to be a mandatory feature of the handling of something labelled a "continuous forest." This notion probably arose because the practice happened to be introduced first in localities where natural regeneration became established almost automatically when needed.

Lack of concern for reproduction also arises from unwillingness, conscious or otherwise, to accept the necessity of allocating growing space to regeneration. As long as an area is kept stocked mainly with the middle and older age classes the current annual increment of merchantable volume remains higher than the average that can be maintained in a stand or forest in which all the age classes are equally represented. This increased increment can be maintained for long periods but, when the large growing stock is ultimately whittled away, posterity is left with the correspondingly reduced harvests available from a stand in which the younger age classes predominate. Sustained-yield forestry without reproduction is in the same category as perpetual motion.

The methods of cutting employed are best described as including both thinning and almost all variants of the shelterwood and selection methods. The tendency is to develop an irregular uneven-aged stand. The principle is of value in emphasizing the importance of skillful and intensive tending of individual trees and the site but is not a separate method of reproduction. The approach is suited only to highly intensive management in situations where a very competent forester has intimate knowledge and control over a relatively small forest for a long period of time. Otherwise affairs may drift aimlessly into chaos as a result of lack of attention to regeneration and distribution of age classes.

Extensive application of the selection method. Although the selection method is frequently thought of as a highly intensive silvicultural technique, it is most commonly applied in North America as a crude method under extensive practice. When markets are poor and logging is expensive, only the biggest and best trees can be cut profitably. Under these circumstances a simple kind of selection cutting may be practiced indefinitely or adopted as a purely temporary expedient until conditions become more favorable. Under extensive application the cutting cycles are long and there are no intermediate cuttings; growth is retarded by close competition, and there is little control over stand composition. Although the results are far from satisfactory, they may be the best that can be secured under adverse conditions.

In a pure stand or in a mixed stand where all species are desirable, an extensive application of the selection method, particularly group selection, may prove reasonably successful. Best results are obtained when the desirable species represent a physiographic or climatic climax. In the ordinary mixed stand, containing one or more inferior species, form and composition usually degenerate under such treatment. The desirable trees and species are cut; the inferior are left. The undesirable species multiply rapidly if they are tolerant. This type of treatment soon results in building up a growing stock of cull trees and poor species at the expense of the better ones.

The poorer forms of selection cutting have been practiced for centuries, without thought of future harvests, in mixed or uneven-aged stands containing only a few trees that were clearly useful. True clearcutting has been employed primarily in even-aged stands where all trees could be used. The main reason why such clearcutting has been thought of as more destructive than "high-grading" is that disastrous fires were much more common after clearcutting. Actually ill-considered partial cutting may do a more permanent and subtle kind of damage to the forest because the poorest trees are left to dominate the site.

Crude application of the selection method is not the only solution to the problems of extensive silviculture in localities where only large saw logs can be cut. If stands are allowed to grow until they have desirable advance regeneration and contain mainly trees of merchantable size, the one- or two-cut shelterwood method of harvesting them is often most advantageous from the standpoints of both logging and silviculture.

In situations where landowners have no interest beyond liquidation of existing merchantable timber, foresters have used one important principle of extensive application of the selection method as a device to discourage heavy cutting. There is always a limiting diameter below which trees cannot be profitably utilized for a given purpose, because the handling costs exceed the sale value of the small material produced. The tree which can be harvested with neither profit nor loss is referred to as the **marginal tree** of the stand or forest in which it occurs. A cutting that removes all trees that can be utilized without financial loss is called a **zero-margin** selection cutting. If a landowner can be induced to recognize the existence of the marginal tree, it becomes clearly desirable to him to leave smaller trees in logging. If the presently unmerchantable trees are sufficiently large and numerous to provide the basis for another harvest in the near future, there is an additional incentive to protect the smaller trees and shift away from a policy of short-term liquidation.

This approach has proven very effective in getting the practice of forestry established, but is hardly an appropriate basis for long-term practice. In fact, as economic factors become more favorable, the size of the marginal tree often drops to the point where virtually every tree in a stand can be utilized at a profit. Under these conditions zero-margin selection cutting may become synonymous with clearcutting. The primary drawback of basing the selection method on the concept of the marginal tree is that the potentialities of different trees for future growth are not taken into account. Although a tree may be logged profitably at a given time, it often can be harvested at a greater profit at some later date.

Once a landowner is committed to retaining small trees for growing stock it becomes desirable to know which trees are best reserved to the next cutting cycle. This can be done by using the concept of financial maturity to detect those trees that will earn an attractive rate of compound interest on their own present value if left to grow (Reynolds,

Bond, and Kirkland, 1944). This procedure usually results in the setting of an approximate diameter limit substantially higher than that which would apply to zero-margin cutting. If the total return to be obtained during another cutting cycle is high enough, the practicability of continuing operations at least to the end of that cycle is demonstrated.

The practices involved in this procedure are often referred to as "selective cutting," although **economic selection method** is a more precise term. The line of financial logic is often sufficient to guide forest practice up from mere mining to a level of extensive practice likely to ensure continuity of management. However, if it is feasible to intensify practice still further to secure optimum production and sustained yield, the suitability of the selection method should be re-examined. The concept of the single tree as a productive unit cannot be translated into continuing application of the single-tree selection method unless the species are sufficiently tolerant to be grown according to that method. When all of the biological and economic factors are considered, it is ordinarily found that some sort of even-aged management or the group-selection method provides the best framework for further intensification of practice.

Choice of Trees To Be Harvested

The marking of trees for harvest cutting is a fine art in uneven-aged stands in which the even-aged aggregations are small. Theoretically the true reproduction cuttings involve the removal of the oldest and largest trees with some predetermined diameter limit being taken as a definition of the smallest trees old enough for such cutting (Fig. 14-4). However, any diameter limit is only a first approximation of the characteristics of trees selected for cutting.

Trees above the limit may be left because they are increasing in value with unusual rapidity or for such reasons as their capacity to provide seed and protection for reproduction. The trees designated for cutting even though they are below the limit are those that increase in value too slowly because of low quality or poor growth, those that interfere with logging or the growth of better trees, or those that are likely to be lost after the cutting. The guiding diameter limit is completely ignored when it comes to determining what trees are removed in the true thinnings among the younger age groups (Fig. 14-4). The diameter limit is also abrogated to whatever extent may be necessary to correct and allow for the effects of imbalances in the diameter distribution of stands or forests being managed as sustained-yield units.

The guidance of such complicated timber marking is sometimes facilitated by tree classifications. These are especially necessary if the various age groups are small, because the standard crown classification is most useful in rather large, single-canopied, even-aged aggregations. In other kinds of stands it must be supplemented by other information although the matter of position in the crown canopy is always important. The other characteristics important in deciding whether trees should be cut or left are (1) age or size, (2) quality, and (3) vigor.

One of the oldest American tree classifications intended for use in uneven-aged stands is that developed by Dunning (1928) for the mixed conifer forests of the Sierra Nevada. He classified the ponderosa pines and other species into seven tree classes on the basis of age (four classes), degree of dominance within each age group (five crown classes), crown development, and vigor (three classes). The seven classes were numbered in order of decreasing capacity for further growth. This classification is presented in abbreviated form in Table 14-2 together with the original cutting recommendations for each class.

Table 14-2.   Dunning's tree classification for the mixed conifer forests of the Sierra Nevada

Tree Class	Crown Class	Age Class *	Vigor	Recommendation for Marking
1	Isolated, dominant, rarely codominant	Young and thrifty mature	Good	Leave when sound
2	Codominant, rarely isolated or dominant	Young and thrifty mature	Good to moderate	Usually leave but cut some
3	Isolated, dominant, rarely codominant	Mature	Moderate	Cut part and leave part
4	Codominant, rarely isolated or dominant	Mature	Moderate to poor	Cut unless no other available seed trees
5	Isolated, dominant, rarely codominant	Overmature	Poor	Cut unless no other available seed trees
6	Intermediate, overtopped	Young and thrifty mature	Moderate to poor	Cut, if merchantable, unless freed from competition
7	Intermediate, overtopped	Mature and overmature	Poor	Cut if merchantable

* **Young**—less than 50 years.   **Thrifty Mature**—50 to 150 years.   **Mature**—150 to 300 years.   **Overmature**—over 300 years.

It will be seen that cutting was done principally in the oldest timber and that merchantable trees of the subordinate crown classes were removed unless "young or thrifty mature."

The more elaborate tree classification developed by Keen for the interior ponderosa pine type was intended primarily for the guidance of pre-salvage cuttings but has also been found useful for other kinds of cutting as well. This and similar classifications for other species were discussed in Chapter 6.

It is highly desirable to adapt tree classifications so that they can be used in assessing the degree of financial maturity of individual trees. This requires a means of estimating the rate of diameter growth from external characteristics. The extraction of increment cores is so slow and sometimes so harmful that it is done only to provide occasional checks on estimates. The best evidence is provided by the size and vigor of the crown but the characteristics of the bark are useful and convenient.

One of the best illustrations of the use of bark characteristics for this purpose is the classification of southern upland hardwoods by Burkle and Guttenberg (1952). While there are important exceptions, trees with smooth bark are growing rapidly and the larger and coarser the segments of rough bark, the slower the growth (Fig. 14-7). Since the bark grows outward from the cork cambium as the wood grows inward from the cambium, there is an ill-defined lag in the manifestation of changes in diameter growth by the bark.

There are a number of instances in which the application of tree classifications has been further refined by incorporation of the concept of financial maturity. This approach is illustrated by the maturity-selection system which was devised for ponderosa pine in the interior of the Northwest and is described in a subsequent section. The same principles have, for example, been applied to eastern white pine and hemlock by Heiberg (1942, 1945) and to a number of hardwood species (Guttenberg and Putnam, 1951; Campbell, 1955).

It is important to recognize that tree classifications are useful in any form of partial cutting, such as the shelterwood system, as they are in uneven-aged management.

A tree classification, like any other classification, can be no better than the assumptions and principles on which it is based. It often conveys a certain air of authority which causes this point to be overlooked. Even some of the details of the famous Keen classification of ponderosa pine were condemned by Pearson (1944, 1946) who pointed

Fig. 14-7. Bark characteristics indicative of different classes of vigor and rate of growth of southern red oak: (*a*) High. (*b*) Medium. (*c*) Low. (*d*) Very low. The pattern depicted is typical of most, but not all, species. As vigor and growth decline the individual bark plates become larger and the fissures between them deeper. A tree of very high vigor would have nearly smooth bark. The stems shown above are not necessarily of the same diameter. (*Photographs by U. S. Forest Service.*)

out some of the pitfalls in the uncritical use of such classifications. One of these is the common error of classifying trees on the basis of their *past* growth and *present* characteristics without making allowance for the effects of release from competition in the projected cuttings. Another is the danger of arbitrarily combining promising trees with distinctly poor kinds in one category.

Advantages and Disadvantages of the Selection Method

Foresters have argued inconclusively for generations over the relative merits of even- and uneven-aged stands, often with the production of considerably more heat than light. Each category of stand and procedure involves so many variations that neither makes a well-defined target that can be attacked or defended effectively.

The range of choice is not a horizontal continuum from clearcutting at one extreme to the most intricate kind of single-tree selection cutting at the other. In a certain oversimplified manner of description, it can instead be viewed as a closed circle split into halves representing even-aged and uneven-aged systems. At one point of union the irregular shelterwood method blends with the single-tree selection method. At the other, the conduct of the selection system in stands composed of large even-aged groups becomes scarcely distinguishable from clearcutting. The earnest partisans of either approach soon find themselves chasing each other endlessly around this circle.

In order to facilitate discussion and set aside some of the shades of gray, the following comparison is drawn *only* between two moderately broad and readily comprehensible samples of the two forms of management. On one hand are the single-tree selection system and those forms of group-selection involving small groups; on the other, those forms of even-aged management that produce distinctly uniform stands from natural regeneration by methods not more complicated than the two-cut shelterwood system.

The difference in potential gross production, whether measured in biological or economic terms, probably lies slightly in favor of the selection system. The growing space is likely to be occupied more nearly continuously and the opportunity to balance more large trees against fewer small ones in a sustained-yield growing stock must somewhat increase the merchantable yield.

The selection method offers a stability of environmental conditions and influences that is not available in even-aged stands which continually change as they grow older. This is an advantage to whatever extent the stable conditions thus created are favorable. Where it is desirable to maintain the nearly continuous cover of a protection forest on steep slopes in order to prevent erosion, landslides, avalanches, or rapid runoff, the selection method is the safest. The danger of fire is usually less than in even-aged stands because the fuels are shaded and concentrations of slash are widely separated. However, crown fires are more likely to develop because the step-like arrangement of crowns always brings some foliage close to the ground.

The selection stand has an appearance that is continuously more picturesque and attractive to the layman because there are always some large trees, small clumps of small trees, and only a few patches with the devastated appearance inevitably associated with regeneration cuttings.

Uneven-aged stands are generally regarded as being less susceptible to damage from biotic enemies because most injurious species do not attack all age classes of a given tree species. Separation of age classes may inhibit the spread of insects and fungi as well as hold their populations in check by restricting the supply of food. However, if all age classes are susceptible, as is true with dwarf-mistletoe, the uneven-aged arrangement can ensure the continuing re-establishment of the pest. Since environmental conditions are maintained in a nearly constant state, the whole plant and animal population of the stand remains in relatively stable equilibrium. The question of whether this equilibrium is satisfactory depends on how well its characteristics coincide with economic objectives. The risk of violent and unforeseen fluctuations is sharply reduced, to say the least.

One protective feature of the uneven-aged form is the permanent vertical closure of the stand. This tends to prevent the wind from entering the stand and diffuses its force if it does enter. The large trees develop greater windfirmness than they would in even-aged stands and the small trees are sheltered. An even-aged stand develops an open stratum below its canopy and has vertical closure only on the edges and then only as long as a curtain of foliage continues to extend to the ground. The security of an even-aged stand against wind is thus no better than the strength of its edges so there is a tendency for the whole to stand or fall as a unit. On the other hand, it should be noted that the creation of openings in uneven-aged stands increases the number of gaps into which the wind can funnel and be accelerated sufficiently to cause serious damage. The wind resistance of uneven-aged stands is not maintained if cuttings are infrequent and drastic. The greatest degree of resistance can be obtained by use of the strip-selection method.

The belief that uneven-aged stands are more resistant to all forms of damage than even-aged stands has sprung, at least in part, from the fact that the same degree of injury is much more obvious in a uniform stand than in one of irregular form. In general, the primary factor that makes uneven-aged management less hazardous is the reduced risk of losing whole stands at once and having to regenerate them with inadequate sources of seed.

The presence of a permanent seed source in uneven-aged stands is highly advantageous. This is especially true in unfavorable climates where adequate reproduction can become established only gradually over long periods or during abnormally favorable years occurring at infrequent intervals.

One disadvantage that limits the use of the selection method is the complexity of all operations conducted in intermingled mixtures of different age classes. Any activity conducted in the stand is diffused over a large area and all the procedures applicable throughout a whole rotation are done simultaneously and continually. This necessitates much more supervisory attention and skill than even-aged management in which different things are done in sequence at different times in uniform stands.

Almost everything that is done in the truly effective handling of an uneven-aged stand must be closely supervised by an experienced forester. There is far less opportunity to delegate such operations as timber marking to subprofessional personnel on the basis of general instructions about particular stands.

The progress of regeneration and the condition of the growing stock are often submerged in an uneven-aged stand. It is consequently more difficult to evaluate the results of operations than in even-aged stands where the different age classes are readily distinguished.

The difficulty and expense of harvesting operations is usually greater than in even-aged stands where each age class is concentrated in space. Under the selection method it is necessary to cover a large area to harvest a given volume in one operation. If any real thinning is involved it becomes necessary to handle many different sizes of trees simultaneously. Because of the mixture of age classes, it is difficult to prevent logging damage to immature trees.

Some of the factors that make selection management a costly proposition are temporarily avoided or at least concealed in the crude, extensive application of the method. The choice of trees to cut may require nothing more than the ability to select scattered trees of sufficient size and quality for profitable utilization. Under such procedures, the costs of handling each unit of harvested volume can be minimized by restricting cutting to the best and largest trees and these savings may entirely offset the high costs of transportation. However, several repetitions of this kind of cutting usually leave the stand in such condition that nothing can be profitably harvested for many decades.

If there is any method of cutting that is likely to reduce the productivity of the forest by eliminating good genotypes, it is the selection method. While this risk is of unknown magnitude, it is probably difficult to avoid even under intensive application of the method.

There are several important considerations about which generalization is probably unwise even when comparison is restricted to the rather specific kinds of even- and uneven-aged stands under consideration.

The environmental conditions under which reproduction becomes established are distinctly different but the question of which is best depends on the species and unalterable site factors. In the uncomplicated even-aged stands under consideration, reproduction is secured in the rather uniform environmental conditions of essentially open areas or those covered by diffuse shade. Such variable factors as shade and root competition are only temporary in their effect. In the mode of selection cutting under discussion, reproduction is sought in small openings and there is no provision for prompt or systematic enlargement of them.

There is probably no species that could not be grown in some sort of uneven-aged stand, although in many instances it would be necessary to shift to those kinds of group-selection management involving distinctly large openings.

The quality of the timber that is produced depends more on the intensity of treatment and the reaction of the particular species than it does on any general differences between even- and uneven-aged stands. Even in the single-tree selection stand, many of the trees develop in even-aged aggregations throughout the early formative period during which the ultimate stem quality is largely determined. The differences that may develop depend on the many kinds of influences that can affect the trees around the edges of the even-aged units. The proportion of trees so affected is greatest when the units are small. Some of the detrimental or even disastrous effects that can take place along such edges have already been considered. On the other hand, if the trees remain straight, their early development may be sufficiently restricted that natural pruning is excellent and no significant core of objectionable juvenile wood develops. When such trees are released by the removal of older, adjacent trees they may be able to grow with unusual rapidity through the stages of middle age when the growth of trees in even-aged stands is most likely to be restricted. The edge trees may thus produce considerable amounts of knot-free wood grown at the uniform rates regarded as most satisfactory for lumber and similar products.

It must be reiterated in concluding this comparison that it dealt almost exclusively with differences between uneven-aged stands consisting of small units and the more uniform kinds of even-aged stands. Sometimes the disadvantages of the even-aged arrangement can be reduced by making the stands smaller or shifting to the more sophisticated kinds of shelterwood cutting. Conversely, some of the drawbacks of uneven-aged stands can be mitigated by making the component even-aged groups larger.

There is no ground for believing that one form of arrangement of age classes is inherently better than the other. The choice depends on careful consideration of the circumstances, not the least important of which is the existing arrangement of the stand. Changes in the age distribution of existing stands are sufficiently difficult and costly that they should not be undertaken unless careful analysis of all factors, economic and biological, shows that alterations are mandatory. The policies of silvicultural management generated by extreme viewpoints are usually the ones that require the greatest amount of tampering and ultimately prove the least rational.

Application of the Selection Method

The selection method has its natural counterpart in forests that are subject to occasional partial disturbances which kill scattered trees or larger patches and thus allow the establishment of different age classes. If all such disturbances have been very small and continued over a long period, the stands are likely to reach or approach the final stage of plant succession, which may be a climatic or physiographic climax. However, if large openings have been created, almost any stage of plant succession may be represented. The only way in which the balanced uneven-aged arrangement could appear naturally would be in the very unlikely event that disturbances of equal severity occurred with uniform periodicity.

Instances of intensive application of the single-tree selection method in North America exist only as isolated attempts, the outcome of which will remain obscure for many years to come. Most American application of the selection method takes the form of a variety of kinds of group-selection cutting or of practices little different, if at all, from high-grading.

"Selective cutting." During the 1930's, extensive application of the selection method was regarded by many foresters as the panacea of all problems of American forest management. It was during this period that the vague term "selective cutting" was coined. The times

were peculiarly appropriate for such proposals. The development of trucks and tractors suitable for use in logging big timber had commenced to displace railroad logging thus making partial cutting possible in old growth. Lumber markets were so badly depressed that only the biggest and best trees could be harvested profitably.

These developments played a highly important role in demonstrating that partial cutting was feasible and that residual stands of usable timber could be profitably left for future harvests. Unfortunately this campaign implanted certain misconceptions in the minds of some foresters and the public which have persisted. Selective cutting is a tool that can be used for good or evil. All too often it has resulted in neither maintenance of the uneven-aged form, establishment of desirable reproduction, nor preservation of residual stands. These errors have arisen primarily from lack of appreciation of the fact that natural laws eventually have economic consequences fully as important as the costs of harvesting and manufacturing the products of the forest.

Although selective cutting is frequently conducted in the name of the selection method, it more commonly bears closer resemblance to other kinds of silvicultural treatment. Many of the best selective cuttings are aimed exclusively at the most effective management of existing stands without provision for regeneration; such operations are definitely in the category of thinnings. Those that are conducted primarily to remove merchantable trees of undesirable form or species from the stand are best termed improvement cuttings and represent advantageous treatment preliminary to the initiation of more standard intermediate and reproduction cuttings. Selective cuttings that remove mostly trees threatened or already damaged by injurious agencies should be regarded as salvage cuttings.

Many selective cuttings, especially those conducted under extensive practice, remove such a high proportion of the merchantable volume that they destroy rather than accentuate any unevenness that may have existed in the age distribution of the stand. This development has also resulted from the deterioration of residual stands left after cutting. Treatments of this kind tend to create even-aged stands and should be regarded as crude variants of the shelterwood method. Finally there are some selective cuttings that create or maintain the inherent characteristics of the uneven-aged stand, and may be correctly referred to as selection cuttings.

It can be readily seen from the foregoing that the doctrine of selective cutting should not be condemned out of hand. The most important drawback is that it often constitutes an opportunistic policy of silviculture which rarely looks beyond the end of the present rotation.

Selection management of irregular cut-over stands. One of the noteworthy outgrowths of "selective cutting" has been the effective application of the selection method in irregular stands inherited from previous high-grading operations. This development has ordinarily been more successful with coniferous species, which tend to remain straight in spite of suppression, than with the malformed remnants of high-grading in hardwood stands.

The best account of such conversion is that of Reynolds (1959) regarding selection cutting in irregular stands of loblolly and short-leaf pine in Arkansas. These species characteristically grow together in even-aged stands so their successful culture in uneven-aged stands is proof of the versatility of the method. The basic objective of the procedure is to develop a good saw-timber growing stock as swiftly as possible from the remnants of high-graded even-aged stands. The same objective could be achieved by liquidating the remnants and replacing them with even-aged reproduction but this would cause serious delay and the needless sacrifice of many small and medium-sized trees of good potentialities.

The guiding principle followed in the cuttings advocated by Reynolds is the concept of financial maturity which is applied in such manner that careful attention is paid to increment of quality as well as volume. Full advantage is taken of the excellent natural pruning of some of those remnants of earlier stands which are capable of returning to full vigor.

The procedure has proven successful as a means of rehabilitation. It also transmits enough of the irregularity of the initial stands to their replacements that some intermingling of age classes remains. However, some of the associated recommendations have been the subject of the kind of debate (Chapman, 1942; Bond, 1953; McCulley, 1953; Wahlenberg, 1960) which shows that silviculture is far from being a stereotyped procedure. These involve a rather deliberate lack of concern for reproduction, intentional suppression of developing saplings, and attempts to develop balanced, uneven-aged stands. When prescribed burning represented the only means of controlling the hardwood understory, selection cutting posed a serious dilemma because of the continual presence of seedlings vulnerable to fire. However, the introduction of herbicides has resolved this problem.

While it has been shown that the pine seedlings can develop satisfactorily in small openings (Wahlenberg, 1948), there is less certainty that reliance on the natural pruning of deliberately suppressed saplings is as economical a method of producing good saw timber as relying on vigorous, artificially pruned trees. It may also be more advisable to shift gradually toward even-aged management than to accentuate the uneven-aged condition. In other words, the procedure that works well in the preliminary stages of management is not necessarily the best permanent policy.

Hardwood types. The selection method is a logical means for handling many of the complex mixtures of hardwoods found in eastern North America (Minckler, 1958). This is partly because so many of the stands have become uneven-aged as a result of natural processes or previous high-grading. There is increasing recognition of the fact that hardwoods develop best form if grown as dominants in even-aged aggregations, so there is a strong tendency to use the group-selection method in dealing with uneven-aged stands. Furthermore, most of the valuable species are relatively intolerant and are able to emerge from the welter of competing vegetation only if there is plenty of light. Of course, there are many even-aged hardwood stands that are best maintained as such. Many of the stands form the stratified mixtures that will be considered from a different point of view in Chapter 16. No silvicultural system provides an automatic solution to the problem of ridding mixed hardwood stands of the residue of all shapes and sizes of defective trees that almost inevitably accumulate.

The old-growth northern hardwood forest, which consists primarily of sugar maple, beech, and yellow birch, is well adapted to the group-selection method, unless the stands are highly defective (Gilbert and Jensen, 1958). Single-tree selection cutting is advantageous if used as a means of improving the growing stock of existing stands, particularly if the stands contain a high proportion of sugar maple (Eyre and Zillgitt, 1953). The birches and, in the Lake Region, hemlock tend to deteriorate after exposure in partial cutting. Single-tree selection cutting also favors reproduction of tolerant sugar maple and beech (a species rarely worth encouraging) to the exclusion of valuable intolerant species like yellow birch and white ash (Cope, 1948). Therefore, those cuttings that are actually intended to promote the regeneration of intolerant species or to release that of tolerant advance growth should be patch-wise clearcuttings, preferably of mature or overmature groups.

Very large openings should be avoided because of the danger of encouraging shrubs and undesirable pioneer vegetation like raspberries, pin cherry, and aspen (Godman and Krefting, 1960). Linteau (1948) found that in Quebec the valuable yellow birch regenerates best on bare mineral soil in openings of ½ acre or less. In the drier climate of the Lake Region, smaller openings, not more than ⅒ acre in size, have been found more satisfactory for yellow birch (Zillgitt and Eyre, 1945). Observations by Hough (1953) indicated that the best reproduction of black cherry, a species which is very valuable if of good form, occurs on small patch or strip clearcuttings. Excessively wide openings do not preclude the eventual establishment of desirable reproduction, but invading shrubs and herbs may prevent the new crop from making any effective growth for 20 years or more (Gysel, 1951). The most desirable treatment for such stands is often a combination of group-selection cuttings for reproduction and improvement cuttings to rid the intervening areas of unthrifty individ-

Fig. 14-8. A stand of redwood on the lands of a lumber company in northern California 5 years after a selection cutting. The stand was cut to a diameter limit of 52 inches. There is good reproduction of seedlings and sprouts, although only the latter are visible. (*Photograph by California Redwood Association.*)

uals. This will lead eventually to stands uneven-aged by groups. Stands that are hopelessly overmature are usually well stocked with advance reproduction and should be "clearcut" according to the one-cut shelter-wood system. Thrifty even-staged stands of second growth may be handled most satisfactorily by some variant of the shelterwood method.

It is significant that the same general procedures, with greatest emphasis on selection cuttings in small groups, are regarded as most appropriate to the management of *uneven-aged* mixtures of southern bottomland hardwoods (Putnam, Furnival, and McKnight, 1960).

Coniferous types. The coast redwood forests of northern California are adapted to the selection method (Fig. 14-8). Redwood is a remarkably tolerant species which regenerates best under shelter and responds to release vigorously even when centuries in age (Fritz, 1951). Since the species is well-nigh indestructible it is possible to retain ancient trees for as long as necessary to create an uneven-aged stand suitable for commerical rotations. Unfortunately the great size of the timber makes selection cutting difficult and results in heavy accumulations of slash. Logging debris presents a serious fire hazard and an impediment to reproduction. Unless performed with unusual care, disposal of slash by burning tends to destroy the young growth essential to uneven-aged management. If this problem cannot be solved effectively, the silviculture of the redwood type is likely to develop along the lines of the shelterwood rather than the selection method. In either case, the protection of an overwood is highly desirable and tends to favor redwood over the associated grand fir and Douglas-fir (Person and Hallin, 1942). The only redwood reproduction that occurs after very heavy cuttings comes from sprouts that develop in dense clusters around the stumps of even the most ancient trees.

The group-selection method is suitable for the management of the ponderosa pine forests that grow in the dry regions east of the Cascade Range and the Sierra Nevada. These stands are characteristically uneven-aged by groups (Fig. 14-9). Although the species is very intolerant, it represents a climax community on all but the best sites. Therefore, the invasion of more tolerant species like Douglas-fir and various true firs is not often a problem. The most serious problems are establishment of reproduction, reduction of losses from bark beetles, and maintenance of satisfactory growth.

Natural reproduction develops very gradually in the stands because of the semiarid climate. It is abundant only in the rare coincidence of good seed years followed by abnormally high rainfall in spring and

Fig. 14-9. A stand of ponderosa pine in the Fort Valley Experimental Forest, Arizona, managed under the improvement selection system. The group of smooth-boled trees (15 to 24 inches D.B.H.) in the foreground was thinned 32 years ago by the removal of 4 trees (positions marked by small white cards) and 2 years ago by the cutting of a 30-inch pine (large card). (*Photograph by U. S. Forest Service.*)

early summer. Therefore, a liberal number of seed bearers must be maintained permanently in order to take advantage of every opportunity for reproduction. Were it not for this requirement the seed-tree method might be used in the same manner as it is in the long-leaf pine region where soil moisture is also an important factor.

The attrition of various damaging agencies, particularly bark beetles, is a very serious problem in old-growth ponderosa pine. The ravages of *Dendroctonus* beetles are often sufficient to bring mortality into balance with growth and are, incidentally, the primary cause of the grouped arrangement. These insects are best held in check by the cutting of the unthrifty trees, which are highly susceptible to attack (Miller and Keen, 1960). This objective can be most easily attained by extending light selection cuttings to remove such trees throughout the whole forest as rapidly as possible. Fortunately most of those that should be cut first are the large veterans, which can be utilized most profitably.

The climate is so dry that root competition is a serious factor limiting the growth of stands throughout life (Pearson, 1950). Once reproduction is established the young clumps soon become so dense that all the individuals grow very slowly. The markets are usually too poor for early thinning of these groups. Consequently the only way that young clumps can be released from competition is by freeing the edges in periodic cuttings of adjacent, older groups. Once the trees in the young groups have reached merchantable size it becomes feasible to thin them at the same time that more valuable trees are cut nearby. It is also advantageous to maintain a good growing stock in order to keep the periodic annual increment at a high level (Briegleb, 1950; Roe, 1952). Although the trees of the virgin forest cannot be retained indefinitely, there is no compelling reason to harvest them so long as they increase in value at a satisfactory rate. The remarkable longevity of the species, the high premium placed on trees of large size, and the low carrying charges on land make this an advantageous course.

The terrain is rarely rugged, so frequent, partial cuttings are readily feasible. However, it was only about 1930 that the shift from railroad logging to use of trucks and tractors made it possible to introduce true selection cutting. Before then the closest approach consisted of removing 75 to 80 per cent of the merchantable volume on a cutting cycle of 35 to 60 years.

The first departure from the old policy was the maturity-selection system developed in eastern Oregon and Washington (Munger, 1941). This represented a carefully planned form of economic selection cutting based on the concept of financial maturity. The ordinary predictions of change in tree value involved in applying this concept were quantitatively adjusted on the basis of predictions of the percentage of mortality caused by bark beetles. The Keen tree classification of vulnerability to beetle attack (Fig. 6-2) was used as a basis of predictions of mortality and growth for trees of different diameter classes. Predictions were based on a 30-year cutting cycle and the cuttings usually removed about 40 per cent of the merchantable volume.

Since the mid-1940's more versatile cutting policies have developed because of increased experience and also because it became feasible to extend very light sanitation-salvage cuttings rapidly over wide areas to save as much timber as possible from the beetles (see Chapter 6). Sharp rises in lumber prices so far exceeded any increases anticipated from growth alone that the wisdom of regulating cutting *entirely* according to financial maturity became doubtful. Present cutting practices are varied according to the vigor of the trees that compose the stands. The range covers everything from light selection cutting to procedures which are really even-aged management, at least from the silvicultural standpoint.

The most completely developed procedure, called **unit area control** (Hallin, 1959), is a program under which the rather small, natural, homogeneous, even-aged "units" or groups are gradually marshalled into uneven-aged stands consisting of large even-aged groups. The various units comprising existing stands are carefully differentiated as to degree of maturity and such characteristics as presence or absence of either brush or advance regeneration. The most decadent units are harvested with whatever form of slash disposal and scarification is necessary for the establishment of either natural or artificial regeneration. In order to alleviate the border effects of root competition and to facilitate operations, attempts are made to create new groups 4 to 7 acres in size, although large "groups" of overmature timber up to 50 acres in area are sometimes clearcut and replaced in one operation. Improvement cuttings may be conducted in the older units not yet ready for replacement; pruning and even precommercial thinning are sometimes conducted in the immature units.

The kind of group-selection cutting involved in unit area control is also used in the mixed conifer type of the western slopes of the Sierra Nevada (Dunning, 1949). These fine forests consist of sugar and ponderosa pine in intimate mixture with more tolerant species like incense-cedar and white fir. Heavy winter precipitation is favorable to the growth of deep-rooted, established trees, but the lack of summer precipitation seriously hampers establishment of desirable regeneration. Root competition from dense brush, which commonly invades cutover areas, is a major problem (Fowells and Schubert, 1951). The brush often must be eliminated mechanically during slash disposal, but the groups thus created are usually not larger than an acre.

Another important variant in the silviculture of the interior ponderosa pine type is the technique of **improvement-selection cutting** developed by Pearson (1942, 1950) in the Southwest (Fig. 14-9). Greatest emphasis is placed on developing a saw-timber growing stock of high quality. One important feature is the release of trees, often with small crowns, that have been well pruned naturally by the effects of competition. Wadsworth (1942) and Pearson demonstrated that such pines had the ability to commence rapid growth. This approach is distinctly different from those aimed at controlling *Dendroctonus* beetles because such devices as the Keen tree classification are predicated on the assumption that trees with deep, vigorous crowns are least vulnerable. Pearson took sharp exception to the idea that the beetles should rule ponderosa pine silviculture and even went so far as to contend that a tree with a live crown ratio greater than 40 per cent had no place in a managed forest. However, this difference in approach is largely the result of the fact that *Dendroctonus* beetles are far less harmful in the Southwest than in localities farthei north. It is also noteworthy that improvement-selection cutting is essentially a kind of thinning or improvement cutting because it rarely leaves vacancies in the soil space large enough for reproduction. Although reproduction of any sort is difficult to secure in the Southwest, the cuttings intended for the purpose are essentially the same kind of group-selection cuttings employed in other uneven-aged stands of ponderosa pine.

The different modifications that have been applied to the use of the selection method in the management of ponderosa pine represent variations in the degree of emphasis placed in particular times and places on the various objectives of all silvicultural management. The maturity-selection method was aimed mainly at making best use of the growing stock in a rather passive manner; improvement-selection, at the active upgrading of the growing stock; sanitation-salvage, at overcoming catastrophic losses; and unit area control, not only at reproducing stands but also at establishing an efficient arrangement for future management. The arguments that have revolved around the management of ponderosa pine provide one of the best illustrations of the conflict in objectives that must be resolved in the continuing development of effective silvicultural systems.

No account of the selection method would be complete without mention of the half-forgotten attempt to apply the economic-selection method in the virgin forests of Douglas-fir and associated species in the Northwest. This policy proved disastrous because partial cuttings in these ancient forests opened the way for accelerated deterioration of residual stands under the attacks of insects, fungi, and atmospheric agencies (Munger, 1950; Isaac, 1956). Furthermore, the method was unsuitable for the regeneration of Douglas-fir, which is less tolerant than its competitors in this particular region. The selection method is applicable to Douglas-fir only in dry situations where it grows as a physiographic climax in relatively open stands.

The failure of the selection method in West Coast Douglas-fir is an outstanding example of the difficulty of attempting to convert overmature stands into productive units by selection cutting. Stands of this kind are often best stored on the stump until needed and then swiftly removed by application of the clearcutting or shelterwood methods.

REFERENCES

Anderson, H. W.   1960.   Research in management of snowpack watersheds for water yield control. *J. Forestry* 58:282–284.

Bond, W. E.   1953.   The case for all-aged management of southern pines. *J. Forestry* 51:90–93.

Bourne, R.   1951.   A fallacy in the theory of growing stock. *Forestry* 24:6–18, 159–161.

Briegleb, P. A.   1950.   Growth of ponderosa pine. *J. Forestry* 48:349–352.

Burger, H.   1942.   Holz, Blattmenge und Zuwachs. VI. Ein Plenterwald mittlerer Standortsgüte. Der bernische Staatswald Toppwald im Emmental. *Mitt. d. Schweizer. Anstalt f. d. forstliche Versuchswesen* 22:377–445.

Burkle, J. L., and S. Guttenberg.   1952.   Marking guides for oaks and yellow-poplar in the southern uplands. *SFES Occasional Paper* 125.

Campbell, R. A.   1955.   Tree grades and economic maturity for some Appalachian hardwoods. *SFES Sta. Paper* 53.

Chapman, H. H.   1942.   Management of loblolly pine in the pine-hardwood regions in Arkansas and Louisiana west of the Mississippi River. *Yale Univ. School of Forestry Bul.* 49.

Cope, J. A.   1948.   White ash-management possibilities in the Northeast. *J. Forestry* 46:744–749.

Davis, K. P.   1954.   *American forest management.* McGraw-Hill, New York.

Dunning, D.   1928.   A tree classification for the selection forests of the Sierra Nevada. *J. Agr. Research* 36:775–771.

———.   1949.   *In:* A sugar pine regeneration cutting experiment. *West Coast Lumberman* 76(3):62, 64.

Eyre, F. H., and W. M. Zillgitt.   1953.   Partial cuttings in northern hardwoods of the Lake States. *USDA Tech. Bul.* 1076.

Fowells, H. A., and G. H. Schubert.   1951.   Natural reproduction in certain cut-over pine-fir stands of California. *J. Forestry* 49:192–196.

Fritz, E.   1951.   Some principles governing the growing of redwood crops. *J. Forestry* 49:263–266.

Geiger, R.   1957.   *The climate near the ground,* Rev. ed.   Translated from German by M. N. Stewart and others.   Harvard University Press, Cambridge. Pp. 350–356.

Gilbert, A. M.   1954.   What is this thing called growth? *NEFES Sta. Paper* 71.

———, and V. S. Jensen.   1958.   A management guide for northern hardwoods in New England. *NEFES Sta. Paper* 112.

Godman, R. M., and L. W. Krefting.   1960.   Factors important to yellow birch establishment in Upper Michigan. *Ecology* 41:18–28.

Guttenberg, S., and J. A. Putnam.   1951.   Financial maturity of bottomland red oaks and sweetgum. *SFES Occasional Paper* 117.

Gysel, L. W. 1951. Borders and openings of beech-maple woodlands in southern Michigan. *J. Forestry* 49:13–19.

Hallin, W. E. 1959. The application of unit area control in the management of ponderosa-Jeffrey pine at Blacks Mountain Experimental Forest. *USDA Tech. Bul.* 1191.

Heiberg, S. O. 1942. Cutting based upon economic increment. *J. Forestry* 40:645–651.

———. 1945. Does economic cutting pay? *J. Forestry* 43:109–112.

Hough, A. F. 1953. Preliminary recommendations for the management of black cherry on the northern Allegheny Plateau. *J. Forestry* 51:184–188.

Hough, A. F., and R. D. Forbes. 1943. The ecology and silvics of forests in the high plateaus of Pennsylvania. *Ecological Monographs* 13:299–320.

Isaac, L. A. 1956. Place of partial cutting in old-growth stands of the Douglas-fir region. *PNWFRES Research Paper* 16.

Jarvis, J. M. 1956. An ecological approach to tolerant hardwood silviculture. *Canada, Forestry Branch, Forest Research Div. Tech. Note* 43.

Knuchel, H. 1953. *Planning and control in the managed forest.* Translated from German by M. L. Anderson. Oliver and Boyd, Edinburgh.

Köstler, J. 1956. *Silviculture.* Translated from German by M. L. Anderson Oliver and Boyd, Edinburgh.

Linteau, A. 1948. Factors affecting germination and early survival of yellow birch (*Betula lutea* Michx.) in Quebec. *Forestry Chronicle* 24:27–86.

McCulley, R. D. 1953. The case for even-aged management of southern pine. *J. Forestry* 51:88–90.

Meyer, H. A. 1943. Management without rotation. *J. Forestry* 41:126–132.

———. 1952. Structure, growth, and drain in balanced unevenaged forests. *J. Forestry* 50:85–92.

———, and D. D. Stevenson. 1943. The structure and growth of virgin beech-birch-maple-hemlock forests in northern Pennsylvania. *J. Agr. Research* 67:465–484.

Meyer, H. A., et al. 1961. *Forest management,* 2nd ed. Ronald Press, New York.

Miller, J. M., and F. P. Keen. 1960. Biology and control of the western pine beetle. *USDA Misc. Pub.* 800.

Minckler, L. S. 1959. Concepts basic to the practice of hardwood silviculture. *Proc. Soc. Am. Foresters Meeting,* 1958:155–157.

———, W. T. Plass, and R. A. Ryker. 1961. Woodland management by single-tree selection: a case history. *J. Forestry* 59:257–261.

Munger, T. T. 1941. They discuss the maturity selection system. *J. Forestry* 39:297–303.

———. 1950. A look at selective cutting in Douglas-fir. *J. Forestry* 48:97–99.

Pearson, G. A. 1942. Improvement selection cutting in ponderosa pine. *J. Forestry* 40:753–766.

———. 1944. Tree classifications. *J. Forestry* 42:49–51.

———. 1946. Age-and-vigor classes in relation to timber marking. *J. Forestry* 44:652–659.

———. 1950. Management of ponderosa pine in the Southwest. *USDA Monograph* 6.

Person, H. L., and W. Hallin. 1942. Natural restocking of redwood cutover lands. *J. Forestry* 40:683–688.

Putnam, J. A., G. M. Furnival, and J. S. McKnight. 1960. Management and inventory of southern hardwoods. *USDA Agr. Handbook* 181.

Reynolds, R. R. 1959. Eighteen years of selection timber management on the Crossett Experimental Forest. *USDA Tech. Bul.* 1206.

———, W. E. Bond, and B. P. Kirkland. 1944. Financial aspects of selective cutting in the management of second-growth pine-hardwood forests west of the Mississippi River. *USDA Tech. Bul.* 861.

Roe, A. L. 1952. Growth of selectively cut ponderosa pine stands in the upper Columbia Basin. *USDA Agr. Handbook* 39.

Sammi, J. C. 1961. de Liocourt's method, modified. *J. Forestry* 59:294–295.

Troup, R. S. 1952. *Silvicultural systems,* 2nd ed. Edited by E. W. Jones. Oxford University Press, London. Pp. 109–120, 185–192.

Wadsworth, F. H. 1942. Value of small-crowned ponderosa pines in reserve stands in the Southwest. *J. Forestry* 40:767–771.

Wahlenberg, W. G. 1948. Effect of forest shade and openings on loblolly pine seedlings. *J. Forestry* 46:832–834.

———. 1956. An early test of levels of growing stock in Appalachian hardwoods. *J. Forestry* 54: 106–114.

———. 1960. *Loblolly pine, its use, ecology, regeneration, protection, growth and management.* Duke University School of Forestry, Durham, N. C.

Walker, N. 1956. Growing stock volumes in unmanaged and managed forests. *J. Forestry* 54:378–383.

Zillgitt, W. M., and F. H. Eyre. 1945. Perpetuation of yellow birch in Lake States forests. *J. Forestry* 43:658–661.

CHAPTER 15

Methods based on vegetative reproduction

A **low forest** is one originating vegetatively from sprouts or layered branches as contrasted with a **high forest** developing from seeds or planted seedlings. These two terms bear only an indirect reference to the height of the stands. Stands of vegetative origin are ordinarily grown on much shorter rotations than those arising from seedlings and are, therefore, of lower stature when harvested. The term **coppice** refers specifically to a stand originating primarily from sprouts; the means of regenerating such forests is called the **coppice** or **sprout method.**

In the **simple coppice method** clearcuttings are carried out at the end of each rotation. The **coppice-selection method,** which is poorly adapted to conditions in North America, is basically similar to the selection method except for the origin of the reproduction. A **compound** or **composite coppice** is a stand in which certain selected trees or standards are carried on a much longer rotation than a simple coppice beneath them. The technique of handling them is the **coppice-with-standards** or **compound coppice method.** The procedure of reproducing stands from layered branches may be referred to as the **layering method** (Nelson, 1951).

Vegetative Reproduction

The ability to reproduce vegetatively is a characteristic of tremendous survival value for many species of woody plants. Only by this means is it possible for a species to maintain itself in the face of catastrophes that occur so frequently that no individuals reach seed-bearing age. Almost every forest region has areas where fires have occurred so often that sprouting species predominate to the exclusion of those that reproduce only from seed. Unfortunately, the characteristic is more commonly a detriment than an advantage from the standpoint of the forester. A high proportion of the woody plants that sprout readily are merely shrubs. The sprouts of desirable arborescent species are almost never as good as trees of the same species originating from seed.

Sprouting is a response to sudden death of the parent tree caused by agencies such as fire or cutting. It may also occur as a result of disease, injury, or serious physiological disorder. In fact, the appearance of sprouts of any form near the base or on the bole of a tree is frequently the first sign of unhealthiness. The process is probably triggered by interruption of the flow of auxins that are produced in the top of the tree and normally inhibit the development of basal buds.

The shoots which arise from portions of an older tree grow much more rapidly in youth than seedlings of equal age. This tendency is to some extent the result of inherent physiological differences that are not clearly understood. It is probable, however, that much of the unusual rapidity of growth of young sprouts can be accounted for by the inheritance of extensive root systems and supplies of carbohydrate from the parent trees.

Cuttings made during the dormant period lead to much more vigorous sprouting than those made during late spring and summer. This difference is traditionally ascribed to the belief that the reserves of carbohydrates in the roots are at a maximum during the winter and at a minimum immediately after the formation of new leaves and shoots. However, there is evidence that the seasonal variations in sprouting are not always related to variations in carbohydrate reserves and that fluctuations in hormones may be a more direct cause (Kramer and Kozlowski, 1960). If cuttings are made late in the growing season, sprouts sometimes appear almost immediately, but they rarely harden before the first frost. Therefore, coppice cuttings are best made in late fall or winter.

If full advantage is to be taken of vegetative reproduction in renewing a stand, all the trees of the species to be reproduced should be cut in one operation in order to stimulate sprouting to the utmost. Trees of the same species in a single stand are often interconnected by root grafts. Therefore, if a few scattered trees are left behind they may draw on the food supply of the common root system or contribute inhibitors of sprouting and thus reduce the vigor of the new sprouts. The reduction is often greater than could be caused by the shade of the residual trees. Therefore, vegetative reproduction obtained after clearcutting is usually superior to that resulting from partial cutting.

Although trees of vegetative origin grow faster during early life than those developing from seed, they do not retain this advantage on long rotations. As a general rule, vegetative reproduction may be expected to attain larger size on a short coppice rotation than trees grown from seed would in the same time. In fact, that is the primary advantage of coppicing stands on short rotations. If the rotations are extended just enough to produce saw logs there appear to be no consistent differences in size which can be related to the mode of origin (Leffelman and Håwley, 1925). McIntyre (1936), however, found that oak sprouts grown beyond a century in age on good sites tended to be smaller than trees originating from seed. He found no evidence that oak sprouts were inherently shorter lived than oaks grown from acorns.

There is a tendency for repeated coppicing from the same root stocks, especially on short rotations, to cause a progressive decline in the vigor of successive crops. The general experience abroad has been that coppice forests must be renewed from seed occasionally to restore the level of production. Bourne (1924), on the other hand, observed that oak coppices in Germany had been worked on short rotations for centuries without declining in vigor or site quality. It is probable that repeated removal of very small branch wood would cause permanent depletion of the inorganic nutrient capital of the site. Loss of vigor may also result from increasing prevalence of fungi or obscure viruses in the root stocks. Declining productivity would occur if there was a progressive decrease in the number of basic sprout clumps which led to understocking. However, if repeated vegetative reproduction were inherently deleterious, this fact would have been observed in certain varieties of woody ornamentals and fruit trees which have been propagated entirely from cuttings for centuries.

Actually the most serious defects of vegetative reproduction are not particularly subtle. The form of the trees is often poor, and the incidence of rot is high. The conditions required for successful reproduction sometimes place serious limitations on the size and spacing of the trees that can be grown. In this connection, however, it is important to distinguish between the different kinds of vegetative reproduction.

Stump sprouts. The sprouts that arise from the root collars of stumps represent the most important type of vegetative reproduction. These shoots almost invariably develop from **dormant buds** that were originally formed on the leading shoot of the seedling and grew outward with the cambium, but previously failed to develop into branches (Büsgen and Münch, 1929). The pith of dormant buds can be traced all the way back to the pith of the original stem. If this connection is broken during the growth of the tree the bud becomes incapable of developing into a new shoot. If the bark over the dormant bud becomes too thick, it may be impossible for the bud to break through and develop into a sprout. Both the thickness of the bark and the possibility of interruption of the bud trace increase with age. Therefore, the sprouting capacity of the tree tends to decline with age.

Dormant buds may be produced at any level on the bole, but only those at the ground line are capable of developing into useful sprouts. Those at higher levels are important only as a source of troublesome **epicormic branches** or "water sprouts." Roth and Sleeth (1939) observed that the sprouts of eastern oaks are subject to butt rot if they arise from the surface of the stump above the ground level.

Roth and Sleeth also found that the incidence of rot in oak sprouts increased rapidly with the diameter of the parent stump. This problem is a serious drawback inherent in vegetative reproduction from stump sprouts. Leffelman and Hawley (1925) found that this difficulty was reduced to insignificance only when the stumps were less than 2 inches in diameter. The cut surfaces of stumps of this size can usually be depended upon to callus over and seal off the xylem before it is infected with wood-rotting fungi. Sprouts arising from stumps less than 2 inches in diameter are given the special name, **seedling sprouts,** because they can be regarded as seedlings for all practical purposes. There are a few species in which the spread of rot from stump to sprout is not a significant problem. The best example is coast redwood, which produces good sprouts from even the most gigantic stumps.

Sprouts can also arise from **adventitious buds,** which develop mainly from callus tissues formed after wounding. If young sprouts originating from dormant buds are cut off a stump, adventitious buds may form in the resulting callus tissue and develop into new sprouts (Woods and Cassaday, 1961). In a few species, like American beech, adventitious buds produce **stool shoots;** these arise between the bark and wood and result in peculiar, usually short-lived rings of sprouts around the tops of the stumps.

Root suckers. Sprouts may also spring directly from the roots of trees which have been cut or damaged. Shoots of this kind, which are called **root suckers** or **root sprouts,** develop from adventitious buds that arise on the surfaces or in the outer layers of roots (Büsgen and Münch, 1929). Few species can be depended upon to reproduce from root suckers. American beech often produces dense clumps of root suckers that are very susceptible to rot. The only American species that are intentionally reproduced from root suckers are black locust and the quaking and bigtooth aspens.

Root suckers are less susceptible to butt rot than stump sprouts. Furthermore, they are not confined to the old stump but may spring up over wide areas around the parent trees. As a result, stands arising from root suckers are stocked much more evenly than those that consist of scattered clusters of stump sprouts.

Layering. This peculiar kind of vegetative reproduction arises from living, low-hanging branches that have been partially buried in moist organic matter. Layering is a process of silvicultural significance mainly in peat bogs where sphagnum moss tends to overgrow the lower branches of trees in open stands. Black spruce and northern white-cedar are the only American species that have been extensively regenerated by natural layering.

COPPICE METHOD

In this method stump sprouts or root suckers are relied upon as the main source of regeneration, although some seedlings and seedling sprouts may form part of the new crop. The stand is cut clear so that nothing is left to reduce the vigor of sprouting (Fig. 15-1). Most

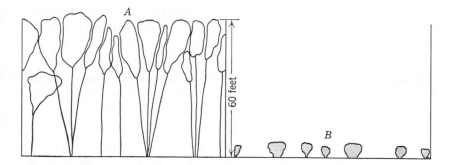

Fig. 15-1. A stand reproduced by the simple coppice method, shown before and after the reproduction cutting. *A.* Stand ready to cut clear. *B.* Same area 1 year later with tall, wide-spaced clumps of sprouts growing from the stumps of the felled trees.

hardwood species can be regenerated by this method, but redwood is the only American conifer for which it might be used with much success. A clear distinction should be drawn between species that sprout from stumps and those that form root suckers.

Most species that can be handled by the coppice method reproduce vegetatively from stump sprouts. The characteristics of this kind of reproduction place certain restrictions on the details of application. In the first place, the rotations must be shorter than those ordinarily contemplated for the production of good saw logs.

The spacing of a coppice stand derived from stump sprouts is controlled by the arrangement of the parent trees. If the rotation is extended sufficiently to produce saw timber, many of the basic sprout clumps will die of suppression. If dependence is then placed on reproduction by the simple coppice method, the new sprout clumps will grow up so far apart that the stems become crooked and branchy before the stand closes. Best results are obtained when the rotation is so short that the final spacing of sprout clumps is acceptable as an initial spacing for a new coppice stand.

The vigor of sprouting from stumps also declines rapidly with increasing age and diameter. The period of satisfactory sprouting is usually coincident with that of most rapid growth and ordinarily ends before the trees become effective seed bearers. The age at which sprouting can be expected varies widely with species. The longest rotation likely to produce satisfactory results varies between 30 and 40 years. Some species will sprout well when much older, but the problem of spacing then becomes the limiting factor.

The incidence and extent of decay in stump sprouts also increase with age (Roth and Sleeth, 1939), although the rate of deterioration varies greatly with species and climate. Some species are affected very slowly and to an insignificant extent; in others, decay spreads quickly and may be so injurious as to preclude use of the method.

The quality of stump sprouts depends in large measure on the height and characteristics of the stumps. Sprouts that arise from the root collar at or below the ground surface are the most vigorous and least susceptible to rot. Therefore, the stumps should be cut as low as possible. The same effect can be achieved by broadcast burning after cutting, which kills the living tissues of the exposed parts of the stumps, or by removing sprouts that originate too high on the stump (Roth and Hepting, 1943).

Little or no site preparation is required for regeneration from stump sprouts. They compete successfully with residual underbrush and are not influenced by the condition of the forest floor. Slash disposal is rarely a problem because the sprouts will come up through a fairly dense cover of debris and any reduction in the number of sprouts per clump causes the growth to be concentrated on fewer stems (Joranson and Kuenzel, 1940).

If repeated crops are to be secured from stump sprouts, the rotations are ordinarily less than 35 years and sometimes only several years long. The logical rotation length is that which will produce the maximum mean annual increment of fuelwood and other small products. The form of the stems is usually so poor that these are the only products intentionally grown under the coppice method. The rotations can be extended to produce saw timber of acceptable quality but this is most often done, intentionally or otherwise, in the process of converting coppice stands to high forests derived from seed. However, even if the coppice method is to be continued, it is still desirable to obtain some reproduction from planting or natural seeding to replace decadent root stocks and improve the spacing. This kind of restocking can sometimes be encouraged by thinning the coppice stand late in the rotation. Another important objective of any thinning is the reduction of the number of sprouts in a clump; the faster this number can be reduced to one, the better is the growth.

As the amount of reproduction from seed and the length of the rotation are increased, the coppice method comes to resemble the shelterwood or clearcutting methods. The best criterion of distinction is the relative importance and value attached to reproduction from sprouts as compared with that from seedlings. With species that occasionally sprout at advanced ages, it is to be expected that scattered trees of sprout origin will appear in many stands managed under high-forest methods.

Application of the coppice method to the management of species that regenerate from root suckers is even simpler than creating a new crop from stump sprouts. Sprouting is not confined to the stumps of the original stand so that spacing is not a problem nor is any care necessary in preparing the stumps. There is no evidence that the ability to produce root suckers declines with age. The maximum length of the rotation is determined largely by the rate at which the losses from decay increase. It so happens that the aspens, the American species most commonly regenerated from root suckers, have an unusually short pathological rotation, although the fungi responsible do not invade the sprouts through the old roots of the parent tree

(Schmitz and Jackson, 1927). Vigorous reproduction from root suckers can be obtained only if the parent stand is cut completely clear.

Advantages and Disadvantages of the Coppice Method

The coppice method is the simplest and most dependable means of approaching the maximum average annual production theoretically attainable from a given species. There is no delay in reproduction and the growing space in the soil remains almost continuously and completely occupied. Furthermore the rotations are confined to the period of most rapid growth in height and diameter. Although the wood produced is usually small and poor, the net return on the small financial investment in growing stock is high and may be obtained in a short period.

The coppice method is usually dependent on the existence of markets for large volumes of fuelwood and other small or specialized products. At least under American conditions and with the exception of redwood and the aspens, it is rarely possible to use the method continuously to grow much saw timber or even trees large enough to be harvested economically for pulpwood. The loss of the appropriate markets is financially disastrous if large areas are under this form of management because little or nothing can be harvested until the trees have grown to substantially larger sizes. The small growing stock does not provide much leeway for meeting extraordinary demands or changes in market conditions. This shortcoming is common to all silvicultural systems involving the production of small trees on short rotations. Consequently the method is poor policy on public forests managed to safeguard the regional forest economy and is at least treacherous as far as private ownership is concerned. Actually the small products secured can usually be obtained readily and with substantial silvicultural benefit from thinnings and other intermediate cuttings in high forests.

The coppice method reduces all operations to the utmost of simplicity. No other method is more certain to produce regeneration or to preserve whatever good genetic qualities existed in the previous crop.

From the aesthetic standpoint the coppice method is the least desirable means of regeneration because the forest is low in stature, monotonously regular, and often full of poorly formed trees.

Application of the Method

The coppice method is applicable only to species that are capable of sprouting satisfactorily and growing into useful material. The locality must ordinarily be one in which small products are readily salable. Under these conditions the small growing stock, low investment, and quick returns appeal to private landowners. The coppice method finds its greatest usefulness abroad in densely populated or poorly forested regions where coal and oil are scarce and wood is an indispensable fuel. Although the method is of small importance on this continent, its role in the world forest economy should not be underestimated.

Japan is one country where the method has been intensively developed, although not to the exclusion of high-forest methods. The rotations on privately owned lands are often as low as 4 to 8 years; Japanese foresters, however, advise rotations of 10 to 30 years, depending on species, site, and market requirements, in order to obtain higher mean annual growth.

One interesting modification practiced with the tolerant evergreen oaks of southern Japan is the coppice-selection method (Mine, 1950). More than half the cubic volume is removed at intervals of 6 to 15 years by cutting the larger stems from each sprout clump. By leaving several thousand stems per acre, at least two age classes are continuously maintained, thus protecting the steep slopes against erosion. However, the method is not suitable for deciduous oaks because they lack the ability to endure shade and to grow rapidly when released.

In the United States, as in many other countries, the coppice method represented the first kind of intentional silvicultural practice. Almost from the time of settlement until the present century, readily accessible parts of the eastern hardwood forest were coppiced repeatedly to produce successive crops of fuelwood and charcoal for both domestic and industrial use.

Intentional use of the coppice method in most eastern hardwood forests has almost vanished except as a means of growing small amounts of specialized products from small trees or for the intensive production of browse on wildlife management areas (Gysel, 1957). It is at least conceivable that coppice management might reappear if it became possible to harvest pulpwood with gigantic mowing machines or similar equipment and to develop a satisfactory means of removing bark from small sticks. As the costs of present methods of handling small sticks of hardwood pulpwood increase, the possibility of using the coppice method to produce this kind of material actually continues to become more remote than ever.

The most important sprouting species of the eastern hardwood forest are the oaks, although many others, such as white ash, yellow-poplar, basswood, and the maples, can also be reproduced from stump sprouts if the rotations are not too long. The species best adapted to the coppice method was the ill-fated chestnut, which sprouted vigorously even from large stumps and grew rapidly into stems suitable for saw logs and telephone poles. If a satisfactory hybrid chestnut resistant to the blight is developed, the coppice method will be the best for reproducing it through successive rotations. Vegetative propagation is the only means by which the proper combination of genetic factors could be economically preserved.

The old practice of coppicing hardwood stands in populous sections of the East has created deficiencies in growing stock which remain serious until the old sprout stands reach saw-timber size and can be reproduced from seed. Fortunately most of the species involved tend to remain sound until they reach appropriate age. Actually they sprout so well that the stands will contain a fairly high proportion of trees of sprout origin regardless of the method of reproduction employed. There appears to be little advantage in discriminating against individual trees solely because they are of sprout origin; although many of them should be eliminated in intermediate cuttings, there are always some worthy of retention through relatively long rotations.

Black locust, which yields very durable fence posts, is an outstanding example of a species which can be planted and managed thereafter by the coppice method (McIntyre, 1929).

Redwood is the only American conifer that can be satisfactorily reproduced from sprouts. Redwood sprouts are straight and highly resistant to decay so they make a remarkably dependable, acceptable, and durable contribution to regeneration after any kind of cutting (Fig. 14-8). The stumps of old-growth stands are so widely spaced that sprouts are sufficient to restock only a small fraction of cutover areas (Person and Hallin, 1942). The spacing of trees in second-growth stands may, however, be close enough to enable use of the coppice method; the techniques remain to be tested and developed.

The only important American species which must, in practice, be reproduced by the coppice method are the quaking and bigtooth aspens. Reproduction from seed is rare but that from root suckers is usually prolific (Fig. 15-2). Fortunately the method can be applied to these species without encountering many of the disadvantages of coppice management of most other species. The aspens occur over a wider range than any other American species but are most important in the Lake Region; there they have invaded vast areas after the destruction of virgin stands of pine or hardwoods by clearcutting and

Fig. 15-2. A well-stocked stand of 4800 aspen root-suckers per acre, which originated after a clearcutting made during the dormant season 11 years previously.
Chippewa National Forest, Minnesota. (*Photograph by U. S. Forest Service.*)

repeated fires. The aspens remain sound until they reach merchantable size only on the better sites (Stoeckeler, 1948). Aspen stands on
poor, sandy soils have an excessively short pathological rotation and
should be converted to conifers whenever possible. Stands on better
soils can be reproduced quite simply by cutting all the trees during
the dormant season (Zehngraff, 1949). Zillgitt (1951) found that
disking after cutting can bring about substantial increases in stocking
at low cost, although this treatment is not always necessary. Rotations
should be no longer than about 55 years on good sites, 45 years on
medium sites, or 35 years on poor sites, being governed by the inroads
of heart rots.

COPPICE-WITH-STANDARDS METHOD

In this method of reproduction, selected trees arising from either
seedlings or sprouts are maintained as standards above a simple coppice stand. This technique differs from the coppice-selection method
in that some of the best stems are reserved for a period as long as one
high-forest rotation. The resulting compound coppice resembles an

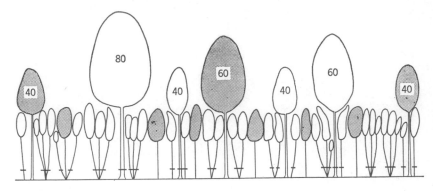

Fig. 15-3. A compound coppice, with three age classes of standards, at the end of a 20-year coppice rotation. All trees of the coppice stratum will be cut except those (*shaded crowns*) chosen for new standards. The 80-year-old standard has reached the end of its assigned rotation and will be cut. The cutting of three younger standards is an operation analogous to thinning by which the number of standards in a particular age class is gradually reduced with advancing age, just as in a balanced, uneven-aged stand.

uneven-aged selection forest superimposed on an absolutely even-aged coppice forest. The underlying coppice is reproduced on a short rotation by cutting all the trees in it except for those chosen as standards. Above the coppice are several different stories of standards, each story representing an age class that is a multiple of the length of the coppice rotation (Fig. 15-3).

The coppice-with-standards method is most easily understood by considering the steps by which a simple coppice is converted into a compound coppice stand. When the coppice reaches the end of the rotation all the trees except for certain carefully selected standards are removed. The individuals reserved should be dominants of good form and species, preferably of seedling origin. The sprouts which arise after the cutting form a distinct story beneath and between the standards.

At the end of the second coppice rotation another age class of standards is selected from the best trees in the coppice and the remainder are cut. Some of the standards left at the end of the first coppice rotation may be harvested, but the better ones are left. This process is continued through as many coppice rotations as desired; the number of age classes increases by one for each cutting of the coppice until the last of the first standards chosen are harvested. The number of standards in a given age class is gradually decreased through successive coppice rotations. If the stand is to be a sustained-yield unit, the distribution of diameter classes of standards should conform to the J-shaped curve that is characteristic of a balanced, uneven-aged stand.

When the old standards are finally harvested, their stumps may be too large to sprout and they may have to be replaced by planting or natural seeding from the remaining standards.

Cleanings are sometimes necessary to bring young prospective standards of seedling origin up through the competition of the faster-growing stump sprouts. The growth of well-established seedlings can also be accelerated by cutting them back to the ground and converting them into seedling sprouts. Plants of this type have the rapid initial growth of true sprouts, combined with the good form and rot-resistance of trees of seedling origin. If the seedling sprouts spring up in pairs or clusters, all but the best one should be eliminated.

The standards and the coppice need not be of the same species. Intolerant species with light foliage are usually favored as standards, but trees capable of thriving under partial shade are desirable in the coppice. The species of the coppice must sprout readily and produce wood that is merchantable in small sizes. The standards do not have to be of species that sprout; therefore, a conifer can be grown over a hardwood coppice, being introduced by planting if necessary.

The standards ordinarily are sufficiently isolated to develop deep crowns so their rather short boles grow rapidly in diameter. It is necessary that the coppice rotations be long enough that the sprouts will grow up and cause adequate natural pruning of the standards. This effect is also necessary to eliminate the epicormic branches that may develop on the naturally pruned boles as a result of the extreme exposure after each cutting.

Epicormic branching is a problem in many species of hardwoods and a few of conifers. It is by no means confined to the coppice-with-standards method but may be encountered after any kind of partial cutting. Artificial pruning is not a useful solution because resprouting is usually prompt, so repeated operations would be necessary to keep the stems clear. The physiological causes for the sprouting of dormant buds into epicormic branches are obscure. However, dominant trees with full, vigorous crowns are less likely to develop new branches after exposure than those that have unthrifty crowns or are from lower crown classes (Wahlenberg, 1950; Brinkman, 1955). The best way to avoid epicormic branching is to develop good crowns by thinnings and to maintain crop trees as dominants throughout their lives.

**Advantages and Disadvantages of the
Coppice-with-Standards Method**

The coppice-with-standards method occupies a position intermediate between the simple coppice and high-forest methods, although nearer to the former. It shares, in lesser degree, the merits and drawbacks of the coppice method.

Individual trees with stems of high quality can be grown rapidly in open stands without risk of creating large vacancies in the growing space. The invasion of undesirable vegetation is prevented by the rapid development of the young coppice which occupies the soil continuously. Trees of given diameter can be grown on substantially shorter rotations than in high forests. The compound coppice does not represent as heavy an investment in growing stock as a normally distributed high forest. Therefore, the net return on the investment is comparatively high, especially if fast-grown trees of large diameter command good prices.

The danger of logging damage to the residual stand is very low. The irregular appearance and the presence of fine individual trees make a compound coppice almost as pleasing aesthetically as a selection forest.

This method permits the production of saw timber and also allows the reservation of a fairly large growing stock for future demands. In these respects it is far superior to the simple coppice but inferior to the high-forest methods. Although saw timber is likely to be the principal product, this method, like simple coppice cutting, cannot be applied unless there is a good market for fuelwood or other low-grade products. As in the selection method, a high degree of skill is required in managing a compound coppice forest, particularly in regulating the cut of saw timber.

Application of the Method

The compound coppice method has an origin almost as ancient as that of the simple coppice method, having been applied in Europe long before 1600 (Troup, 1952). For centuries it was the most common method of managing hardwoods, especially oak, but most compound coppice stands are being transformed to high forest (Knuchel, 1953). The decline of markets for fuelwood as well as the difficulties of silviculture and management inherent in the system have been the main reasons for its abandonment.

In North America the method has been applied in intensive management of oak and associated hardwoods only in rare situations where there is some reason to produce substantial volumes of fuel-wood. It may still have some place as a means of managing small woodlots or areas where timber management is distinctly secondary to production of browse for wildlife. If it ever became desirable to produce large quantities of small hardwood for uses not now in exist-ence, the compound coppice method might well provide a form of management superior to the simple coppice method.

Otherwise the only importance of this rather archaic method is that it provides an idea of the possibilities of other techniques of growing isolated, deep-crowned trees above a matrix of shorter trees. In this respect, the method bears similarities to the reserve seed-tree method, the irregular shelterwood method, and the procedures for handling stratified mixtures that will be considered in the next chapter.

REPRODUCTION BY NATURAL LAYERING

In the peat swamps of the northern forest, regeneration of black spruce and northern white-cedar by layering is an important supple-ment to that from natural seeding. Although these species bear seed in abundance, a high proportion of the seedlings are suppressed by the relatively fast-growing sphagnum moss which is the main constit-uent of the ground cover. The seedlings have the best chance of sur-vival on scattered, elevated hummocks and on decaying wood, a seed-bed which should not be abundant in the managed forest. As time progresses the peat grows up and engulfs the bases of the trees, cover-ing any low-hanging branches that remain alive. The adventitious buds of buried portions of the branches develop into roots while the living ends of the branches turn upward and grow into separate trees. Young shoots of this kind are sturdier and more vigorous than seed-lings, but their form is not as satisfactory.

Reproduction of black spruce by layering is most readily achieved in peat bogs by the use of a modification of single-tree selection cut-ting (LeBarron, 1948; Heinselman, 1959). If continued reproduction from layers is to occur the uneven-aged form must be maintained so that the living crowns of the trees will remain in contact with the ground long enough for layers to become firmly rooted. It is possible that this kind of management provides a greater yield of pulpwood than even-aged systems because the site is more continuously occupied and any sort of reproduction is slow to start. However, Heinselman concluded that clearcutting in patches gave a higher proportion of the more desirable seedling reproduction greater freedom for the growth of the new crop. It may be that clearcutting with main reliance on regeneration from seed is best in the dense stands of better sites while selection cutting aimed at more layering is superior in the open stands of the poorest and wettest sites. It is significant that the residual stands are surprisingly resistant to wind because the peat is so resilient that the force of the wind tends to be dissipated in agitating the soil itself rather than in damage to the trees. However, black spruce growing on the firmer soils of uplands lacks windfirmness and rarely layers; therefore, it is best reproduced by clearcutting after advance regeneration has become established.

In northern white-cedar, reproduction from layers is fully as important as that from seed. Although normal layering from low-hanging branches is the most common form of vegetative reproduction, it is also possible for new, upright stems to develop from the branches of windthrown trees (Curtis, 1946). Appreciable amounts of reproduction may also arise from the rooting of small branches that become partially buried after being severed from the parent tree by browsing animals or during logging (Nelson, 1951). The species is important not only for the production of posts and poles but also as a favored winter food of deer. Nelson recommended that stands being managed primarily for wildlife be cut clear on short rotations according to the "layering method" in order to encourage a low growth of vegetative reproduction easily browsed by deer. Where wood production is also desired, he proposed use of a method of "layering-with-standards." In this method selected trees would be left to grow to merchantable size and a fair proportion of the reproduction would come from seed borne by the standards.

CONVERSION FROM COPPICE TO HIGH FOREST

Both in Europe and America the problem of transforming low forests into high forests is of far more importance than the creation and maintenance of coppice or coppice-with-standards. In Europe, it is primarily a case of converting from a compound coppice (Troup, 1952); in America, the starting point is usually a simple coppice, which has come into being as a result of repeated fire or clearcutting. The most outstanding examples of this problem are to be found in the vast forests of worthless aspen which dominate most of the old pine lands of the Lake Region (Heinselman, 1954). A similar situation is encountered in the coppice stands found in various parts of the eastern hardwood forest, especially in the Northeast. The extensive brushfields that have developed after heavy cutting and repeated burning in some western forests are different only by virtue of the fact that they are rarely thought of as coppice stands.

The most expeditious method of conversion is to destroy the old coppice and replace it by artificial regeneration. This was formerly a very difficult process because of the vigorous sprouting that almost invariably followed cutting. With herbicides and heavy mechanical equipment it is now ordinarily possible to kill or disrupt the roots of the old coppice sufficiently to prevent excessive sprout competition. This method of conversion is usually expensive but is distinctly cheaper than any other quick method.

If the old coppice includes desirable species that will develop acceptably it can be left to grow, and converted to high forest by shelterwood cuttings after the period of vigorous sprouting. This technique is applicable chiefly in the conversion of coppices in the eastern deciduous forest, except for those composed of aspen. The coppice rotations usually must be extended to 70 years or more, and even then a limited amount of sprout regeneration must be expected in the new crop.

The procedure consists in thinning the coppice stands at repeated intervals, saving the more promising stems. The thinnings must not be so heavy that the stand is converted into a new coppice with one age class of standards, unless this is regarded as a desirable stage of transition. The shelterwood cuttings are initiated near the end of the extended rotation to secure establishment of seedling reproduction. If necessary, the stumps can be killed with herbicides or any unwanted sprouts can be removed in subsequent cleanings or thinnings.

REFERENCES

Bourne, R. 1924. A note on a recent forest tour in Germany. *Quart. J. Forestry* 18:319–320.

Brinkman, K. A. 1955. Epicormic branching on oaks in sprout stands. *CSFES Tech. Paper* 146.

Büsgen, M., and E. Münch. 1929. *The structure and life of forest trees*. Translated from the 3rd German edition by T. Thomson. Wiley, New York. Pp. 53–79.

Curtis, J. D. 1946. Preliminary observations on northern white cedar in Maine. *Ecology* 27:23–36.

Downs, A. A. 1947. Losses from high stumps in sprout oak stands. *J. Forestry* 45:903–904.

Gysel, L. W. 1957. Effects of silvicultural practices on wildlife food and cover in oak and aspen types in northern Michigan. *J. Forestry* 55: 803–809.

Heinselman, M. L. 1954. The extent of natural conversion to other species in the Lake States aspen-birch type. *J. Forestry* 52:737–738.

———. 1959. Natural regeneration of swamp black spruce in Minnesota under various cutting systems. *USDA Production Research Rept.* 32.

Joranson, P. N., and J. G. Kuenzel. 1940. Control of sprouting from white oak stumps. *J. Forestry* 38:735–737.

Knuchel, H. 1953. *Planning and control in the managed forest.* Translated from German by M. L. Anderson. Oliver and Boyd, Edinburgh. Pp. 233–241.

Kramer, P. J., and T. T. Kozlowski. 1960. *Physiology of trees.* McGraw-Hill, New York. Pp. 388–390.

LeBarron, R. K. 1948. Silvicultural management of black spruce in Minnesota. *USDA Circ.* 791.

Leffelman, L. J., and R. C. Hawley. 1925. Studies of Connecticut hardwoods. The treatment of advance growth arising as a result of thinnings and shelterwood cuttings. *Yale Univ. School of Forestry Bul.* 15.

McIntyre, A. C. 1929. Black locust in Pennsylvania. *Penn. AES Bul.* 236.

———. 1936. Sprout groups and their relation to the oak forests of Pennsylvania. *J. Forestry* 34:1054–1058.

Mine, I. 1950. Improved management of coppice forest. *Japan, Ministry of Agr. and Forestry, Meguro Forest Exp. Sta. Forestry Tech. Series* 7.

Nelson, T. C. 1951. *A reproduction study of northern white cedar.* Michigan Department of Conservation, Game Division, Lansing.

Person, H. L., and W. Hallin. 1942. Natural restocking of redwood cutover lands. *J. Forestry* 40:683–688.

Roth, E. R., and B. Sleeth. 1939. Butt rot in unburned sprout oak stands. *USDA Tech. Bul.* 684.

———, and G. H. Hepting. 1943. Origin and development of oak stump sprouts as affecting their likelihood to decay. *J. Forestry* 41:27–36.

Schmitz, H., and L. W. R. Jackson. 1927. Heartrot of aspen with special reference to forest management in Minnesota. *Minn. AES Tech. Bul.* 50.

Spaeth, J. N. 1928. Twenty years growth of a sprout hardwood forest in New York: A study of the effects of intermediate and reproduction cuttings. *Cornell Univ. AES Bul.* 465.

Stoeckeler, J. H. 1948. The growth of quaking aspen as affected by soil properties and fire. *J. Forestry* 46:727–737.

Troup, R. S. 1952. *Silvicultural systems,* 2nd ed. Edited by E. W. Jones. Oxford University Press, London. Pp. 129–171.

Wahlenberg, W. G. 1950. Epicormic branching of young yellow-poplar. *J. Forestry* 48(9):417–419.

Woods, F. W., and J. T. Cassaday. 1961. Sprouting of sandhills scrub oaks following cutting. *SFES Occasional Paper* 186.

Zehngraff, P. J. 1949. Aspen as a forest crop in the Lake States. *J. Forestry* 47:555–565.

Zillgitt, W. M. 1951. Disking to increase stocking in aspen stands. *LSFES Tech. Note* 357.

CHAPTER 16

Silviculture of mixed stands

Most of the principles of silvicultural treatment have been developed on the basis of experience with pure stands and do not entirely fit the more complicated structure of some kinds of mixed stands. The techniques considered in previous chapters have generally involved the tacit assumption that an even-aged aggregation of trees forms a crown canopy in a single stratum. It has, of course, been noted that understories of shrubs or advance growth commonly appear beneath the main canopy and comments have been made about the use or control of such subordinate vegetation.

Mixed stands are, however, most readily understood if it is recognized that many of them do not form a single crown canopy. It is rare that any two associated species grow in height at precisely the same rate throughout life even when they are not actually competing with each other. If they are intimately intermingled, the species with the most rapid rate of juvenile growth in height will gain ascendancy over the slower growing species which will lag even farther behind because of lack of light. If the slower growing species is not sufficiently tolerant of shade and competition, only the random individuals that penetrate to the top of the main canopy will survive and a nearly pure stand of the faster growing species will remain. However, if the slower growing species is sufficiently tolerant, it will persist as a lower story beneath the main canopy formed by the other species. This is the simplest kind of **stratified mixture,** a kind of mixed stand in which the different species ultimately tend to become arranged in different strata of the total crown canopy (Fig. 16-1).

There are numerous possibilities for variations on this pattern. In

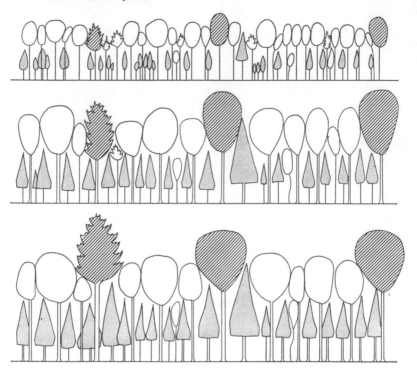

Fig. 16-1. Stages in the natural development of an untreated stratified mixture in an even-aged stand of the eastern hemlock-hardwood-white pine type. The upper sketch shows the stand at 40 years with the hemlock (*gray crowns*) in the lower stratum beneath an undifferentiated upper stratum. By the seventieth year (*middle sketch*) the emergents (*hatched crowns*) have ascended above the rest of the main canopy, except for the white pine which has only started to emerge. The lower sketch shows the stand as it would look after 120 years, long after the end of a commercial rotation for the upper strata, with the ultimate degree of stratification developed.

general, there will be as many strata as there are groups of species that differ from one another in height growth and tolerance. The stratification is not always perfect or readily apparent. Even when the stratification is well differentiated a few individuals of species that go with one stratum may by chance have grown upward into a higher stratum or have been left behind in a lower one. Furthermore, the observer standing beneath a stratified mixture will have to look closely and exercise some imagination to perceive the different strata. Finally there are some simple mixtures of two or three species which grow enough alike that they can be regarded as single-canopied stands.

The concept of the stratified mixture originated in the wet evergreen and moist deciduous tropical forests, which are practically incomprehensible without this means of analyzing their structure (Richards, 1952). In these forests, which normally have scores of species of trees per acre, it is usually possible to distinguish at least three canopy strata, exclusive of any of shrubs or lesser vegetation that may be able to persist beneath. In the terminology of Richards, the different strata are designated A, B, and C downward. Stratum A may be continuous but it is more often composed of scattered and isolated emergents that either grow faster or continue growing in height longer than their associates. The most valuable timber species, such as the famous Honduran mahogany and Spanish cedar of Central America, are usually emergents and relatively intolerant. If stratum A is discontinuous, stratum B forms the main upper canopy of the stand and often contains the most heterogeneous mixture of species. The subordinate stratum C is composed of the most tolerant species.

This mode of analysis appears to provide part of the key to successful treatment of some of the rather complicated mixed stands that abound in the moister regions of North America and other parts of the temperate zones. There are few items of unfinished business in silviculture that are more important than the development of techniques for harnessing the productive potential of such complex mixtures. The more favorable the climate and soil the greater is the number of species and the theoretical capacity of the sites to produce wood. At present the difficulty of dealing with all the different species restricts efforts to make highly effective use of such stands.

The wholesale conversion of these forests to pure stands and other simple forms is technically possible. It is not, however, always economically desirable because the conversion is expensive and because such wide departures from natural precedent have often had unfortunate consequences. Simple silviculture has important virtues, but the forest cannot always be torn down and replaced with stands suited to the most elementary kinds of treatment.

Natural mixed stands are found in most parts of North America but the more complicated ones usually occur in regions of abundant precipitation and favorable soils near the coasts. The most outstanding example is the eastern deciduous forest which, with its admixture of conifers, constitutes the most complex forest formation outside the tropics (Braun, 1950). The most complicated mixtures of conifers on

earth are the coastal forests of the Pacific Northwest with their out-
liers in the Northern Rocky Mountains; those of the west slope of the
Sierra Nevada are only slightly simpler.

Mixed forests in these regions sometimes have definite emergents
and distinction can usually be made between upper- and lower-story
species. However, a species that can behave as an emergent in one
part of its range may elsewhere occupy the *B* stratum in mixture with
different associates. Douglas-fir, for example, has the ability to develop into an emergent in mixtures in the Pacific Northwest but may
form the *B* stratum with emergents of coast redwood in northern
California or under the species with which it is normally associated in
the Rocky Mountains. Some valuable intolerant species, like yellow-
poplar, black cherry, and black walnut in the eastern hardwood forests, can scarcely exist in mixture unless they are emergents. Very
tolerant species, like the hemlocks and beech, are almost always to be
found in the bottom story of those stratified mixtures in which they
occur.

One of the well-differentiated stratified mixtures is that of eastern
white pine, various hardwoods, and eastern hemlock occasionally
found in the Northeast and the Lake Region. In old stands, the scattered white pines are the emergents simply because they continue
growth in height after the hardwoods have ceased. The mixed hardwoods form stratum *B*; the very tolerant eastern hemlocks, stratum
C, such that the two layers of conifers are separated by one of hardwoods. If the stands are viewed casually from a long distance to the
side, the few pines may appear to form a nearly pure stand; from
above, they would look like nearly pure hardwood stands; the observer beneath the stand would see mostly hemlocks, some hardwoods,
and scarce pines.

Of course, many mixed stands are less complicated. The two-
storied mixture of some fast-growing pioneer species, like aspen or
red alder, over more tolerant species is very easily recognized for
what it is and handled accordingly. In some mixed stands the different species vary so little in height growth that stratification does
not really develop and the stands remain single-canopied. For example, the height growth of shortleaf pine is not sufficiently slower than
that of loblolly pine for the two to differentiate into stratified mixtures.
In other mixtures, like those of spruce and fir, where both components are tolerant, either group may form either stratum and the
two are often intermingled.

Origin of stratified mixtures. It is important to note that *it is entirely possible and common for mixed and perfectly even-aged aggre-*

gations of trees to develop into stratified mixtures (Fig. 16-1). There are instances in the Northeast where the white pine–hardwood–hemlock mixtures just described have apparently arisen after very heavy cuttings which left little but low advance regeneration. Stratified mixtures of hardwoods in the southern bottomlands and elsewhere throughout the East often develop from the even-aged aggregations that appear after sizable holes are opened in the forest. In their early stages such mixtures usually seem to be hopelessly chaotic brush patches destined for complete domination by shrubs or tree species of low value. However, if there is adequate light, the valuable, long-boled, and relatively intolerant species almost miraculously arise un-aided above the confusion as emergents or main canopy trees (Putnam, Furnival, and McKnight, 1960). It is not unlikely that many of the mixtures of conifers now appearing on clearcut areas in the Pacific Northwest will form stratified mixtures with Douglas-fir above and tolerants, like red-cedar and hemlock, beneath.

Some species grow upward more quickly and at different times than others. The simplest kind of true emergents, exemplified by yellow-poplar (Hough and Taylor, 1946), shoot up quickly or not at all. The same is true of the fast-growing species that often form a full and even top canopy. Others resemble northern red oak which, in regions of its best development, remains merely at the same level as the associated hardwoods during the sapling stage; it then forges ahead so successfully that it may actually accelerate in diameter growth at middle age without aid from thinning. Some, such as the white pines and spruces, may linger below the top of the canopy and ultimately rise above it simply because they survive or continue growing in height longer than their associates. These examples serve to indicate that mixed stands cannot be handled successfully without determining the development of each species with respect to its associates.

Once a mixed stand has become stratified the total range of height and diameter classes becomes very wide even though the distribution of diameters for any one species continues to conform to the bell-shaped normal curve. The diameter distribution of the whole stand may even come to resemble the J-shaped curve associated with balanced uneven-aged stands, although the very small sizes are usually lacking. It is, therefore, not surprising that even-aged, stratified mixtures are commonly mistaken for uneven-aged stands. Even if the arrangement of age classes is correctly identified, it is still tempting to assume that the stand can be treated as if it were uneven-aged and entirely suitable for selection management.

This kind of misconstruction, like most of the others possible in silviculture, leads to mistakes. In this instance it is simply incorrect to assume that the whole mixture will magically replace itself during a series of successive cuttings of the largest trees as they grow beyond a certain diameter limit. The largest and most valuable species initially present are almost invariably the fast-growing intolerants confined to the upper layers. If they are all witlessly cut in the early stages, the seed source is eliminated and few real openings are made in which they could become re-established anyhow. Part of the difficulty is that the different size classes are arranged one above the other rather than intermingled horizontally as they are in truly uneven-aged stands.

Of course, not all stratified stands are even-aged. New age classes can develop beneath a long-established overstory and, as they grow up, additional ones can appear beneath. However, if this happens, each wave of reproduction usually represents a later successional stage than the preceding one. If the upper story is still complete the growth of the younger trees is distinctly restricted until openings develop above. In any event, it is not often that the same species would be equally represented from top to bottom in such a vertical arrangement of age classes. The result is usually the same as in an even-aged, stratified mixture; the least tolerant species occupy the upper story and the most tolerant are found beneath.

In other words, the truly uneven-aged arrangement of age classes is best regarded as something generally existing in the horizontal and on a larger dimensional scale than the arrangement of different species in a stratified mixture (Fig. 16-2). In fact, there are a number of instances in which stratified mixtures are most logically managed by a modification of the group-selection system in which stratified, even-aged aggregations representing different ages and stages of development are interspersed with one another. This is sometimes the most effective way to keep a seed source of desirable species close to all groups where regeneration cuttings are in progress.

Treatment of Mixed Stands

If the different species in a mixed stand develop at varying rates, as they usually do, the treatments must be conducted with due regard for these differences. If the overstory is undesirable and the better species are at the lower levels, it is obviously advantageous to eliminate the upper strata as quickly as possible and preferably in such manner that the unwanted species do not reappear. If the re-

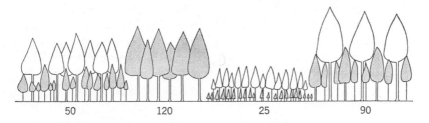

50   120   25   90

Fig. 16-2. Part of an uneven-aged stand being managed by the group-selection system and composed of a stratified mixture of two conifers arranged in even-aged groups. The trees with the *light crowns* are of an intolerant species that grows comparatively rapidly when young and attains greater size than the more tolerant (*dark-crowned*) species of the mixture. The numbers indicate the ages of the groups. The upper stratum is ready for the first thinning at 25 years of age and, at 50 years, most of the crowns of this stratum have been freed around most of their perimeter. This stratum is harvested soon after 90 years; this re-leases the lower stratum which has been left untreated in the meantime to fill any gaps. The remaining stratum is managed for the rest of the rotation as a simple, single-canopied, even-aged group. After 120 years, it is ready for uniform shel-terwood cuttings designed to replace the mixture. The trees reserved in these cuttings provide the seed of the tolerant species; that of the intolerant species comes from adjacent groups. There is no silvicultural reason why either stage of the rotation could not be prolonged or terminated earlier; the timing indicated here is purely an example.

verse is true, the lower stories should be discriminated against when-ever opportunity offers. If good species are found in all strata, more sophisticated treatment is necessary. However, if a mixture contains many species, it is inevitable that some will be of more harm than benefit, so some effort toward reduction of the number of species is usually desirable.

If the uppermost species are the most desirable, as is usually the case, the stands have one very useful attribute not found in pure stands. In pure, even-aged aggregations there is a tendency for all the trees to grow at the same rate so that the crown canopy is apt to become congested and tightly closed all at one level. If the trees are kept far enough apart to remain vigorous, there is little oppor-tunity for the effects of competition to cause straight, well-pruned boles to develop. If they are close together they are very likely to develop good boles but very small crowns; one must then choose be-tween expensive precommercial thinnings or the loss of growth sus-tained awaiting natural expression of dominance. In mixed stands, on the other hand, the trees that ultimately rise above the majority are far more likely to remain crowded from the side during the formative period and then automatically emerge and develop good crowns at the proper time. This kind of self-thinning can cause substantial improvements in diameter growth and is a very useful process in an economy where early thinnings are not profitable. The fine dominants often found in undisturbed stands of mixed hardwoods are probably the result of this kind of development.

If the uppermost stratum consists of scattered emergents or of a canopy that never becomes fully closed, the component trees continue to grow rapidly in diameter for a long period because their crowns remain deep and well exposed to sunlight. The trees of the lower strata act as trainers, causing some continued natural pruning as well as the suppression of any epicormic branches. The general effect is much the same as that achieved in the coppice-with-standards method, except that the lower strata do not have to be cut repeatedly and are usually more effective and salable than a coppice would be.

It may, of course, be desirable or even necessary to aid and hasten the development of the upper story by cleanings in the early stages. Once the upper strata have developed, their treatment during the period of intermediate cuttings is comparatively simple. They can be thinned as occasion arises and thinned much more heavily than would be possible in a pure stand because any gaps are quickly utilized by the lower strata (Fig. 16-3).

If the lower strata include an adequate number of trees of good species capable of responding to release and if their form is not harmed as a consequence of growing beneath other trees, stratified mixtures can be handled very effectively. The overstory trees may be removed in whatever pattern is most logical from the standpoint of financial maturity, the need for reserving sources of seed, and similar considerations. As the upper strata are removed the lower strata take command of the growing space and can be carried to the end of their normal rotation more or less as even-aged stands.

The previously mentioned mixtures of white pine, hardwoods, and hemlock in the Northeast provide a good illustration of how this process might proceed. The most crucial component is the lower stratum of hemlock, a species sufficiently tolerant that it can grow right up to the bases of the crowns of the trees above. It thus trains the boles of the hardwoods which have a propensity for developing forks, crooks, large branches, and short merchantable boles. The understory hemlock is practically the only kind of vegetation that can maintain a stand atmosphere at all conducive to the natural shed-

Fig. 16-3. A stratified mixture, consisting of a 60-year-old upper story of various hardwoods above a somewhat younger lower story of eastern hemlock, in Connecticut, 2 years after the third thinning of the hardwood stratum. The straight yellow-poplars tend to project as emergents above the less erect red oaks and other hardwoods. If the hemlocks were as old as the hardwoods, they would extend up to the bases of the hardwood crowns. (*Photograph by Yale University School of Forestry.*)

ding of dead branches from immature white pines. It also precludes the development of the thickets of shrubs that normally occupy the growing space beneath hardwood stands and quickly claims any gaps made in the overstory. Once the high-quality timber of the overstory has been carried to the end of a 60- to 90-year rotation, the hemlock is left for several decades. During this second stage of the rotation the hemlock grows very rapidly, producing large volumes of material that is suitable for construction timber if the trees are not allowed to become so large that they develop rot and shake. This procedure appears to work only in a belt extending from southern Maine to northern Pennsylvania; outside this belt, eastern hemlocks are more likely to respond to sudden release by dying of exposure rather than by vigorous growth (Graham, 1943).

In any such procedure it is necessary to retain a seed source of the overstory species so that they can be regenerated at the end of the two-stage rotations involved. The least complicated way of doing this is to handle the stands on a group-selection system such that the overstory of trees of younger age classes are close to the groups that are cut clear (Fig. 16-2). If ecological requirements dictate securing regeneration in smaller gaps or if the whole stand is to be kept as nearly even-aged as possible, a modification of the irregular shelter-wood method can be employed (Fig. 16-4). In this approach some of the overstory trees are retained throughout the rotation and openings are made in the understory when and where reproduction is desired.

If the trees of the lower stratum are too poor to be left for further growth or cannot withstand exposure, one useful approach is something more closely akin to the uniform shelterwood system. The overstory trees are temporarily reserved in whatever numbers are necessary for seed, shelter, and the suppression of undesirable pioneer vegetation; the understory is reduced enough to provide the proper environmental conditions for re-establishment of the desired mixture. If the proper species will appear after clearcutting in the presence of a seed source and need no protection, the new crop can be established simply by clearcutting in patches. If advance growth of the proper species is already present beneath the various strata, the one-cut shelterwood method may suffice. If any or all of the trees of the lower strata are potentially worthless, there is no silvicultural system sufficiently magical to make them otherwise; if they will not die of exposure and are likely to hamper future growth, the only logical thing to do is to kill them.

The best species for the lower strata are those that are sufficiently geotropic that they continue growing straight and do not bend toward the light. They must also be resistant to rot and all the other vicissitudes that may befall them during long periods of slow growth. Tolerant conifers are ordinarily more satisfactory understory species than hardwoods. American beech is, for example, a species with a bad reputation because of the deformities and rot that develop in it while

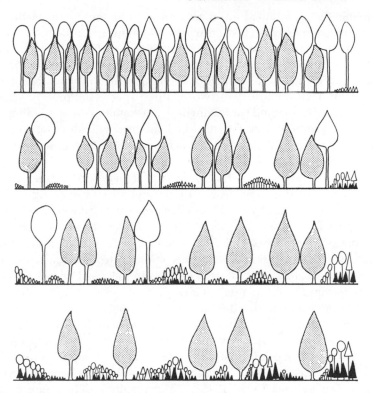

Fig. 16-4. Reproduction of an even-aged stratified mixture of eastern hemlock (*dark crowns*), hardwoods (*rounded white crowns*), and white pine (*pointed white crowns*) by the irregular shelterwood method. The upper sketch shows a 75-year-old stand prior to treatment. Successive sketches, from top to bottom, show the stand at 15-year intervals, just before each cutting. They indicate how the upper stratum is opened up rapidly, releasing the hemlock but leaving some of the upper stratum for seed and extra increment. The hemlock stratum is opened more slowly and only to the extent necessary to allow regeneration of the intolerant species of the upper stratum. The bottom sketch shows the stand at 120 years, just before the last of the old hemlocks are removed; this leaves a new stratified mixture of somewhat broader range of age than the previous stand.

it grows in its characteristic position in the lower stratum of northern hardwood stands. Like most hardwoods, it develops very well if it is continuously dominant.

Planting of Mixed Stands

Stratified mixtures can be created by planting. This is indeed about the only basis on which intimate mixtures of species can be permanently maintained in plantations. The most successful mixtures are composed of fast-growing intolerant species above slower-growing tolerant species. If there are species that differ sufficiently in rate of growth and tolerance it is possible to create stands with several different strata, although it is rare that much advantage is gained by having more than two or three species. Properly selected species can be planted simultaneously at random or according to a variety of patterns and the stratified mixture will develop automatically. Sometimes the fastest growing can be planted several years after those destined for the lower strata.

The larches are among the most satisfactory overstory species for plantations because they grow rapidly and usually cast light shade. The very intolerant pines that so often appear as pioneers are almost equally useful. The best species for the lower strata are very tolerant conifers, notably spruce, fir, hemlock, and others characteristic of late successional stages. Species of intermediate tolerance, such as Douglas-fir and most of the pines, can be used for either story depending on the associated species.

It is practically impossible to find two species that will grow at the same rate and thus develop into single-canopied mixtures. The one with the more rapid juvenile growth will go to the top and the other will either lapse into an understory or die of suppression. Even small differences in initial height growth will cause such a development (Hawley and Lutz, 1943). The resulting self-thinning effect may enhance the growth of the ascendant species, but the other species may prove to be a rather expensive filler and trainer if it does not grow to useful size. If mixtures of closely similar species are desired it is necessary to separate them into groups and strips wide enough to allow space for mature individuals of the particular species. However, if horizontal mixtures of this sort are planted the arrangement should be laid out either to expedite future harvests or conform to variations in site and existing vegetation.

Mixed stands are not appreciably more expensive to plant than pure stands. The extra trouble of handling two or more species, and controlling their arrangement, may be offset by the lesser cost of the stock of one of the species.

Examples of Silviculture of Mixed Stands

There is scarcely any locality in which the details of managing and maintaining mixed stands have been completely developed. In fact, the concept of the stratified mixture is borrowed from the moist tropical forests mainly as a device for reducing the silvicultural confusion generated by the simpler mixtures found in temperate climates.

The forests of the moist parts of the tropics are themselves so chaotically variable that it is almost foolhardy to attempt any brief synopsis of developments in their treatment. Three main avenues of approach may be distinguished (Haig, Huberman, and Aung Din, 1958). The simplest but most expensive of these is clearcutting and planting of the more valuable species. The control of pioneer weeds is so much of a problem that agricultural crops are sometimes interplanted with the trees which benefit from the subsequent cultivation; this combination is the so-called **taungya** method of planting. The second technique is that of "enrichment" which usually involves the planting of the most valuable species in lanes opened through the natural forest; this works only if followed by frequent cleanings of the aggressive climbers and weed trees that inevitably appear in openings. Ever-increasing interest is directed toward natural regeneration, a third alternative which requires exceedingly skillful treatment but is least likely to depend on small armies of laborers with machetes.

It was once taken more or less for granted that light selection cutting was most likely to ensure the perpetuation and increase of the small minority of valuable species. However, this was usually found to be a very cumbersome approach requiring repeated release of feeble trees growing in small holes in the stands. In recent years there has been an increasing trend toward essentially even-aged management in which some reliance is placed on the ability of the valuable intolerant species to rise above their competitors when an adequate amount of light is admitted. A considerable amount of cleaning is still necessary, but it does not have to be continued indefinitely.

Some of the best success has been achieved with the dipterocarps of Southeast Asia which are sufficiently tolerant to become established as advance regeneration. They are also capable of developing into stands in which the useful species predominate, an uncommon situation in the moist tropical forests. In Malaya it was found that heavy unregulated cuttings of all merchantable trees made during World War II actually gave better regeneration than the lighter selection cuttings previously attempted. Consequently attention shifted to a version of one-cut shelterwood method in which the reduced cover left by unmerchantable subordinate trees is used to ward off the invasion of grass and other weeds while the valuable species in the advance growth are brought up by means of release cuttings. The technique does not differ greatly from the heavy cuttings that can sometimes be used to rehabilitate defective stands of eastern hardwoods (Jemison, 1946).

In tropical Africa and America there appear to be only a few species that develop equally useful advance regeneration; these are usually heavy-seeded and tend to grow in pure stands (Budowski, 1956). In the complex mixed forests where light-seeded intolerant species are most valuable the "tropical shelterwood method" seems most highly regarded. This is a kind of irregular shelterwood cutting in which the seed cutting is accomplished mainly by harvesting or killing trees of the middle canopy strata. Most of the valuable trees of the upper strata are temporarily reserved for seed and the lower strata are kept in place long enough to keep the jungle of climbers and weedy pioneers in check. So many of the trees are unmerchantable that the method is economically successful only because of the availability of herbicides that can be applied by injection.

On the good sites where eastern hardwoods grow satisfactorily, mixed stands usually become stratified with the better species ascending to the upper strata. The manipulation of the upper strata is not especially difficult. The main problem is dealing effectively with the lower story, which will usually respond to release, although the result is often an enhanced growth of malformed, short-boled trees that impede regeneration of the good species (Trimble, 1961). Markets become so quickly glutted with the low-quality products available from the trees of the lower strata that greater use of tree-killing techniques seems desirable.

Mixed stands of conifers, whether stratified or not, are much easier to handle than those of hardwoods because the trees grow straight. There are a number of examples of productive stratified mixtures of conifers in the West and North. Among these are the Douglas-fir–western hemlock–western red-cedar mixtures of the Pacific Northwest; the so-called western white pine type of the Inland Empire; the mixtures of jack, red, and white pine in the Lake Region; the western larch–Douglas-fir type; and the mixtures of eastern white pine with eastern hemlock or balsam fir in the Northeast. Although the principles according to which these stratified mixtures might be managed are reasonably clear, the details remain to be developed. In some instances the mixtures are not necessarily as satisfactory as pure stands of the more valuable intolerant species. Oddly enough the resistance of understory conifers to foliage spraying with herbicides is coming to make them more difficult to control than the sprouting hardwoods once viewed as the main impediment to successful management of some conifers.

There are, of course, some mixed forest types that may or may not become stratified. Among these are the various mixtures of spruces and true firs as found in eastern Canada, adjacent parts of the United States, and the Rocky Mountains. The best-known samples are the upland mixtures of red, white, and black spruce with balsam fir found from the St. Lawrence Valley southeastward (Westveld, 1953). The firs grow more rapidly than the spruces and also reproduce more prolifically (Place, 1955). However, any stratified mixtures that develop ultimately break up because the firs are comparatively short-lived. The proportion of residual spruce thus gradually increases in the upper stratum but the advance regeneration that simultaneously begins to appear beneath the stand is predominantly of fir (Ghent, 1958). The result is that the fir is sometimes on top and sometimes under the spruce, but more often the two are intermingled at all levels.

The maintenance of both spruce and fir is usually regarded as desirable; although the fir grows to pulpwood size more rapidly than the spruce, it is distinctly perishable beyond the sixtieth year and also invites the catastrophic outbreaks of the spruce budworm (Blais, 1958). The chief problem is maintaining the proper proportion of spruce, which usually finds its way to the upper crown levels simply by outliving the fir. The "clearcutting" or one-cut shelterwood cutting so common in the region (see Chapter 13) has the same effect as the budworm outbreaks; that is, it releases the advance regeneration which grows up into stands of nearly pure fir (Hatcher, 1960).

It has long been recognized that the best solution is to reduce the balsam fir by cutting it heavily for pulpwood before it becomes rotten and releasing spruce in the process. This often means that the fir is cut to a minimum diameter limit of 8 or 9 inches and the spruce to an approximate limit several inches larger. The fir is thus carried on a shorter rotation than the spruce. While there is no argument about the desirability of this general procedure, there is the option of conducting it within the framework of the single-tree selection method or that of the irregular shelterwood method (Westveld, 1946; McLintock, 1947; Place, 1953; Baskerville, 1960). The selection method would be aimed at the ultimate creation of balanced uneven-aged stands by frequent light cuttings; the irregular shelterwood, at the development of stands of not more than two age classes with the cuttings coming at longer intervals during the last portion of a long rotation.

Relative Merits of Pure and Mixed Stands

The question of whether mixed stands are superior to pure stands is fully as controversial as that of the relative merits of different kinds of age distribution in stands. In this case, comparisons need not be made over long periods and the evidence is more plentiful. Nevertheless broad generalization is deceptive if not impossible.

Mixed stands containing several different species are usually more resistant to damage by biotic agencies than are pure stands (Graham, 1952). The reasons for this superior resistance are in general the same as those which tend to apply in uneven-aged stands. The physical separation of food plants tends to inhibit the spread of all but the most mobile pests and also keeps their populations in check. The intimate mixture of susceptible and resistant species provides, for example, a good means of combatting root rots like *Fomes annosus* and *Poria weirii*, pathogens which are becoming increasingly important and are difficult to control by other means.

In fact, mixture of species probably reduces danger of loss to biotic enemies somewhat more than does mixture of age classes. However, this kind of protection is more effective against the less dangerous indigenous pests than it is against virulent introduced diseases like the white pine blister rust or serious native enemies like the spruce budworm. Furthermore, there are numerous instances of pure stands that are more resistant to certain pests than are mixed stands composed of the same species together with highly susceptible ones. Pure stands of spruce are more resistant to the spruce budworm than spruce-fir stands with overmature balsam firs which serve as brood trees (McLintock, 1947). The presence of susceptible black birch and dogwood in eastern hardwood stands increases the danger of infection of other species by Nectria canker (Kienholz and Bidwell, 1938).

There are numerous exceptions to the generality that mixed or other allegedly natural kinds of stands are more resistant to damage than pure stands (Peace, 1961). The resistance of any stand to its biotic enemies depends on the susceptibility of its individual components and not on doctrinaire generalizations. The relative resistance of mixed or pure stands to damage from fire and from mechanical agencies such as wind and snow depends on the physical characteristics of the stands and the nature of the injurious agencies. A mixed stand of both resistant and nonresistant species is bound to be more secure against injury than a pure stand of a nonresistant species, but there is no reason why it should be as secure as a pure stand of a resistant species. Often the only value of mixed stands in this respect is the rather dreary consolation that risk of losing whole stands at once is reduced.

The question of whether mixed stands are more productive than pure stands depends on (1) the units of volume or value on which comparison is based, (2) relative vulnerability to losses, and (3) relative degree of utilization of the growth factors of the site.

As far as total production is concerned, horizontal single-canopied mixtures are bound to yield less than pure stands of the most productive member (Jackson, 1960), except to whatever extent the mixed stands suffer lower losses. The productive potential of the fastest growing species is simply diluted by intermingling with the less productive.

Stratified mixtures, however, are likely to have greater total productivity than pure stands of the overstory species. The species of the lower strata are, by their very nature, more efficient in photosynthesis than the overstory species. Furthermore, they must to some extent use solar energy not absorbed by the overstory. They also utilize some of the component of total productivity that would be wasted on any lesser vegetation that might otherwise be present. It is, however, probable that a pure stand of the tolerant species of the subordinate stratum would have a greater total productivity than a mixture of which it could be a part.

Mixed stands probably utilize the soil more effectively than pure stands, although the extent to which they do so is not clear. It is not likely that the root systems of different species become stratified like the crowns, but some penetrate more deeply than others and thus extract soil nutrients and water from a thicker stratum than is available to the other species. The nutrients ultimately return to the forest floor in fallen leaves and thus become available to the whole community. Some species are also more efficient than others in extracting soil nutrients. A mixed stand including such a species might thus become more productive than a pure stand of one with less efficient roots but not necessarily more than a pure stand of the most efficient.

Another slightly different question is whether mixed stands are more effective than pure stands in preventing loss of nutrients through leaching; this seems at least theoretically possible. Actually, comparisons made by Lunt (1941) in the humid climate of Connecticut indicate that losses from leaching beneath both mixed hardwood stands and pure red pine plantations are insignificant. Scott (1955) has also found that the shrubs and herbaceous plants which commonly grow beneath "pure" stands play an active role in the nutrient cycle of the forest. It is probable that, in most forests, any nutrients which are in temporary surplus are soon captured by new plants established in the vacant growing space. However, some of this surplus may be lost if the soil is too cold or too dry to allow the vegetation to respond rapidly. The activity of micro-organisms and the adsorptive capacity of soil colloids also resist such losses.

If stand composition is such that the litter of the forest floor decomposes very slowly, much of the nutrient capital of the site may be bound up in unavailable form in thick layers of humus. This is most likely to occur under extremely dry, wet, or cold conditions. The best means of dealing with this problem is to render the microclimate more favorable to decomposition; this can be done by appropriate cuttings or by shifting to a kind of composition that does not shield the ground surface so thoroughly. Sometimes the decomposition of coniferous litter is enhanced by an admixture of hardwood litter which supports a more abundant and versatile population of decomposing and disintegrating organisms.

It must be borne in mind that no manipulation of vegetation can bring about any increase in the total nutrient capital of a site. The fact that poor soils tend to support pure stands whereas mixed stands are associated with good soils is an effect rather than a cause of the condition of the soil.

Gross production and vulnerability to losses are not the only relevant considerations because other factors are also involved in determining the value of utilizable production. The highly efficient shade-tolerant species that occupies the site most fully and offers the greatest total productivity may, for example, be a deep-crowned tree that produces very knotty wood of low technical quality.

The choice between pure and mixed stands most often comes to issue as one between pure stands of conifers and mixed stands of conifers and hardwoods. Evergreen conifers are generally capable of producing substantially more wood substance than deciduous hardwoods and a higher proportion of it is deposited in the usable bole. Furthermore, the growth of conifers is diminished less by unfavorable site conditions than that of hardwoods. Consequently, a pure coniferous stand plagued with some ills might still be superior to the alternative of a mixture of conifers and hardwoods when all relevant factors were considered. It is, therefore, logical that the conversion of hardwood stands on poor and mediocre sites to pure stands of conifers is usually regarded as desirable.

The whole question actually comes into prominence on relatively favorable sites which are the only ones where hardwoods grow well and where natural mixed stands of acceptable quality are most likely to occur. Here the margin of difference in basic productivity between conifers and hardwoods is not as great and the greater unit value of high-quality hardwoods becomes an important factor. Furthermore, the techniques of controlling stand composition are not yet sufficiently cheap or effective that the forester has complete freedom of choice on these sites.

REFERENCES

Baskerville, G. L. 1960. Conversion to periodic selection management in a fir, spruce, and birch forest. *Canada, Forestry Branch, Forest Research Div. Tech. Note* 86.

Blais, J. R. 1958. The vulnerability of balsam fir to spruce budworm attack in northern Ontario, with special reference to the physiological age of the tree. *Forestry Chronicle* 34:405–422.

Braun, E. Lucy. 1950. *The deciduous forest of eastern North America.* Blakiston, Philadelphia.

Budowski, G. 1956. Regeneration systems in tropical American lowlands. *Caribbean Forester* 17:75–90.

Ghent, A. W. 1958. Studies of regeneration in forest stands devastated by the spruce budworm. *Forest Sci.* 4:135–146.

Graham, S. A. 1943. Causes of hemlock mortality in northern Michigan. *Univ. of Mich. School of Forestry and Conservation Bul.* 10.

———. 1952. *Forest Entomology,* 3rd ed. McGraw-Hill, New York. Pp. 177–193.

Haig, I. T., M. A. Huberman, and Aung Din. 1958. Tropical silviculture, Vol. I. *FAO Forestry and Forest Products Studies* 13.

Hatcher, R. J. 1960. Development of balsam fir following a clearcut in Quebec. *Canada, Forestry Branch, Forest Research Div. Tech. Note* 87.

Hawley, R. C., and H. J. Lutz. 1943. Establishment, development, and management of conifer plantations in the Eli Whitney Forest, New Haven, Connecticut. *Yale Univ. School of Forestry Bul.* 53.

Hough, A. F., and R. F. Taylor. 1946. Response of Allegheny northern hardwoods to partial cutting. *J. Forestry* 44:30–38.

Jackson, D. S. 1960. World experience with forest monotypes. *In: Proc., Fourth Conf. on Southern Industrial Forest Management, Duke Univ. School of Forestry.* Pp. 12–19.

Jemison, G. M. 1946. Rehabilitation of defective Appalachian hardwood stands. *J. Forestry* 44:944–948.

Kienholz, R., and C. B. Bidwell. 1938. A survey of diseases and defects in Connecticut forests. *Conn. AES Bul.* 412.

Lunt, H. A. 1941. Forest lysimeter studies under hardwoods. *Conn. AES Bul.* 449.

McLintock, T. F. 1947. Silvicultural practices for control of spruce budworm. *J. Forestry* 45:655–658.

Peace, T. R.   1961.   The dangerous concept of the natural forest.   *Quart. J Forestry* 55:12–23.

Place, I. C. M.   1953.   "Selective cutting" and the all-aged stand.   *Forestry Chronicle* 29:248–253.

———.   1955.   The influence of seed-bed conditions on the regeneration of spruce and balsam fir.   *Canada, Forestry Branch Bul.* 117.

Putnam, J. A., G. M. Furnival, and J. S. McKnight.   1960.   Management and inventory of southern hardwoods.   *USDA Agr. Handbook* 181.

Richards, P. W.   1952.   *The tropical rain forest, an ecological study.*   Cambridge University Press.

Scott, D. R. M.   1955.   Amount and chemical composition of the organic matter contributed by overstory and understory vegetation to forest soil.   *Yale Univ. School of Forestry Bul.* 62.

Trimble, G. R., Jr.   1961.   Managing mountain hardwoods—a ten-year appraisal.   *NEFES Sta. Paper* 143.

Westveld, M.   1953.   Ecology and silviculture of the spruce-fir forests of eastern North America.   *J. Forestry* 51:422–430.

Common and scientific names of trees and shrubs mentioned in the text

Common Name	Scientific Name *
Alder, red	*Alnus rubra* Bong.
Ash, white	*Fraxinus americana* L.
Aspen, bigtooth	*Populus grandidentata* Michx.
quaking	*Populus tremuloides* Michx.
Basswood, American	*Tilia americana* L.
Beech, American	*Fagus grandifolia* Ehrh.
European	*Fagus sylvatica* L.
Birch, black	*Betula lenta* L.
gray	*Betula populifolia* Marsh.
paper	*Betula papyrifera* Marsh.
yellow	*Betula alleghaniensis* Britton
Blackberry	*Rubus* spp.
Cedar, Spanish	*Cedrela mexicana* Roem.
Cherry, black	*Prunus serotina* Ehrh.
choke	*Prunus virginiana* L.
pin	*Prunus pensylvanica* L. f.
Chestnut, American	*Castanea dentata* (Marsh.) Borkh.
Cottonwood, eastern	*Populus deltoides* Bartr.
Currant and gooseberry	*Ribes* spp.
Dogwood, flowering	*Cornus florida* L.
Douglas-fir	*Pseudotsuga menziesii* (Mirb.) Franco
Fir, alpine	*Abies lasiocarpa* (Hook.) Nutt.
balsam	*Abies balsamea* (L.) Mill.

* Scientific names of North American trees based on: E. L. Little, Jr., *Check list of native and naturalized trees of the United States (including Alaska)* U. S. Dept. Agr., Agr. Handbook 41, 1953.

Fir, grand	*Abies grandis* (Dougl.) Lindl.
silver (European)	*Abies alba* Mill.
white	*Abies concolor* (Gord. & Glend.) Lindl.
Hemlock, eastern	*Tsuga canadensis* (L.) Carr.
western	*Tsuga heterophylla* (Raf.) Sarg.
Hickory	*Carya* spp.
Hinoki	*Chamaecyparis obtusa* Endl.
Hop-hornbeam, eastern	*Ostrya virginiana* (Mill.) K. Koch.
Incense-cedar, California	*Libocedrus decurrens* Torr.
Larch, western	*Larix occidentalis* Nutt.
Japanese	*Larix leptolepis* (Sieb. and Zucc.) Gord.
Locust, black	*Robinia pseudoacacia* L.
Mahogany, Honduran	*Swietenia macrophylla* King.
Maple, big-leaf	*Acer macrophyllum* Pursh
red or soft	*Acer rubrum* L.
sugar	*Acer saccharum* Marsh.
vine	*Acer circinatum* Pursh
Oak, bear	*Quercus ilicifolia* Wangenh.
black	*Quercus velutina* Lam.
bur	*Quercus macrocarpa* Michx.
interior live	*Quercus wislizenii* A. DC.
northern red	*Quercus rubra* L.
pin	*Quercus palustris* Muenchh.
post	*Quercus stellata* Wangenh.
scarlet	*Quercus coccinea* Muenchh.
southern red	*Quercus falcata* Michx.
white	*Quercus alba* L.
Pine, Aleppo	*Pinus halepensis* Mill.
bishop	*Pinus muricata* D. Don
eastern white	*Pinus strobus* L.
jack	*Pinus banksiana* Lamb.
jelecote (Mexican)	*Pinus patula* Schl. & Cham.
loblolly	*Pinus taeda* L.
lodgepole	*Pinus contorta* Dougl.
longleaf	*Pinus palustris* Mill.
Monterey	*Pinus radiata* D. Don.
pitch	*Pinus rigida* Mill.
pond	*Pinus serotina* Michx.
ponderosa	*Pinus ponderosa* Laws.
red or Norway	*Pinus resinosa* Ait.
sand	*Pinus clausa* (Chapm.) Vasey
Scotch	*Pinus sylvestris* L.
shortleaf	*Pinus echinata* Mill.
slash	*Pinus elliottii* Engelm.
sugar	*Pinus lambertiana* Dougl.
Virginia	*Pinus virginiana* Mill.
western white	*Pinus monticola* Dougl.
Poplar	*Populus* spp.
Raspberry	*Rubus* spp.

Red-cedar, eastern	*Juniperus virginiana* L.
western	*Thuja plicata* Donn
Redwood, coast	*Sequoia sempervirens* (D. Don.) Endl.
Sassafras	*Sassafras albidum* (Nutt.) Nees
Spruce, black	*Picea mariana* (Mill.) B.S.P.
Engelmann	*Picea engelmannii* Parry
Norway	*Picea abies* (L.) Karst.
red	*Picea rubens* Sarg.
Sitka	*Picea sitchensis* (Bong.) Carr.
white	*Picea glauca* (Moench.) Voss.
Sugi	*Cryptomeria japonica* D. Don
Sweet-gum	*Liquidambar styraciflua* L.
Walnut, black	*Juglans nigra* L.
White-cedar, Atlantic	*Chamaecyparis thyoides* (L.) B.S.P.
northern	*Thuja occidentalis* L.
Yellow-poplar	*Liriodendron tulipifera* L.

APPENDIX II

Abbreviations in reference lists

Standard abbreviations are used in the names of serials and periodicals, with the following exceptions, most of which involve publications of the regional experiment stations of the United States Forest Service:

AES—Agricultural Experiment Station
Alleg. FES—Alleghany Forest Experiment Station
Appal. FES—Appalachian Forest Experiment Station
CFRES—California Forest and Range Experiment Station
CSFES—Central States Forest Experiment Station
FAO—Food and Agriculture Organization of the United Nations
IMFRES—Intermountain Forest and Range Experiment Station
LSFES—Lake States Forest Experiment Station
NEFES—Northeastern Forest Experiment Station
NRMFRES—Northern Rocky Mountain Forest and Range Experiment Station
RMFRES—Rocky Mountain Forest and Range Experiment Station
PNWFRES—Pacific Northwest Forest and Range Experiment Station
PSWFRES—Pacific Southwest Forest and Range Experiment Station
SEFES—Southeastern Forest Experiment Station
SFES—Southern Forest Experiment Station
USDA—United States Department of Agriculture
USFPL—United States Forest Products Laboratory
USFS—United States Forest Service

AUTHOR INDEX

SUBJECT INDEX